Inside Macromedia Director 5 with Lingo for Macintosh

Lee Allis

John Chambers

Robert Connolly

Matt Davis

Scott Kildall

Gretchen MacDowall

David Miller

with

Sasha Magee

Noel Rabinowitz

New Riders Publishing, Indianapolis, Indiana

Inside Macromedia Director 5 with Lingo for Macintosh

By Lee Allis, John Chambers, Robert Connolly, Matt Davis, Scott Kildall, Gretchen Macdowall, Sasha Magee, David Miller, and Noel Rabinowitz

Published by:
New Riders Publishing
201 West 103rd Street
Indianapolis, IN 46290 USA

Printed in the United States of America 1 2 3 4 5 6 7 8 9 0

Library of Congress Cataloging-in-Publication Data

Inside Macromedia Director with Lingo for Macintosh / Lee Allis ... [et al.].

p. cm.

Includes index.

ISBN 1-56205-567-4

1. Multimedia systems. 2. Macromedia director. 3. Lingo(Computer program language) 4. Macintosh (Computer) I. Allis,Lee, 1969-.

QA76.575.I57 1996

006.6--dc20

96-16336

CIP

Warning and Disclaimer

This book is designed to provide information about Macromedia Director and Lingo. Every effort has been made to make this book as complete and as accurate as possible, but no warranty or fitness is implied.

The information is provided on an "as is" basis. The author(s) and New Riders Publishing shall have neither liability nor responsibility to any person or entity with respect to any loss or damages arising from the information contained in this book or from the use of the disks or programs that may accompany it.

Publisher Don Fowley

Publishing Manager David Dwyer

Marketing Manager Mary Foote

Managing Editor Carla Hall

Product Director
Alicia Buckley

Development Editor
Steve Weiss

Project Editor
Jennifer Eberhardt

Copy Editors
Lillian Duggan, Danica Matthew, Cari Skaggs Phil Worthington

Technical Editors
Jeff Buell, Brian Schmidt

Associate Marketing Manager
Tamara Apple

Acquisitions Coordinator
Stacey Beheler

Publisher's Assistant
Stephanie Layton

Editorial Coordinator
Karen Opal

Cover Designer
Karen Ruggles

Cover Production
Aren Howell

Book Designer
Anne Jones

Production Manager
Kelly Dobbs

Production Team Supervisor
Laurie Casey

Illustrations
Casey Price

Graphics Image Specialists
Steve Adams, Daniel Harris, Clint Lahnen Casey Price, Jeff Yesh

Production Analysts
Jason Hand, Bobbi Satterfield

Production Team
Heather Butler, Terrie Deemer, David Garratt, Krena Lanham, Joe Millay, Beth Rago, Erich Richter, Pamela Volk, Megan Wade, Christy Wagner

Indexer
Craig Small

About the Authors

New Riders is proud to present Lee Allis and the authoring team for *Inside Director 5*. Their efforts during the development of this book truly reflect their dedication to craft, creativity, and professionalism.

Lee Allis

Lee Allis has worked in a variety of positions at Macromedia, all focusing around Director. Many developers know her as the Director sysop on the Macromedia CompuServe forum. She most recently spent time away from technical support on the Director 5 Quality Assurance team and returned to become the Technical Support Supervisor. Prior to joining technical support, Lee produced the Director 4.0 *Lingo Dictionary* and *Using Lingo* manuals, and at one time was the assistant product manager for Director and Authorware. Prior to Macromedia, Lee worked for other small multimedia and data-compression software companies. Lee graduated from the University of Michigan and lives in San Francisco.

John Chambers

John Chambers is a full-time instructor at Art Center College of Design, in Pasadena, California. He is currently teaching half a dozen different multimedia classes using Macromedia Director as the key authoring environment, as well as other related digital media classes. John also owns and operates Conceptual Designs, a Southern California computer consulting firm that specializes in training Macintosh applications. His client list includes: Walt Disney Consumer Products, Walt Disney Imagineering, McDonalds, Turner Entertainment, The Six Flags Corporation, Southern California Edison, Southern California Gas Company, and Lawrey's Foods. John can be reached via e-mail at john@macsos. com or by phone (500) 675-3701. Feel free to visit his Macintosh help Web site at http://www.macsos.com.

Bob Connolly

Bob Connolly lives in Toronto, Canada, and currently produces interactive CD-ROMs for the travel industry. He also is the multimedia editor of the *Graphic Exchange*, a Canadian trade publication that is targeted toward desktop publishers. His past experience includes the production of 12 record albums and several travel television series. He and his wife are the writers and producers of "The Search for Ancient Wisdom," a commercial CD-ROM title about their latest TV series, "Timeless Places." You can reach Bob via e-mail at bconnolly@sympatico.ca.

Matt Davis

Matt Davis, full name Matthew Robert Davis, born November 6, 1966, in Wiltshire, UK. After school and college—initially photography, switched to film studies, which led to graduation film via Fuji Film Scholarship in 1986 shown at British Academy of Film and Television Arts (BAFTA)—went straight into television via film editing. Matt switched to video editing, then moved into video graphics (though he spent 12 months in Floor Management and puppeteering). Matt also did some freelance video graphics, and then in 1989 was offered the position of Creative Director with Autocue (the teleprompt company), where he set up their video graphics division. He left Autocue to start Manor Multimedia in 1990, which was bought by and merged with Project Multi Media shortly afterward. Matt's primary achievement was to convert established conventions from specialist Broadcast equipment such as Quantel Paintbox and Aston 4 to the Macintosh platform while retaining broadcast video quality. Matt remains Director of Graphics & IT with Project Multi Media. He also created "Power Presentations" CD-ROM, a collection of tools and material for presentation software, and "ClickTracks," a software toy.

"I use Director because here's a tool that works at many levels—it copes with almost everything you care to chuck at it. It also has a history, which protects your investment in time spent with the tool. But above all, if you make friends with Director, you can meet C++ eye to eye whilst enjoying the scriptor's quality of life—care about users, content, and interface—not APIs, memory leaks, and pointers.

"VideoWorks was brought to my attention by a distinguished and respected man whom I dined with in 1989. He pressed an article in my hand afterwards and stated that this was something that was to be investigated, and it was a good investment in time and resource. This chap controlled a research center in Palo Alto (I didn't realize its significance at the time!!!) and that article was a 'perfect Xerox' of a Director Interactive review from *Byte,* if I remember correctly. Yes, I was told to get into Director by the boss of Xerox. It was the 'New Dimensions' seminar in Vienna. When I'm sans teeth, sans eyes, I will still remember that moment!"

Scott Kildall

Scott Kildall was raised in the mean streets of Pebble Beach and was one of the lucky few who escaped. He went to Brown University as undergraduate, focusing his studies on biology, Marxism, and Russian history, and received a degree in political philosophy in 1991. After graduating, he moved to San Francisco where he found a part-time job as a general systems operator and arduously worked his way up to the position of systems operator specialist. In 1992, he was hired at Macromedia in the technical support department where he learned how to write Lingo scripts, use Director, and became interested in programming. In 1994, he founded Red Eye Software, which now specializes in writing XObjects, Xtras, and other C/C++ code for custom multimedia applications. Scott currently lives in Seattle and in his copious free time enjoys snowboarding, playing snooker, and combing the beach with a metal detector. You can visit the Red Eye Software Web site at http:www.halcyon.com/redeye.

GRETCHEN MACDOWALL

Gretchen Macdowall spent nine years in traditional software development before discovering Macromedia Director. She has been programming in Lingo ever since. Gretchen's credits include the CD-ROM titles *Multimedia IQ Test* and *BodyPark*, product demos, award-winning interactive marketing pieces, and corporate Web sites. She maintains her own Web site for Director developers at http://www.xensei.com/users/gcm/. She holds a degree in psychology from Emmanuel College.

"Sometimes I feel like Director *is* my life! I have worked at Brueckner interactive, the interactive division of the advertising agency Duval Woglom Brueckner and Partners, for the past year doing demos on CD for client products, sales tools, animatics (mockups for TV commercials), and enhancements to client Web sites. The majority of my work there is in Director and Shockwave, although I now also do some HTML and Perl programming.

"When I'm not doing that, I'm maintaining my own Web site of information on Director development. At my last job I started keeping a list of all of the problems I had come across—and the solutions, to hand off to the next person we brought on board so they wouldn't have to bang their head on the desk over the same things. The Web site idea was born from that list.

"Before Brueckner Interactive, I worked for Virtual Entertainment, programming CD- ROM titles in Director. That was a startup when I came on board. At the very beginning it was five guys and me. It's a much bigger company now. Part of their success is due to the ability to turn an idea into a cross-platform title quickly. That would not be possible without Director. Yesterday I went to a computer superstore and got a little rush when I saw that one of the titles I worked on for Virtual—*Multimedia IQ Test*, is still on the shelves. IQ Test took less than six months from concept to shipping product.

"For quite a few years I did Director programming as a sideline, waiting for multimedia to take off. Then it finally did, and I've been doing Director work full time ever since. I feel extremely fortunate to be doing something I love all day long."

David Miller

David Miller is an Instructional Technology Specialist at the School of Education and New Media Center, Stanford University, where he helps faculty integrate new technology into the classroom. He also provides multimedia application development, World Wide Web site management, design, and CGI programming services and instruction in the San Francisco Bay area. Dave is finishing up his Ph.D. at Stanford. Prior to that, he was a lecturer at California State University, Chico.

"I've used Director since 1991. I like Director's media integration features, ease of cross-platform development, and its object-oriented scripting language, Lingo. Lingo enables me to create class libraries of reusable interface objects and to use features such as dynamic binding to provide user modeling and other sophisticated runtime behavior."

Sasha Magee

Sasha Magee failed the only computer science course he ever took, because he cut class to write Excel macros for his job. Despite that, Sasha received a B.A. in Semiotics from Brown University in 1990. He spent most of college raising hell, producing documentary videos, and working various computer jobs. Since then, in addition to his stint as head of Quality Assurance for Director 4.0 Macintosh at Macromedia and other computer jobs, Sasha has worked as a community organizer, network technician, dishwasher, word processor, cashier, and short-order cook.

In addition to his partnership at InfraRed, Sasha continues his activism for affirmative action, a higher minimum wage, against Prop. 187 and Three Strikes, and against the dismantling of the safety net in our society.

NOEL RABINOWITZ

Noel Rabinowitz's earliest memories are of peace demonstrations, picket lines and folk concerts. A sometimes Renaissance man, Noel has tried his hand at film making, guitar making, songwriting, stage acting, sculpture, painting, physics, and applied revolutionary philosophy. After graduating from Brown University with a B.A. in Physics and Visual Arts in 1991, Noel then moved to San Francisco. He has been a graphic designer, video editor, multimedia production manager, documentary film producer, and is now Partner of InfraRed Communications.

Noel continues his commitment to social change movements, working with grassroots community organizations such as the Jobs for Youth Campaign, Californians for Justice, the People's Unity Center, and People United for a Better Oakland.

Noel and Sasha formed InfraRed Communications in 1993, which has since distinguished itself as a leader in Shockwave innovation, total multimedia solutions, and a socially responsible business.

In June 1995, InfraRed produced the first Shockwave movies ever shown for the Macromedia-Netscape announcement of Shockwave at Digital World in Los Angeles. In March 1996, New Riders released its best-selling *Macromedia Shockwave for Director User's Guide.*

InfraRed features Internet multimedia, deep Lingo, and project management. InfraRed has produced for clients such as Macromedia, Netscape, Apple, Infonautics, Organic Online, Acclaim Technologies, Great Plains Software, Action Technologies, and others. InfraRed's first mission is cutting-edge solutions, on-target delivery and full-service support.

InfraRed actively supports youth action projects in mass media, equipment access, and job training for youth in working class people of color communities. It is clear that the fruits of the information revolution are becoming the sole private property of corporate elites. InfraRed helps develop resources and institutions to assert more public control over the information resources of our country.

Trademark Acknowledgments

Dedications

Lee Allis

This book is dedicated to my parents, Susan and Harry Allis, for their love and the knowledge that anything is possible.

John Chambers

To my wife, Paula, for her love and understanding. Also, to my two little girls, Courtney and Aubree, who wanted very badly to draw pictures for "Dad's book" and many times asked, "Dad, how many more days until your book is done?"

Gretchen Macdowall

This is dedicated to my parents, Robert and Stephanie Macdowall, for instilling the kind of values and work ethic necessary to get somewhere in life.

From New Riders

New Riders would like to express thanks to everyone involved in creating *Inside Macromedia Director 5 with Lingo* for Macintosh. It was a pleasure to work with such a great collections of Director professionals.

Special thanks go to principle author Lee Allis: for her enthusiasm from project-start to finished-book; for her courage in making her authoring debut in such an auspcious project; for her awe-inspiring dedication to detail and perfection; for here good humor through the long hours; for her patience in understanding the publishing process; for her professionalism; and for being such a pleasure to work with.

Lee, you are truly awesome. (And we'll miss the e-mail…<g>.)

Kudos, also are owed to technical editors Jeff Buell and Brian Schmidt, both of whom went the extra mile to make this book the best it could be. Thanks, guys.

Acknowledgments

Lee Allis

A special thanks to my family for their support: Tom, Bob, Carol, Melissa, Shelly, Emily, Ashley, Katie, and Scott Allis. You should now understand where I was when you called.

A special thanks to James Hayes, the Burrito guy, for his loving support and patience. I could not have done this without you.

Thanks to the following Macromedians: John Dowdell for his infinite knowledge; Karl Miller, Kevin Mullet, Aric Rubin, and Alex Zabatone for ideas for the book; Diana Wynne, Joe Schmitz, Ben Melnick, Lalit Balchandani, Mark Shepherd, John "J.T." Thompson, Peter Grandmaison, Mike Seery, Buzz Kettles, Doug Wyrick, John Ware, Joe Dunn, Phil Schiller, and Kevin Ellis all for their help with Director 5; to Bud Colligan, Miles Walsh, Sherry Flanders-Page, and Ed Krimen for giving me the opportunity; to Victoria Dawson, Sasha Magee, and Jason Yeaman for their support and for doing it first; David Mendels, Carolyn Hyland, Kate Jordan, Stephanie Dworkin, Fred Green, John Lorance, Scott Williams, and Pete Caban.

And especially, thanks to the Macromedia technical support department; the Director Engineering team; and the members of the Macromedia CompuServe forum.

At New Riders Publishing, thanks to Alicia Buckley, Steve Weiss, David Dwyer, Don Fowley, and Jennifer Eberhardt for talking me into this and not letting me give up.

John Chambers

A special thanks to Lynda Weinman for her support and telling New Riders about me; Lee Allis for all of her extra and timely help; all of my students who had to listen to the endless stories about "The Book;" the fun people at New Riders: Alicia Buckley, Steve Weiss, Jennifer Eberhardt, David Dwyer, and the group that made the little marks all over my chapter review, I thank you all.

Bob Connolly

As always, all my love to my wife and partner, Bea, who keeps me focused, inspired, fed, and who eases the workload so I can concentrate on my writing. As a MacHead, I must also extend many thanks to Jeff, our resident Windows PC Master, who can always figure out how that darned machine works!

Matt Davis

Eternal thanks and respect to John Dowdell, Lee Allis, and the crew at Macromedia; Alex Gollner for expanding my Lingo and Musical vocabulary; Vegard Brenna and Gretchen Macdowall for demystifying the infinitely mysterious; and David Sloss and the many video engineers in the BBC and ITV for patiently teaching me all the scary stuff about video.

Scott Kildall

Thanks to Astrid Javier, Noel Rabinowitz, Sasha Magee, Erich Strom, Tasha (Femme) Fatale, Peter Vanags, Terry Schussler, David Calaprice, J.T., Lee Allis, and any other helpful Macromedia folks.

Gretchen Macdowall

Thanks to Duval, Woglom, Brueckner and Partners—especially Rob Brueckner—for accommodating me with a flexible work schedule while I was writing my chapters.

David Miller

First, I'd like to thank the editors at New Riders, Steve Weiss and Jennifer Eberhardt, for their great work on a tight deadline; and to Alicia Buckley, Stacey Beheler, and Tracey Turgeson for timely support. Thanks to Brian Schmidt for his technical editing. I'd also like to thank Lois Brooks for being the most supportive boss in the world during the writing process. Thanks to Alan Garber and Mary Goldstein for providing great multimedia projects and being willing to push the frontiers in Director, and to Charles Kerns and the rest of the New Media Center staff for providing a rich developer community within which to work.

Sasha Magee and **Noel Rabinowitz**

We would like to thank our families for making us who we are (it's their fault) and to all of you who have shown us good faith and support. We thank you!

Contents at a Glance

Table of Contents

Introduction

Lee Allis

All the world's a stage.

—William Shakespeare

Inside Macromedia Director 5 with Lingo for Macintosh is not just another Director book. In fact, it's more like a Director production. It is a compilation of work by a group of artists, teachers, programmers, videographers, and just plain crazy people who select Director as the means for their career. Look at *Inside Director* as a seminar, given by seven experts in the field. The cast of authors for *Inside Director* has been using Director for years, some since 1985, when Director was still the product VideoWorks. These experts have posted thousands of online messages, worked through thousands of issues with other developers, and are here to share their knowledge and love for this product with you.

Why "With Lingo"?

When I was first approached by New Riders to do the *Inside Director* book, "with Lingo" was not a part of the title. New Riders wanted to publish an intermediate-to-advanced, beyond-the-tutorials Director book. Like many people, they saw a number of basic Director books out there and knew people wanted more. The trouble with writing a book on Director is that there's so much information to cover. You can write 800 pages on the basic information and never touch Lingo or you can write an entire book on Lingo. That's what you find today—basic Director books or Lingo-specific books. But never the two together. Even the Director documentation divides its books between the basics and Lingo. Once you come to the intermediate level with Director, however, you end up using Director with Lingo each step of the way. Hence, *Inside Macromedia Director 5 with Lingo for Macintosh* was born.

The Director basics take a while to understand. After you learn how to place cast members in the Score and In-Between them over time, you need to learn the real facts about how Director is using those cast members. Understanding the operating systems and the memory that cast members use, and managing that memory, takes the use of Lingo. Try playing your 650 MB CD-ROM in a 4 MB RAM partition. The most effective ways to manage your system memory are to scale the production back and to use more Lingo.

With Lingo, you can craft a production to fit any environment whether you distribute to a 14.4 modem, a floppy disk, or a Windows 95 machine with 8 MB of RAM. Scanning 24-bit images, using 16-bit, 44 KHz sounds, and capturing 80 MB QuickTime files is fun. The real test, however, is learning how to use the right tools to edit down those media elements to a manageable size without decreasing quality. *Inside Director* shows how to bring them all together, use the Score or Lingo to control them, and deliver your movie onto a low-end machine. This book covers each step in the Director development process, and shows how Lingo can help you achieve some of the best results. There is much to learn, which is why the authors of *Inside Director* have written this book.

Who Should Read This Book

Inside Director is for those of you who are serious about Director. It is for those of you who need to know all the little-known facts about Director, but who do not necessarily have time to learn them on your own. This book assumes you're familiar with the Macintosh or Windows environment and Director, or at least have access to the basic Director tutorials. You might have already taken a class in Director, or worked through the tutorials, but still have many unanswered questions.

If you are new to Director, this book gives you a jump start in Director development. It offers background information about each step of the Director development process and is written with the intention of being a companion to the basic Director 5 documentation set.

How This Book Is Organized

Inside Director covers every part of a Director development process—from pre-planning projects and prototyping, and working with each media type, to delivering the production. Five parts make up the main text:

- Part 1: Director Inside and Out
- Part 2: Pre-Planning a Director Project
- Part 3: Director's Multimedia Components
- Part 4: Lingo
- Part 5: The Final Phase: Beyond Director

The final part, Part 6, consists of five appendices, discussed later in this introduction.

Part 1: Director Inside and Out

The first part of the book, "Director Inside and Out," introduces Macromedia Director and the role it plays in the multimedia industry. You'll learn all that's new in Macromedia's new release, Director 5, and how to set up your Director authoring station. The final chapter in Part 1 introduces ways of working with Director and guidelines for understanding Director's metaphor.

Chapter 1, "Multimedia and Director"

By Lee Allis

Chapter 1 discusses Director's role in the multimedia revolution. It features some of the most successful Director developers and the different ways they've used Director. You'll learn why Director is the standard for multimedia authoring and the Internet, as well as read a background and perspecitve on cross-platform development.

Chapter 2, "Introducing Director 5: New Features Overview"

By Lee Allis

This chapter introduces all the new features in Director 5, a short description of each, and where the new features are in relation to the rest of the text.

Chapter 3, "Configuration and Working Environment"

By Lee Allis

In this chapter, you'll learn everything you need to know about setting up your multimedia studio as well as tools for working with Director.

Chapter 4, "Working with Director: Understanding the Metaphor"

By Lee Allis

This chapter is an introduction to Director, setting the scene for the application and how different parts work together. Whether you're new to Director or still having doubts about the program, Chapter 4 also provides background information for new to intermediate users, and provides useful tips on how to work with each part of Director.

Part 2: Pre-Planning a Director Project

Part 2 covers topics not typically addressed in Director books—the planning stages. Before you break into the tool, there is a lot of groundwork to cover that will save you time in the long run. David Miller covers both a strategy to taking on a Director project and ways of staging a multi-person Director project.

Chapter 5, "The Strategy"

By David Miller

You just found out that your boss wants to convert all your company's training materials to CD-ROM. Or maybe the Chamber of Commerce wants you to produce a kiosk for the city's main tourist attraction. You have a budget, a delivery date, and a design team. Now what do you do? In this chapter, a design strategy is for Director projects. The strategy borrows from software engineering, film and television development, and publishing. Although geared toward large Director projects, you can apply the suggestions and methods outlined here to any development project.

Chapter 6, "Staging Your Production"

By David Miller

Coordination and organization of a multi-person Director project can be like herding cats. It's easy for the process to run away from you. This chapter discusses some production tips you might find helpful, and is based on experience trying to organize and streamline multi-person development groups.

Part 3: Director's Multimedia Components

Use Part 3 as a reference for every multimedia element in a Director project. If you have a question about sound, for example, turn to Chapter 12, "Sound: The Soundtrack." If you want to add three-dimensional animations to your Director piece, turn to Chapter 13, "Director in 3D."

Chapter 7, "Import Options: The Casting Call"

By John Chambers

Everyone wants to be an actor…

Actually the line should be: Everything can be an actor, authoring in Director that is.

When you are the producer of a multimedia project, you will need to put out a casting call—a call for all of those media elements for Director includes pictures, videos, sound effects, music, backdrops, and don't forget those cool credits at the end. (You do sit through the credits don't you?) This chapter deals with importing all of these media elements into Director. Starting with the programs that you probably use every day, we will take a step-by-step tour of the options available in Director to give these media elements their 15 minutes of fame.

Chapter 8, "New in Director 5: Multiple Casts"

By John Chambers

Faster, better, and more of it. Earlier upgrades to Director brought us to 48 channels of information—this was up from 24 channels—then another push upward brought us a whopping 32,000 cast members to a cast file, up from a measly 512. Well, they've done it again. Macromedia's latest upgrade to Director now brings us the capability to create and manage unlimited cast member files. This new cast technology brings us not only multiple internal cast member files to easily sort and keep track of large groups of cast members inside a Director document, but also the capability to create and maintain external cast member files that are stored outside of the Director file. Externals cast member files can be shared over a network or swapped out with other cast member files instantly. Be it a large or small Director project, multiple casts will help everyone to be more organized.

Chapter 9, "Graphics: The Visuals"

By John Chambers, with Lee Allis

Grab your paintbrush and easel as we take a tour through the visual creation process of Director's Paint window. Explore an array of tools, effects, and of course, don't forget the shortcuts. We will cover all of the rules of working with graphics in Director, especially when importing them from tools other than Director.

Chapter 10, "Paint Window Enhancements"

By Lee Allis

This chapter features all the new features of Director 5's Paint window, including Photoshop-compatible filter support, support for multiple color depth editing, and the true animation capability: onion skinning. See how powerful the Paint window has become in the latest release.

Chapter 11, "Text: The Story"

By John Chambers

Words, sentences, paragraphs, chapters, books. They all start with the one common element—the typed character. Line these characters up in some orderly fashion, and you can make people laugh, make them cry, and make them think. The textual information contained in a document is as important, if not more important, than its visual design. The document might look great, but not say anything. Text and graphics are used together to relay your message. This chapter will take you through the many different ways of creating and using the textual elements in the new Director 5.

Chapter 12: "Sound: The Soundtrack"

By Bob Connolly

I am often asked why the sound found on some interactive CD-ROM's is so bad—or worse, the sound doesn't work at all! There could be several reasons, but we usually will find the improper use of Lingo or the wrong sampling frequency to be the culprit. Standard procedures need to be followed, especially if you are planning a Mac/Windows hybrid CD-ROM. This chapter will provide the basics of getting good audio into your Mac, making it interactive, and finally, making sure it works on all the many different kinds of computers.

Chapter 13, "Director in 3D"

By David Miller

The creation of computer-generated 3D worlds, once the exclusive domain of super-computers and high-end workstations, is now possible on typical desktop computers.

System-level integration of 3D graphic libraries, hardware advances, and technologies such as VRML (Virtual Reality Modeling Language) and QuickTime VR promise to bring more interactivity and realism to desktop 3D graphics. The open architecture of Director 5 and the integration of Extreme 3D into the Director Multimedia Studio should make it even easier to plug 3D graphics into your Director presentations. This chapter provides an overview of 3D graphic techniques and provides some tips on how to incorporate 3D graphics in Director.

Chapter 14, "Digital Video: The Movie within the Movie"

By Matt Davis

Digital video can be a dark subject, full of folklore, secret tricks, and special words, as well as many pitfalls to catch the unwary. On the other hand, digital video provides many useful solutions to the Director user. This chapter explains the mysteries, exposes the secrets in getting smooth digital video and demonstrates uses of digital video beyond the "talking head."

Chapter 15, "Director as an Animator"

By John Chambers

This is where it all started many years ago. They called it VideoWorks, a very cool black-and-white program that enabled users to move objects around a tiny, eight-inch screen, measured diagonally of course. Years later, things just keep getting better.

Macromedia has added an arsenal of new features to Director 5. In this chapter, you'll find many step-by-step instructions to help get you up to speed in creating cool animation quickly. Also included are some troubleshooting tips to help out with some of the more common mistakes when creating animations in Director.

Part 4: Lingo

Gretchen Macdowall conquered the entire Lingo section of *Inside Director* on her own. Gretchen's repertoire includes lead Lingo programming of Kenwood Stage 3 Product Simulation, Multimedia IQ Test, Virtual Entertainment 1995 Product Line Demo CD, and Body

Park Director projects. Gretchen hosts her own Web page, update Stage, a bi-weekly chronicle of her Director adventures.

Chapter 16, "Lingo: The Basics"

By Gretchen Macdowall

There is nothing as satisfying as seeing a concept that minutes before existed only in your head take shape on screen. No tool out there quite matches Director's ability to help you realize ideas quickly. If this is your first programming experience, you've made the right choice. Lingo shields you from much of the complexity of other computer languages. Just one or two lines of Lingo can *make something happen*! It's almost magic.

Chapter 17, "Managing Your Data"

By Gretchen Macdowall

One of the most valuable enhancements to Director was the introduction of lists. Lists can sort data and act like arrays. Lists are fast. If you get nothing else out of this chapter, make sure that you learn how to use lists.

Chapter 18, "Movie in a Window"

By Gretchen Macdowall

Movies in a Window (MIAWs) offer many creative possibilities. They can help you add novelty to your interface, overcome the 48 sprite barrier, or make tools for yourself and others. On the other hand, having more than one Director movie running at a time requires some orchestrating on the part of the programmer. Make sure that you test the MIAW portions of your project early, often, on both platforms, and in projectors. You have been warned.

Chapter 19, "Advanced Concepts"

By Gretchen Macdowall

It's one thing to read and understand the manuals and quite another to figure out what combination of the 600+ commands, functions, and key words applies to your problem. This section covers some of the situations you're likely encounter taken from my own experience—and their Lingo solutions.

Chapter 20, "Object-Oriented Programming in Director"

By Gretchen Macdowall

I think that a lot of attempts to present object-oriented programming lose the audience because they stay at a very academic level. For some reason all OOP books illustrate OOP concepts with little personified animals that bark or oink depending on what kind of animal they are. After reading a couple of books like this I decided that there weren't any real-world examples because the whole thing was a big hoax.

Then Macromedia introduced support for objects in version 4.0 of Director and I slowly changed my mind. Used at the most basic level, objects help you organize your code. As you progress, you will find that code structured around multiple objects can save you time if you have to make changes later.

If you're looking for object-oriented design theory I'm afraid you won't find it here. What you *will* find are simple, clear explanations of how to create and use objects in Director. The examples center around tasks you might want to accomplish in real life and explain how coding with objects helps accomplish your goal.

Chapter 21, "How Do I . . . : The Top 20 Lingo Support Questions"

By Gretchen Macdowall

Macromedia's various support forums receive hundreds of new posts every week, but most of the questions center around the same areas. If you're new to Director and you run across a problem or have a question, check this chapter first.

Part 5: The Final Phase: Beyond Director

There is much more to know beyond Director. Part 5 outlines what it takes to distribute your Director project to your audience. It also covers the "Xtra" step you can take. With Xtras and the Macromedia Open Architecture, there are no limits to Director's capabilities.

Chapter 22, "Delivering the Goods"

By Lee Allis

Chapter 22 covers all the issues you'll need to know when putting together a Director piece for distribution. This chapter covers testing your Director production, setting up the Director projector, and the Director files and projector you need to include with your Director projector.

Chapter 23, "Macromedia Open Architecture: All About Xtras"

By Scott Kildall

Previous versions of Director offered the capability to write extensions written in C or C++ using the XObject protocol. Although XObjects can be powerful, they have virtually no access to Director's internal information such as cast data, the Score, Director's off-screen buffer, and so on, and are essentially communicating blindly with Director. Many exist and these XObjects are often outdated, buggy, or not very useful.

With Macromedia Open Architecture (MOA), a C or C++ programmer can write Xtras, a new external type. Not only can Xtras get access to and manipulate many pieces of a movie's data, but they also can define Lingo commands, establish new cast member types, make custom transition types, and be used not only with Director but with Authorware, SoundEdit, and other Macromedia products.

In this chapter, I discuss all of the new Xtra types and provide simple-to-use examples of each, as well as cover how to use XObjects.

Part 6: Appendices

The five appendices include:

- Director on the Internet: Shockwave!
- Hot URLs: Favorite Director Web Sites
- New Lingo Terms in Director 5
- Contacting Macromedia
- The Inside Director 5 CD-ROM.

The Director 5 Challenge

Writing about a software package under development is difficult. It's never clear how the new features will turn out, or how to think up ways in which you will use them. It would have been much easier for all of us to write about Director 4—now that it's been out more than two years—but then you wouldn't have bought this book.

As with all new software, Director 5 will certainly undergo its share of changes, updates, tweaking, and the like. So keep in mind that you might find errors in *Inside Director*, just as you would with any software-dependent publication. Please do not call Macromedia's technical support about this book. Instead, please contact the authors (through New Riders) with suggestions of ways to update the next version.

Thanks for buying *Inside Director 5 with Lingo for Macintosh!*

PART I

Director Inside and Out

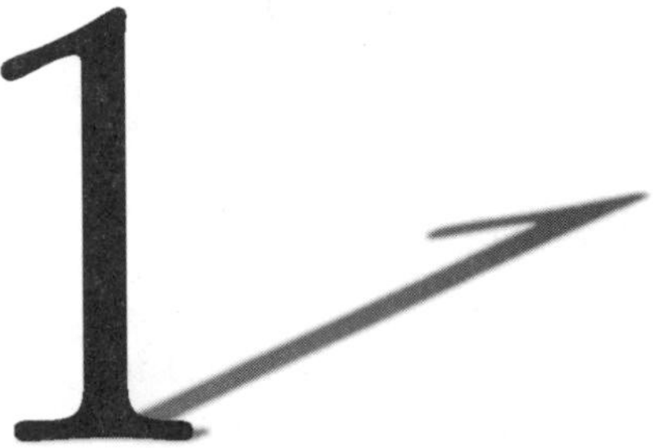

Lee Allis

Multimedia and Director

Think of any idea. Think of how you could pass along that idea and make it come alive. This is the power of multimedia. Black-and-white overhead transparencies, chalk boards, and (in some cases) printed books, are becoming a thing of the past—unless, of course, the printed book has a CD-ROM in the back, like this one.

The multimedia revolution is here. Magazines dedicated to multimedia abound, and multimedia is the topic of discussion in every standard computer magazine. Thousands of companies are creating their own multimedia presentations and products. Multimedia presents a practical and robust tool for communicating ideas. The global popularity of multimedia reaches the entire world—from Japan to Europe, across the United States, and down to Australia. It's literally a multimedia revolution we're witnessing, and Director is playing a significant role in that revolution.

Macromedia Director's Role

If you take the text of your idea and add brilliant images, accompanying music, digital video, and animations, think of the impact the project will have. That is Macromedia Director's role.

Director is the industry-standard authoring tool for multimedia production and the Internet. Director not only combines multimedia elements into a portable movie, but backs them up with Lingo, its own interactive scripting language.

Lingo enables a Director developer and the movie's audience to control any situation in the production. The audience may interact with any of the media elements presented, navigate through volumes of information, play an interactive game, and so on. Using Director with Lingo, the only limitation is your imagination.

With Director 5, Macromedia introduces the most sophisticated version of Director to date (see fig. 1.1).

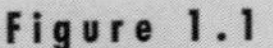

Figure 1.1

Director 5 is the most powerful authoring tool for multimedia and the Internet.

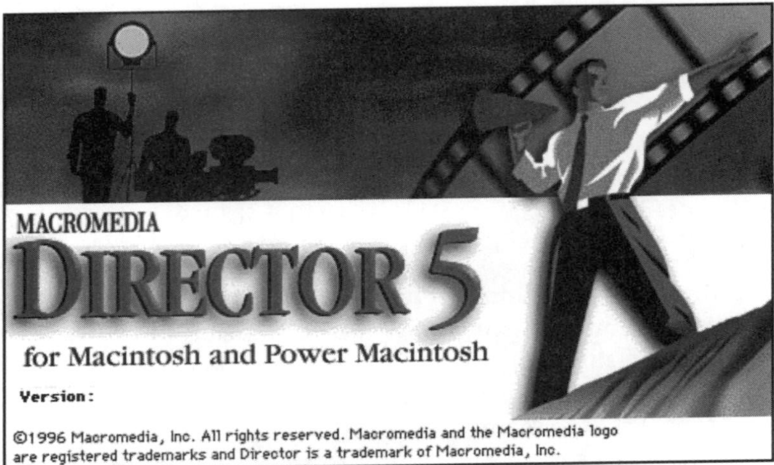

Director is a key component for producing multimedia Web pages, CD-ROM titles, and persuading business audiences to understand your products and ideas. You can do it all with Director.

This chapter describes how Director and the multimedia industry developed together, what people have done with Director, why

Director is the standard, and how the Director community can assist you as a developer.

Shockwave for Director

The World Wide Web is the hottest method of communication today—the information superhighway—the frontier that changes every minute. The Internet offers a low-cost solution for distributing ideas to millions of people and multimedia is taking over. Shockwave for Director helps you develop Web pages that display Director movies full of rotating logos, animations, transitions, sound effects, interactivity, and more.

Figure 1.2

Shockwave for Director provides for the creation of multimedia Internet solutions.

Blinking text is no longer the hit of HTML. Check out Macromedia's Web page at http://www.macromedia.com. Macromedia's Shockwave area hosts the Shockwave Epicenter with the Shocked Site of the Day, featuring the coolest sites in the world (see fig. 1.3).

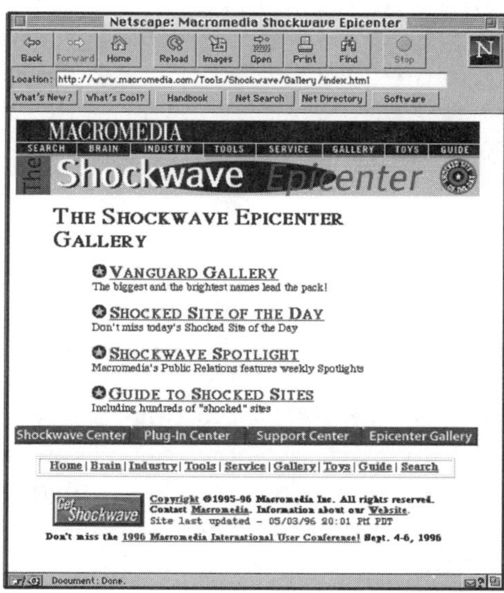

Figure 1.3

The Shockwave Epicenter is a guide to all of the Shockwave sites. It features a new site of the day every day.

Corporations using Shockwave include CNN, Apple, @Home, General Motors, Netscape, Pepsi, MTV, *New Media Magazine*, Intel, Maytag, Nissan, and more. The list of corporations and developers using Shockwave grows every day. Shockwave for Director is truly changing the face of the World Wide Web.

Figure 1.4

The Vanguard Gallery on the Macromedia Shockwave page features the top Shockwave sites, how they're using Shockwave, and what they have to say about Shockwave.

What is the trick to this Shockwave for Director technology? It's actually quite easy—use Director. You'll need to learn some details of the Internet delivery platform, but Director is the key. If you already have Director and know everything about it, turn to Appendix A, "Director on the Internet: Shockwave!," for information about Shockwave—unless, of course, you want to know more about Director 5.

The Shockwave Plug-In is a playback engine for Macromedia Director movies. Shockwave is currently available for Macromedia Director, Authorware, and FreeHand. The Plug-In integrates flawlessly into a Web browser, such as Netscape Navigator, (on both Macintosh and Windows). The AfterBurner, a post-processor compression utility, compresses a Director movie by approximately 60 percent. Shockwave and the AfterBurner are both free from Macromedia at their Web page at http://www.macromedia.com. The actual address for the Plug-In Center and what the site looks like are shown in figure 1.5.

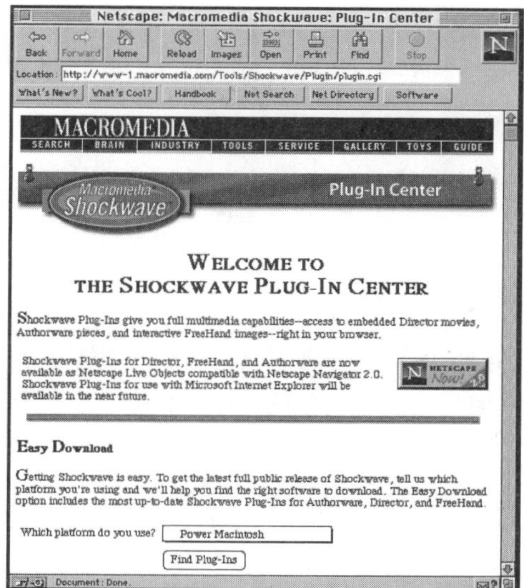

Figure 1.5

The Plug-In Center is where you can obtain Shockwave and the AfterBurner for both Macintosh and Windows.

NOTE

Shockwave for Director 5 was still under development at the time this book was published. By the time you read this, it should be available at http://www.macromedia.com.

Complete your movie, compress it with the AfterBurner, and put it on a Web server. You can refer to it in your HTML document like any GIF or JPEG file. That's the basic concept, but many more techniques exist. The Shockwave-specific HTML commands and Lingo syntax are covered in Appendix A, "Director on the Internet: Shockwave!" The most up-to-date information on Shockwave is on Macromedia's Web page.

The key to Shockwave for Director development is to understand Director. The most successful Shockwave developers have been using Director for years. They understand the different media elements and how to use Lingo to create an animation in a very tight Internet environment. It's easy, but even easier when you know Director. That's why you're reading this book.

Director and the CD-ROM Industry

CD-ROM drives are standard on personal computers today. A look at the statistics tells you that CD-ROM drive sales have increased six-fold in the last three years. More and more software companies ship their products on CD-ROMs and prices have fallen on CD-ROM drives. Whether families purchase CD-ROM drives to play educational titles for their children, or a programmer listens to an audio CD on one machine as he compiles his code on another, more users than ever have common access to CD-ROM drives. The market is there. Last Christmas, it was reported that a four-year-old girl wanted nothing from Santa but CD-ROM games.

Is the future of multimedia success on the World Wide Web or in CD-ROMs?

Perhaps the two of them could work together. One option is using the Web for low-cost advertising of CD-ROM titles. Another option is to eventually use the Web and CD-ROMs together—the Web holding the information that changes and the CD-ROM holding the bulk of the static information. The good news is that Director movies can play on both: CD-ROMs and the World Wide Web. It's really up to you.

Technologies develop all the time to better suit the needs of multimedia productions. What could be better than a CD-ROM with 650 MB of free space to fill up with *stuff*? And soon, the new DVD-ROM drives promise 4.7–8.5 gigabytes of storage space. Floppy disk distribution is still possible, and many developers continue to pursue that avenue. With CD-ROM drives on most machines, though, a floppy cannot compare to a CD-ROM when it comes to potential storage space. Finally, with the future promise of cable connections for interactive television and a wider bandwidth for the Internet, you as multimedia developers are in the hot seat of the future.

Director and the CD-ROM industry developed together. Director was actually around first and Director titles have helped define the interactive CD-ROM world. Last year, 75 percent of the *New Media Magazine* Invision Awards were given to CD-ROM titles created with Director.

Examples of Director CD-ROM titles include museum and hospital kiosks, sales and marketing presentations, educational titles, children's games, grown-ups' games, annual reports, family picture albums, and so on. Take any idea, and you can make it come alive.

The Future of Multimedia

No one knows where the future of multimedia will take us. We do know that it will be an exciting ride with many changes. The mode of distribution for Director movies changes all the time: CDs, DVDs, Shockwave over the Internet, the future with interactive television, and so forth. One thing is certain—it will become easier and faster to get the same idea across with each new technological breakthrough.

Director has proven itself again and again as the leader in multimedia. It lends itself to working with the finest media creation tools on the market and hitting every mark for delivery platforms. When new platforms grow to the size of the Macintosh and Windows, you can bet that Macromedia and Director will be there.

How Do People Use Director?

The ways to use Director are endless. One method is to categorize into four groups the main ways people use Director:

- Edutainment
- Interactive reference materials
- Custom multimedia
- Business and personal

The following sections feature people successfully using Director in the marketplace.

Edutainment

Director educational products typically teach the user a subject in a fun and entertaining way. Most of these "edutainment" products include children's learning applications for reading, writing, learning the alphabet, learning to play the piano, math, and much more.

Big Top Productions

Big Top Productions of San Francisco is a leading producer of children's interactive titles. One of their latest productions is Big Top's Cartoon Toolbox, starring Felix the Cat (see fig. 1.6). With this title, children design their own animated cartoons, much like creating a Director title itself. The application contains many editing features, backgrounds, props, sound effects, original soundtracks, and The Toon Transformer. The Toon Transformer is a separate application that makes it easy to send cartoons over the Internet via e-mail.

Figure 1.6

Big Top's Cartoon Toolbox, starring Felix the Cat.

Other products from Big Top include Hello Kitty Big Fun Deluxe and Keroppi Day Hopper. Hello Kitty Big Fun Deluxe stars the popular children's character Hello Kitty and presents fun lessons in reading, arithmetic, art, music, shapes, colors, and more. Keroppi Day Hopper is an interactive journal, calendar, and address book that makes writing fun for kids. Figure 1.7 shows an example of a child's journal.

According to Big Top, "We want children to see that writing is a form of creative expression. We've made our product for boys and girls alike to express their own thoughts and create their own 'stories.'"

To see how Big Top uses Shockwave for Director to advertise their products, and for more information on Big Top, take at look at http: //www.bigtop.com/. You also will find a demo of the Big Top products on the *Inside Director* CD-ROM.

Figure 1.7

A child's journal in Big Top's Keroppi Day Hopper.

Interactive Reference

Director often is used to create complete multimedia reference materials. Photographs, narratives, text, and interactivity can be combined to bring any book or experience to life. Some examples of what people have created in this category include interactive encyclopedias, multimedia documentaries, or campus orientation CDs with maps and student life information. This section features two Director projects: Passage to Vietnam and the Breast Cancer Lighthouse. Both of these projects are exceptional examples of how people have used Director to produce rich multimedia versions of their own wealth of information.

Passage to Vietnam

Winner of the "Best of Show" 1995 *NewMedia* INVISION Award, Passage to Vietnam is one of the most highly-acclaimed interactive reference pieces created with Director (see fig. 1.8).

The Passage to Vietnam CD-ROM is based on Rick Smolan's most recent book by the same title. Smolan, best known for his "Day in the Life" book series, took seventy of the world's best photojournalists to Vietnam to document this little-known country for the first time in twenty years. The project has been responsible for a large format coffee-table book and HDTV documentary special. An interactive CD-ROM was created with Director and developed by Against All Odds Productions in conjunction with ad•hoc Intertactive, Inc. and produced by Against All Odds Productions in association with Interval Research.

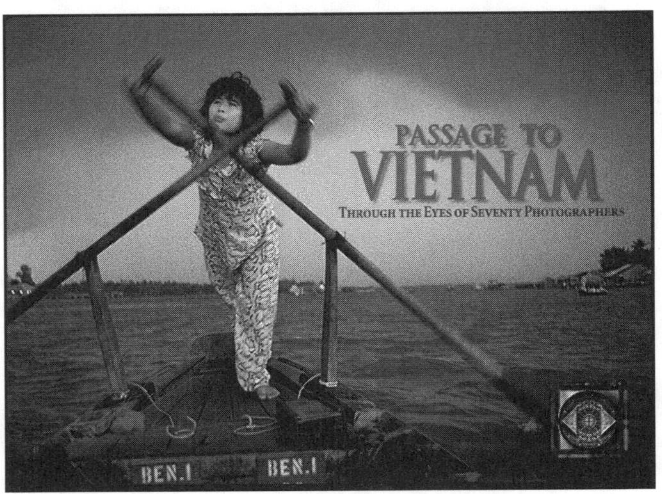

Figure 1.8

Passage to Vietnam by ad•hoc Interactive, Inc.

According to Megan Wheeler, Co-Founder and Creative Director of ad•hoc Interactive, Inc.:

> *The CD was based around what we felt was a fairly unexplored concept—how does one create an interactive documentary format? What are the rules for documentary in multimedia? We decided that the piece should be based on the idea of a conversation with the user, or viewer, as we like to think of ourselves. Bringing the personalities of Rick [Smolan] and the photographers into direct interaction with the people on the other side of the monitor. We wanted this lush Vietnamese experience to translate into a direct experience for the viewer, one where their feedback becomes part of the experience, but also one where a beautiful, emotional, fascinating story is still being told.*
>
> *We also were very concerned about having the photographs tell their own stories. The tremendously exciting thing about this multimedium is that all the tools are available to let us do exactly the same thing.* (See figure 1.9.)
>
> *We featured the photographs full-screen to maximize the visual stage; then we incorporated video and audio interview footage in a very seamless way graphically. By incorporating certain elements of the interface into the overall image, the photographs stood on their own, then were able to speak to us when and if we wanted.* (See figures 1.10.)

Figure 1.9

Passage to Vietnam, letting the photographs tell the story.

Figure 1.10

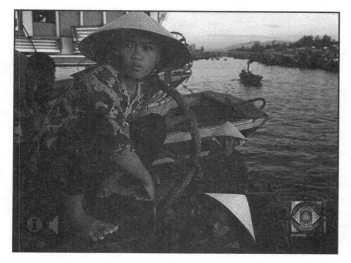

The Quebe Interface, designed by Megan Wheeler and programmed by Shawn McKee, allows for this concept of full-screen exploitation of space without losing the ability to navigate the dense content of the CD-ROM intuitively. (Photo by Natalie Forbes, USA.)

Along with your travels through the Passage CD-ROM, you are invited to join two of the world's leading picture editors in an interactive photo session. Video footage of Mike Davis of *National Geographic* and Michelle McNally of *Fortune Magazine* describe to you why some photos are chosen for the CD-ROM and why others are not. (See figures 1.11 and 1.12.)

According to ad•hoc:

> *The Passage to Vietnam CD-ROM was a particularly challenging project because of the technical hurdles it posed. From the very*

beginning it was envisioned that photographers would be walking around within their own photographs. Making the arresting images shot by 70 of the worlds best photo-journalists look as much like the actual prints as possible in a 256-color environment was also an interesting problem. Cutting edge technologies in both digital video and imaging were employed by ad•hoc to achieve the beautiful images present in the CD.

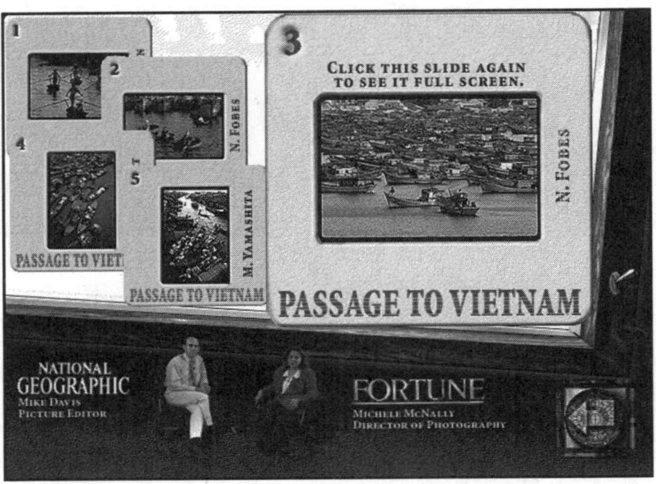

Figure 1.11

Sit with two of the world's leading photo editors in an interactive photo-editing session.

Passage to Vietnam is one of those few products whose audience spans across age groups, gender, and even politics. The Passage to Vietnam CD is an enduring look into the human face of Vietnam. The CD appeals to young adults only now learning about the Vietnam War, as well as older Americans for whom Vietnam represents a tragic time in American History.

With the coming of the 20th anniversary of the end of the Vietnam War, interest in the country is more intense than ever before. The Passage to Vietnam CD-ROM lifts a veil of mystery that has surrounded this country for more than 20 years.

To order the Passage to Vietnam CD, please call 415-331-6300.

Figure 1.12

Two boatmen ferry a precious cargo on a tributary of the Bac Dan River in Quand Ninh Province in northeastern Vietnam. (Photo by Barry Lewis, United Kingdom.)

Breast Cancer Lighthouse

Breast Cancer Lighthouse is a CD-ROM project and Web site that enables women who are newly diagnosed with breast cancer to explore medical information and survivors' personal stories about breast cancer and treatment options—a virtual support group. According to Dr. Carrie Heeter, Director of the Communication Technology Laboratory at Michigan State University, this software will shape how medical communication will be provided to health care consumers in the future.

The software can be used at home or in a clinic, where the woman (alone or with her family) can spend as much time as she wants going through the information. The following are some questions answered by Dr. Heeter about this exciting new way to use multimedia in medical treatment.

What can the Breast Cancer Lighthouse offer that a health care provider cannot?

Unlike a health care provider, the computer will repeat itself as many times and go into as much detail as desired. Also, unlike a health care provider, our software lets women explore in-depth the experiences of other women who faced the same diagnosis. Both choices lead the user out to a particular part of the island where the women or the medical information can be found.

How is the Breast Cancer Lighthouse software different from a pamphlet?

The overall interface design was developed to carry a strong feminine, calming, and friendly tone. (See figure 1.13.)

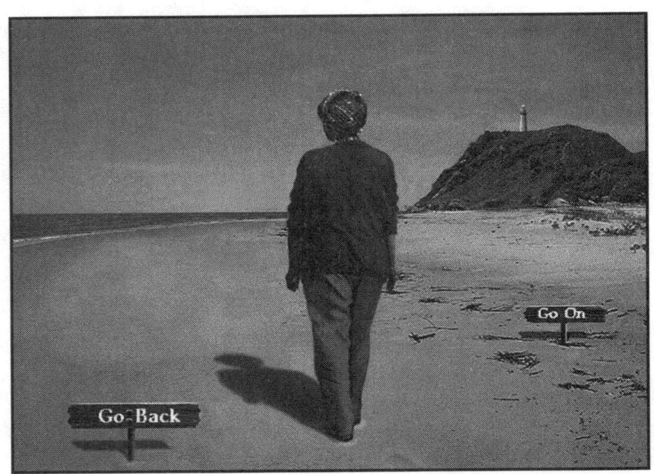

Figure 1.13

Wooden signs offer options for navigation as patients walk down the beach by the lighthouse.

We use the metaphor of a lighthouse on an island—a beacon to guide you.... The interior of the island has a garden path, with wooden signs offering different menu options for diagnosis, treatment, and recovery information. A competent and friendly nurse presents information. Music and environmental sound effects accompany the audio content and interface sound effects. The user can also choose to go for a "walk on the beach" to hear women who have survived breast cancer talk about their personal stories. Oceans are both calming and somber—the mood here is pensive but strong.

How is Breast Cancer Lighthouse different from a TV documentary?

A two- to three-hour documentary could be created which contains the exact same content—the same audio and images as does our CD-ROM. But it would not be made. Documentaries present content in a single, linear order. When people are quoted, it is typically a 10- to 30-second sound byte making exactly the point the producers are seeking. With our interactive CD-ROM, we include 20 to 30 minutes of audio quotes. The user chooses and listens to the stories of most interest to her.

What sort of safeguards did you have to take with this sort of medical guidance?

By separating personal stories from medical facts in the opening menu choice, we were able to skirt liability issues which might arise if personal experiences were construed as medical advice—but still include the experiences, both good and bad, of the real women.

How does the CD-ROM technology used help bring across your story?

The Breast Cancer Lighthouse World Wide Web site also makes a contribution to CD-ROM version development through visual artistry and emotional tone. By giving women time to explore their options in a self-paced, self-directed format where they can take as long as they want and repeat as often as they want, we hope to enhance the likelihood of reaching them at this highly emotional moment. The software is designed to be personal and intimate, with heavy reliance on photography, artwork, and personal stories.

For more information on The Breast Cancer Lighthouse and the Michigan State University Communication Technology Laboratory, refer to their World Wide Web site at http://commtechlab.msu.edu/.

Entertainment and Custom Multimedia

On the entertainment front, developers use Director to combine sound, graphics, and video to create games and multimedia experiences. Games are the top selling interactive CD-ROMs today. Some of those you might recognize that were made with Director include "Iron Helix" by Drew Pictures, "The Star Trek Interactive Technical Manual" by Simon & Schuster Interactive, and "Total Distortion" by Pop Rocket. The following sections feature Headbone Interactive, one company making a mark for itself with games made in Director, and Canter Technologies, a company that uses Director to create custom multimedia pieces and define new art forms.

Headbone Interactive

Headbone Interactive uses Director to produce their critically-acclaimed "What the Heck Will Elroy Do Next?" CD-ROM series. According to Headbone Interactive, Elroy Goes Bugzerk, the first episode of the Elroy series, is an Interactive Comic Adventure for ages 7–97. Elroy Goes Bugzerk introduces Elroy and his sidekick, Blue, in a race against time, trying to find an incredible bug to defeat mega-jerk Gordon Smugs in the 10th Annual Big City Insectathon (see fig. 1.14).

According to Headbone Interactive, "A world of obstacles stands between Elroy and the Technoloptera—the bug of his dreams. He'll need your help every nerve-tingling step of the way! To win, you'll need to muster courage, smarts, determination, and a sense of humor (and pick up dozens and dozens of insect facts as you go)!"

Figure 1.14

Elroy and his trusty bloodhound, Blue.

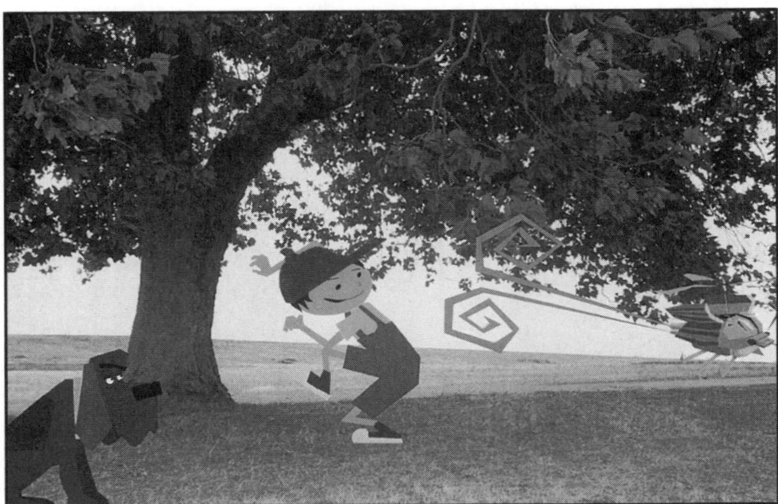

Elroy Goes Bugzerk won *PC Gamer*'s "Best Educational Software Title of 1995," the *MacUser* list for Top 50 CD-ROMs of the Year, and critical acclaim from many publications, including *PC Gamer*: "...this is the best I've seen. Because of its fresh and clever graphics style, as well as its well-told story, Elroy Goes Bugzerk takes the prize." (See figure 1.15.)

The latest title in the Elroy series is Elroy Hits the Pavement. In Pavement, according to Headbone Interactive, Elroy and Blue are back, and their pal Syd has joined the team. Someone swiped their Canine Revitalizer, and our heroes need that gizmo back. Weave a perilous path through a booby-trapped, bad-guy hideout. Rely on your wits and use basic science principles to fashion a makeshift battery, calibrate a laser, and repair a broken gear system. Surf the Net with Elroy and Syd to get the goods on Big City's biggest crooks and unmask the Big Boss. Elroy needs your help—the outcome of this relentlessly inventive, map-cap thriller is in your hands! Elroy Hits the Pavement is the recipient of the Family Channel's Seal of Quality.

Figure 1.15

Hoe-down with the Technoloptera.

You will find a demo of Elroy Goes Bugzerk and Elroy Hits the Pavement on the *Inside Director* CD.

Meet MediaBand

Developers on the cutting edge of multimedia development use Director in completely original ways. The best example of this application is the Meet MediaBand CD by Canter Technology. Marc Canter, the creator of VideoWorks (which later became Director) now heads up Canter Technology creating interactive music videos with Director.

According to Marc Canter, "We wanted to help define a new class of Interactive Music—beyond liner notes and repackaging—material that is intrinsically created from day one to be interactive. Interactive technology is a new art form, and Canter Technology's mission is to merge the musical and visual worlds, while breaking down the barriers between performer and audience."

Canter Technology's first CD-ROM is Meet MediaBand (see fig. 1.16). The following section is from Marc Canter, on Meet MediaBand:

> *Meet MediaBand has two sections: UnDo Me and HouseJam. The two hits offer very different approaches to interactivity in a music video. UnDo Me is the tale of a woman's search for romance and the user actually controls the search and the choices* (see fig. 1.17).

Figure 1.16

Meet MediaBand is the first interactive music video CD-ROM with totally original content.

Figure 1.17

The UnDo Me interface on the Meet MediaBand CD-ROM.

In HouseJam, the user becomes a DJ or VJ in an MTV video game-like environment. (See figure 1.18.)

Figure 1.18

HouseJam enables the user to become the DJ or VJ of the visual and musical experience.

In addition to the two music videos, Meet MediaBand enables you to explore six separate environments within its aetherRAVE cyberspace: The Stage, Smart Bar, Archives, Tekno Room, Kid's Room, and Swag Shop. Each room offers another peek into the MediaBand mythology. (See figure 1.19.)

Figure 1.19

The AetherRAVE Stage, one of six rooms in which a user can explore the MediaBand mythology.

Several of the rooms enable the user to "perform the space" by moving or clicking the mouse. "The more you click, the weirder it gets."

MediaBand is the multimedia performance ensemble begun in 1992 to create original interactive music videos that are scaleable to any distribution platform, for example, CD-ROM, Cyber Clubs, or Interactive TV. All of the songs are created with "live" performance in mind, as well as Interactive TV.

Meet MediaBand is the first CD-ROM version of the MediaBand's ever-growing "database" of material, designed to eventually be a server of interactive media and available to any traveler of the info highway. The MediaBand database evolves by adding more rooms to the aetherRAVE and by adding lots of new interactive pieces. In other words, it's really an Interactive TV show! For more information on Canter Technology and the MediaBand, check out http://www.mediaband.com/.

Business

Corporations use Director for prototyping new products and creating sales and marketing demos, as well as educational courseware. Director is used for trade show kiosks, advertisements on the World Wide Web, annual reports, and so on. The business aspect of using Director is probably the widest growing market.

Mattel

Mattel, Inc. is one corporation using Director to develop some of its creative marketing tools. Following is an interview with Clark Dugger, Manager of Digital Studio Services at Mattel.

How did the idea of Hot Wheels® Computer Cars™ computer disks come about?

The Hot Wheels Marketing and Design groups at Mattel wanted to produce an interactive computer disk that would be sold with a Hot Wheels car. They asked our in-house Digital Studio Services department to design and produce it. We produced a demo for our Pre-Toy Fair, and it was enthusiastically received. (See figure 1.20.)

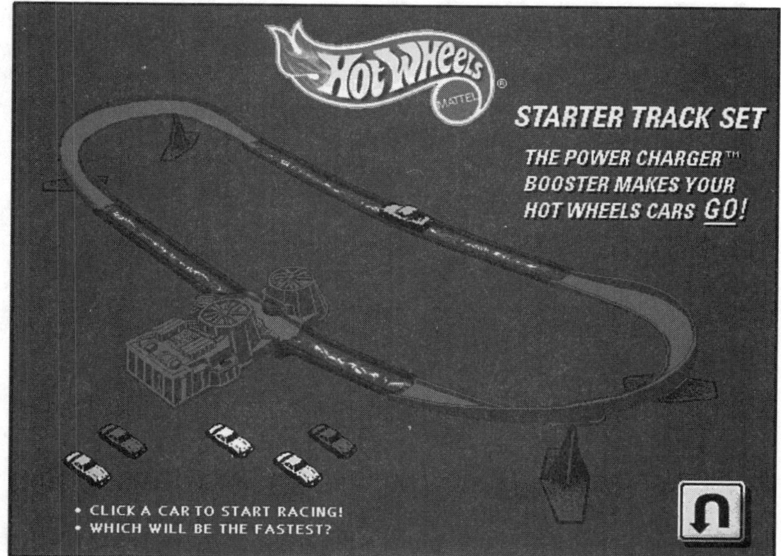

Figure 1.20

One of the activity screens in Computer Cars. You can race cars on the track and find the fastest one. (Hot Wheels and associated trademarks are owned by and used with permission of Mattel, Inc. ©1996 Mattel, Inc. All rights reserved.)

I understand that your product is produced for floppy disk distribution. Why did you decide to go this route?

Considering our market (boys between 6 and 10), it was decided early on to produce this on a floppy disk rather than CD-ROM in order to keep things as simple as possible. Also, for a typical CD-ROM, budgets tend to be higher and development times much longer than what we had to work with. It was also decided that the self-running file would not be compressed in order to minimize the steps necessary to play with it.

What is included on the floppy disk?

Each floppy disk (currently there are six) has three "worlds:" a comic strip story, an activity area, and a trading card section. Also included is either a puzzle or other fun activity. Each of these worlds relates to the particular car sold with the disk, kind of like a "digital trading card." (See figure 1.21.)

What technical challenges did you face?

The challenge in designing the disks was to put as much fun and entertainment as possible onto each disk. Most of the graphics end up in 4-, 2- or even 1-bit elements. Sound elements were carefully edited to create the smallest files. Wherever possible, elements were reused.

Figure 1.21

Frame 1 of the interactive comic strip for Hydroplane. (Hot Wheels and associated trademarks are owned by and used with permission of Mattel, Inc. ©1996 by Mattel, Inc. All rights reserved.)

It sounds quite successful. How did you manage the different processes in creating a Director production?

Because the production department and the Hot Wheels Marketing and Design groups were all in close physical proximity, most brainstorming and approval meetings included everyone. This greatly reduced the development and approval process schedules.

Personal

Director also opens the door for those people who want to use it as a personal creative tool. Think of those family pictures and albums. With a scanner, you could scan all of your family picture album photos and import them into Director. Add sounds, buttons to flip back and forth between the pages, transitions between scenes, and voilà, you've got yourself a keepsake for your entire family to enjoy. Another popular way to use Director is to create a multimedia version of a résumé.

How Do They Put It Together?

The way you use Director is entirely up to you. An empty Score and a blank stage for your movie appears when you launch the application.

This can be a bit daunting for some people, but for some reason, many people see that blank stage and create a similar framework for their Director presentation. If you're in the predicament of not knowing where to begin, the following section should help.

Most commonly, Director files, or "movies," begin with a main menu screen. This is completely controlled by you, the movie's director. The audience progresses through the show in a linear or non-linear fashion with a number of buttons or options to select. Lingo allows for this navigation as Director follows its commands and holds the media together. This, of course, is only one way to use Director. Like most things, the more you learn about Director, the more uses you'll find. If you know one way to use Director, this book helps you learn another way—to use Director with Lingo.

A completed Director movie can be turned into a self-running executable, called a projector. A projector runs on any machine that fits the Director playback requirements, whether or not Director is installed. Chapter 22, "Delivering the Goods," covers how to set up a projector and what to include with a Director projector.

A movie production metaphor with a stage, a cast of characters, and a Score in the background continues throughout the development process to help you understand how it all comes together. The commercial potential of a Director production is that of creating, distributing, and selling a software application. Therefore, a Director user is automatically called a developer, or sometimes, an author. Chapter 4, "Working with Director: Understanding the Metaphor," covers in detail working with Director and understanding the metaphor in which its different parts work together.

What Is Director's Secret?

So what is Director's secret? Why is it the industry-standard multimedia authoring tool? Why do more than 300,000 people use it? The words "really cool" come to mind, but for cold hard facts, you can break up its advantages into three categories

- Ease of use
- Power
- Presence

Ease of Use

It is possible to compare Director to the C programming language and Java because all three create software applications. Java and C are programming languages. Director, on the other hand, offers a powerful scripting language called Lingo, in addition to an easy-to-use development environment similar to standard applications.

The Director Score provides a visual interface where you can examine movie elements at every moment in time. According to Marc Canter:

> *Time, as represented by the Score in Director, is the single aspect that differentiates multimedia from flat media, such as paper. After all, time is what animation, sound, and video are all about. Combining the time-line Score and WYSIWYG (what-you-see-is-what-you-get) layout capabilities, you create an intuitive system for multimedia composition.*

There might be times when you program Lingo routines to occur only when the movie is playing. If this is the case, it is quick and easy to prototype, preview, and debug Lingo code before you finalize the presentation. Lingo is easier to use than Java or C. There is only a handful of terms you'll use most often and their syntax is easy to understand. English-like events such as `on mouseUp` or `on enterFrame` and simple `go to` commands make it easy for an artist to learn how to program. On the other hand, a programmer can take Lingo to the extent of a complete programming language, like C.

If there is a feature you would like to add to Director that Lingo doesn't provide, you can create external C modules called Xtras. Xtras communicate with Director 5 through the new Macromedia Open Architecture (MOA). With MOA, Xtras now show up under a pull-down menu, right in the Director interface. In the past, you had to script most of the interaction with XObjects, the predecessors to Xtras, yourself. Director 5 ships with a number of third-party Xtras as well as an Xtras Development Kit on both platforms. There is practically nothing you can't do with Director, Lingo, and Xtras.

For the non-programmers in the group, Director gets easier to use with each new version. Among many other features, Director 4 introduced a reference to all cast members by number rather than Octal code of A11-H88. The interface changed considerably and it allows for the dragging and dropping of cast members onto the stage, around the Score, and around the Cast window.

Director 5 introduces grids on the stage and an alignment palette. Information about anything in the Director movie or interface is a Control-click or right-mouse click away. By Control-clicking a sprite on the stage, for example, a shortcut menu pops up with all the commands and options for that sprite. Every window has a toolbar; and every toolbar has tool tips. The new Macromedia User Interface (MUI) gives Director 5 a standard interface similar to most other software applications.

Power

The first thing you notice about a Director movie is the powerful media it presents. The audience might not know what's going on in the background, but if your product is authored well, they see a production with moving animations, brilliant images, sounds, and quick interactive control.

The time-based Score of Director allows for a true cel animation, updating the movements of 48 visual elements in each frame. Behind the stage is the Director engine capable of 120 frames per second. Director authors also can test for any user interaction and, given the interaction, change the production in a multitude of ways.

Director is where the media comes together. It accepts and integrates media elements created in specialized tools for sound, digital video, and graphics. Director 5 also offers Photoshop-compatible filter support and onion skinning support in the Paint window for creating specialized content within Director. Director 5 has a closer relationship with SoundEdit 16, where sounds can be edited and updated directly from the Cast window. The new Macromedia User Interface (MUI) gives an author the power of jumping between applications in the Director Multimedia Studio and quickly creating complete multimedia productions.

For power users, Director 4 introduced Movie in a Window (MIAW), the capability to open child Director movies in their own window at the same time that the main movie plays. Director 5 offers more support for MIAW during authoring time, so MIAWs can more easily be used as authoring assistants. The Animation Wizard that ships with Director 5 is a good example of this. The Auto-Animate features in previous versions of Director are all available through this separate Director file now. They are available under the Xtras menu. The Animation Wizard acts as a Tool Xtra, but also as a Director movie opened as a Movie in a Window.

Xtras and the MOA have opened the door to a whole new world of powerful features for Director. Those shipping or in the works when Director 5 shipped, include MPEG, custom transitions, QTVR, QT3D, palette manipulation, MIDI, and many more. Chapter 23, "Macromedia Open Architecture: All About Xtras," covers Xtras in more detail.

Presence

Director 5 ships on five platforms: the Standard Macintosh, Power Macintosh, Windows 3.1, Windows 95, and Windows NT. All five operating systems are available for both playback and authoring. Director files are binary-compatible, meaning that the same file opens on both the Macintosh and on Windows. Once the file or set of files is complete and ready to distribute, use the specific platform that you are targeting to create the Director executable, or "projector." For example, you'll need to have Director for Windows and a Windows machine in order to create a Director for Windows projector. The same file or set of files used to create a projector for the Macintosh might be made into a 16-bit or 32-bit Windows projector as well. This is how Macromedia has coined the "Author once, publish anywhere" slogan. No other application on the market provides this binary-compatible authoring solution.

The Player Alternative

If you are new to Director, you might wonder why Director Macintosh movies can't be converted through a playback-only converter for Windows. If you prefer the Windows platform, you might ask the opposite question for the Macintosh. Developers who used Director before version 4 have learned the hard way how painful a playback-only solution can be.

Macromedia (Macromind at the time) released its first version of a Windows player, Director Player for Windows 1.0, in 1991. Prior to that, they worked with Microsoft on the Multimedia Extensions for Windows 3.0. Microsoft's kit included a converter similar to the final Gaffer of Director Player for Windows. It worked with Director Macintosh 2.0 Movies to convert them to Windows Players that could be played back with MCI calls and the MCIMMP.DRV. Microsoft is no longer shipping the converter, nor is the converter compatible with Director for Macintosh version 3.0 or higher.

The first Macromind Windows Player 1.0 worked with Director 2.0 or 3.0 movies on Windows 3.0. Through further incarnations of Director Macintosh and the Windows Player, the final version of Director Player for Windows 3.11 worked with Director for Macintosh 3.1.3. Even though these final versions made the road to Windows that much easier, there were still many battles to overcome. The movies would look perfect on the Macintosh, but horrible on Windows. Palettes would have to be reversed manually, and font-mapping was a nightmare. It could take an extra six months to iron out the details.

Director for Windows

It was not until the release of Director for Windows 4.0 in July 1994 that the Windows world was truly opened to the Director community. Most of the cross-platform conversion issues were handled in the new, authoring version of Director for Windows. If there was anything strange in the movie on Windows movie, you could (and still can) troubleshoot and fix it within the Windows *or* Macintosh environment.

The marketplace for Director Macintosh productions opened up to the much wider Windows market. The future for the multimedia producer was solidified and Windows users found themselves with a mature, easy-to-use, multimedia authoring tool for both markets. Today with Shockwave for Director and Internet authoring, Director movies work on both platforms through the use of Director's binary-compatible file format introduced in Director 4.

The cross-platform development gives teams of Director producers a choice. Content for the Director movies can come from either the Macintosh or Windows, even if their intent is for the other side. Graphic artists and animators might prefer the Macintosh; CAD designers might prefer Windows NT, and the sound composers and programmers can work on whatever platform they prefer. Director brings it all together in one unified file that opens on both platforms. Platform-specific testing and delivery are other steps to take.

The Secret to Cross-Platform Authoring

The secret to cross-platform authoring is this: you need to open and test your production in the target environment from the very beginning of development. Director takes care of almost everything, but the last thing you want is to develop for six months on the Macintosh and at the last minute decide your movie should play on Windows. You might be lucky and have no problems, but why take that chance? Testing your Director production and the famous quotation of Macromedia's John Dowdell: "Test early, test often, test on all of your target machines" is covered in Chapter 22, "Delivering the Goods."

Director for Macintosh and Director for Windows are virtually the same application. The interface is exactly the same, Lingo works exactly the same, and it should not be a big transition. After Director users set up the dual platforms, it is amazingly easy to transfer a file to the other platform, open it and make sure it runs well. Director takes care of almost everything, but there are still some differences.

Taking on a cross-platform project requires learning another operating system. Director needs to be on the platform you distribute to and you need to have an IBM-compatible PC or a Macintosh system. Currently, the Macintosh machines with Soft Windows do not hold up to Director's minimum requirements on the PC. For more information on the system requirements on both platforms, refer to Chapter 3, "Configuration and Working Environment."

An Interview with Two Director Developers

The release of Director for Windows created an interesting time in the Director community. With Director's roots on the Macintosh, many Director developers had to get used to the Windows operating system.

Windows developers new to Director had to get used to Macintosh-centric books and training materials, and a general consensus that the Mac was the platform of choice. Little did everyone know that Director for Windows would take off as well as it did.

Windows experts came on the scene to help many of the Macintosh users along. David Goldsmith and Tab Julius, both volunteer sysops on Macromedia's CompuServe forum, became the resident Windows gurus in the forum. David Goldsmith taught me a lot about the Windows video and sound cards, and informed users which installer programs and sound utilities the Windows world was really using. Tab Julius started his *Lingo Users Journal* and told of his DLLs he wrote that week. David often mentioned his requisite Macintosh in the corner that he used for testing.

The following are some questions and answers from both David and Tab about Director for Windows and Director development.

Why did your company choose Director for its development platform, David?

I did an extensive evaluation of multimedia tools available at the time and found Director to be the most cost-effective solution for JourneyWare Media's multimedia development projects. Director was the only authoring tool that allowed us to develop on both of our target platforms: Windows and Macintosh. With our developers' expertise in Windows, and with 80 percent of our target audience running Windows, we were delighted that Macromedia had come up with a solution that let us develop on Windows and easily port to the Mac.

A key feature for us was the ability to use object-oriented techniques in our development. With Director, we were able to get a good start on building a class library that we can reuse in future projects.

What can you tell me about working cross-platform? How hard was it to go from Windows to the Macintosh?

We had no problem at all. In my opinion, it's essential that you begin authoring on whatever platform the majority of your audience will have. We encountered none of the problems usually associated with Windows multimedia development using Director. And going to Director for Macintosh was easy.

In speaking with Tab Julius, I asked him a few questions, too:

How long have you used Director?

I honestly didn't start using Director until Director for Windows came out, but immediately decided to make it my development system of choice.

What did you do before you used Director?

I'd been doing commercial software for many years, but usually for other people who would hire their own Mac engineers to do the Mac version. However, as my business (Penworks Corporation) started growing, I'd get requests to provide both Windows and Mac versions. See, nowadays many products have both Mac and Windows versions on the same CD, and this perception has taken root that all you do is recompile for one or the other. Obviously it's not so, at least not in C, so when I heard about Director for Windows I became immediately interested.

Why do you like Director?

I like Director because it abstracts me from the gritty details specific to each platform and lets me write programs that run, basically unchanged, on Windows, the Mac, and now the Web. It's hard enough being at the top of the learning curve for just one platform (Windows); there's no way I could be at the top of three platforms. Now, I just try to write good programs and I let Director do the porting for me.

As a C programmer, what do you think about Director?

I was willing to accept Director as my development environment of choice because it is still extensible if I need it. I can still write C code and plug it in if I need to, so effectively I get the best of both worlds.

The initial investment of a cross-platform authoring environment might seem a bit high at first. The long-term rewards are much higher, though, with royalty-free distribution of commercial titles to the entire PC market and a chance for creating a multimedia version of any idea you have. Hybrid CD-ROMs and Internet authoring for both platforms is a short time away. Once you become proficient in Director, your imagination is the only limiting factor.

The Director Community

Director has a great supportive developer community. *Inside Director 5 with Lingo for Macintosh* is actually a book by a whole group of developers wanting to pass along what they've learned about Director to you. If you ever have a question about anything, someone is there to help. Your first course of action is to get online! The Director Internet Mailing list, called Direct-L, has developed into a respected community of high-level Director users. The Director engineers "lurk" this forum to see what people are saying all the time. There also are many Director-specific Web pages created by third-party developers. A list of useful Director Web sites and information on subscribing to Direct-L is in Appendix B, "Hot URLs: Favorite Director Web Sites."

There are Macromedia Users Groups all over the world. A current list of the groups is on http://www.macromedia.com. To contact Macromedia technical support directly, you can access them on their CompuServe and America Online forums, the Microsoft Network, or the phone and fax number provided in Appendix D, "Contacting Macromedia." The online forums publish library files with product updates, sample movies, and techNotes from Macromedia technical support and Macromedia's technical database of information, the KnowledgeBase.

Summary

Macromedia's Web page keeps you up-to-date with all the Macromedia, Director, multimedia, and computer industry trends. As the product information, third-party information, and Shocked sites change, you can find the news first on http://www.macromedia.com.

If you are new to the Director community, welcome. You are definitely not alone. If you've come from an artistic background, you'll feel right at home. If you are a programmer, you'll find Lingo easy to learn and the artistic aspects of Director intuitive. A world of exciting technology and opportunities, with a supportive development community, awaits your artistic genius.

Lee Allis

Introducing Director 5: New Features Overview

Introducing Director 5, the premiere authoring tool for multimedia production and the Internet. This chapter introduces Director's new features, briefly describes each feature, and tells you where to find more information about each feature elsewhere in *Inside Macromedia Director 5 with Lingo for Macintosh*.

Macromedia divides Director 5's numerous new features into four basic categories: power, productivity, performance, and platforms. The following chapter discusses these categories in turn. I hope you enjoy the new release.

Power: New Capabilities

This section describes Director 5's completely new features that add new capability not available in any form in earlier versions. These features and the rest bring Director to new heights as the most powerful authoring tool for multimedia and the Internet.

Rich Text Support and Anti-Aliasing

Director 5 supports importing and creating high-quality anti-aliased text. You can work with both rich text format (RTF) and ASCII text cast members. With rich text, you can create anti-aliased headings, import pages of formatted text, and adjust the text's leading and kerning (see fig. 2.1).

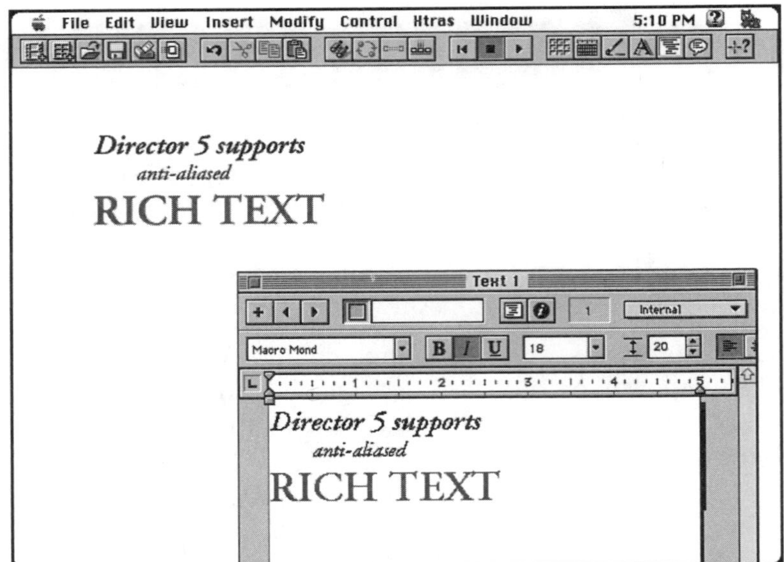

Figure 2.1

Director 5 supports the rich text format (RTF), useful for anti-aliased headings and importing stylized text.

The "Productivity" section later in this chapter discusses Director 5's changes to text editing, and Chapter 11, "Text: The Story," covers using text in Director.

Multiple Casts

You can maintain cast libraries of up to 32,000 cast members each by using multiple casts. Multiple casts enable you to organize large projects by making casts of different types, and new Lingo terms for working with multiple casts let you manipulate multiple casts in the Score (see fig. 2.2).

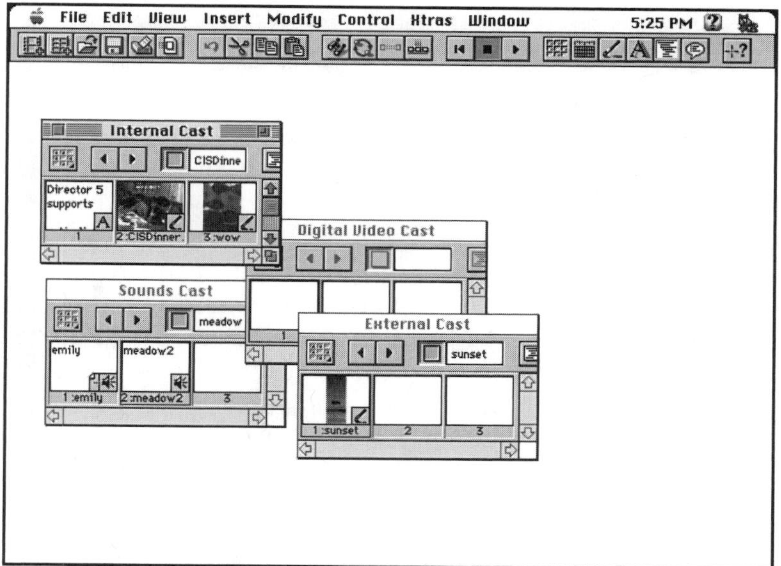

Figure 2.2

Multiple casts allow for better organization of a movie's cast, the capability to switch movie casts on the fly, and share cast members between movies.

You can store casts internally or externally, as well as linked or unlinked. When linked to the Director file, you can share external casts across movies—similar to how shared casts work in Director 4.0.4. Multiple casts enable groups of Director developers working on the same project to divide work easily into separate casts and then integrate them later. It also would enable localization teams to create one version of a Director project and then swap the cast depending on the language of the target country. Multiple casts will eliminate reworking the core of the project for each language.

Chapter 8, "New in Director 5: Multiple Casts," covers multiple casts in-depth.

True Color Support on 32-Bit Windows

Director 5 for Windows supports true color, which means that when you author on the Windows 95 or Windows NT platforms, you now can edit in the Paint window at a color depth higher than 8-bit. You also can display 16- or 24-bit true color images on the stage, greatly simplifying color management. For a Macintosh developer, this also is a breakthrough for cross-platform development.

> While working in Windows 3.1, editing in Director's Paint window and images on the stage are restricted to 256 colors.

Onion Skinning

Artists now can create cel animations more easily in Director's Paint window using the new Onion Skinning tool. Onion skinning takes its name from the traditional animation technique of using thin "onion skin" paper to create movie animations. Just as a stack of thin onion skin paper in traditional hand-drawn animation enables other pages of the animation to show through, Director's Paint window can display cast members before and after the one being created as exact reference points.

In figure 2.3, you can see that the tree is being displayed in the Paint window as the artist creates the snake winding it's way around it.

You no longer need to cycle through cast members to view your animation, nor do you need to place them on the stage for precise positioning. Onion skinning enables you to view the background artwork and draw your characters to scale. You no longer have to guess the outcome or flip through cast members when using certain ink effects, such as Reveal. You can now use the Reveal ink effect to see the preceding cast member and bring out only a certain part of it in the new bitmap. The applications are countless.

Chapter 10, "Paint Window Enhancements," covers onion skinning and the other Paint window enhancements.

Figure 2.3

The Onion Skinning tool allows for cel animation without leaving Director's Paint window.

Photoshop-Compatible Filter Support

Photoshop-compatible filter support in Director's Paint and Cast windows enables you to apply special effects to bitmaps without switching tools. You can now touch up your images and apply powerful effects to parts of the images or the entire images.

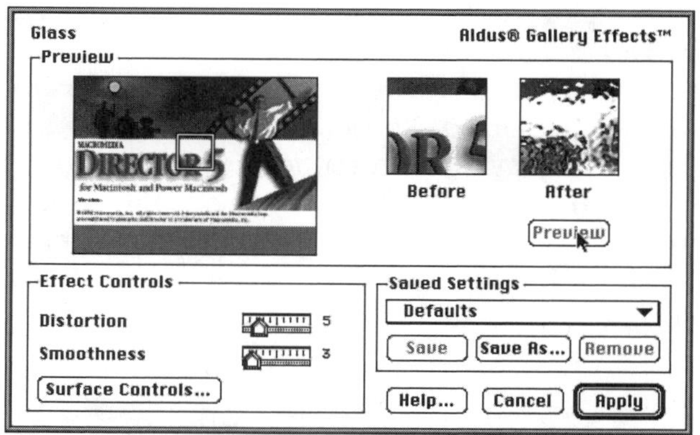

Figure 2.4

Photoshop-compatible filter support in Director 5, enabled by the Macromedia Open Architecture (MOA).

Depending on the filter you use, Director lets you use the Auto Filter command to create a series of new cast members. Auto Filter enables you to create a tweened effect over the series of cast members, yielding an animated effect.

Chapter 10, "Paint Window Enhancements," covers Photoshop-compatible filter support in detail.

IMA-Compressed Sound Support

Director 5 for Macintosh and Windows can work with IMA-compressed sounds. Macromedia's SoundEdit 16 version 2 supports creating IMA-compressed sounds for the Macintosh and Windows, a breakthrough for 16-bit sound compression that significantly changes the way you use sound in Director.

The "Productivity" section later in this chapter covers integrating Director 5 and SoundEdit 16. Chapter 12, "Sound: The Soundtrack," covers using sound in Director.

Digital Video Compositing on Windows

You can turn the `Direct to Stage` property of a digital video sprite on and off in Director for Windows. Turning Direct to Stage off enables you to use Director's Score ink effects and composite digital video on the stage. In the previous Director for Windows versions, Direct to Stage was always enabled. You might want to keep Direct to Stage enabled, as it then plays directly to the screen buffer, atop all the other Score channels. The audio and video of the digital video will synchronize more accurately this way. Disabling Direct to Stage might slow down the video, but will allow for non-rectangular animations via digital video.

> The capability to disable Direct to Stage in Director 5 for Windows is only available for Audio Video Interleaved (AVI) files and not QuickTime for Windows (MOV) files—at this time. As QuickTime for Windows changes, this capability may be enabled for use in Director.

Chapter 14, "Digital Video: The Movie within the Movie," covers using digital video in Director 5.

Powerful New Lingo Features

Director 5 introduces many new Lingo terms, including new families of terms for new Director capabilities. A complete list of all the new terms by category is included in Appendix C, "New Lingo Terms in Director 5."

Scriptable Authoring

New Lingo functionality has been added to Director 5 to enable score generation. You can add and delete new frames, cast members, and sprites. You also can edit and store frame and sprite properties programmatically rather than manually setting them up in the Score. Almost everything you can do during authoring mode now is available in Lingo.

A good example of score generation is the Animation Wizard that ships with Director 5 (see fig. 2.5).

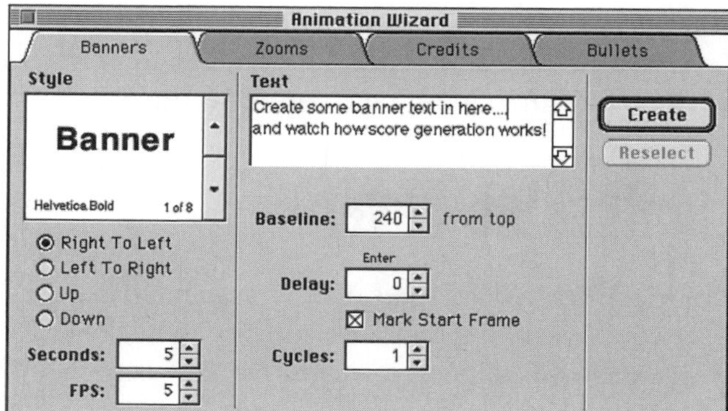

Figure 2.5

The Animation Wizard uses score generation to create new frames in the score.

The Animation Wizard generates new text sprites and score information given the instructions the user provides. To access the Animation Wizard, select it from the Xtras menu. To view the scripts of the Animation Wizard, open the animation wizard movie within Director; it resides in the Director application's Xtras folder.

You can use Lingo's `new` command to create new cast members in Director 5. Scriptable authoring enables you to define and change cast members of all types, their content, and their properties on the fly. This new feature adds even more power to Director's dynamic run-time environment.

Chapters 19, "Advanced Concepts," and 20, "Object-Oriented Programming," cover advanced Lingo concepts.

QuickTime Track Control

Lingo can now turn on and off extra tracks stored internally to a QuickTime movie. This capability enables dynamic control of QuickTime audio and video track playback from a single file. In the past you would have to use multiple iterations of the same QuickTime file.

A good example of who would use QuickTime track control offers would be a company that localizes Director titles. In the past, such a company would need to distribute a French, German, and Japanese version of the QuickTime file for each of those target markets, whereas now it could use one QuickTime file and use Lingo to control which of the different audio and video tracks play.

Chapter 14, "Digital Video: The Movie within the Movie," covers using digital video in Director. Appendix C, "New Lingo Terms in Director 5," covers the new QuickTime track control terms.

Built-In Desktop Cover

Director for Macintosh developers no longer need to use an XObject to cover the area outside of the stage area during playback. The Macintosh Projector Options dialog box now offers a Full Screen option. This capability was only available on Windows in previous versions of Director. When you select the Full Screen option, Director covers the desktop area behind the stage with whatever color to which the stage is set in frame 1. If you'd like a black background, you can set the stage color to black in the Movie Properties dialog box or you can use Lingo to set the color.

> To view the Full Screen option on the Macintosh without making a projector, press Shift+Return. On Windows, you will need to select the Full Screen option in the Projector options dialog in order to preview this effect.

The Full Screen feature will save developers hours, especially those unfamiliar with XObjects. Chapter 22, "Delivering the Goods," covers projector options and delivering a Director project.

Shockwave Integration

Shockwave for Director has changed the face of the Web by enabling interactive, multimedia Director movies to play on the Internet. Director 5 will soon support the launch of the AfterBurner compressor from within its Xtras menu for automatic World Wide Web creation.

> By the time you read this book, Shockwave for Director 5 should be available at http://www.macromedia.com.

You currently can play back Shockwave movies with Netscape Navigator on Macintosh and Windows but soon should be able to do so as well on the Microsoft Internet Explorer, Microsoft Network, SGI WebForce, and CompuServe. For the latest information on Shockwave versions and playback opportunities, stay tuned to Macromedia's Web page (http://www.macromedia.com).

Appendix A, "Director on the Internet: Shockwave!" features the Shockwave technology.

Xtras and the Macromedia Open Architecture

Xtras are the third-party plug-in applications that take advantage of the Macromedia Open Architecture (MOA). Xtras in Director's Xtras folder appear as menu items in Director 5 and offer specialized functionality not currently available in the Director. Many Xtras are available across multiple Macromedia applications. You could, for example, use the same transition Xtra within Director and Authorware.

Four kinds of Xtras are available in Director 5: Sprite Xtras, Transition Xtras, Lingo Xtras, and Tools Xtras. Current Xtras capabilities include MPEG, QuickDraw 3D support, MIDI control, custom transitions, printing enhancements, database connectivity, and more.

The Director Xtra Development Kit (XDK) ships with Director for Macintosh and Director for Windows. It contains all the files, documentation, and samples you need to begin developing Xtras (providing you're familiar with C or C++ programming languages).

Chapter 23, "Macromedia Open Architecture: All About Xtras," covers the Macromedia Open Architecture and Xtras.

Productivity: Ease-of-Use Enhancements

Director productions can take from weeks up to months to develop and often require coordinating the efforts of many people. Director 5 introduces many new features to enhance productivity, facilitating each step of the way, especially for development teams.

Macromedia User Interface (MUI)

The first thing you notice after you launch Director 5 is the new Macromedia User Interface (MUI). MUI defines a common look and behavior that Macromedia plans for all of its products to eventually share. Other tools that currently ship with the MUI include Macromedia SoundEdit 16 2 and Macromedia xRes 2. The intended purpose of the MUI is to make switching between Macromedia applications easier for creative professionals, so they don't have to adjust to a completely different environment when using a studio of tools.

Many of the following new features in this section stem from the MUI. Other features relate to how Director works with other programs. It also includes several new ease-of-use enhancements within the traditional Director framework.

The Toolbar

The main Toolbar in Director 5 provides fast access to commonly used commands in menus and dialogs (see fig. 2.6).

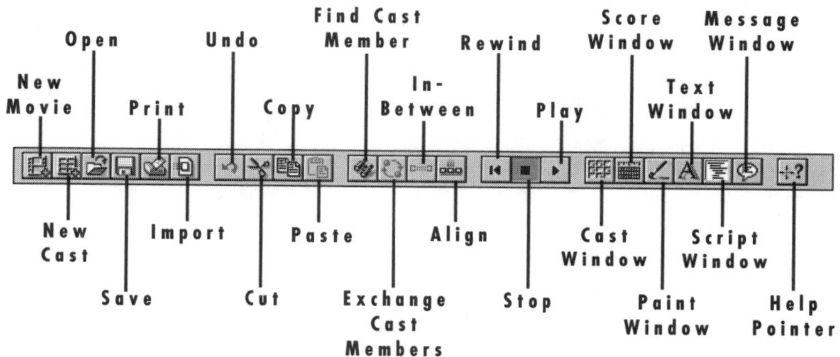

Figure 2.6

The Director 5 Toolbar.

If you cannot see the Toolbar beneath the main Director menus, make sure it's enabled in the Window menu.

You now can execute many File and Edit menu commands; perform common score routines; rewind, stop, and play the movie; and open the most important Director windows, simply by clicking on a button. The most useful button in the Director 5 Toolbar is the Help button, on the far right.

Online Help

The online Help system in Director 5 is one of its best new features. If you ever have a question about Director, click on the Help button and search for the topic you have in mind (see fig. 2.7).

Director 5's Help system has been enhanced tremendously over previous versions. It includes context-sensitive definitions for every tool, descriptions of how to work everything in Director, and FAQs about Director and Macromedia.

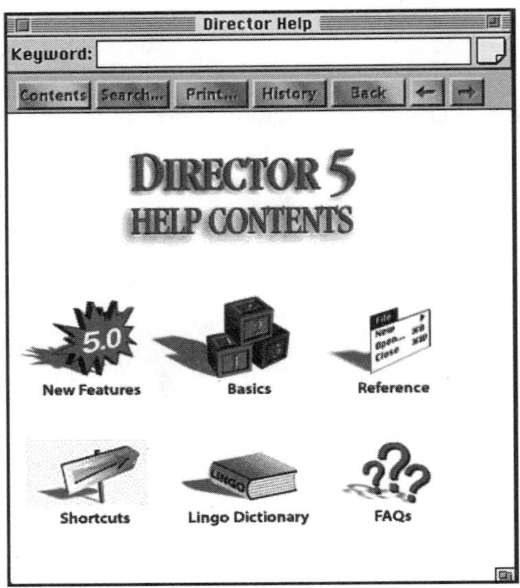

Figure 2.7

The main screen of the Director 5 Help system.

For an example of Help's helpful power, try the following:

1. Open the Message window from the Window menu and type `member`.
2. Select the text you typed and click on the Help button in the toolbar. The Help system automatically launches the definition of "member," the new way to refer to a cast member with Lingo in Director 5.

If you search under the word "Lingo" in the Help system, Director's Help system provides you with Lingo concepts, and categorizes each Lingo term alphabetically and by functionality. You can create bookmarks in Help, copy a sample script and paste it into Director, print topics, and more. The Macromedia instructional media department deserves a round of applause for this new feature.

Tooltips

Tooltips are a new feature of the MUI, helpful for new and old users alike. If you have the Show Tooltips box enabled, which it is by default, in Director 5's General Preferences dialog box, the name of each tool pops up when you hold your cursor over it (see fig. 2.8).

General Preferences

Stage Size: Use Movie Settings
Match Current Movie
Center
Reset Monitor to Movie's Color Depth
Animate in Background
User Interface: Classic Look (Monochrome)
Dialogs Appear at Mouse Position
Save Window Positions On Quit
Message Window Recompiles Scripts
Show Tooltips
Text Units: Inches
Memory: Use System Temporary Memory
OK
Cancel
Help

Figure 2.8

You can enable Tooltips in the General Preferences dialog box.

Tooltips are helpful for new Director users for getting to know the tools and for experienced Director users for getting to know what's new and where to find familiar commands.

Window Enhancements

Almost every window in Director 5 contains new features, a toolbar, and a new way to execute old routines. The Message window is one good example (see fig. 2.9).

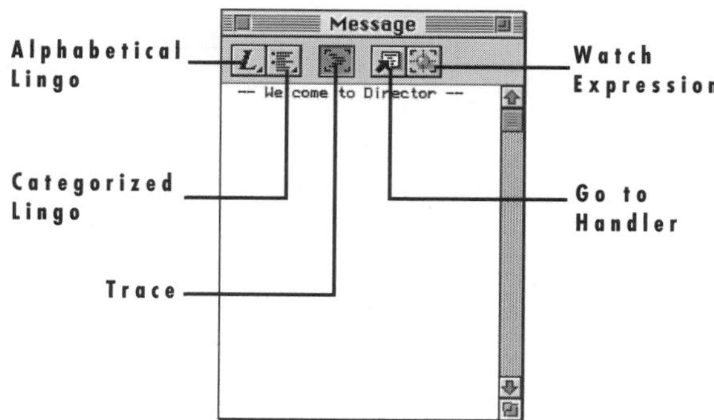

Figure 2.9

The Message window in Director 5.

The new Message window has its own toolbar, with pop-up Lingo menus and built-in debugging tools. If you're looking for the Message window's Trace control, you can find it on the toolbar, three tools from the left.

To make sure you can view and access a given window's toolbar, you need first have the window selected. Then, enable the toolbar option in the View menu for that particular window.

Script Windows Enhancement

Director 5's Script window offers many new enhancements for speeding up the creation and management of your Lingo code. A new pop-up of all the handlers in your movie is available, as well as Lingo pull-down menus for all Lingo terms (alphabetically and by category). You can comment and uncomment your scripts in the Script window toolbar. The Toggle Break points and Watch Expression buttons work with the new Debugger and Watcher windows. And the lightning bolt button enables you to recompile all your scripts (see fig. 2.10).

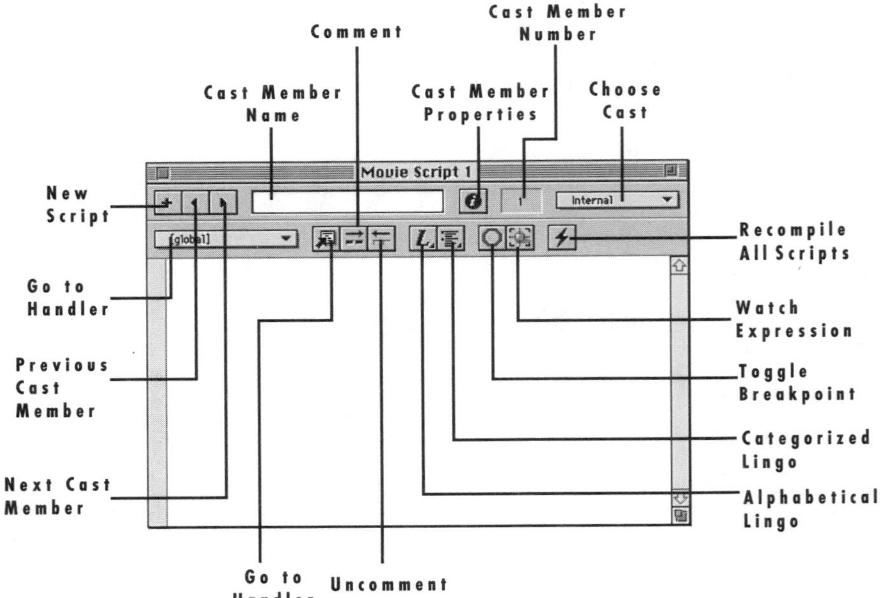

Figure 2.10
Director 5's Script window has many new enhancements.

You can set break points in a script by clicking in the Script window sidebar, in the gray area to the left of the script. To access help on a certain term, you can highlight a Lingo term or expression in your script and click on the Help button to have Help open the definition and furnish a syntax example for that term.

Part 4, "Lingo," contains the Lingo-specific chapters.

Paint Window Enhancements

The Paint window has a new face and the effects are in the Paint window toolbar. You can apply effects to graphics without using pull-down menus and quickly repeat and undo the changes as you like (see fig. 2.11).

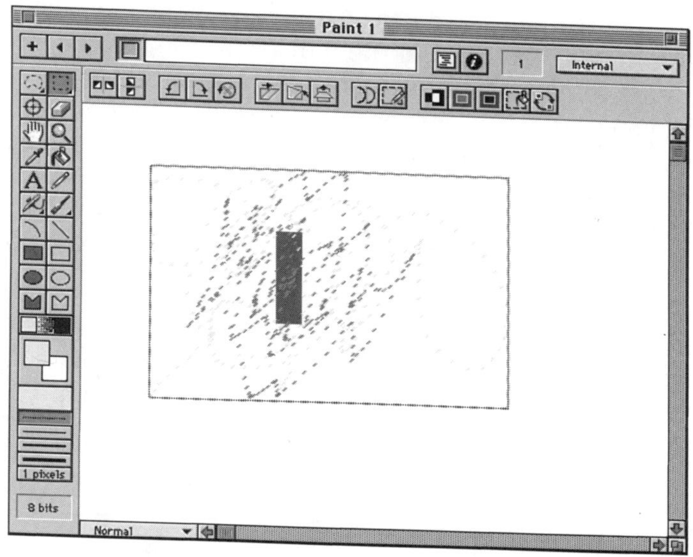

Figure 2.11

Director 5's Paint window.

The Paint window displays the cast of which the active bitmap is a member in the top right corner. When you create a new bitmap in the Paint window, Director automatically places that cast member in the internal cast. To place the bitmap in a cast other than the internal cast, make another cast and make it active in the Paint window pop-up menu.

You can edit at any color depth in the Paint window in Director for the Macintosh and Windows, regardless of the color depth to which your monitor is set.

Notice that the Paint window ink modes have moved to the bottom of the Paint window.

Chapter 9, "Graphics: The Visuals," covers using graphics in Director, and Chapter 10, "Paint Window Enhancements," covers the new Paint window features.

Keyboard Shortcuts

Keyboard shortcuts are always fun to discuss with a new release of a software product. The good news is that if you're confused about any of the shortcuts, you can use the buttons in the various toolbars to perform the commands until you're used to the new keyboard combinations. Veteran users will once again have to relearn some commands, particularly those who routinely used the keyboard to rewind and play the movie. You will now also need to press the Option key more often. These keyboard combinations are part of the MUI, and you'll become familiar with them as you work across Macromedia applications.

You might be happy to know that some of the keyboard commands are the same. You can still use Command+4 for Score and the basic window commands. Some of the keyboard shortcut changes that could trick you at first, however, include Rewind, Play, Print, and Import (see the following table).

Command	Director 4.0.4	Director 5
Rewind	Command+R	Command+Option+R
Play	Command+P	Command+Option+P
Print	Nothing	Command+P
Import	Command+J	Command+R

For a list of all of the new keyboard commands, look in Director 5's online help. Typing **`keyboard shortcuts`** into the search field brings up the 13 sections available for different keyboard accelerators. If you would like a printed list, you can print them from the help system.

As always, the numeric keypad, Option, Control, and Command keys hold specific keyboard acceleration features. These are outlined on the back cover of the *Learning Director* manual that ships with Director 5.

Shortcut Menus

Get ready for quicker access to information in Director 5. Director 5 offers shortcut menus for almost everything on the stage and the interface. To access a shortcut menu for a sprite, Control-click on a sprite on the stage. If you Control-click on the stage itself, you'll access the movie shortcut menu. Control-click on a cast member will access the shortcut menu for that cast member, and so on. You can access a number of commonly used commands for any object directly from the user interface by using a keyboard shortcut.

NOTE

> In Windows, you can access the shortcut menus by right-clicking on an object.

This new functionality definitely enhances productivity and shortens the development time of the Director production.

Recent Files List

Director offers access to the four most recent movies as options on the File menu, like other standard applications—it was a highly requested feature in previous versions of Director. You still can have only one movie open at a time, but you can easily open recently used movies more easily, directly from the File menu.

Long Filename Support on 32-Bit Windows

Director supports long file names on Windows 95 and Windows NT, so you can name your files descriptively on 32-bit Windows and the Macintosh. Windows 3.1 is limited to the DOS 8.3 file format—the name can consist of eight numbers, letters, or an underscore, followed by the extension DIR. So if your Director for Macintosh movie will eventually be played back on Windows 3.1, you will still need to conform to the 8.3 DOS standard. If you are authoring for 32-bit Windows only, you can enjoy long, descriptive filename support.

Preferences and Properties

The Macromedia User Interface (MUI) has changed the way Director sets up its preferences and properties for all the objects in a movie. The following sections provide a brief description of the changes.

Four Preferences Windows

Director 5 has four Preferences windows, located under the File menu. These include the General, Score, Cast, and Paint window preferences. These four Preferences windows have replaced the Preferences and Movie Info dialog box available in Director 4.0.4. Figure 2.12 shows the General Preferences dialog box.

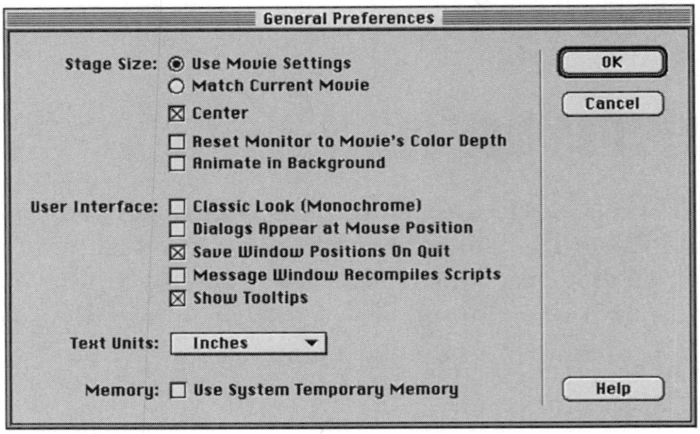

Figure 2.12

The General Preferences is one of the four new Preferences dialog boxes in Director 5.

Look at each of the dialog boxes to view all of the settings available. Chapter 4, "Working with Director: Understanding the Metaphor," as well as Director 5's Help, offers some tips on using these new dialog boxes.

Properties

Every object in Director has properties that you can edit during authoring mode. You can access the Properties window for any object from Director 5's new Modify menu. You can also Control-click (on the Macintosh) or right-click (in Windows) on any object to access its shortcut menus and properties. You can open the cast member properties, sprite properties, or movie properties dialog boxes, depending on the object you select.

Director 4.0.4 developers might be surprised to find the Movie Properties dialog box under the Modify menu instead of the File menu as it used to be. The movie is an object that has properties you can modify, so those settings have moved to the Modify menu, where you now set up your stage size, stage location, and stage color.

The Insert Menu

The new Insert menu offers a fast, convenient way to insert objects into your Director movie. It automates frame insertion, media elements, control items, and film loops. As new member types are supported by added Xtras, you also will find them in the Insert menu.

Import Enhancements

Importing media elements into Director has changed drastically. Director 5 sports an entirely new Import dialog box, with a keyboard shortcut of Command+R instead of Command+J, along with many new capabilities. Figure 2.13 shows the new Import dialog box.

Drag-and-Drop Import

Drag-and-drop import is new in Director for Macintosh and Director for Windows. You can drag and drop cast members directly from the desktop to the Cast window.

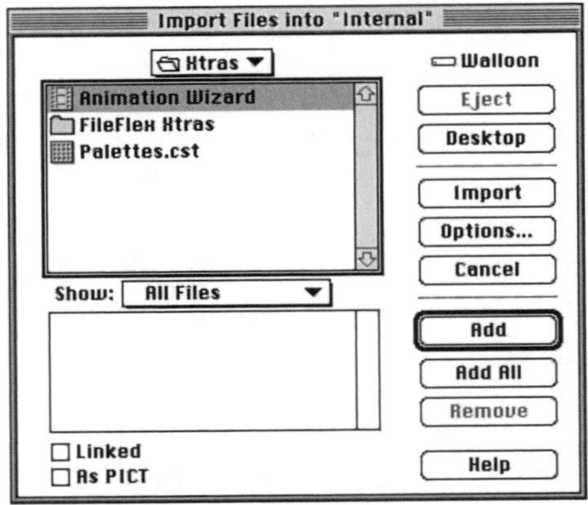

Figure 2.13

Director 5's import capabilities have been enhanced considerably.

Importing Text

Text can now be imported into Director 5 in the rich text format (RTF). To bring ASCII text into Director 5, you can copy and paste the text from the Clipboard—similar to the procedure in previous versions of Director. *Text cast members* refer to rich text cast members in Director 5. ASCII text fields of Director 4.0.4 and earlier are referred to as "Fields." Chapter 11, "Text: The Story," describes the differences between the two types of text.

Multiple Media Type Import

You can import multiple cast members of different types in a single operation. You can add a digital video, three text cast members, some sounds, and some graphics to the list and import them all at the same time. These groups of cast members no longer need to be in a folder for multiple-item import.

Import at Different Color Depth

Director no longer dithers bitmaps to the active color depth of the monitor when you import them. Rather, it prompts you to see what you want to do and offers the capability to import bitmaps at different color depths at the same time.

Text Editing Enhancements

Director 5 offers a variety of new ways to create and edit text. You no longer need to create text externally and import it as a bitmap to get high-quality results. Now you can import and create a rich text cast member within Director. The text fields of Director 4.0.4 and earlier now use the new Field window, and remain for Lingo accessibility and run-time editing.

Text Inspector

The new Text Inspector is a floating palette that you can use to edit any text on the stage, be it rich text or ASCII field text (see fig. 2.14).

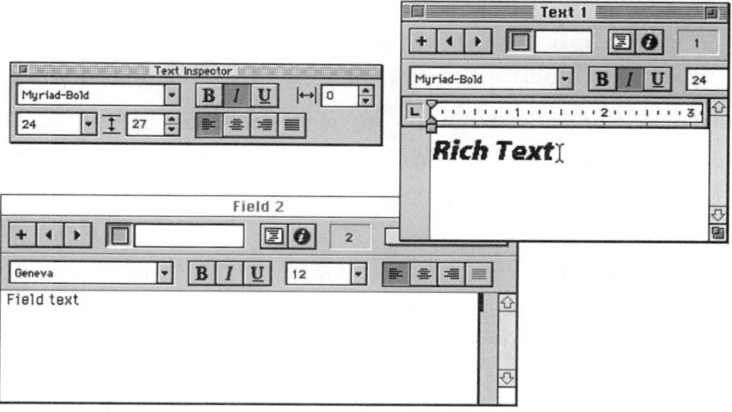

Figure 2.14
The Text Inspector will edit both field and rich text.

If the text is rich text, the Text Inspector lets you adjust the kerning and line spacing, two popular feature requests from users of previous versions.

Font Dialog Box

You now can use a specific dialog box to apply font settings by selecting the Font submenu from the Modify menu (see fig. 2.15).

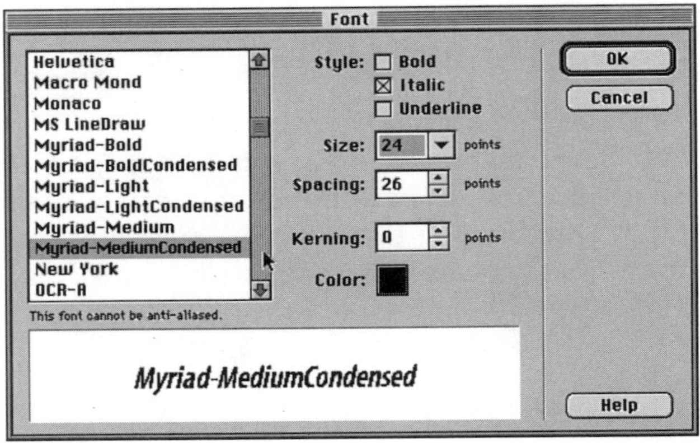

Figure 2.15

The Font dialog box enables you to preview fonts and set their style, as well as see whether they may be anti-aliased.

The Font dialog box replaces Director 4.0.4's text pull-down menus. If you select text on the stage, you can open the Font dialog box from the Modify menu to set the font's style, size, and color here and preview it. The preview option saves time and the need for accessing menu items repeatedly, like in previous versions of Director.

The Font dialog box also can help you use Director 5's new anti-aliasing feature. When you select a font in the Font dialog box, Director indicates whether that font, with the style you select, can be anti-aliased.

If a font may be anti-aliased, Director states, "This is an outline font." If the font may not be anti-aliased, Director states, "This font cannot be anti-aliased," as shown in preceding figure. You must have an outline version of the font installed on your system before you can anti-alias it.

Paragraph Dialog Box

A new Paragraph Formatting window also is available to enable you to adjust the margins and paragraph attributes of rich text cast members.

Chapter 11, "Text: The Story," covers text in more detail.

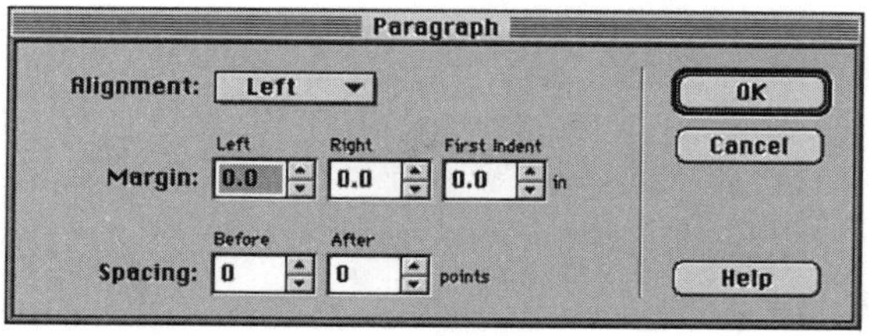

Figure 2.16

The Paragraph dialog box enables greater control over editing rich text cast members.

SoundEdit 16 Integration

Director 5 launches SoundEdit 16 from the Cast window on the Macintosh when you double-click on a sound cast member. Director also automatically updates any changes you make to the sound.

OLE Support for Windows

Director for Windows now supports OLE during authoring mode so you can dynamically update data from other OLE-compatible applications before distributing the movie. This will save time in merging data from Microsoft Excel spreadsheets and graphs, for example, into Director where you can update the data at a later time.

Grids on Stage

Grids on the stage are available to help decrease the time you spend in Director on stage layout work. You can find the Grid settings from the View menu (see fig. 2.17).

You can change the color and spacing of the grid, as well as determine whether it consists of dots or lines. You can toggle the grids—as well as the snap-to-grid feature—on or off.

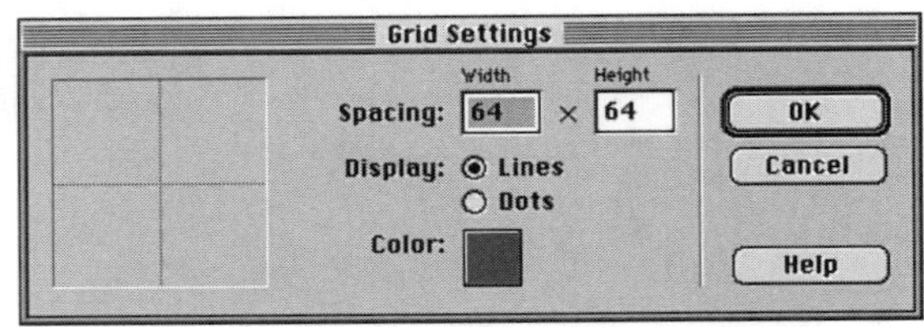

Figure 2.17

Grids decrease the time you spend laying out objects on the Director stage.

Align Dialog Box

The Align dialog box saves Director authors hours of work in laying out sprites on the stage. To open the Alignment dialog box, choose the Align command from the Modify menu or click on the Align button on the main Toolbar (see fig. 2.18).

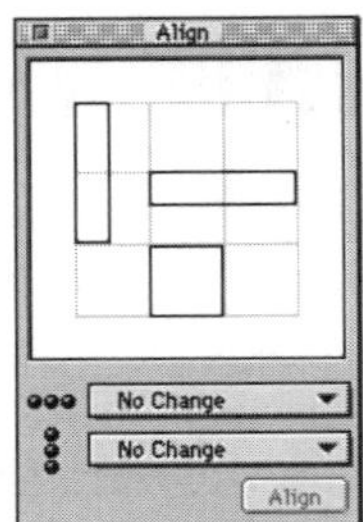

Figure 2.18

The Align dialog box helps align sprites on the stage both horizontally and vertically, without the need to adjust the sprite properties manually.

When you select multiple sprites on the stage, you can hold down the Control key and access the Alignment palette from the shortcut menu. You can quickly update the sprites' positions relative to one another and keep the Alignment palette open for further changes.

Lingo Case Statements

Case statements are a new way to structure Lingo logic in a more readable way. You can create multiple branching case statements rather than deeply nested if-then-else structures as an easier way to specify control flow.

Debugging Tools

Lingo programmers now have the kind of debugging tools similar to Integrated Development Environment (IDE) available for conventional programming languages. Director 5 introduces the Debugger window and the Watcher window to work with the Message window for troubleshooting Lingo code Director movies.

The Debugger window enables you to step through your Lingo code. The Debugger window works with the Script window to run through lines of code, stop at break points, examine parameters and variables, and monitor how the scripts execute (see fig. 2.19).

The Watcher window enables you to view variables or expressions as the movie progresses (see fig. 2.20).

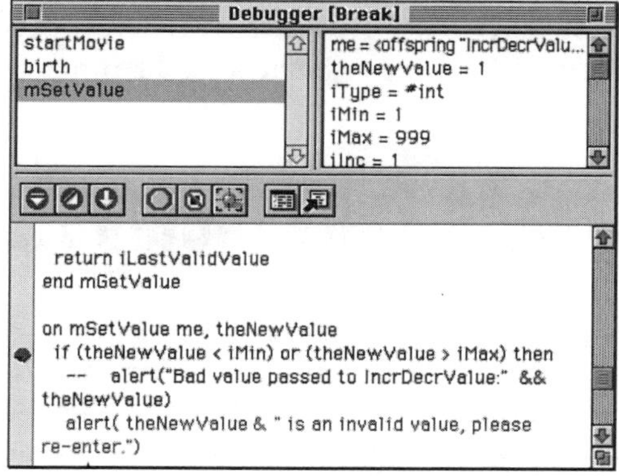

Figure 2.19

The Debugger window enables you to step through your Lingo code, like utilities available in conventional scripting languages.

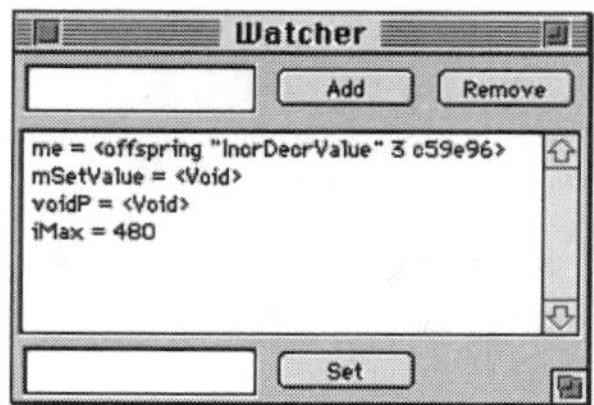

Figure 2.20

The Watcher window watches any variable or expression as the Director movie progresses.

The Watch Expression button is available in the Script window, the Debugger window, and the Message window to add new expressions to the Watcher window list from all three windows.

Part 4, "Lingo," covers the debugging tools.

Batch Processing

Director 5 enables batch processing of updating movies, meaning you can update complete projects while keeping folder and linking relationships intact. You can update an entire CD-ROM project using just one command.

When protecting movies, this feature works the same. For those who are unfamiliar with this feature, protected movies are made uneditable, and their size is reduced by stripping out cast member thumbnail images and script text. The Director file, when protected, is given an extension of DCR and can only be accessed from a projector.

Performance Enhancements

With each new version of Director, the engineers work to enhance Director's performance. An experienced Director developer knows, however, that to take advantage of Director's speed you must learn how to use it well. The movie's performance deals considerably with how you use the tool. *Inside Director* will help you learn that using Director and Lingo's memory management tools along with the enhanced internal memory manager of Director is the key.

New Lingo: Memory Management Terms

Director 5 offers new Lingo terms to help manage memory and determine what happens behind the scenes as the movie plays. Memory management has been improved with the new Lingo commands that define how cast members are loaded into memory. The interval and duration of these memory loads may now be set to virtually eliminate animation discontinuities. Background loading of animations is available, because you can define how you use the processor idle time between frames.

New `preload` and `unload` commands offer support for loading full casts and movies into memory, which will help make smoother transitions between scenes.

Chapter 17, "Managing Your Data," covers memory management with Lingo, and Appendix C, "New Lingo Terms in Director 5," covers the new Lingo elements.

Platforms

The following section discusses the authoring and playback platforms for Director 5. This is a small, but important section, setting Director apart from all of its competitors.

Authoring Platforms

Don't take this final section lightly. Director 5 ships concurrently—for the first time—on five platforms: Power Macintosh, Standard Macintosh, Windows 95, Windows 3.1, and Windows NT. In addition to shipping in English, Director also ships in three localized languages: French, German, and Japanese. The Quality Assurance engineers who had to test each feature on every platform deserve a huge round of applause!

Director 5 for Windows is 32-bit native for Windows 95 and Windows NT. Director is Windows 95-compliant and projectors made using Director for Windows are eligible for the Windows 95 logo. The complete information on the Microsoft certification can be found on Macromedia's Web page at http://www.macromedia.com.

Playback Platforms

The playback list of platforms available for Director expands constantly. You can author on one of the five previously mentioned platforms, and you can make that file into an executable to play back on those five platforms and more. This is the basis of Macromedia's

"Author Once, Publish Anywhere" statement. You should understand, however, that you can author your movie once on whatever platform you want, but you need to use Director on the platform to which you intend to deliver before you can create the executable.

Shockwave for Director on the Internet currently is the most exciting additional playback platform for Director. Right now, you can view Director for Macintosh or Windows movies using the Netscape Navigator 2 browser. Other technologies underway from Macromedia include: CD+, OS/2, OS/9, the Microsoft Internet Explorer, Microsoft Network, SGI WebForce, and CompuServe.

Stay tuned to Macromedia's Web site for the latest developments.

Summary

If you're new to Director, you should enjoy a complete, powerful, multimedia authoring tool. If you've used Director before, welcome to Director 5 and all its new features. Either way, *Inside Macromedia Director 5 with Lingo for Macintosh* will help you take advantage of this powerful new release.

Lee Allis

Configuration and Working Environment

Your system for authoring in Director most likely differs from your audience's system. You need to think about both systems: the system on which you'd like to work and the minimum system necessary for running your production. Ideally, you want the best system you can afford, as well as systems similar to those for which you author.

The Authoring System

Deciding on the authoring machine depends on your priorities and budget. Because Director and the multimedia applications you will use along with Director require the most of your system resources, the better system you can afford, the easier your job will be.

Minimum Requirements

The following are the minimum system requirements for a Director authoring system on both the Macintosh and Windows, as defined by Macromedia.

Director 5 for Macintosh:

- ◆ 68040 processor or faster, including PowerBook, AV, and PowerPC
- ◆ System Software version 7.1 or higher
- ◆ Minimum 8 MB of RAM or more
- ◆ 40 MB available hard disk space

Director 5 for Windows:

- ◆ 486/66 or faster with 8-bit or higher video
- ◆ Windows 95, 3.1, 3.11, NT 3.5.1, or higher
- ◆ 8 MB of RAM
- ◆ Hard disk with 40 MB free disk space

These are the baseline requirements. You can enhance your system in many ways to make working in Director that much easier.

Recommended Enhancements for Macintosh

Working with Director under the minimum system requirements will work, but might be somewhat painful. Again, these are minimums set by Macromedia to *run* Director only. As Director works with files from any other application, you often have more than one application open at a time. If Director finds itself in a low-memory situation, it quits gracefully, but it certainly lets you know. While playing a movie, Director either warns you that you've used all of its system resources or simply purges cast members from memory and doesn't play them. The following sections discuss the recommended system enhancements that make working with Director easier.

RAM

The more physical (real) RAM you have on the system, the better. Unfortunately, this is the most expensive component to buy. You quickly learn that performance in Director derives directly from the amount of RAM allocated to the application and how the system uses its RAM.

A realistic *minimum* RAM is 16 MB for a reasonably friendly authoring environment. You really want more if you want to run Director, Photoshop, and other editing tools at the same time. Some development systems have as much as 100 MB of RAM.

CPU Speed

Processor speeds increase all the time. The faster the CPU, in conjunction with RAM, the faster you can work in Director. A Power Macintosh processor would be an excellent choice.

Recommended Enhancements for Windows

If you're doing cross-platform development, you need to use Director for Windows and a Windows machine. Director for Windows doesn't run on SoftWindows on the Macintosh. Although this could change in the future, the current version of SoftWindows emulates a 286 Windows processor, whereas authoring in Director for Windows requires at least a 486 Windows processor.

The same applies to your Windows system: the better your machine, the easier you can work in Director. If you do most of your work on the Macintosh and simply test on Windows as you go along, your Windows machine should match your target machine as closely as possible. Again, this means you realistically need to have a system that supersedes the suggested minimums.

Your Testing Environment

You can save Director files, or movies, as self-running executables, called projectors. You might be creating a full-blown software package for distribution. Your audience might eventually include all the Macintoshes and IBM-compatible machines on the market. If you have such intentions for this product, you need to do a great deal of testing.

Operating Systems

Director 5 on the Macintosh and Windows supports five platforms: 68 KB Macintosh, Power Macintosh, Windows 3.1, Windows 95, and Windows NT 3.51. If you intend to access each of these markets, you need to test on each one of these platforms. You might even want to test for differences between Windows 3.1 and 3.11.

If you have friends giving away their old Macintosh or Windows machines, find out if they will give the machines to you. I recommend collecting as many systems as possible for testing. For example, if you are authoring for the Macintosh market, you'll need to test your production on both a PowerPC and 68K machine. On Windows, you'll want to test on a 386, 486, and Pentium, if they are all within your market.

System Software and QuickTime

When you work with Director, you want to keep up with the goings-on at Apple and Microsoft. New versions of the system software will affect your Director movie and the media elements it contains. Be sure to test your Director movie with the latest version of the system software and Sound Manager. Start collecting versions of QuickTime and the Sound Manager from Apple for testing with your Director movie. Apple frequently releases new versions of QuickTime.

Director ships with the most current version of QuickTime available at the time it is released. Director 5 was tested and ships with version 2.1 of QuickTime on both Macintosh and Windows. Macromedia and Apple work closely together, but idiosyncrasies usually crop up with each new release. To ensure that the product you're creating is compatible with the latest version of QuickTime, you'll need to stay in contact with Apple for the latest update information.

Chapter 22, "Delivering the Goods," covers distributing QuickTime and contacting Apple and Microsoft.

Windows Video and Sound Systems

Before you distribute your Director projector on Windows, it would be best if you and your beta testers test it with a number of video and sound cards. As a minimum, you will need to test your projector under the Microsoft standard driver set: Standard VGA (640×480×256) and VGA (16-color) drivers. These and many third-party video card drivers ship on the Windows 95 CD-ROM. For the latest versions of specific vendor's drivers, you will want to contact the sound or video card manufacturer directly.

Macromedia publishes a list of tested and recommended video and sound cards that it has tested with Director. You can find it on the Director 5 for Windows CD-ROM. You should test most popular systems. Many people take their final titles to testing houses, or even a local computer store to test on the different systems. Chapter 22, "Delivering the Goods," contains more information on distributing your Director production.

Complementary Software

Director productions usually are created by teams of people. Your team might include graphics artists, programmers, a producer, a videographer, a photographer, and more. The artists might prefer a certain favorite tool on the Macintosh or Windows machine, and Director can accept media from almost every tool. Director is where it all comes together: integrating the media, and putting it all together for final distribution.

Director does contain media creation tools, but a specialized software package often works better for creating content for your movie. Much of the content brought into Director production comes from external creation and editing tools. This is the basis for Macromedia's new product strategy.

Macromedia's Strategy

Macromedia has designed a new product strategy around the studio approach to multimedia development. They offer three studio bundles: the Director Multimedia Studio, the FreeHand Graphics Studio, and the Authorware Interactive Studio. They know you need a number of tools during development, so they offer them all together at a discounted price.

The Director Multimedia Studio is designed to bring together all the tools you need to create an entire multimedia application with Director. The FreeHand Graphics Studio includes Macromedia's imaging products: FreeHand, Extreme 3D, Fontographer, and xRes. The Authorware Interactive Studio includes Authorware Professional and the entire Director Multimedia Studio.

The Director Multimedia Studio currently ships on both Macintosh and Windows and includes the following software:

- Director 5: Macromedia's most powerful and complete tool for multimedia and the Internet (see Appendix A, "Director on the Internet: Shockwave!" for more info)
- SoundEdit 16 version 2 plus Deck II 2.5 (Macintosh), the desktop tools for audio production, or Sound Forge XP (for the Windows version), an award-winning general-purpose sound editor

- Extreme 3D 1.0, Macromedia's 3D solution for design and multimedia
- Macromedia xRes 2.0, Macromedia's creative tool for high-resolution images

To support the studio initiative, Macromedia has introduced a restructuring of all of its tools with the new Macromedia User Interface (MUI). MUI will eventually span across *all* of the Macromedia products so that you can feel comfortable as you switch between them. MUI supports common toolbars, menus, and keyboard shortcuts across Macromedia tools as well as other desktop products. It is designed to make you feel like you're in the same product as you complete your multimedia productions. If you've used Director prior to version 5, I'm sure that you'll notice the changes.

Sound Editors

Before you can edit sounds for your movie, you need to have a sound editing tool. You might want to edit sounds from an audio CD-ROM, or you might want to record your voice or sounds in nature. Director supports the recording of sound, but does not include sound editing features.

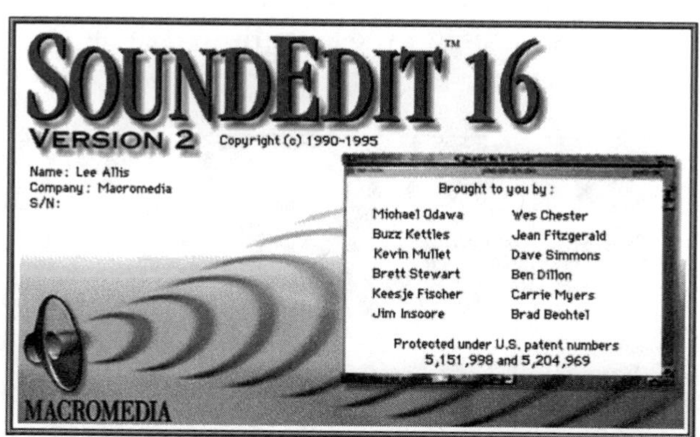

Figure 3.1
SoundEdit 16 is the standard sound editing tool on the Macintosh for Director authors.

Almost every Director user uses SoundEdit 16, available from Macromedia on its own or in the Director Multimedia Studio. SoundEdit, on the Macintosh only, lets you edit sounds up to 16-bit, 44 KHz sounds (if you have 16-bit sound hardware). It's also useful for editing QuickTime files for audio and video synchronization. You can select key frames in the QuickTime file and synch them to specific places in the wave form, resave the movie, and then import it into Director.

Director now launches SoundEdit 16 from the Cast window whenever you double-click on a sound cast member. SoundEdit 16 version 2 is one of the only tools that supports the creation of IMA compressed sounds, especially designed for compressing 16-bit sounds. And Director now supports these IMA-compressed sounds on both the Macintosh and Windows.

In Windows, many people use Sound Forge from Sonic Foundry which is quite similar to SoundEdit 16 on the Macintosh. Sound Forge ships in the Windows version of the Director Multimedia Studio. Some people also use a shareware utility called COOLEDIT.ZIP, for basic sound editing. You can find COOLEDIT.ZIP on Macromedia's Web page at http://www.macromedia.com.

Deck II is a new addition to the Macromedia product line, and a new addition to the Director Multimedia Studio. Award-winning for professional quality multitrack music and sound production, Deck II is a digital audio workstation for the Macintosh (see fig. 3.2).

Figure 3.2

Deck II is Macromedia's digital audio workstation for the Macintosh.

Deck II is a software-based multitrack recording studio that enables you to record and edit up to 999 16-bit digital audio tracks. It enables you to play back as many as 32 tracks in real time on Power Macintosh computers, with no additional hardware required. It offers SYMPTE sync to all frame rates, including 29.97 drop and non-drop, and many more features. Director developers may not have gotten to know Macromedia's new sound product yet, but with both SoundEdit 16 and Deck II included in the Director Multimedia Studio, they'll soon learn all about it.

Illustration Tools

Graphics artists typically have their favorite tools, including Macromedia FreeHand, Adobe Illustrator, Fractal Design Painter, and others. When you save these graphics files for use in Director, you should save them in a PICT format at 72 dpi. Director requires a bitmap format and screen resolution for compositing its animations. To import vector graphics created in FreeHand, you can copy and paste the graphic from the Clipboard into Director's Paint window.

Macromedia now offers FreeHand for Macintosh and Windows, along with the FreeHand Graphics Studio of tools. Director 5 and FreeHand both support the Macromedia Open Architecture (MOA) and the support for third-party Xtras. The same Xtras, such as Adobe Photoshop-compatible filters, can now appear in both Director 5 and FreeHand 5.5 and later. FreeHand provides a complete page-layout environment and currently ships with 500 fonts and 10,000 images.

> To find out more about how to get in touch with Macromedia, see Appendix D, "Contacting Macromedia."

One new feature in FreeHand 5.5 that helps Director users is the Create PICT Xtra, which converts vector graphics to bitmapped PICTs within FreeHand itself. It's perfect for Director, because you cannot animate EPS files on-screen.

Graphics Editors

Director can process graphics in regard to color depth and palette manipulation with the Transform Bitmap command. It can scale bitmaps, create effects in the Paint window and now supports onion skinning and Photoshop-compatible filters. For many graphical processes, however, you still want to use a dedicated graphics editing tool to do much of the work. If you have a number of graphics to process or you have scanned artwork to edit down for Internet distribution, you'll want to do that outside of Director and then import the graphics into your movie as cast members.

Adobe Photoshop is the standard graphics editing tool today. Most Director users become proficient in both tools for a number of graphical applications. Macromedia has just introduced xRes (see fig. 3.3) to its product line as the perfect companion to Photoshop. Macromedia xRes automates creating and editing high-resolution graphics and now ships with the Director Multimedia Studio.

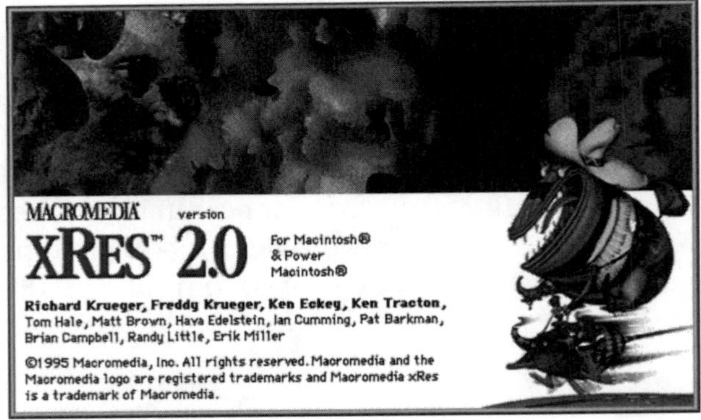

Figure 3.3
The splash screen of Macromedia xRes 2.0 is the most powerful creative tool for high-resolution images.

Whichever tool you choose, you need a graphics editing tool as a companion to Director's Paint window. The Paint window is perfect for creating sharp-edged bitmaps that are perfect for animation, previewing imported graphics and applying Photoshop-compatible filters to them. It also has a whole new role in creating animations with the onion skinning tool. For processing scanned artwork or creating high-resolution images, you will want to used the specialized tools and then import them into Director.

Digital Video Editors

Director can cut, copy, and paste frames in a digital video movie, as well as export to QuickTime on the Macintosh and AVI on Windows. You need to use a dedicated digital video editing tool, however, for editing digital video files and doing post-production work.

Adobe Premiere is the standard digital video editing tool today. Macromedia currently is developing its own digital video product to make the studio complete.

3D Modeling Tools

Real-world interfaces, three-dimensional buttons and controls, and animations add another dimension to your Director movie. They also can add a rich, professional appeal to your project.

Extreme 3D's interface conforms to popular illustration, animation, and rendering standards, enabling new users to be productive right away (see fig. 3.4). For power users, Extreme 3D offers sophisticated functionality and integration with Macromedia FreeHand, Director, and Authorware.

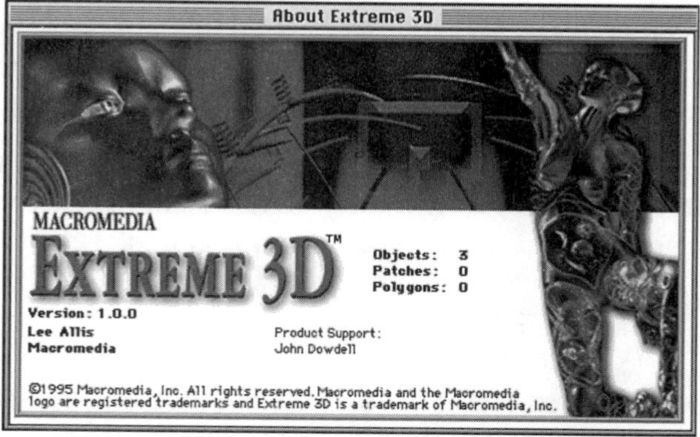

Figure 3.4

Extreme 3D 1.0, a powerful 3D solution for design and multimedia.

With identical environments and file formats on Windows and Macintosh, Extreme 3D allows transparent file exchange and supports built-in distributed rendering across platforms.

Word Processing Software

With Director 5's new support for the Rich Text Format (RTF), you want to have a powerful word processor for generating large amounts of text. Most of the RTF testing for Director 5 has been done with RTF from Microsoft Word.

Compressors and Installers

When your Director production is ready for distribution, there are a few other tools you will need to use in order to distribute your movies to the audience. If you would like to distribute on a floppy disk or a series of disks, you will definitely need to use a compression utility. And for larger applications, you will most likely use an installer. Here are a list of some of the most popular ones used.

Compression Software

For floppy distribution, you often need to compress your Director movies to fit on one or a number of floppies.

Stuffit Deluxe from Aladdin Systems is a Macintosh-only application, most commonly used for compressing small Director projects. Stuffit enables you to create self-extracting archives and segment those archives across multiple floppies.

In Windows, PKZip from PKWare is used quite often, although the word from the Director community is that Windows users are getting used to more sophisticated installation programs.

Installers

If your Director production includes many files, you need to use an installation package.

For the Macintosh, Aladdin Systems offers Installer Maker and Stuffit, as previously mentioned. Macintosh users usually expect to drag a folder or file from a floppy or CD-ROM onto their hard drive.

Windows installer programs are much more involved. Chapter 22, "Delivering the Goods," covers what you need to distribute with your Director for Windows projector. As for Windows installation programs, you can choose from a wide variety, including, among others, the following:

- Install Shield from Sterling Technologies
- EDI Install Pro from Eschelon Development
- Wise Installation System from Great Lakes Business Solutions
- Installit by Helpful Programs, Inc.
- Freeman Installer by Freeman-Teresa Software
- Setup Factory 3.0 by Indigo Rose Corporation

Chapter 22 contains information on contacting these companies.

Complementary Hardware

The multimedia software you use will use your system to its fullest potential. There are many hardware enhancements you can invest in to make your multimedia authoring experience that more enjoyable. See the section titled "The Authoring System" at the beginning of this chapter for more information.

Large or Multiple Monitors

Many Director developers use a large monitor or even a multiple-monitor setup. If you will be using one monitor, a 17-inch monitor or larger is worth the investment. It is nice to use a high resolution so that the Director stage does not fill the entire screen.

On the Macintosh, adding additional video cards will allow you to access more than one monitor. When developers use a two- or three-monitor setup, they typically keep the Score, Cast, and editing windows on the first or second monitor and preview the stage on the other monitor. In Windows, video cards that support multiple monitors are rare and finding them is difficult. Two manufacturers providing this capability include Tridium Research, Inc. (http://www.accessone.com/~tridium) and Intergraph Computer Systems (http://www.ingr.com/ics/accel/glz.html).

Be sure to set both monitors to the same color depth in the Monitors control panel to minimize palette confusion in Director.

16-Bit Sound Card

CD-quality sound is 16-bit, 44 KHz. Before you can edit 16-bit sound files on your system, you need a 16-bit sound card. The original Macintosh systems and many of the more recent Performas and Quadras have 8-bit monophonic sound. If you have a newer Mac model, it may have 16-bit stereo input/output capability built into it.

The highest-end Macintoshes come without cards, ready with slots for expanding with peripheral cards. For the latest 16-bit sound cards, refer to Macintosh and multimedia magazines, such as *New Media*, or a reseller in your area.

Video Capture Cards

As with the sound input on your Macintosh, you should purchase a video capture card for creating digital video. The AV-Macintosh systems support video-in. The first flavors of the AV-Macintoshes were the 660AV and 840AV, both of which Apple has discontinued. The Power Macintosh line carries AV models, and the 8500 Macintosh is the "AV" of its line. The Video Vision Studio card has become a standard in the Director authoring studios.

As third-party hardware changes all the time, check with the latest magazines and resellers for the most current video capture cards.

Camcorders and VCRs

A camcorder enables you to capture your own video before you digitize it for Director. Depending on your camcorder, you also might want to use a VCR to preview the video and help make the conversion from NTSC to RGB for the computer.

Scanners

Scanners can save lots of time when creating content. You can scan photographs for a slide show, or diagrams or other art work from an analog source.

Laser Printers

Printers can prove useful for previewing the stage, printing Lingo scripts and printing information about your movie. Director can print a number of useful reports during authoring mode. To print the stage, you also might want to invest in a color printer.

High-Capacity Hard Drives

A high-capacity disk drive is useful while authoring, as well as to store your project before you transfer it onto a CD-ROM. The current size of a CD-ROM is 650 MB. If you use an inexpensive CD burner, you will need at least 1300 MB of total disk space, with at least 650 MB on a single "image" drive.

CD-ROM Burners

Depending on the size of your company, purchasing your own CD-ROM burner might be cost efficient. Service bureaus can create CD-ROMs for you, but paying them to do so can get quite expensive. Eventually testing your CD-ROM project from a CD is important, and you might go through many *one-offs*, or single copies, throughout testing.

Setting Up the Director Environment

Within Director, there are certain settings you might choose to customize your working environment. Most important, you need to know what's going on with your system and the memory used by Director and the other applications you use. There also are Director-specific settings you will want to consider.

Director Memory Settings

Depending on how you are using Director, you may want to adjust the memory the Director application is using. If you are importing 500 bitmaps, for example, you will want to have more memory available for Director than if you are testing your movie for distribution. On the Macintosh, you may need to alter the amount of memory allocated to Director in these different scenarios. On Windows, it's the other way around. Director will take the memory available on the system, so you may want to alter how much is available to Director on the system.

Memory Management

On the Macintosh, you get to know the About This Macintosh window quite well during development. Knowing how much RAM is available on the system and how much you can allocate to Director becomes important. To access the About This Macintosh window, click on the Macintosh desktop to make the Finder active and select About this Macintosh from the Apple menu (see fig. 3.5).

Figure 3.5 shows a system in which the largest unused block on the system is around 45 MB. You could easily allocate 20 MB of RAM to Director and work quite smoothly.

If you want to allocate memory to Director, be sure to close Director—if it's open—then find the Director application on your hard drive. Select the application icon (but don't launch it) and choose Get Info from the File menu. Figure 3.6 shows the Director 5.0 Info dialog box.

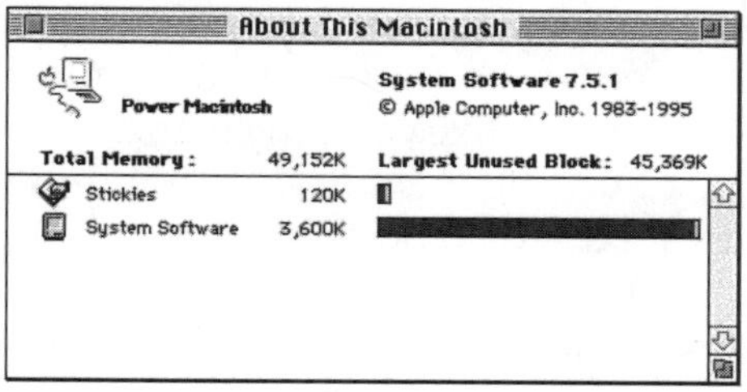

Figure 3.5

The About This Macintosh window provides useful information about your system's memory and how much each active application is using.

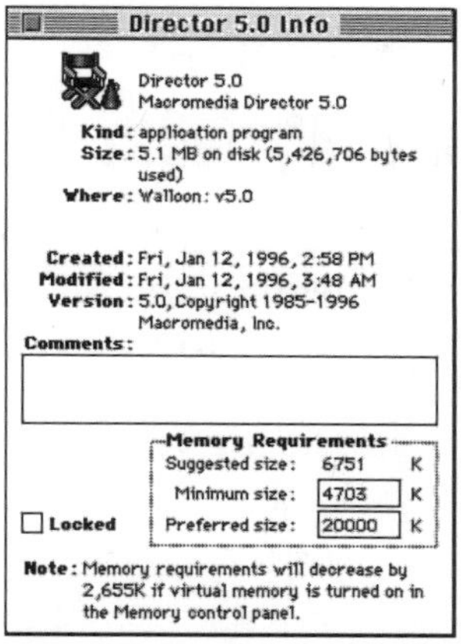

Figure 3.6

Get Info, when accessed for an application, provides a means by which you can adjust the amount of memory allocated to that application.

You can change the Preferred size setting to whatever you want to allocate to the application. The Suggested size to allocate to Director on a Power Macintosh is 12288 KB, and the Minimum size is 8192 KB. On a 68 KB Macintosh, the Suggested size is 9467 KB and the Minimum size is 5371 KB.

Consider changing the memory allocated to the Preferred size to something close to what you have available on the system (as indicated by the Largest Unused Block in the About This Macintosh window), but not too close. You'll want to take into account that QuickTime takes system memory to load. Some developers recommend at least 1 MB free to load QuickTime. If you plan to run multiple applications, you need to change this allocation accordingly, depending on how much memory Director and the other applications require.

In addition to monitoring memory allocation during authoring mode, you will want to take care and test different memory settings when you distribute a projector. Just like you can get information on the Director application and adjust the memory partition to the application, you can do the same for a projector. When testing, you should lower the memory partition to what you expect the target machine to have. If your target machine has 16 MB of RAM, for example, you can assume that the system software will take up 4–5 MB. Therefore, allocating 8 MB to your projector would be a conservative test.

New Memory Management Settings

Director 5 introduces a new memory management feature. Select Preferences from the File menu to find the new setting for Director to Use System Temporary Memory. (By default, this feature is turned on.) If you've allocated 10 MB of RAM to Director and the system has 15 MB free at that time, for example, it gives Director some of its temporary memory.

If Use System Temporary Memory is selected, it will use as much of the system memory as it can. This may prohibit QuickTime from launching. If by chance a QuickTime file does not play from a projector, it may be that you'll need to deselect the Use System Temporary Memory option.

This setting is saved for Director projectors as well. You should think of this as a bonus feature of Director movies. You still should set the Preferred size of a projector to the lowest value you would permit the system to use to play your production to your liking. It's good to know that it might even run a little faster with this option turned on.

Virtual Memory

Director runs with virtual memory turned on, on both the standard and the Power Macintosh. The system uses hard disk space as virtual memory to emulate physical RAM. You can make an 8 MB RAM machine think that it has 16 MB of RAM, for example, by turning on virtual memory in the Memory control panel.

Virtual memory is slow, though, and cannot handle the multimedia processing that Director requires. It often can cut out media elements from your Director movie at inappropriate times, because it doesn't anticipate what the software will use next. Macromedia doesn't recommend using virtual memory with Director movies or projectors.

New Preferences Windows

Director 5 introduces a new way of organizing the Preferences settings within the product. If you select Preferences in the File menu, you see four new options for Preferences: General, Score, Cast, and Paint, Preferences.

The Director 5 online help file explains every option in these dialog boxes. This section focuses on some of the options that make working in Director easier.

You can experiment with the Director windows to set them up the way you like. Director automatically remembers where you've placed your windows at the time you quit and maintains their position when you relaunch the program. You can turn off this behavior in General Preferences by disabling the Save Windows Position on Quit option.

The window location information is stored in the Director 5 Preferences file in the Preferences folder of your System folder. If you like, you can throw away your Director Preferences file to return to the default settings. Be sure to quit Director before doing so, however. After you throw away your Preferences, Director writes a new Preferences file for the next time you launch it.

Trashing your Preferences file often is recommended if your system has crashed at any time during development.

In Windows, the Director windows sometimes can get pushed out of reach, beneath the main menu bar. You might not be able to access the title bar of a window such as the Control Panel. Trashing the Director.PRF file in the Windows directory is the only way to reset the Director window positions when that happens.

Likewise on a Macintosh, if a second monitor is removed or fails, windows that were positioned on that screen will be inaccessible. Tossing the preferences will bring the windows back to their original position.

The General Preferences

Open the General Preferences dialog box (see fig. 3.7) by choosing the File, Preferences, General menu. This dialog contains some of the most commonly used settings for a Director file.

Tips on Using the General Preferencs

1. If you plan to open other applications from Director using the Open command, you should enable the Animate in Background option.
2. Switch your display to Classic Look (Monochrome) if you deal with a number of custom palettes, to eliminate the user interface flashes that occur when you switch between palettes.
3. You can toggle the new Show Tooltips option to turn on and off the new Tooltip helpers (new in Director 5). You should turn on Show Tooltips to start out, because the new Macromedia user interface has changed many of the interface buttons and controls.

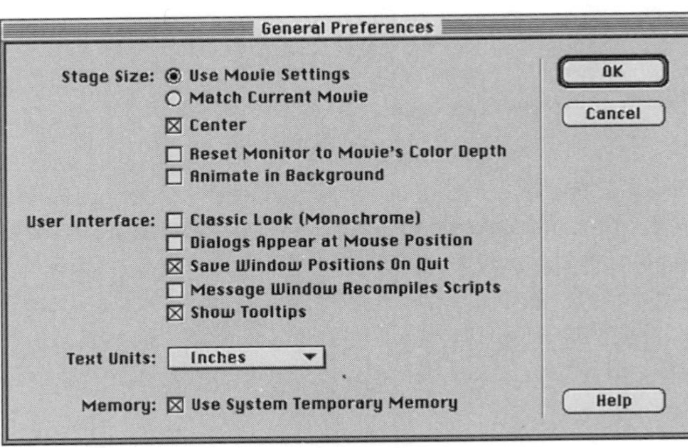

Figure 3.7

The General Preferences dialog box contains a variety of options to change the behavior of the Director movie.

Again, the Director online Help file provides a hot-link definition for every option in these dialog boxes.

The Score Preferences

For the most part, the Score preferences (see fig. 3.8) determine how the Score window displays sprite information. To view the Score Window Preferences dialog box, select File, Preferences, Score Window. The display options to Allow Colored Cells or Enlarged Cells can help you organize and follow the movie along in the score.

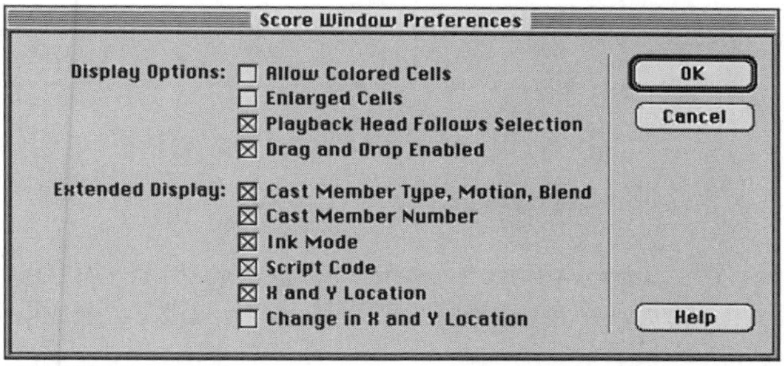

Figure 3.8

The Score Window Preferences determine how the Score shows sprite information.

The Extended Display options let you analyze certain characteristics about each sprite in the score. You can adjust these to your liking, depending on what you're testing. If, for example, you are testing the performance of different ink modes, you may select the "Ink Mode" option. In the Score, if you select "Extended" in the display, the ink mode for each sprite in the score will display. Enabling few statistics at a time will make the score more comprehensible.

Cast Preferences

Similar to the Score Window Preferences dialog box, the Cast Window Preferences for "Internal" dialog box (see fig. 3.9) enables you to define how Director displays the cast members in the Cast window. (Select File, Preferences, Cast to view the dialog box.) You should set up a system in which you're used to organizing your casts, especially if you create large Director projects that involve teams of people. A rule, such as having a row width of ten thumbnails at all times, can eliminate confusion and wasted development time.

You may not access the Cast Window Preferences very often, but it is useful in customizing the Director environment. If you have a large monitor, you may use the large thumbnail size for cast members. If you are limited in monitor space, you may want to use the small thumbnail size setting.

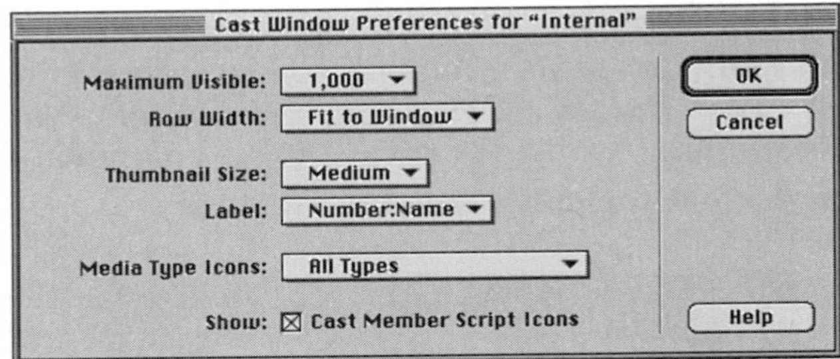

Figure 3.9

You use the Cast Window Preferences dialog box to define how Director displays the cast members in the Cast window.

Paint Preferences

The Paint Window Preferences dialog box (see fig. 3.10) enables you change the way certain paint tools work in the Paint window, along with the ways certain drawing methods behave. (To view the dialog box, select File, Preferences, Paint Window.) The settings in this dialog box give you greater control over the Paint window.

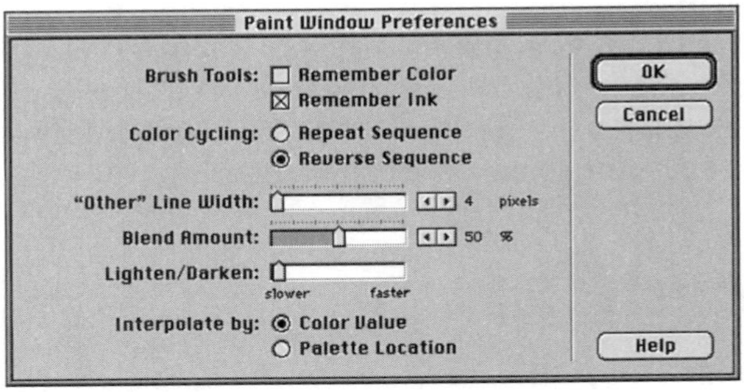

Figure 3.10

The Paint Window Preferences dialog box contains options you can use to determine how certain paint tools work in the Paint window, as well as how certain drawing methods behave.

One useful way to use the Paint Window Preferences is if you are working with multiple paintbrushes. If you would like to set each paintbrush with a different color, for use with onion skinning for example, you can select the Remember Color option in the Paint Window Preferences dialog box. Afterward, when you select each brush, the foreground and background colors you originally selected for that brush will appear. The Paint Window Preferences enable you to set the speed at which the Lighten and Darken effects take place, as well as set the opacity of a color used with the Blend ink effect. Paint window enhancements are covered in Chapter 10, "Paint Window Enhancements."

The Movie Properties

You set the properties for the active movie in the Movie Properties dialog box by selecting Movie and then Properties from the Modify menu (see fig. 3.11).

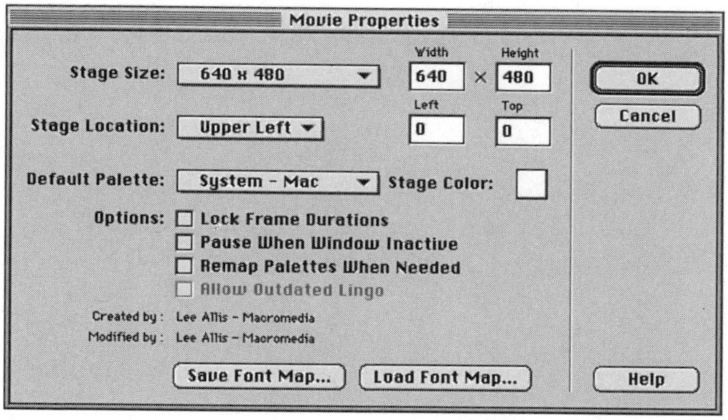

Figure 3.11

The Movie Properties dialog box is where you define the settings for the active movie.

The Modify menu offers a new way to alter any object in your Director movie. These options are covered as you work through the book, but since they were held in the Preferences and Movie Info dialogs in previous versions of Director, they are also mentioned here. (This might confuse some users, but not those of you reading this book.) After you learn where to find these settings for stage size, stage color, stage location, and more under the Modify menu, you'll get used to them.

A quick way to access the Movie Properties dialog box is to Command-click on the stage and select the Movie Properties option in the pop-up menu that appears.

Summary

After reading this chapter, you should understand the options you have for setting up your Director environment. Within Director, there are many settings for the application—as well as for the file you're creating outside of Director—and there are system settings of which you will need to be aware. Authoring a multimedia application takes computer savvy in both hardware options and a number of software applications. Director touches on all of it, and none of it stays the same. Welcome to the Information Superhighway.

Lee Allis

Working with Director: Understanding the Metaphor

When I was thinking of how to explain how to work with Director, I asked John "JT" Thompson, the lead Lingo engineer at Macromedia, what he would say. I asked him how he would explain that Director offers many ways to do everything.

He said, "Director is a like a lived-in house. It has been reworked and reworked since 1985, and each new version has built upon the last. There are some hidden things, and many things remaining from past versions. With each version of Director, Macromedia has introduced a more standardized way of working."

Thompson also said to "sit back, relax, have a cup of tea." Start by reading others' advice on working with Director, such as this book, and an online community. You'll quickly begin building your own approach to create the most powerful multimedia applications for desktop computers today.

If you're experienced with Director, this chapter might be a review. If you've already worked through the tutorials, this chapter might clear up some concepts. If Director is new to you, this chapter should serve as background for the more advanced chapters that follow. Even if you've worked with Director for years, this chapter might spark some new ideas.

Check under the Window menu for an overview of Director's windows. If you're accustomed to earlier versions of Director, you're likely to notice that many features have moved. This chapter doesn't describe each window and what it does—the Director documentation and the expanded, context-sensitive, online Help system conspire to do that.

Rather, this chapter describes how the Stage, Internal Cast, and Score windows work together, as well as furnishes tips for using each of them and using Lingo to work with them. Once you understand how it all works together, you're well on your way to authoring your first movie—with Lingo!

The Stage: What the Audience Sees

Everything the audience sees on the monitor in a Director movie occurs on what is called the *stage*. The stage serves a function in Director parallel to that of a theatrical stage. Your characters exit on and off of it, and can say lines or dance to music on it. Keeping this theatrical stage metaphor in mind should help you understand how to work with Director.

When you first launch Director (see fig. 4.1), the three most important Director windows appear (after the splash screen): the Internal Cast, the Score, and the Control Panel.

If the Cast, Score, and Control Panel windows aren't open after you launch Director, you can open them from the Window menu.

The white canvas in the background is the stage on which your movie takes place.

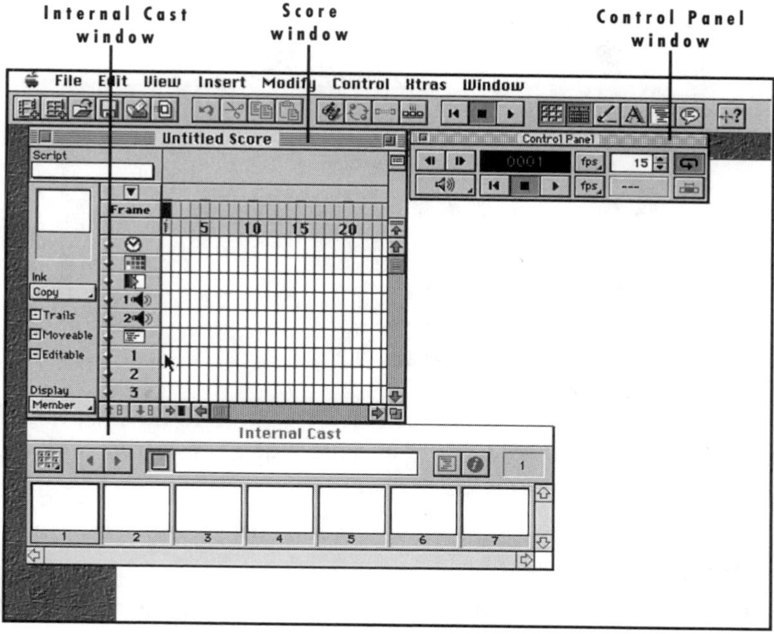

Figure 4.1

The opening screen that appears when you launch Director.

Setting the Stage Color

If you'd like to change the stage's color, you can do so in the Movie Properties dialog box (see fig. 4.2).

You can access the Movie Properties in Director 5 in three ways:

- Choose the Modify menu, then Movie, then Properties
- Press Command+Shift+D
- Control-click the stage on the Macintosh (right-mouse click the stage in Windows 95)

Click on the white color swatch next to the Stage Color setting in the Movie Properties dialog box. (This swatch is where the cursor is in figure 4.2.) After you click on the color swatch, a pop-up palette will appear and you can select a color for the stage. You can select any of the 256 colors in the movie's active palette for your stage's color.

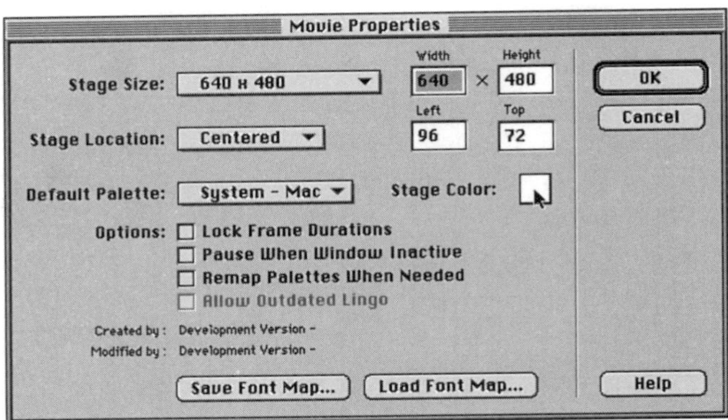

Figure 4.2

Use the Movie Properties dialog box to change the color of the stage, as well as other movie settings.

If you'd like to step on the gas and try out Lingo to do this, here it is: you can change the color of the stage using the Lingo `stageColor` property. The following is an easy example:

1. In Director, open a new movie by selecting New, then Movie from the File menu.
2. Open the Score window and double-click in the Script channel of frame 2. (The *Script channel* is the channel above channel 1.)
3. Type the following in the Script window that appears:

```
on enterFrame
      set the stageColor to random (256) - 1
end
```

The preceding three lines set the stage color to a random color in the active 256-color palette each time the playback head enters that frame.

```
on exitFrame
      go to the frame
end
```

The preceding three lines tell the playback head that when it leaves the frame it needs to return to that same frame. Figure 4.3 shows the sample script as it appears in the Script window.

4. Close the Script window.
5. Open the Control Panel from the Window menu, then rewind and play the movie. (If you have the toolbar displayed under the Window menu, these commands are available there as well.)

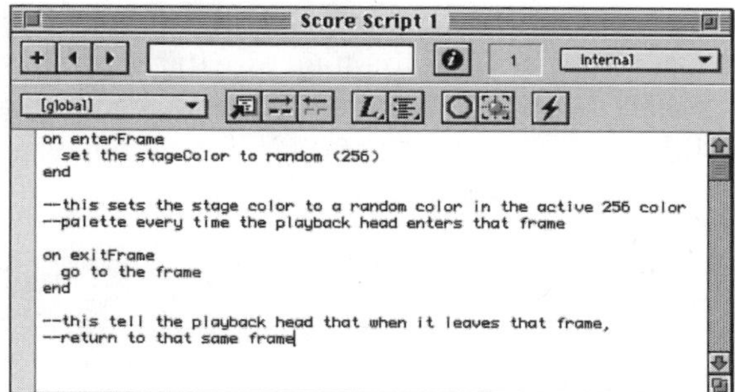

Figure 4.3

The sample script as it appears in the Script window.

You also can find this movie on the accompanying *Inside Director* CD in the Chapter 4 folder.

Defining the Stage Size

One of your first steps as a Director author is to define the movie's stage size. You do this in the Movie Properties dialog box. Remember the theatrical stage metaphor? How else could you set up the lighting and tell the characters where to go? It's best to think of this from the very beginning. Technically, if you draw animated characters to scale for a large stage size and at the last minute decide that the movie should run with a smaller stage, you will not be able to automatically resize everything easily.

Director opens with a default stage size of 640×480 pixels, probably the correct setting for you if you're trying to learn more about the product or are targeting a basic system. A typical multimedia presentation is authored for the standard monitor: 640×480 pixels, with 256 colors.

> The rest of this section targets those of you authoring for distribution. Even if you aren't doing that, however, defining the target audience is an important issue to understand for developing good authoring skills. It also might be news to you that you can use different stage sizes and work with multiple movies.

An easy mistake to make is to develop an entire project without thinking of the final audience until the last minute. They, and the system they will run, should be the focus of your development from the very beginning. Does your audience have a 9- or 13-inch monitor? You need to arrive at answers to these sorts of questions at the beginning of the project. You can work with the stage size in two main ways. You can make one project with the smallest stage size necessary or design multiple versions of the project for different target systems.

Regardless of the size you choose to make the stage, the horizontal dimensions must be divisible by 16, because of the way Director draws the stage internally.

Make Only One Project

If you intend to make only one version of the movie, you need to set the stage size to the least common denominator of monitor dimensions for your intended audience. Cases for which you may need to make only one version include:

- Your project needs to be small enough to fit on a floppy disk
- You're authoring for the Internet
- You have limited time (most common reason)

Suppose you're creating a CD-ROM title for mass market distribution. Your project team decides every school computer around the world—even those with 9-inch monitors—must be able to view your movie. You need to make the dimensions of your movie for the 9-inch monitor (512×342). If the 512×342 movie also is going to be played on monitors that exceed nine inches, you can cover the desktop area behind the movie before you distribute it.

You can distribute Director movies as run-time modules, called *projectors*. Director 5 includes a new feature that enables you to play your projector Full Screen, which covers the desktop area behind the stage with the stage color of the first frame of your movie. Setting up your projector for distribution is covered in Chapter 22, "Delivering the Goods."

Before Director 5, the Full-Screen Projector option was available only in Director 4 for Windows. In the Macintosh version, you had to use the Rear Window XObject that shipped with Director, or a commercial product called Finder Hider, to do this for you.

Make Multiple Copies of the Same Project

If you decide to make more than one version of the same project, you could make both a 9-inch (512×342) and a 13-inch (640×480) movie, or more. On occasion, you will need to make two completely separate movies or a series of movies. Doing so forces many extra steps because you have to resize each bitmap to fit the proportions of the different stage sizes.

After you complete two (or more) projects, you can easily use Lingo to test for the monitor size and play one movie or another. The following example shows how to do this and assumes you already have made two movies, one called SMALL.DIR and another called BIG.DIR.

1. Create a third movie and call it INTRO.DIR. Make sure the INTRO.DIR movie's stage size is small enough fit on any of the target monitors.

   This movie will use Lingo to call out and play one of the two movies, given the size of the monitor.

2. Under the Window menu, select the Script window and type the following movie script:

```
on startMovie
  global monitorHeight, monitorWidth

  set monitorHeight = the stageTop + the stageBottom
  set monitorWidth = the stageLeft + the stageRight

  if monitorWidth < 640 then go to movie "small.dir"
  else
  go to movie "big.dir"
  end if

end
```

The preceding code plays one of the two movies, depending upon on the monitor size. Line 5, for example, determines that when the monitor's width is less than 640, the SMALL.DIR movie will play. If the monitor width is greater than 640, the BIG.DIR movie will play.

3. In the Script channel of Channel 1, type the following Lingo script:

```
on exitFrame
  go to the frame
end
```

4. Save the movie.
5. Select the Create Projector command from the File menu and add INTRO.DIR to the projector list.

   Clicking the Options button in the Create Projector dialog will launch the Projector Options dialog box.
6. In the Projector Options dialog box, select the Full Screen option to fill the area behind the stage with the color of the stage.
7. Click the Create button.
8. Name the projector and choose Save.

The projector you just created will appear in the active directory or wherever you decide to save it. When you launch the projector you just created, it will first launch the INTRO.DIR movie. The Lingo you scripted will decide the size of the monitor and play one of the movies.

The Cast: Behind the Scenes

To display the items on the stage, Director works behind the scenes to access a database of cast members. As in motion pictures, cast members come in many different shapes and sizes. In computer-generated movies, cast members include a number of computer-generated media elements, such as graphics, sounds, text, 3D files, digital videos, and other Director movies. Other types of cast members, such as custom palettes, film loops, transitions, and scripts, are imported or generated while working in Director. These types of members might or might not be media elements, but you can access them from the Cast window (see fig. 4.4). Therefore, they still qualify as cast members.

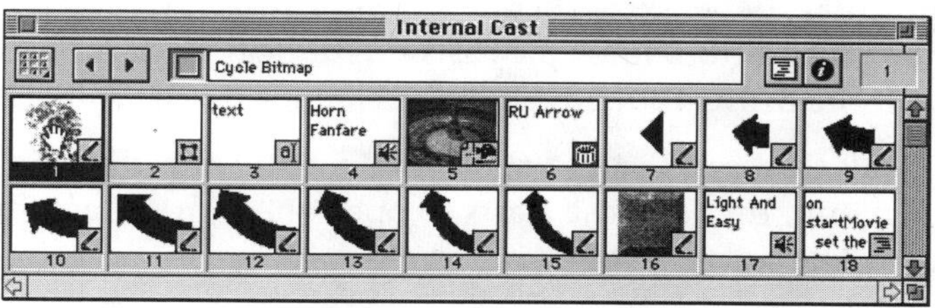

Figure 4.4

The Cast window is where all of your cast members are stored. The default cast is the Internal cast. With multiple casts, you might have additional internal and external casts.

Infinite Number of Cast Members

Director 4 introduced the capability to include up to 32,000 cast members in each movie. In Director 5, you now can have multiple casts in the same movie, each of which can contain up to 32,000 cast members. This means you have virtually millions of possible cast members in each movie file.

By default, Director 5 stores casts internally; hence, *internal casts*. If you want to create a new cast, select the Choose Cast button in the top left corner of the Cast window to open the New Cast dialog box (see fig. 4.5). This dialog box enables you to specify whether the cast is internal or external.

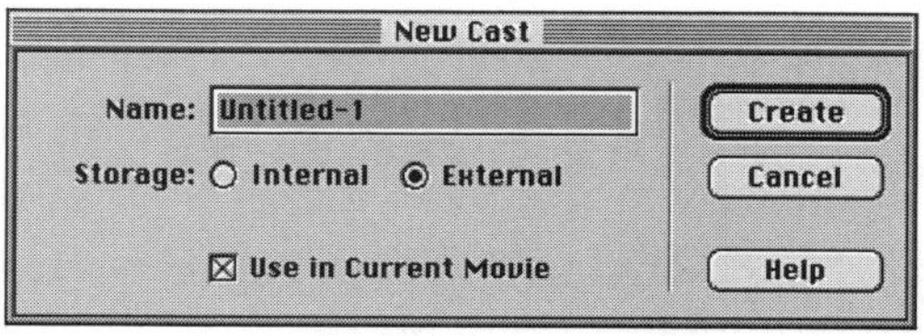

Figure 4.5

The New Cast dialog box enables you to name the new cast and determine whether it is stored as an internal or external cast.

If you select the External option, Director automatically links the new cast to the movie. By default, the Use in Current Movie option is selected for external casts. If you deselect this option, you can generate a cast in one Director movie for use in another Director movie, without ever using the cast in the first movie.

You can share external casts between movies. In Director 5, a shared external cast works the way the SHARED.DIR file did in Director 4. In Director 5, this file is called the SHARED.CST. Using multiple casts can be helpful to organize your cast members by type. You can have a cast of bitmaps, a cast of digital videos, and so on, and you can access all of them in the same file. You might use multiple casts to swap libraries of graphics files, depending on the resolution of the target machine's monitor. In addition, multiple casts might be used to group members by use in the Score, for convenient preload, unload management.

To view all the casts used in the active movie, select Movie from the Modify menu, then choose Casts to open the Movie Casts dialog box (see fig. 4.6).

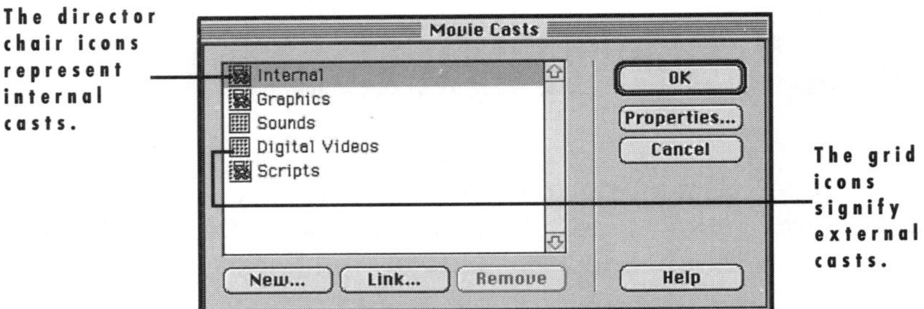

Figure 4.4

Use the Movie Casts dialog box to modify the movie's casts.

You can modify the movie's casts in this dialog box as well as view the names and types of all the casts. The icon that looks like a director's chair indicates an internal cast and the "grid" icon signifies an external cast. For more information on working with multiple casts, refer to Chapter 8, "New in Director 5: Multiple Casts."

Tips on Using the Cast Window

Working in the Cast window is easy. You can drag and drop cast members in the window to organize them as you please. Director automatically updates the other cast member positions and all references to them in the movie.

You can drag and drop cast members directly onto the stage from the Cast window. In Director 5, you even can drag and drop cast members into the cast from the desktop. The Cast window is your reference for everything you create or import in your Director movie.

Finding Cast Members

You can find specific cast members by selecting Edit, Find, Cast Member. When you do, the Find Cast Member dialog box appears (see fig. 4.7).

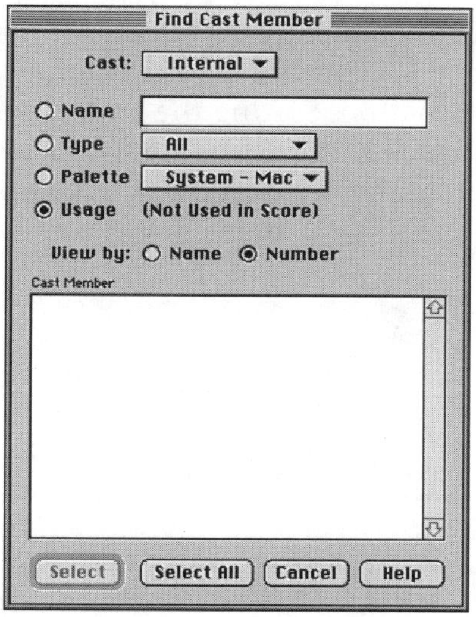

Figure 4.7

Use the Find Cast Member dialog box to locate specific cast members.

You often use the Find Cast Member dialog box before finalizing a project to find cast members you haven't used in the Score. You can then delete any unused cast members to optimize the file.

If you use Lingo to puppet sprites in your movie, those sprites might not appear anywhere in the Score. One way to handle this is to set up an unused frame that contains all the puppetted sprites. That way, when you use the Find, Cast Member, Usage, (Not Used in Score) commands, they will find those cast members not used in the movie at all and cleared from the cast.

Sorting Cast Members

You can use the Sort command from the Modify menu to sort the cast members in the Cast window. To open the Sort window (see fig. 4.8), first select a range of cast members in the Cast window and select the Sort submenu from the Modify menu.

When you select Usage in Score in the Sort window, you optimize your movie for faster playback. This is especially important when you author for CD-ROM distribution. Sorting the cast by media type will enable you to organize the cast. If you end up with a large internal cast with mixed media, you might first sort the internal cast by media type and take all the graphics, for example, into a cast of their own.

Figure 4.6

Use the Sort window to sort the cast members in a particular cast.

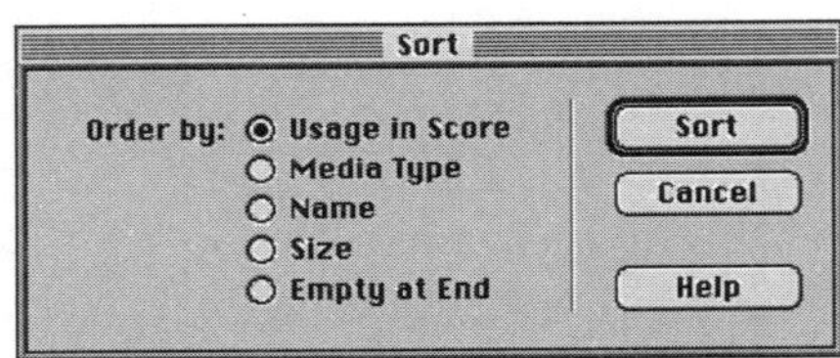

Previewing Cast Members

After you import cast members into a Director file, make sure to preview them from the Cast window—especially sound and digital video cast members.

Table 4.1

Previewing Cast Members

For	In the Cast Window, Do This
Graphics	Double-click on the cast member to preview it in the Paint window.
Sounds	Select the cast member and use the Information button or press Command+I to open the Sound Cast Member Properties dialog box. Click on the Play button to preview the sound.
Digital Video	Double-click on the cast member to launch the Video window and preview it. Use the Information button or press Command+I to open the Digital Video Cast Member Properties dialog and make sure that Direct to Stage is turned on.

You often import media elements that have been created or edited in another program into Director. Director often gets used as a media-integrator, rather than as the tool for creating the media. Frequently, one team of people creates a set of cast members and then sends it over a network or via an external medium to the Director author. Obviously enough, things can go wrong under such an arrangement. This is why previewing a cast member after it's imported is important.

Using other software programs often amounts to only half the battle. After you import cast members into Director's cast, you need to test them in the Cast window before you work with them in the movie to prevent many troubleshooting issues later. If the media element doesn't work properly in the Cast window, you can bet it won't work well in the movie. You might need to return to the digital video editing, sound editing, or graphics editing tool you used to create the piece of content for further editing.

> If you double-click on the sound cast member, Director prompts you to launch an external sound editing program, like SoundEdit 16. You can then edit the sound as necessary and return to Director with the freshly edited sound.

After you import or create a cast member, open the Cast Member Properties dialog box. This dialog box contains all the information on the cast member. You also can select special Director settings for cast members in these dialog boxes. For example, figure 4.9 shows the Cast Member Properties dialog for a digital video cast member. This is where you will set up if the digital video is looped, plays Direct to Stage, or plays sound along with many other options.

To open the Cast Member Properties dialog box, select the cast member in the Cast window, then do one of the following:

- Click on the blue "i," or Information, button in the window
- Press Command+I

Experiment with different types of cast members to see the different options.

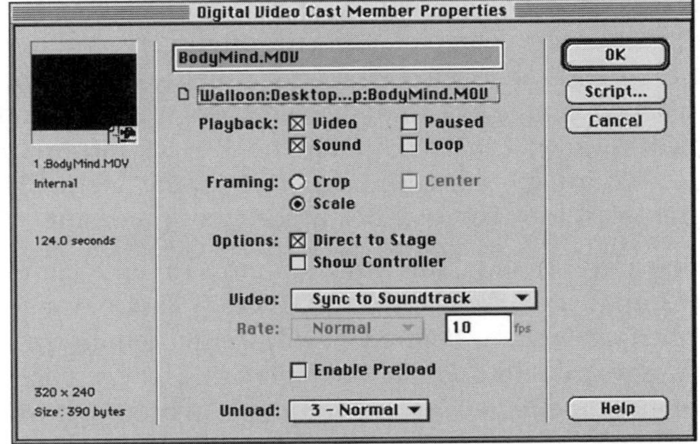

Figure 4.9

The Digital Video Cast Member Properties dialog box is where you select many of the settings for that particular cast member.

Naming Cast Members

Name your cast members after you import them so that if you move them in the Cast window, your Lingo scripts still can find them. Your Lingo scripts generally should refer to a cast member by name and a sprite by number. You can name a cast member in the Cast Member Properties dialog box, the Cast window when it's selected, and many of the preview and editing windows. The initial member name of an imported file is the original name of that file on the hard disk.

If you run speed critical Lingo scripts that refer to a cast member many times consecutively, you can enhance performance by using the number of the cast member rather than its name. Director accesses the cast member faster by number than by name. You can use the `number of member` Lingo function to find a cast member's number value, and then you can pass that value to your repeat loop, animated button, or other routine.

The Sprites

A *sprite* is an instance of a cast member on the stage. And each sprite occupies its own rectangular area on the stage. In the background, the Director Score keeps track of which cast member is on the stage, and the sprite information for that cast member at every point in time.

Sprite-based animation is the key to Director's power. As the Director playback head advances through the Score, it first reads the sprite information in the current frame. As it advances to the next frame, Director only updates what has changed. For example, think of an animated character walking across the stage. In the first frame of the animation, Director would read in the background bitmap, and other things on the stage. As the character walks across the stage and the Director playback head advances to the next frame, it only has to update the small rectangular area of that one sprite. This way, Director can maintain a fast animation engine and a complete multimedia scene at one time.

Director supports the use of 48 sprites on the stage at any one time. The sprite's *location* refers to the stage coordinates, in relation to the top left corner of the stage. Director's Score keeps track of all of the sprite information at all times. Each time you place a cast member on the stage, it becomes a sprite.

A sprite can assume several different shapes and sizes during a movie. These properties can change as the movie advances, still referencing the same, unchanged, cast member in the cast. One cast member can be represented in many instances, or sprites, in the movie, yet still occupy only one cast position.

You typically use Lingo to examine or change the properties of a sprite as the audience interacts with the movie. Given a certain interaction by the audience, like the click of a button, you might change the properties of a sprite to look like it's been pressed. You refer to these sprites by sprite number and change their properties however you want.

The Lingo chapters will explain how you use Lingo to "puppet" a sprite and take control of it away from the Score. You can use the Lingo commands to reference the Score information and change it however you want. The analogy of the Hollywood sound stage, or Broadway production, shifts to a puppet show when you start to use Lingo. This concept is covered in Chapter 16, "Lingo: The Basics."

The Score

The most important window in Director is the Score. The Score window is your mission control tower. It's similar to a spreadsheet, in which a sprite occupies one instance, or *cel*, in the Score at a time. The Score reflects the stage contents and other items across specific frames.

A sprite that is placed in the Score may occupy one of the 48 sprite channels in the Score window (see fig. 4.10). Sprite 1 is in channel 1, sprite 17 is in channel 17, and so on. Therefore, cast member 10 could be represented in sprite 1 and 17 at the same time.

Figure 4.10

The Score is where everything is controlled in the Director movie.

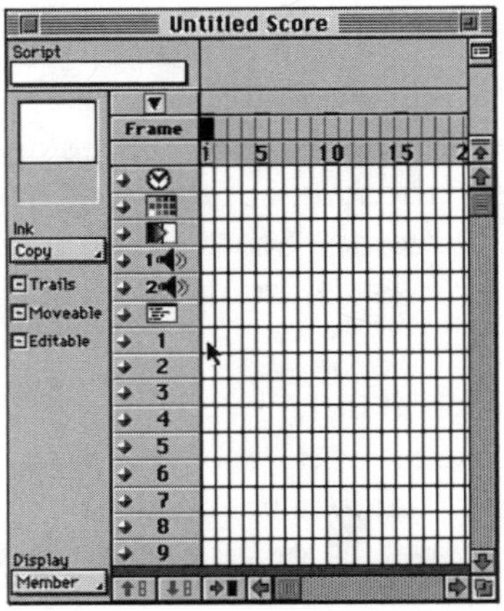

The Frames

Director advances over time across frames in the Score. You can have an infinite number of frames in your movie. Each frame can represent a new scene in the movie or introduce an animation over time as the playback head advances. Chapter 16, "Lingo: The Basics," covers how you can use Lingo to control which frames Director's playback head advances to in non-linear, interactive projects.

By default, Director's playback head runs through the Score until it reaches the end of a movie. You could develop a linear movie that has many frames, each representing a moment in time. You also could create an entire Director movie in one frame, in which case you would use Lingo to make all necessary changes. You nearly always need to find a proper medium for your projects that falls between these two extremes.

The 48 Sprite Channels

Every time you place a cast member on the stage, a sprite appears in the Score. Likewise, every time you place a cast member in the Score, it appears on the stage. The Score contains 48 vertical sprite channels, allowing up to 48 visual sprites on the stage at one time.

One technique you could use if you wanted to have more than 48 sprites on the stage at one time would be to use Movie in a Window. Movie in a Window lets you open another Director movie in its own window. The Movie in a Window has its own stage, with its own 48 sprite possibilities. Chapter 19, "Advanced Concepts," covers Movie in a Window techniques.

Ink Effects

The sprite channels increment in layers—channel 1 being in the background, channel 2 being on top of it, and so on. Ink effects are available in a pop-up menu in the Score for creating layering effects between the vertical channels of the Score. Director 5 ships with a nice ink effects lab in the tutorial files on the Director CD that enables you to view the effects of each ink.

To apply an ink effect to a sprite on the stage, first select the sprite in the Score and select one of the inks from the pop-up menu. One of the most commonly used ink effects is Background Transparent. Applying the Background Transparent ink effect wipes out the background color of the sprite. You can use it to eliminate the white bounding box behind a bitmap on the stage.

Sometimes you might like to drop out a color other than white with the Background Transparent ink effect. To do so, select the sprite on the stage, and in the Tools window, select a different background color for that sprite. Background Transparent then removes whatever color you've selected.

You also can change the sprite ink effect with Lingo during the movie. Table 4.2 shows all the inks available through Lingo.

Table 4.2

Inks Available Through Lingo

0*–Copy	6–Not reverse	34–Add
1–Transparent	7–Not ghost	35–Subtract pin
2–Reverse	8–Matte	36–Background Transparent
3–Ghost	9–Mask	37–Lightest
4–Not copy	32–Blend	38–Subtract
5–Not transparent	33–Add pin	39–Darkest

**The number before each ink effect is the number you will use when you assign an ink effect to a sprite with Lingo.*

To see how easy it is to use Lingo to set the ink of a sprite, open the INKS.DIR movie from the *Inside Director* CD-ROM.

1. Within Director, open the control panel and rewind and play the movie (see fig. 4.11).

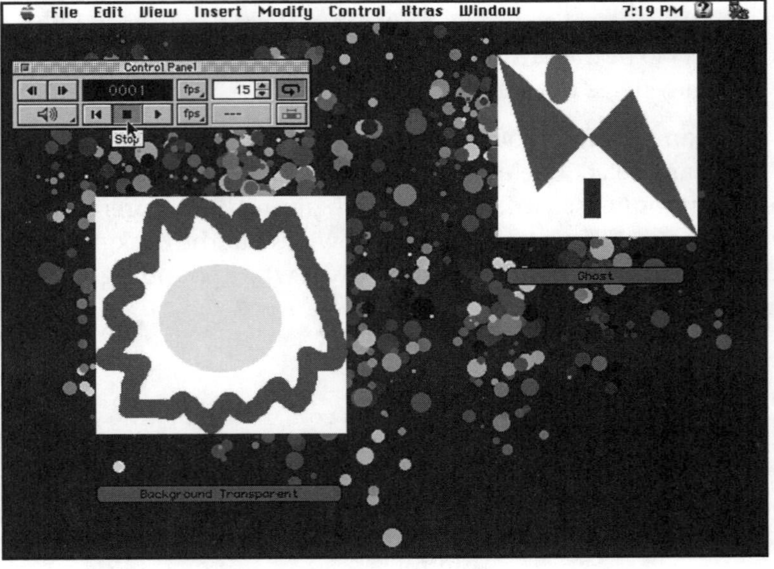

Figure 4.11

The INKS.DIR movie on the Inside Director *CD-ROM.*

2. Click on the two buttons and notice the how the sprites change. With Lingo, you are changing their ink effects.
3. Stop the movie, open the Cast window and find cast member #6.
4. Double-click on Cast member #6 and take a look at the Score script (see fig. 4.12).

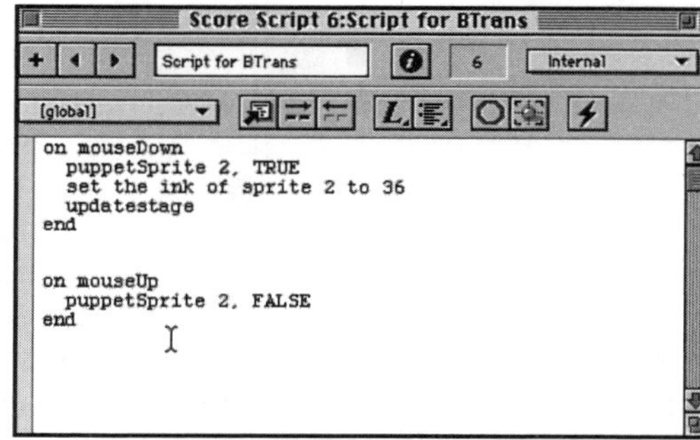

Figure 4.12

Score script to change the ink of a sprite to Background Transparent.

The script should read:

```
on mouseDown
   puppetSprite 2, TRUE
   set the ink of sprite 2 to 36
   updatestage
end
on mouseUp
         puppetSprite 2, FALSE
end
```

The preceding script sets the ink of sprite 2 to Background Transparent when the mouse is clicked down, and turns it back when the mouse is released. You could change the `36` in the third line of the script to any of the inks listed in table 4.2. Open cast member #7 to see the script to turn the ink effect to Ghost.

Other Effects

A few other buttons in the Score enable you to quickly change the properties of sprites, including the Trails, Moveable, and Editable buttons (see fig. 4.13).

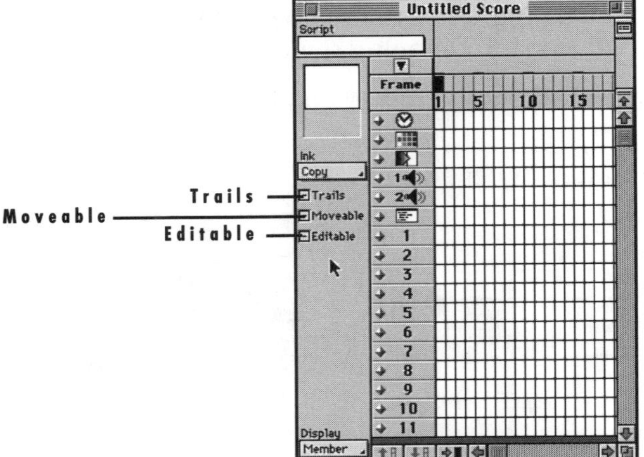

Figure 4.13

You can set the Trails, Moveable, and Editable properties of a sprite by selecting the sprite and clicking one of these buttons.

Like the ink effects, you can apply these effects to specific sprites by selecting the sprites in the Score and clicking on these buttons. Again, you can dynamically turn these sprite properties on and off using Lingo.

The Director Score settings are quick and easy to use, but you might have more control over your movie if you use Lingo to control the settings. (Never forget that you can do the same thing many ways in Director. Part of your development as a Director author simply entails finding which ways are best for you.) Chapter 16, "Lingo: The Basics," begins the Lingo section of the text. Eventually, once Director developers start using Lingo, they prefer to use Lingo exclusively.

Controlling the Playback Head with Lingo

As you become more familiar with Director and begin to work on larger projects, you'll begin to use Lingo to control the course of the movie.

Looping with Lingo

With Lingo, you can set up loops to wait for a particular action to occur before allowing Director to advance to the next frame. You don't need to In-Between, or repeat, copies of frames of static images or QuickTime movies over the course of time it takes the user to view them when you can do it using just one or two frames with Lingo.

Pause Versus Go to the Frame

The most important Lingo loop you should learn is as follows:

```
on exitFrame
  go to the frame
end
```

The preceding handler also works if you use `go the frame` in the second line. Either way, it tells Director's playback head to go back to the same frame when it exits the frame.

Users new to Lingo might learn the `pause` command and figure they should pause the Director playback head in that frame until the user clicks a button. The fact is, however, you can get yourself in trouble using `pause` because you can end up pausing other Director functionality that you want to keep running.

A `go to the frame` loop, on the other hand, allows animations, Movie in a Window, and user event processing to continue to run while the movie still looks paused to the audience.

You then can have a button with a script that executes the following to exit the loop:

```
on mouseUp
  go to the frame + 1    --or "go to the frame - 1"
end
```

Any text with a -- in front of it in a Script window is called *commented text* and will not execute. It's available so you can comment your code.

Memory is an important issue in multimedia. If you learn to use Lingo successfully, you can learn how to manage how the cast of your movie is used in the Score. Using Lingo to loop the playback head is the first step to controlling the Score with Lingo. Chapter 17, "Managing Your Data," offers more information on memory management and using Lingo.

The Special Channels

In addition to the 48 sprite channels, there are six special channels in the Director Score (see fig. 4.14). You use these to determine a movie's tempo and active palette, when to add transitions and sound, and for which specific frames of the Score to use Lingo.

These special channels are perfect for linear, slideshow-type presentations. If you have a board meeting in two hours and you don't know what Lingo commands to use, these channels are perfect for setting up your controls.

If you design an interactive CD-ROM or kiosk that's supposed to have user-controlled navigation, you want to use Lingo to script everything in the upper channels of the Score. The syntax is easy and enables the end user to interactively control the course of the movie at run time.

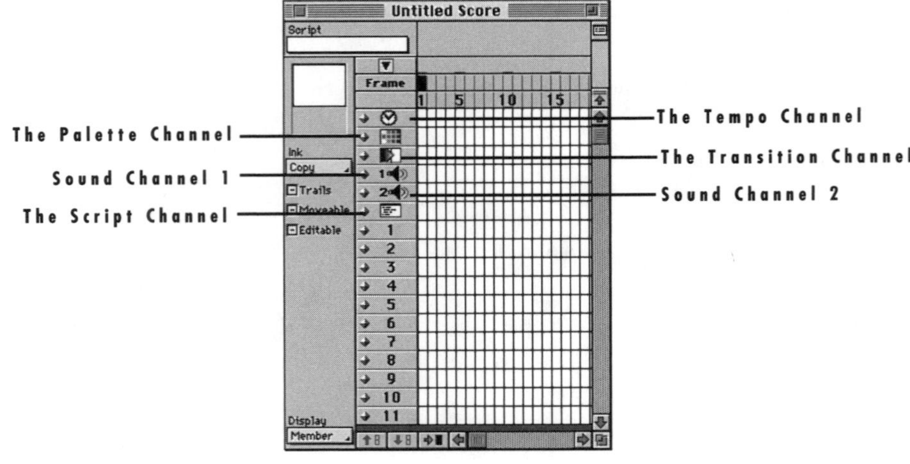

Figure 4.14

The special channels in the upper part of the Score define a number of attributes for the course of the movie.

The Tempo Channel

You use the Tempo channel to set up the tempo and establish tempo changes for the movie. You also can use certain Tempo dialog box settings to direct the Director movie to wait a specified amount of time until a specific event happens on the system. Figure 4.15 shows the events for which you can have Director wait. Double-click in the Tempo channel of one of the frames to view the available options.

Although the Wait settings in the Tempo channel are quick and easy controls you can set up in the Score, you also can script these same wait commands using Lingo. So which should you do?

Figure 4.15

Use the Tempo slider to establish a frames per second movie speed, and optionally, use the Wait settings to have the movie wait in that frame until the specified event occurs.

A Test Case

Imagine a scenario in which you would like the movie to pause on a particular frame until a sound or narration has stopped playing. The sound is in sound channel 1. You can choose the Wait for End of Sound in Channel 1 option in that frame's Tempo channel to tell Director's playback head to stay until the sound finishes, and only then advance to the next frame in its natural procession.

Suppose you've also created buttons available throughout your whole movie that enable the user to advance or go back between scenes at any time. If the sound is still playing in sound channel 1 and the user clicks on the button to go back a frame, Director doesn't know what to do.

If you use Lingo and interactivity, letting the audience control the navigation of the movie, you want to use Lingo to script these Wait commands, not use the Tempo channel. Doing so is easy and overcomes the potential fight for control of the Score between the Tempo channel and Lingo. You'll want to arrange a situation in which you use a wait that still lets the user exit the loop in the movie.

In this example, the script would be as follows.

In the Script channel for that frame:

```
on enterFrame  if soundBusy(1) then      --If the sound is playing
    go to the frame               --Go back to the same frame
  end if
end
```

In the Score script for the Step Back button:

```
on mouseUp
  go to the frame - 1
end
```

Chapter 21, "How do I...: The Top 20 Lingo Support Questions," covers this Lingo syntax for the remainder of the Tempo channel.

The Palette Channel

You use the Palette channel (see fig. 4.16) to set up the active palette, palette changes, and color effects over time in the movie. Double-click in one of the frames of the Palette channel to view the available settings.

Palette manipulation in Director might be new to you. Chapter 9, "Graphics: The Visuals," covers palettes in greater detail.

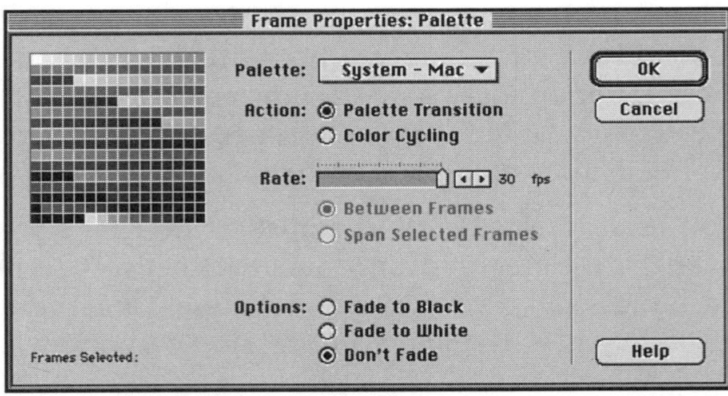

Figure 4.16

Use the Palette channel to set up the active palette, palette changes, and color effects over time.

Color Depth

Palettes refer to the colors available on the monitor at any one time in an 8-bit environment or less. Palettes work hand in hand with your monitor's display settings. On the Macintosh, you would set your monitor to 256 colors for 8-bit; you'd select a 256-color video driver with Windows.

An easy way to test for the active color depth of the monitor is to open the Message window (see fig. 4.17) and type the following script:

```
put the colorDepth
```

Press Return (or Enter) and the active color depth will be returned to you.

Figure 4.17

Testing the color depth in the Message window.

The range of color depths depends on your system. Table 4.3 breaks down these possibilities.

Table 4.3

Range of Color Depths per System

Color Depth	Number of Colors
1-bit	black and white
2-bit	4 colors
4-bit	16 colors (VGA on Windows)
8-bit	256 colors (SVGA on Windows)
16-bit	32,768 colors (Thousands on the Macintosh)
24-bit	16,777,216 colors (Millions on the Macintosh)

Typically, you author Director movies for 8-bit environments, 8-bit being the basic system today. Just like the size of the stage, the lowest common denominator factor becomes an issue again. You cannot, for example, display a 24-bit graphic in an 8-bit display with any success. If the machine you target has a limit of 256 colors, you need to author in 8-bit. And you need to deal with palette issues, as well.

True color, or 24-bit, movies are available in Director 5 on both platforms now—a big breakthrough for Director 5 on Windows. Now that Director 5 for Windows is a 32-bit native application, it can take advantage of the new architecture of Windows 95 and Windows NT. Director for Windows on Windows 3.1 is still limited to 256 colors, but can enjoy true color on Windows 95 and Windows NT.

You still need to think of that target, 8-bit machine, though. Animation, combined with the system capabilities and the effects possible in Director, usually is best viewed in 256 colors. Palette transitions are ignored with more than 256 color screens, and performance is much faster with less information to process.

Switching between Palettes

If you target an 8-bit environment and you scan 100 photographs to use in a Director movie, you need to transform each scan down to 256 colors. You can use Photoshop, xRes, or your favorite graphics editing tool, and each graphic will have its own custom palette. Custom palettes estimate the closest 256 colors that an image uses. Because your target machine may have a 256 color display, and your scanned artwork may be 24-bit, or 16,777,216 colors, the image you display will need to be edited to use only 256 colors.

When you edit graphics, be sure to save them at 72 dots per inch (dpi). Director, when animating images across the screen requires that they are 72 dpi, or screen resolution. If you happen to bring in an image with 300 dpi, or anything higher than 72 dpi, you'll notice that Director will reduce their resolution to 72 dpi, and they will dramatically shrink in size. Chapter 9, "Graphics: The Visuals," covers working with graphics.

When you import a graphic that contains a custom palette into Director, a dialog box appears prompting you with a couple options. One option is to import the graphic's palette as a cast member (see fig. 4.18). To maintain that the graphic uses the custom palette you've made for it, select that option and make that palette cast member active in the palette channel of the Score.

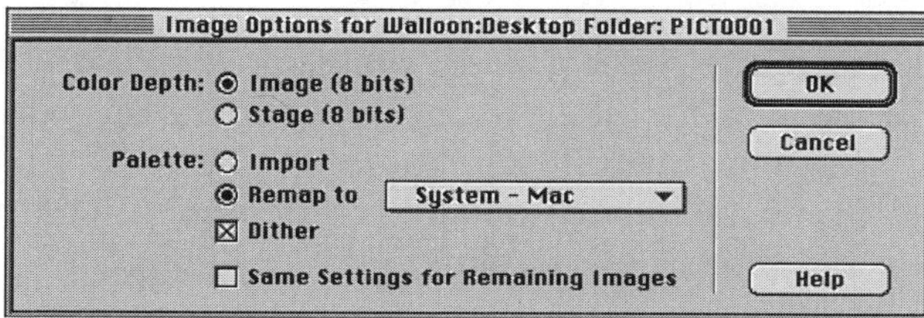

Figure 4.18

When importing an image with a palette that is not currently in the Director movie, you will be prompted with the Image Options dialog box.

Another option you have for importing images is to remap the color depth and palette of the image to one of the palettes already within Director. This is sometimes called *auto remapping*. What this does is use Director to replace the image's colors with the most similar colors in the palette you select from the pop-up menu. This can be done for images of all color depths. When you select the dither option, Director blends the colors in the new palette you choose to approximate the original colors in the graphic.

Only one palette can be active on the monitor at one time, so if you have multiple palettes in your movie, you need to work with switching between them.

Director offers a couple options for dealing with multiple palettes. You can use the Palette channel's Fade to Black option or Fade to White option before displaying the next graphic. To avoid switching between palettes, many developers use editing tools from outside Director to make a common palette, or "super palette," that the images all could share.

Tools that can help you create a super palette include the following:

- DeBabelizer from Equilibrium Technologies (Macintosh only)
- Brenda (Windows)

See Appendix E, "The *Inside Director 5* CD-ROM," for information on tools and utilities included with this book.

After you create the super palette, you can activate it in the palette channel of the Score for the entire movie. Applying the palette to frame 1 will cause it to remain in effect for the entire movie. Alternatively, you could select it as the movie's default palette under the Modify menu and Movie and Properties submenus.

To change the palette dynamically using Lingo, you can use the `puppetPalette` command. When you puppet the palette, the palette you specify remains in effect until you use the `puppetPalette 0` command to turn it off. Director doesn't obey any more subsequent palette changes in the Score so long as the puppet palette stays in effect.

Chapter 9, "Graphics: The Visuals," offers more information on using palettes in Director and Chapter 16, "Lingo: The Basics," discusses puppets in detail.

The Transition Channel

In the Transition channel (see fig. 4.19), you set up the special effects between the scenes of your movie. For example, if you'd like to dissolve one scene into the next, you will set up the Dissolve, Pixels Fast transition in the frame of the Score in which you would like it to take place. You usually can tell that a movie was created using Director because of its really cool transitions. The Transition channel is easy to use, and, used properly, can add the extra impact your movie or business presentation needs.

To set a transition in the Score, first double-click in a cel in the Transition channel.

Director 5 now assigns transitions by category. Selecting different categories in the Categories scroll box gives you different sets of transitions in the Transitions scroll box. In turn, selecting different transitions in the Transitions scroll box offers different settings you can determine. One transition might enable you to adjust duration, smoothness, and stage area, whereas another transition might let you change the transition effects.

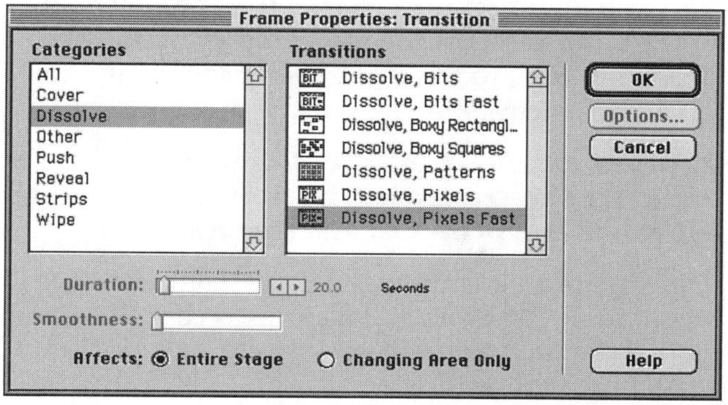

Figure 4.19

Use the Transition channel to create special effects for transitions between scenes in your movies.

You can use transitions to add effects to the whole stage as you enter a new section of the movie. On the other hand, you can apply them to only the part of the stage that changes as you enter a new frame. Applying a transition to the changing area allows you to highlight specific areas of the stage to add a special emphasis to just one part or another in your presentation. For example, you might create bulletted text to "push" on from the left, each line "pushing" on in each new frame.

Tips on Using the Transition Channel

The following includes some tips for using the Transition channel. Transitions are easy to use, but there are a couple of common mistakes people make. These tips should help you avoid those mistakes.

- **Set a transition in the frame to which the playback head is going, not from which it's leaving.**

  A transition occurs between frames, as the playback head enters a new frame. You would put a Dissolve Pixels Fast in the Transition channel of frame 3, for example, if you wanted the effect to occur when the movie reached frame 3.

- **Never loop in a frame with a transition.**

  You might have the following loop set up in the Score to loop in a particular frame:

```
on exitFrame
   go to the frame
end
```

You also might set up a wait in the Tempo channel. You don't want to repeat the transition every time the playback head goes back to the frame, because it would cause performance problems and crazy visual disturbances.

- **If other elements on the stage drop out of a movie, turn off the transition in that frame and see whether the problem disappears.**

  Transitions are memory and processor intensive. They are the hardest tasks for the machine to complete. You might notice the time a transition takes to execute increases significantly on a low-end system.

- **Don't start a sound, test for mouse events, or try to apply palette effects in the same frame as a transition.**

  Transitions, like Lingo repeat loops, monopolize the processor, do their job, and get out. Apply the transition and move on.

- **Be sure to delete transitions that you don't end up using in the Score from the cast because they take up memory.**

  After you use a transition in the Score, Director stores it in the cast (new in Director 5). You now can reapply the same transition settings easily and share it with other movies in an external cast.

Transition Xtras

Director 5 introduces a whole new way of working with transitions. Developers now can develop their own transitions in addition to the ones that ship with the product. These are called *Transition Xtras.*

Chapter 23, "Macromedia Open Architecture: All About Xtras," covers Transition Xtras and the Macromedia Open Architecture.

The Two Sound Channels

Director provides two sound channels in the Score, but you actually can play more than two sounds at a time. The Macintosh can support up to eight sound channels. On Windows, Director for Windows can mix multiple sounds together into one with its MACROMIX.DLL, a technology built into Director. Chapter 12, "Sound: The Soundtrack," covers sound techniques and cross-platform sound considerations in detail.

To use the two sound channels directly, double-click in the sound channel of the frame in which you would like to start the sound. The resultant Frame Properties: Sound dialog box (see fig. 4.20) contains a list of the sound cast members in the cast.

Figure 4.20

Use the Sound channel to assign sounds to a frame.

Before you can view sounds in this window, you must first import sounds into Director's cast. Audio Interchange File Format (AIFF) is the most common sound format used in Director, as it is can play back on both the Macintosh and Windows.

Selecting the sound in this list sets the sound in that frame. You also can drag and drop a sound cast member from the Cast window to one of the two sound channels in the Score.

If you use Lingo to control sounds, you can have a movie play a sound when a user clicks a button, as well as initiate a sound at a certain time during the movie. Using Lingo sometimes can work better than using the Score if you're playing the movie in a low-memory situation. If you place the sound in the Score, the sound might be purged from memory if memory runs low. If Lingo tells a sound to play at a certain time, the sound might have a better chance at playing successfully than a sound simply waiting in the Score. Chapter 12, "Sound: The Soundtrack," covers using Lingo with sounds.

Tips on Using the Sound Channels

The following are some tips for using the two sound channels in the Director Score.

- You usually use sound channel 2 for background sounds. Reserve sound channel 1 for Lingo's `puppetSound` command.
- Avoid placing large sounds in frame 1 of your movie. Director loads the movie, its scripts, and other elements at that time. If possible, start the sounds after frame 1.

After you set your sounds in the Score, turn off the Score's sound channel. One way to do so is to click on the diamond to the left of the channel. You'll want to turn the sound channel back on for testing, but until then, you won't have to grow tired of the movie's sounds from hearing them over and over.

The Script Channel

You use the Script channel (see fig. 4.21) to enter Lingo scripts in effect only while the playback head is in that particular frame. The scripts in the Script channel are called *Score scripts*, but calling them *frame scripts* might be easier to remember, since they're intended for events that take place specifically in that frame.

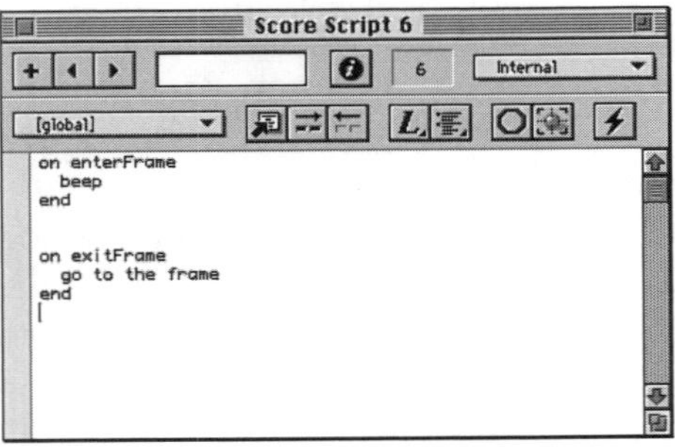

Figure 4.21

Enter Lingo programming for a frame in the Script channel.

To enter scripts for a particular frame, double-click on the Script channel for that frame and type the script. By default, the Script channel contains an empty `on exitFrame` handler. The two handlers that any frame can have are the `on enterFrame` handler and the `on exitFrame` handler.

Director executes the `on enterFrame` handler when the playback head enters that frame. Likewise, it executes the `on exitFrame` handler when the playback head exits the frame. Every script in the Script channel can contain one, none, or both of these handlers. For example, if the tempo of your movie is set to 10 frames per second, the exitFrame message will be received 1/10 second after the enterFrame message.

The Script channel is only one of four places you put your Lingo scripts. To find out more about the four places to put your scripts and the Script channel, see Chapter 16, "Lingo: The Basics."

Lingo

Almost everything you can do in the Score, you also can do using Lingo. The tutorials teach you about animating sprites, adding sounds and digital video, and changing cast members on the stage—you can do it all using Lingo. The trick is to find a nice balance between using Lingo in your movie and using the Score.

Many people say they know Director, but don't feel comfortable with Lingo yet, because they see a large learning curve with Lingo. And yes, the learning curve is high for learning *everything* about Lingo. What you might not realize is that you mainly use only a handful of Lingo terms. After you master these few terms, you're well on your way to high-quality Director work. Chapter 16, "Lingo: The Basics," contains a list of these essential Lingo terms.

Beyond the essential Lingo terms, Lingo becomes a robust scripting language. For the true programmers, it offers a complete interpretive language. Using the Director and Lingo, you are virtually unlimited in what you can do. And if you can't do it with the two together, you can use Lingo to communicate to C code compiled into Xtras.

Director 5 ships with many Xtras. Like XObjects before them, you can expect to see third-party Xtras, advertised on Macromedia's online services. If you can't find an Xtra that performs the functionality you seek, you can always develop your own using the Xtras Development Kit that ships with Director 5 Macintosh and Windows. Chapter 23, "Macromedia Open Architecture: All About Xtras," covers Xtras and the Macromedia Open Architecture in detail.

Interactivity and Navigation

Lingo is essential to interactivity and navigation within a Director movie. *Interactivity* is an oft-heard buzzword, right up there with multimedia and the information superhighway. *Interactivity* means just what it sounds like: the user interacts with the movie, which describes the beauty of how Director and Lingo work together. Director combines the multimedia elements; you decide where they should appear on the stage in the Score. Then, you use Lingo to tell Director what to do when a particular event occurs, such as when the user clicks on a button.

You can use Lingo to navigate around the Director Score, between Director movies, and launch other applications. The commands for this navigation are as easy as `Play`, `Go`, and `Open`. Examples of using these commands are covered in Chapter 16, "Lingo: The Basics."

Special Effects

You can create special effects and feedback in your movie using Lingo, saving time in Director because you don't have to set up each and every new scene in the Score. You can keep track of a user's path in a game you create that contains a maze to complete. If the user travels down the right corridor in your maze, you can play a particular sound. You can switch the color of the stage on the fly, initiate a transition, change the volume of a sound, or even quit the application.

Managing Media

Lingo provides many elements for managing the media in your Director movie. Director has memory management built into it, but you might need to issue some explicit memory management commands, depending on what you include in your movie and the system on which you intend to run your movie. Some of these commands include `Preload`, `Unload`, `PreloadRAM`, and so on.

You can use Lingo as a tool for testing the target machine and for testing the movie before you distribute it. It's a powerful tool in a Director project, as well as other Director movies designed as testing modules. Examples of Lingo tools and managing media with Lingo is covered in Chapter 17, "Managing Your Data."

Extending Beyond Director

Director 5 introduces the Macromedia Open Architecture (MOA) as a way to extend beyond Director. If you find you would like to add something to the basic functionality of Director, you can use C programming modules to extend the capability of Director. These modules in C are called *Xtras* in Director 5, and they are easy to use. Xtras currently available include the functionality for database connectivity, expanded printing, additional transitions, and more.

> Xtras are an updated and expanded replacement of the XOjects used with previous versions of Director. Director 5 still supports XObjects, but most of the current XObject developers are working with Macromedia to update their XObjects for the Director 5 Xtras architecture.

Director 5 also ships with an Xtras Development Kit (XDK), if you would like to develop these Xtras yourself. Chapter 23, "Macromedia Open Architecture: All About Xtras," covers Xtras and the Macromedia Open Architecture.

For those of you who simply use Xtras, your job is easy. After you place the Xtra in the correct place on your system, it appears in the appropriate menu. Depending on the Xtra's function, it could appear in a number of the menus. If, for example, the Xtra creates a new cast member, it will show up in the Insert menu. If it doesn't fit into one of the menu categories, it appears in the Xtras menu.

To install an Xtra, all you have to do is drop the Xtra in a folder called Xtras in the Director application folder. You use the Xtras folder in a folder called Macromedia in your System Folder. The Xtra then appears in all the Macromedia applications that support that Xtra.

The Projector

After your movie is complete, you can save it as a self-running executable file, called a *projector*. This projector can run on any machine that meets your movie's system requirements. The target machine doesn't need to have Director on it. The beauty of it is that it is royalty-free to Macromedia.

Director projectors are platform-specific. A Macintosh projector can play only on the Macintosh and a Windows projector can play only on Windows. You need to obtain a separate version of Director for each platform to which you want to distribute in order to create the platform-specific projector.

You can put a number of movies in a projector and distribute only one file to your customer. For larger projects, though, creating one small file to put in the projector that in turn calls to a number of smaller movies in the same folder or out on the CD works better, and also is a popular setup for creating hybrid CDs. You can have a CD-ROM with a Macintosh and Windows projector, each calling the same set of Director movies in a separate folder.

Depending on what media types your movie uses, you need to distribute certain files with the projector. On the Macintosh, your main concern if you are using QuickTime movies is to install QuickTime on the target machine. Chapter 22, "Delivering the Goods," covers file distribution, and distributing QuickTime and your relationship with Apple.

Royalty-Free

Macromedia stopped thinking about charging a run-time royalty on all of its products in 1994, when it introduced the Made with Macromedia program. Rather than a royalty, commercially distributed products require that you place the Made with Macromedia logo (see fig. 4.22) somewhere on the packaging and somewhere on the product.

The Made with Macromedia logo and licensing information is easy to obtain on the *Inside Director* CD-ROM or on the Macromedia Web site at http://www.macromedia.com. Frequently asked questions can be answered at the Made with Macromedia FAQ voice mail: 415-252-2171. Chapter 22, "Delivering the Goods," and Appendix D, "Contacting Macromedia," covers additional information on the Made with Macromedia program.

Figure 4.22

Macromedia requires that you include the Made with Macromedia logo on the packaging and the product if you commercially distribute any products you create using its products.

Using the New Director Assistants

The following sections are just a few of the features new to Director 5. They fit into this chapter because they change some of the ways you work with Director. Chapter 2, "Introducing Director 5: New Features Overview," covers these and other new features in greater detail.

The Toolbar and Tooltips

If you've worked with previous versions of Director, one of the first things you might notice in Director 5 is the Toolbar. Director is moving ever nearer to becoming a standard desktop product. You might even forget some of your keyboard shortcuts when you start using it, because you now can click on a number of tools in the Toolbar to do many of the same things you formerly had to dig to find.

If you select Show Tooltips in the General Preferences dialog box under the File menu, Preferences, General, you can move your mouse over each tool to find out its name. You also can turn off the Toolbar at any time from the Window menu.

The Right Mouse Button

Another new Director assistant to Director 5 is the capability to access shortcut menus all over the interface. You can access these menus within Director 5 with the right mouse button. You might wonder what "right mouse button" is supposed to mean, seeing as the Macintosh has only one mouse button. Clicking the right mouse button on the Windows interface typically reveals properties about whatever you click on. Well, Macromedia presents the same benefit on the Macintosh in Director 5, but you use the Control key.

In Windows, you can use the Control key or the real right mouse button to access information about properties.

Click on anything in Director 5 with the mouse while pressing the Control key to open a pop-up menu of options. You can get sprite properties when you click on a sprite, movie properties when you click on the stage, and more. Try clicking on a position in the Cast window and see all that you can do.

After you become accustomed to using the Control key, you can use it to automate many operations in Director.

The Inspectors

The marriage of Altsys and Macromedia in 1995 helped Director inherit some of FreeHand's helpful features, including the inspector palettes, grids, and alignment tools.

FreeHand calls its floating windows "palettes;" Director calls them "windows." We'll call them inspectors.

The Text Inspector

The new Text Inspector (see fig. 4.23) enables you to edit any text on the stage. To open the Text Inspector, select Inspectors from the Window menu and then the Text submenu, or press Command+T.

Although a basic feature, the Text Inspector saves time over the old menu routines used to edit text in previous versions of Director. Double-click on a rich text cast member or text field on the stage if you want to edit almost anything about its text.

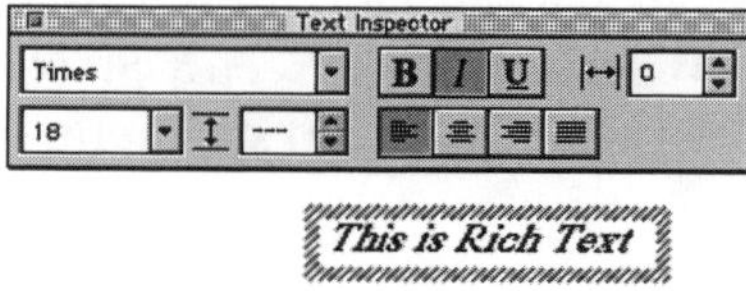

Figure 4.23

The Text Inspector enables you to edit any sort of text on the stage.

The Memory Inspector

Those of you familiar with previous versions of Director will recognize the Memory Inspector window (see fig. 4.24). To open the Memory Inspector, select Inspectors from the Window menu, and then the Memory submenu.

The information available now in the Memory Inspector used to be available in the About Director dialog box. This window shows a thermometer of the types of memory Director and the different parts of your movie are using at any given time. If you click on the Purge button in this window, the thermometer should drop, if you saved recently. If it does not drop, you'll want to select the Save and Compact command from the File menu to optimize the file. You can fill up Director's thermometer in a number of ways, mainly by working for a long time without saving. Using the Save and Compact command from time to time is a good way to keep your Director file optimized.

Figure 4.24

The Memory Inspector enables you to monitor how your system uses memory.

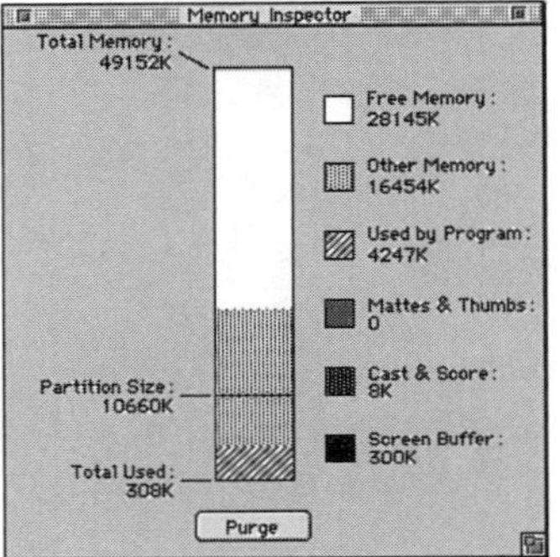

Grids and Alignment

Previous Director users should be happy to see the new addition of Grids and Alignment settings in Director 5. To view all of the Grid settings (see fig. 4.25), select the Grid submenu from the View menu.

Figure 4.25

Grids and alignment settings are new in Director 5.

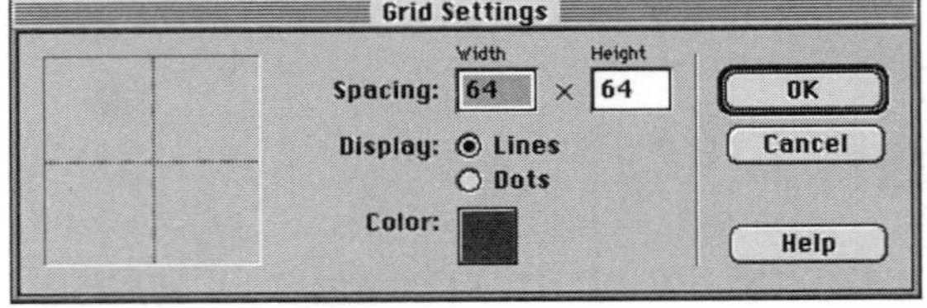

You can change the grid's color and spacing, as well as whether Director uses lines or dots for it. Experiment with these grids; they're quite easy to use.

The Align window (see fig. 4.26) enables you to select sprites on the stage and align them in a number of ways, both horizontally and vertically. You can find the Align command for opening this window under the Modify menu.

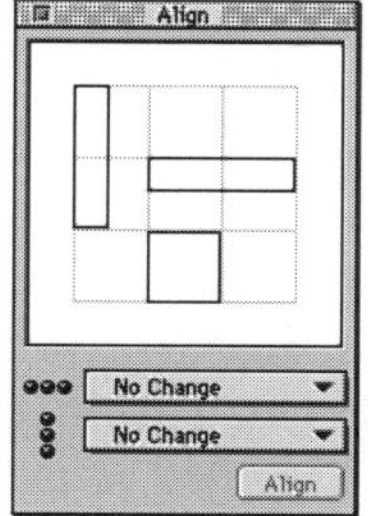

Figure 4.26

The Align window is yet another of Macromedia's brilliant new Director 5 features.

No longer do you need to use the Sprite Properties information to make sure that all the sprites line up to the same pixel on the stage.

NOTE

> You also can access the Align menu by Control-clicking any sprite on the stage.

To align a group of objects on the stage, Shift-select them all and open the Align window from the Modify menu. Select the alignment options you would like and click the Apply button. This feature is easy to use, and will save you hours of development time.

Director References

Any time you're working in Director and aren't sure what to do next, you have several options for finding additional help. The following three sections offer advice on where to go and who to ask for help.

Using the Online Help

Director's online Help system has undergone a complete overhaul and can help you considerably in version 5. Check out the FAQs, the bookmarks you can set up, and the copy-text capabilities of the Help system. It is a preview of Macromedia's move toward online documentation and should be applauded!

Using the Director Documentation

If you haven't previously worked with Director, consider progressing through the tutorials and sample files. The Learning Director and Learning Lingo can complement the Using Director manual, and you should never write a line of Lingo without the Lingo Dictionary nearby. The online Help file contains all the Lingo Dictionary contents, as well. The New Lingo Terms in Director 5 are listed in Appendix C, "New Lingo Terms in Director 5."

The Director Community

The Director community is strong and supportive. If you're just starting out with Director or you feel all alone with many seemingly insurmountable obstacles before you, here's some good news.

Nearly everything you might ever need to know about Director has been tried before. Although Director 5 does offer new features that everybody's going to have to get used to, you've still got a wealth of knowledge available. Every developer has particular ways of doing things in Director, but many people understand any number of common issues. Tapping into the knowledge and experience of other developers can help tremendously.

Get online. Download two weeks of CompuServe messages in the Macromedia forum (GO MACROMEDIA) or lurk on AOL (keyword: MACROMEDIA). Subscribe to the Direct-L mailing list and participate in the forum. If you're open to learning, you'll find many sources of information. For information on subscribing to Direct-L, check out Macromedia's Web site at http://www.macromedia.com.

Summary

This chapter merely scratches the surface of what you use in Director. As with any other product, the more you experiment, the more you discover and the easier it becomes.

Working with Director is easy after you get the hang of it. Some people jump right in with no problems, whereas other people look at all the cool things other people have made using Director—and at Director itself—and decide they'll never be able to learn how to create such things. The fact is, doing so really isn't that difficult.

You're now in the Director's chair of your own production outfit. You'll need to get to know the sets, the crew, and your cast of characters. You'll need to understand the target audience. Most important, though, you'll need to have fun. And you will!

PART II

Pre-Planning a Director Project

David Miller

The Strategy

This chapter looks at some of the issues you should consider before you begin authoring. What does the product do? Who is it for? What platform will it run on? Defining these issues at the outset will save you much grief and hair-pulling later on. This chapter also outlines a strategy for Director project development from concept to prototype.

Director projects can take many forms, and no development strategy will fit every project. Projects are developed by single authors in garages or by production teams with seven-figure budgets. Each project has its unique design requirements and creative solutions. Still, all projects share the goal of trying to communicate information using rich, multimedia content. This chapter outlines a development strategy and provides a framework you can adapt to the goals of your specific project.

The road from concept to prototype consists of three main steps:

1. Analysis: What are you doing?
2. Design: The way in which you are going to do it.
3. Prototype: Now do it!

The steps are followed in chronological order. The goal of each step is to produce a set of design documents that provide a road map and reference point for the next step. While you are in the middle of each step, bounce ideas off colleagues; be creative; brainstorm. Do not be afraid to try new ideas. But at the end of each step, come to a consensus and freeze the design. If necessary, revise the budget and time line. Do this early in the development process before "feature creep" and "design drift" consume your resources. At the end of this process you should have a well-defined, working prototype that forms the basis for production and a set of documents that form the basis for manuals and user documentation.

Feature creep is the tendency to tack on features to your software that go beyond its core functionality. A lot of commercial software suffers from this syndrome, where the pressure to create upgrades produces software with unnecessary complexity and a feature set that most people don't need or use.

Design drift happens when you start changing your design in ways that don't support your design goals; for example, adding a richly textured 3D interface just because it's the cool thing to do and not because it adds value or functionality to your product.

In general, the initial analysis, design, and prototyping should make up about a third of the total development time. Final authoring, production, and content creation should take another third, and quality assurance testing another third (if you're lucky!).

The project development strategy and design guidelines presented here are just that, guidelines. Know the rules—but know when to break the rules if it suits the design goals of your project.

Analysis: What Are You Doing?

During the analysis phase, nail down the goals and project specifications. What exactly do you want the product to do? For whom? On what platform? After the user is finished with your project is he entertained, educated, or informed? Or all three?

Define Goals

The first step in goal definition is to ask yourself, "What is this product trying to accomplish? Why does the product exist?" Are you trying to sell something, provide access to reference material, or reduce the client load for the customer support division? Write down these goals. In many ways, this is the most important part of the design process. At every decision point in your project, you should ask yourself, "Does this help me accomplish my goals?"

Another way to look at goal definition is to define the message that you want to convey. What story are you trying to tell? Why does the user want to use the product? What is the hook?

Write down a list of goals on a sheet of paper and make sure everyone on the development team has a copy. Every element of the project, including graphics, layout, and information design, should reflect these goals.

Define the Audience

To define your project's audience, create a list of the demographics of typical users. These might include education, age, and familiarity with computers and the subject matter, among others. Is the product for twelve-year-old gamers or computer-naive elders? What do these typical users want from your product? What assumptions and attitudes do they bring with them? Your design follows one track if the product is an in-house corporate training module, but follows another if it is a mass-market consumer product.

Talk to your users. A little informal market research cannot hurt, especially if you do not have access to market research data. Ask them what they like about products similar to the one you will be creating, why they do not like them, and what they wish they could do. If your product doesn't fill a perceived need, no one will want to use it.

After you define your audience, you might want to change your product's goals. Do it now. Rip up your list of goals and start over. It is easier to make changes early in the development process. The assumptions you make about your audience will affect every decision you make. If you reach the prototyping stage and your target audience finds the product unusable, annoying, or silly, you've just wasted a lot of time and money.

If your product distributes internationally, then start keeping track of cultural and language-specific items. You might need to leave extra space on the screen for the text of different languages. Be aware also of the cultural assumptions about visual symbols and colors. In some cultures, colors have special significance. For example, in Islamic countries green is often a holy color, and in Japan, white is associated with death. With Director 5 you can create multiple casts—each designed for a specific culture or language. Then you can switch casts at run time based on the user's culture and background. Managing multiple casts is covered in Chapter 8, "New in Director 5: Multiple Casts."

Is the product accessible to people with hearing loss, sight impairments, or limited motor skills? Designing for maximum accessibility often improves the design for everyone. You could make your product more accessible, for example, by choosing fonts that make text more legible or creating buttons that are bigger and easier to click on.

Define Delivery Platform and Delivery Media

Decide on the minimum system requirements for running your project. Director 5 projects run on a broad range of operating systems and hardware. Macromedia provides a list of supported hardware, video cards, and sound cards. Although Macromedia has done a great job of making Director files transparently cross-platform, you still need to be aware of cross-platform differences in such elements as fonts, palettes, and the gamma values of monitors. The "Tips and Tricks" booklet that comes with the Director documentation has a lot of helpful information in this regard.

TIP

If you are developing for delivery on Windows 3.1, then your file names must follow the 8.3 DOS naming conventions. Refer to the Director documentation "Tips and Tricks" for a detailed description of DOS naming conventions.

If your project delivers on an ISO 9960 CD-ROM, then naming conventions are even more restrictive. The only non-alphanumeric character allowed in file names on ISO 9960 CD-ROMs is the underscore "_".

Your minimum system places drop-dead design constraints on authoring and content creation. If your project has scrollable 1024×1024, 24-bit graphics and your clients have 386s with VGA monitors, then you have trouble. Macromedia states that Director projectors need a minimum of 4 MB of RAM, a 68020 processor, and System 7 on Macintosh machines and 4 MB of RAM and a 386/33 processor on Windows 3.1 machines. If you use 24-bit graphics and a lot of digital video, these requirements will increase. Make a list of the minimum system configuration you will support, including:

- Operating system
- Device drivers
- CPU
- Memory
- Monitor size and color depth
- Drives
- Network bandwidth

Test your project on your minimum systems from the start, especially under low memory conditions. Director 5 ships with a suite of new Lingo commands for memory management. Whenever possible, place your minimum systems in the same room as your authoring workstation and network them. When you are developing for multiple platforms, parallel development on the target platforms is generally more efficient than porting a finished product to a new delivery medium or platform.

Another critical design constraint is the delivery media. Will you deliver the product on hard disk, diskette, CD-ROM, videotape, kiosk, corporate intranet, or global Internet? Will you deliver it on more than one media? You should always design with reuse and repurposing in mind. The content from the CD-ROM you develop today might soon wind up on your company's Web site.

If you intend to output the project to videotape or display it on a television set, then test the project on your output system. The edges of your Director screens may be cut off. You might need to move screen objects so that they fall within what is called the action-safe or title-safe area. The *action-safe area* is generally 10 percent smaller than the area you see on the computer screen, or about 576×432 on a 640×480 Director stage. The *title-safe area* is generally 20 percent smaller than the area you see on the computer screen, or about 516×384 on a 640×480 Director stage.

Content Inventory

Now is a good time to take stock of your content, such as text, digital audio and video, videotapes and audio tapes that you will need to digitize, graphics, and all other collateral material. If you can use existing content, then you might be able to save a lot of time and money. Obtain high-quality originals of the content when you can.

Start a content inventory by making a list of existing content (see fig. 5.1). Next to each content element, indicate what additional work needs to be done to modify or repurpose the content for your project. Break text up into digestible chunks for the computer screen. Graphics, animation, and video might need to be edited or compressed so they can be displayed on your minimum system. Do you have the copyright or license to use the material? If not, can you get a copyright or is the material in the public domain?

Next, make a list of the content that you will need to create from scratch. Indicate media type, dimensions, resolution, time length, and anything else you think is important. Do not worry about accounting for all the content in your project now. Just give a general picture of what needs to be done. Keep this list nearby as you continue the development process and update it frequently. Your minimum system requirements place limits on what kind of content you can use. You should be aware of the technical limits of the media and playback systems you are using and how they restrict what is possible.

Content Inventory

Project interactive brochure Date 4/5/96

Content	Screen	Source	Format	Copyright	Processing
corporate video of headquarters	Intro	Company archives	VHS tape	Own	Digitize opening 10 sec; no audio
logo	Intro	Graphics Dept.	FreeHand	Own	Create PICT, no dither 256 system palette
product catalog	various	Publications Dept.	Quark	Own	Extract and edit text for each screen; find source for product photos

Figure 5.1

Example of a content inventory.

Beware of gratuitous media that can bloat a project. Creating original animation, video, and 3D graphics can quickly eat up time and budget. Whether you create original content or use stock content, it can consume memory and processor time, degrading the overall performance. Do you really need a CD-quality soundtrack to accompany the virtual reality tour of the company's main lobby?

Consider devising a coding scheme to name content. If the dimensions of your graphics are an important element of the content, then include the dimensions in the file name, such as HOUSE280.PIC. If color or black-and-white versions are available, then call it HOUS280C.PIC.

Organize content into categories, which makes it easier to update later. Also, it will make it easier to use the powerful new multiple cast features of Director 5. You could define a separate cast for each content category, making the content easier to find, organize, update, and change. If you are working on a large project with multiple authors, consider using a server to store content. Keep a log of edits you make to each content element. In Photoshop 3.0, use the File Info command from the File menu to store information about the file, such as what fonts are used or the location of the high-resolution original.

If you have tons of content, then you might want to create a content database to organize it all. You can use a general purpose database program, such as Claris' FileMaker Pro, or several other solutions designed specifically for multimedia, such as the Cumulus Network Image Database from Canto Software. Your content database should include such information as:

- File name
- Keywords
- Copyright and licensing
- Size
- Dimensions
- Color depth
- Resolution
- Compression
- Edit history
- Source file
- Projects in which you use the content

Information Design and Structure: Flowchart

In this step, you design a structure to lay over your information. What is most important about this information? Go back to your statement of goals and try to organize the information into manageable chunks based on these goals. Start writing down topic headings and subheadings. Arrange them hierarchically and draw links between topics. What relationships in the information do you want to emphasize? The hierarchy should not be too deep, maybe three or four levels. Links between sections will become the paths that a user follows to access the information. Generally, links should flow logically between sections without unexpected jumps or leaps. The user should find it easy to get to the most important information. Does it take more than three jumps to get to any place in your information structure? At the end of this process, you should have a flowchart, which will be the information map for your project. Figure 5.2 illustrates two very simple flowcharts.

Do not worry about the way in which this will all fit on a computer screen or the way you will do this in Director. That part of the design process will come in the next step. By breaking down the information into sections, drawing links, and creating a flowchart, you are setting the stage for the storyboard.

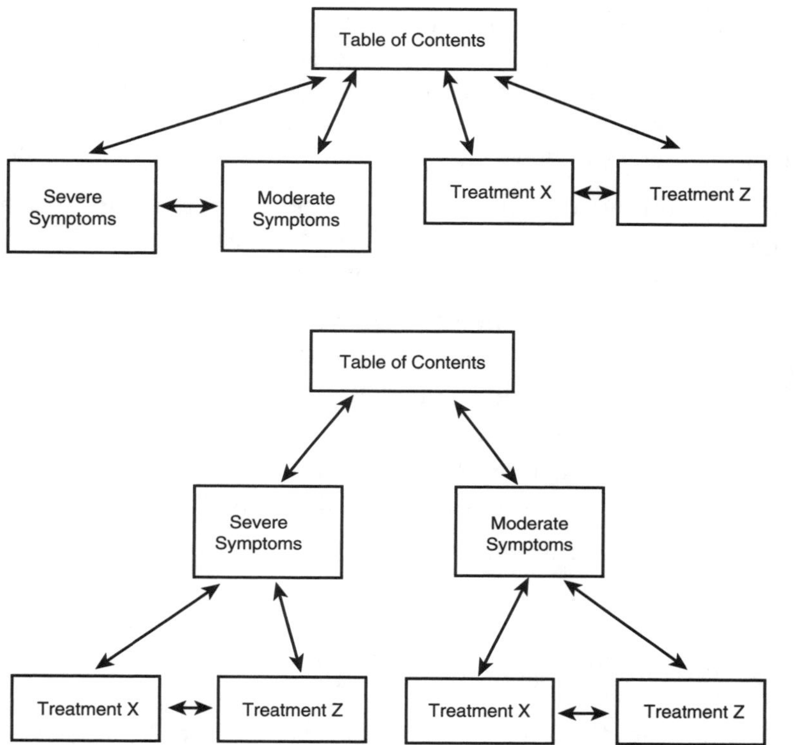

Figure 5.2

Examples of two different flowcharts for the same information in a health-care education product.

You can break down the information into sections and subsections in several ways. These ways include:

- By Category
- By Scaled Quantity
- Spatially
- By Time
- Alphabetically

One way to subdivide information is by category. Categories are anything appropriate to the content. Be aware of the underlying assumptions in your categories. Are you inadvertently emphasizing one aspect of the information at the expense of another?

Another way to organize information is by a scaled quantity, such as from cheap to expensive or from easy to difficult. A catalog of real estate properties might be organized by price, or educational software might be organized by level of difficulty.

Spatial organization, such as a map, is perfect for geographical data, but other kinds of information can be organized this way, with spatial proximity emphasizing relationships. You don't have to be constrained to two dimensions, either. Three-dimensional spatial interfaces are becoming increasingly popular.

Another common organization scheme is to organize information temporally, such as in a time line. This scheme is good for historical information or if your information takes a narrative form.

If text searching is important, then you can arrange information alphabetically. An alphabetized hypertext index or glossary is a handy, familiar way for users to find topics and jump to specific sections.

If you are repurposing existing material, such as the script of a corporate video or a training manual, then look at the underlying information structure and see the way in which it applies to the goals of your project.

For each section and subsection of your flowchart ask these two questions:

- What tasks is the user going to perform in this section?
- What is the goal of this section?

Write down the tasks and goals for each section. The tasks and goals will form the basis for the navigational design and interface design. If you cannot articulate a task and a goal for a section, then rethink your information structure.

End Result

At the end of this step you should have the following design documents:

- Statement of Goals
- Audience Definition
- Delivery Platform and Delivery Medium Specifications

- Content Inventory
- Flowchart

Make sure every member of the design team has a copy of the statement of goals, audience definition, and delivery platform specifications. These documents will guide every design decision you make.

Design: Which Way Are You Going to Do It?

In the design phase, you merge the flowchart with content and sketch out the user interface, screen layouts, and navigational controls. You determine the number of screens for each section of the flowchart and what content is displayed on each screen. When designing screen layouts and interfaces, do not worry about the details. Just block out the positions of the main interface elements, such as buttons, text, graphics, and digital video. You can use paper and pen, a draw program like FreeHand, or Director to sketch out the interface—whatever works best for you.

Using a computer to design your storyboard can help you figure out the quantity of text that will fit within a particular space and the way on-screen colors will look. Screen objects also are easy to move and resize on a computer.

At the end of the design phase, you have a storyboard to use when you start creating your product in Director.

User Interface Principles

The way in which you design your interface depends on your product goals. Making your product easy to use is usually one of those goals. The easiest-to-use interfaces are transparent; they get out of the way and let the user get work done.

Users like to feel in control of the computer and be able to directly manipulate objects on the screen, so do not take control away from the user. Be consistent in the ways that you indicate to the user which objects he can click, drag, or edit. When the user manipulates something, provide visual and aural feedback. If a user starts a process that will take more than a few seconds to complete, then show a watch or other "busy cursor."

Also, design a consistent interface. A particular button should always have the same function and be in the same place. It should not disappear unexpectedly or suddenly do something different.

Let the user make mistakes and undo actions. Do not be rigid in your design. Consider enabling the user to customize the interface in some way.

Apple Computer has made their excellent user interface guidelines available free of charge on the Internet. You can find these guidelines—along with a lot of other useful material—at http://www.info.apple.com. "The Macintosh Human Interface Guidelines" can usually be found in the Developer Services-Technical Documentation-Human Interface directory.

Help

The interfaces you design are always completely transparent and intuitive, right? Even so, it is often a good idea to provide some kind of on-screen help. A help feature is especially important if your users are unfamiliar with computers. You can provide a help feature in several ways. You can create a separate help screen, a floating Movie in a Window (MIAWs are covered in Chapter 18, "Movie in a Window"), or create help balloons or pop-ups like Director's Tooltips (see Chapter 2, "Introducing Director 5: New Features Overview," for a description of Tooltips). You also can use Director's animation features to provide guided instruction and task emulation.

Navigation and Interactivity

On each screen the user should be able to answer the following questions: Where am I? Where can I go? In what way do I get there? Navigation should be simple, consistent, and intuitive. Or, if you are designing a game, you might want the navigation to be difficult. An immersive, virtual reality environment will have different navigation than the navigation needed for a sales demo. Again, your design goals define your navigation.

How deep is your information structure? Does it take more than three clicks to get anywhere? If so, you should probably rethink your structure.

Also, it is a good idea to make all navigation reversible. If the user jumps somewhere, then he should be able to jump back. You might want to include a list of the screens that the user has visited, which helps him keep track of where he has been. You can use Director's List data structure to keep track of user actions. If the user visits your product more than once, then consider creating an external preference or bookmark file.

Generally, you should group buttons and controls that have related functions. Try to keep these groups in a consistent screen location. If for some reason a button is inactive or unavailable, then it is better to show this by dimming, or some other way, than by having the button disappear.

Make sure the function of each button and control is clear. Do not create similar-looking buttons that do different things. If the button that takes you to the next screen is a right-pointing arrow, then do not use a similar right-pointing arrow for another function, such as playing digital video. If you use an icon for a button in one screen, then do not reuse the icon as part of a non-clickable graphic somewhere else in the product. If you use drop-shadows or 3D, chiseled edges to indicate clickable regions, then do not incorporate these elements in other graphics. The user will think they are buttons.

Consider using both icons and text to label your buttons. Clear, easy-to-understand icons can be hard to design for certain functions. If you use text labels, then it is generally best to capitalize the first letter of each word and have the rest of the word in lowercase. Usability studies indicate that text is more readable on-screen this way.

Besides navigational elements, what other screen elements will the user be able to manipulate? What media controls will you provide? Is it necessary for the user to have frame-by-frame control of digital video? Of sound volume? In what way will the user interact with large chunks of related text that will not fit on one-screen? Will she, for example, jump to a new screen, use scroll bars, or turn pages?

Creating a Storyboard

This section outlines the steps to take when you create a storyboard. The *storyboard* is the main outline for the project. It merges the flowchart, script, screen layout, and navigation design into a single document.

Script

Gather together the narration and text (other than labels and buttons) and put them into one document in the order that they will appear in the product. This document is your *text script*.

Director's Score gives you control of the flow of events over time. If your project is heavily time-based and requires synching audio, video, voice narration, and screen display, then a good idea is to create a time line for each screen. Use your text script as a basis and insert audio, video, and animation cues when they should occur. If your project contains extensive animation or digital video, then consider writing out separate screenplays to give animators and videographers.

Screen Layout

Grids provide consistency, balance, and structure in page design and layout. Consider using a grid as a framework for your screen layout. An alternative to a grid is to use a 3D metaphor, such as a theatrical stage or desktop.

Sketch the grid or other framework. Then start sketching all the navigation controls and screen objects that will be common to all screens. These might include such objects as headings and labels. Do you have any room for the content?

Try several different layouts. At the bare minimum, you should create seven or eight sketches for each type of screen in your product. Then, you can narrow down your sketches to two or three basic designs. Do not worry about getting the screen layouts perfect. You will have time to do that during the prototyping phase.

Storyboard

Now it is time to create the storyboard. Get the project team together. (If you are the only person working on the project, then invite yourself to a meeting.) Make sure you have a whiteboard, blackboard, or slips of paper, thumbtacks, and a corkboard. Determine the number of screens for each section of the flowchart and what content you want to display on each screen. Sketch each screen on a separate sheet of paper with references to content and script, and thumbtack the papers to a corkboard. Try to visualize the big picture. Focus on the screen level and question the functionality of every element. In what way does each element help you meet your design goals?

Show your storyboard and flowchart to potential users, colleagues, and friends. Potential users might reveal logical inconsistencies in your information structure and flowchart. If so, go back and revise your flowchart and navigational design. Make your changes early. If you reveal design flaws and inconsistencies early in the process you will not need to spend extra time and money later on trying to fix them.

End Result

At the end of this step you have your project outline—the storyboard (see fig. 5.3). This design document is the road map for production and provides a visual overview of the entire project. By updating the storyboard as the project progresses, you can get a quick idea of how the development process is going. The storyboard also will provide a reference point for all team members. By sticking to the storyboard, you can help avoid potential design side trips that can throw your project off course.

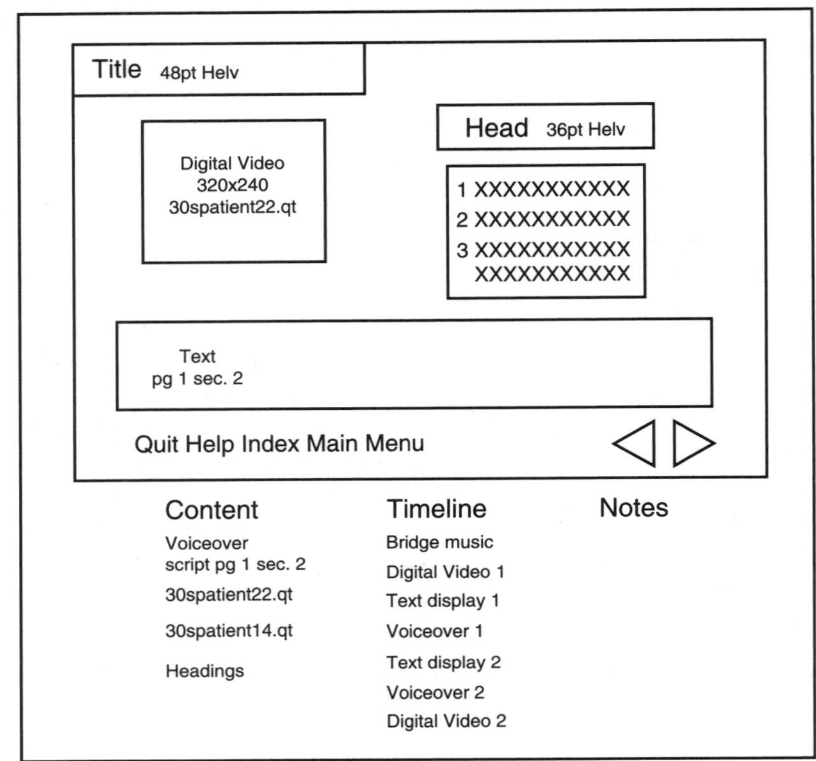

Figure 5.3
Sample page from a storyboard.

Implementation: Do It

During the implementation phase, use the storyboard and Director 5 to create a working model of your project. The working model is called a *prototype*. Director 5 has many new features to help you create a prototype, including grids (Chapter 4, "Working with Director: Understanding the Metaphor"), multiple casts (Chapter 8, "New in Director 5: Multiple Casts"), scriptable authoring and Lingo control of the Score (Part 4, "Lingo").

If you are developing for cross-platform delivery, then you need to develop a prototype for each platform. Windows and Mac programs typically follow certain interface conventions that users have come to expect from software. Quick and dirty ports from one platform to another are usually easy to spot for their non-Mac-like or non-Windows-like behavior. By developing a prototype for each platform, you can tailor the interface and functionality to the users of each platform and avoid the headache of incorporating interface and design changes late in development.

If you are developing cross-platform, then the following Lingo function will return the correct path delimiter for the current system.

```
on GetPathDelimiter
  if the machineType = 256 then
       return "\"
  else
       return ":"
  end if
end
```

You can build platform-independent path names, such as the following:

```
"MYDRIVE"&GetPathDelimiter()&"MOVIES"
```

Make sure your file and path names conform to the naming conventions of your minimum system.

Use the basic principles of user interface design and navigation design discussed in a preceding section as you create your prototype. Prototyping may reveal serious design flaws and you might need to go back and revise your storyboard or flowchart, but that is OK. Better that you find out now, rather than a week before the ship date when changes could put you weeks or months behind deadline and thousands of dollars over budget.

Prototypes

This section describes different prototyping strategies. Your prototype will probably be a mix of these types. The goal of prototyping is to reproduce the functionality of the final product as much as possible, without actually creating it. Also, prototyping enables you to test the most design-critical elements of your product before you begin serious authoring.

Proof-of-Concept

Sometimes, you might want to try something that has never been done before. For example, you might want to implement an artificial intelligence algorithm in Lingo or use a voice-recognition Xtra in a crowded computer lab. Can you do it? Who knows? One thing that is certain, however, is that it is time to create a proof-of-concept demo. You need to isolate the elements of the system that you need to test and begin a mini-design process.

Content

When you create your prototype, choose an extreme or end-member example from each of your content categories so that you can test playback and display. If the color-fidelity of 24-bit graphics is critical to your design goals, then make sure you include at least one 24-bit graphic in your prototype.

Broad Prototypes

In a *broad prototype*, you extensively develop a single layer within the information hierarchy. Screens in this layer are prototyped as fully as possible, and layers above and below are developed less completely.

Deep Prototypes

A *deep prototype* tunnels through your information structure. A screen from each layer is prototyped as fully as possible while adjacent screens on that layer remain sketchy.

Look-and-Feel Prototypes

A *look-and-feel prototype* emphasizes screen and interface design. Choose a representative screen or group of screens and bring them as close to the final version as possible. Adjacent or similar screens do not have to be as completely developed or as functional.

Using Director as a Prototyping Tool

This section discusses specific ways you can use Director to help you create your prototypes, including:

- Transforming a storyboard into a Director project
- Linking content
- Using grids, multiple casts, and scriptable authoring

Transforming a Storyboard into a Director Project

Authoring in Director generally falls between two extremes, Score-based and Lingo-based. *Score-based authoring* maps out everything in the Score with markers and frame sequences. *Lingo-based authoring* uses Lingo scripts and puppeted sprites to make everything happen in one frame. Most projects use a mix of Score-based and Lingo-based techniques. The Score provides a visual overview of your project that you cannot get from using a Lingo-based style. Often it is easier, however, to change a line of Lingo code than to march through 1,000-frame, Score-switching cast members. Whether you use Score-based authoring, Lingo-based authoring, or a combination of both depends on your experience, project performance, and how easy and efficient it is to author and make changes.

In any case, it is generally a good idea to use modular design principles to construct your Director project. *Modular design* means breaking up the project into self-contained chunks based on functionality and purpose. In theory, each chunk is a separate unit that has limited interaction with other chunks. If you need to change something or extend functionality, then you only have to change and extend one small chunk. The rest of the product is isolated from the change.

Your flowchart and storyboard already use modular design principles. The way in which you transform this modular design into a Director project is up to you. Director has several features that help you implement a modular design. One feature is Director's basic file type, the movie file. A natural way to implement a modular design is to treat each section of your flowchart as a separate movie file.

Next, you need to create a modular design for each screen. A single screen can be implemented as a two- or three-frame loop in the Score. Use the marker feature to name the frame loop. If you want, you can use Lingo to initialize the screen on the first frame. Then loop on one or two frames, waiting for the user to perform some sort of action, such as clicking on a button. After the user has done that, perform any clean-up functions, such as resetting buttons or graphics to their initial state, and jump to a new frame loop or movie.

Director's new multiple cast features also provide ways to create modular casts. Chapter 8, "New in Director 5: Multiple Casts," focuses on using multiple casts in this way.

Lingo is a powerful object-oriented scripting language. *Object-oriented* means, among other things, that Lingo has built-in modular code structures. Chapter 20, "Object-Oriented Programming," focuses on using Lingo in this way.

Linking Content

Do not worry about plugging in final content at this point. Just create low-resolution proxies, dummy graphics, or one-frame QuickTime movies to act as placeholders. If you develop a naming scheme for your content, then give the placeholders the same name as your final content. Keep the dummy files external to your Director file and link them into the cast. You can easily update the project with its final content by dragging and dropping the final content into the same folder as the proxy content. Importing and linking cast members is discussed in Chapter 7, "Import Options: The Casting Call."

Grids, Multiple Casts, Scriptable Authoring

Director has several new features that help you create prototypes. With the Grid and Alignment features, you can modify the underlying grid and align groups of sprites with one command. You can quickly create several different screen layouts and then test which layout users like the best.

Another powerful prototyping feature is the capability to include multiple casts. You can create sets of casts with different fonts, colors, and graphic styles. During prototyping you can quickly switch between different casts to compare and contrast different interface styles.

With the new Lingo features of scriptable authoring and Lingo control of the Score, it is even possible to create a prototyping tool that enables you to build prototypes on the fly, based on user input. Scriptable authoring and Lingo control of the Score provide new levels of programmatic control over development, prototyping, authoring, and playback.

Testing

Testing should be incorporated in all phases of the project from the beginning. Early testing can reveal design and implementation flaws that can be real show-stoppers if they turn up later. Catch problems early, when design and implementation are still fluid, before they become frozen in the final product. Test information flowcharts and storyboards on potential users before you even begin coding. If your project will depend heavily on digital video or other resource intensive media, get playback machines configured to your minimum system and create a quick prototype to test playback. Will the graphics cards you support handle your 24-bit illustrations? Does your printing Xtra conflict with a standard printer driver? Can you composite sprites on QuickTime movies in Windows? Will your FileIO routines work cross-platform? You won't know the answers to these questions until you run real-world tests. If you can, set up a room with several machines configured to minimum system and typical user system setups. Test early and test often on these machines to reveal potential bugs and bottlenecks.

As delivery dates slip, you might feel the pressure to spend less time on testing and quality assurance. Do not do this. Doing so sacrifices both your integrity and the quality of your final product.

Use your prototypes on every kind of hardware and software you can get your hands on and run them through their paces. In addition, have all the members of the development team do the same. Be sure to make a projector of your prototype and test outside the authoring environment, testing with the target audience, if possible. Whenever you include testers from outside the development team, try to shield them from non-functional parts of the prototype, for example, by providing a friendly dialog box indicating a feature is not implemented, or instruct them that they are testing a prototype and that not all of the functionality of the final product has been implemented.

Also, be sure to encourage them to be critical of the product and to provide feedback on how to make the product better. A good test subject should be articulate and opinionated about his user experience. One testing strategy is simply to encourage a test subject to continually verbalize about the user experience as he uses the product, while you sit nearby taking notes. Often a little compensation, such as money or a T-shirt, can help a test subject become more engaged.

Another testing strategy, which requires a little more work on the part of your test subjects, is to have them fill out written bug reports (see fig. 5.4). These reports should include details of hardware and system configuration, the severity of the bug, what screen the bug occurs on, the exact sequence of steps leading up to the bug, whether the buggy behavior is reproducible, and so on. A special bug report form is a good way to focus your testers on providing the detailed information you need.

Figure 5.4

Sample bug report.

Bug Report

Project__________________ Version ________ Date ________

Hardware:

Operating System:

Other software:

Severity of bug: 1 2 3 4

Description of bug:

Screen with bug:

Error codes or alerts:

Detailed steps leading to bug:

Reproducible:

End Result

Now that you have reached the end of your implementation phase, you should have a well-defined prototype and a set of design documents to guide authoring and content creation. By following these design and implementation steps, you should save yourself a lot of trouble later and be able to create a product of which you can be proud.

Summary

Before you begin creating a multimedia project in Director, it's important to clearly define product goals, characterize your target audience, and specify the minimum hardware platform you will support. These initial specifications will guide every subsequent design decision you make. Create a series of design documents that will provide a clear outline of the information structure and interactivity. These documents lay the foundation for content production and programming. Don't be afraid to make radical changes early in the process, but define milestones at which the design process becomes frozen and then move to the next step. Following the sequence of steps and other suggestions outlined in this chapter will help keep you on time and on budget.

David Miller

Staging Your Production

This chapter provides some tips on production management. Large multimedia projects involve the coordination of programmers, interface designers, content experts, writers, graphic artists, audio specialists, videographers, and animators. At the outset, it's important to set standards for file naming, version control, documentation, and editing. Also, it's important to clearly define who has responsibility for the different parts of the production, such as graphic content, video content, audio content, script writing, programming, interface design, and so on.

The model for multimedia production borrows from the publishing model, with authors and editors who compose and revise information respectively; the movie studio model, with a core staff of administrators, marketers, and creative directors who contract production to freelance talent; and the software development model, with full-time staff that supports multiple systems, performs system integration, and creates new versions and upgrades.

The following main subject areas are covered in this chapter:

- Setting the stage
- Managing content
- Code documentation
- Development issues by project category

Setting the Stage

This section discusses some general considerations for production authoring. Although geared toward larger projects, it also contains tips for smaller projects.

Document Everything You Do

Documentation of procedures is important. Documentation provides a database of tips and techniques that saves you time and money in future projects. Do not reinvent your workflow every time you want to burn a CD or retouch a scan. Carry a notebook with you and, as you perform different tasks, jot down the steps you take, the problems that arise, and the solutions you derive. Set aside an hour or two a week to organize and write up these notes and keep them in a three-ring binder for other team members to access. Provide a style sheet or form for documentation. If you are truly ambitious, you can create an online knowledge base that is accessible over a network.

For an online knowledge base or documentation form, include fields for date; name of person; functional category such as "Lingo programming," "Digital video editing," or "CD-ROM burning;" the purpose of the task, such as reducing 24-bit digital video to 8-bit; hardware and software used; a detailed list of steps taken; problems encountered; and results. For an online knowledge base, devise a consistent keyword scheme to facilitate searching and data normalization.

Naming Conventions

At the outset, determine a file-naming scheme for the Director movies, external casts, and final directories. If you are developing a hybrid HFS/ ISO 9660 CD-ROM, then the shared data must conform to the ISO 9660 naming conventions. Be sure you create directories for Mac-specific data, PC-specific data, and shared data. Create directories and subdirectories for external content and casts. The directory structure should mirror the organization of Director movies and Score sequences. When you reference movies from Lingo, leave off the DXR and DIR extensions. If file names change, you can use Director's search-and-replace feature to change the names within Lingo scripts. Use a MacPerl, AppleScript, or Frontier script to change multiple file names at the System level on a Macintosh.

Also, you should devise a coding scheme for naming content. Choose whatever works for you, but be consistent. Make sure all team members use the same scheme. To make sorting easier, the first letter(s) of the file name should be a code for the most important aspect of that file, such as media type, color depth, or client name. Include a code for version tracking, which can be the initials of the person doing the current work, a version number, or an identifier such as "prototype1" or "final." If an intermediate step generates numerous auxiliary files or alternate versions, then append an appropriate identifier, such as "edit1.1," and place them all in the same folder or directory.

If you are not constrained to the 8.3 DOS naming convention, for example, you could code QuickTime files as "qt;" the color depth as "8," "16," or "24;" movie dimensions as "160," "240," "320;" presence of foreign language text tracks as "engl," "span," "fren," "germ;" and use an extension such as ".v1" for a version number. Then, if you want to arrange files on disc based on color depth, you could name your files something like 24qt160span.v1. If external media, such as digital video, will be delivered on Windows, you'll have to conform to the DOS 8.3 naming convention.

Divide and Conquer

Consider dividing development responsibilities into manageable chunks based on functionality and content type. For example, one person can create interface elements, another can create digital video, and another can code the interface using proxy casts for the interface elements. Have the content developers create content as external casts that can link to Director movies for testing during development.

Refer to your flowchart and storyboard (discussed in Chapter 5, "The Strategy") and divide programming tasks based upon functional groups. Decide early the way in which the functional groups will interact. For example, if the project consists of three main sections, each of which contains 20 Director movies, then decide first the way in which the main sections interact at the top-most level and work your way down. Implement the most general data structures and most important features first, such as the basic navigation or help systems. Consider creating a "shell" or generic template into which you can add additional functionality as needed.

If you are working with the information flowchart, for example, you could decide to make each section of the flowchart a separate Director movie. First, code the navigation functions for the top-level "Table of Contents" screen. Then, create generic templates for the "Symptoms" screens and "Treatment" screens. These templates would provide basic navigational functionality and maybe a "shell" for a help system. The next step would be to add content, interface details, and context-specific help features to individual screens.

An alternative to this "top-down" approach, would be a "bottom-up" approach. In this approach, the lowest-level screens and Director movies are worked on first and the higher-level functions are overlaid on top of lower-levels later in the development process. What works best for you depends on your project, the number of people working on it, and their own particular preferences and programming styles.

Production Infrastructure

If you have several workgroups working on different parts of a project and sharing files that are in different stages of development, then you need to establish procedures for workflow, project tracking, and version control. A multimedia database on the back end helps manage content. You also need to set production criteria and milestones to ensure that the project remains on time and on budget. Production plans can be shared verbally by small workgroups or shared in writing by recording task lists and process flowcharts for large workgroups.

The enterprise network can be an important productivity enhancer or bottleneck. The speed, bandwidth, and storage requirements of a multimedia production network can quickly overwhelm Ethernet-based local area networks (LANs). You might need to isolate the production network from other traffic on your network. Fast Ethernet, Fiber Distributed Data Interface (FDDI), Asynchronous Transfer Mode (ATM), and Switched Multimegabit Data Service (SMDS) help reduce bottlenecks. Intelligent hubs enable individual workstations to optimize available bandwidth. Disk arrays and near-line optical jukeboxes can solve huge storage requirements.

The following is a possible model for a production infrastructure solution:

- Store master content on a near-line optical jukebox.
- Use a high-end Macintosh server or Silicon Graphics workstation as a production server.
- Attach a 9 GB disk array to your server with a 1 or 2 GB partition for each workgroup.
- Store edits and intermediate files in the workgroup partitions.
- Store personal archives on the local drives of client machines or on removable drives.
- Where necessary, mirror the directory structure of the final product on production drives.
- At the end of each day, move the material that meets the production criteria or milestone to a separate production archive that is a special drive with restricted write permissions. The material is now eligible for further production processing by other workgroups or is frozen.
- Use file permissions to restrict who can "check out" material from any drive or storage archive.
- Create disk images for test CDs from the production archive.

- Designate one person in each workgroup as the information "shepherd" to enforce version control and to make sure files are moved to correct locations.

Backups

A consistent and comprehensive backup strategy is critical. The backup system you choose depends on the amount of material you have to back up, the speed it takes to back up, the cost of drives and media, ease of use, and accessibility. Your back up system should be scaleable and expandable to accommodate the ever-increasing storage requirements of multimedia. The capability to perform unattended network backup is important for large networks. Having a centralized backup system is probably better than depending on each team member to back up his own workstation. You might consider using a dedicated server that backs up nightly to tape.

Think of backups as a cheap insurance policy. Disasters happen. The first time you use one of your backups due to hardware failure, fire, earthquake, and other disasters, it will pay for itself. Nobody thinks *their* system will be hit by a fire (or whatever) until it happens. Then it's too late. Don't trust "fireproof" data safes. Store your backups in a location separate from your originals. If the building in which you store the backups burns down, you can still make new backups from your originals.

The software you use for backups should support scheduling, multiple volumes, remote network backups, and the capability to perform incremental and full backups. Retrospect backup software from Dantz Development Corporation is a popular choice. Keep a copy of your backups off-site.

Removable drives such as Syquest drives, Zip drives, Jaz drives, and magneto-optical drives or external hard drives are generally cost-effective for backups in the 1–4 GB range or less. The removable drives also provide fast backup rates and easy access to files. The removable drive market is changing rapidly. Read trade magazines for reviews of the latest technology and see whether it meets your current and projected requirements.

The following trade magazines frequently review storage devices: *MacWeek*, *MacWorld*, *PC Magazine*, *InfoWorld*, *Byte*, and *New Media Magazine*.

Digital audio tape (DAT) drives provide up to 8 GB storage capacity per cartridge with transfer rates around 20 MB per minute. DAT loaders provide higher storage capacities with multiple cartridges.

Digital linear tape (DLT) drives are more expensive than DAT but can back up files at rates up to 100 MB per minute. A single cartridge holds up to 30 GB of data using 2-to-1 hardware compression. DLT drives are designed for the backup of large files—as opposed to several small files. DLT loaders provide higher storage capacities with multiple cartridges.

You can use recordable CD-ROMs for backups, but they have limited capacity and speed, and are write-once. CDs are good for archiving purposes.

Automation and Batch Processing

Scriptable authoring and Lingo control of the Score are new productivity enhancements in Director 5 and are used to streamline many tedious authoring tasks.

A *macro utility*, such as CE Software's QuicKeys, can automate repetitive processes or ensure consistency in editing. An example of this might be when you want to repeatedly enter the same value in an editing dialog box.

With a Macintosh, scripting languages such as AppleScript, Frontier, or MacPerl provide even greater control over processes along with some control over the system and other applications. All three languages support drag-and-drop and batch processing.

To batch process bit-depth reduction, resizing, file conversion, and many other image processing tasks, you can use Equilibrium Technology's Debabelizer. To batch process audio processing, use Macromedia's SoundEdit16 or Wave Technology's WaveConvert. Programs such as Adobe After Effects and Macromedia Extreme3D enable you to set up batch renders that you can schedule to run at night or on weekends when computers are not being used for other tasks.

Managing Content

This section discusses general issues regarding content management. Managing content for a large project involves balancing the competing constraints of time, quality, and money. To produce a quality enhancement of 10 percent may take 50 percent of your budget and 80 percent of your time. Only you can decide whether it's worthwhile.

Multi-Purposing

You should try to use existing content. This has the potential to save a lot of time and money, which you could then redistribute to other parts of your project. Snoop around for public domain material or collateral material to which you have the rights. Often, different departments in a large organization have collateral materials you can use. Many companies have media archives that contain videotapes, brochures, and training manuals. Maybe the facilities department has CAD-based maps of the company headquarters or perhaps there's a library where someone saved old photographs.

The downside of using existing content is that it often requires substantial investments in time and money to bring it up to acceptable quality. Corporate videos may be poorly lit or contain large areas of solid color that do not digitize well, making them unusable. Conversely, the video might be usable but you need additional footage. If you need to add material, such as additional video footage or voice-overs, then it might be impossible to match the style, production values, or to obtain the same talent used in the existing version.

When you have to create from scratch, you should design your original content with repurposing in mind. *Repurposing* means using the same content in different projects or on different media and delivery platforms. The content you create for your Director project might wind up in print, broadcast video, CD-ROM, or the Internet. You can create the content once, then modify copies for a specific delivery platform. This usually is more efficient than creating new content for every project. Creating content once and repurposing it also helps to enforce a consistent look across multiple platforms and projects. Generally, a good idea is to create original content at the highest resolution you can afford in time and disk space. By using the highest resolution, the content survives the conversion to different formats and media. Consider such issues as what 24-bit graphics will look like dithered to 256 colors, what downsampling does to audio, and the tradeoffs in different video compression formats.

Also, you can edit copies of high-resolution originals. Keep your digital assets on a locked volume, such as a CD-ROM, to prevent accidental editing. A good idea is to keep an edit log as you edit your content. An edit log can be a text file in the same directory as the content and with the same name but has the extension TXT. For example, grphc24.txt would be the edit log for the file grphc24.pic. Also, you can use an application-specific feature, such as Photoshop's File Info command from the File menu, to record information regarding the file.

You should always save intermediate versions of edited files, in case you have to reconstruct a file after a bad edit. Save copies of your Premiere or After Effects projects because they provide a record of filters, effects, and compression settings. If you need to compress, reduce bit depth, resize, or in any way reduce the amount of actual information in your file, then save this edit for last.

Master Content and Archives

Master content is the high-resolution, high-quality source that you use to create content for your Director project. A good idea is to create or obtain high-quality master content because it ordinarily is easier to repurpose, edit, and—if it is in analog form—digitize. You should never edit or directly change master content; only edit copies.

The reason you want to spend time and money to create, digitize, or obtain high-quality master content is to save time and money when you need to generate derivative content for multiple products. If all you plan to do is create a one-shot, animated Shockwave banner, then don't waste time and money creating 24-bit graphics. On the contrary, if you intend to create corporate identity elements to use in different media and products, then it pays to create high-quality, master content. Look at the return on investment and evaluate whether it justifies the extra expense. Consider the "shelf life" of the content—the length of time before the material becomes dated. If you create and own original, high-quality content, consider licensing it to others.

Determine also the file formats you want to support based on compatibility and storage space. Save files in the format that preserves the most information. Devise a file-naming scheme that encodes information such as file type, file characteristics, client, and project name in the file name itself. Be sure to give the master content files a special extension or identifier. For example, indicate master files with a capital "X," such as 24qt160span.X. On the Macintosh, you also could use the Label feature to give a common label to your master content files.

If you use a multi-layered Photoshop or Painter file, save the file in its native format to preserve the layering. The same is true for FreeHand artwork or other object-based drawing files. Make a copy of these files as PICT (or another format) for use in Director.

The resolution of a computer monitor is only 72 dots per inch (dpi), so you might think that you do not need to create files with more than 72 dpi. Still, at some point in the future, you might use your digital assets in product packaging or the company's annual report. If repurposing for print is a possibility, then you might want to create content at higher than 72 dpi. Also, reducing the size and bit depth of graphic files usually works best if you start with high-resolution and high bit-depth originals. Another situation where you might want to use a higher dpi is in scanning. Reduce the material to 72 dpi when you are ready to import it into Director. If you do not reduce the material to 72 dpi, a 144 dpi file, for example, will appear twice as large in Director.

At 72 dpi, a 640×480, 24-bit graphics file is approximately 900 KB in size. At 144 dpi, the same file is four times as large, or about 3.6 MB. For information about using graphic content in Director, see Chapter 9, "Graphics: The Visuals."

Digitize video at full-screen, 30 frames per second (fps), and reduce the size and frame rate for your Director project. (Chapter 14, "Digital Video: The Movie within the Movie," contains more information.) The file size of digital video depends on many factors, but 2–6 MB for every second of digital video is not unreasonable.

File sizes for one minute of uncompressed, digital audio range from 0.7 MB for telephone quality (8-bit, 11 KHz, mono) to 10.6 MB for CD-quality (16-bit, 44 KHz, stereo). Chapter 12, "Sound: The Soundtrack," discusses digital audio in more detail.

Also, you need to determine in what way you will store your master content. Maintaining libraries of videotapes, audio tapes, photographs, and printed source material can be costly and the materials can degrade over time. Digitized versions are more durable and easier to edit, but require vast amounts of storage. After you spend the time and money digitizing material, you probably will want to archive it. One solution is to use one of the backup options discussed in the "Backups" section later in this chapter. Storage on one-off CD-ROMs or a PhotoCD is one solution. CDs provide fast random access, write-protection, and are accessible on any computer with a CD-ROM drive. (Remember to store a copy of the master content off site.) Media servers and fast networks are another archive option, provided you have a lot of money.

Organization, storage, and retrieval issues might require that you create a content database. If so, you can use a general purpose database program, such as Claris' FileMaker Pro, a content browser such as Adobe Fetch or Kudo Image Cataloguer, or an industrial-strength database designed specifically for multimedia content, such as the Cumulus Network Image Database from Canto Software. Your content database should include the following types of information:

- File name
- Keywords
- Licensing and copyright
- Size
- Dimensions
- Color depth
- Resolution
- Compression
- Edit history
- Project tracking information
- Source file
- Projects it is used in.

Copyright and Intellectual Property

Copyright and intellectual property laws are murky, especially for digital media. The easiest way to handle copyright and intellectual property issues is to only use materials you own. If you do not own the material, then purchase the material and all rights to use it. If you cannot buy the material outright, then you will have to obtain a license agreement, permission letter, or release form. If you use so-called public domain material, then make sure it is really free for you to use.

Even though you use material in one project, do not assume you can use it freely in subsequent products. As long as material is in the public domain, do not assume that all forms of it also are in the public domain. A piece of music may be in the public domain, but a recording of it by the San Francisco Symphony Orchestra probably is not. Also, you need to obtain a model release form when you use someone's likeness in a product.

Copyright and intellectual property issues are worth books in themselves and several good books are available in the market.

A good book that covers copyright issues and many other legal issues surrounding multimedia is *The Multimedia Law and Business Handbook* by J. Diane Brinson and Mark F. Radcliffe, Ladera Press.

The opinions set forth in this section do not constitute legal advice or counsel. Be nice to your lawyer friends; you might want to discuss it with them beforehand.

Code Documentation

Lingo has become an industrial strength, object-oriented scripting language. Although probably not suited for coding an airplane guidance system, you can do almost anything else in Lingo. Large projects generate a lot of code. The more code there is to maintain and debug, the more important it is to document your code.

Code documentation consists of the following:

- Specifications and requirements for the project code
- Descriptions of the algorithms and data structures
- Descriptions of overall design and architecture
- Comments and documentation within the code itself

Typically, maintaining an existing code base consumes the most time and effort in a large programming project. Consequently, it is important to make code readable and easy to maintain. For a big project, it is helpful to have a dictionary of the data structures used in the project.

The dictionary should list the names, data type, and purpose of the most important data structures. For example, the global variable `glUserHistory` is a list containing the names of the movies the user has visited. The list is modified by the `SetUserHistory` function in the `startMovie` handler of every movie. The `DisplayUserHistory` function takes the list and creates a pop-up menu, when the user clicks on the Go button.

Also, it is helpful to have a written overview of the program design and architecture. The overview should indicate where important scripts reside in Director (Score, frame, cast, movie), what these scripts do, and the way to implement an important feature like navigation. The overview also should list any external files or Xtras you use. If you use object-oriented techniques, then prepare a class diagram that illustrates the relationships among classes.

In each movie, for example, the Score is divided into short frame loops. Each frame loop corresponds to a single screen. The first frame contains initialization code. Then, the program loops on the remaining frames, waiting for user input. A frame script in each frame tests rollover conditions to provide interface feedback.

Self-Documenting Code and Comments

A good idea is to make your code self-documenting. *Self-documenting* means that variables and functions have names that describe their purpose. Make your variable names reflect what the variable stands for, for example, `ButtonSprite` or `NextMovie`. Nothing is more confusing than trying to read code where all the variables are named x, y, z. Your functions should have names that reflect what they do, such as `HiliteButton` or `ProcessMouseDown`. Capitalize words in multi-word names. The goal is to make your code readable and understandable to someone else or to remind yourself, months later, what a variable stands for in case you forget.

A common variable naming technique, is to start every global variable with a lowercase `g`, such as `gMyGlobalVariable`. You also can start each variable name with a lowercase letter that stands for the data type of that variable. For example, use `sTodaysDate` for a variable that contains the date as a string; `iAge` for a variable that contains the user's age as an integer; or `lMovies` for a variable that contains a list of movies. Variables in Lingo can contain a string, integer, object, or any other data type, which helps to prevent the assignment of the wrong data type to the variable. You can extend this technique to multiple characteristics. For example, `piAge` could be the property of an object that is an integer.

Comments are statements in your code that begin with a double dash (--). Director ignores these statements. Adding comments to your code is essential for readability, but you can overdo it. Don't clutter your code by commenting the obvious. The goal of comments is to make the code readable and maintainable. In general, it is a good idea to provide comments for the following:

- New variables
- Code structures such as if-then statements and repeat loops
- Functions
- Any non-obvious or obtuse code (of course, no one ever writes obtuse code!)

Include the following information in comments about a function:

- What information and data types are sent to the function
- What the function does
- What data the function returns
- Where the function is used in the overall program design

Because Lingo scripts can contain styled text, you can use colors and text styles to highlight different parts of your code. You can make all comments italicized, for example, or all references to a particular object a shade of red. To colorize your text, select the text you want to colorize and choose a new foreground color from the pop-up palette in the Tools palette.

Version Control

Document any changes you make to existing code. Create a comment section in a prominent place; for instance, the beginning of the `startMovie` handler, where programmers insert comments as they make changes. The comments should indicate the date, the programmer's initials, and the changes the programmer makes. Another good idea is to insert comments with the same information in the code itself, at the location where major changes are made.

Development Issues by Project Category

This section discusses development issues for some specific project categories. These include the following:

- Presentations
- Sales and marketing
- Enhanced CD and CD Plus
- Educational software
- Corporate training
- Kiosks
- Games
- Consumer titles
- World Wide Web
- Interactive art

Presentations

If you use Director to create presentations, tailor your presentation for the target audience. Use external, linked casts so you can easily change content to suit your audience.

Test your presentation on the display system beforehand. Make sure audio and video can be heard and seen from the back of the room. Have a backup, such as slides, transparencies, or a complete second system.

Design easy navigation. Consider including a way to jump directly to any screen in the presentation, which is useful when you want to illustrate a point in a question-and-answer session.

If the presentation is running on a laptop, what are the screen size and bit-depth of the laptop's screen? Will you have to support video mirroring to a second display device?

If the display device is a television set or the presentation is output to videotape, the edges of your Director stage might get cut off. Make sure your presentation fits within the action-safe and title-safe areas. The *action-safe* area is about 576×432 on a 640×480 Director stage; the *title-safe* area is about 516×384 on a 640×480 Director stage

Sales and Marketing

Sales and marketing projects include demos, advertisements, interactive business cards, catalogs, portfolios, and promotional pieces—to name just a few. Delivery can be on a wide range of platforms, including floppy disk, CD-ROM, broadcast video, and the Internet.

Clever packaging or cover art is a good hook. Whenever possible, provide one-step installation. The interface should be simple and fun, and not distract from the product message. Provide information in short, digestible chunks. The users should be in control and able to skip over sections when they want. The user should be able to reach contact and purchasing information easily.

You can use Director's animation capabilities for task emulation in a demo. Reuse existing content, such as print and video material, in advertisements and promotional pieces. Catalogs provide a way to look at an object from different views or in different situations.

Enhanced CD and CD Plus

The enhanced CD is based on audio CD. Audio CDs follow a standard industry format called the Red Book and hold about 74 minutes, or 650 MB, of digital audio data. Typically, audio CDs contain less than 74 minutes of music. If a CD has 50 minutes of music, then there is about 24 minutes, or about 200 MB, of unused space. Use the unused space to provide interactive content that follows the Yellow Book standard industry format.

NOTE

You can obtain the technical specifications of the Red Book and Yellow Book standards by contacting ANSI at the following:

ANSI
Attn: Sales
1430 Broadway
New York, NY 10018
212-642-4900

The first enhanced CDs placed the interactive content in the first track of the CD (Mixed-Mode) or before the first track (Pre-Gap). One problem with these formats is that users inadvertently rewind or play the interactive content on their audio CD player that creates a horrible noise.

In 1995, Apple, Microsoft, Sony, Philips, and the Recording Industry Association of America (RIAA) defined a new standard industry format, called CD Plus or Blue Book, for enhanced CD. CD Plus is a multisession standard, so computers will need to have multisession-capable CD-ROM drives. Most recent drives are multisession-capable.

Apple Computer is shipping its QuickTime Music Toolkit for Enhanced CD development. Macromedia and Brilliant Media have announced plans for Enhanced CD tool kits.

Educational Software

Educational software consists of a broad range of products, including electronic textbooks, collaborative learning environments, simulations, and teacher support materials that are used in school, work, and home. The benefits of educational software include consistent message, rich content, self-paced learning, audio and visual reinforcement, and the capability to simulate problems and environments that might be too expensive or dangerous in the real world.

User tracking is one of the most important issues in educational software. Director has two excellent, built-in data structures that you can use to store user data—lists and property lists. (You can find more information about lists and property lists are discussed in Chapter 17, “Managing Your Data.”) Property lists are similar to associative arrays in other computer languages. A property list to track user data might look something like "[#name: "Jessica", #answer1: "yes", #answer2 :23]". Use Director to write this data to an external text file for storage. Provide a way to read the data back in, to provide support for multiple sessions by the same user.

Corporate Training

Corporate training projects include standalone individual instruction materials, support for classroom training and on-demand training, and have many of the same production issues as educational software. You can develop a "shell" or template for corporate training projects that you can reuse and update, in order to present a consistent corporate identity.

Kiosks

Kiosk applications are commonly developed for a specific delivery platform. Test your project from the beginning with the kiosk hardware and system software.

A kiosk typically contains an attract loop or snazzy introduction that runs repeatedly to attract people's attention. After you grab the user, you need a way for that user to interface with the product. Should you use a touchscreen or a keypad? Test the response of a touchscreen to Lingo `mouseUp` and `mouseDown` handlers. If you use a touchscreen, then make the buttons bigger than a person's fingertip and leave plenty of space around each button. Use a `timeout` handler to drop back into the repeat loop after a certain amount of time.

You also need to determine whether the kiosk will support transactions or printing. Consider the way in which you will update material for the kiosk. Can the people who maintain the kiosk access the CD-ROM drive to perform updates? If the kiosk is networked, you might be able to perform updates and maintenance over the network yourself. Keep material that requires updating in linked, external casts.

Be sure to consider what the lighting in the kiosk environment is like. You might need to adjust the brightness of the monitor and the saturation and contrast in your graphics. Check kiosk placement to minimize glare. If the environment is noisy, then you may need to provide headphones and create your attract loop visually.

Games

Games must have fast response times and usually require performance testing to optimize playback. Although a thorough discussion of the critical aspects of game development are beyond the scope of this book, a sampling of game programming techniques are discussed in Chapter 19, "Advanced Concepts."

Consumer Titles

Developing a consumer title is a complex process that requires having time, money, high-production values, marketing knowledge, and distribution channels.

Typical development times range from nine months to one year. If you are developing a consumer title, many of the suggestions in this and the previous chapter will help. Define the product goals, know your audience, and define the delivery platforms you will support. What platforms you support will place critical design constraints on your product. Unlike most presentation, training, and educational software, consumer's are not a captive audience. Therefore, your title should be easy to use, easy to install and absolutely bulletproof.

Generally, there are three publishing models for consumer titles. Each publishing model has varying barriers to entry. You can sell your work outright to an established publisher and receive royalties or a flat fee. You can sign with an affiliate label that has exclusive publishing rights where you retain more control over the product. Or you can publish, distribute, and market the title yourself.

World Wide Web

With Shockwave for Director you can deliver multimedia over the World Wide Web. For first generation Shockwave titles, the user must download the entire Shockwave movie completely before the client computer can play it. The critical issue in Shockwave titles is movie size and download time. If users are connecting over high-speed Ethernet, a movie in the 400–600 KB size range might be acceptable. For users connecting via modem over phone lines, a movie of the same size would take several minutes to download. Streaming technology, where the Shockwave title starts playing first and then downloads the rest in the background, wasn't available for Shockwave at the time of this writing, but it was under development and plans were underway to implement it soon. For more on Shockwave development, see Appendix A, "Director on the Internet: Shockwave!" More thorough coverage is available in *Macromedia Shockwave for Director User's Guide*, published by New Riders.

Macromedia has a useful online developer's guide for Shockwave called "Shockwave Developer's Guide." You can find it at http://www.macromedia.com/Tools/Shockwave/sdc/Dev/.

Interactive Art

Interactive artists are expanding the multimedia aesthetic and are blurring the lines among performance, video, visual art, music, and sculpture. Adaptive interaction enables an audience to mold and change an interactive performance.

Many interactive art pieces rely on external device control and feedback. You can control external devices through the Macintosh's serial port or use an external control device such as a CNX box. A CNX box has features including analog-digital, digital-analog, and digital I/O ports. CNX boxes connect to a Macintosh via LocalTalk. Director control is through XCMDs.

For more information call Engineers Express, Inc. at 1-800-882-3797.

Other options for external control include the MIT Miniboard (http://cherupakha.media.mit.edu), and devices from Alcorn McBride Inc. (http://www.alcorn.com/) and IBVA Technology (1-212-754-IBVA).

Summary

There are no hard and fast rules in multimedia development. The main points to get out of this chapter are the importance of procedure documentation, and the organization of media and processes such as file naming, editing, and backups. Also, it's important to not let deadlines slip.

There are few road maps to guide developers. Borrow what you can from television, film, computer software, and publishing development models, but realize it's a new frontier. Just do what works. Rapid changes in hardware and software tools make multimedia development a continuously evolving process. The skills and tools you have today might not be used in two or three years. Don't stop educating yourself.

PART III

Director's Multimedia Components

John Chambers

Import Options: The Casting Call

This chapter covers how to import media elements into Director. Starting with the programs that you probably use every day, you'll take a step-by-step tour of the options available in Director to give these media elements their 15 minutes of fame. The information in this chapter helps smooth the way to a better understanding of how you acquire, integrate, and save media elements, as well as how to make them behave correctly after you introduce them to Director's authoring environment.

This chapter covers the following material:

- Importing essentials
- Matching imported media with screen colors
- The Import window
- Image options
- Format options for importing

There is no one way to perform a task—you always have options. Bearing that in mind as you work with other applications, be sure to check out all of any application's available export options. You can use Macromedia FreeHand, a PostScript drawing program normally used to create files for high-resolution imagesetters, for example, to create text boxes formatted as Rich Text Format (RTF) as well. You also can save FreeHand files as PICT files. You can move a PICT file into Adobe Photoshop, where you could add a drop shadow airbrush effect, resave the file, and import it into Director. Experimentation is key in designing creative images and a single application might not solve all your imaging roadblocks. Mix, match, and explore.

Importing Essentials

Any media elements you import are added to a cast file and become cast members. When you import media elements into a multiple cast Director project, you must first select the Cast window into which to import the media. Figure 7.1 shows two available windows, with only one active. Imported media are placed only into the active Cast window. In this example, the topmost Cast window is the active window. You also need to choose the storage method for the imported data. Two options are available, the first is non-linking (the default) and the other option is linking. A Director document containing non-linking media elements makes the entire Director project larger.

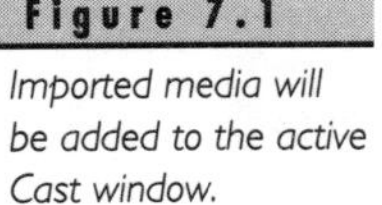

Figure 7.1

Imported media will be added to the active Cast window.

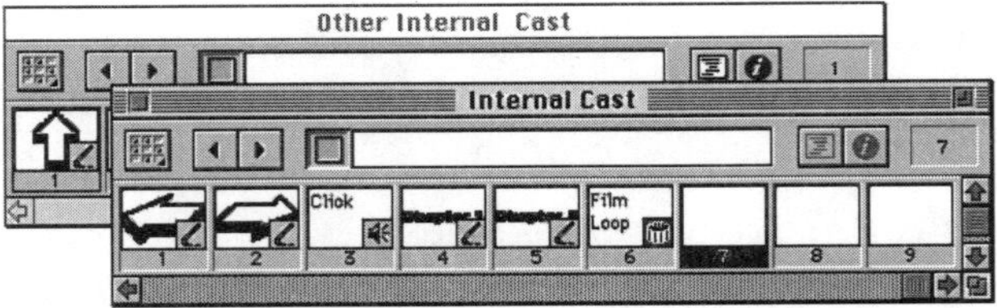

If you had to import a 300 KB graphic into the current file, the Director file would increase in size by 300 KB. Non-linked media elements work very well for smaller media projects. (A small media project might fit on a single disk or on a set of three or four disks.) You would then need to segment and compress the file. Your user could load the multiple disks to a hard disk drive and then join and expand the project.

A program that works very well for compressing and segmenting files is StuffIt Deluxe from Aladdin software. With this type of stuffed file, your recipient can easily join and expand the file automatically.

The second option for storing imported data would be to use a linked file. A linked media file is located outside the actual Director file. Using the linked file option makes for a smaller Director file. A linked graphic about 300 KB in size adds only about 1 KB to the file, as opposed to about 300 KB if you were to use the non-linked media file method. The only downside to using the linked option is that you have to keep track of the media files you use. Director uses a path name to locate the original media files, so be sure to keep the original media available for the document. One advantage of linking media is that it enables you to view a large project on a computer that has a limited memory capacity, so you could show a 400 MB project on a computer that has only 16 MB of RAM. A 400 MB Director project would be pressed onto a CD-ROM with linked media.

When the CD is loaded into the machine and the project is run, the linked media of the Director file loads on demand as the project plays. Another advantage to linked media files is that the files are not contained inside the Director project. Since these linked files are stored outside the Director file, the linked files can be modified individually. Maybe change the theme song of a movie or update an employee list. After the individual file is updated, the Director project will automatically update due to its linking properties.

You can modify a linked file without opening its parent Director document. You could use a set of dummy media or slug files, for example, before the actual art files become available. After the media does become available, you just rename the new art files with the dummy file names. Remember, Director uses the path name for linked files. Also, note that the dummies and newly added media files should match in size and resolution.

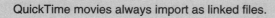

QuickTime movies always import as linked files.

Matching Imported Media with Screen Colors

When you open a file in Director, it first checks your monitor's Color bit depth setting, which affects the number of colors displayed on-screen. *Color depth* refers to the amount of color the computer screen is displaying, which can be adjusted in the Monitors control panel. You can check and modify the Color bit depth setting by choosing the Monitors icon in the Macintosh's control panels folder. Select Apple Menu, Control Panels, Monitors to display the Monitors preferences dialog box (see fig. 7.2).

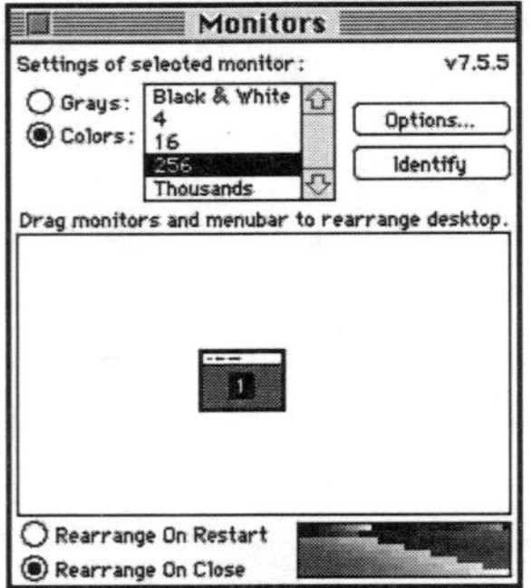

Figure 7.2

The Monitors control panel settings.

When you launch Director, it automatically sets its palette to the color depth of the monitor's control panel. A Director movie can play at any number of bit depths, ranging from 1-bit black-and-white, 8-bit in either 256 colors or 256 levels of gray, all the way up to 24-bit, which is more than 16 million colors. When you import media into Director, you actually are dealing with two different types of color depth information. The first type of color depth information is the amount of color available in the Monitor's control panel during launch. The second type of color depth information is how much color is in the file being imported.

The number of colors the monitor was set to at launch should match the amount of color contained in the file being imported. Otherwise, your file looks rather odd on-screen and might not run at its optimal playback speed. Chapter 9, "Graphics: The Visuals," covers using Adobe Photoshop to adjust the bit depth of a media file outside of a Director document. Adjusting the bit depth of a media file that you're importing is discussed below.

The Import Window

To import a media element into Director, choose File, Import (Command+R) or select the Import button in the toolbar, to open the Import dialog box (see fig. 7.3). The list at the top of the dialog box contains all the files—within the currently displayed folder—Director can import. As you select elements from the top list, review pictures appear in the dialog box's upper left corner (that is, assuming that the QuickTime extension has been loaded properly). Sometimes you need to push the Create button if you want to be able to view a poster image of the incoming media. You can turn off the Preview feature by disabling the Show Preview check box.

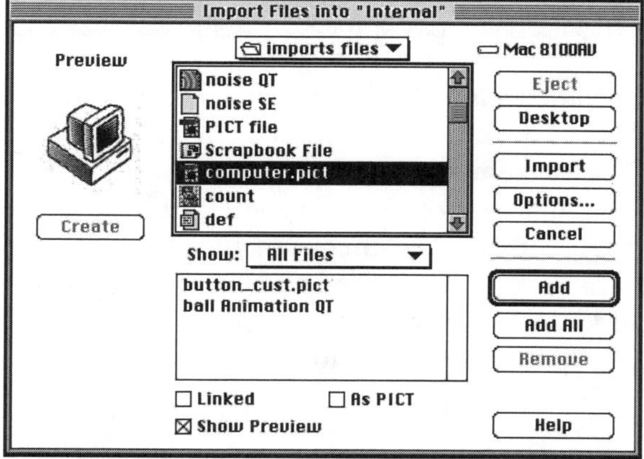

Figure 7.3
Director's Import dialog box.

You can import a single media element by selecting the media element in the upper list and then clicking on the Import button. To import multiple media elements, select a media element from the top list and click on the Add button or double-click on the element. Clicking on the Add button places the selected media elements into the lower list. The lower list is called the *import list*. The import list is very helpful for gathering media elements from different folders, because by using it you don't have to keep opening the Import dialog box every time you select a different target folder.

Clicking on the Add All button places all available media from the current top list into the lower import list. Only single files are added to the lower list, not folders. You use the Show pop-up menu box (see fig. 7.4) to narrow your selection of media elements. Choosing QuickTime from the Show pop-up menu, for example, makes only QuickTime movies visible and leaves all other file formats hidden in the top list.

Figure 7.4

The Show pop-up menu in the Import dialog box.

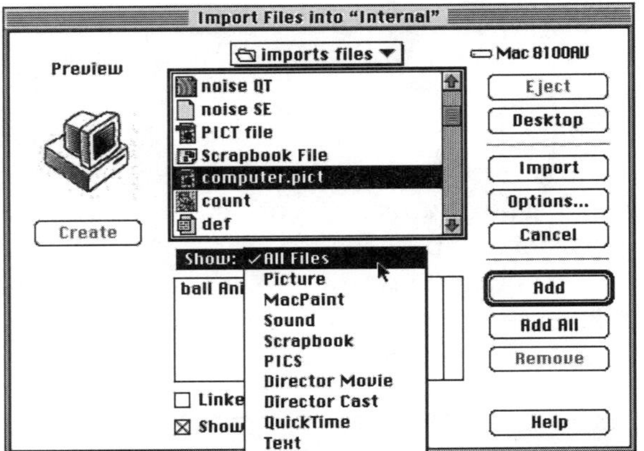

Next, you need to decide whether you want to link the files. If you click on the Import button while the Linked check box is enabled, Director imports all media elements listed in the lower import list as linked files. So, if you want the Director file to contain the media as non-linked files, be sure to disable the Linked check box before you click on the Import button. You cannot import linked and unlinked files at the same time. To import linked and non-linked media files, you would need to use the Import dialog box twice—once for linked files and a second time for non-linked files.

Image Options

Director offers the capability to change the bit depth and palette setting of a media element as it is being imported. Say that for a certain project, you are given a media element that has a higher bit depth than that project requires. The project is being compiled with a bit depth of 8 bits per pixel (256 colors), for example, and the media element you are supplied arrives as a 16-bit image (32,768 colors). After you import the file, the Image Options dialog box appears (see fig. 7.5).

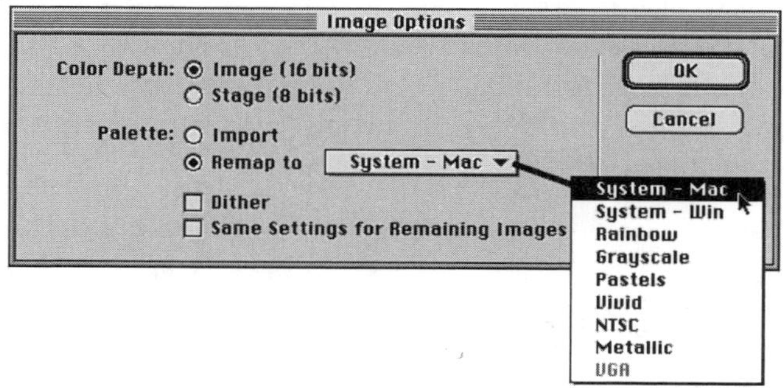

Figure 7.5

More options are available when selecting the Options button within the Image Options dialog box.

Your choices are to keep the file color depth as is, Image (16 bits), or to change the image to the color depth of the Director file, Stage (8 bits). In the preceding example, you would use the Stage (8 bits) radio buttons to change the image's bit depth so that it matches the project's bit depth. Although Director does offer the capability to dither the incoming image, programs such as Adobe Photoshop or Equilibrium's DeBabelizer are much better suited for dithering.

In some painting applications, you can apply a modified color palette (called a *custom color palette* or an *adaptive palette*) to an image. This option is great for making an 8-bit image that contains 256 colors look more like a 24-bit image. A 24-bit image contains millions of colors.

You convert a 24-bit image into an 8-bit image by creating an index color palette. Chapter 9, "Graphics: The Visuals," covers creating an index color palette for an image outside of Director.

When you import an image that already contains a custom color palette, the Image Options dialog box offers you a choice. You can import the custom palette as is or remap the image to another Director palette. *Remapping* is the process of finding a range of color from the incoming images palette and swapping these colors with colors in the Director's palette. The Remap option sometimes causes very strange effects owing to the colors of one palette not exactly matching with the colors of a second palette. Your best bet is to keep the incoming image and its palette together or create an adaptive palette.

An adaptive or common palette is created in an application like Photoshop to combine the most used colors of multiple images into a single 8-bit palette (256 colors). An adaptive palette can make 8-bit imagery look almost as good as 24-bit. The downside to using adaptive palettes is that only the images that were included when the adaptive palette was created can be used in the same frame as this palette.

You can apply a dither effect when you import an image. The Image Options dialog box's dithering command enables you to add new pixels to an image to create the illusion of color pixels that don't actually exist in the new palette. You dither by mixing white pixels into a group of colored pixels to create an in-between color value. When you import multiple media elements that share the same attributes into Director, such as a group of 1-bit black-and-white PICT files, you can enable the Same Settings for Remaining Images check box. The Same Settings for Remaining Images check box uses the current settings in the Options dialog box for the remainder of this import group. In other words, if the screen bit depth is set to thousand and a group of 10 black-and-white PICT images are imported with the Same Settings for Remaining Images check box checked on, you would not have to OK the Options dialog box 10 times. All 10 PICT images would change to the original option settings.

A commonly made mistake when importing media files into Director is forgetting to make sure that file bit depth matches the monitor setting. If you fail to check the monitor setting each time you launch the program, you can end up with a mixture of 8-, 16-, and 24-bit images. Remember: Director checks the monitor's setting every time you open a document.

If you want Director to automatically change the monitor setting when you open a file, choose File, Preferences, General, then select the Reset Monitor to Movie's Color Depth check box (see fig. 7.6). Now, whenever you open the Director file, the monitor changes to the color depth you had at the time you set the Preferences.

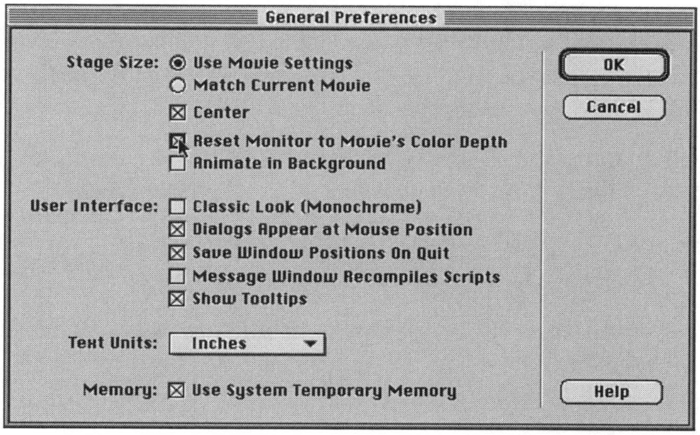

Figure 7.6

Set the Color Depth check box in the General Preferences dialog box.

Another way to solve the problem of color bit depth switching is to create a movie script that changes the color depth of the monitor every time you run the movie. You need to remember to actually run the movie when you open the file for the change to take place.

The following Lingo script could be entered in the movie script (located in a `StartMovie` handler):

```
on StartMovie
set the colorDepth = 8
end
```

The `colorDepth` setting can be one of the following:

- 1 = black-and-white
- 2 = 4 colors
- 4 = 16 colors
- 8 = 256 colors
- 16 = 32,768 colors
- 32 = 16,777,216 colors

Some of the newer Macintosh monitors cannot be set to 2 or 4 bits.

The above Lingo command will execute when the Director movie starts to play.

continues

Another way to change the color bit depth of an opened Director file is to use the Message window. The message is like a Lingo script scratch pad, a place to run script tests.

Select Message from the Windows pull-down menu or press Command+M. Enter the following Lingo script, followed by the Return key.

```
set the colorDepth to = 8 (RETURN KEY)
```

This command will change the color depth of the monitor without running the movie.

The Formats

The next section deals with all of the different types of formats that can be imported into a Director file. Some might think that the number of formats Director imports is very limited, but you will see in the following section that if it can be shown on the computer screen, it can be imported in a Director file. So don't let what seems to be a short import list keep you from importing any type of document into Director.

All Files

Setting the Show pop-up menu to All Files helps you find all available media in a given folder. You can import different files from different folders at the same time.

The Show pop-up menu setting, All Files, is the default setting in the Import Options dialog box. Be aware that enabling the All Files setting in the Show pop-up menu even displays files that Director can't import correctly. If the Show pop-up menu is set to All Files, for example, an Adobe Illustrator file imports as an Encapsulated PostScript file—a very large text file—not a graphic at all.

Pictures

There are actually two types of PICT (Macintosh Picture Format) files, and Director works with both of them.

One type of PICT file is based on Macintosh QuickDraw routines called Draw PICT (object-oriented or rastered). Draw PICT files generally are smaller in kilobytes, print and scale better than bitmap, but tend to move very sluggishly when animated on-screen. Also, you cannot edit Draw PICT files in the Paint window. The other type of PICT file is a bitmapped image (like a Photoshop file), and these files tend to be larger but animate much more quickly than draw-type files. You also can edit bitmapped PICTs in the Paint window using standard paint tools.

Director automatically converts imported picture files to bitmapped unless you enable the As PICT check box in the Import dialog box (refer to fig. 7.3, shown earlier in this chapter).

Converting a Draw PICT to Bitmapped

You can convert an already-imported Draw PICT cast member to bitmapped by copying that Draw PICT cast member in the Cast window and then pasting it into a Paint window paint canvas. Converting a Draw PICT to a bitmap is a one-way route because you cannot convert the cast member back into a Draw PICT. The only way you could restore the bitmap back to a Draw PICT would be to reimport the element, as a Draw PICT.

How to Import Any File into Director

Multimedia artists always ask how to import files from an application that doesn't save in a PICT format. QuarkXPress, PageMaker, and Illustrator generally are at the top of the "No PICT" list. Hope springs eternal, however. You can import the image of *any file* into Director.

Since day one of the Macintosh interface, you have been able to take a screen snapshot. A *screen snapshot* is a bitmapped picture (PICT) of the entire computer screen, or if your computer has a multiple monitor setup, both screens will be captured. To take a snapshot, hold down the Shift and Command keys and press the 3 key (Command+Shift+3). The number 3 on the number key pad will not work in the sequence. Actually, a screen shot is no more than a picture of the current screen. In other words, again, you can import the image of *any file* into Director.

When you take a snapshot, Director saves the file on the hard disk drive as picture 1, picture 2, picture 3, and so on. You need to modify the files a little in Director's Paint window or some other paint application. The menu bar appears at the top of the file, as well as cursors, guidelines, and other program elements that you might not want to show in your media project. Hiding some of these elements before you take the snapshot can help. Also, remember that a snapshot is always actual size, so be sure to scale the page if necessary before you use the Command+Shift+3 sequence to capture the screen image.

Several commercial screen capture applications are available. ScreenShot for Macintosh from The Beale Street Group, Inc. is a great, easy-to-use, to-the-point screen capture utility program. Instant Replay from Strata, Inc., takes screen snapshots and records screen activity, as well as saves the files in a QuickTime format.

MacPaint

A MacPaint file is a 1-bit, black-and-white image. With a maximum file size of 7 1/2×10 1/2 inches in a vertical orientation, that's it. Today, very few graphics are saved in a MacPaint format, but you would be surprised to know how many people and companies still have stacks of old MacPaint format clip art libraries lying around. Maybe a diamond in the rough? It's nice to know that if you need to import one of these small black-and-white media elements, you can do so using Director.

Don't forget the introduction of Shockwave, a Macromedia format that enables a Director document to be played in its entirety in a Web page. Using black-and-white images in a Shockwave file can keep a document small in size and reduce download time.

Sound

When you select a sound in the Import dialog box, a Play Sound button appears in the Preview area (see fig. 7.7). If the Show Preview check box is enabled, pushing the Play Sound button plays a sound.

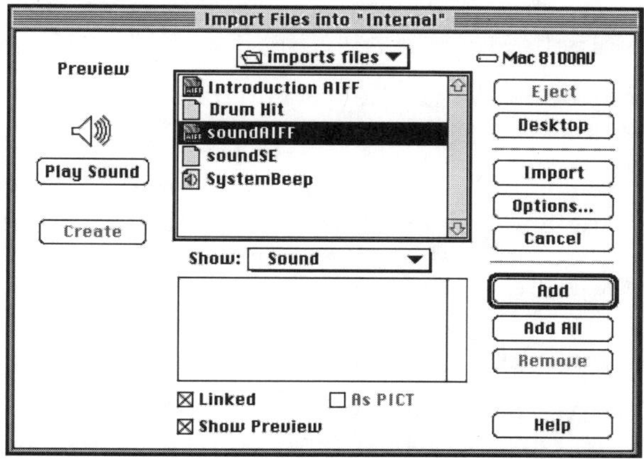

Figure 7.7
The Play Sound button in the Import dialog box.

Director imports the sound formats SoundEdit 16, System 7 sound, and Audio Interchangeable File Format (AIFF). An AIFF sound file can have an internal loop. An *internal loop* is a way to mark a position inside of a sound. You can play the marked part of a sound over and over again. Looping a sound in Macromedia SoundEdit is called *setting a loopback*. If you import the looped AIFF sound into Director unlinked, you can control when and how many times the sound loops.

Scrapbook

A *Scrapbook file* is a collection of items from different documents such as graphics, text, sounds, movies, and just about any other type of data, that can be copied and pasted from the Edit pull-down menu and stored in one convenient place. You could easily build a Scrapbook file of just family photos and create a quick and easy screen saver-like application in Director.

The following steps show how you can import a Scrapbook file full of graphics into Director to use as a screen saver:

1. In a new Director file, select Import from the File pull-down menu and choose Scrapbook from the Show pop-up menu.
2. In the System folder locate the Scrapbook file and choose the Import button. To bring the Scrapbook file into Director, two choices are available in the Import Options dialog box (see fig. 7.8):
   - **Range.** How much of the Scrapbook, in frames, are to be imported.
   - **Scrapbook.** What the placement is to be for the incoming images.
     - If you select the Original Position radio button, cast members you import appear in the Paint window in their original position relative to the other scrapbook images. In other words, you should take the largest image in the series of Scrapbook images and center the remaining images to it.
     - If you select the Centered radio button, cast members you import appear centered relative to elements in the Paint window; incoming Scrapbook images are centered in the Paint window in relationship to the other paint images in the Director file.

     After the Scrapbook file is imported. The cast members can be placed out onto the Stage, aligned to one other and over time automatically, in the Score window.
3. Press and drag the single Scrapbook cast member file out onto the Stage. The single file contains the location of all the other images located in the Scrapbook cast member. Placing this single cast member will display all the images when the movie is played.

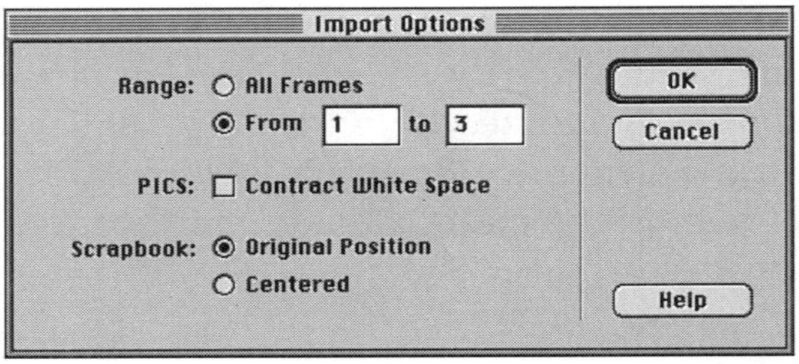

Figure 7.8

Set choices in the Import Options dialog box.

4. Open the Control Panel (Command+2). The button in the upper right corner, the Loop Playback button, should be down. Otherwise the multiple Scrapbook images will not appear.
5. Play the movie.

PICS

A *PICS file* is a single file that contains multiple PICT images. Macromedia developed the PICS format for Director for use in animation. You cannot compress PICS files like QuickTime, but you can extract a single PICT image of a PICS file. This technique is very helpful, something that can't be done with QuickTime. The maximum size of a PICS file is 16 MB.

When you import a PICS file, you can select a range of frames by choosing the Options button in the Import dialog box. Enabling the Contract White Spaces check box in the Import Options dialog box (see fig. 7.8 shown previously) removes the white area around all PICS images as they are imported.

> A Director document can contain a PICS file as an unlinked file, whereas a QuickTime file must be linked and travel with the Director project. As an alternative to using linked QuickTime, a small PICS file stored inside (unlinked) a Director document can be played back almost as fast as a QuickTime and the trouble of keeping track of a linked QuickTime file can be avoided. See the Blur Movie Using PICTs example in folder Chapter 7 of the accompanying CD.

Director Movie

You can import an entire Director file into another Director file. The imported Director file is placed in the Cast window as a looped cast member. All the original cast members of the movie you import are added to the Cast window. When you use the imported movie in the current movie, only a single cel is used in the Score window. Importing a movie into another movie does pose certain drawbacks. The following options do not carry over: tempos, transitions, markers, or resources.

A better way to play a movie within a movie is to use a `play movie` Lingo script. You can use a `play movie` script within a button or a frame script. The script instructs another movie to play when a user pushes a button or advances to a scripted frame.

The following Lingo script could be entered in a sprite, cast or frame script:

```
play movie "chapter2"
```

The `play movie` script causes the current movie to close, then Director opens and plays the movie named chapter2. To return the user to the original movie, use a `play done` script. A `play done` script returns the playback head to the point at which the play command was issued.

You can always extract the cast members contained in a Film Loop. To extract all of the locations and layers of a looped cast member, select the looped cast member in the Cast window and then copy and paste it into a blank cell in the Score window. All of the cels and channels are restored to their original positions.

Director Cast

A cast member file can contain 32,000 cast members. You can create libraries of media elements in external cast files and then import these external cast files on demand. Also, you can share the external cast files over multiple Director movies.

To keep an external cast file from loading all of its cast members into a movie at one time and filling up memory, you can use the `preLoadMode` Lingo script.

The following Lingo script could be entered in a `movieScript`:

```
set the preLoadMode of castLib "arrows" = 0
set the preLoadMode of castLib "boxes" = 2
```

The `preLoadMode` script performs two functions. First, the cast file named `"arrows"` loads only when the playback head encounters a frame that contains a sprite from the external cast file. Second, the cast file named `"boxes"` loads into memory after the playback head leaves frame 1, which enables the user to view the artwork in frame 1 while the external cast named `"boxes"` loads. You can use the following settings for preLoadMode:

- 0 = When Needed
- 1 = Before Frame One
- 2 = After Frame 1

QuickTime

A QuickTime or Digital Video is a sequence of video frame contained in a single. These Digital film clips can be captured at different sizes and levels of compression. Even though the Digital Video format contains many different frames of information, only a single Digital Video cast member has to be dealt with. A Digital Video movie always imports as a linked file, even if the Linked check box is not selected.

Remember to always transport the Digital Video movie file with its linked Director document. If you move a linked Digital Video movie file from one folder on your hard disk drive to another during the development of a project, you must update the Digital Video cast member paths. If you don't, Director prompts for the correct location of the Digital Video file every time a user tries to play the movie.

Any modifications made to Digital Video movies inside a Director document automatically update the external Digital Video movie files. Be sure to have full-length backup copies of your Digital Video movies stored in another folder, away from the modified files, so you have a master file just in case.

Text

Director 5 imports text formatted as Rich Text Format (RTF). RTF contains paragraph formatting and defines Tab settings. Page breaks and section breaks in an RTF document cause Director to place the text after the break into a separate cast member. Most word-processing applications save in a standard RTF. Macromedia's FreeHand also saves text in RTF. Text saved in a text-only format can still be imported into the document, except the formatting vanishes. Text is the only import option that cannot be linked to a Director document.

Drag-and-Drop

New to Director 5 is the capability to drag an acceptable file format from the desktop directly into a cast member file (see fig. 7.9).

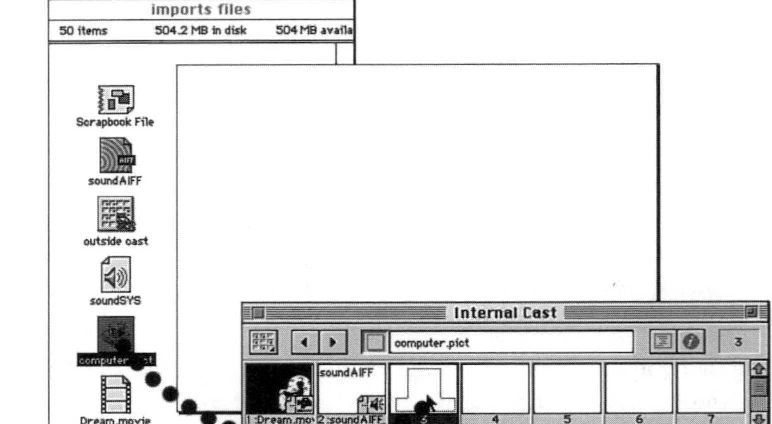

Figure 7.9

What could be easier than just dragging a media element from the desktop into a cast member file?

This is almost too easy. What happened to the good-old days of opening and closing all those windows when importing something? The one thing that you will need to be aware of with the drag-and-drop importing feature is the linked status of the incoming file. Director uses the Linked check box in the Import dialog box to set the link attributes of an incoming file. Choosing Import from the File pull-down menu to set the Linked status.

The Original Import Option: Copy and Paste

Even though copying and pasting isn't an import option, you can forget how easily you can just select an element, whatever the format, and paste it into a document. If you have enough memory installed, you can launch multiple applications at the same time, and with a Macro program such as QuicKeys from CE Software, you can record the actions of a copy, switch applications, and paste the sequence into a single button command. Then all you have to do to move an element into Director is select an element in another application, push a button and the macro copies the element to the Clipboard, switches to Director, and pastes.

Adobe Illustrator is a PostScript drawing application. You can convert PostScript shapes into PICT objects by holding down the Option key as you make a copy. Using this feature copies only the PICT shape information but not the underlying PostScript information. You then can paste the PICT shape element into one of Director's paint canvas windows or cast members.

Summary

As stated earlier, there are very few things that can't be imported into Director, such as data from an Excel document. Or can it? Even though Excel doesn't export as a PICT file, you could export the file as a Tab-separated text file and then import it into Director as a Text cast member, where the cel data could be modified further. A screen capture could be made from the spreadsheet data, imported as a bitmapped cast member, and then all you need to do is add some animation to show. Or, you could videotape someone explaining how to create an Excel spreadsheet, capture this file as a QuickTime, and import the file into Director to make an interactive training demo. This list can go on and on, but you get the point.

This chapter showed how media can be saved outside of Director and how to get what's been saved outside inside.

By now, you've put out the casting call and the actors are ready to perform. The next chapter shows how to store all of the elements you learned how to import.

John Chambers

New in Director 5: Multiple Casts

A good analogy for explaining the Cast Member window is that it's like a green room in a theater, a place for actors to hang out. So when you need your talent, you know where to find them. Not only does this green room hold actors, it also contains the props, sets, colors, scripts (Lingo), scene changes (transitions), and quite a few other elements to be used on your stage. Plain and simple, the cast member file contains everything that is seen or heard in your document, serving in all but name as a database of media elements.

This chapter covers the following areas:

- Overview of the Cast Member window
- External cast members files
- Unlinked external cast member files
- Linking unlinked cast member files
- Unlinking or removing attached files
- Using cast files

New in Director 5 is the capability to use multiple casts within a document. These multiple cast files come in two flavors—internal and external. In earlier versions of Director, if you needed to use more than one cast file, you had to create a shared cast. Shared casts worked well for using the same cast member in different movies. Multiple casts files take this concept a great deal further. Now you could have, for example, a cast file just of navigational images, such as arrows, buttons, or icons. Think of this navigational cast file as a library from which to choose media elements.

You could have different casts libraries to hold different types of media or often used media elements. Figure 8.1 shows an example of multiple cast windows.

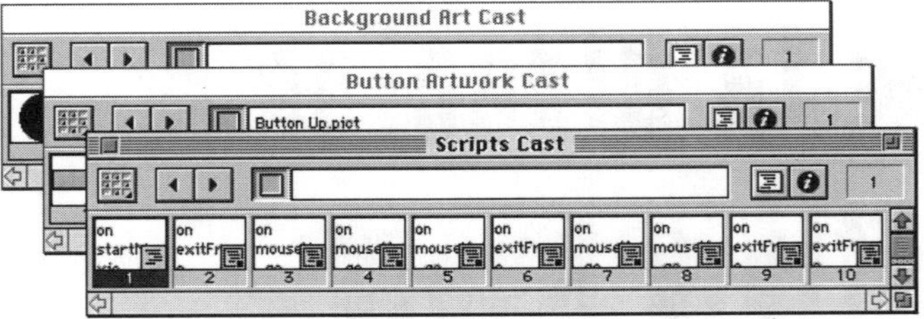

Figure 8.1

Director's new multiple cast windows.

You could, for example, create a cast library of transitions. When you need a transition, you just drag the cast member from one cast file to another cast file, as shown in figure 8.2. Another great advance to multiple cast windows is the capability to load a cast library onto a server so a group can share the media.

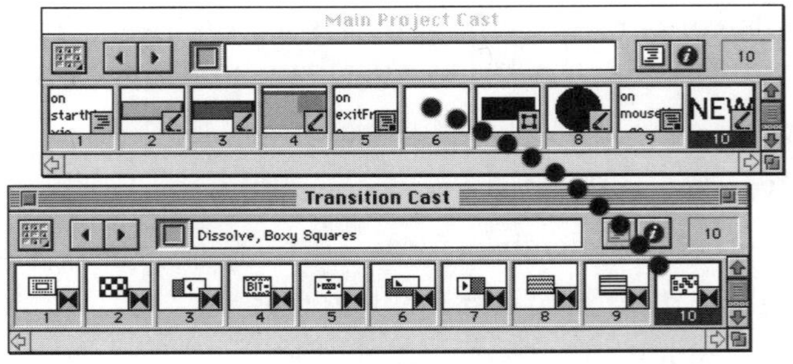

Figure 8.2

A Cast Member window used as a transition library.

An Overview of the Cast Member Window

The Cast Member window in Director 5 contains a couple new options and updated icons. Figure 8.3 shows the layout of the new cast window. Cast member files are stored on a hard disk. The Cast Member window is used to view the cast member files.

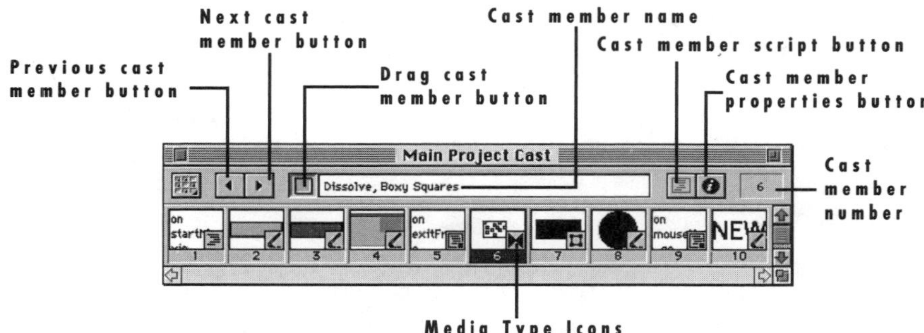

Figure 8.3

Director's new Cast Member window.

- **Display Cast button.** Press this button, located in the upper left corner of the Cast Member window, to bring up a pop-up list of currently available internal and external cast files. A new Director document shows only one cast file in this list, the default internal cast file. Naturally, the list grows as you add new cast files to the document. Adding internal and external cast files are explained later in this chapter in the section "Creating an Internal Cast Member File."
- **Previous and Next buttons.** These enable you to select cast members one at a time within a cast window. Holding down one of these arrows enables you to scan through the cast window very quickly.
- **Drag cast member button.** You can place a selected cast member onto the stage using the Drag cast member button. To use this feature, select a cast member in the cast window, then use the Drag cast member button to press and drag the cast member out of the Cast Member window and onto the stage. You then can position the cast member on the stage.

You also can use the Drag cast member button to drag a selected cast member to a cel in the Score window, and thus, create a sprite. By default, this sprite is centered on the stage.

When you place a cast member in a cel of the Score window, it officially becomes a sprite. It still exists in the cast window, but now its presence in the Score window is referred to using the alternative descriptive term, "sprite."

- **Cast member name.** The cast member's name appears to the right of the Drag cast member button. The name of an imported media element automatically appears in the name box of the cast member you select. You can change the name of a cast member you select by selecting and reentering that name in the text box.

Even though Director's cast members can share the same name, you really don't want to do that. A Director document could become confused when cast members of the same name are called using a Lingo script. If two cast members share the same name and you use a `castName` Lingo script, the script chooses the cast member that has the lowest cast number.

- **Cast member Script button.** This is the second button from the right in the Cast Member window. You use this button to open a selected cast member's script. If the selected cast doesn't have a cast script, opening this dialog box sets up an `on mouseUp` handler. Here, you can enter your Lingo script on the blank line between the `on mouseUp` and end statements. A cast script is located inside the selected cast member (see fig. 8.4).

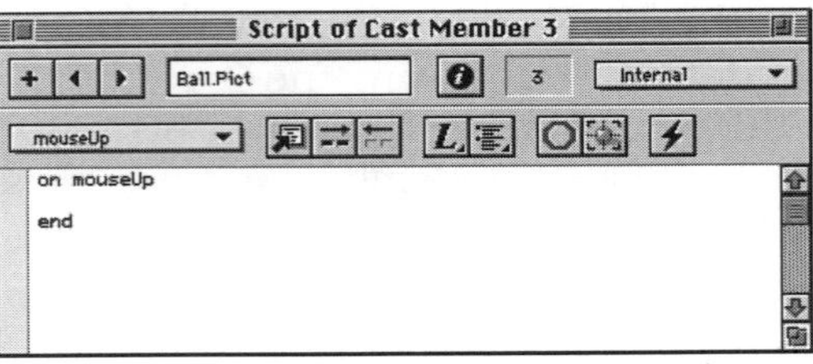

Figure 8.4

Selecting the cast script button will open the cast script window. Here, Lingo code can be entered or modified.

- **Cast member Property button.** This is the last button on the right of the Cast Member window and is covered in the section "Property Options of Cast Members" later in this chapter (see fig. 8.5).

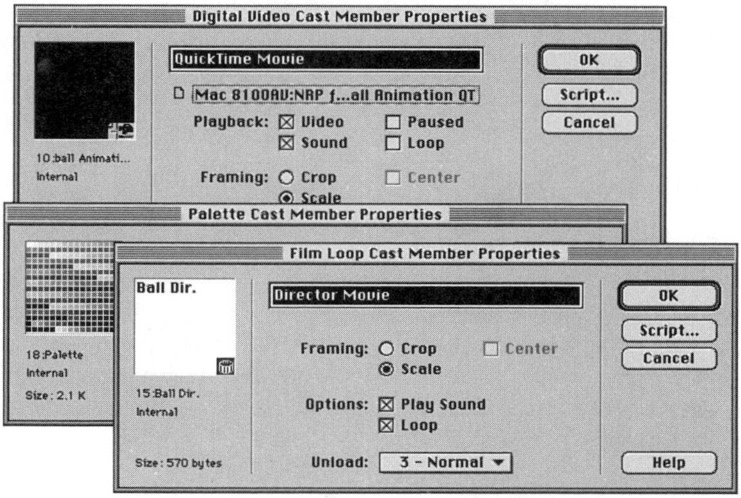

Figure 8.5

One of many different Cast Member property dialog boxes displays depending on which type of cast member you select.

- **Cast member number.** The area in the upper right corner of the cast window is the number of the selected cast member. Double-clicking in this area launches an editor for the selected cast member, if the element can't be edited inside the Director document. The launch editor is great for easily opening an application like Macromedia SoundEdit 16 or other sound application to make a quick modification to a sound cast member.

To launch an application editor, double-click on a cast member that you can't edit in Director, such as a sound file, or select Launch External Editor from the Edit pull-down menu. If an editor has not been selected, a dialog box prompts you to search for the correct editor for that media type.

The cast members appear as icons in the Cast Member window. You can customize how the icons appear by choosing Preferences, Cast from the File pull-down menu (see fig. 8.6). Each Director document can contain up to 32,000 cast members per cast file. The Cast Preferences dialog box enables you to set the number of cast members contained in each cast window.

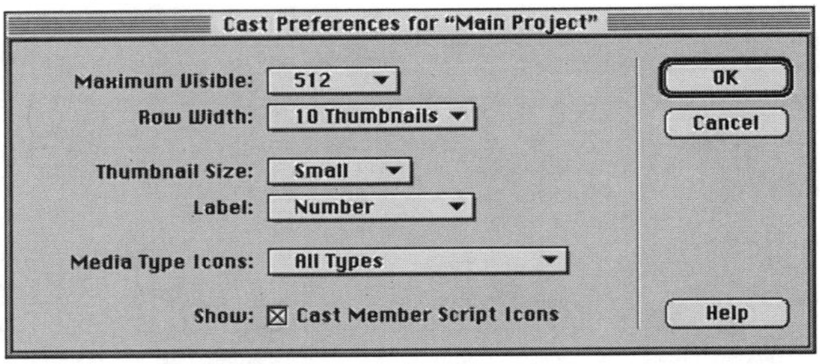

Figure 8.6

The Cast Preferences dialog box.

Do not set the maximum visible setting to 32,000 if you use fewer than 512 cast members per window. Higher-than-needed numbers tend to slow down both playback speed and load time.

The cast member preferences are:

- **Maximum Visible.** Enables you to set how many cast members are seen in a Cast Member window (512 to 32,000).
- **Row Width.** Limits how many cast members are visible from left to right in the Cast Member window. A small number will keep you from having to scroll two different directions on a small monitor.
- **Thumbnail Size.** Adjusts the size of the cast member tile. If a great deal of cast members are needed to be viewed, a setting of small could be used, though it might be difficult to see.
- **Label.** Cast members can be viewed by name, number, or both.
- **Media Type Icons.** Graphics icons displayed in the bottom of cast member tiles can be turned on or off.

This preference change affects only the active cast member file. You would need to change the remainder of the cast windows separately to apply the same settings.

Getting back to the Cast member window, Cast member icons also contain Media type icons in the lower corners, which helps distinguish the type of cast member they are, such as whether the cast member has been linked or has an embedded script attached to it. Figure 8.7 shows the different types of icons that you can view in a cast member icon.

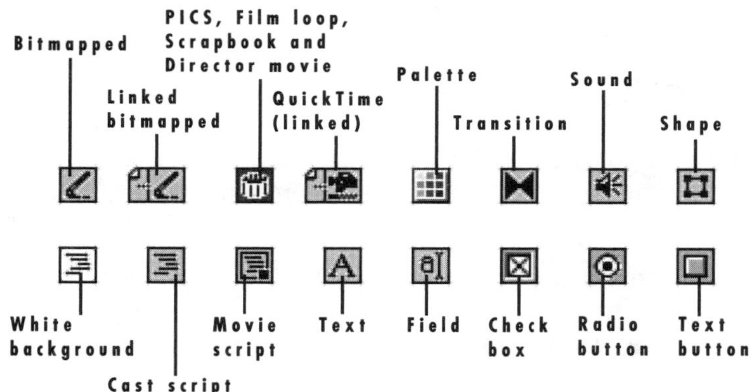

Figure 8.7

Media type icons shown here are located in the bottom corners of the cast members and are used to quickly identify the type of cast member it is.

Using Multiple Casts

A Director document can contain two types of cast member files—internal and external. Internal cast member files are stored inside of a Director document. These cast member files tend to make the document file size larger, whereas an external file is stored outside of the document, making for a smaller document. The drawback to an external cast member file is that the actual cast file needs to travel with the Director document. External cast member files act just like imported linked media.

The positive side to an external cast member file is that the external cast member file, like linked media, can be updated or modified outside of the parent document. You could create a calendar in Director, for example, and save the file as a projector, a self contained application. Then, each year, a new external cast member file with updated art and data could be sent to your users. All the user has to do is replace the old cast member file with the new one.

Creating an Internal Cast Member File

An internal cast member file actually is part of the Director document. A Director document can have an unlimited number of internal cast member files per document. The benefit of using multiple internal cast files would be that it can cut down on the time you spend scrolling through a large cast file, for example, one that has a hundred or so media elements, or having to drag cast members around a large window to organize them into smaller groups.

You could use multiple internal cast files to create a file that contains only background art and another cast file of buttons. Perhaps you could even add a cast file of just Lingo scripts to your document to help speed up the scripting process. You could then open all of these cast windows on-screen at the same time for easy viewing (as seen previously in fig. 8.1). Director's new drag-and-drop feature enables you to drag a cast member from one cast file to another. After you finish a project, you can remove unwanted cast member files from the document.

After you create an internal cast file, you cannot convert it back into an external cast file. The internal cast file always remains part of the document. The only way to delete an internal file is to remove it from the current Director document. To remove an internal cast file, choose Movie, Cast File from the Modify pull-down menu. Select the unwanted cast file and click on the Remove button.

To create a new internal cast member file, the default Cast Member window must first be opened. After the Cast Member window is available, the Choose Cast button can be selected to create a new internal cast member file (see fig. 8.8).

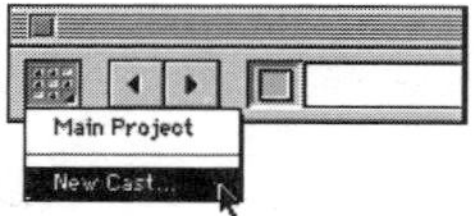

Figure 8.8

Select the choose cast pop-up list to create a new cast member.

You would follow these steps to create a new internal cast member:

1. In the Cast Member window, press and hold the Choose Cast Member button to access the pop-up menu.
2. Select New Cast from the choose cast member pop-up list.
3. Name the new internal file.
4. Enable the Internal radio button, as shown in figure 8.9.

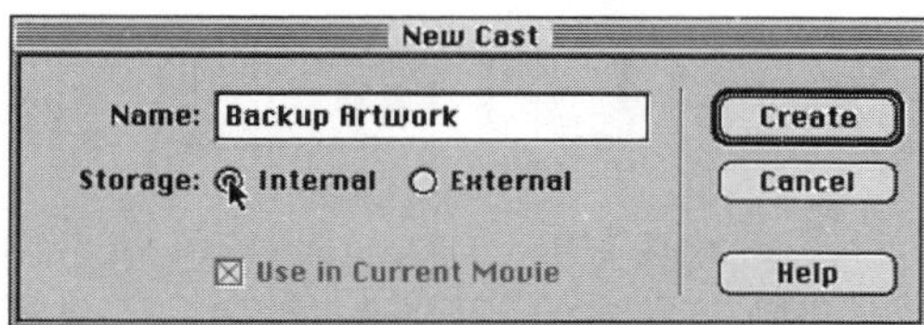

Figure 8.9

Setting up an internal cast member file.

You should enable the Use in Current Movie check box. Otherwise, the file won't link.

Another way to create a new internal cast file is to choose New, Cast from the File pull-down menu. Name the new cast file and enable the Internal radio button.

The new internal Cast Member window opens and the default cast window closes. You can view the default window again by choosing the Choose Cast Member button pop-up list and selecting the default file from the list (see fig. 8.10).

Figure 8.10

Opening a closed default Cast Member window.

To have a new or existing cast window open on top of the default cast window (viewing both windows at the same time), hold down the Option key while choosing the Choose Cast Display pop-up list. The cast window you just opened is stacked on top of the first cast window. You need to move this newly opened second window so you can view both windows. To move the top-most window, press and drag the title bar of the top window to another location. Also, remember that only one Cast Member window can be active at a time. When you edit cast members in a paint or text modification window, be sure to know which cast window is active. The selected cast member of the active window is the element to be modified.

Using External Cast Member Files

External cast files are stored outside the current Director document and come in two different types—linked cast members and unlinked cast members.

Linked External Cast Files

A linked cast file behaves the same as an internal cast file, only it is stored outside the current document and Director then uses a path name to access it. A linked cast file makes the document smaller than a document using an internal cast member file. Remember, an internal cast file is stored inside the document. Storing the cast member inside the document is similar to linking a media element when importing. Director only needs to keep track of the location of the linked external file. Figure 8.11 shows an external cast member file in the same folder as the Director document that uses it.

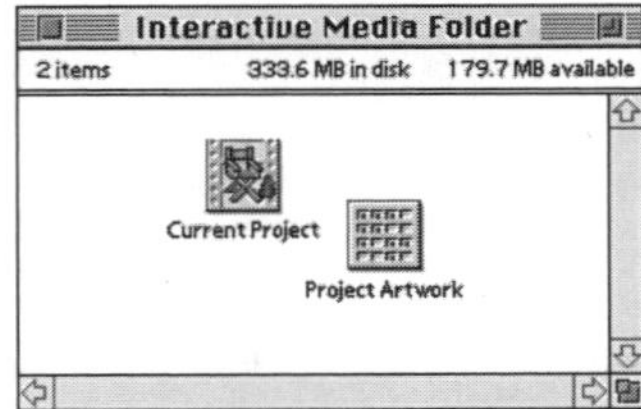

Figure 8.11

The external cast member file named Project Artwork is stored outside the Current Project Director movie and is viewed as an independent file.

Creating a Linked External Cast Member File

You would use the following steps to create an external cast member:

1. In the Cast Member window, press and hold the Choose Cast Member button to access the pop-up menu.
2. Select New Cast from the choose cast member pop-up list.
3. Name the new file.
4. Choose the External radio button, as shown in figure 8.12.

Make sure that the Use in Current Movie check box is not enabled. Otherwise, the file won't be linked.

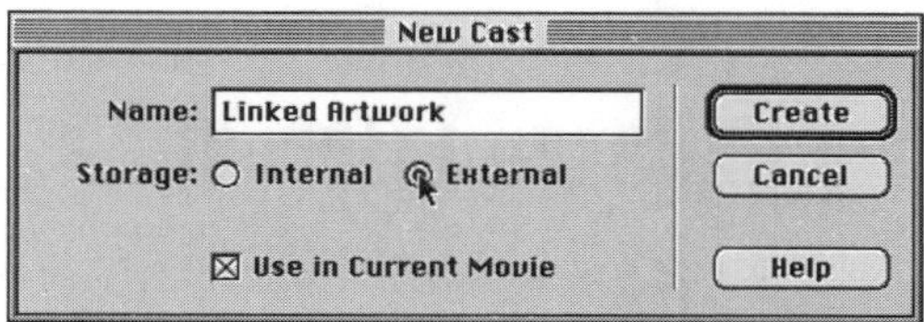

Figure 8.12

Creating a linked external cast member file.

Another way to create an external cast file is to choose New, Cast from the File pull-down menu. Name the new cast file and choose the External radio button.

The new external Cast Member window opens and the default cast window closes. You can view the default window again by selecting it in the Choose cast display pop-up list.

If you want Director to open the newly selected cast window on top of the default window, hold down the Option key while you select from the Choose cast display pop-up list. The cast window you just opened stacks on top of the first cast window. You'll need to move it if you want to view both windows at the same time.

Using Unlinked External Cast Member Files

The other type of external cast member is an unlinked external cast member file. An unlinked external cast member file has no ties or links to a Director document, by default—it's a free-standing file. Like the Macintosh Scrapbook utility, you can drag media elements out of the unlinked cast file to the cast file of the current Director document to quickly copy media elements. An external unlinked cast member file is easy to spot—it appears darker in color than a normal Cast Member window. After you link this file, its color lightens to match other Cast Member windows.

Creating an Unlinked External Cast Member File

You can create new unlinked external cast member files in three ways. Each of the following methods produces the same results:

Method 1:

1. Choose New, Cast from the File pull-down menu.
2. In the New Cast dialog box, enter the name of the new external file in the Name text box.
3. Enable the External radio button, as shown in figure 8.13.
4. Disable the Use in Current Movie check box. If you leave this check box enabled, you end up with the new cast file being linked.

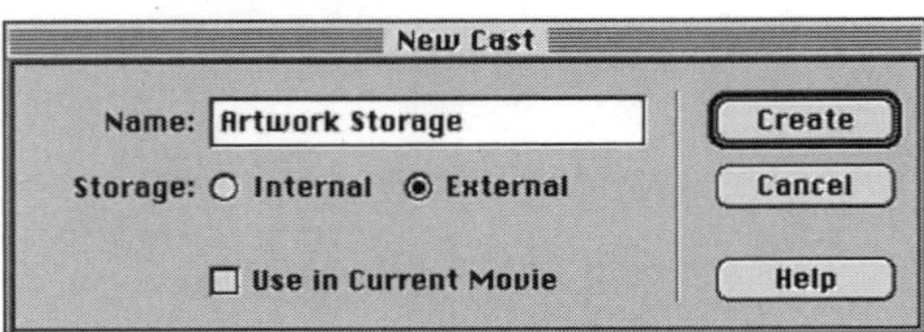

Figure 8.13

Creating an unlinked external cast member file.

Method 2:

1. Choose the Choose Cast pop-up list of the active cast window.
2. Select New Cast and name the new external file.
3. Enable the External radio button.
4. Disable the Use in Current Movie check box.

Method 3:

1. Choose Movie, Casts from the Modify pull-down menu.
2. Click on the New button.
3. Name the new external file.
4. Enable the External radio button.
5. Disable the Use in Current Movie check box.

This unlinked cast file saves independently of the current Director movie. You can store unlinked cast files on a local drive or on a server for easy access.

To open an unlinked cast file, choose Open, Cast from the File pull-down menu. After you open the unlinked cast file, you can copy the cast members and paste them into and out of the current Director document's cast file. You also can link the unlinked cast file to the current Director document. Linking an unlinked file is covered in the section "Linking an Unlinked Cast Member File" later in this chapter.

Before you can copy a media element from an unlinked external cast file to the current Director cast file, the unlinked cast file must be available to the current document.

> You cannot select an unlinked cast file from the Choose Cast Display pop-up list, because the external cast file is unlinked and has no ties to the current Director file.

With the unlinked external cast member open, notice the cast window appears darker in color than the other internal or linked Cast Member windows, which indicates that it is an unlinked cast file. Use Director's new drag-and-drop feature to simply drag a cast member from the unlinked cast window into another Cast Member window of the current Director document, as shown in figure 8.14. A copy of the media element remains in the unlinked file.

Figure 8.14

Copying an unlinked cast member to the current Director document.

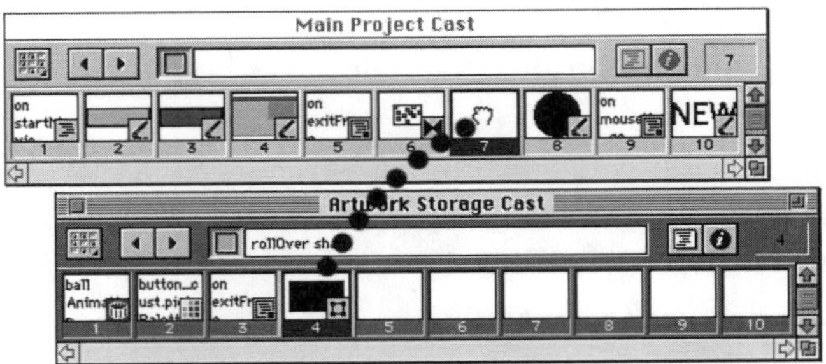

Linking an Unlinked Cast Member File

Sometimes, you need to link an unlinked file to the current Director document. By dragging a cast member from the unlinked cast window to the stage or a cel in the Score window of the current Director document (see fig. 8.15), you cause the unlinked file to link to the current document.

Figure 8.15

Dragging an unlinked cast member to a cel in the Score window links the cast member file to the current Director document.

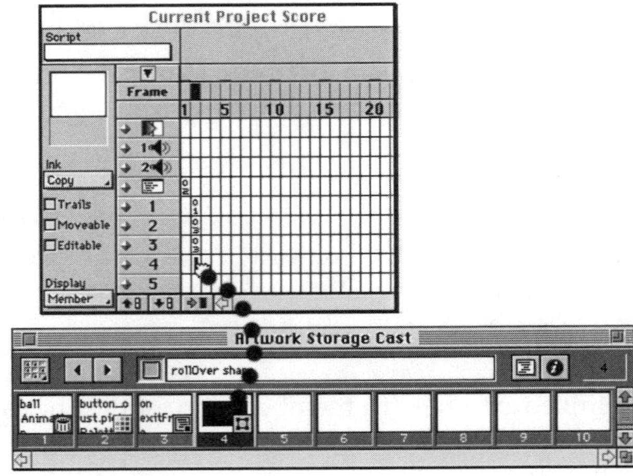

You also can attach an unlinked cast file to the current document by selecting Movie, Cast from the Modify pull-down menu. Choosing the Link button in the Movie Cast dialog box will bring up a standard Macintosh Find dialog box. Once the correct file is found, click the Open button and the cast file will be added as a linked cast member file to the current movie. (See fig. 8.16.)

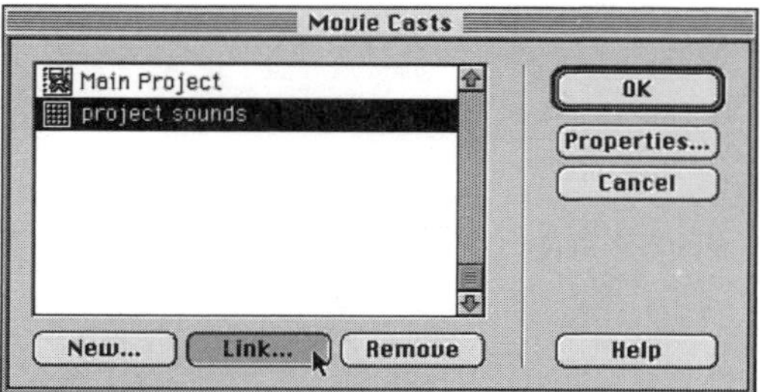

Figure 8.16

A cast member file also can be linked using the Movie Casts dialog box.

Unlinking or Removing An Attached File

You can remove linked cast files from the current Director document, and you might want to do so after you copy the necessary cast members to a more frequently used cast member file.

Choosing Movie, Cast from the Modify pull-down menu opens a dialog box in which you can select the cast member file you want to remove from the current Director document. An alert message appears, informing you of the consequences of removing this cast member file.

Be very careful when you use the Remove button. Using it removes all media elements contained in the soon-to-be-removed cast file from the Score window. If you remove the linked cast file, for instance, you also delete a sprite located in the Score window of the current document from the stage *and* the Score window at the same time. You should copy cast members over to another cast member file before you select the remove button.

Using Cast Files

A Cast member file can contain any of the following media elements:

- PICT and PICs files
- Sound
- Scrapbook
- QuickTime
- Shape
- Text
- Field
- Transition
- Color palettes
- Film loops
- Director casts and Director movies
- Sprite scripts and movie scripts

You can control the way all of these media elements behave in a Director document. The following is a discussion of cast member property options in a cast file. The cast member Property button is located in the upper right corner of the cast window. Choose the Options button of a selected Cast Member to open the options dialog box for that type of cast member (see fig. 8.17).

Figure 8.17

The Properties dialog box of two different cast members.

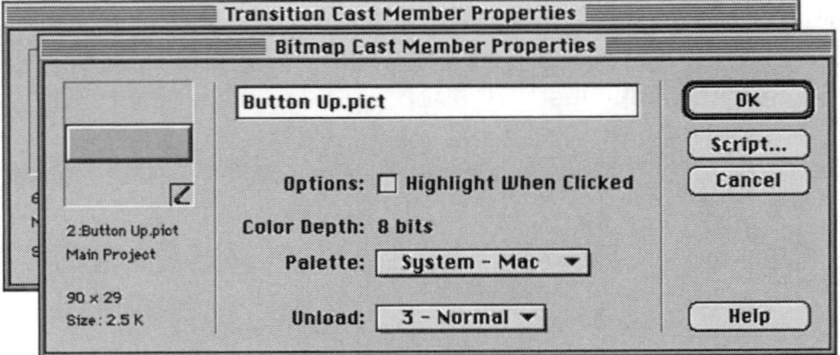

Property Options of Cast Members

The following is a quick tour of the cast member property options. This short list contains common options shared between the different cast members (see fig. 8.18). Later in the chapter, the remanding options for each cast member are discussed. The shared cast member property options are:

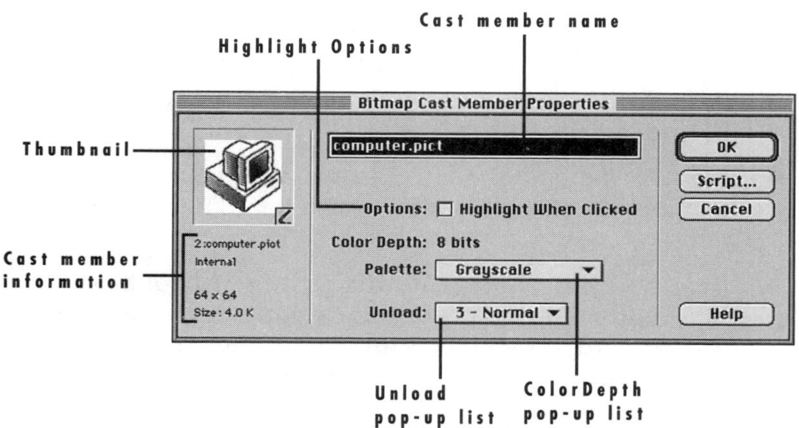

Figure 8.18

The Bitmap Cast Member Properties dialog box shows some of the shared options available for most of the cast members.

- **Thumbnail.** A small version of the selected cast member.
- **Cast member information.** Located on the left side of the option dialog box. Here you can quickly view the cast member number and name, what type of palette the cast member is located in, and the size in pixels and in kilobytes.
- **Cast member name.** For imported media the name of the original file will display here. The name can be changed by entering new text. Cast members will retain their names if moved to another location in the cast window.
- **Options.** Highlight When Clicked will allow for a scripted cast member to flash when clicked. A non-scripted cast member will not highlight.
- **Color Depth.** This pop-up menu will enable you to change the palette of the selected cast member to any of the available defaults or custom color palettes.

- **Unload.** Director enables you to set when cast members are to be removed or unloaded from memory to make room for other cast members. Sometimes, a large cast member is only shown on the screen for a frame or two and then not again for the remainder of the movie. This large cast member can be removed for the project to make room for other cast members that might be used more often. The following is a list of unload options:
  - **Normal.** This setting causes Director to unload this cast member first.
  - **Next.** Cast members with this setting will be removed from memory after the cast members set to normal are purged.
  - **Last.** Cast members set to Last will be unloaded from memory after the cast members are set to normal and next.
  - **Never.** Cast members with this setting will not be removed from memory. Use these settings to make Director keep the cast members used most often loaded in memory and the seldom-used cast members unloaded or purged from memory when you no longer need them.

Bitmapped Cast Member

Bitmapped cast members can have a highlight option. Choosing the highlight option causes the cast member to highlight when a user clicks on it. Using the pop-up menu, you can change color palettes to preset or imported palettes. You also can adjust the purge setting here. When you click on the Script button, an embedded Script window for this particular cast member opens.

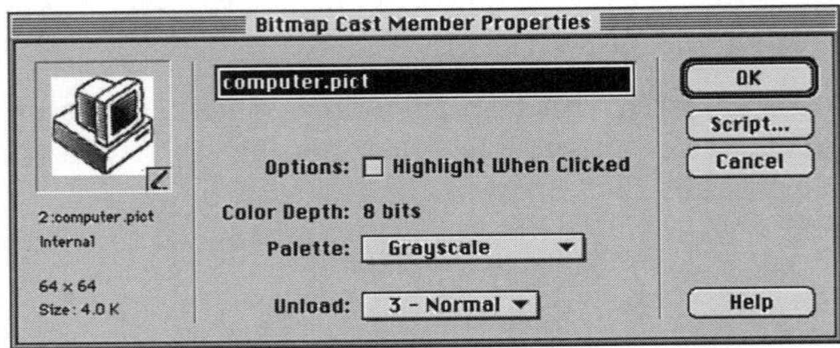

Figure 8.19

The Bitmap Cast Member Properties dialog box.

You can use Lingo to access some parts of the Bitmapped Cast Member property dialog box. The following are some of the Lingo scripts that pertain to this dialog box.

The following script sets the purge property of the cast member `keyboard` to never remove from memory: 0 = never. Other options: 1 = purge last, 2 = purge next, 3 = purge normal.

```
set the purgePriority of member "keyboard" to 0
```

This script switches the sprite in channel 2 with cast member 11.

```
set the memNum of sprite 2 to 11
```

Note that `puppetSprite` must be true for a `memNum` switch.

Shape Cast Member

You use the Tools palette (Command+7) to create a variety of shapes. In the properties dialog box, shapes can changed to other shapes like Oval, Rectangle, Rounded Rectangle, and Line—if needed. Shapes can also be filled or unfilled.

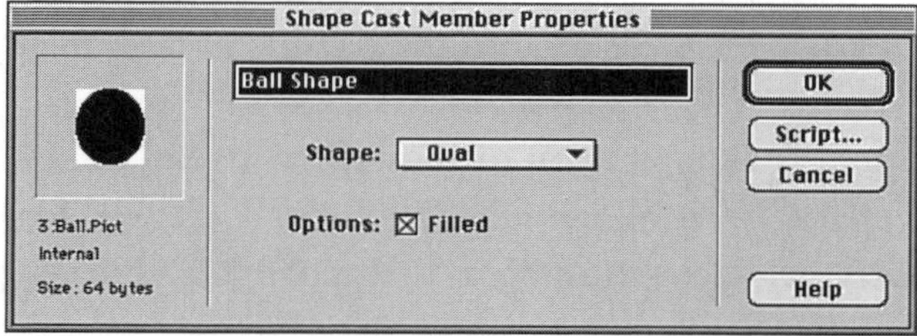

Figure 8.20

The Shape Cast Member Properties dialog box.

PICS Cast Member

An imported PICS file actually consists of two parts. The first part is the container file and the second part is the actual data or individual PICTs that make up the container.

Figure 8.21
The PICS Cast Member Properties dialog box.

The container file serves to place the PICS file onto the stage. The container holds the cast numbers of the individual elements that comprise a PICS file. In other words, the container helps keep you from having to place multiple PICT files onto the stage over time. When you place a PICS container onto the stage, you actually are moving all the internal PICTs elements at once.

Never delete the individual elements of a PICS file while in the cast window. The PICS container needs these files. Removing the single elements causes dropouts when you play the project.

The property options also enable you to create framing effects for a PICS cast member. The options are:

- **Cropping.** Areas around the outside of the image are trimmed off. This does not affect the image.
- **Scaling.** Enables you to change the size of the PICS on the stage. This effect can distort the sprite from its original size.
- **Center.** Keeps the scaled or cropped PICS file centered inside its frame.
- **Sound.** If available, can be turned on or off.
- **Loop.** Enables the sound of a PICS file to play over and over.
- **Purge setting.** Also can be adjusted. Covered earlier in this chapter.
- **The Script Button.** Allows for a script to be added to the PICS cast member.

Film Loop Cast Member

The property options also enable you to create framing effects for a Film looped cast member. (See figure 8.22.) The options are:

- **Cropping.** Areas around the outside of the image are trimmed off. This does not affect the image.
- **Scaling.** Enables you to change the size of the Loop on the stage. This effect can distort the sprite from its original size.
- **Center.** Keeps the scaled or cropped Looped file centered inside its frame.
- **Sound.** If available, can be turned on or off.
- **Loop.** Enables the sound of a Looped file to play over and over.
- **Purge setting.** Also can be adjusted. Covered earlier in this chapter.
- **Script button.** Allows for a script to be added to the Looped cast member.

Figure 8.22

The Film Loop Cast Member Properties dialog box.

Scrapbook Cast Member

A Scrapbook cast member uses properties that are very much the same as the PICS cast members, except it deals with an imported Scrapbook file. (See figure 8.23.) The options are:

- **Cropping.** Areas around the outside of the image are trimmed off. This does not effect the image.
- **Scaling.** Enables you to change the size of the Scrapbook image on the stage. This effect can distort the sprite from its original size.
- **Center.** Keeps the scaled or cropped Scrapbook file centered inside its frame.
- **Sound.** If available, can be turned on or off.
- **Loop.** Enables the sound of a Scrapbook file to play over and over.
- **Purge setting.** Also can be adjusted. Covered earlier in this chapter.
- **Script button.** Allows for a script to be added to the Scrapbook cast member.

Figure 8.23

The Scrapbook cast member properties dialog box.

Director Movie Cast Member

A Director Movie cast member uses the same properties as the PICS cast member, except it deals with an imported Director movie. (See figure 8.24.) The options are:

- **Cropping.** Areas around the outside of the image are trimmed off. This does not affect the image.
- **Scaling.** Enables you to change the size of the Director movie image on the stage. This effect can distort the sprite from its original size.

- **Center.** Keeps the scaled or cropped Director movie file centered inside its frame.
- **Sound.** If available, can be turned on or off.
- **Loop.** Enables the sound of a Director movie file to play over and over.
- **Purge setting.** Also can be adjusted. Covered earlier in this chapter.
- **Script button.** Allows for a script to be added to the Director movie cast member.

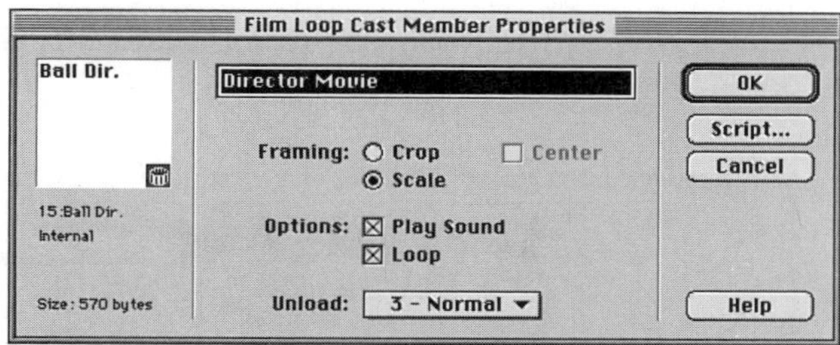

Figure 8.24

The Director Movie cast member properties dialog box.

Sound Cast Member

In addition to the basic information, like cast name modifying and file size, the attributes of the selected sound are displayed at the lower left side of the dialog box. The Loop option enables the sound cast member to play over and over. You can play the sound cast member from the properties dialog box's Play button (see fig. 8.25).

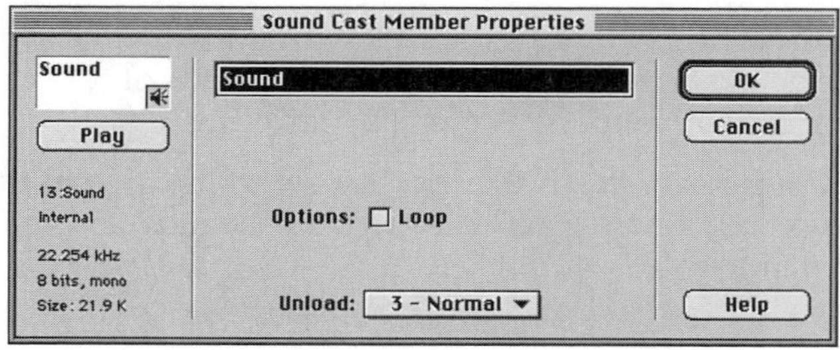

Figure 8.25

The Sound Cast Member Properties dialog box.

Selecting the Looped check box, located in the center of this dialog box, causes a sound to play over and over within a project. Sound cast members that contain a preset loop or loopback—created in applications like Macromedia SoundEdit 16—loop their internal preselected loop section. Sound cast members also can have Purge properties. You can add embedded scripts to this cast member by selecting the Script button.

Text Cast Member

During playback text, you cannot edit these cast members. Options for Text cast members deal with two areas—framing and anti-aliasing. (See figure 8.26.)

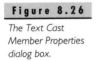

Figure 8.26

The Text Cast Member Properties dialog box.

Framing

Framing refers to how you draw text boxes on stage. The following options are available within the framing pop-up menu:

- **Adjust to fit.** Expands the text box as the user enters text.
- **Scrolling.** Presents the user with a scroll bar down the right side of the text box. Here, large amounts of text can be read in a small amount of space by scrolling.
- **Cropping.** Keeps the text box set to its original size—the text box doesn't expand when a user adds text to the cast member.

Anti-Aliasing

The anti-aliasing options are new in Director 5. Anti-aliased text renders smooth on-screen, not jagged. The process of anti-aliasing creates colored pixels around an object. For instance, a black letter will have a gray edge around it to anti-alias to a white background. A red letter on a white background would have a pink anti-aliased edge to smooth the letter out on the screen. You can set the following anti-alias features:

- **All Text.** Sets all the text in the cast member to render smoothly on the stage regardless of size.
- **Text over a certain size.** This setting will anti-alias only text over the indicated size. Be careful. Small text can be very hard to read when smoothed on the screen. Generally, you shouldn't anti-alias text under 11 points.
- **None.** No anti-aliasing will be applied to the text on the screen of this cast member, regardless of text size.

NOTE

Anti-aliasing degrades Director performance slightly. Director must smooth the text on the fly and this will slow down the playback speed. To keep Director from having to do all the work, import painted or bitmapped text that has already been anti-aliased in an application such as Adobe Photoshop. This type of cast member will animate faster on-screen due to the fact that it comes in smoothed to begin with and Director does not have to smooth it in each frame of the movie.

Field Cast Member

During playback, the user can edit Field cast members. The Field cast members properties are very similar to the Text cast member properties. The Field cast members deal with two areas: framing and options. (See figure 8.27.)

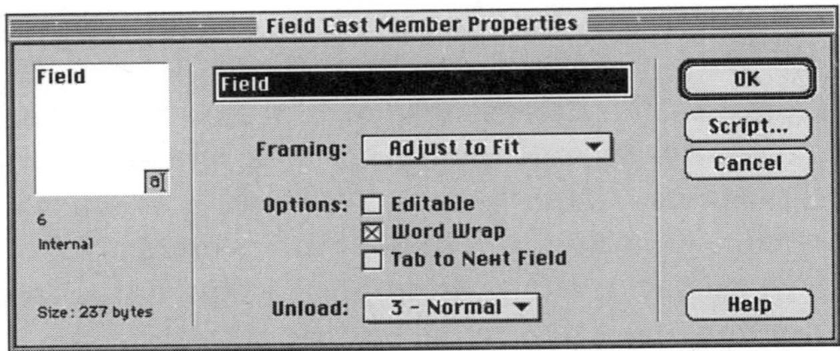

Figure 8.27

The Field Cast Member Properties dialog box.

Framing

Framing refers to how you draw text boxes on stage. The following options are available within the framing pop-up menu:

- **Adjust to fit.** Expands the text box as the user enters text. Scrolling presents the user with a scroll bar down the right side of the text box.
- **Fixed.** Keeps the text box set to its original size and newly entered text continues down the text box unseen.
- **Scrolling.** Presents the user with a scroll bar down the right side of the text box. Here large amounts of text can be read in a small amount of space by scrolling.
- **Limit to field size.** Keeps the text box set to its original size and ignores any newly entered text located outside of the text box.
- **Options.** The options area of the Field cast member properties deals more with the entering of data as opposed to the physical box configuration, which framing deals with.
- **Editable.** Enables the user to enter text as the project is running.
- **Word Wrap.** Causes text to return to the next line automatically. With Word wrap off, the text continues past the right side of the text box until the user presses Return.
- **Tab to next field.** Advances the text entry point—if any—to the next editable text box.

When you convert a Director movie to a Projector field, text remains as text and also remains editable. Text cast members convert to bitmapped or painted images.

Don't confuse *anti-aliasing*, the smoothing or blurring of text cast members, with rasterizing of large text sizes in a document. *Rasterizing* is the process of reading the outline information of a font, which has no real size only coordinates, and creates a bitmapped character to a desired point size on the screen. Director's text rasterizing enables you to create large text sizes, including even a 300-point letter, without the aid of Adobe Type Manager.

You can use Lingo to access most of the settings in the Field cast member property dialog box. Following are some of the Lingo scripts that pertain to this dialog box.

This script sets the font of cast member to Times:

```
set the textFont of member 6 = "Times"
```

This script sets the font size of cast member 6 to 24 point:

```
set the textSize of member 6 = 24
```

This script sets the line spacing or leading of cast member to 48 points:

```
set the textHeight of member 6 = 48
```

This script sets the alignment of cast member to centered:

```
set the textAlign of member 6 = "center"
```

This script sets the text wrap of cast member 6 on:

```
Options: Left, Right and Center.

set the textWrap of member 6 = TRUE
```

Button Cast Member

You can change cast member's properties for buttons in the Button cast members properties dialog box. (See figure 8.28.) The only choices available are radio button, check box, or text buttons.

- **Radio Button.** Radio buttons enable one item within a group of items to be selected true or false (on or off).
- **Check Box.** Check boxes enable multiple items within a group to be selected true or false (on or off).
- **Text Button.** Text buttons are used in the standard Macintosh interface for OK, Apply, Cancel and so on. Any text can be given to a text button in Director to make your buttons in the project more Mac-like.

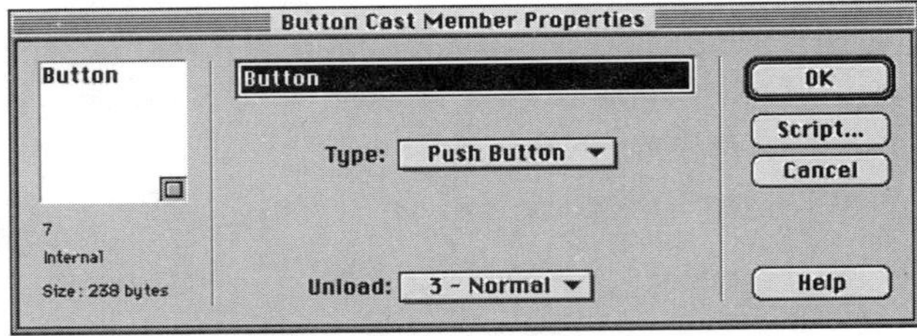

Figure 8.28

The Button Cast Member Properties dialog box.

The setting in the Button Cast Member Property dialog box can be accessed using Lingo.

```
set the buttonType of member 9 = "radioButton"
```

This script changes the button type of cast member 9 to a radio button.

```
Other lingo button options: radioButton, checkBox and
pushButton.
```

Palette Cast Member

You can change only the Name and Load properties of a palette cast member. (See figure 8.29.)

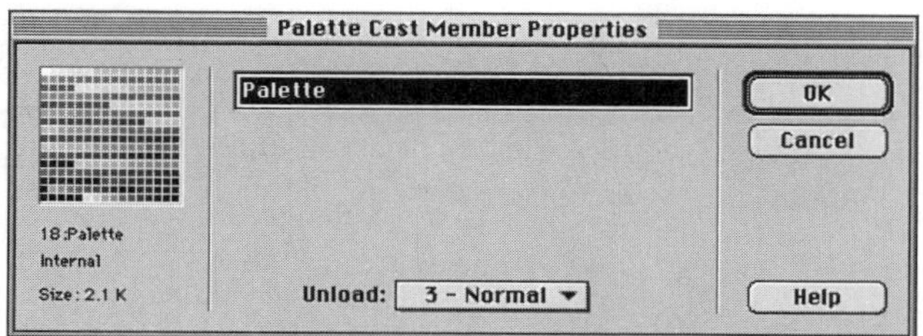

Figure 8.29

The Palette Cast Member Properties dialog box.

Transition Cast Member

You can change only the Name and Load properties of a transition cast member. Xtra Transitions choices might include options for a more customizable look and information about the Xtra transition cast member and its third-party developer. (See figure 8.30.)

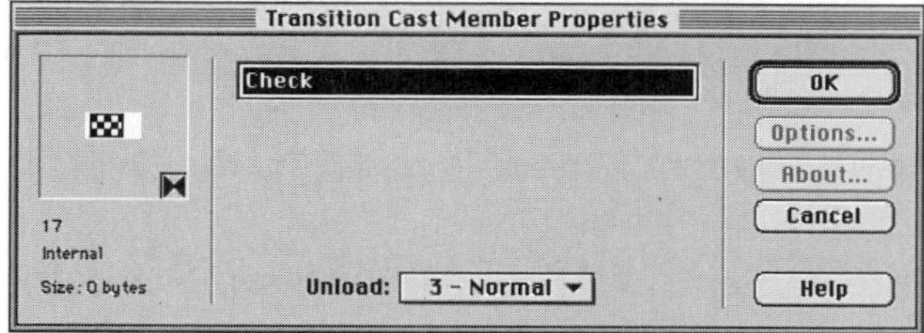

Figure 8.30

The Transition Cast Member Properties dialog box.

QuickTime Cast Member

The dialog box for the property of a QuickTime movie or digital movie is quite large (see fig. 8.31). You can give a considerable amount of control to a QuickTime movie within the cast member property dialog box. In addition to the basic information, such as cast name modifying and file size, the time of the QuickTime movie you select appears at the left side of the dialog box.

Figure 8.31

The QuickTime Cast Member Properties dialog box.

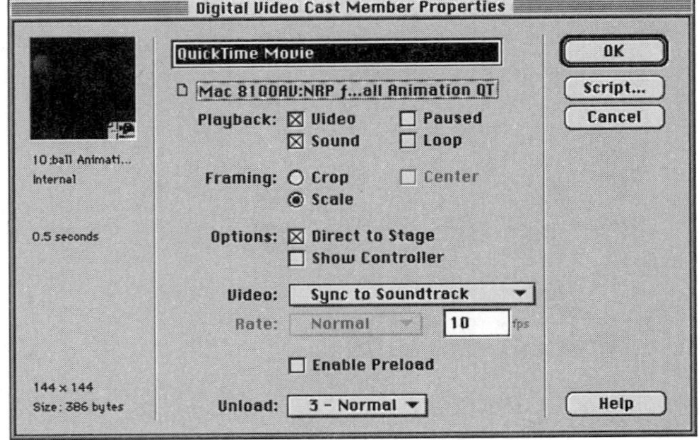

Remember that QuickTime movies are always linked to a Director document. QuickTime movies are located outside a document. When you transfer a Director Project from place to place, the QuickTime movie must travel with the project.

The following options can be accessed in the Digital Video Cast Member Properties dialog box:

- **File name.** This area contains the path name (the location of the cast member). The path can be changed or updated by double-clicking the file name box and reselecting the movie. The new path will be visible in the file name box.
- **Playback.** The four checkbox options in the playback area set:
    - **Sound.** Sets the sound of the cast member on or off.
    - **Video.** Sets the video of the cast member on or off.
    - **Paused.** Causes the movie to wait until a Lingo script such as the following:

      ```
      set the movieRate of sprite 4 to 1
      ```

      This script plays the digital cast member in channel 4 to play a normal speed forward.
    - **Loop.** The digital video cast member will play over and over.

- **Framing.** The framing area of the digital video cast member properties adjusts the manipulation of the image on the screen.
- **Cropping.** Areas around the outside of the image are trimmed off. This does not affect the image.
- **Scaling.** Enables you to change the size of the Director movie image on the stage. This effect can distort the sprite from its original size.
- **Center.** Keeps the scaled or cropped Director movie file centered inside its frame.

When a QuickTime movie pauses and the playback head enters a frame that contains the QuickTime movie, the QuickTime movie doesn't play. You can use the following Lingo command to play the QuickTime movie.

```
Lingo Script: sprite script
on mouseUp
set the movieRate of sprite(1) to 1
end
```

This script makes the QuickTime movie in channel 1 of the current frame play at normal speed when the user releases the mouse.

Options: 2 = play twice as fast; –2 = half as slow (sound also plays back at this speed).

A QuickTime movie placed on the stage can be cropped, scaled, and centered; however, scaling a QuickTime movie is not advisable.

Scaling really isn't the best thing to do with a QuickTime movie. Always try to retain a QuickTime movie's original proportions. This is a must for option viewing. Not only does scaling make the movie look bad, it also slows the computer's performance.

- **Options.** The options check boxes deal with how the digital video cast member behaves with other sprites on the screen and user input on the screen. The available options are:

- **Direct To Stage.** The Using the Direct To Stage option of a QuickTime cast member is like placing a QuickTime cast member in the 49th channel of the movie. (Director has only 48 channels). This imaginary 49th channel comes before all the other channels. The option enables the QuickTime movie to play more efficiently, because Director can play the QuickTime file without worrying about layering other elements in front of the QuickTime movie.
- **Show Controller.** This check box enables the user to start, stop, pause, and step the movie forward and backward within a running project by displaying a control bar at the bottom of the digital video cast member.

- **Video.** The video options adjust how the digital video cast member plays back on the screen. The options are:
  - **Sync Soundtrack.** This option plays the video and its contained sound at normal speed.
  - **Play Every Frame (No Sound).** In normal playback of a QuickTime movie, frames are dropped to keep up with the sound. This is a normal occurrence for a slower computer. Play Every Frame does just that, plays every frame of the video, but no sound will be heard. The video can now be played at different speeds. Normal is the speed of the video at time of capture. Maximum will play the video as fast as the computer is capable. Fixed will enable you to set how fast the video plays back (to the maximum).
  - **Enable Preload.** The last check box for the QuickTime property options, Enable Preload, is used to load the selected QuickTime movie into memory all at once. By default, QuickTime movies load in small chunks for playback on all configurations of machines. This Enable Preload setting will really speed up the playback speed of the QuickTime movie.

- **Unload.** This pop-up menu enables you to set when cast members are to be removed or unloaded from memory to make room for other cast members. Sometimes a large cast member is only shown on the screen for a frame or two and then not again for the remainder of the movie. This large cast member can be removed from the project to make room for other cast members that might be used more often. The following is a list of unload options:

- **Normal.** This setting causes Director to unload this cast member first.
- **Next.** Cast members with this setting will be removed from memory after the cast members set to normal are purged.
- **Last.** Cast members set to Last will be unloaded from memory after the cast members set to normal and next.
- **Never.** Cast members with this setting will not be removed from memory.

Most of the settings in the QuickTime cast member property dialog box can be accessed using Lingo. The following is a list of Lingo scripts pertaining to this dialog box.

Playback Scripts:

This script will not play the video portion of the QuickTime movie named My Movie:

```
set the video of member "My Movie" FALSE
```

This script will not play the audio portion of the QuickTime movie named My Movie:

```
set the sound of member "My Movie" to 0
```

This script pauses the QuickTime movie named My Movie:

```
set the pausedAtStart of member "My Movie" TRUE
```

This script loops a QuickTime movie named My Movie:

```
set the loop of member "MyMovie" to 1
```

Framing Scripts:

This script crops the QuickTime movie to the sprite rectangle:

```
set the crop of member "My Movie" TRUE
```

This script adjusts the centering of the QuickTime movie named My Movie:

```
set the center of member "My Movie" TRUE
```

Options Scripts:

This script sets the option of the QuickTime movie named My Movie to directToStage:

```
set the directToStage of member "My Movie" to 1
```

This script sets the option of the QuickTime movie named My Movie to show controller:

```
set the controller of member "My Movie" to 1
```

Video Scripts:

This script plays every frame in the movie named My Movie at its preset rate:

```
set the frame rate of member "My Movie" to -1
```

Options: a number between 0 and 255 plays the movie at that rate; –2 forces the movie to play every frame as fast as possible.

Rate:

This script preloads into memory the QuickTime movie named My Movie:

```
set the preLoad of member "My Movie" TRUE
```

Script Cast Member

Within the properties of a Script cast member, you can change the type of script to a sprite script, movie script, or parent script. (See figure 8.32.)

Figure 8.32

The Script Cast Member Properties dialog box.

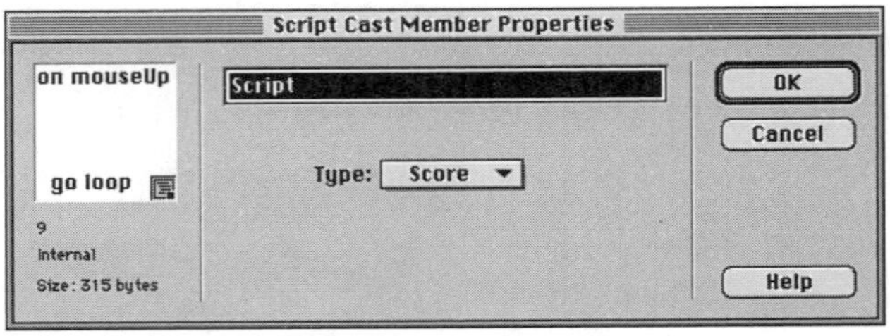

Working with Multiple Casts

The fastest way to learn Director 5 is to experience it. In the next part of the chapter, you build an interactive document. The project uses multiple cast files, both internal and external, linked and unlinked. This project shows the convenience of using multiple cast files to quickly assemble interactive media projects.

You can find the demo for this exercise on the accompanying CD-ROM in the DEMOS folder in Chapter 8 Demo. The CD Chapter 8 Demo folder contains six files. The Multiple Cast Demo file is the finished project; the file Multiple Cast Demo.empty is the unfinished project you use to build up to a finished project.

> You might have heard this caveat many times before, but it always bears repeating: *Remember to save your work often.* If you save every two minutes, you can lose only two minutes of work. If you save every two hours, however, you can lose two hours of work.

Building the Project

First, copy the Chapter 8 Demo folder from the CD-ROM to your hard disk.

Open the Chapter 8 Demo folder and look at its contents. It should look like figure 8.33. This is the finished Director document Multiple Cast Demo. The unfinished Director document Multiple Cast Demo.empty contains four external cast files, as follows:

- Project sounds
- Often-used scripts
- Favorite buttons
- An alias of the cast file located in the temp_server folder

This temp folder contains a cast file named PAGE ART, which is to serve as a make-believe server to show how you can share multiple cast files over a server environment.

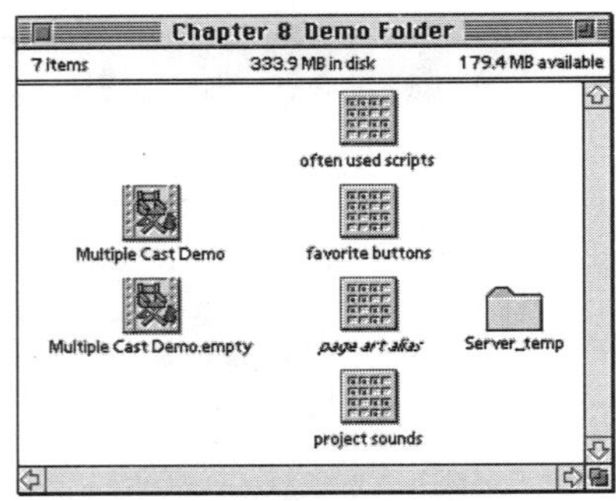

Figure 8.33
The contents of the Chapter 8 demo folder.

Open the file Multiple Cast Demo.empty (the unfinished document).

To Open the Score Window

Select Score from the Windows pull-down menu (Command+4).

This file contains only four frame markers and a `go loop frame` script used four times. The `go loop frame` script keeps the playback head from continuing to the next frame or marker until it is instructed to do so. The frame markers have been spaced apart just to give some visual separation. The document would play no differently if the markers were located only one frame apart or one hundred frames apart.

To Open a Cast Member Window

Select Cast from the Windows pull-down menu (Command+3).

Director automatically created this internal cast window when you first opened the document (the default cast window).

To Name the Default Internal Cast File

Select Cast Properties from the Modify pull-down menu. Name the internal cast file **`main content`**. Media elements will be added to this empty "main content" cast window from other cast windows.

To Save the Document

Select Save from the File pull-down menu (Command+S).

Instead of writing scripts from scratch, let's assume we have a library of scripts stored in an external cast member file. As other projects are developed, useful scripts can be added to this file. Then, to take advantage of these useful scripts, the external cast member file only needs to be opened.

To Open an External Cast Member File

Select Open from the File pull-down menu. In the Open dialog box, select the often used scripts file, which is an unlinked external cast member file. The scripts cast file opens on top of the current cast member file named main content. Drag the often used scripts cast window to another location so you can more easily view both windows. You need a copy of the loop script for the current project.

To Copy the Loop Script from the Unlinked Cast to the Current Cast Window

Drag the loop script (cast member 1) from the often used scripts cast window to the cast 1 position of the main content cast window. Notice that a duplicate cast member was created. Duplicate cast members are created when you drag a cast member from an `unlinked` cast file to the current cast file. Dragging a cast member from a `linked` file to the current cast file would remove the cast member from the linked cast file and move it to the current cast file.

To Close the "Often-Used Scripts" Cast Member File

Select Close from the File pull-down menu (Command+W), then save the document.

Drag the loop script, now located in cast member 1 of the main content cast window, from the cast window to frame 1 of the Script channel in the Score window. Also, place the same loop script in frames 5 and 10 of the frame Script channel, as shown in figure 8.34. When played, the project waits at each looped frame until further instructions.

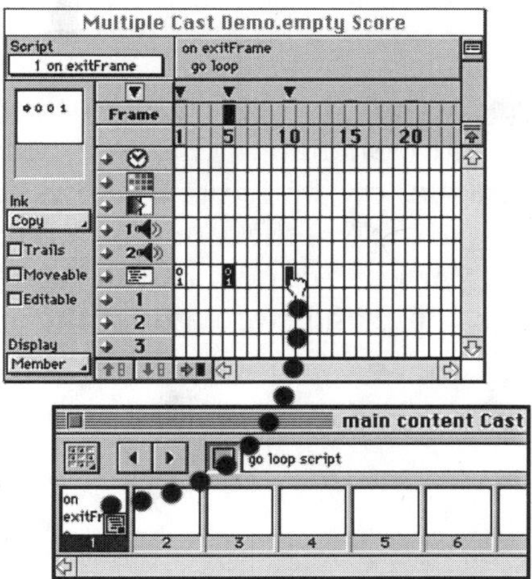

Figure 8.34

Dragging a previously unlinked cast member to different locations of the Score window.

An introduction sound should play when the movie starts, as well as play click sound effects when the user pushes and releases the mouse throughout the movie. The sound library cast file contains all the sounds necessary for the project. This sound cast file right now is unlinked, but because all the sounds in the file are used throughout the project, the sound cast file should be linked.

To Link an Unlinked Cast Member File to the Current Project

Open the cast file named project sounds. Choose Open from the File pull-down menu and select project sounds. The sound cast file opens as a dark gray window, indicating an unlinked file. To link the file, simply drag the Intro Music.AIFF, cast member 1, to sound channel 1 of frame 1 of Score window, as shown in figure 8.35. An alert dialog box explains that the file isn't linked and lets you link the file.

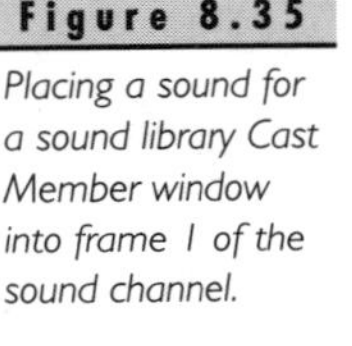

Figure 8.35

Placing a sound for a sound library Cast Member window into frame 1 of the sound channel.

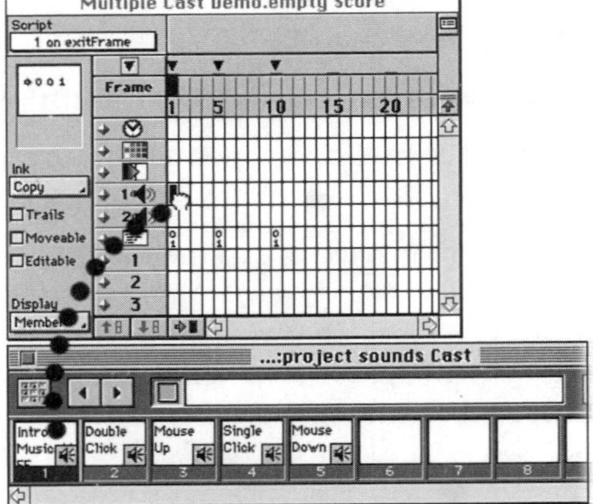

Select the OK button to link the project sounds cast file to the current document. The sound cast file attaches and becomes light gray to match the other cast window. Both cast windows now are open. When the document plays, so too will the sound Intro Music.AIFF. The other sound effects in the "project sounds" cast file can be used for `mouseUp` and `mouseDown` Lingo commands throughout the document.

Save the document.

To Make a Cast Window Active

Select the window to make a cast window active. You also can select either of the cast windows by choosing Cast from the Windows pull-down menu. Closing a cast window makes it unavailable from the Cast, Windows list. Close the Project Sounds Cast Member window.

To Reopen an Attached External Cast File

Choose project sounds from the choose cast display pop-up list in the current cast window (see fig. 8.36). The Cast file reopens.

Figure 8.36

Reopening a closed cast member using the display cast pop-up list.

A new internal cast member file will be created to store incoming navigational icons for the current project.

To Create an Additional Internal Cast File

Select New Cast from the choose cast display pop-up list. In the New Casts dialog box, name the new cast file **`navigational icons`**. Since you want this new cast to be internal, enable the Internal radio button (see fig. 8.37).

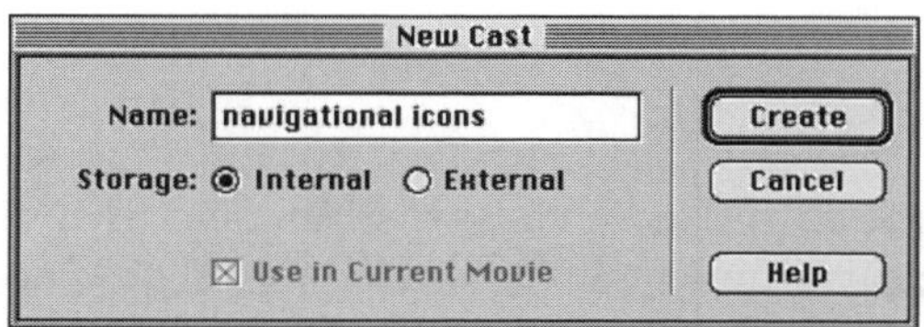

Figure 8.37

Creating a new cast library to hold often used media elements.

> An internal cast file is part of the Director document and cannot be viewed or selected in the finder the way you can an external cast file.

To Open a Cast Library Named Favorite Buttons

Select Open from the File pull-down menu. Select the cast file named favorite buttons.

To Transfer a Cast Member from the Favorite Buttons Cast to the Navigational Icons Cast Window

Simply drag cast members 1 and 2 from the favorite buttons cast window to cast members 1 and 2 of the navigational icons cast window.

To Transfer a Cast Member and Leave a Copy of the Cast Member Behind

Press and hold the Option key during the press-and-drag operation.

After both arrows transfer to the second internal cast file named navigational icons, you can close the favorite buttons cast window.

You now can place the right and left arrow on each of the three pages. You can script these arrows to "go" to other pages throughout the document. To complete this Demo script, you can add the Lingo commands contained in the "often used scripts" cast "go marker(1)" and "go marker(-1)" to the right and left arrows.

Maybe during the production of the project, an unlinked cast file is linked and then needs to be removed. In the last step from the demo, an unlinked cast file named favorite buttons cast was opened, cast members were copied, and then the unlinked cast file was closed. This time the unlinked cast member file named favorite buttons was linked to the current document and then unlinked after finishing. First, you need to link the cast file named favorite buttons to the current document.

To Link an Unlinked Cast Member File

This is the same as in the previous section. Select Movie, Cast from the Modify pull-down menu. In the Movies Cast dialog box select the Link button, then choose the cast file named favorite buttons. Favorite buttons will be added to the linked cast file list. Select OK to close the Movies Cast dialog box. Cast members can now be copied to the navigational icons cast file.

Now it's time to remove the favorite buttons cast member file from the current document.

WARNING

Removing a cast file can be very dangerous if cast members are being used in the current document. The cast members must first be transferred over to another attached or internal cast file before removing the unwanted cast file. Removing a cast member file from a Director project will also remove their corresponding sprites from the Score window. Removing a cast member file could remove hundreds of active sprites.

To Unlink the Linked Cast Member File

Select Movie, Cast from under the Modify pull-down menu. In the Movie cast dialog box, select the favorite buttons cast member file and select the Remove button. An alert box will appear explaining the consequences of removing a cast with references to a document. Since the cast member media was only dragged from cast file to cast file, this alert box can be ignored. Also, if changes have been made to the outgoing cast file, Director will ask whether the cast file should be saved to disk. The cast file is now unlinked from the current document and the cast window will close.

Unlinked external cast files also can be shared over a network—either by opening the file directly from within the Director document or by creating an alias of the original cast member file, which is sometimes more convenient.

To Create an Alias of a Cast Member File

From the finder level, find and select an external cast member file. This file can be stored anywhere on a local disk or network. With the target cast member file selected, choose Make Alias from the File pull-down menu. Move the alias to a folder containing other files used in the Director project. Opening an alias is exactly the same as opening the original cast member file.

The cast file named page art, which is an aliased cast member file, can now be opened and linked to the Multiple Cast Demo.empty. Placing the page art onto the four pages and saving the document as Multiple Cast Demo.finished will complete this demo.

Summary

Multiple cast member files can speed up the production time of a project. Scrolling around a cast window with hundreds of elements can take quite a lot of time. Breaking the cast element into smaller groups using multiple cast is much easier. Also, as projects are created, the cast library can be continually updated with new elements and shared with other members of a project team or network.

Now that you understand the workings of the Cast Member window and its functions, you are ready for the next logical step. In the next chapter, you will learn how to deal with images in Director and will be taken step-by-step through some cool special effects and tricks used in Director's Paint window. Also covered in the next chapter is the process of importing and manipulating artwork, as well as creating something from scratch to dazzle your audience.

John Chambers
with Lee Allis

Graphics: The Visuals

Most of what the audience sees in a Director movie is made up of graphic elements. The backgrounds, the characters, the interface, the buttons, almost everything the audience sees is a graphic of some sort. The Score ink effects, transitions, text, and even the Lingo you use, work with graphics to tell the story of your Director movie. Understanding graphics, color depth issues, palettes, memory issues, and ways to work with graphics in Director is a large part of successful Director authoring.

Director has a paint program for creating and editing graphics built into it—the Paint window. To look at it, the Paint window has changed very little from the early days of VideoWorks, but the new capabilities of the Paint window in Director 5 bring it to a new level of maturity. Coverage of these new capabilities fill their own chapter, Chapter 10, "Paint Window Enhancements." This chapter will explore graphics concepts, information on importing graphics into Director, and how Director works with graphics. It also will provide thorough coverage of the Paint window tools, some of which you might use more often now, with Director 5.

Topics covered in this chapter include:

- Director and Photoshop
- Bitmapped graphics and palettes
- Importing graphics into Director
- Graphics sources
- How Director 5 uses graphics
- The Paint window

Director and Photoshop

Adobe Photoshop is the standard graphics editing tool on the market today. Most Director users are well-versed in Photoshop. Macromedia has recently released its own image editing tool, called xRes, and distributes it with the Director Multimedia Studio. xRes is marketed as a companion to Photoshop, for quickly editing high-resolution images. Whichever image editing tool you use, you will find the need to use both Director and Photoshop, or xRes, or even FreeHand for creating artwork for your Director movie.

Some people try to compare Director's Paint window to Photoshop. They ask why they should use Director's simple Paint window when powerful programs like Photoshop are available. The answer is that you need the right tool for the right job. You will use both. Director's Paint window is simple and easy for those new to creating computer graphics; the learning curve for Photoshop is much higher. It's also easy to stay within Director to make a basic edit or create a simple graphic, without exiting to Photoshop. Just select the cast member, open the Paint window, make the changes, and away you go. To make the same changes in Photoshop would take a great deal longer to accomplish.

Photoshop users and most Director users know why they choose to use Photoshop. If you were to scan hundreds of images for a Director movie, you would first edit those scans in Photoshop before bringing them into Director. Director is oftentimes used as a media-integrator—rather than a media creator—for graphics, digital videos, and sounds.

Bitmapped Graphics and Palettes

All elements created in the Paint window or imported from an image editing application are bitmapped graphics—"just a bunch of pixels." A *pixel* is the smallest element that can be viewed on the screen. These pixels are clustered in groups to create areas of color, your graphics.

The colors used in a graphic with an 8-bit color depth and less are contained in palettes. A *palette* is a table of colors stored in the computer color look up table (CLUT). These tables can be as small as 1 bit.

- A 1-bit palette contains only black-and-white pixels.
- A 4-bit palette contains 16 colors. On the Macintosh, you can customize these 16 colors. In Windows, you can only use one 16-color palette, the Microsoft VGA palette. Therefore, if you are making your Director movie for a 4-bit machine and intending to distribute it cross-platform, you'll want to use the Windows VGA palette.
- An 8-bit color palette contains 256 colors. This palette contains black, white, a small range of grays, and a general selection of basic colors. You can customize an 8-bit palette on both the Macintosh and Windows. Director ships with a number of 8-bit palettes built into it. You also can import custom 8-bit palettes into your Director movie with images. They are then stored as cast members.
- The 16-bit, or thousands of colors, color depth contains 65,536 colors. This color depth was created to closely match the color values of a normal television set. This color depth does not have a palette associated with it.
- The 24/32-bit, or millions of colors, color depth contains 16,777,216 colors. This is the maximum numbers of colors that can be viewed on a Macintosh. This number is actually overkill because a person with normal vision can only perceive about nine million different colors. This color depth does not have a palette associated with it. When Director displays an image on the stage, it not only has to deal with the 16,777,216 colors in that one 24/32-bit graphic, but it also has to deal with graphics or the media elements in the other 47 channels. Each frame in a Director movie can contain up to 48 channels of graphics information, and Director can run up to 120 frames per second.

> Now not only does Director have to deal with showing 48 channels, 120 times per second, but it also has to dispose of the information. This process is very taxing on any speed of machine. When designing your graphics, always try to create and work with them in the smallest color depth. To figure out what color depth to use, all you have to do is think of the numbers. Because an 8-bit image uses 256 colors and a 24/32-bit image uses 16,777,216 colors, it will take less processing power to move the 8-bit graphic around. The fewer colors used in the images, the faster the animation.

If you edit an image to an 8-bit palette or less, it will use either one of the system palettes or its own custom palette. The problem is that the monitor can only display one palette at a time, so everything on the stage will need to use the same palette. Switching between palettes and managing multiple palettes can be difficult in large projects. One of the most common techniques when working with multiple palettes is to create a "super palette" with third-party image processing software.

Some of the most commonly-used packages for processing palettes include:

- DeBabelizer for the Macintosh by Equilibrium Technologies
- graphicsConverter, a Macintosh shareware application
- HiJaak Pro on Windows
- Brenda, a Windows shareware application

Once you have created a super palette in one of these applications, you can import it into Director and make it active for the entire movie. Some developers choose to create one super palette for each movie and switch between palettes as they transition between movies. Director's Fade to Black command is commonly used when switching between palettes. To change palettes on the fly, use Lingo's `puppetPalette` command.

Importing Graphics into Director

All the bitmapped graphics used in a Director file on the Macintosh are PICT files. A *bitmapped graphic* is a "bunch of pixels." Almost all painting applications will save your file in the PICT format. The PICT format was developed by Apple Computer for the Lisa, and later for the Macintosh operating system, as a way of transferring bitmapped graphics from one application to another.

Since its creation in the early '80s, the PICT standard has changed very little. When the color Macintoshes were introduced, the PICT file format was separated into two: a PICT format for black-and-white graphics and a PICT II format for color graphics. Today the term PICT means both types of PICT data.

Director for Windows imports a number of different Windows graphics file formats, not only PICT. Once imported, Director handles the file internally so that both Macintosh and Windows can read it. If you would like to export a Director frame, Director for Macintosh will export the frame as a PICT file, and Director for Windows will export the frame as a BMP file.

Many people wonder why Director doesn't accept EPS files. That's easy: Encapsulated PostScript (EPS), developed by Altsys Corporation, is used for printing to PostScript printers at varying resolutions without losing quality.

Altsys, located in Richardson, Texas, is now a part of the Digital Arts Group of Macromedia. Altsys developed the first PostScript drawing application, Fontographer, which later inspired the development of FreeHand. Fontographer and FreeHand are both Macromedia products.

A Director movie is an on-screen, multimedia experience and works in screen resolution only, or 72 dots per inch (dpi). Some of the new Macintosh monitors can be set to higher or lower resolutions, but they still remain at 72 dpi. A machine with a lower resolution will display larger pixels (fewer pixels per inch) and machines with a higher resolution will display smaller pixels (more pixels per inch). So a file set to 640×480 pixels will stay the same dimensions in pixels, only the pixels could be smaller or larger depending on the monitor settings.

Multimedia artists often ask how to import a file from an application that does not save in a PICT format. QuarkXPress, PageMaker, and Illustrator are generally at the top of the No PICT list.

FreeHand 5.5 on the Macintosh has a new feature called the Create PICT Image, where you can save your vector graphic selection as a PICT file to be imported into Director. This Xtra also enables you to adjust the level of anti-aliasing you would like to apply to the image.

For the other programs, though, there is hope. Any file can be imported into Director. Let me say that again. *Any file* can be imported into Director. Since day one of the Macintosh interface you have been able to take a screen snapshot. A screen snapshot is a bitmapped picture (PICT) of the entire computer screen(s).

To take a screen snapshot, press Shift+Command+3. Actually, a screen shot is just a picture of the current screen. So in other words, any file can be imported into Director. When a snapshot is taken, the file is saved on the hard disk drive as picture 1, picture 2, picture 3, and so on.

When you take a screen shot, you capture the entire monitor. The files might need to be modified a little in Director's Paint window or another paint application. The menu bar appears at the top of the file as well as cursors, guidelines, and other program elements that you might not want visible in your media project. Hiding some of these elements before taking the screen shot is helpful, and remember that it is always actual size, so scale the page if needed before you use the screen shot command.

There are a number of commercial screen capture applications available. ScreenShot for Macintosh from The Beale Street Group, Inc., is a great, easy to use, and to the point, screen capture utility program. Instant Replay from Strata, Inc., takes screen snapshots as well as records screen activity and saves the files in a QuickTime format.

Things to Remember When Importing

The three main things to remember when creating and importing graphics, regardless of the application they where created in are anti-aliasing, resolution, and bit depth.

Anti-Aliasing

An anti-aliased graphic has a fuzzy edge surrounding it. The edge is created automatically in a program like Photoshop, where its number one goal is to smooth everything into everything else for a high-quality photo image.

Let's say, for example, you create a circle graphic in Photoshop. The circle is red with a white background. If you look very closely at the graphic, the edge on the circle is made up of pink pixels where the circle touches the white background. This is the anti-aliased edge. Save the file as a PICT and import it into Director.

Problem 1—Halos

If the red cast member is placed onto the stage with a white background, no problem, the pink edge blends into the Director background fine. But if you to create a black background, things are going to change a little. The pink anti-aliased edge of the red circle glows pink against the black background, creating a "halo."

If the red circle/white background is not going to move during your movie, you might not notice the "halo." But if the circle is to move about your stage and pass over other different colored sprites, you'll need to do a few things to the Photoshop graphic file before importing it.

> This is one instance where you would use Director's Paint window to create hard-edged images without the anti-aliased "halo" effect. If you were really creating a red circle, you should create that in Director to avoid this problem. But, like most of your images, they will be more complicated than a circle. You'll have a person's body or face, or your company's logo. You will then need to work on the "halo" effect, back in Photoshop, before importing the image into Director. You should apply this red circle example to your more complicated artwork.

When working in a painting program like Photoshop, be sure to turn off the anti-aliased features of the tools you will be using. If the graphic has already been created, use a selection tool with its anti-aliased and/or feathering features turned off before copying or cutting and pasting it into Director.

To edit the "halo" effect within Director, you can use the Switch Color tool in the Paint window. The Switch Color tool is very helpful in removing unwanted pixels from an 8-bit graphic. Here, you can select the unwanted colors within an exact area and swap them with pixels of another color, including white. The Switch Color tool is covered in more detail later in this chapter.

Resolution

One of the joys of teaching Director is finding out how many ways something can be done. People try to solve problems in so many ways—not always right and not always wrong, but it's great to witness them all. If I were given a dollar for every time I heard this one: "I saved the file at 144 dpi so it would look better, but the file comes in too big. Why?"

Problem 2—Image Size

The resolution of a Director file is *always* 72 dpi—not 72 dpi for graphics and 300 dpi for photographs. It's *always* 72 dpi. Photographers, graphic designers, and film people will have the most problem with this concept. These types of people, including myself, are all accustomed to 300 dpi for high-end printers like Iris and Splashes, and 150 linescreens (lpi—lines per inch) for printing presses at the local print shop. For these types of people, 72 dpi images are low resolution images. But because the Macintosh monitor is 72 dpi, we're stuck with it. And to tell you the truth, images saved at 72 dpi look great for computer presentations. Saving a file at 144 dpi will not make the file twice as good, only twice its actual size. A 2×2-inch image saved at 144 dpi in a paint program will import as a 4×4-inch image in a Director file *always*.

When changing an image size to be larger or smaller, the application that is doing the scaling will have to add or remove pixels to the image.

When enlarging an image, the computer will look at two adjoining pixels and create a new one to match the original two. This made-up pixel will cause the image to look out of focus. When reducing the size of an image, the program is removing pixels and the image will stay fairly sharp.

The moral to the story: try to scan, create, work, and save the image at the size it will be used in the presentation if you can. Reducing an image is generally acceptable, but enlarging an image is going to be a problem for sure.

Problem 3—File Size

One major concern of a Director author is the file size of the Director movie. And what do you think helps to make a Director's file size larger? You guessed it. The graphics.

One trick to cutting down on the size of graphic cast members is a technique you can use in Photoshop or xRes. When editing an image, make sure you save the image in Indexed Color mode. Typically, your image when scanned or acquired elsewhere will be in RGB mode. One graphic could take up more than 500 KB. In Photoshop, if you save the image in Indexed Color mode, one indexed color will replace the R (red), G (green), and B (blue) colors associated with each pixel. The file size of the image could be reduced from 500 KB to 77 KB with a single command.

Bit Depth

The bit depth is the amount of color available in a graphic file. It's not the actual amount of color used to make the graphic, but how many choices of colors are available in the palette, or range of colors. You could, for example, draw a black-and-white happy face picture. Even though the artwork is only black and white, the bit depth of the file could be 24/32 bits (millions of colors).

Figure 9.1 shows the bitmap cast member properties of two identical files, one saved in 1 bit (black and white), the other file saved in 24/32 bit (millions of colors.) The 1-bit image is 2.4 KB in size while the 24/32 bit image is 75 KB—a very substantial difference. This might not seem like very much, but it could be very critical when trying to develop a project that has to fit on a floppy or you have a CD that is too full to place just two more small images on. When importing an image from another program, such as Photoshop, the image should have its bit depth set before the import takes place.

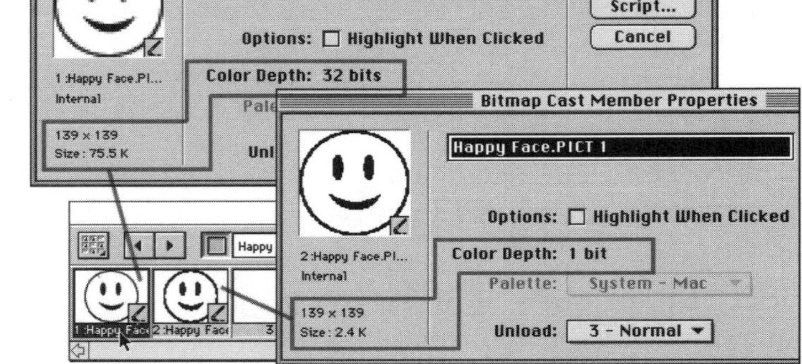

Figure 9.1
The same cast member imported with two different bit depths and their kilobyte size differences.

NOTE

When explaining bit depth, the highest bit depth on a Macintosh is written as 24/32. The reason for this is that the bit depth 24/32 is actually 32 bits of information; 24 bits of this setting is for your everyday normal colors. The next 8 bits deal with alpha channel information or other special effects. The fact is, you can't work in 24 bits, so when someone says 24-bit they are actually referring to a 32-bit resolution.

When an image is imported into Director and the image resolution doesn't match the project color depth, Director will ask how to import the image (see fig. 9.2). You can either keep it as is or sample it up or down to match the project's bit depth.

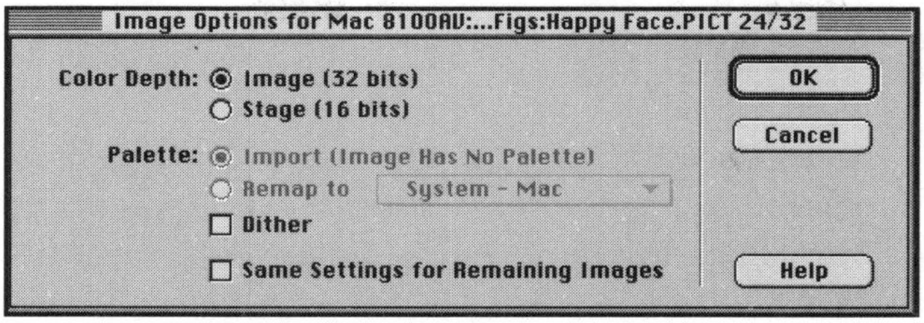

Figure 9.2

The import options for an incoming image that does not match the screen depth of the current project.

The project bit depth is the setting of the monitor in the Monitors control panel in the System Folder (see fig. 9.3). Any time an image is imported, Director checks the settings of the Monitors control panel and gives you the option of what bit depth the incoming image can be—either the setting of the incoming image or the setting of the monitor.

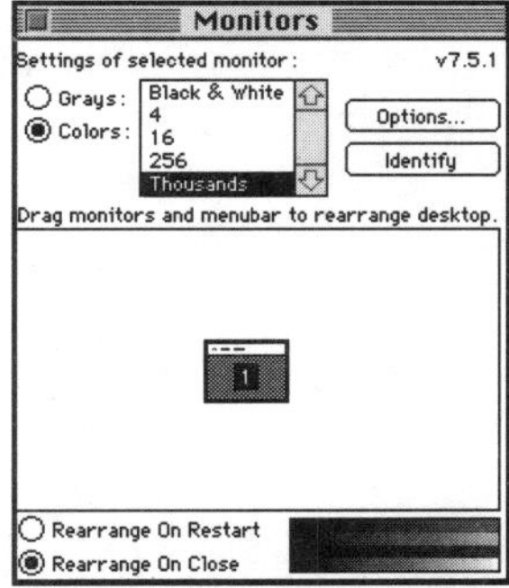

Figure 9.3

The monitor settings in the Monitors control panel.

Even though Director is capable of converting one bit depth to another, this task is best handled by the program that created the graphic.

Graphic Sources

Besides creating your own graphics for use in a Director project, you can use graphics from at least two other general sources: scanning images and using stock photography and imagery.

Scanned Images

So let's say you're not too keen on painting or drawing, or you'd like to use a group of photographs you've shot. Media elements don't have to be just drawings, scanned images can be imported as well. Scans, too, are bitmapped images. Layered photos with text effects overlaid can make a very impressive presentation. A scanned image can be helpful for digitizing your company logo. A black-and-white cartoon could be scanned in and then electronically colored.

One of my students had a great story of needing a woodgrain pattern for an interactive project. After rolling his computer table over to a heavy pitted wooden door and hitting the scan button, he quickly held the scanner up to the door and scanned the surface. Not only did the project turn out well, but the story that goes along with the project always causes a second look at the file. Because a scan is a bitmapped image, the image can be modified just like any other image, using filters and effect options.

Scan photographs at a resolution of 100 dpi. Earlier I said that 72 dpi is the correct resolution, but for the best-looking scans, scan the image at a resolution of 100 dpi. Set the scanner to scale the image to the size it will be in the project. Save the scan and import the file into Photoshop. In Photoshop, select Image Size from the Image menu and change the resolution to 72 dpi. Scanned images look better when the resolution is modified in Photoshop as opposed to setting the scanner to scan at 72 dpi. With this technique, there seems to be no gain in image quality by scanning at higher than 100 dpi.

Stock Photography and Clip Art

Okay, so you don't like to draw or paint and you don't have a scanner. Many services provide stock photography, like Image Club Digital stock photography from Adobe. Here you can buy a CD full of images such as sunsets, skies, and weather, or textured backgrounds. Image Club offers dozens of CDs to choose from. Each disk contains about 100 ready-to-use images that can be easily copied and pasted into your project.

If you're looking for clip art, you'll find volumes upon volumes of clip art CD-ROMs in any software store. Be sure to check the licensing agreements on the clip art before using it in a Director movie you intend to distribute. Many companies publish royalty-free clip art you can use.

How Director 5 Uses Graphics

Following is a basic list of how Director uses graphics and all cast members. This will be a review for experienced users, but some of the terminology has been changed with Director 5. When working with graphics and other media elements, it's often necessary to review the basic functionality of Director. This way, when you're lost in your Lingo code, you can remember where you are and what you're referring to. For those of you new to Director, the following can be a good way to remember how Director "works."

- When a graphic is created or imported into Director it becomes a cast member.

> The main terminology change in Director 5 has to do with the new feature of multiple casts. Cast members are now referred to as "members," because they can be stored in one of many casts.

- Members are stored in the Cast window. (Basically, the Cast window is a database of all the media elements used in the movie.)
- For Director to use these media elements, the members are placed onto the stage.
- When a member is placed onto the stage, it appears as a sprite in the Score window.
- A sprite is just a member located on the stage. The sprite also appears as a cel in the Score window.
- A cel is where a channel and frame meet (see fig. 9.4).
- The member is the original and the sprite is a copy of the original with information contained within it to tell the Score window where, when, and how the sprite should be viewed on the stage.

- A cel can only contain a single sprite. The Score window has 48 channels per frame. This gives you a maximum of 48 cels or graphics per frame for creating complex scenes.
- By adding and removing graphics from cels and advancing the playback head at a high speed, you get animation.

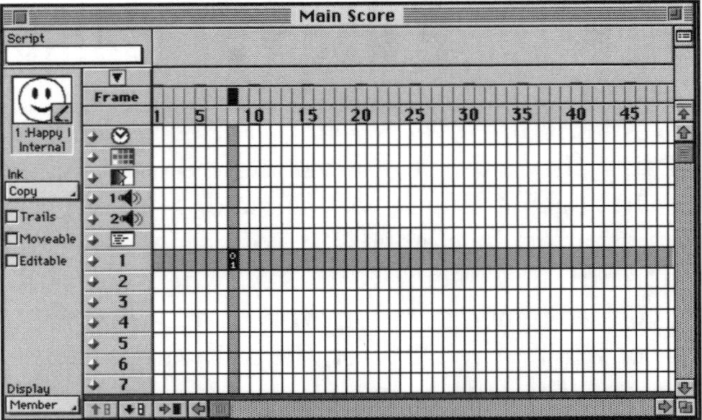

Figure 9.4

In the Score window, cels are where frames and channels meet.

With Lingo, you can control sprites on the stage, cast members, the speed of the playback head, transitions, and a great deal more.

The Director 5 Paint Window

Director's new Paint window, as shown in figure 9.5, has had a complete makeover from the earlier version, with its clean updated tool palette and function buttons, manageable text options, rulers, unlimited filters, and onion skinning. What more could you ask for? These new features will have Director users using the Paint window much more often for media creation and editing. In fact, many of the old features might become new to you if you begin to use the Paint window more. The next chapter, Chapter 10, "Paint Window Enhancements," covers all of the new features. This section of the chapter gives you a solid background to the functionality of each part of the Paint window that you'll use in conjunction with the new features in Chapter 10.

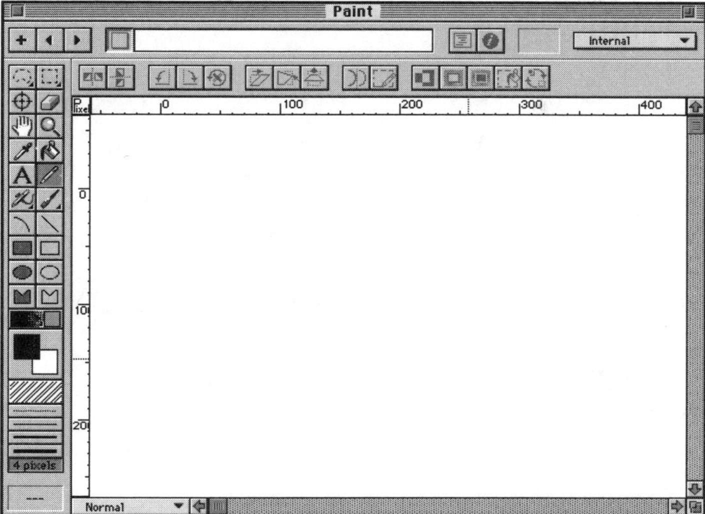

Figure 9.5

Director's new Paint window.

This section covers the following features of Director's Paint window:

- Tool palette
- Gradient selector area
- Color selector chips
- Pattern selector area
- Line thickness buttons
- Paint ruler
- Paint window button bar

Tool Palette

The following are descriptions of Director 5's Paint tools.

> If an arrow appears in the lower right corner of a tool, click the tool to display a pop-up list of options.

Selection Tools

Between the two selection tools, the Lasso and the Marquee tool, you have a choice of seven different selection options. Pressing either of these tools will invoke a pop-up menu selection as shown in figure 9.6. After an element or part of an element is selected it can be cut, copied, or moved to another location on the canvas.

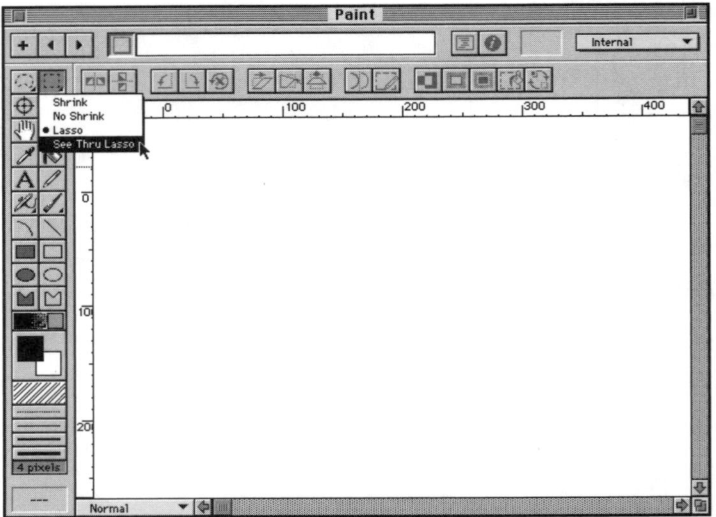

Figure 9.6

Seven different pop-up options are available between the two selection tools.

NOTE

After making a selection, the up, down, left, and right arrows on the keyboard will move the selection one pixel in that arrow's direction.

- **Marquee, Shrink.** On selection of an element, the selection marquee will shrink up to the outside edges of the artwork, to create a flat-sided selection. All white pixels contained within this selection will be seen as opaque white.
- **Marquee, No Shrink.** On selection of an element, the selection marquee remains in the dragged position as a flat-sided selection. All white pixels contained within this selection will be seen as opaque white.
- **Marquee, Lasso.** On selection of an element, the color of the pixel and all same colored touching pixels where the drag was started will be ignored, all other colors within the selection will

be selected within a flat-sided selection. All white pixels contained within this selection will be seen as opaque white.

- **Marquee, See Thru Lasso.** This option behaves the same as Marquee, Lasso except all white pixels contained within this selection will be seen as transparent (no value).
- **Lasso, No Shrink.** The area drawn with the lasso tool retains its shape and selects all of its content. All white pixels contained within this selection will be seen as opaque white.
- **Lasso, Lasso.** On selection of an element, the color of the pixel and all same colored touching pixels where the drag was started will be ignored, all other colors within the selection will be selected within the drawn area. All white pixels contained within this selection will be seen as opaque white.
- **Lasso, See Thru Lasso.** This option behaves the same as Lasso, Lasso, only all white pixels contained within this selected area will be seen as transparent (no value).

Have you ever tried to select one colored item inside of another in Photoshop? Not an easy thing to do. With Director's Lasso, the process is easy. Using either selection tool, with its pop-up option set to Lasso, drag around an object of one color within another colored object and release. Like magic, you will have a selected color within another.

Registration Point Tool

A registration point is a set position within a cast member. By default, the registration point is set to the center of a newly created, imported, or pasted cast member (see fig. 9.7). This position is used for aligning with other cast members on the stage. For example, to create the spinning hands of a clock, the registration point would be placed at the pivot point of each of the clock hand cast members. The Cast to Time command in the Score menu would align all of the hands to a central location on the stage.

Figure 9.7

The registration point of a cast member.

Double-clicking the Registration tool will reset the registration point of the cast member back to its center.

Eraser Tools

This one-size-fits-all tool does one thing—gets rid of whatever it's drawn over. Actually, it changes the colors it touches on the canvas to white. Doubling-clicking on the eraser tool will remove all of the art contained on the canvas, not just the viewable area.

Due to the block shape of the Eraser tool, the Paintbrush tool or other small-tipped tools set to white can make the job of erasing pixels or correcting a little easier.

Eyedropper Tool

The Eyedropper tool is a handy tool used to pick up a color used in a piece of art. The color under the eyedropper at the time of the mouse click will be placed into the Foreground Color chip.

Pressing the Option key while clicking on a colored pixel with the eyedropper tool will fill the Gradient destination color chip with the color under the clicked cursor (see fig. 9.8).

Figure 9.8

Clicking on a color with the Eyedropper tool while the Option key is pushed will cause the Gradient destination color chip to change.

Hand Tool

The Hand tool is used to move artwork around in the Paint window. As you use the Hand tool, the scroll bars at the top and right sides of the Paint window update to show where the artwork is in relation to the window frame.

Pressing the Spacebar will invoke the Hand tool even with another tool selected in the Tool palette. For obvious reasons, this tip will not work if the text tool is selected.

It is possible to temporally lose artwork in the Paint window. This could be done by dragging the artwork beyond the top or side rulers. This will put the artwork in a no-man's-land, until the Paint window is closed and reopened or the next or previous cast member buttons are used to return to the lost cast member.

Zoom Tool

To get a closer look at your artwork, use the Zoom tool (magnifying glass). Starting at the actual size of the image, the Zoom tool will double the magnification for each click of the mouse, up to 800 percent. Clicking in the upper right actual size mini-window will return you to actual size. The Zoom features also can be accessed by using the Zoom submenu from the View menu.

Pressing the Command key and clicking the mouse will quickly zoom into the artwork. Pressing the Command and Shift keys while clicking the mouse will zoom out from the artwork. These shortcuts will help you get a better look at your artwork without changing tools in the palette.

Many people new to the computer will sometimes confuse the difference between scale and magnify. The Zoom tool only changes the magnification of your view—the way you *look* at the artwork. The actual size of the artwork is not changing when you zoom in or out on an image.

Paint Bucket Tool

Use the Paint Bucket tool to pour a color onto the canvas. First, select a color from the Foreground color chip, and click on the Paint Bucket tool. Then click on a pixel within the artwork, and the pixel and all of the pixels touching it with the same color will change to the selected Foreground Color chip's color.

The *hot spot* or *target spot* of the Paint Bucket tool is the tip of the pouring paint. Careful—this hot spot is only three pixels in size and it is sometimes difficult to select the right pixel. Zooming in might help. Or you might need to Undo if you click on the wrong pixel.

Text Tool

The Text tool is used to enter bitmapped text into the Paint window. Clicking in the paint canvas with the Text tool will create a text box; here you can enter text from the keyboard to fill the selected area. As long as the box is active, the text can be modified.

With the text box active, double-click the Text tool in the tool palette and the Font dialog box will appear (see fig. 9.9). Here, all the attributes, such as font, size, and color of the text, inside the active text box can be modified. Click away from the active text box or select another tool from the tool palette to deselect the text box.

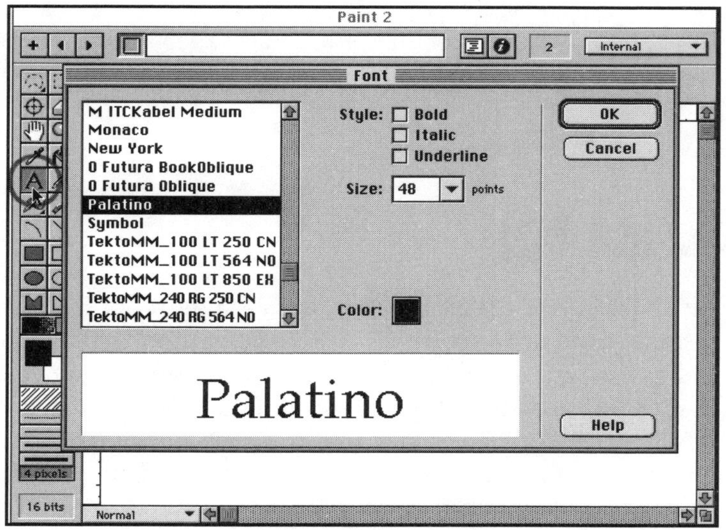

Figure 9.9

Double-clicking on the Text tool will bring up the Font dialog box.

The text entered into the Paint window is only text until it is deselected. Deselected text turns into a bitmapped graphic. In other words, be sure the spelling is correct before deselecting the text.

Pencil Tool

One of the many great things about the Director Paint window is the simplicity of the tools. The Pencil tool only draws a one-pixel-thick line in the color of the Foreground Color chip. The word "only" used in the preceding sentence is not a bad thing. Drawing a one-pixel line in Photoshop can be accomplished, but the line weight has to be set, the anti-aliasing has to be turned off, and the transparency has to be checked—not to mention a handful of other settings. In Director we have a "line," plain and simple.

Pressing the Shift key and dragging a pencil line constrains the line to a horizontal or vertical direction. The Pencil tool does not have a snap-to function. In other words, the Shift key must be depressed before the drag is started. Pressing the Shift key after the line is started yields no effect.

Air Brush Tool

The effect the Air Brush tool creates, at first, might not look like paint being sprayed out of an air brush. To get a very smooth spray, the pixels would have to be smoothed out or anti-aliased, something you generally don't want to do in a Director animation. The Air Brush can create some fun patterns all the same. The Air Brush has five fixed settings, ranging from small to large, and a custom setting dialog box to set up your own air brush pattern (see fig. 9.10). Click on the Air Brush tool to activate the pop-up menu. Choose Settings (or double-click on the Air Brush tool) to open the Air Brush Settings dialog box.

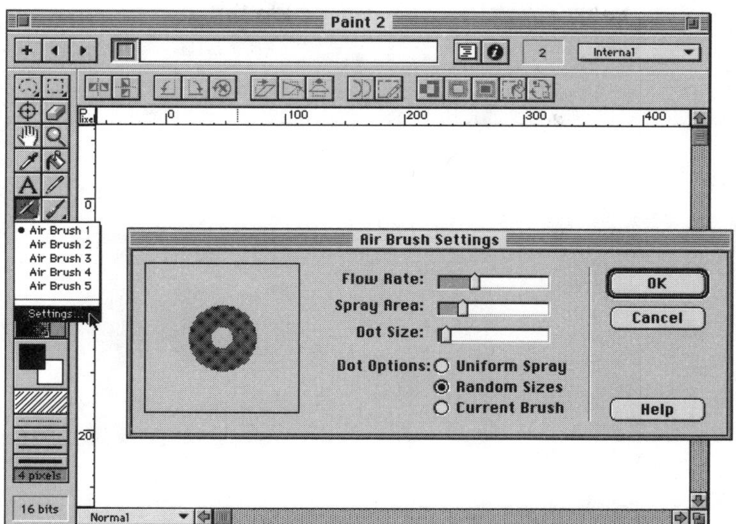

Figure 9.10

The Air Brush tool has five presets and a custom settings dialog box.

The following settings are available for the Air Brush tool.

- **Flow Rate.** Sets how fast the paint comes out of the gun. The higher the setting, the more paint dots.
- **Spray Area.** How much area the dots can cover for each click of the mouse. If the mouse was to be clicked and held in one place for a period of time, the paint dots would fill the entire spray area.
- **Dot Size.** Size of the paint dots that hit the canvas.

Brush Options:

- **Uniform Spray.** Even amount of paint is sprayed from the tool.
- **Random Sizes.** Paints dot of random sizes.
- **Current Brush.** Sets the paint dot to the shape of the paintbrush tool. Double-click the Brush tool to set this option.

Brush Tool

The Brush tool draws the color of the Foreground Color chip. You can use one of five preset brushes in the Paint window at any one time. Click on the Brush tool to select one of the five brushes. To adjust the settings for a brush, first select the brush you'd like to alter and select Settings from the list or double-click on the Brush tool (see fig. 9.11).

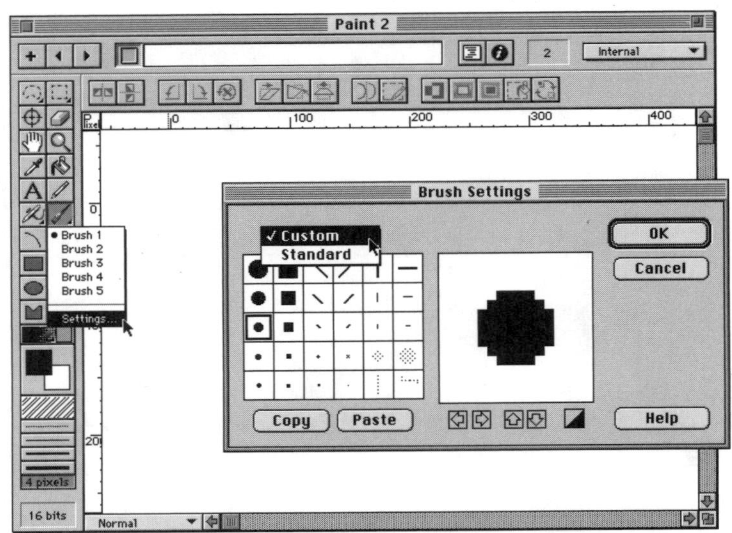

Figure 9.11

The Brush tool has five presets and a Standard and Custom settings dialog box.

In the Brush Settings dialog box, you can choose from the Standard settings or click on the pop-up menu at the top of the dialog box to create custom settings. The Standard settings offer a preset palette of brush styles (see fig. 9.11).

The Custom settings has a fully customizable palette of brushes. Within the Custom Brush Settings dialog box, pixels can be added or removed from the enlarged brush creation canvas on the right of the dialog box. Pixels can be shuffled up, down, right, and left one pixel by using the move arrows buttons below the brush creation canvas. The pixels in the blown-up area also can be swapped or inverted: white to black or black to white. Brushes also can be copied to or from the Macintosh Clipboard.

With the Custom Brush Settings open, select an area outside of the dialog box and a black-and-white image of what is under the cursor will be placed in the custom brush creation canvas.

Arc Tool

The Arc tool draws an arched line on the canvas the thickness of the line set in the line weight selection area of the tool palette. The color of the line is the same as the Foreground Color chip.

> Pressing the Shift key when an arc is created causes the arc to constrain to the 1/4 circle dimension.

Line Tool

The Line tool creates straight lines. The width of a line in the Paint window can be between one and 64 pixels. Click on the default one-, two-, and three-pixel line width settings, or double-click on the Other Line Width setting to select a larger width. A line takes on the color of the Foreground Color chip.

> Pressing the Shift key as a line is being created will cause the line to constrain to a 45-degree angle.

Shape Tools

The Rectangle and Ellipse tools create basic shapes on the canvas. These bitmapped shapes can be filled or unfilled, depending on which tool you select. The line weight of the shape is set with the line weight selectors and the fill color is set with the Foreground Color chip.

> Pressing the Shift key as the bitmapped shapes are being created will constrain the shapes to square or circular.

The Polygon tools create both filled and outlined polygons. Each click you make in the Paint window with the Polygon tool becomes a corner of the desired shape. The shape can be finished by either double-clicking to close the shape or by clicking the last position over the top of the first position.

Gradient Colors Settings

This cluster of three boxes sets the behavior of a graduate fill (see fig. 9.12).

Figure 9.12

The Gradient Selector.

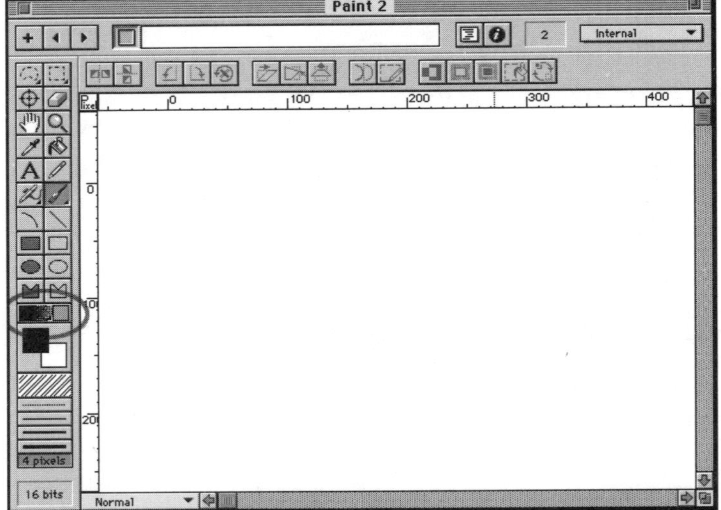

The box on the left sets the start color for the gradient. The box on the right set the destination color for the gradient. The pop-up menu box in the middle sets the style of the graduate effect. Figure 9.13 shows the many different combinations of gradations.

To set one of the tools in the tool palette to fill with this graduate effect, choose a tool in the tool palette, set the Paint window ink effect to Gradient (see fig. 9.14) and either create a new element or recolor an existing element with a graduate fill.

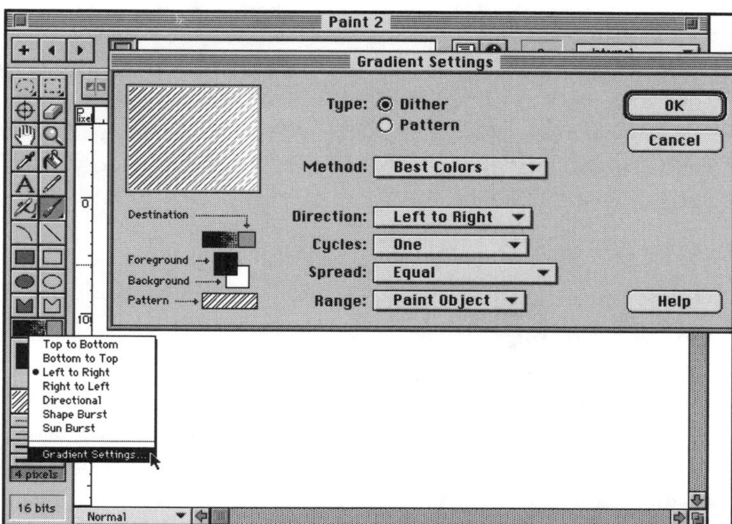

Figure 9.13

The many options of the Gradient Settings.

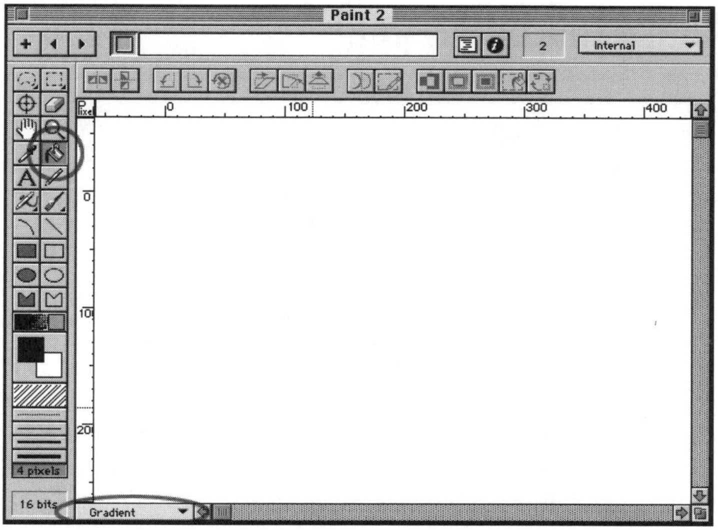

Figure 9.14

Setting the Paint Bucket to fill with a gradient fill.

Color Selection Chips

Pressing on the mouse over the Foreground or Background Color chips will pop up a selection of 256 colors. White is always the top left chip and black is in the lower right corner. To choose a color, press and drag to a preferred color and release. The color chip will change to this newly selected color.

Director's Paint window can draw from any of the 256 colors in the active palette. Corrections can be made to a 16- or 24-bit image in Director's Paint window, but only with its palette of 256 colors. If more colors are needed to correct the image, you will need to edit the image in another image editing application.

Foreground Color Chip

The Foreground Color chip is on the top left, overlapping the Background Color chip beneath it. The Foreground Color chip is used most often to set the colors of most items, such as fills, lines, text color, and start location for a graduated fill effect.

Background Color Chip

The Background Color chip is located below and to the right of the Foreground Color chip. The Background Color chip is used in conjunction with the Pattern tool just below the color chip selection tools. The background color is the color that shows through the foreground color.

Pattern Selector Area

Patterns add texture to the fill of an image. Pattern styles in the Paint window range from very little to a lot of the background color showing through the foreground color. The pattern selector is very helpful in creating a color effect when a limited color palette has to be used. The patterns selector has a great deal of options.

Patterns

Pressing and holding the pattern selector will display the Selector menu. Choose from a palette of 56 styles and eight tiles as shown in figure 9.15. The pattern style with its corresponding foreground and background color will be shown in the pattern selector. As the foreground and background color chips change, the pattern selector will update to show the new pattern colors. Custom patterns can be created by selecting Pattern Settings from the bottom of the pattern selector pop-up menu. The Pattern Settings dialog box allows for the use and creation of custom and standard patterns.

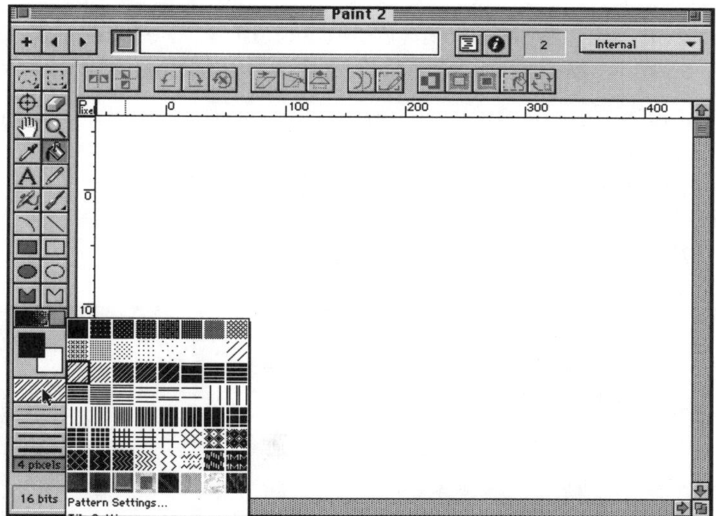

Figure 9.15

The many choices of patterns in the Pattern pop-up selector.

Tiles

Tiles are located on the bottom row of the pattern selector pop-up menu. You can select from eight different colored tiles or define your own. Tiles are perfect when authoring for the Internet when file size is an issue. They are 1-bit and take up very little disk space.

Tiles are used as repeatable patterns for fills. To create a custom tile, first create an image you would like to use for the tile. Next, choose Tile Settings from the pattern selector pop-up menu. In the Tile Settings dialog box, select Cast Member for the source and click the arrow keys until you find the cast member you created.

Click on the image to define the area for the tile. You can adjust the width and height of the selection in the pop-up menus at the bottom of the dialog box.

The new tile you create replaces one of the default tiles. If you delete the cast member you used for the tile, the tile is removed from the tile palette and replaced with the default tile.

Line Weight Settings

Select from one of the four preset line weights in the Paint window. The line weight is applied to any non-filled element created in the window.

Double-click on the fifth button in this series, the Other Line Width button, to open the Paint Window Preferences dialog box. Here, you can define the line width from 1 to 64 pixels (see fig. 9.16). The Other Line Width setting will retain its setting until you change it in the Paint Window Preferences once again.

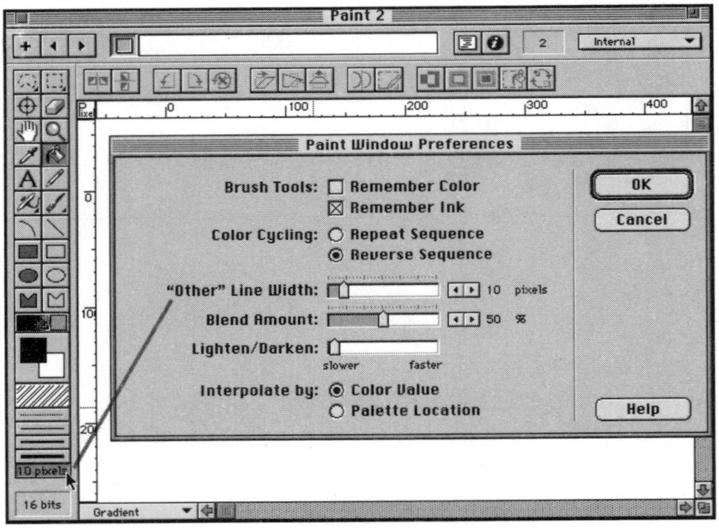

Figure 9.16

To preset a heavy line in the Paint window, double-click the "Other" Line Width button and adjust the line's thickness in the Paint Window Preferences dialog box.

Paint Ruler

With the Paint window open and active, select Ruler from the View menu to activate the Paint window rulers. Click in the upper left corner of where the rulers meet to change the type of measurements. The display changes between Inches, Centimeters, and Pixels. To assist in accurate editing, dotted lines follow your mouse on both of the rulers as you move it around the Paint window.

Effects Toolbar

All of the effects have moved onto their own toolbar in Director 5's Paint window. The effects will become available as a valid selection is made with one of the selections tools. A button will be grayed out if an effect will not work with the current selection. For example, the smoothing button is only available when an 8-bit object is selected; 16- and 24-bit elements cannot be smoothed.

For more about the new effects toolbar, see Chapter 10, "Paint Window Enhancements."

- **Flip.** The grouped Flip Horizontal and Flip Vertical tools will flip a selected element across a horizontal or vertical axis.
- **Rotate.** Selected elements can be rotated 90 degrees clockwise or counterclockwise. The Free rotate tool will enable the selected element to rotate freely around its center. The selection will place handles on each of the element's corners. Drag these handles to a new position to produce the rotation.
- **Distort.** The next three buttons can create some fun effects. The Skew tool will skew selected elements by slanting the sides of an element equality, leaving the top and bottom of the element perpendicular to one another. The Warp tool will enable handles of the selected element to be pulled around to create a smashed or twisted effect. Last, the Perspective tool will shrink or expand the edges of the selected element to give the illusion of depth.
- **Smooth.** Enables smoothing of pixels within a selected area of artwork. The smoothing effect will only function when the bit depth of the cast member is set to 8 bits.
- **Trace Edges.** Creates a new 1-pixel thick line around the edges of the original pixels of the artwork, leaving the original pixels white.

The last group of buttons in the effects toolbar deals more with the color of a selection rather than the shape or orientation of it.

- **Invert.** When clicked, the selection will change to where its black pixels will change to white and white pixels will change to black. Colors in the active 8-bit palette will flip to the opposite side of the palette. To see the exact place a color occupies in a palette, open the Color Palettes window from the Window menu. If a image has a color depth higher than 8-bit, the Invert command will replace the colors with their RGB complement colors.

- **Lighten and Darken.** Selected elements will grow lighter or darker in its palette of colors. This command is unavailable in a 16-bit color space.
- **Fill.** Fills any selected area with the current foreground color or pattern.
- **Switch Colors.** Changes the color of a group of identical touching or not touching pixels. Use the Eyedropper tool to click on the color in the image you would like to change. This will set the Foreground Color chip to color correctly. Then set the gradient destination color chip to the new color you'd like to use. Using one of the selection tools, make a selection. Click the Switch Colors tool and any pixels inside of the selected area that match the destination color chip will be replaced with the foreground color.

Switch color will work only when the cast member is set to a palette of 256 colors or less.

Summary

This chapter described how to use the most common type of media elements used in Director—the graphics. It has touched on graphics concepts and some techniques in third-party image editing tools, necessary to understand when working with graphics in Director. For more information on the third-party tools discussed, check out the books dedicated to those products.

You can turn back to this chapter for a reminder of the most important factors when working with graphics in Director: palettes, importing issues, and how Director uses graphics in the movie. Should you decide to create your own graphics from within Director, this chapter provides a reference to all that the Paint window offers. You can do more than ever in Director 5's Paint window, and you'll find out more about all of the new features of the Paint window in the next chapter, "Paint Window Enhancements."

Lee Allis

Paint Window Enhancements

Director 5's Paint window, at first glance, looks quite similar to that of Director 4.0.4—the effects moved onto a new toolbar; the inks moved to the bottom of the window; the buttons at the top changed color and moved around a bit. But all in all, it looks very much the same. It's not until you start *using* Director 5's Paint window that you realize it has received a full feature upgrade.

The Paint window always has been useful for creating sharp-edged, screen-resolution images that are perfect for run-time animation. Working around anti-aliased edges for Score ink effects and channel layering are never a problem as they are with images imported from other graphics editing tools. Director 5 expands on the Paint window's three major new features:

- The capability to edit graphics at multiple color depths
- Photoshop-compatible filter support
- Onion skinning

This chapter describes the new organization of the Paint window and ways to take advantage of each one of the major new features.

New Window Elements

Before we explore the new capabilities of Director 5's Paint window, you should first notice the new window elements available to you: the Paint window toolbar and cast information.

The Paint Window Toolbar

The Paint window toolbar offers easy access to the effects previously found in pull-down menus. With the click of a button, you can flip an image, rotate it, warp it, apply perspective, invert, darken and lighten its colors, and much more (see fig. 10.1).

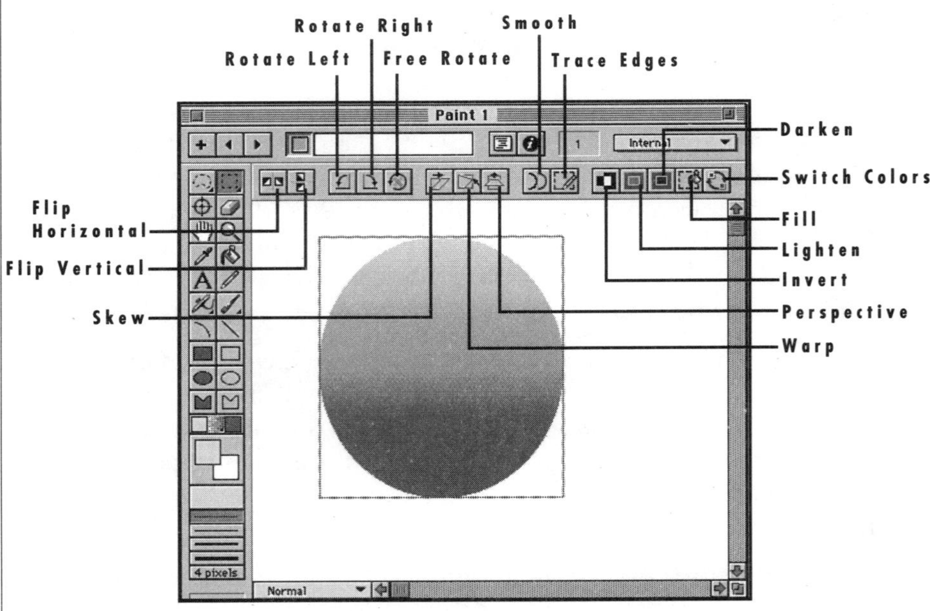

Figure 10.1

Director 5's Paint window toolbar holds all of the effects previously found in the Director 4 menus.

Having the effects in a toolbar enables you quicker access to them and automatic feedback to the effect you've made. You now can easily click on the button again to repeat or undo the effect you've chosen—without navigating through a long pull-down menu.

To try out these effects, do the following:

1. Launch Director 5 and open the Paint window by pressing Command+5.
2. Select the Airbrush tool to the left of the Brush tool (see fig. 10.2).
3. Select Cycle from the inks at the bottom of the Paint window.
4. Choose a wide range of colors for the start and end colors of the Gradient Colors and spray some ink in the window.
5. Double-click the Marquee tool. This selects the entire bitmap.

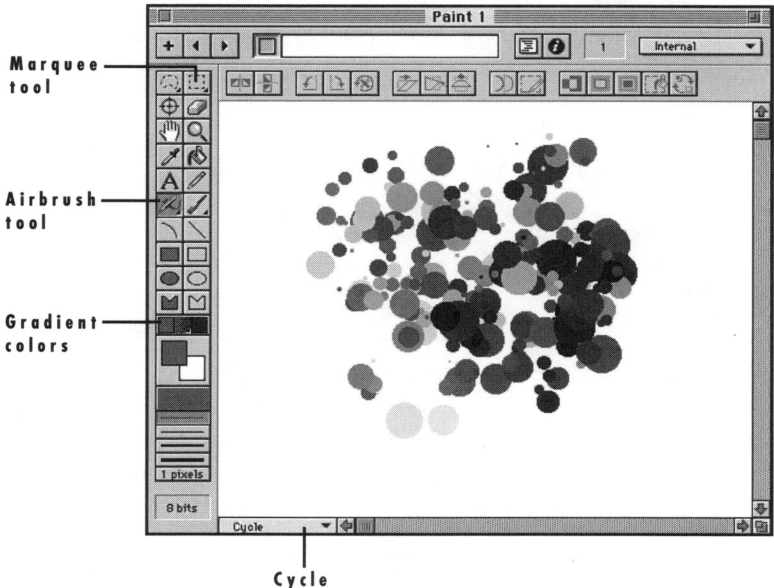

Figure 10.2

A quick way to select the entire image in the Paint window is to double-click on the Marquee tool.

If you would like to erase the entire image in the Paint window, press the delete key after you've selected it with the Marquee tool, or double-click on the Eraser tool.

6. In the Paint window toolbar, click the Invert button. Flip the image with the Flip Horizontal or Flip Vertical button, warp it, and darken it.

Congratulations! You've successfully made programmer art. You now are ready to apply these same effects to the real art for your project.

Cast Information

To help you work with multiple casts, Director 5's Paint window displays the cast that the active graphic is a part of in the top right corner of the window (see fig. 10.3).

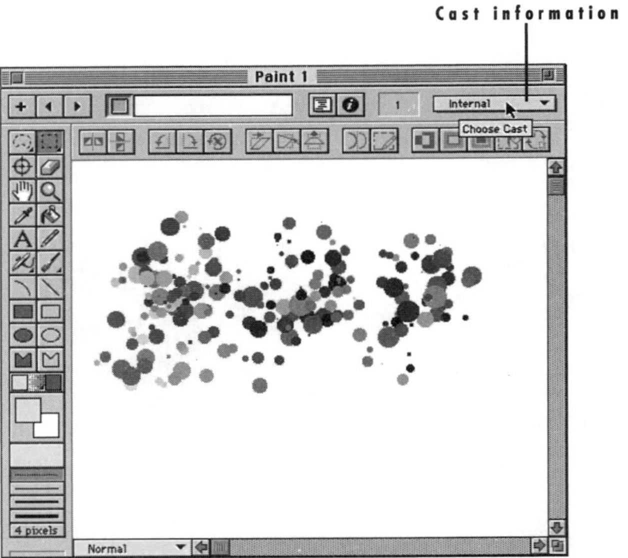

Figure 10.3

The top of the Paint window helps keep track of which cast you are working with by displaying the current cast name.

To create a graphic for a different cast, you must first have another cast created. For information on creating a new cast, refer to Chapter 8, "New in Director 5: Multiple Casts." In the Paint window, select the different cast in the cast pop-up menu and a new graphics cast member is created in the cast you select.

To view the bitmap members of a particular cast one-by-one in the Paint window, make sure the cast you are interested in is active in the cast pop-up menu. If you would like to display the graphics of a different cast, simply select that cast in the pop-up menu and one of the graphics in the new cast appears. Chapter 8, "New in Director 5: Multiple Casts," covers multiple casts in greater detail.

New Editing Power

Watch out, because many of the limitations to editing in the Paint window in previous versions of Director have disappeared in version 5. Director 5 now supports the editing images at multiple color depths, as well as high color editing on 32-bit Windows.

Multiple Color Depth Support

Director 5 supports the editing of multiple color depths in the Paint window. What this means is that your monitor can be set to millions of colors and you can edit in 256 colors, or vice versa. When you're done, you can open another graphic that is of a different color depth and edit that graphic as well, without switching the resolution of your monitor or the graphic.

Director 5 batch imports cast members of different types like digital videos, sounds, and graphics. It also batch imports a group of graphics that are of a different color depth. Upon import, Director 5 prompts you to maintain the original color depth of the graphic or remap it, with or without dithering, to the current monitor resolution (see fig. 10.4).

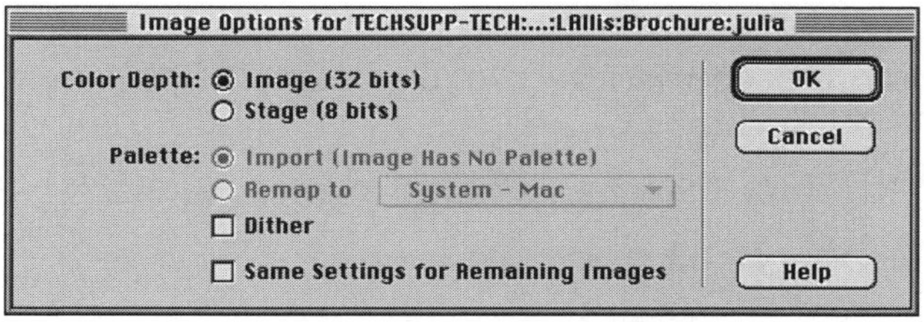

Figure 10.4

Director 5 prompts you for instructions if the image you import is of a different color depth than your monitor.

This dialog box also appears when the image uses a palette that is not currently a part of the Director movie. Notice the Same Settings for Remaining Images option at the bottom of this alert. This option is helpful when you want to import a number of images and you want them all to take on the same settings. If you do not select this option, Director will prompt you with each image and you can choose the instructions for each graphic separately.

Working in multiple color depths adds flexibility to the Director editing session. The color-depth mismatch alert box provides added control over how each image is handled. You can save hours of switching between tools and reediting graphics with this new capability.

True Color Support on Windows

On Windows 95 and Windows NT, you have the same Paint window editing capabilities as on the Macintosh. You can edit in the Paint window in a 1-bit, 4-bit, 16-bit, or 24-bit space—regardless of the monitor's resolution. The Windows 3.1 authoring environment is limited to an 8-bit editing space in the Paint window.

Photoshop-Compatible Filter Support

The Macromedia Open Architecture (MOA), enables Director to open its architecture to third-party Photoshop-compatible filters. Hundreds of filters are available on the market. Director 5 ships with demo filters from:

- Andromeda's Series 1 Circular Multiple Images and Series 2 Three D Filter
- The Human Software Company, Inc.'s Squizz
- MetaTools, Inc.'s Kai's Power Tools
- Multimedia Marketing GmbH's HoloDozo
- Xaos Tools' Paint Alchemy, Terrazzo, and TypeCaster

The filters are accessed by the Photoshop Filters Xtra, which communicates to Director through MOA. Filter support enables developers to update, edit, and create special effects directly in the Paint window.

Installing Photoshop-Compatible Filters

To have a Photoshop-compatible filter appear in Director 5's Xtras menu, Director must first find it or a reference to it in the appropriate Xtras folder. You can install third-party filters in four ways:

Place the filter or a folder of filters

- in the Xtras folder in the Director 5 folder.
- in the Xtras folder in the Macromedia folder in the System Folder.

Place an alias to the filter or a folder of filters

- in the Xtras folder in the Director 5 folder.
- in the Xtras folder in the Macromedia folder in the System Folder.

When you create an alias to the filters, you are able to store the filters where you currently have them stored on your hard drive. For example, you may make an alias of the Filter folder in the Photoshop program's Plug-in folder in order to make all the filters available in Director. Placing the filter or other Xtras in the Xtras folder in the Macromedia folder in your System Folder enables Xtras to appear across Macromedia applications. The same Photoshop-compatible filter, for example, can be used in Director 5 and FreeHand 5.5 for Macintosh.

Once you place the filter or an alias to the filter in the appropriate place, launch Director. If Director was running when you set up the Xtras folder, you'll need to quit Director and relaunch it. Director reads the filters or other Xtras and places them in the appropriate menu.

> If the filters you install do not show up in Director, you might be missing the Photoshop Filters Xtra. When Director is properly installed, you should find this Xtra in the Xtras folder in the Macromedia folder that's in your System Folder. If you do not find this Xtra in the correct place, reinstall Director.

To find out about Xtras in more detail, see Chapter 23, "Macromedia Open Architecture: All About Xtras."

Applying Photoshop-Compatible Filters

Third-party image filters for use with Director 5 offer a variety of controls and effects. Within Director, you'll be able to use one of three main commands: the Filter Bitmap command, the Recent Filter command, or the Auto Filter command. This section describes how the filters and the three new commands work together.

To apply a filter to a graphic cast member, you may select it either in the Cast window or the Paint window. If you select the cast member in the Cast window, the effect you choose is applied to the entire cast member. Applying a filter to a bitmap from the Cast window also enables you to apply the same effect to a range of cast members at the same time.

You usually apply a Photoshop-compatible filter in the Paint window. The Paint window enables you to use the Marquee or Lasso tools to select part or all of the image to which you would like to apply the filter effect. In contrast to the Cast window selection, the Paint window enables you to view the area you will affect before and after you apply an effect, zoom in on specific areas, and use the other Paint window tools.

Filter Bitmap Command

To apply a Photoshop-compatible filter to a single bitmap member or a series of bitmap members, use the Filter Bitmap command. The Filter Bitmap command is available in Director 5's Xtras menu. To activate the command, you must select either the Paint window or a bitmap in the Cast window. The images to which you apply filters might be scanned images, work created by your art department, art you created in the Paint window, and so on. As an example, you'll create some specialized text in the Paint window.

Creating Specialized Text

Use the Filter Bitmap command to create specialized text.

In order to step through this example, you must have the desired Photoshop-compatible filter installed in the correct place. For information on installing Photoshop-compatible filters, see the previous section.

1. First, launch Director 5 and open by choosing the Paint window from the Window menu or pressing Command+5.
2. In the Movie Properties dialog box, under the Modify menu, set the stage color to black.
3. Double-click on the Text tool in the Paint window (see fig. 10.5).

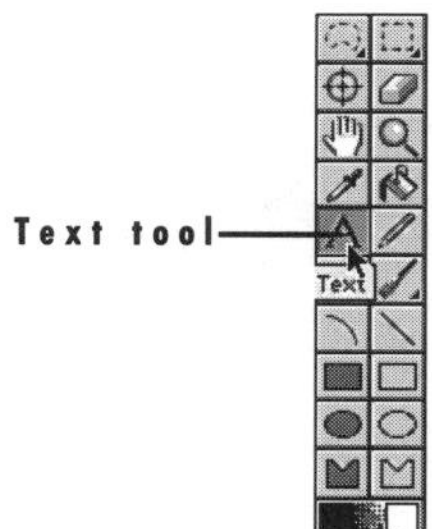

Figure 10.5

Double-click on the Text tool to open the Font dialog box.

4. In the Font dialog box, select a font, size, style, and color for your text. In this example, I've selected Monaco, 36 points, bold, and pink (see fig. 10.6).

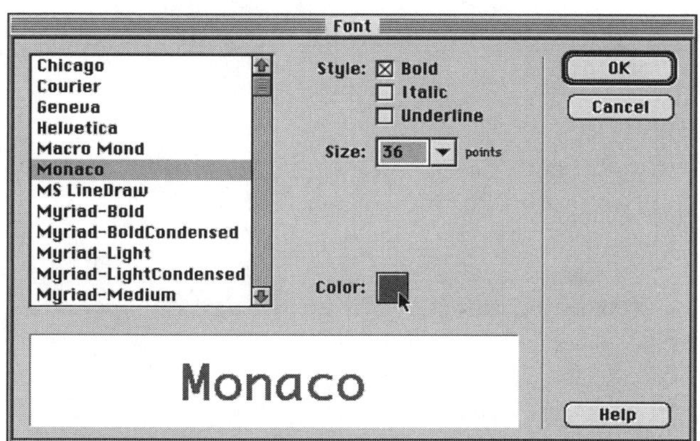

Figure 10.6

The Font dialog box is where you define the text you use in the Paint window.

5. Click OK.
6. Next, click somewhere in the Paint window and type **`Director 5 Filters!`** as shown in figure 10.7.

Figure 10.7

Creating specialized text in the Paint window.

7. Select the Marquee tool and draw a box well outside of the words you typed.

Make sure the Marquee tool is set to No Shrink mode so that you are able to make this selection.

You might be tempted to simply double-click the Marquee tool to select the entire graphic, but be aware that a number of filters grow the image dimensions. A tightly fitting selection will "clip" the filtered image.

8. From the Xtras menu, select the Filter Bitmap command. The Filter Bitmap dialog box appears (see fig. 10.8).

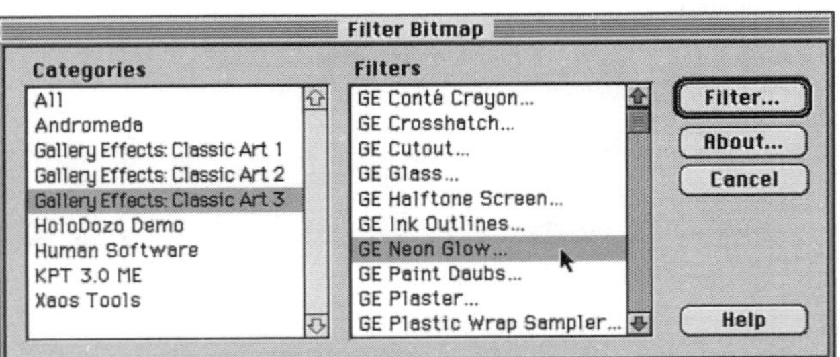

Figure 10.8

The Filter Bitmap dialog box displays the filters installed on your machine that are available to Director.

9. Select the desired filter and click the Filter button. When you do, the filter Preview dialog box appears (see fig. 10.9).

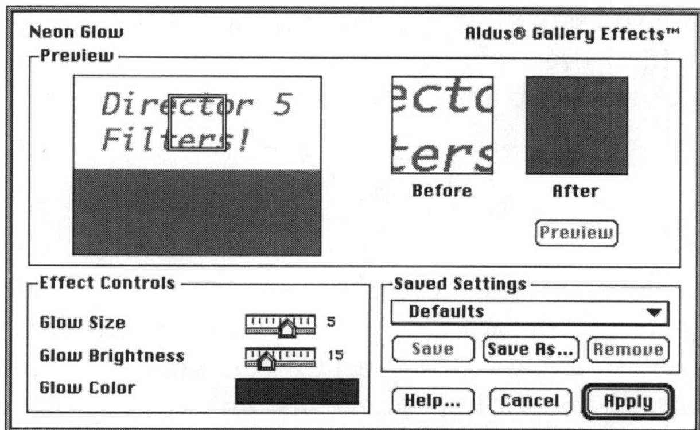

Figure 10.9

The Preview dialog box for filters enables you to adjust the filter settings and preview the before and after effects of the filter.

10. Preview and adjust the settings, then click on the Apply button.

You return to the Paint window with the filter applied to the marqueed region.

11. Now, drag the filtered text onto the stage. Apply some Score ink effects such as Ghost, and Not Copy to it against a non-white background to see the different looks you can achieve.

Repeating the last effect applied in the Paint window is easy by using the Repeat command in the Edit menu, or by pressing Command+Y. To pick from several previously used filters, use the Recent Filters command, described in the following section.

Recent Filters Command

After you use a particular filter, Director places it into the Recent Filters submenu of the Xtras menu. This way, you can apply the same effect at a later time without setting it up again.

To use the Recent Filters command, after you select all or part of the graphic in the Paint window to which you want to apply the filter. If you know you want to apply a filter to the entire bitmap, you may apply this to the cast member in the Cast window as well.

Whether you use the Paint window or the Cast window, to select a filter from the Recent Filters list, Director launches the filter Preview dialog box for that filter. The Recent Filters command opens the filter you used before with the same settings. You can click on the Apply button to apply the filter the same way as before or adjust the settings in this dialog box before you apply the effect again.

Auto Filter Command

In addition to the Filter Bitmap command, Director 5 introduces the Auto Filter command for creating filter animations across a series of images. You can apply a filter effect to a series of images that are already created or tell Director how many cast members you would like it to generate with the interpolated effect. All you have to do is adjust the filter parameters for the start and end positions of the animation and tell Director how many cast members to generate between the positions.

Not all filters support the Auto Filter command. If the filter you're using supports this feature, it appears in the Auto Filter dialog box.

Creating a Filter Animation

To create a filter animation, do the following:

1. Select a bitmap cast member in the Cast window or double-click on a bitmap cast member in the Cast window to open it in the Paint window.

Make sure not to select anything in the Paint window. At the time this book was published, the Auto Filter command could only be applied to the entire image, and if applied in the Paint window, only if nothing is selected.

2. Choose the Auto Filter command from the Xtras menu. When you do, the Auto Filter dialog box appears, as shown in figure 10.10.

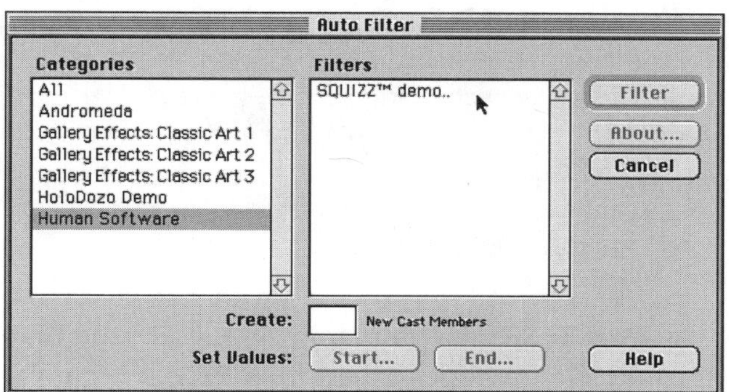

Figure 10.10

The Auto Filter command enables you to animate filter effects over a series of cast members.

3. Select the filter you want to apply and click on the Start button in the Set Values settings.
4. In the filter Preview dialog box, select the settings you want for the initial image in the animation and click on the Apply button.
5. When you return to the Auto Filter dialog box, select the End button. Next, select the settings you want to finish with and click on Apply.
6. Type the number of cast members you want to generate in the animation and click the Filter button.

A progress bar appears as Director creates a new series of cast members. After the effect is finished, cycle through each image in the Paint window to preview the animation by clicking on the right- and left-arrow buttons. If the effect was not what you expected or if the filter animation did not work for some reason, take a look at the "Tips on Working with Filters" section later in this chapter.

Score Applications of Filter Animations

After your filter animation is complete, use the Cast To Time feature to bring that series of cast members to the stage. Cast To Time tells Director to place the images in subsequent frames, one on top of the other when the animation plays.

Before you bring an animation to the stage, make sure that the registration points for each image is in the same place. An easy way to do this is to open the Paint window with the first image in the animation. Double-click on the Registration tool and Director sets the registration point to its center for that image. Repeat this step for all of the images and they all register at the same location.

To apply the Cast To Time command, first select the first cell in the Score you would like the series of cast members to occupy. Then select the range of cast members in the Cast window, and from the Modify menu, select the Cast To Time command (see fig. 10.11).

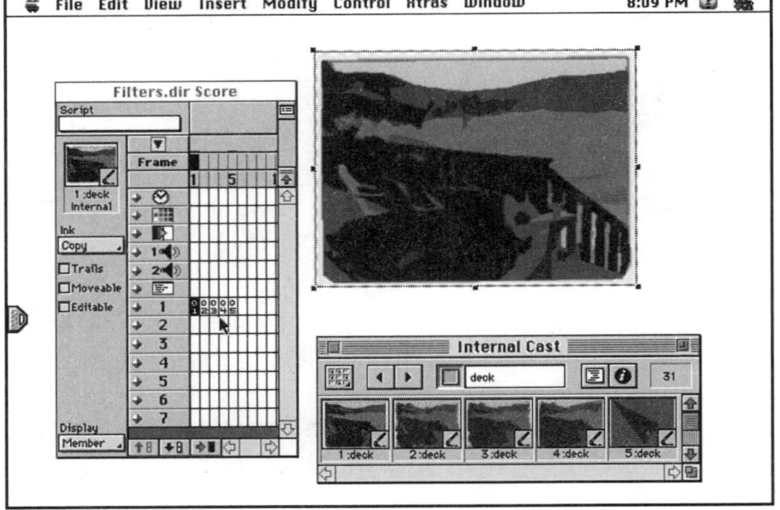

Figure 10.11

The Cast To Time animation command is an easy way to bring a filter animation to the stage.

In this example, cast members 1–5 were brought to the stage with Cast To Time. Rewind and play the movie. Looping Director's Score in the control panel enables you to view the entire animation.

After you've created this animation, you might want to create a film loop or export it to a QuickTime movie. Using the QuickTime technology, instead of using full-bitmapped animations, enables you to compress the animation and link it to the Director movie. When exporting to QuickTime, establish the desired QuickTime movie dimensions before exporting. Repeat the Cast To Time sequence described previously, and export to QuickTime from Director's File menu. The QuickTime file can then be imported into your main Director movie as a cast member.

For more information on digital video, refer to Chapter 14, "Digital Video: The Movie within the Movie." For information on creating a film loop, refer to Chapter 15, "Director as an Animator."

Tips on Working with Filters

If the effect you selected does not work or you experience troubles when working with Photoshop-compatible filters and Director 5, here are some things to try:

- Allocate more memory to Director when you work with filters. Some of the filters take more memory than you might expect. You should compensate for the processing and memory needed for the cast members you generate with the Auto Filter command.
- If your machine freezes when you're working with filters, restart your machine. Before you launch Director again, find the Director 5.0 Preferences and Director 5.0 Xtra Cache files in the Preferences folder of your system folder and throw them away. Now when you launch Director, these files are rewritten for you.
- Make sure you read the Read Me files for each of the filters before you use them. Many need specific system and extension requirements in order to run. You must have QuickDraw 3D installed on your PowerPC, for example, in order to use the HoloDozo filters.
- If the Auto Filter command generates the number of cast members you specify, but no effect is applied to the new cast members, make sure you have nothing selected in the Paint window before using the Auto Filter command. Future versions of Director might support applying the Auto Filter command to only part of an image, but version 5 does not.

Onion Skinning

Director 5 gives the Paint window a whole new dimension with the new Onion Skinning tool. Onion skinning enables animators to create cel animations completely within Director's Paint window.

Onion skinning takes its name from the traditional animation technique of using thin "onion skin" paper to create movie animations. Just as a stack of thin onion skin paper in traditional hand-drawn animation allows other pages of the animation to show through, Director's Paint window displays cast members before and after the one being created as exact reference points. This new feature drastically improves an artist's productivity within Director and control over the creative process.

The *Inside Director* CD contains three movies that were created with onion skinning. These were made by Mark Shepherd, the Director engineer at Macromedia who is responsible for the onion skinning technology. You'll find Mark's movies in the Chapter 10 folder on the CD. Take a look at all three movies before you experiment with onion skinning.

The following sections will work through Mark Shepherd's movies on the accompanying CD as they describe the new onion skinning tools.

Enabling Onion Skinning

You can easily learn the onion skinning technology by stepping through an animated Director movie that's already created. You'll use Mark's BLAH.DIR movie in this example.

1. Open the BLAH.DIR movie in the Mark Shepherd folder located in the Chapter 10 folder on the accompanying CD (see fig. 10.12).

Figure 10.12

The BLAH.DIR movie, by Mark Shepherd, was created with onion skinning.

2. Open the Paint window and choose Onion Skin from the View menu. The Onion Skin floating toolbar appears (see fig. 10.13). Do not close the BLAH.DIR movie; you will use it in the next section.

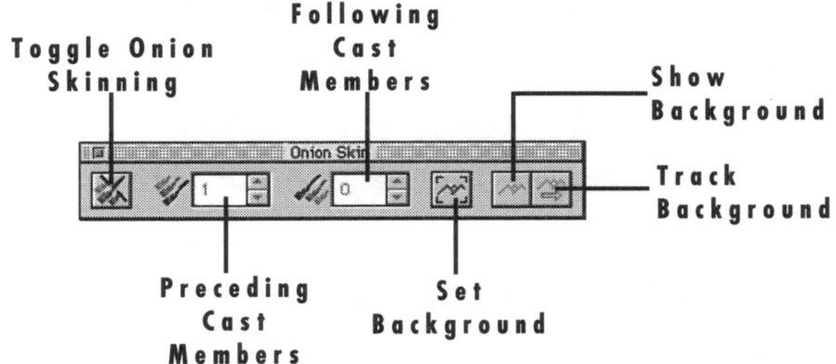

Figure 10.13

The Onion Skin tool enables the creation of cel animations within Director 5's Paint window.

The Toggle Onion Skinning button is the button on the far left of the toolbar (see fig. 10.13). With the Paint window open, you can toggle this button to enable or disable onion skinning. When enabled, dimmed images of cast members before and/or after the active cast member are blended into the Paint window's drawing area as you create the new cast member. To turn off those reference images, toggle the Toggle Onion Skinning button to the off state.

To enable and disable onion skinning, use the shortcut key Command+Option+K. If you have the CloseView control panel installed, you will need to remove it in order to use this keyboard shortcut normally in Director.

Preceding and Following Cast Members Settings

To determine which cast members display along with the current cast member in the Paint window, adjust the Preceding Cast Members and Following Cast Members settings.

The Preceding Cast Members setting indicates the number of cast members in cast positions immediately before the current one in the Cast window that blends into the current image. The Following Cast Members settings indicate the number of cast members immediately following the current one that displays in the Paint window. Cast members farther away from the active image appear dimmer than ones closer to the image.

1. With the BLAH.DIR movie still open, make cast member 2 active in the Paint window.
2. The Onion Skin toolbar should still be open, but if not, open it again from the View menu and click the Toggle Onion Skinning button.
3. Type 1 in the Preceding Cast Members setting to see how Mark used the previous cast member to create the new one that makes the man look like he's talking (see fig. 10.14).

If you cycle through the remaining images in the Paint window, you see the entire animation.

4. Press Command+1 to close all the windows or select Stage from the Window menu. Then rewind and play the movie to see the final effect.

Figure 10.14

Director's Paint window, displaying a previous cast member, as you create a new one in the animation.

Creating Key Frames

The basic advantage to the Onion Skinning tool is the capability to view other images while you create new key frames in an animation. For this example, you'll create a new movie—use the example of drawing an animation of a character walking across the stage. You import or draw the first cast member as he begins to walk. To create a subsequent pose of the same character using onion skinning, complete the following steps:

1. Select the initial cast member in the Paint window.
2. Open the Onion Skin tool from the View menu.
3. Click the Toggle Onion Skinning button on the Onion Skin toolbar and set the Preceding Cast Members setting to `1`. Make sure everything else is disabled or set to `0`.
4. Click the + button in the Paint window.

You should now see a dimmed version of the original character. Next, you'll create the second version of the character—in a new pose— and a key frame for your animation. Keep repeating these steps, adjusting the Preceding Cast Members and Following Cast Members settings accordingly. The next section demonstrates how easy it is to use onion skinning to create an element in an animation in-between two extremes already created.

Creating Animations

Open the SNAKE.DIR movie in the Mark Shepherd folder from the Chapter 10 folder on the *Inside Director* CD and play the animation. This example shows how to create an entire animated movie with the help of onion skinning (see fig. 10.15).

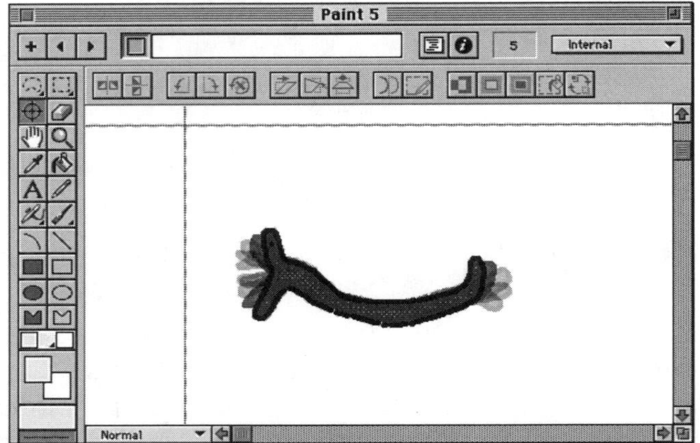

Figure 10.15

With onion skinning enabled, you can view the entire snake animation within the Paint window.

Step through the Paint window to preview the animation. By adjusting the onion skinning settings for Previous and Following Cast Members, you see how helpful it is to view other key frames in an animation while creating a new character.

Now try it yourself. Open a movie you are working on, or create a new movie. After you create the extreme key frames, you can use the Preceding and Following Cast Members settings to view the key images when creating the in-between states of the animations. The following steps illustrate one way to create an in-between version of two extreme key frames using onion skinning:

1. In a new movie, open the Paint window and select Onion Skin from the View menu.
2. Click the Toggle Onion Skinning button so that it's depressed and turn off all other settings if they aren't already off.
3. In the Cast window, drag the two key images to cast positions 1 and 3.
4. To open cast member 1 in the Paint window, select it in the Cast window and double-click to make it active in the Paint window.

5. Click on the + button in the Paint window.

If you leave the Cast window open beside the Paint window, you notice that Director creates a new graphic cast member in cast position 2.

6. From the Onion Skin toolbar, set both the Preceding and Following Cast Members settings to `1`.
7. You now can draw a new version of the cast member as an in-between version of the two extremes as the two extremes display dimly in the same canvas.

Creating Special Effects with Reveal Ink

Use the Onion Skinning tool along with the Paint window inks to create special effects on the graphics you are using currently.

If you have a scanned image or graphic you like, import it into Director and make it active in the Paint window.

1. Open the Onion Skin toolbar from the View menu, and click on the Toggle Onion Skinning button.
2. Set the Preceding Cast Members setting to `1` and set everything else to `0` or disabled.
3. With your image active in the Paint window, click on the + button in the Paint window. When you do, a new painting canvas appears with a dimmed version of the first image in the background.
4. Next, select the Paintbrush tool and the Reveal ink effect.
5. Brush part of the preceding image to create a new, partial image of the original.

You now have created a new cast member—a copy of part of the image. You can use the Score ink effects to layer that partial image as a mask on top of the original.

Background Settings

There are three different background settings in the Onion Skin toolbar, as shown previously in figure 10.12.

Set Background and Show Background are fairly straightforward techniques. In contrast to the Previous and Following Cast Members settings, the Set Background and Show Background settings are used behind all images in the Paint window, regardless of cast positions. The Track Background feature is covered later in this section.

Set Background and Show Background

To set a particular cast member as the background for other images, select the Set Background button in the Onion Skin toolbar. The active cast member displaying in the Paint window becomes the Background reference cast member. The Show Background button is a toggle to show or hide the background image.

Director remembers the background image you set and can display it behind any subsequent images. To set a different cast member as the background cast member, click on the Set Background button again with the new cast member active in the Paint window.

Drawing Images to Scale

The background settings are useful for creating new cast members in relation to the background you will later have on the stage. You can use the Sprite Properties scaling feature after the images are on the stage, but you generate higher-quality images if you first create them to scale in the Paint window.

Like many Director authors, you might create a custom interface or main menu in which your audience navigates to and from different scenes in the production. If you display the interface image as a background in the Paint window, you can create buttons to scale directly in the Paint window. This can all be done before you place anything on the stage.

Setting the Scene

Perhaps you would like to create an animation with characters drawn to scale in relation to one another while the background is active. Use the Preceding and Following Cast Members settings and toggle the

Show Background setting to view the entire scene in the Paint window. You can then cycle to a new cast position and work on another active image.

Using Track Background

The Track Background setting is useful when you want to use a series of images as subsequent backgrounds and create another series of foreground images. A good example might be to create an animated character giving a walking tour through various European cities.

To begin, you might have a series of scanned photographs, each of a different European city. The Track Background feature enables you to cycle through the different background images as you create a new version of the foreground image, or, in this case, a character.

You'll try this in following steps:

1. If you have a series of images you would like to use as a series of backgrounds, import them into a new Director movie.
2. In the Cast window, make sure that the backgrounds you want to use are in adjacent cast positions.

> The Track Background feature of onion skinning only follows along a series of images if they are in consecutive order in the cast.

3. Select Onion Skin from the View menu and click on the Toggle Onion Skinning button of the Onion Skin toolbar. Make sure all other settings are set to 0 or disabled.
4. Open the first cast member you would like to track as a background in the Paint window.
5. From the Onion Skin toolbar, click on the Set Background button. Click on the + button in the Paint window to create a new bitmap cast member.
6. Click on the Show Background button to display the background cast member you set and click the Track Background button.
7. Draw your initial foreground cast member.

8. Click the + button in the Paint window once again to create a new bitmap cast member. The next background in the series appears as the background for the new foreground. You then can draw a new version of the foreground character.

There is no limit to the number of cast members you can create in a series. Repeat step 8 until you finish your series of cast members.

Onion Skinning—with Lingo

For a good example of combining onion skinning with Lingo, open Mark Shepherd's FACEHAT.DIR movie. You will find it in the Mark Shepherd folder in the Chapter 10 folder on the accompanying CD. Open the movie. Then rewind and play it (see fig. 10.16).

Figure 10.16

The Facehat movie, by Mark Shepherd, is a great example of combining animations created with onion skinning and Lingo.

When you play the movie, roll your mouse over the character and notice the cast members change and follow the mouse as you move it. Check the script cast members in the Cast window to see how this was done.

Thank you, Mark, for the onion skinning feature and the sample movies.

Summary

You can use Director 5's Paint window to create custom buttons for your movie, or touch up or add effects to images with Photoshop-compatible filters. You also can create real-life animations with onion skinning or simply enjoy the ability to edit at different color depths. The Paint window has had its share of enhancements. The new techniques are endless with the addition of new color-depth flexibility, third-party filters, and true animation capabilities. Enjoy!

In the next chapter, John Chambers will explore different ways to combine text with the images you create to pass along the story of your movie. Chapter 11, "Text: The Story," also covers all the new ways to use and edit text in Director 5.

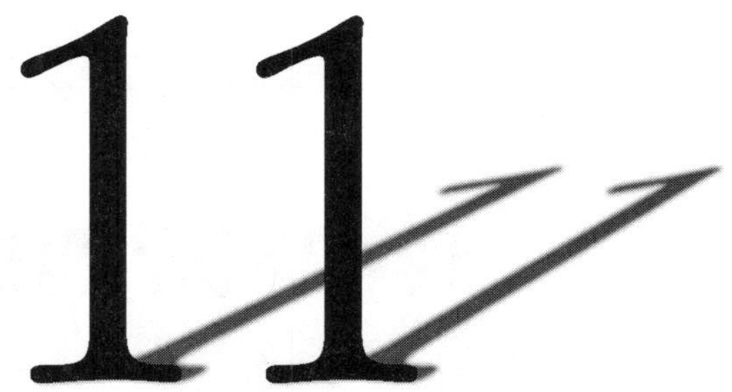

John Chambers

Text: The Story

Macromedia has made sweeping changes to the way in which text is created, viewed, and imported into Director 5. Text objects placed onto the stage are anti-aliased or blended with underlying sprites to create a beautifully merged graphic. New text windows have been added for easy modification of type and paragraph information. Also, the words tab and indent have been added to Director's vocabulary of text attributes for accurate placement of text characters. Preformatted text documents with style sheets can be imported while retaining all internal formatting. Now, dealing with text within a Director document is a pleasant experience instead of a typesetter's nightmare.

This chapter covers the following topics:

- New in Director 5: Rich Text Format
- Text verse fields
- Text inspector
- The Modify menu
- The Text Modification window
- The field buttons

- Text sprites selection
- Bitmapped text
- Using the new text options

New in Director 5: Rich Text Format

The Microsoft Corporation developed the Rich Text Format (RTF) to enable the exchange of text documents among different operating systems. With Rich Text Format, you can set paragraph formats such as tabs, colored text, text of different sizes and styles, groups of fonts, and header and footer information along with many other types of document format data. Currently, Director 5 does not take advantage of all of RTF's specifications. Thus, revision marks and summary information do not carry over to your Director document and probably never will. An RTF document contains literally hundreds of different code calls, most of which will never be needed by us regular folks. The information Director reads from a Rich Text File has more than enough control data to create an information rich screen.

RTF Importing: Writers and Readers

Most of the newer word processing applications, such as Microsoft Word, save to a Rich Text Format. Programs that save in an RTF format are called writers. A *writer* creates control codes for changes in text data, similar to typesetter's marks within a galley of text. The control codes contain control information for style, point size, color, and font usage. The codes are saved separately from the document's text and only are used to format the data. The following is the shortened RTF document containing the text:

```
{\rtfl\mac\deff2 {\fonttbl{\f0\fswiss chicago;}{f21\fswiss
Helvetica; }{\f22\fmodern couier;}{\f23\ftech
Symbol;}{\colftbl\red0\green0\blue0;
\red0\green0\blue255;\red0\green255\blue255;\red0\green255\
```

```
blue0;\red255\green0\blue255;\red255\green0\blue0;\red255\green
255\blue0;\red255\green255\blue255;}{\stylesheet{\sbasedon222\snext0
Normal;}{{\infor{\title Chapter12}\author John W. Chambers}}
{\widowctrl\ftnbj \sectd
\sbknone\linemod0\linex0\colsl\endnhere \pard\plain
{\f21 Here is a line of text.}\par}
```

In the preceding code, the last line (the one that starts with `{\f21`) is the control code for the font Helvetica. The actual text `Here is a line of text.` and the paragraph return `\par` follow the control code. RTF documents contain hundreds of control codes to format a single document. In order to save space, the previous code was shortened a great deal. RTF documents encode all the fonts loaded into the current operating system. Therefore, you might want to create a minimal system font set before you create an RTF document.

Macromedia Director is a reader. A *reader* translates an RTF file into a formatted text file. The translation takes place when you import an RTF file into a Director 5 document. Imported RTF files become cast members. Each time Director encounters a hard page break or section break during the import process, Director places the text following the break into a new cast member. The name of the incoming text document uses the name of the cast member followed by the number of each break, such as 0, 1, 2, and so on.

Text Versus Fields

Text created in Director 5 now breaks down into two different types: text and fields. A text cast member now can contain paragraph information such as indents, tabs, kerning, tracking, custom leading, and line justification. Text cast members now have full paragraph control. Text cast members are anti-aliased by default and blend smoothly with underlying sprites. *Anti-aliasing* is the process of smoothing the hard edges of an object. Smoothing the hard edges of an object is accomplished by changing pixels on the outside edge of a graphic to blend with the underlying color of another image or background (see fig. 11.1).

Figure 11.1

Magnified view of Director's new anti-alias text.

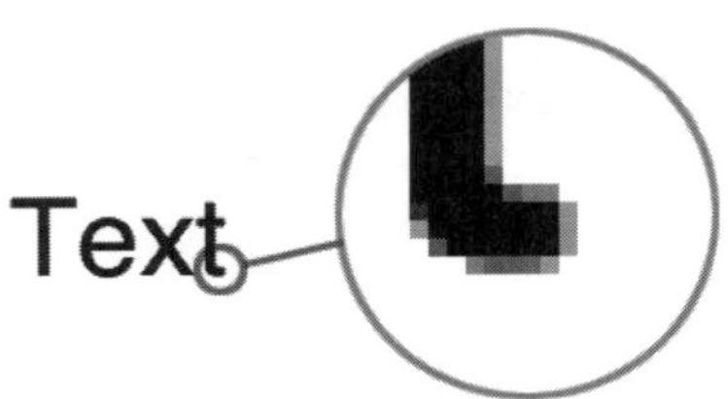

You can turn on or off the anti-alias feature depending on the size of the text. The anti-alias feature can be turned on and off by Selecting a Text cast member, then choosing the Cast members property button in the cast member window. When you place a text cast member on the stage and deselect it, Director temporarily converts the text cast member from a text or drawn object to an anti-aliased graphic or bitmap. This feature is great when you're dealing with animation, due to the fact that bitmapped objects render much faster than drawn objects. Director only has to work with a group of pixels instead of groups of text characters. When you reselect the graphic object for editing, the object reverts to its text object state and you make modifications with the keyboard the same way you originally created it. When you deselect the object, it again returns to a bitmapped object.

When you create a projector of a Director 5 document, text objects permanently change into graphics. If user text entry (editable text) is needed during playback of the projector, then be sure not to use a text cast member. Text cast members are changed to graphics when a projector is created. A Field cast member will remain as editable text.

The other type of text element is a field cast member. Field cast members do not contain paragraph information, such as tabs and indents. You use Field cast members mostly when users need to type in data (keystrokes from the keyboard) during the playback of a Director movie. A Field cast member can be set to allow editable text. The editable status of a Field cast member can be turned on or off by selecting the Field cast members Property button in the cast member window. Lingo Scripts added to a field cast member can be used to retain font color, size, alignment and style information.

An empty field does not retain font and style information. For example, you can create a field for a user to enter his name. Director creates a blank text field so that the user can enter text when the movie plays. Use a movie script to permanently set the parameters of a field.

The Lingo script (located in a `startMovie` handler) is as follows:

```
set the textFont of member "userName" = "Times"
set the textSize of member "userName" = 24
set the textHeight of member "userName" = 48
set the textAlign of member "userName" = "center"
set the textWrap of member "userName" = TRUE
put "" into member "userName"
```

The preceding Lingo script, sets the contents of a Field cast member named `userName` to 24-point Times, with 48-point line spacing. The content centers within the field, and the newly entered text wraps to the next line when the contents extend past the edge of the field box. The last line of the script `put "" into member "userName"` sets a placemark so the preceding script has a point to set to. Without this last line, the formatting of the field cast member returns to Director's default settings.

Text Inspector

You can use Text Inspector to easily edit text on the stage, regardless of whether the text is a text object or a field object. The Text Inspector is a small, floating palette that you use to modify text on the stage or in one of the text windows. The use of this small palette cuts down the clutter of multiple windows when you need to edit text directly on the stage. Within a text object, the Text Inspector enables the manipulation of the font, size, style, kerning, leading, and alignment. The Text Inspector only modifies the font, size, style, and alignment of a field object due to the limited format information within a Field cast member. One place the Text Inspector does not modify text is within the Paint window because these attributes are part of the painting mechanism.

The Modify Menu

You can view and set font, paragraph, and border information from under the Modify pull-down menu. A discussion of the Modify menu options follows.

Font Options

A display list of available fonts and areas to view the selected font can be seen in the Font dialog box. Select Font under the Modify pull-down menu. (See figure 11.2.) You can select the three style check boxes to alter standard font attributes. You have two ways to select the size of the font. You can enter the point size with the keyboard or use the pop-up menu to select the point size from a preselected list of popular sizes.

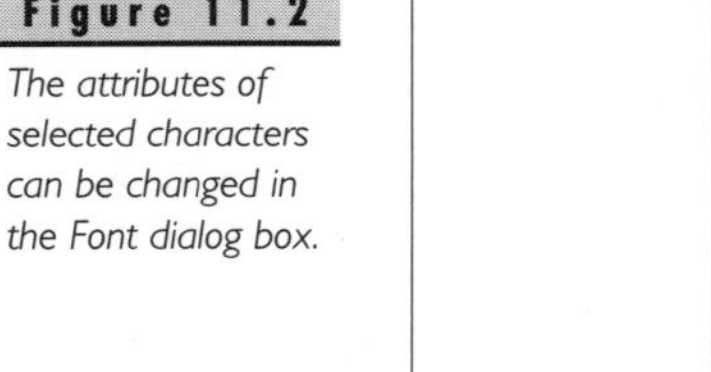

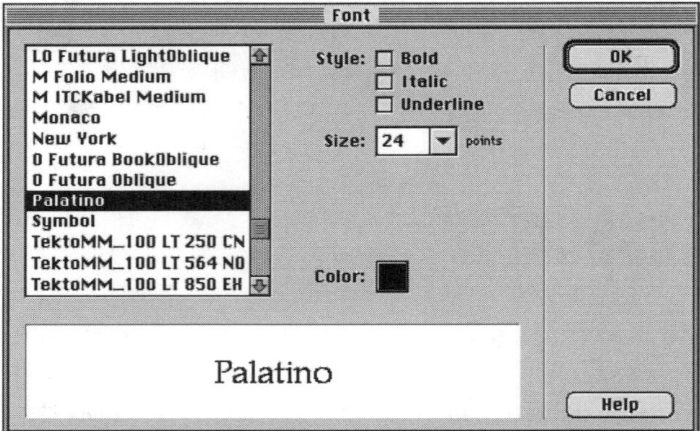

Figure 11.2

The attributes of selected characters can be changed in the Font dialog box.

Spacing is the distance from the bottom of a letter, excluding descenders, in one line to the bottom of a letter in the next line. (*Descenders* are the tails of letters like, y and g.) The point where the bottom of the letters align, excluding descenders, also is known as the *baseline*. The baseline is measured in points. With the Font dialog box open, you can change this number by entering a number from the keyboard or using the arrow buttons to move up and down in one point increments.

Kerning is the spacing between letters. The measurement also can be set two ways in the Font dialog box: by the keyboard or text entry. The color of the selected font can be set to one of 256 different colors from the color palette. To select a new color, press on the color chip and drag out into the palette to a desired color and release. Between the font select list and the font viewing area is a message bar that informs you of the smoothing status of the selected font. The messages can be: This is an outline font, which can be anti-aliased (smoothed) or This font cannot be anti-aliased.

Paragraph Option

Choosing Paragraph from under the Modify pull-down menu will bring up the Paragraph dialog box (see fig. 11.3). From the Alignment pop-up menu, you set the alignment of any selected paragraph to left align, center align, right align, or justify within a text block. A justified setting expands the space between letters to make the line fit from margin to margin. The margin setting enables you to indent both right and left margins, as well as indent the first line. Use first-line indents to create hanging indents. A hanging indent is an indent in which the first line in a paragraph aligns to the edge of the text box and all others line up to a hard return. Indents can be measured in inches, centimeters, or pixels. To set the measuring units for indents, tabs and rulers, select Preferences General from the File menu or press the Control key and press in the ruler of a Text or Field cast member. The spacing before and after sets extra spaces before and after the Return key when you use keyboard entry. The space before and space after can only be measured in points.

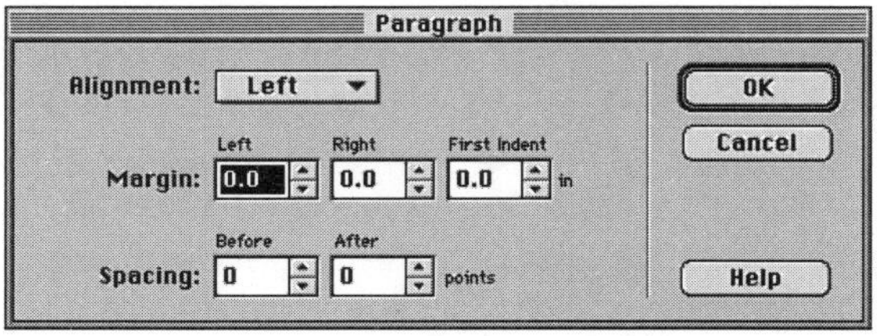

Figure 11.3

The Paragraph dialog box adjusts how the content of a text cast member is viewed.

Border Options

Border information is only available for field objects and can be selected from the Modify menu (see fig. 11.4). The border deals with the area around the field object. The Border options are as follows:

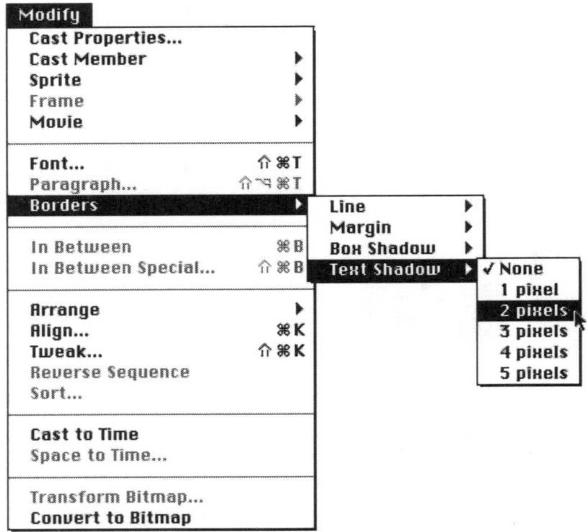

Figure 11.4

Many different border attributes can be applied to a Field cast member.

- **Line.** None to five pixels thick. Line sets the thickness of the field frame.
- **Margin.** None to five pixels thick. Margin is the white space or air around the text and border line.
- **Box shadow.** None to five pixels thick. Box shadow adds a black drop shadow to the bottom right edges of the chosen field box.
- **Text shadow.** None to five pixels thick. Text shadow adds a gray drop shadow underneath the selected text.

The Text Modification Window

In Director 5, you can easily and quickly edit text in the Text Modification window. You no longer have to make a number of pull-down menu choices to edit text. Most of the attributes of a text box, such as indent, margins, tabs, leading, type font, color, size, spacing, and kerning can all be changed within a single Text Modification window. You can open a new text window by choosing the Text button located on the toolbar as shown in figure 11.5. If you don't see the toolbar, select Toolbar from the Window pull-down menu.

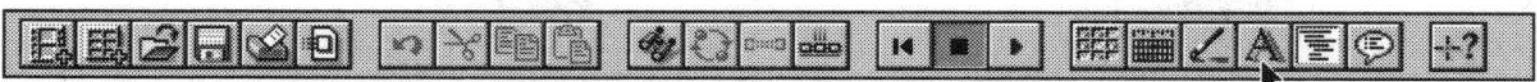

Figure 11.5

Use the toolbar's Text button to create text boxes quickly.

The Field Buttons

The Tools palette has a new addition called the Field button (see fig. 11.6). The Field button is used to create Field objects drawn directly onto the stage and are used for editable text fields. The Text object button creates text boxes just like earlier versions of Director.

Figure 11.6

The new Field button is used to create Field objects directly on the screen.

Text Sprites Selection

The selection of text elements (a type of *sprites*) in Director 5 is very different from earlier versions. You can move a text object about the stage by clicking on and dragging it, just as you did in earlier versions. But when you need to edit the contents of a text object, you have to be double-click on the object with the Tools palette's Arrow tool. A double-clicked text or field object outlines the text with a pattern of diagonal lines, indicating the contents are in the process of being edited (see fig. 11.7).

Selected Text Box

Figure 11.7

A text box selected for text editing.

A *sprite* is a cast member that has been placed onto the stage and shows up as a cel in the Score window.

Remember that to actually change the text contained inside a text or field object, the information that you need to change first must be selected with the I-beam cursor. If you do not select the information requiring the change, then only newly entered data will have these attributes applied.

Bitmapped Text

Text cast members and Field cast members explained above are defined areas in which you type data in from the keyboard. Text can also be entered in the Paint window. Text in the Paint window or bitmapped text is very different from Text and Field cast members which are QuickDraw text objects. QuickDraw text objects retain their text data for easy modification from the keyboard. Everything created in the Paint window is comprised of pixels, this includes text. Bitmapped text can be stretched, scaled, distorted and rotated as opposed to Text or Field cast members which remain horizontal. The most that can be done to a Text or Field cast member is change its size, color and font.

Creating bitmapped text in the Pant window is easy once you understand the text selection process. The Text Tool in the Paint window palette is used to select a position for new text to be entered. Once a position is clicked in the canvas area, a small gray boxed selection will appear. At this point one of two things could be done.

With the selection made, Font can be selected from the Modify menu and the soon-to-be-entered text can be given its attributes such as font, color, and size. After the attributes are made and the Font dialog box is closed, any newly entered text will conform to the attributes just set.

The second option is, after the Text tool is used to make a selection, to enter text. Then the Font dialog box can be opened and the attributes of the selected text can be set. Here's the catch: once the text is deselected, the text is no longer text. Text is deselected when the Text tool is clicked somewhere else in the canvas area or another tool is selected in the Paint window tool palette. The letters on the screen are bitmapped; graphics can no longer be edited with the text tool. Another tool, such as the Pencil of Paintbrush, would have to be used to modify the letters on the canvas. As long as the text stays selected, the font, size, and color can be changed with the Font dialog box. Once deselected, a different group of tools will be needed to make changes.

The Paint Window contains many built-in paint modification tools for rotating and distorting graphics elements. New to Director 5 is the use of plug-ins. A plug-in can be a filter the Paint window used to modify bitmapped elements. Use the filters to create bitmapped text that can blur, slant, mosaic, spherize, tile, and even lens flare. (Be careful, though. This last filter might make for difficult reading.) You can find the plug-ins inside the Xtras folder in the Macromedia folder located in your system folder.

Using the New Text Options

This section of the chapter familiarizes you with Director 5's new text features by showing how to create, import, and manipulate text elements.

Importing RTF Files

For these exercises, you'll need to use the simple RTF document found in the Chapter 11 folder on the accompanying CD to see firsthand how an RTF file imports into Director.

1. Choose Import from the File pull-down menu or press Command+R.
2. Set the Show pop-up menu to either All types or text as shown in figure 11.8. Text files not saved in RTF still import as in earlier versions of Director.

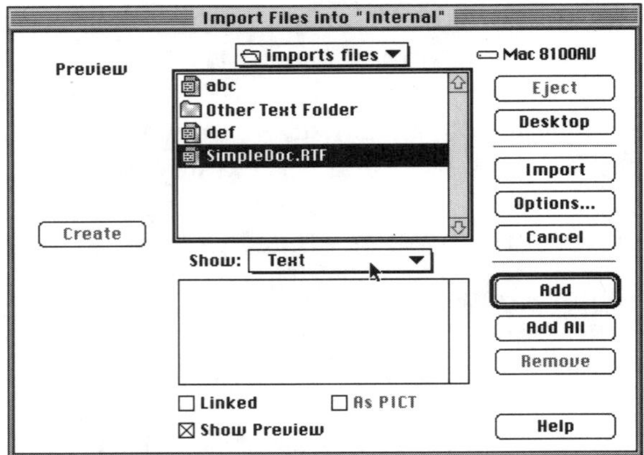

Figure 11.8

Select text or all files in the import dialog box to import text.

3. Locate the file SIMPLEDOC.RTF on the CD. Select it, then choose the import button.

   The simple document has one page break after the first paragraph, which causes the incoming file to be placed into two different cast members.

4. Double-click on cast member 1—now named SIMPLEDOC. RTF 0—to view the formatting of the RTF file. The RTF file contains colored text, text of different sizes (within the same paragraph), and a number of different fonts using multiple line spacings. (See figure 11.9.) The content of this cast member can be used as is or modified further.

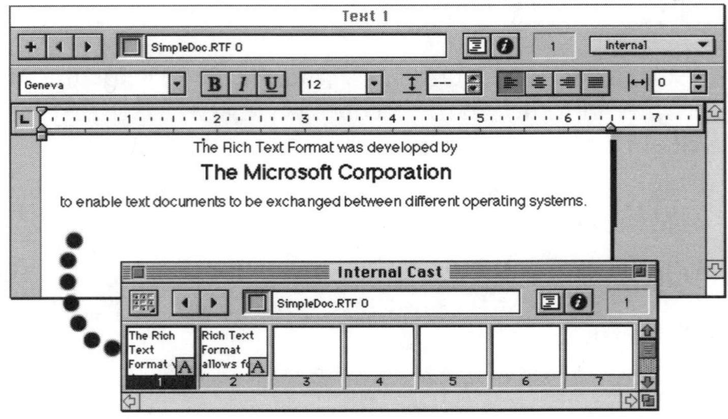

Figure 11.9

Text boxes can contain multiple fonts, styles, sizes, and tab information.

The benefit of an RTF document is that you can format a text file outside of the Director environment and import it. Even though Director has the capability to format text, someone not familiar with Director can create, spell check, and format text in another (more familiar) word processing program. At that point, the user can save the file and hand it over to someone more proficient in Director who can then import it. The capability to format outside of the Director environment is very helpful when working in design groups.

Creating Text Objects—Directly on the Stage

These following steps will use the Tool Palette to create text directly on the stage. Sometimes creating text on the stage rather than in a text window can speed up the visual design of a project.

1. Open the Tool palette by pressing Command+7.
2. Choose the Text tool (see fig. 11.10).

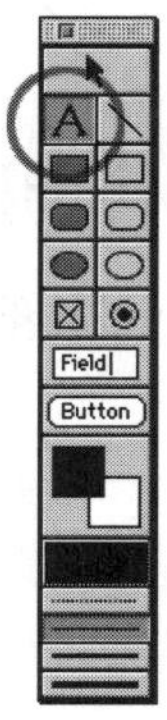

Figure 11.10
The Tool palette Text tool.

3. On the stage, with the mouse, press and drag out a small rectangle and release. The rectangle will appear in a preset size and will expand as type is entered. The object outlines the text with a pattern of diagonal lines.
4. Enter text.

Click outside of the newly created text box with the Arrow tool to deselect it.

Resizing Text Boxes

After text boxes are created on the stage, the size of the text box might have to be adjusted.

1. Choose the Arrow tool in the Tools palette. Click and drag the handles of the text box to change its size. The handles on the top and bottom of the box adjust the height; the handles on the left and right adjust the width. The corner handles adjust two axes at the same time (see fig. 11.11).

Figure 11.11

Adjusting the size of a text box by clicking and dragging on its handles.

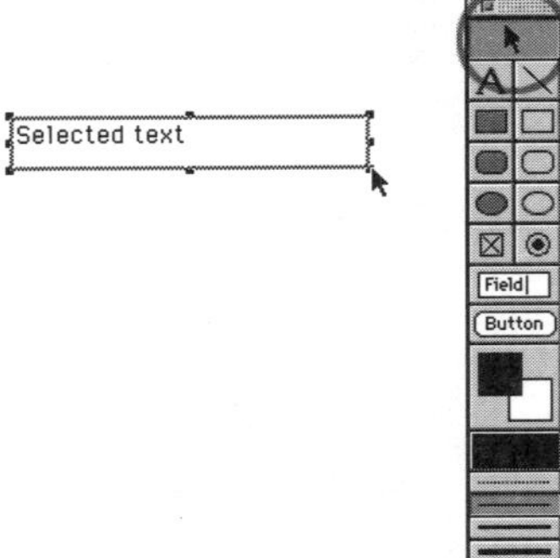

Adding More Text to Text Boxes

With the Selection tool, double-click on the text box. Diagonal selection lines appear around the box.

Select an insertion point and enter the text.

A single click on a text box with the selection tool does not make its contents active; it only selects the box. A double-clicking on the text box with the arrow tool enables text modification, which is shown by a diagonal, dashed line around the field box.

Clicking inside a text box with the Text tool does not select its text. The Arrow Tool will be needed to select the text box. Two clicks with the Arrow in the text box selects an entire word; three clicks will select the content of the entire text box.

Creating a Push Button

A push button is a quick and easy way to mimic the Macintosh interface. The rounded corner rectangles found on push buttons actually highlight when a user clicks on them—all without the use of Lingo scripts. You can automate the process of highlighting the element, but you'll need to use a Lingo script in order for the button to truly *do* something.

1. Open the Tool palette by pressing Command+7.
2. Choose the Push Button tool (see fig. 11.12).

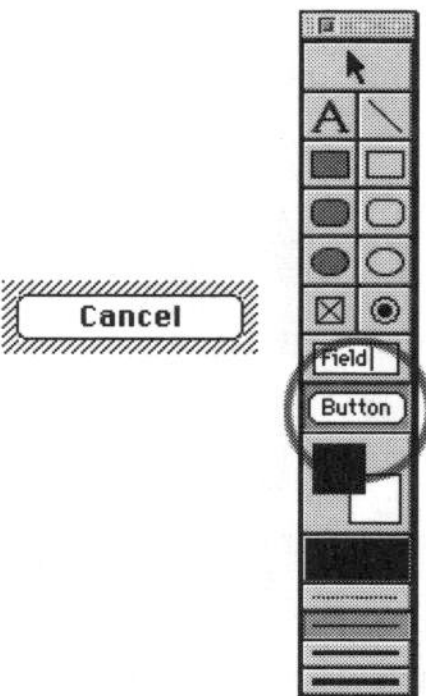

Figure 11.12

The Push Button tool selected in the Tool palette.

3. On the stage, with the mouse, press and drag out a small rectangle and release. The rectangle will appear in a preset size and will expand as type is entered. The object outlines the text with a pattern of diagonal lines along with a black button shaped outline.
4. Enter text.

Use 12-point Chicago to create a button that matches the text buttons of the Macintosh interface.

5. Click outside of the newly created push button to deselect it.

Creating a Radio Button

Use radio buttons to turn on or off one function from within a group of functions, as in printing a document. Use radio buttons to select either paper cartridge or manual feed; here you can have only one choice, not two.

1. Open the Tool palette by pressing Command+7.
2. Choose the radio button tool (see fig. 11.13).

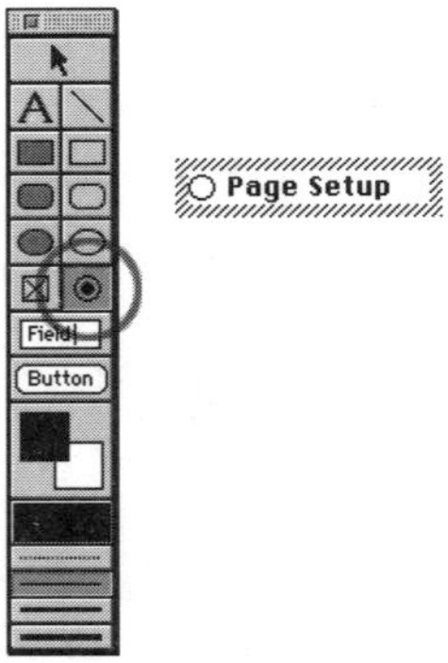

Figure 11.13

The Tool palette radio button tool.

3. On the stage, with the mouse, press and drag out a small rectangle and release. The rectangle will appear in a preset size and will expand as type is entered. The object outlines the text with a pattern of diagonal lines along with a round radio button graphic.
4. Enter text.
5. Click outside of the newly created radio button with the Arrow tool to deselect it.

Creating a Check Box

Use check boxes to turn on or off functions from within a group. This is similar to modifying the page setup for a document that you need to print. Use check boxes to set the functions by turning on font substitution *and* faster bitmap printing but not turning on graphics smoothing. Here you can have multiple choices from a group.

1. Open the Tool palette if it is not already opened by pressing Command+7.
2. Choose the check box tool (see fig. 11.14).

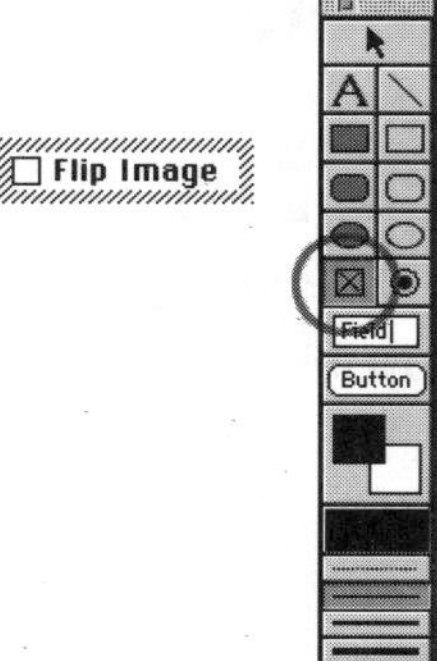

Figure 11.14

The Tool palette check box tool.

3. On the stage, with the mouse, press and drag out a small rectangle and release. The rectangle will appear in a preset size and will expand as type is entered. The object outlines the text with a pattern of diagonal lines along with a square check box graphic.
4. Enter text.
5. With the Arrow tool, click outside of the newly created radio button to deselect it.

You'll need to understand the functions of the check box and radio buttons in order to operate them correctly. When a push button is used on the stage, the user must push it for something to happen. With a check box or radio button, a user turns on the item and the item stays in the "on" state until it is checked off. If you want to use a check box in a frame to "go to another frame," then your user will not able to return to the starting frame until he turns off the check box. At this point, the user cannot turn off the check box because he can't return to the first frame.

Creating Text in the Text Window

Earlier in this section text was created directly on the stage. The text window also can be used to enter text in a more page-like environment and then later placed on the stage.

1. Open the Text window by choosing Text from the Window menu or pressing Command+6.
2. The entered text appears at the text insertion point.

To place the new text cast member into the stage quickly, press and hold on the Drag Cast Member button and move the Cast member out onto the stage as shown in figure 11.11.

Creating Field Objects—Directly on the Stage

The Field object behaves very much the same as the text object above only this type of text object is used for editable text. An editable text field is where a user can type data in as a Director file plays. In other words the text you enter in this exercise, if used in a real project, would be overwritten at some point: (Your Name Here) or (Today's Date).

1. Open the Tool palette by pressing Command+7.
2. Choose the Field tool (see fig. 11.15).

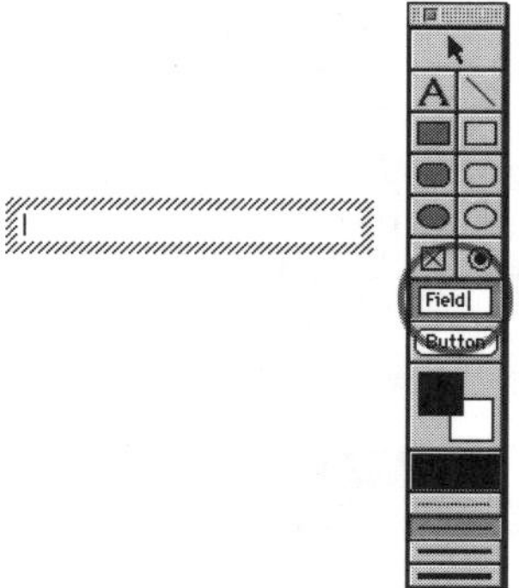

Figure 11.15

The Tool palette Field tool.

3. On the stage, with the mouse, press and drag out a small rectangle and release. The rectangle will appear in a preset size and will expand as type is entered. The object outlines the text with a pattern of diagonal lines.
4. Enter text.
5. With the Arrow tool, click outside of the newly created text field to deselect it.
6. To edit the field, follow the directions on resizing and adding text in the previous section. You edit both the text and field objects the same way.

Creating Text in the Field Window

Open the Field window by choosing Field from the Window menu or pressing Command+8.

The entered text appears at the text insertion point.

> To place the new field cast member onto the stage quickly, press and drag the place to stage button of the cast member out and onto the stage.

You also can edit Text objects and Field objects by opening their cast member icons. The cast members' icons are shown in figure 11.16.

Figure 11.16

Text and field icons shown in the Cast Members window.

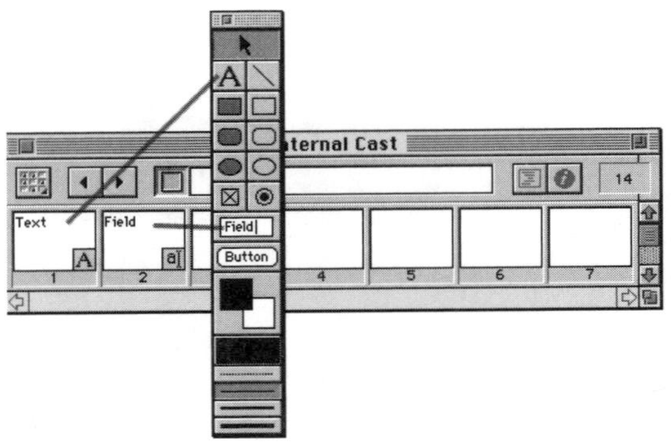

Using the Text Window to Edit Text

Director has added a ribbon of tools to its Text window. The upper part of the Text window deals with the cast member attributes; the lower part of the window deals with the attributes of the data contained inside the text box.

Open a text object by double-clicking on its cast member icon. When you do, the Text window opens.

Figure 11.17 shows the position of the many different Text window options that are explained in the next section.

Figure 11.17

The layout of a new Text window.

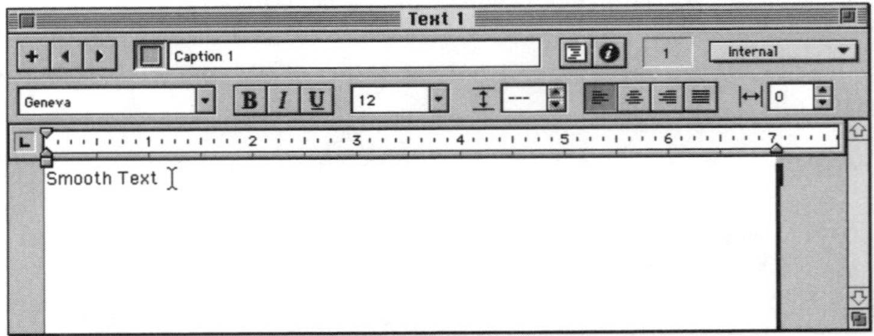

Upper Text Window Elements

The following section contains the descriptions of each of the elements located in the Text window.

- Choose the new cast member button to create a new empty text cast member.
- Choose the previous cast member button to back up one text cast member, if one is available.
- Choose the next cast member button to view one text cast member forward, if one is available.
    - Use the drag cast member button to move the currently opened text cast member out and onto the stage. When released, the Text cast member appears as a sprite on the stage and a cel in the Score window.
    - Use the cast member name area to name the selected cast member. Imported text cast members import with the file's given name. You can leave the file name as is or update it.
- Choose the cast member script button to access its embedded cast script. The Script window opens with an empty `on mouseUp` handler. You can add scripts at this time by using the cast member script button.
- Choose the cast member properties button to adjust the properties of the text cast member. The property settings deal with the way in which the text box behaves, which is different than, for example, paragraph information that deals with character placement. The options for the Text cast member properties are covered in the following sections.

Framing

Use framing to set and view the outside of the text box. The framing pop-up menu contains the following options:

- **Adjust to Fit.** Enables the text box to expand as the user enters text.
- **Scrolling.** Brings up a scroll box on the right side of the text box. View large amounts of text by scrolling this text box.
- **Cropped.** Causes the text box to remain the same size even when you enter text past the bottom right side of the text box. This text is unseen by the user.

Anti-Alias

Anti-aliased text blends smoothly with sprites located below it. The options for the Anti-alias radio buttons are:

- **All text.** Causes all the text in the text cast member to anti-alias. No matter how small the text, this setting is not recommended for text smaller than 12 points. Anti-aliased text under 12 is very difficult, if not impossible to read due to the blurring effect added to the edges of text.
- **Larger than (number) points.** Enables you to select the size of the anti-aliased characters in the current text cast member. The default size is 12 which works well for most fonts. Still, some decorative fonts might be hard to read, even though they are anti-aliased at higher sizes.
- **None.** Prevents Director from smoothing any text in the current cast window. The "none" radio button does not have to be selected to gain speed in a Director document. The smoothing of text is done at the time of cast member closing and not at playback, so a slowdown of the project does not occur.

The cast member number is located to the right of the properties button. Cast numbers are assigned at the time of creation. As cast members are dragged from one position to another within the Cast window, the cast member number updates accordingly.

The Choose Cast pop-up menu selects internal and external cast files.

The Lower Text Window Elements

The Font pop-up menu will display all of the available fonts.

To the immediate right of the font pop-up menu are three buttons. Choose one or more of the three buttons to set the style of the selected text to bold, italic or underscore, respectively.

You can use the size area two ways. One way is to use the pop-up arrow to select a size. Or you can enter a size in the size box and press the Return key.

Click on the up or down arrows to increase or decrease the line spacing for the selected lines of text. For a description of line spacing see the "Modify Menu: Font Options: Spacing" section earlier in this chapter.

Choose one of the four alignment buttons, just below the Cast member number to set the selected text to left or right align, center, or justify the selected text.

Click on the up or down arrows to increase or decrease the kerning of the selected text.

Always select text before you set tabs. If no text is selected, then the tab set appears only on the line where the cursor is located instead of on multiple lines.

To set a tab, first select the tab type from the tab well in the left of the Text window. (See figure 11.18.)

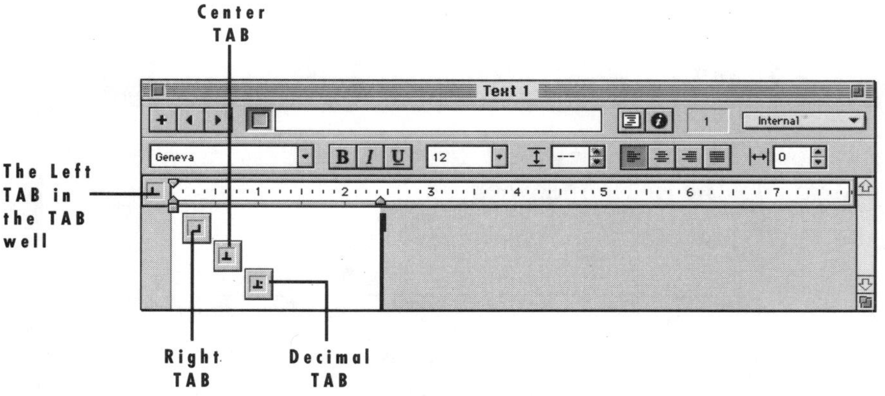

Figure 11.18

The available tab settings in the Text window.

Click on the ruler to set a tab position.

To delete a tab, drag the tab up and out of the ruler.

Drag the indent arrows across the ruler to set indents for the selected text. The settings include First indent, Left indent, and Right indent.

Modify the text box width by dragging the vertical black line to the right or left. The black width line is located at the far right side of the text box, as shown in figure 11.19.

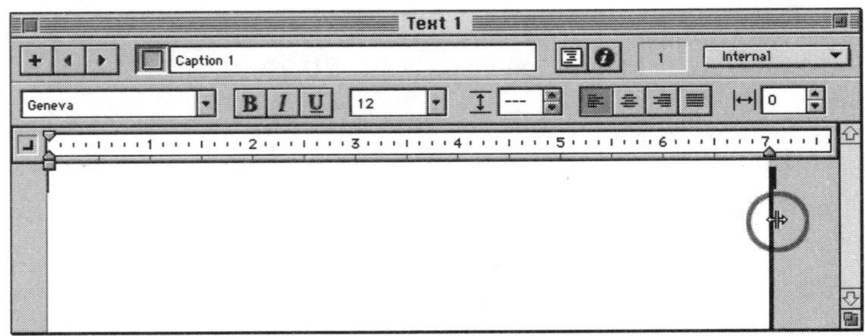

Figure 11.19

Dragging the width line of a text or field increases or decreases the width of a cast member on the stage.

When you want to modify text, be sure to actually select some text. If you make a modification without a selection, any newly entered text takes on these new attributes and the text you intended to modify remains unmodified.

Using the Field Window to Edit Field Text

You can open a field object by double-clicking on its cast member icon. When you do, the Field window opens.

Figure 11.20 shows the layout of the new Field window.

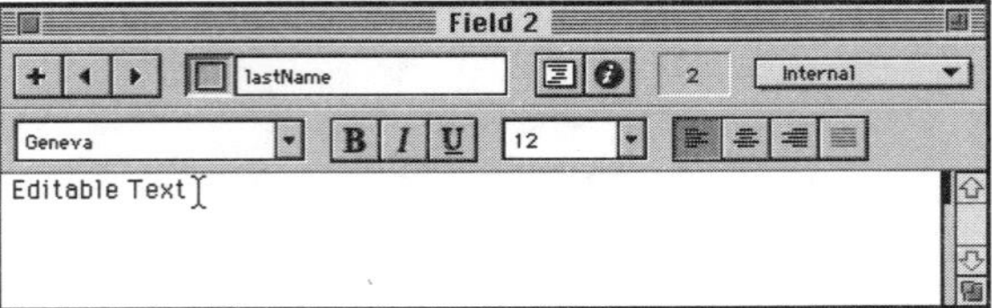

Figure 11.20

The layout of the new Field window.

Notice that there are not as many options available for a field object as there are for the text object. Rich Text Format (RTF) deals only with text objects and not fields.

The following is the explanation of the field attributes that are not covered or that are different than the preceding text attributes.

The Upper Field Window: Text Property Options

Framing

In the framing options: Adjust to fit, Scrolling and Fixed are the same as the "Upper Text: Text Property Options" described earlier in the chapter. The additional option for Field Properties is:

- **Limit to field size.** Keeps the text box set to its original size and entering text stops when the bottom edge of the text box is reached.

Options

Because the Field text can not be anti-aliased, the following options replace the anti-alias section of the field properties:

- **Editable.** Enables the user to enter text as the project is running.
- **Word Wrap.** Causes text to return to the next line automatically. With word wrap off; the text continues past the rightside of the text box until the user presses the return key.
- **Tab to next field.** Advances the text entry point (if any) to the next editable text box.

Using the Text Inspector

To open the Text Inspector, choose Inspectors Text from the Window menu or press Command+T.

Figure 11.21 shows a great little window that can modify text just about anywhere in a Director document—on the stage, in the text window, field window, text buttons, or radio and check boxes. A text selection should be made in any of the previously mentioned text editing areas in order to use the Text Inspector. All of the options in the Text Inspector are duplicates of the modification tools in the lower ribbon of the text manipulation window.

Figure 11.21

The Test Inspector—small in size and easy to use.

Using Pull-Down Menus to Modify Text

You also can modify selected text by choosing Font from the Modify menu or pressing Shift+Command+T. The Font dialog box enables you to modify and preview the attributes of the selected text before committing the changes to the document (see fig. 11.22). In the Font dialog box all of the following attributes can be accessed from the same area: font, style, size, kerning, line space, and text color. Under the font selection area, a message informs you about the anti-alias status of the selected font. These font options have been explained in greater detail earlier in the chapter in the section "Font Options."

Figure 11.22

The Font dialog box enables modify and preview text attributes.

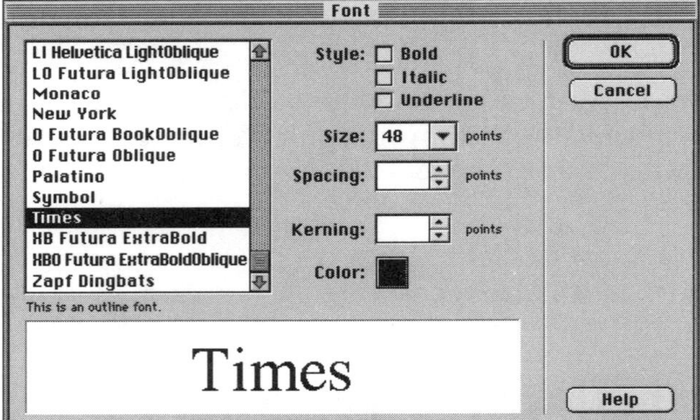

The anti-alias status of fonts is as follows (see fig. 11.23):

- *Message: This is an outlined font.* The selected font will anti-alias due to the fact Director has access to the outline information for this font.
- *Message: This font cannot be anti-aliased.* The selected font will not anti-alias due to the fact Director can not find nor has access to the outline information for this font.

Figure 11.23

The area of the Font dialog box showing both the types and the effects of the anti-alias messages of selected fonts.

Text in the Paint Window

Text in the Paint window is only text for a short period of time. When you deselect text in the Paint window, the text becomes a bunch of pixels, or a bitmapped image, and the ability to modify text characters is lost. Until you deselect the text, however, you can still modify it.

Creating Text in the Paint Window

To open the Paint window, choose Paint from the Windows menu or press Command+3. Figure 11.24 shows the Paint window's Tools palette with the Text tool highlighted.

Choose the Text tool and click on the paint canvas. A gray outline with a flashing I-beam appears.

Deselecting the text now causes it to be uneditable. You need to make all modifications to the text before you deselect it.

Figure 11.24

The Paint window's Tool palette with the Text tool selected.

Double-click on the Paint text tool to bring up the Font dialog box. In this dialog box, there is a display list of available fonts and an area to view the selected fonts. The three check boxes available to choose the styles of the font include bold, italic, and underscore. The size of the font in points is where you can enter a number select from a preselected list of number sizes. You can set the color of the font to one of the color palette's 256 different colors. Between the font select list and the font viewing area is a message bar that informs you of the status of the selected font.

Modifying Text in the Paint Window: Using Filters

After you deselect the text in the Paint window, you lose the ability to modify the text. The reason is that the text is no longer text; it is a graphic. Therefore, as long as the spelling is correct, a whole new world of effects opens. Text can be somewhat plain at times, or text can be bold, italic, or bold italic. With the addition of filters, however, your bold text can acquire a melting stone or broken glass text effect. Filters apply effects to graphics such as blur or sharpen. The filters move and change pixels to cause an effect. The following example takes a single text word and turns it into a graphic effect.

1. With the Paint window open, choose the Text tool from the paint tool box as shown in figure 11.20.
2. Double-click on the Text tool to bring up the Font dialog box. Select a 96 point size and a thick-bodied font such as Helvetica bold, then press and hold on the color pop-up menu, drag to a red color, release.

   Any newly created text will now display in these attributes.
3. Move your pointer into the canvas area and click. A type selection box that contains a flashing text insertion point appears.
4. Enter the word Wrap (see fig. 11.25).

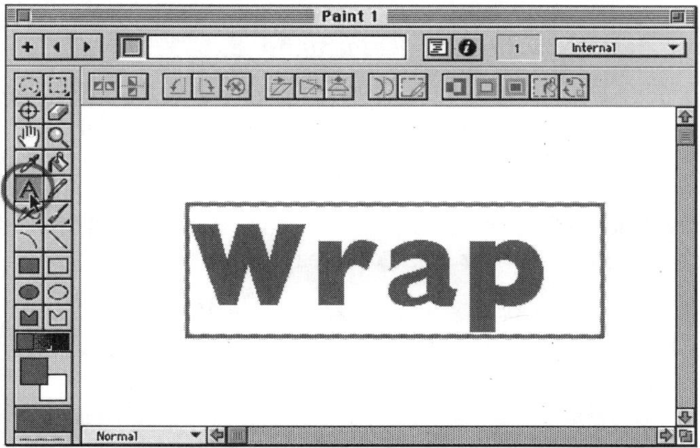

Figure 11.25

The beginning of the Text effect starts with a regular type style.

5. Choose the Lasso tool to deselect the text selection.
6. Save the document as "Text Effect" to the hard disk.
7. Choose the Lasso tool from the Paint tool palette. Press and hold the Lasso to select the Lasso option (see fig. 11.26).

   The effect that is going to be used on the text looks better when the letters in the word are closer together.
8. Drag a selection all the way around the letter "W."
9. Pressing the right Arrow Key on the keyboard will move the selection to the right 1 pixel. Move the letter "W" over closer to the letter "r."
10. With the Lasso tool, select the letters "Wr" and using the right arrow key, move both or these letters closer to the "a." Kern (move together) all the remaining letters in the word "Wrap."

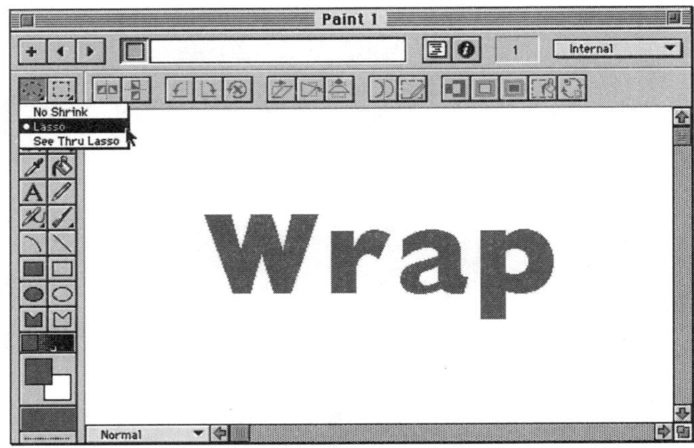

Figure 11.26

Choosing the Lasso tool's Lasso option in the Paint window Tool palette.

11. Save the file by pressing Command+S.
12. Select the non-filler rectangle tool in the tool palette and draw a box, that will be filled, around the word "Wrap."

To set the Foreground color to black:

13. Press and hold the foreground color chip, drag down to the bottom right corner (black) release.
14. Draw a box around the Word. Leave a little space around the outside (see fig. 11.27).

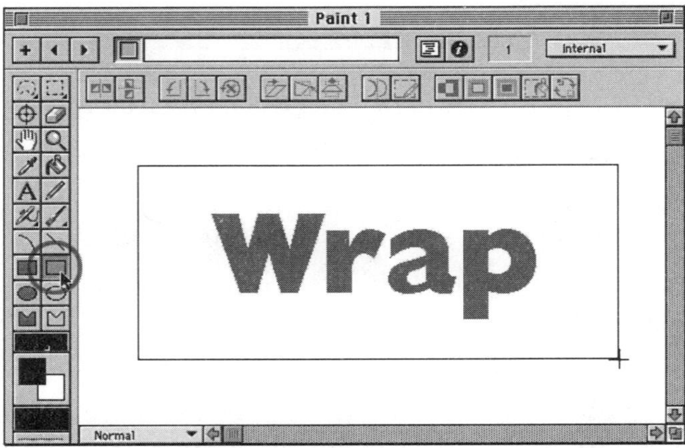

Figure 11.27

Dragging an unfilled box around the word.

15. Select the Paint Bucket tool in the Tool palette and click inside of the newly created black box. Don't click any of the letters or they will change to black.

    The interior of the box will fill, except for the center of the "a" and "p."

16. Click inside of the unfilled letters to complete the fill.

17. Save the File (Command+S). An Undo command used later will return you back to this point of progress.

18. Using the Marquee selection tool with its option set to shrink, drag around the entire black box and word.

    The selection will shrink up to the box.

19. Choose Filter Bitmap from the Xtras menu. The Filters dialog box opens.

The Filter Bitmap dialog box is divided into two halves: categories and filters. The categories side displays filters grouped into areas such as sharpen. On the right side of the dialog box, a list of filters pertaining to a sharpening effect is displayed. The Xtras folder (located in the Macromedia folder in the System folder) reads the list of filters. The contents of this folder can be the alias of another plug-in folder, such as Photoshop or Painter. Literally hundreds of filters are available from software developers such as HSC software (formerly known as Kai's Power Tools), Gallery Effects from Adobe, Alien skin effects from Andromeda Software, and of course, good old reliable Adobe Photoshop filters. To easily add filters to your existing Macromedia Director 5 document, just drop aliases of the plug-in filters into your Macromedia Xtras folder and filter away.

20. On the category side of the dialog box, select Gallery Effects: Classic Art 2. On the Filters side of the dialog box select GE Plastic Wrap sampler. Select the Filter button.

    The Filter dialog box will open explaining two options of this filter, click OK.

21. The setting arrows can be adjusted and the Preview button clicked to see the effect.

    Set the adjustment to figure 11.28 and click the Apply button.

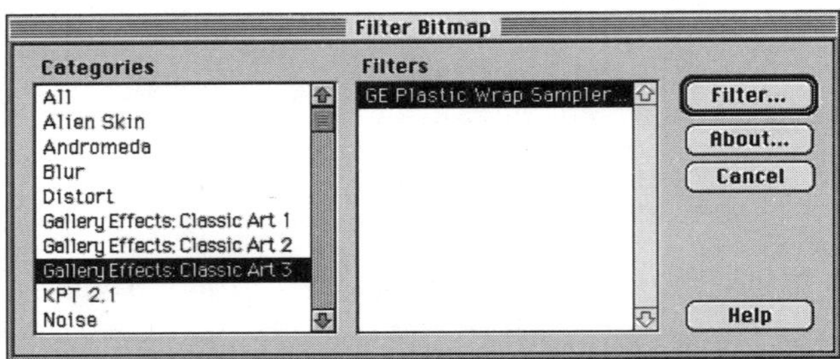

Figure 11.28

Settings in the GE Plastic Wrap Sampler dialog box.

Due to the complexities of filter effects the last step, applying the filter can not be undone if the filter was not quite right. Choose Revert from the File menu to get back to the last saved version of this file.

Filter can be very specialized or very general. Lots of experimentation is needed to achieve the right look when filtering text or any graphic for that matter.

Summary

Text, the words that we read on-screen, can play a very important role in the success of the project. If the text is too small, it can't be read. If the text is too large, it can overpower the design of the project. And if the text is moving around the screen, even more rules for readability may apply. If the project is created for very small children, maybe graphic icons should be used instead of words, or words could be used to back up graphics icons. All the same, the text creation tools provided in Macromedia Director are very powerful, and best of all, they're easy to use.

Bob Connolly

Sound: The Soundtrack

In this chapter you explore the procedure of adding sound to your Director movies. If you plan to develop your production to run on both Macintosh and Windows computers, then consider careful preplanning in the sound department. The Macintosh supplies standard built-in sound from its internal architecture, but the PC world is dominated by add-in sound cards such as the "Soundblaster" and its current version, Soundblaster 16. Various other incompatible sound cards for Windows PCs might add to a list of problems you will face, unless you follow the golden rules of cross-platform authoring. These rules will be addressed in this chapter along with the basic fundamentals of preparing your sound files so that they can best be incorporated into a Director movie.

We have included Director movie files on the accompanying CD that are examples of the many various ways to use Lingo to play your sound files. This chapter focuses on the following areas:

- File formats
- Sources
- SoundEdit 16
- Utilities

- Technical choices
- Considerations: internal and external sound files
- Techniques
- Troubleshooting

File Formats

Just as there are several digital file formats for photographs (EPS, PICT, TIFF, GIF, and so on), the same is true for digital audio. Director is compatible with the following sound files: AIFF, WAV, System 7 Sound, QuickTime, Video for Windows, MIDI, and Macromedia's native version, SoundEdit.

Unfortunately, not all sound files are compatible on Macintosh and Windows computers. Sound file format is a concern when initially importing the sound into Director, or when the sound is used as an external linked member. Once a sound file has been imported into an internal sound member, that sound will be compatible with either Mac or PC. The following sections introduce you to the pros and cons of the following digital audio files.

AIFF

Audio Interchange File Format (AIFF) is the workhorse of the digital music industry and is most favored by the multimedia industry because of its universal standard. You can play AIFF files on Macintosh (see fig. 12.1) and Windows computers, and even on TV-set top boxes like 3DO.

WAV

WAV is the PC standard and is not playable by Director on Macintosh computers. This book is targeted toward users who develop on the Macintosh platform and unless you intend your production to be Windows-only, the WAV standard is not applicable.

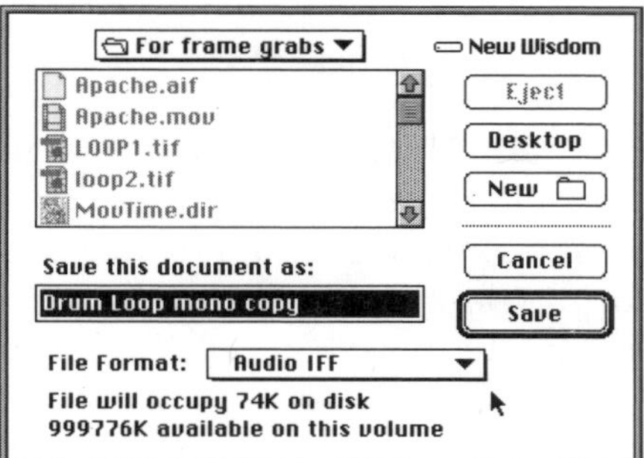

Figure 12.1

Saving AIFF files with the Macintosh.

System 7 Sound

System 7 Sound is Macintosh's standard sound file format. The System 7 Sound format is called a *resource* and is commonly used for the Mac's internal warning sounds, start-up sounds, and so on. These sound files are stored in the Macintosh's System Folder. In Director 4.0, it was very difficult to incorporate these sounds into Director productions that were meant to be distributed to other end users. The installer program had to put these sounds in the user's System Folder, and now, that practice is usually frowned upon.

In Director 5, you now import System 7 Sounds as a file. If it is used as an internal sound, this format will also play on a Windows computer.

Digital Video Sound

Macintosh's QuickTime and Microsoft's Video for Windows are formats that are usually used for digital video movies. Creating sound-only movies, however, is possible. Digital Video Sound format enables you to use Lingo to fast forward or jump to a part of the audio and play from that designated point. You can also use Lingo to pause the playback head at certain specified points, while allowing the audio to continue, which is a great way to obtain tight, sprite to audio, animation synchronization.

MIDI

Musical Instrument Digital Interface (MIDI) is a universal standardized computer language developed for manufacturers of digital music equipment and music software. Director manages MIDI sound files and routes MIDI information to digital MIDI sound modules or MIDI keyboards. Sound Xtras have been developed that use Lingo and MIDI to turn the Macintosh computer into a Wave-tabled sound generator without additional add-in sound cards. Instead of using AIFF audio files for music, Lingo now generates music directly from the computer. By using Lingo, QuickTime MIDI files have the capability to change the tempo of a song without pitch change. This use of Lingo greatly saves disk space and is ideal for distributing productions with music on floppies.

Sources

If you are a graphic artist who has little experience with audio, fear not. To master the world of sound design is a lot simpler than you would think. The use of computers has revolutionized the music industry and it is now a common practice to use a computer to produce the hit songs that are popular today. The Macintosh computer is found in almost all professional recording studios and the music applications that have been developed for them have now been adapted by the multimedia industry.

Most Macintosh computers have the built-in capability to record sound. The latest Power PCs can record very high-fidelity stereo sound. With the addition of add-in sound cards, the Macintosh becomes a professional multitrack recording studio capable of producing finished digital CD masters. Macromedia's Deck II audio recording software offers multitrack recording and mixing capabilities without the need for additional hardware. The speed of your computer determines how many separate tracks will be available for your final mix.

Let's explore the various ways to obtain audio that can be used in your Director productions.

Voice-Over

In using the Mac, there are several details to consider when attempting to record your own narration. First, the microphone that comes with the computer is of poor quality and produces a poor-quality sound. You would be better off to invest a few dollars to purchase or rent a good quality condenser microphone for your project. Even better would be to gain access to a recording studio that is capable of providing you with digital files on a removable Syquest, Zip drive, or write-once CD-ROM.

Redbook Audio (CD-ROM)

Many sources of stock music have been produced on CD over the past few years. Video, film, and multimedia production companies often license CD music and sound effects libraries. Some sound effects libraries come with a buy-out license allowing you to use the music or sound effects for as long as you want; others require you to pay an annual fee. The majority of users play these CDs from a standard CD player in Redbook audio format and record it to audio– or videotape. To use this material in Director, the audio must be re-digitized or converted because the data of audio CDs is stored in a format that is not compatible with Director. Macromedia's SoundEdit 16 version 2.0 can import Redbook audio and convert it to several different compatible audio file formats especially developed for Director.

Music Programmers and Session Musicians

If you have the funds to hire talent that can produce final digital music files, then you have a great opportunity to create interactive audio sections (bridge, chorus, verse, and so on), which Director can control to create interactive music.

Instead of mixing the parts that make up an entire song to a stereo master track, edit the parts of the song, the bridge, the chorus, and the verse into portions that you can loop. Macromedia's SoundEdit 16 can create looped music that will repeat a bar of music.

Record only the drums or the rhythm track. For button sounds, record a cymbal splash, snare roll, tom toms, and so on. Guitar slides and short melody lines using various instruments are perfect audio enhancements for visual transitions, such as dissolves and animation. With all these separate parts, playing in the same key signature at Lingo's beck and call, your audio moves with the visual and creates a truly interactive experience.

SoundEdit 16

Macromedia's sound editing application, SoundEdit 16, is a necessity for sound editors who need to prepare sound files for Director productions. SoundEdit 16 has the capability to record sound by using the Macintosh's built-in audio capabilities. SoundEdit 16 can then resample the sound to different frequencies and bit depths, add effects, edit unwanted portions of the audio, convert to different file formats, mix stereo files to mono, and most important for Director users it has the capability to create "loop points." (See figure 12.2.)

Loop points are internal markers that tell Director where to begin and end in a piece of imported audio that repeats. With the loop points function, you can repeat or loop a bar of music so seamlessly that it sounds like a long verse, bridge, or chorus of a song. You also can loop sound effects, such as crickets, to create an ambiance of background sounds. The loop points function saves disk space and creates an interesting opportunity to overdub additional sounds interactively using Lingo.

SoundEdit 16 version 2.0 has the capability to batch process audio files. If you want to convert 200 AIFF files to IBM PC WAVE files, for example, then this program works unattended, automatically opening, converting, and then saving the new files.

SoundEdit 16 edits the audio portion of QuickTime video. The CinePac compression format, usually used for CD-ROM playback, combines the video and audio tracks. This combination of video and audio tracks is called *interleaving* and enables smooth playback from single-speed drives. SoundEdit 16 strips out the audio track, adds processing, and then replaces the original interleaved track.

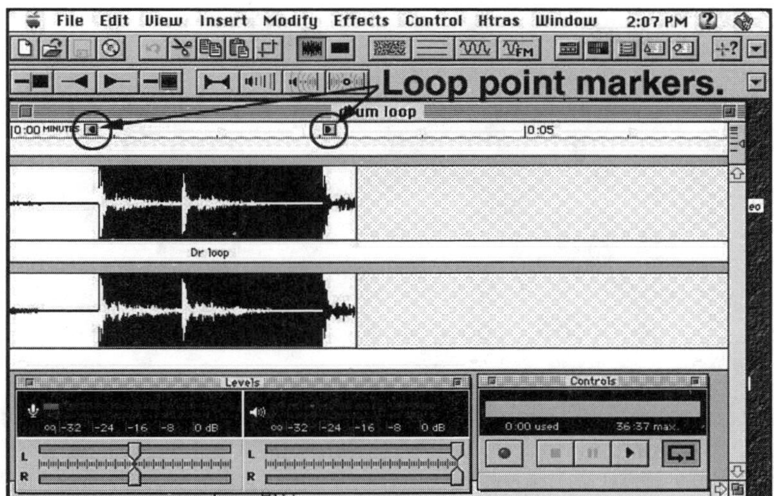

Figure 12.2

SoundEdit 16 edit window with loop points.

NOTE

Director 5 for Macintosh and Windows now works with IMA-compressed sounds (see fig.12.3). Macromedia's SoundEdit 16 version 2.0 supports the creation of IMA-compressed sounds for both the Macintosh and Windows, which is a breakthrough for 16-bit sound compression and changes much of the way you use sound in Director. Although this compression scheme only supports 16-bit sounds, it works wonders with projects that require high-quality sound and limited disk space.

Director 5 launches SoundEdit 16 from the Cast window on the Macintosh when you double-click on a sound cast member. The changes you make to the sound will automatically update in Director.

SoundEdit 16 version 2.0 includes a plug-in Xtra that enables users to directly export to RealAudio formats from SoundEdit 16 version 2.0. You can use RealAudio with SoundEdit 16 version 2.0 to digitize sound streams from Internet Web sites.

Progressive Networks' RealAudio client-server software system enables Internet and online users equipped with conventional multimedia personal computers and voice-grade telephone lines to browse, select, and play back audio or audio-based multimedia content on demand, in real time. Playback in real time is a breakthrough for audio over the Internet because typical download times of audio using conventional online delivery methods are five times longer than the actual program.

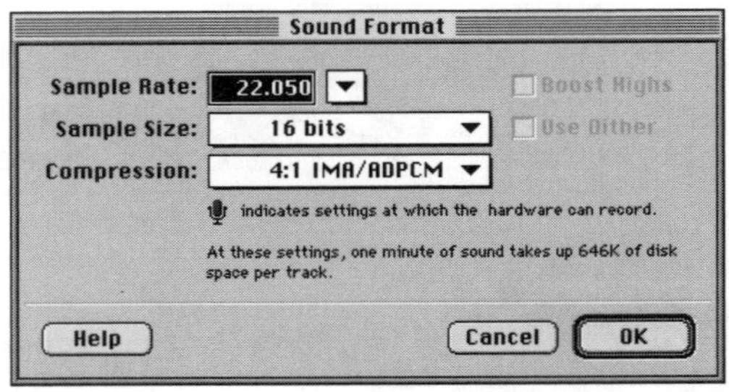

Figure 12.3

The Sound Format dialog box.

The listener must wait 25 minutes, for example, before listening to just five minutes of audio.

If you use Director to create Shockwave Internet Web sites, you might want to supply a link to a RealAudio format file. If the user has RealAudio client software, he will hear playback of your sound almost immediately.

Utilities

A few ways to create digital audio files from audio CDs exist. Apple's QuickTime MoviePlayer 2.0 can open CD audio files and convert them into QuickTime sound digital movies (see fig. 12.4).

You then can export these files as AIFF and System 7 Sound files. Also you can use MoviePlayer to convert AIFF files to QuickTime sound-only files.

SoundConverter is a utility from Apple (included on the accompanying CD) that can change the sampling frequencies and formats of sound files.

SoundEffects (also found on the accompanying CD) is a powerful shareware sound editor. Its strength resides in the capability of applying many digital effects to recorded sounds, and because the effects are plug-in modules, you can enhance the program at any time by just adding any new modules as they become available. Not only can SoundEffects change sounds in many ways through its variety of effects, but it can also handle multichannel sounds, sampled at any rate up to 64 KHz and with any sample size between 1 and 32 bits. Recording rate and sample size are only limited by your Mac or your sound input device.

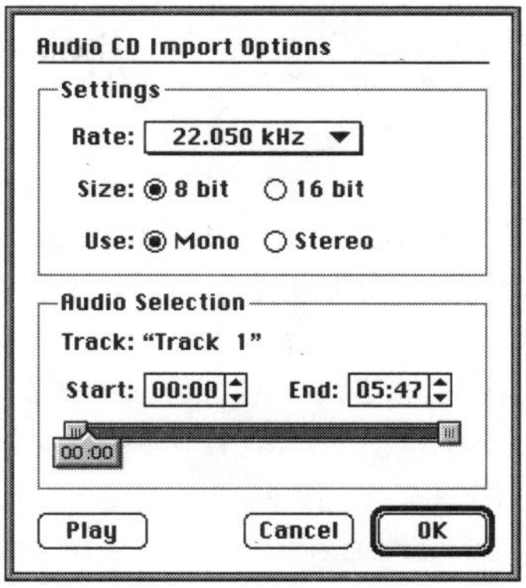

Figure 12.4

Audio CD Import Options.

Optical Media's Disc to Disc program is a good addition to have in your tool chest when you need to convert many Redbook audio files for playback in Director. The Disc to Disc program enables you to select several songs, or portions of songs from a CD, and then automatically batch process the audio to the format you request.

Technical Choices

The rich CD sound from your stereo that you have grown accustomed to is a far cry from the poor sound quality found on the majority of CD-ROM titles on the market today. The reason is not that the CD-ROM producers don't care or don't know how to produce high quality, but rather that some prefer to sacrifice good quality sound for speedier interactive performance. If you use a great deal of digital video in the production, which uses tremendous amounts of disc space, then you might want to opt for lower sound quality in favor of more content. Also, you need to consider the issue of incompatibility with old, 8-bit sound cards or outdated Macintosh Sound Manager System Extensions, that are still in use by a significant portion of the general public.

To play Director sounds immediately when the user pushes a button, the sound file must sit waiting in RAM. Looped audio files also must load into RAM. Audio "hits or stingers" that sound at a precise time during an animation need to be in RAM. It takes time to load sounds into RAM and the user does not like to wait sitting idle while Director loads cast members into RAM.

On the other side of the coin are those long pieces of music and narration that spool from your hard drive or CD-ROM. The files are frequently too large to load into RAM and instead play back directly from the disc. If the audio is streaming from a CD-ROM, then there is a wait time involved because the playback head of the CD searches for the data files. If there are additional graphics that must load at the same time, then serious problems can occur, such as sluggish performance and even sound dropouts. The CD-ROM's playback head has to move to different parts of the disc to search for graphics and audio. Still, there are ways to manage this data flow, for example, by managing the size of the audio files by changing the bit depth and frequency.

Bit Depth

Professional quality CD sound is sampled and stored at 16 bits, 44.100 KHz. Storage of one minute of stereo digital audio consumes roughly 10 MB of disc space. If you resample this audio to 8 bits, then you cut in half the disc space to 5 MB. The bit-depth resolution of a sound establishes its dynamic range, or signal-to-noise ratio measured in decibels (db). Eight-bit sounds have a maximum signal-to-noise ratio of 48 db. This is similar to a cheap cassette recorder. Sixteen-bit sounds have a maximum signal-to-noise ratio of 96 db. This beats the best analog tape recorder.

Most multimedia producers start with the highest possible sound quality for safety backup masters and then resample the final product to 8 bits. When recording 8-bit sounds, some care must be taken to keep the signal levels up over the noise, without excess clipping distortion. To the average person, it is hard to tell the difference between 8- and 16-bit sound, especially when it is played back on the speakers supplied with most computers. In addition to this, there are many computers still on the market that are not capable of producing 16-bit sound. If you are planning a standalone kiosk or multimedia presentation that plays back through large, high-fidelity speakers, 16-bit sound might be a consideration.

Frequency

The frequency area of sound design must follow a critical path when you want your production to run quickly as well as sound good.

Although the latest PowerMac computers can record 44.100 KHz audio, it is virtually useless to use this frequency for playback because it takes too long to load into RAM. Professional developers prefer 22.050 KHz because it has lots of high frequency response, low noise level, loads fairly quickly into RAM, and is compatible with most sound cards for the Windows PC platform. The average computer can process this sound and still enable loading of additional cast members from a CD-ROM without too long of a wait... if the file is mono!

Remember, stereo files are twice as large and take twice the time to load. It is best to use small mono files for internal sounds. Large, high-fidelity stereo files are usually external sounds.

The 11.025 KHz audio files are another preferred standard. At this frequency the sound is a little scratchy and there is a loss of clarity in the high end. Speech can sometimes sound like the person has a lisp. The background noise and hiss are quite noticeable on good, high-fidelity sound systems.

The following sample rates will provide a guideline when sampling or resampling audio for multimedia.

- **5.564 KHz.** Very poor quality speech only.
- **7.418 KHz.** The lowest recommended quality for speech.
- **11.025 KHz (CD).** A good choice for playback on Windows and the new Mac computers. Some distortion and background noise. Use for low quality music or medium quality speech.
- **11.127 KHz.** This was the original standard frequency for older Macintosh computers. New Macs have adopted the IBM 11.025 KHz frequency. This frequency (11.127) is not recommended if you are producing a cross-platform production. Some IBM compatible computers' sound cards will not play this frequency.
- **22.050 KHz.** The most popular choice for Mac and Windows. Good quality music and narration.
- **22.225 KHz.** The old, high quality Mac standard.
- **44.100 KHz.** Standard compact disc (CD) audio rate.

Considerations: Internal and External Sound Files

When you import a sound file into Director, you must decide whether the sound will become an internal or external sound cast member. Internal sounds are loaded into RAM and are saved as data inside the Director movie; external files remain outside the Director movie. For narration and music, many professional CD-ROM developers create audio that is 8-bit, 22.050 KHz stereo or mono that spools, or as Director terms it "links to file," from the disk. Using 16-bit, 22 KHz compressed IMA AIFF files also are another possibility. The external files usually reside in the same folder with Director's movie files on the computer's hard drive or CD-ROM. (See figures 12.5 and 12.6.)

You should name your audio files with the same name of your Director movie. If you name your movie MAIN.DIR, for example, then save your narrated audio files with the names MAINNAR1.AIF, MAINNAR2.AIF, and so on. Using this naming procedure will keep your Director and audio files close to each other on the disk when you copy the data and sound files to another disk or CD-ROM. The files are usually copied in alphabetical order unless specified otherwise by your CD-ROM authoring software. This will speed up Director's performance because the files that are linked to a particular movie can be found by the CD-ROM drive almost immediately.

As internal sound files become part of Director's movie file, use caution. Do not create large movie files that prohibit playback on computers with 8 MB of RAM. Sounds that you must load into RAM are commonly 8-bit, 11.025 KHz mono sounds. The files load quickly, use less available system RAM, and still sound good on an average home computer. Sound effects, mouseDown sounds and short musical selections for animation are popular choices for internal sounds (see fig. 12.7).

As mentioned earlier, SoundEdit 16 can create "looped" internal sound files. If the looped music quality is important, then 8-bit, 22 KHz mono sound is the way to go.

Productions that require rapid-fire sprite animation and many different sounds that play simultaneously from internal RAM should stick to 8-bit, 11 KHz mono.

Figure 12.5

The speakers show whether the files are linked. On the left, the Apache cast member is "Linked to file."

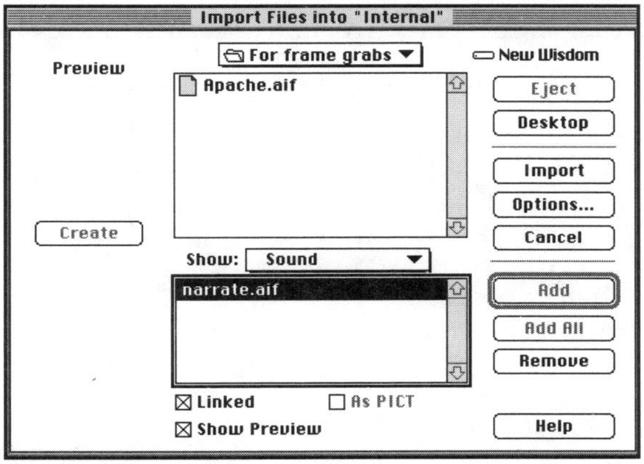

Figure 12.6

The Import Files dialog box.

Techniques

There are a variety of ways to incorporate sound into your production. Every Lingo programmer will have his own preferred method that depends on his particular style of authoring. In this section you will address the many options that are available. Each method has its pros and cons. Finding the right mix that will give you fast performance and high-fidelity sound can only be found by experimentation.

Sounds in the Score

Director has two sound channels in the Score. The Macintosh and Windows versions of the sound channels might look similar but there are differences in the way in which the internal architecture of the two platforms handle and mix the sounds together.

Most users who are new to Director attempt to stay away from Lingo commands that trigger the audio files. By using the two audio channels in the Score, you can drag and drop audio cast members into the sound

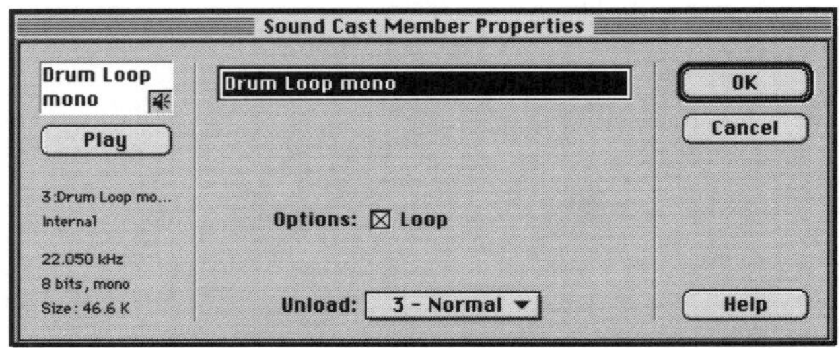

Figure 12.7

Make sure the Loop box is selected in the Sound Cast Member Properties dialog box. If it is not selected, the loop points are ignored.

channel cels. When the playback head reaches a frame containing a sound file, Director plays that sound. If there is a sound in channel 1 and another sound in channel 2 of the same frame, then Director mixes the sound. The sounds will play simultaneously as long as they are not both linked files. The drive cannot read from two places on the drive at once when spooling the audio.

After you learn a bit of sound Lingo, you can then begin to use a combination of channel sounds and puppet sounds by mixing them together or "overdubbing" the audio.

Generally speaking, most programmers prefer to use channel 2 for music and narration. These audio files may be "linked to file" and they play directly from the disk. Channel 1 is then used for internal sounds that must be stored in RAM.

If you want the sound to play while you load a new movie, then it must be internal (not linked to file), and you must place the sound in the same Score frame where you called the Lingo function `go to movie`. You also can play a sound while loading a new movie by using a `puppetSound`.

PuppetSound

Quite often a situation arises where music is playing in the background, and users push a button to go to a different movie or a different part of the movie they are currently playing. Users need some sort of immediate feedback to know that the computer recognizes their selection, which is a good opportunity to use `puppetSound` with the mouse command.

To accomplish this, attach the following script to the button:

```
on mouseDown
   puppetSound "music"
end
```

The preceding command causes the cast member that is named `music` to play immediately from RAM in sound channel 1. This sound must be an internal sound. If you have audio playing in the Score in sound channel 1, then that sound stops and the sound called `music` plays in its place. Therefore, make sure you reserve sound channel 1 for `puppetSounds` when you plan to use this method of mixing sounds interactively. After you take control of sound channel 1 with `puppetSounds`, sound channel 1 is no longer available for use in the Score unless you apply a Lingo command such as the following:

```
on mouseUp
   puppetSound 0
end
```

The `0` function will return sound channel 1 to its original state and will also cancel any current `puppetSound`. If there was sound playing in sound channel 1 before the mouse was pushed, then the sound returns and this channel is now under control of the Score's playback head.

Sound PlayFile

Use the Lingo function `sound playFile` to call and play an audio file that was not imported as a Director cast member. Make sure that the audio file (preferably AIFF) and the Director movie file are in the same folder.

> Although there are two audio sound channels in the Score, on the Mac there are six additional audio channels available. Windows PCs do not have these additional channels.

Now take a look at an example of the ways to use `sound playFile`.

Look for the file named SOUND.DIR in the Chapter 12 folder on the accompanying CD-ROM. Open it and follow along with the steps that follow.

A series of 10, 3D PICS files that produce a spinning globe sit in 10 frames of one channel and loop over the 10 frames. We want to have this globe speak to you when you click the mouse. Looped background music also is playing as the globe is spinning.

The internal looped music is set in sound channel 2 in 11 frames directly above the animated sprite channels. As the playback head loops over and over in these frames, the globe spins and the music plays continuously.

The 10 sprite cels in the Score that contain the world animation have a Score Lingo script attached to them.

The Lingo script reads as follows:

```
on mouseUp
   sound playFile 1, "narrate.aif"
end
```

When the globe is clicked, the animation continues to spin; the background music keeps playing; and the narration that resides on the disk, called NARRATE.AIF, plays in channel 1 along with the music and spinning globe. Notice that the audio file NARRATE.AIF is in the same folder as the movie file. If this is not possible in your production, then you must supply a path name, such as the following:

```
on mouseUp
   sound playFile 1, the pathName & "narrate.aif"
end
```

Digital Video Sounds

Obtaining a precise sync for audio to animation is sometimes difficult because of the various playback performances of computers. The operating system seems to be playing sounds at exactly the correct speed, in order to maintain musical pitch tuning. On the other hand, Director animation speed can be affected by the processor, disk drive speed, and screen depth setting of the user's system; *synchronization* consists of making the animation either catch up with or wait for the music to catch up to it. If you need to synchronize narration and pictures, you can accomplish this by breaking up the narration into separate files or sound cast members. By using the Score's "wait for sound 1 to finish," you can transition pictures between the pauses. When you transition pictures between pauses, however, you break up the speech and this sometimes sounds unnatural. If there are sound effects or music in the track, then you hear breaks when Director loads the linked audio files.

Another way around this is to produce a QuickTime movie that is sound only and times animation events to its `movieTime`. To accomplish this, you need to write a Lingo script that starts a timer at the beginning of a QuickTime movie. Next, write additional scripts in the Score channel that holds the playback head in that frame until a specified time is reached.

When you import a QuickTime sound file into the Cast window, for example, the digital video sound cast member is placed into a sprite channel not the sound channel.

A sample `movieTime` script is included on the CD-ROM in the SOUND.DIR movie. Press the QuickTime Sound Move button to see the effect.

The QuickTime sound cast member is duplicated across three frames in sprite channel 1. Just under the QuickTime sound sprite, three sprite cels supply text. In frame 1 of the Score channel, you set the Lingo script as follows:

```
on exitFrame
   startTimer
end
```

The preceding Lingo command `startTimer` starts Director's internal clock ticking, counting 60 ticks per second. The QuickTime sound file should be set in the frame 2. Above it, in the score's Script channel, we have placed a Lingo script to pause the playback head for three seconds. The script should read as follows:

```
on exitFrame
   if the movieTime of sprite 1 < 180 then go to the frame
   end if
end
```

The previous script tells the playback head to wait for 180 ticks to pass (180 ticks divided by 60 = 3 seconds). After 180 ticks pass, the playback head moves to the next frame and encounters the following score script:

```
on exitFrame
   if the movieTime of sprite 1  < 600 then go to the frame
        end if
end
```

The playback head waits until 10 seconds have passed (60 ticks × 10 seconds = 600 ticks).

The trick is to time the audio and visual so that they match. For transition points, you can use QuickTime's MoviePlayer to time the seconds of the movie and then multiply by 60. Another way is to use Lingo to read the `movieTime` script (see fig.12.8).

A sample of the `movieTime` script is supplied on the CD-ROM in the sound chapter. It is called MOVTIM.DIR.

The following script displays the current time of a digital video movie that is in sprite channel 1 in the Message window and is in the Score in frame 1.

```
on exitFrame
   go to the frame
   put the movieTime of sprite 1
end.
```

Make sure the digital video also is in frame 1. Open the Message window, click the Trace box and start your movie. In the Message window, you see a series of numbers pass by. Stop your movie and write down the last number. This number is the current running `movieTime`, given in ticks.

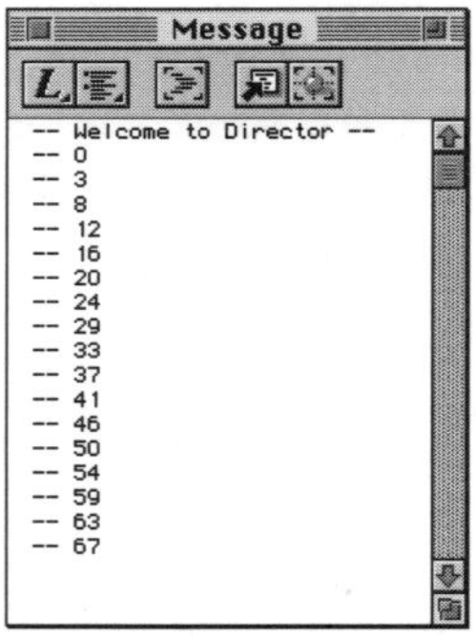

Figure 12.8

The Message window displays the current running movieTime in ticks.

Controlling the Volume

You can use Lingo to control the overall volume of the computer, fade audio in and out, and adjust the volume of individual sound channels.

The volume level of your computer is controlled by a property called `soundLevel`. `soundLevel` is defined as a value from 0–7, where 0 gives no sound and 7 is the maximum sound. Using Lingo to control the volume in this method is the same as changing the volume slider in the Sound control panel.

1. The following Lingo `mouseUp` button script turns up the volume of the computer to full:

   ```
   on mouseUp
        set the soundLevel to 7
   end
   ```

   To turn down the sound to half volume, use the following script:

   ```
   on mouseUp
        set the soundLevel to 4
   end
   ```

2. To fade in the sounds in the Score, use the following handler in the Score script in the frame before the sound starts:

   ```
   on exit Frame
        sound fadeIn 1, 1 * 60
        sound fadeIn 2, 1 * 60
   end
   ```

   The audio in sound channels 1 and 2 fades in, in one second. `sound fadeIn 1` specifies channel 1. `1 * 60` is the time (one second), measured in 60 ticks per second. This is channel-specific and you can independently fade the sound channels in and out over different periods of time.

   To fade out the sound:

   ```
   on exitFrame
        sound fadeOut 1, 3 * 60
        sound fadeOut 2, 3 * 60
   end
   ```

   The audio fades out in sound channels 1 and 2 over a period of three seconds.

3. To adjust the volume of an individual channel, use the `volume of sound` property. Set a value for the volume; the 0 is silent and 255 is the maximum.

The following script turns the volume of sound channel 1 to half volume:

```
on exit Frame
     set the volume of sound 1 to 127
end
```

To control the volume of a digital video sound, the word `sprite` is used instead of `sound`. The script turns the volume of the digital video cast member in sprite channel 10 to half volume.

```
on exitFrame
     set the volume of sprite 10 to 127
end
```

Troubleshooting

Testing on various computers is a must if you plan to release your production to other users. Your product might work flawlessly on your computer and it might fail on others. If you encounter a problem, try to discover first whether it is a hardware malfunction. If other titles work, then you know it is a software problem.

No Sound

Are your speakers still plugged in? The tiny miniature phone jacks that supply sound input and output can become disconnected by accident.

Is the volume on the computer turned off?

Are your headphones plugged in? This will disconnect your speakers.

Make sure you and your end users have installed the latest versions of Sound Manager. At the time of this writing, the latest version of Sound Manager is version 3.1, which enables the playback of 16-bit sound files. You can get this update free from Apple or an Apple dealer. You will need a license from Apple to distribute Sound Manager to your end users.

Intermittent Sound

Turn off virtual memory in the Control Panel. Director uses its own memory management protocols and conflicts can occur.

Stay away from RAM Doubler. Once again, Director is a RAM-intensive application and it is best to stay away from any system INIT that optimizes RAM use.

Are you trying to play two audio files that are linked to file at the same time? Remember that the drive's pickup head cannot be at two places at once.

Loud Hum

If you are going to be digitizing sound, make sure you ground everything in your computer editing suite. If you have a microphone mixer, keep it away from the computer. Quite often, the motors in the fans and hard drives will create a hum if placed too near to the input transistors of microphone mixers.

Distortion

When recording sound, make sure that none of the sound channels are being driven to excessive high levels (in the red). A limiter is a good thing to rent or purchase when processing sound. It limits the amount of sound from the microphone, while keeping the volume up loud without overloading your computer's input amplifiers.

Noise

If you live close to an airport or highway, a noise gate will stop the background room sound from being recorded during breaks in the narration. As we mentioned before, try to re-create a recording studio atmosphere. The professional studio has sound absorbing acoustics on the wall and an isolated control booth to stop unwanted noises from being recorded.

If you are on a budget and have decided to record the narration yourself, try to re-create the studio environment. Keep the microphone far away from the fan noises of the computers and hard drives. Place rugs on the floor. Hang some sound blankets or even sleeping bags on the walls. Try to deaden the room ambiance so that the voice does not have that hollow "hallway" sound.

Authoring Mac and Windows Hybrid CD-ROM Titles

Use AIFF audio files where possible because they play on both computer platforms.

If you use QuickTime digital video sound files, make sure that the Windows computer has QuickTime for Windows installed or supply QuickTime for Windows on your CD-ROM. QuickTime for Windows is free from Apple. You will still need to obtain a license to do this, but it's just a formality. QuickTime for Windows is included with Director 5.

Consider several issues regarding sound when producing a Mac/Windows hybrid disc. Try to use `sound stop` in your Score scripts. Strange things can happen on Windows PCs when you `go to a new Movie`. Sometimes the sound from the previous movie just keeps playing over your new movie. Test your movies in progress on both computer platforms.

The following Lingo in the Movie script will stop the preceding audio from playing over your new audio.

```
on StartMovie
      if soundBusy(1) then sound stop 1
end startMovie
```

Summary

Most users who are new to Director create the pictures, add animation, program the interactivity, and then add some sound bites to fit the piece. This is a big mistake. Interactive pictures need interactive sound. Consider the style of music video editors; they edit the pictures to the music. Select your music in advance and let your imagination experience the mood of the song. Letting your musical soundtrack drive your production will have a definite effect on your Lingo scripting, which is certainly one of the most important aspects of creating musical multimedia.

If you are working in a team situation, play the music to the members of your group in the preplanning stages. You will be surprised at their creativeness when they hear and feel the emotions the music creates. Ideas for animation jump out at you when you hear sparkles in the melody. Your choices of color, text styles, and size will flow and harmonize with the production. Then, when all of the elements are brought together, the job of programming the Lingo that keeps the production in sync is fun and creative. A good Lingo programmer can be compared to the conductor of a live orchestra in a Broadway musical!

Productions that feature narration instead of music probably will have the opportunity (and hard drive space) to produce quality, 8- or 16-bit, 22.050 KHz audio files. If there are pictures or animation to accompany the narration, you might have to first record the narration and then have the art department create the graphics. Once these artists hear the tone, accent, and manner of the voice, images regarding style and content suddenly pop into their heads.

Audio should not be an afterthought.

David Miller

Director in 3D

The advent of the PowerPC and Pentium processors brought high-quality 3D graphics to the desktop. The PowerPC processor, with its excellent floating point math performance, is particularly well-suited for the computationally intensive algorithms that are used in 3D computer graphics. New technology, such as QuickTime VR and QuickDraw 3D are bringing 3D visualization and interactive capabilities to a broad range of desktop systems. Now, all your clients want chrome flying logos and virtual reality tours in their next interactive.

This chapter discusses the creation of 3D graphics and animations for your Director projects. This chapter is not meant to replace reading the manual of your 3D program. It provides a brief overview of the 3D design process for beginners, tips on how to integrate 3D graphics and animation into Director, and how to add interactivity to 3D animations. The chapter discusses the use of relatively inexpensive, desktop 3D graphics software with a special emphasis on Extreme 3D, the 3D modeling, animation, and rendering component of the Macromedia's Director Multimedia Studio.

This chapter covers the following general topics:

- Why use 3D graphics?
- 3D tools
- Creating 3D graphics
- Using 2D programs to create 3D effects
- 3D interfaces, backgrounds, and objects in Director
- 3D animation in Director

Why Use 3D Graphics?

When you create a 2D drawing of a 3D object, you use your illustration skills and imagination to give the image depth and realism. When you create the same object in a 3D program, it exists within a fully realized 3D world and the computer calculates the perspective, shadows, reflections, atmospheric effects, and object overlap. The computer does a lot of the work for you, enabling you to experiment with your illustration.

Once created, a 3D world is the ultimate reusable graphic asset. You can re-create it with different perspective and lighting for different projects. You can use objects in the 3D world over and over again in different contexts. In some respects, the creation of 3D graphics is similar to sculpture, photography, videography, set design, and stage design—in that you manipulate and work with composition, lighting, and 3D objects in a controlled 3D environment. You never have to strike the set; it always exists inside your computer, ready to be changed or reused whenever you need it.

Many 3D programs create 3D animations. Three-dimensional animation has many advantages over traditional 2D cel animation. To animate and rotate objects over time, 3D programs use key-frame or time-based animation, similar to key-frame animation in the Director Score, but much more powerful. Extreme 3D enables you to animate almost every editable parameter, including shape, position, texture, lighting, camera view, motion paths, and so on. After you set up your key frames, the computer automatically generates the intermediate frames.

Three-dimensional programs also make it easier to provide alternate views of a scene or object for your users. You can simulate real-world, dynamic processes and illustrate complex motions with 3D animation. 3D graphics make the spatial and functional relationships of objects and interfaces more clear. Navigable 3D worlds provide visualization of 3D environments that are impossible or dangerous to see in the real world.

High-quality 3D graphics and animation on the desktop are subject to the same limitations on playback and file size as 2D graphics and animations. To create 3D graphics invest in time and equipment. 3D programs have a steep learning curve, but intuitive interfaces, such as Extreme 3Ds, are making it easier. The creation of 3D content takes many times longer than the same content elements in 2D. Final rendering of a long, complex 3D animation can tie up computer resources for hours and even days. 3D workstations require a lot of RAM and a fast CPU with good floating point math performance.

3D Tools

This section discusses some of the hardware and software that you need to create 3D graphics. The advent of faster processors, consumer-level hardware acceleration, and system-level 3D support on desktop computers is changing the 3D landscape. Some of the information provided here might be dated by the time you read it. Keep tabs on recent trade magazines for the latest information.

> Trade magazines that cover 3D issues include *MacWeek*, *MacUser*, *MacWorld*, *New Media*, *3D Design Magazine*, and *3D Artist Magazine*.

System Requirements

Three-dimensional graphics programs require a lot of RAM. The more complex your models and animations and the more texture maps you use, the more RAM you need. You might want to have other programs, such as Photoshop, open while you work in your 3D program. You also might want to leave room to expand your system's RAM to accommodate changing memory requirements. In short, get as much RAM as you can afford. Most 3D programs perform best with at least 16–20 MB of RAM for the program, although you can get by with less. A machine with 32 MB of total RAM makes a serviceable 3D graphics workstation, and workstations with 100 or 200 MB of RAM are not unusual.

Your CPU should be the fastest possible. The PowerPC is a good chip for 3D work because of its superior floating point math performance. Many 3D programs for the Macintosh are PowerPC-native and are typically optimized for the PowerPC chip. If you have an older Macintosh, make sure it has an FPU or floating-point unit.

Also, consider purchasing a 3D accelerator board. Many companies have low-cost 3D accelerator boards for desktop systems. Consider the video-out capabilities of your system if you want to output animations to videotape.

You'll also need a lot of disk space. As a rule of thumb, a 1 MB 3D animation easily generates 10 MB of intermediate and scratch files.

3D Software

The 3D design process involves several different tasks. These tasks include modeling, animating, rendering, and compositing. 3D software programs handle one or more of these tasks. You may use more than one program to create your 3D graphics.

Macromedia Extreme 3D, Strata StudioPro, Specular Infini-D, VIDI Presenter Pro, Hash's Animation Master, Byte by Byte's Sculpt 3D, and Ray Dream (now part of Fractal Design) Designer Studio are integrated programs that provide modeling, animation, and rendering to a varying extent. auto-des-sys formZ is primarily a modeler. Virtus Walkthrough Pro, Gryphon Morph, The Valis Group PixelPutty, and Metaflo provide specialized modeling, animation, or rendering features. MetaTools' Bryce is a unique naturalistic terrain modeler with detailed control of procedural textures and ray-traced rendering. ElectricImage Animation System is a high-end animation and rendering system for the Macintosh that is commonly used with the formZ modeler. If you have a lot of money, you can use high-end tools on Silicon Graphics workstations.

Specular Logomotion and Strata StrataType are inexpensive programs for creating and animating 3D type. Fractal Design Poser is a tool for modeling and rendering the human form.

POV-Ray is a free ray-tracer with a built-in scene description language and many powerful features. You can download it from http://www.povray.org/.

Extreme 3D is the integrated modeling, animation, and rendering program that is part of the Macromedia Multimedia Studio. It's a very capable and relatively inexpensive package for desktop multimedia. Extreme 3D provides CAD-accurate, spline-based modeling with an easy-to-use, intuitive interface. You can animate just about any editable parameter using key-frame and time-based animation. The Extreme 3D file format is compatible across Macintosh and Windows systems and comes with a built-in, cross-platform, production-quality, distributed renderer. The demos and tips in this chapter use Extreme 3D but the same concepts should be applicable to other 3D programs.

Even if you're using an integrated 3D program, such as Extreme 3D or StudioPro, you might want to exchange files between different 3D and 2D programs during the production process. On the Macintosh, it's easy to exchange files between different programs. Be sure that the 3D program you choose is able to export animations as QuickTime movies, as a sequence of numbered PICT files, or as PICs. Your 3D program also should support DXF import/export. DXF is a common, though limited, format used to exchange 3D models between different programs. EPS or EPSF import enables you to import 2D Bezier curves and graphics from FreeHand and Illustrator. TARGA and TIFF are useful cross-platform image formats. Virtual Reality Modeling Language (VRML) export and 3DMF (3D Metafile or QuickDraw 3D format) import/export are starting to turn up in some programs. These formats are useful if you plan to create 3D graphics for the World Wide Web or if you plan to take advantage of the new QuickDraw 3D graphics architecture.

File Type	Extension	Description
QuickTime	MOV, QT	Cross-platform digital video and animation format
Audio Video Interleave	AVI	Windows digital video format

continues

File Type	Extension	Description
DXF	DXF	ASCII-based 3D format
3D Studio	3DS	Autodesk's 3D Studio format
3D Meta-File	3DMF, 3MF	Cross-platform QuickDraw 3D format
VRML	WRL	Virtual Reality Modeling Language for Web
TIFF	TIF	2D graphics format
Targa	TGA	2D graphics
PICT	PICT, PIC	2D graphics format
Bitmap	BMP	2D graphics format
EPS, EPSF	EPS, EPSF	Encapsulated PostScript; 2D format for programs such as FreeHand and Illustrator

Supporting Software

The same programs that you use for 2D graphics and digital video editing can be used to create the building blocks for 3D graphics and texture maps, to post-process and composite 3D graphics for final output, and to add effects to 3D animations. Macromedia FreeHand, Adobe Illustrator, Adobe Photoshop, Fractal Design Painter, Adobe Premiere, Adobe After Effects, Avid Videoshop, and Equilibrium's Debabelizer all provide supporting functions in 3D graphics production work.

Use FreeHand and Illustrator to create 2D profiles for importing into your 3D program for extrusion, lathing, sweeping, or skinning (lofting).

Photoshop and Painter add dimensionality to 2D images and provide many useful image editing and compositing features. Painter is a powerful paint program that emulates natural media such as oil paint and charcoal. Painter also includes 2D animation features such as onion skinning and support for animation formats such as QuickTime. Premiere is a QuickTime-based, digital video editing program. After Effects is a digital video and animation post-processing tool that supports alpha channels for compositing and has powerful key-frame and time-based animation controls. After Effects also provides effects such as motion blur and fully editable Bezier curve motion paths with sub-pixel positioning. Final Effects is a series of plug-ins for After Effects that includes a particle animation system for special effects such as rain, fire, smoke, and explosions. Painter, Premiere, and After Effects export compositions as a sequence of PICT files or as QuickTime movies.

Equilibrium's Debabelizer saves a lot of time whenever you do any kind of animation work. Debabelizer is an essential tool for palette optimization and batch processing animation files. It can also create QuickTime movies.

QuickTime VR and QuickDraw 3D

QuickTime VR (QTVR) is a breakthrough, cross-platform "virtual reality" technology from Apple Computer. With QTVR movies, users of QuickTime-capable Macintosh and Windows systems can interact and navigate through 3D environments on their computers. QTVR movies are special QuickTime movies that enable users to move through 3D environments, pick up and manipulate 3D objects, and activate hot spots embedded in the 3D scene. Interaction is with a mouse and keyboard. Users don't need high-end workstations, special headsets, goggles, or other peripherals. QTVR movies are characterized by high-quality, photographic images, fast playback, and small file-size. QTVR is optimized for photographic images but also works with computer-generated images.

You'll need a QuickTime-capable Macintosh or Windows computer to view QTVR movies. The minimum system requirements for the Macintosh include:

- 68030, 25 MHz processor
- 8 MB of RAM
- QuickTime 2.0
- System 7.1
- 8-bit video

The minimum system requirements needed to view QTVR movies with Windows include:

- 386SX, 33 MHz processor
- 8 MB of RAM

- QuickTime 2.0 for Windows
- Windows 3.1
- 8-bit video
- A QTVR-capable playback application

You can download free samples of a QTVR player for Macintosh and Windows systems as well as sample QTVR movies from Apple Computer's web site at http://qtvr.quicktime.apple.com. You can add cross-platform, QTVR playback, and Lingo control to Director by using XCMDs, XObjects, and Xtras.

Currently, creating QTVR movies requires the QTVR Authoring Tools Suite from Apple Computer. Contact Apple Computer or visit Apple's Web site for details.

Apple Computer's QuickDraw 3D (QD3D) is a cross-platform, software-based, 3D graphics architecture. QD3D provides real-time, workstation-quality rendering, interactivity, and animation of 3D graphics on PowerPC and Pentium-class PCs. As of this writing, Apple is enhancing QD3D to support more platforms and features, including 3D game programming and hardware acceleration.

Check out http://product.info.apple.com/qd3d/QD3D.HTML for all the latest developments and free downloads of the software and development kits.

Users don't need to add accelerators or peripherals to existing systems to use QD3D, but QD3D supports hardware accelerators and peripherals when they are present. QD3D consists of user interface and programming tool kits for MacOS, Windows 95, and a cross-platform file format called 3DMF. Apple Computer, Netscape Communications, and Silicon Graphics have agreed to incorporate the 3DMF format into the next generation VRML that provides interactive 3D graphics on the World Wide Web.

QD3D requires a PowerPC Macintosh with System 7.1.2 or later, 16 MB of RAM, and the QD3D system extension. Microsoft Windows support also might be available in the near future. A few 3D programs on the Mac support the 3DMF format. Macromedia announced that 3DMF support will be added to Extreme 3D. A QD3D Xtra for Director also is expected. With a QD3D Xtra you can import 3DMF files into the Director cast and provide realtime 3D interactivity and rendering from within Director as long as the QD3D system extension is installed on the playback machine.

For the latest on the availability of QTVR and QD3D Xtras, check out http://www.macromedia.com/.

Plug-In Filters

Director 5 now supports Adobe Photoshop plug-in filters. The Director 5 CD ships with several plug-in filters that enable you to add 3D effects to your graphics from within Director. Some plug-ins require the QD3D system extension. To use the plug-ins within Director, install them with the included installer. To apply a plug-in to a bitmap cast member in Director, select the cast member in the Cast window, choose Filter Bitmap from the Xtras menu, and select the desired plug-in from the Filter Bitmap dialog box.

Creating 3D Graphics

As you make the move from computer-based 2D illustration to 3D graphics and animation, the change can be daunting at first because it involves a different way of creating computer graphics. The creation of 3D graphics is an iterative process that involves several different tasks.

- In the modeling step, you create the basic structure of your objects and place them in a 3D world.
- In the animating step, you typically assign different key-frame positions to objects along a timeline. The computer generates intermediate frames between key frames ("tweening") to simulate motion in your 3D world and does all the work of creating perspective, lighting, shadows, and environmental effects. This step is similar to key-frame animating in the Director Score, only more powerful.

- In the rendering step, the computer paints your 3D world based on the lighting, material properties, and camera views you created. Material properties define an object's color, texture, and surface properties. Lights and atmospheric effects define the environment of your world.
- Often, the final step is to merge or composite 3D graphics with other graphics elements using programs such as Photoshop, Debabelizer, Director, After Effects, or Premiere.

Designing a 3D world isn't a simple, linear, step-by-step process. It usually involves alternating between modeling and animation; performing test renderings at different stages to see whether all the various aspects of your world look just right; and performing a final, high-quality render that might take many minutes, hours, or even days! The following sections provide more detail on the process and provide some tips on how you can create 3D graphics and animations for Director.

The 3D World

In 2D programs, such as FreeHand and Director, the screen is divided into an X-Y, 2D coordinate system. You might be familiar with FreeHand, which enables you to set precise X and Y values for the positioning and alignment of objects. 3D programs add a third dimension to this coordinate system. The third axis, or Z axis, extends into the computer screen. Programs such as Extreme 3D enable CAD-accurate positioning and alignment within the 3D coordinate system.

You view your 3D world through a window on the computer screen. This view has editable parameters such as perspective and orientation. At first, it's easy to become disoriented as you construct your 3D world. Become familiar with the way you change and edit view parameters in your 3D program. In the beginning, it may be easiest to stick with a set of default views (such as Front, Back, Top, Right, and so on) if your program provides them.

The camera is a special object. The view you use to edit your 3D world can be the same view as the camera view, but it doesn't have to be. Camera position and look-at points are animated to provide panning, dollying, tracking, zooming, and fly-throughs.

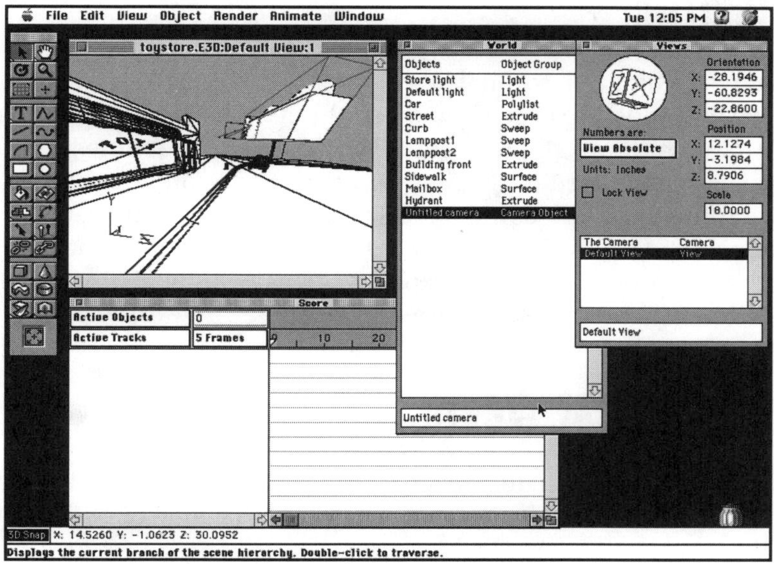

Figure 13.1

A typical interface of a 3D graphics program, in this case, Extreme 3D. Note the animation Score in the lower part of the screen and the camera object in the upper right of the View window.

Modeling

Modeling is the process in which you construct your 3D objects or models and create the basic structure of your 3D world (also called a model). Many 3D programs provide a set of primitive shapes (such as cube, sphere, and cone) from which you can create more complex models. Most 3D programs provide a rich set of tools to construct 3D models from 2D profiles. The tool set usually includes extrusion, lathe, sweep, and skin (loft) tools. Extreme 3D models are built up from true Bezier curves. You can edit and animate models at the vertex or point level to create complex organic shapes.

You position objects in your 3D world by using the mouse or by entering 3D coordinates. Many programs, such as Extreme 3D, enable you to place an object at precise points in your 3D world. It can sometimes be hard to tell exactly where your object is within the 3D coordinate system. When you first create an object, you might want to align it to the (0, 0, 0) point in your world and then move it at right angles along the X, Y, and Z axes just to get a feel for how the object is oriented in the 3D space.

Animating

You create animation through a sequence of still images or frames that are played rapidly in succession so that the eye is fooled into perceiving continuous motion. 3D programs with animation capabilities typically use a key-frame based time line—similar to the Score in Director—to create animations. The computer calculates all the intermediate frames between key frames. In Extreme 3D, you can animate almost every editable property, including texture maps and individual vertices or control points. Motion paths are fully editable curves as well.

The Material World

To make your 3D world look realistic, assign different material properties to objects, and create lights and atmospheric effects.

Shadows and Light

The lighting in a 3D world is similar to the lighting of a stage or movie set in the real world—except you can place lights anywhere in 3D space, and you can easily change the properties of each light, such as color or dustiness. Light sources in 3D programs include distant lights, spotlights, and ambient light. *Distant lights* simulate the sun and throw parallel light rays. *Spotlights* are typically cone-shaped lights that focus on specific points. *Ambient light* is the global, environmental light that suffuses your scene from all directions.

Light in the 3D world doesn't have to follow the laws of physics! You can have lights that don't cast shadows. Anyone who has done photographic, stage, or film lighting can appreciate this feature. Lights can even have *negative intensity*. This means that it takes light out of the area instead of illuminating it.

Procedural Textures and Texture Maps

The surface properties of your 3D objects reflect the materials they are made of and the lighting and environment of your 3D world. Texture mapping and procedural textures are two common ways to simulate materials for your objects.

Texture mapping is the process of applying a bitmap image, such as a PICT file, to a 3D surface. At the simplest level, texture mapping is similar to stretching a decal or placing a label on the surface of an object. You can animate textures, tile textures, and project and place textures with different orientations. You can simulate surface roughness, lighting effects, and transparency settings with texture maps. You can overlay several texture maps on the same surface. Some programs even support QuickTime movies as texture maps.

Procedural textures use mathematical equations to generate surface properties. Because procedural textures are mathematical calculations, they don't require as much disk space or memory as texture maps. They also are resolution independent. You can get very close to an object with a procedural texture and the texture won't become pixellated. Because procedural textures extend through an object, you also can carve into objects and still see the texture. Procedural textures can take a lot of time to render and sometimes require a lot of tweaking to look realistic. Bryce is a 3D program that uses procedural textures extensively to re-create natural forms and textures.

Rendering

Rendering is the process by which the computer generates an image based on all the material properties, positions, lights, and models that you have in your 3D world. The following list describes several different rendering methods. Naturally, the highest-quality methods take the longest time to render.

- **Bounding box rendering.** This type of rendering represents 3D objects as boxes that enclose each object. This method is the fastest and is used to show the basic positions of objects.

- **Wireframe rendering.** This method represents the underlying structure of 3D objects as a grid of interconnected lines and is commonly used for interactive rendering of animations.
- **Flat-shading method.** Flat shading renders objects with faceted polygons.
- **Gourand shading.** Gourand shading provides semi-realistic shading and smoothness and is a good intermediate quality rendering method for test renders during modeling.
- **Phong shading and ray-tracing.** These are the highest quality render methods, take the longest time, and are generally used for final output. Of the two, ray-tracing takes the longest time, because each pixel is calculated based on the simulated light rays from every light source, including reflections.

Interactive rendering is the rendering used to display your 3D world on the screen while you work on it. You want the screen display to be fast, but you also want enough information to be able to create your model and see what you're doing. Many programs use the wireframe rendering method for interactive rendering.

Extreme 3D provides very fast interactive rendering. In Extreme 3D you can assign different render modes to different objects. This feature can save a lot of time during interactive rendering, for example, if you want to see detail in one object but only want to see the rough positions of other objects in a scene. QD3D provides system-level support for fast interactive rendering.

At several stages in your project you might run high-quality test renderings using final output settings. Most programs can render high-quality test renderings to the screen instead of to disk. You might want to render selected key frames at the highest possible setting to make sure your 3D world is shaping up the way you want. You also can render short but critical parts of animations to see what they look like at the final output settings.

Final rendering at high quality settings usually takes a long time. Many programs enable you to distribute rendering across multiple machines on a network. Extreme 3D has a built-in distributed renderer.

You also might want to render images at larger sizes and higher color depths than needed for a particular project, and reduce size and color depth during post-processing using programs such as Photoshop, Debabelizer, or After Effects. Consider rendering against a solid color background to make compositing easier.

Compositing

Compositing is the process of merging or layering separate graphic elements into a single image or animation. Sometimes it is better to render 3D objects and animations separately. In Director, for example, several simultaneous small animations generally have better playback performance than one large animation that takes up the whole screen. You can use After Effects, Photoshop, Premiere, or Director to composite separate 2D and 3D graphics elements against different 2D backgrounds enabling you to re-use the graphics elements in different projects. Compositing enables you to add different backgrounds, change motion paths, or add and delete individual elements without having to re-render the entire scene. Also, you might want to render one object at a higher level of detail and quality (and corresponding longer render time) compared to other objects in a scene. You could then composite the high-detail and low-detail objects to save rendering time.

Alpha Channel

If you plan to composite your 3D graphics, render them with an alpha channel. An *alpha channel* is an invisible, 8-bit, grayscale image that most 3D programs create automatically when you render for final output. An alpha channel is very useful for compositing in such programs as After Effects and Photoshop. Use the alpha channel for masking, transparency, and selection. A file has an alpha channel if it has a color depth of Millions+ or 32 bits (24 bits plus an 8-bit alpha channel).

To load the alpha channel as a selection in Photoshop, choose the alpha channel (typically channel 4) with the Select, Load Selection command.

Director supports layering but doesn't support alpha channels; Photoshop supports layering and alpha channels. Premiere has an A-B roll editing system and multiple superposition layers with alpha channels. After Effects supports layering and alpha channels, and has powerful masking, transparency, compositing, and animation controls. Director, Premiere, and After Effects export animations as a sequence of PICT files or as QuickTime movies.

Using 2D Programs to Create 3D Effects

You don't need a dedicated 3D program to add dimensionality to 2D graphics. Many 2D graphics programs provide ways to add shadows, surface textures, and extrusions to 2D graphics. This section teaches you to use 2D programs to create 3D effects and textures.

Adding Dimensionality to 2D Graphics

In Photoshop and Painter, you can paint in shadows and highlights by hand using tools such as the Dodge, Burn, or Airbrush tools. You also can use several different techniques to add drop shadows to objects. If you add drop shadows, create them on a separate layer in Photoshop or Painter so you can composite and animate them separately.

Painter has a rich set of lighting effects that adds dimensionality to graphics. You can use the Apply Surface Texture command in Painter to texturize your graphics and add dimension to type. Photoshop also has lighting effects. Using lighting effects with grayscale images to create 3D graphics is described in the next section.

Grayscale Bump Maps

Both Photoshop and Painter use grayscale images to create 3D surface textures and lighting effects. The idea is simple. To create a textured 3D surface, these programs interpret the white areas of a grayscale image to be the "bumps" or raised areas of the surface. The black areas of the grayscale image correspond to the pits or the lowest points of the surface. Gray areas have intermediate heights depending on the gray level. Grayscale images used in this way are sometimes called *grayscale bump maps* or *height fields*. Adding lighting effects to an image with a grayscale bump map shades the image based on the "bumps" in the grayscale bump map. This effect is similar in some respects to the emboss filter, but is much more powerful. You can use this feature to create intricate, detailed surface textures. You also can use this technique to create 3D interface objects, such as buttons.

In Photoshop, you can use the Filter, Render, Lighting Effects command and any grayscale image to create quick 3D textures and surfaces. You can texturize and emboss any image by using a grayscale version of the image in conjunction with the Filter, Render, Lighting Effects command. In Photoshop, create a grayscale image from any other image or channel with maximum options and control using the Image, Calculations command. If the transitions between gray values are too sharp, add blur to smooth out the grayscale image.

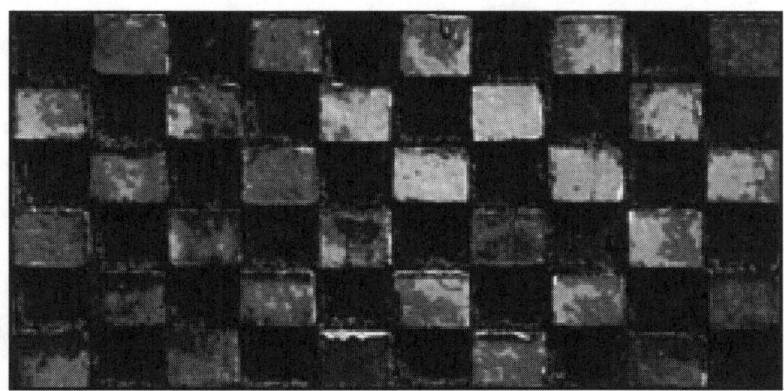

Figure 13.2

The upper image is the grayscale bump map used to create the lower image using Photoshop's Lighting Effects filter.

Creating Textures

Painter, Photoshop, Director, and most 3D programs come with libraries of textures. You can use dedicated texture creation programs or Painter and Photoshop to create original texture maps for your 3D models. Any bitmap can become a texture map. Instead of creating intricate detail in a 3D model, draw the detailed look you want in a 2D program, then import it as a texture map into your 3D program. Sometimes, adding a little noise to texture maps in Photoshop gives them a less sharp-edged, computer-generated look. Scanning and video capture are other ways to create real-world texture maps.

Creating 2D Bezier Curve Profiles

Extreme 3D provides spline-based drawing tools, similar to tools in FreeHand and Illustrator, that create 2D curves or profiles. Various 3D object tools turn your 2D profiles into 3D objects. It is sometimes easier to create 2D profiles directly in FreeHand or Illustrator and import them into Extreme 3D.

Extreme 3D imports FreeHand 4.0 or 5.x files directly. It also imports 2D files saved in EPSF format. Extreme 3D creates profiles from the Bezier curves in your 2D files. It ignores such elements as the fill patterns and bitmaps in your 2D drawing.

If you create your 2D profiles in FreeHand, here are some tips for using FreeHand with Extreme 3D.

- Before you save your FreeHand file for import into Extreme 3D, choose the Document Inspector and drag your page to the lower left corner of the pasteboard.
- After you import your FreeHand file into Extreme 3D, select the View, Fit to Window command to see the profiles in the Extreme 3D workspace.
- Align the profiles in the workspace using the Object, Align command.

- If the sharp corners of your 2D profiles look rounded in Extreme 3D, press the B key while you manipulate the handles of the corner points. Pressing the B key "breaks" the point handles and enables you to create sharp corners in your profiles.

Director

Director provides some built-in tools that help produce the illusion of depth. These tools won't replace a dedicated 2D or 3D graphic program, but they do provide a quick way to simulate a third dimension on a flat computer screen.

To distort a bitmap so that it looks like it's being viewed in perspective, you can use the Perspective tool in the Paint window. Select the bitmap with the rectangular Marquee tool, and click the perspective tool button in the Paint window toolbar. Drag the handles of the selection rectangle to squish the bitmap so that it looks like it's receding toward a vanishing point.

Another way to produce the illusion of depth is to lighten or darken bitmaps that are farther away from the viewer in the 3D world. To lighten or darken bitmaps, choose the Lighten or Darken button in the toolbar of the Paint window.

To produce the illusion of a sprite or bitmap moving into a 3D space and getting smaller and farther away from the viewer, use the Scaling command with Director's Auto Distort command.

Now that Director 5 supports Photoshop plug-in filters, you can use your 3D plug-ins on Director bitmaps. The *Inside Director 5* CD comes with several for you to try out, such as HoloDozo (which requires QuickDraw 3D) and Xaos Tools' TypeCaster for 3D type.

3D Interfaces, Backgrounds, and Objects in Director

Adding 3D elements to Director is as simple as adding 2D bitmaps and involves many of the same issues such as file size and palette optimization. Bitmaps are discussed in Chapter 9, "Graphics: The Visuals." You can look at adding 3D elements to Director in several ways. You can create a background or interface in a 3D program, for example, and composite 2D graphics on top of it. You can create a background or interface in a 2D program, and use Director to composite 3D elements on top. The key to integrating 3D elements in Director is to composite the various 2D and 3D graphic elements as seamlessly and stylistically consistent as possible, even though the elements are created in different programs.

3D Interface Design

Chiseled gray buttons and dialog boxes are commonplace in user interfaces. Just look at the standard Macromedia User interface. 3D graphics and textures appeal to the tactile sense and enhance the feeling that you are directly manipulating objects on the computer screen. A well-designed 3D user interface looks better organized and gives a clearer visual impression of interface functions.

3D user interface design uses the same principles as 2D user interface design. 3D interfaces have the tendency to accentuate bad interface design, so design carefully. The list that follows includes a few points to keep in mind:

- When you create 3D interfaces, don't overpower the content with sumptuous textures.
- Don't compete with the dimensionality of other 3D elements on the screen.
- Restrict the height of 3D interface objects to two or three levels.

- Avoid closely packed, chiseled buttons which create distracting grids.
- Subdue the tonal range of shadows and highlights in the interface. Just a few tens of percent difference in the gray values of shadows and highlights is enough to give the impression of a third dimension.
- Depending on the kind of interface you are designing, keep the shadows and light sources consistent across your interface.
- Use parallel lighting (distant lights in Extreme 3D) to reduce banding, especially if you need to restrict your interface to a few colors.
- Use numeric positioning of objects to ensure consistent placement.

Use 2D programs, such as Photoshop, or 3D programs to create your interface elements. Draw your interface as 2D Bezier curves in FreeHand, for example, leaving holes for the content. Then, import the curves into Extreme 3D and extrude them slightly. Another way to create intricate, molded interfaces is to use a grayscale bump map with the Filter, Render, Lighting Effects command in Photoshop, as discussed previously.

3D Backgrounds

An easy way to add dimensionality to your Director project is to use a 3D background over which you composite graphics and animations. A 3D background can be as simple as a picture frame for a QuickTime movie or as complex as a fully realized stage set for a character animation. By creating your background as a model in a 3D program, it's easy to change perspective, lighting and atmospheric effects, or render different parts of the scene separately.

The following list provides a few basic techniques and tips to keep in mind:

- Set up an interesting perspective for your background by using the camera and view parameters in the 3D program.

- Avoid flat surfaces parallel to the computer screen. Dramatic, low-angle lighting and shadows add a sense of depth.
- Consider rendering your background model in foreground, middle-ground, and background layers. Then, use Photoshop to composite them.
- A simple technique, such as adding a slight Gaussian blur to the background layer using Photoshop's Gaussian Blur filter, creates a sense of depth in a scene.
- Most important, make sure your background doesn't compete visually with the content and interface; make sure your background has a graphic style similar to the rest of the project.

3D Objects

When you composite 3D elements that are rendered separately, it's important that they have stylistic consistency so the elements don't look out of place.

- All elements should be lighted from the same directions so that shadows fall consistently. The lights should be of similar intensity and color.
- Global environment settings such as ambient light and fog, should be the same in your rendered 3D graphics, unless you are designing for a particular effect. Use similar colors and surface properties to give your graphics stylistic unity.
- Before you start rendering, determine the layering order of your 3D graphics in Director and plan your compositing accordingly.

At the outset, decide how to composite shadows in Director. Are you going to render the shadows with the 3D object, add them later as a separate layer in Photoshop, or paint them directly on the background with the Photoshop Airbrush tool? Shadows aren't sharp-edged; they are blurry. Therefore, it can be a challenge to merge them realistically with the background.

Often, it's a good idea to render your 3D images with larger dimensions than you need. Resize the image to the dimensions you want for your Director project. The quality of resized graphics is better if you start with a large graphic and reduce the size, rather than start with a small graphic and increase the size.

Most 3D programs render images at a color depth of 24 bits. You'll need to reduce the color depth to use them in an 8-bit Director project.

A common problem with reducing color depth in 3D graphics is that a smooth gradient, such as a smooth, shadowed surface, becomes banded when it's reduced from 24 bits to 8 bits. Before you reduce the color depth, use Photoshop to add a small amount of noise to smooth gradients and to see whether it helps reduce banding. You also can render the image in your 3D program at a color depth of 8 bits.

Anti-Aliasing

Aliases are the stair-stepped, jagged edges of color fields in computer-generated imagery. Aliasing is a consequence of the pixel-based, discontinuous nature of computer images; rounded edges and color shifts have to be resolved into square pixels. To see aliasing, draw a circle in the Director Paint window and zoom in. The edge of the circle isn't smooth, but jagged. Aliasing is a dead give-away of computer-generated imagery.

Anti-aliasing uses different techniques to blend or blur the jagged edges in computer images so that computer imagery looks more like a continuous-tone photograph. You can perform one of these anti-aliasing techniques in the Director Paint window. Use the jagged circle you just created and scale it 25 percent using the Transform Bitmap command. Now, use the Transform Bitmap again and scale the image up by 400 percent. The edges of the circle are now blurred. If the circle you created is dark-colored, drag the circle onto a dark-colored stage and set the ink type to Background Transparent or Matte. A halo of anti-aliased pixels around the circle shows.

In most 3D programs, you can control the amount of anti-aliasing in your renders. Anti-aliasing can take up a lot of computer time, so it's a good idea to use only as much anti-aliasing as necessary. Anti-aliasing generally makes computer-generated imagery appear more realistic. Be sure you render your anti-aliased images with an alpha channel. Alpha channels are used in such programs as Photoshop and After Effects to composite anti-aliased images against varying backgrounds.

Figure 13.3

Illustration of aliased and anti-aliased graphics in Director.

Director is a hard-edged world—it doesn't support alpha channels. If you plan to composite irregularly shaped, computer-generated imagery in Director, choose some way to deal with the dreaded anti-alias fringe or halo.

One way to work with these problems is to render the image without anti-aliasing. This compromise might not be acceptable, though, if all you want to do is remove the anti-aliasing from the edges of the object. The following sections discuss different ways to handle anti-aliasing.

Removing Anti-Aliased Edges in Photoshop

In Photoshop, there are several ways to remove anti-aliased edges from objects. Most involve modifying the selection outline, and copying and pasting selections into new files or against new backgrounds.

If you use these processes on a sequence of PICT files in an animation, preserve the registration points when you copy and paste. After you have the selection outline the way you want it—but before you paste the selection into a new file—press the Shift key to add two small rectangular selections in the upper left and lower right corners of the image. This ensures that the images's original size is preserved.

If the file has an alpha channel that corresponds to the object's edges, you can use the Threshold command to modify the alpha channel and create a selection outline that removes the anti-aliased edges:

1. Select the alpha channel in the Photoshop Layers palette.
2. Choose Image, Map, Threshold and adjust the slider so that the white area shrinks.
3. Select the RGB channel in the Layers palette and load the alpha channel as a selection.
4. Repeat this process until you have a clean-edged selection outline.

Another technique is to select the object by loading the alpha channel, using the Magic Wand tool or Color Range command, or by painting the selection mask in QuickMask mode:

1. Select the outline around the anti-aliased object, then choose Select, then Modify, Contract with a value of 1 pixel. This command shrinks your selection outline by one pixel and removes most of the anti-aliased halo.
2. After you remove the anti-aliasing to your liking, copy and paste the object into the Director cast or into another Photoshop file for compositing.

After you paste an object into a new file (while it's still a floating selection) use the Select, Matting, Remove White Matte; Select, Matting, Remove Black Matte; or Select, Matting, Defringe commands to remove extraneous pixels you rendered against a white, black, or a colored background.

Which one of these techniques works best for your images depends on the shape and color of the object and its background. Experiment with a test render to see which one works best.

Rendering Against a Neutral Background

Another way to handle anti-aliasing is to render your 3D graphics against a neutral, solid-color background. If the tonal values and colors of your Director background are similar, such as all dark grays and blues, try to render the object against a solid-color background in your 3D program. The solid-color background should be in the mid-range of the tonal values and colors of the Director background. A medium gray, solid-color background, for example, would work well if your Director background contains a range of different grays.

Rendering Against the Final Background

You also can render the image against the actual background. In Extreme 3D, you can import any PICT file to use as a background for your 3D world. This technique can provide the highest quality seamless compositing, but also can require a lot of work, render time, and planning.

3D Animation

Three-dimensional animation can be more than adding morphing chrome logos to your interactive project. 3D animation can provide visualization of complex objects and environments and illustrate dynamic processes. By adding interactivity to 3D animations, you can create navigable "virtual reality" experiences.

General Considerations

The use of 3D animations involves the same issues as 2D animations. As always, plan ahead for 3D graphics. Before you begin rendering in your 3D program make sure you understand how the animation fits into the Director project, and how the animations interact with and overlay other graphic elements.

Animation Formats

Animation formats for 3D animations are the same as for 2D animations—PICs, Director film loops, imported Director movies, sequences of frames in the main movie, sequences of frames in an MIAW, or QuickTime. If you want to add interactivity to animations, create them as a sequence of separate PICT files or as QuickTime movies. Compositing 3D animations can be more of a challenge, so you'll need to decide on layering and compositing strategies.

If you want to add interactivity, you'll probably want to output your animation as a sequence of separate PICT files or as a QuickTime movie. The same issues regarding importing and playback performance of 2D animation and digital video apply to 3D. See Chapter 15, "Director as an Animator," for a discussion of animation in Director; see Chapter 14, "Digital Video: The Movie within the Movie," for a discussion of use of digital video and QuickTime.

Compositing and Post-Processing Animation

All the compositing and post-processing issues for static 3D graphics also apply to 3D animation—except they're multiplied by the number of animation frames!

You can use the symmetry of your 3D object to reduce the render time, and the number of separate frames and cast members in your animation. If you want to rotate the letter "A" 360 degrees about its vertical axis, for example, you only need to rotate it through 180 degrees because of the mirror-plane symmetry along the vertical axis.

Determine the layering order of your 3D graphics in Director before you start rendering and plan your compositing accordingly. Animated 3D graphics look more realistic if they throw shadows across the Director stage. The shadows change shape as the element animates and they fall on different surfaces and objects. Plan from the start how to composite animated shadows.

As you post-process separate animation frames, you might want to preserve the original size of each frame in order to preserve its registration points. Outline each frame with a solid line or paint small, solid-color squares in the upper-left and lower-right corners of the image. When you import these graphics into the Director cast, the original size and registration points are preserved. Remove these marks after you've set up the animation in the Director Score. Crop your frames to reduce file size as the last step, after the animation is set up in Director, so that you don't lose your registration points.

Color depth reduction of 3D animations can cause banding of smooth gradients and pixel drift of dithered patterns. The quality of a color-depth reduction depends on the particular palette and the colors you use in the 3D world. Sometimes, adding a small amount of noise in Photoshop, before you reduce the color depth, helps.

Large areas of flat, solid-color in animations also can have annoying pixel drift when dithered to 8-bit color. Avoid dithering solid-color areas when you reduce color depth. It's a good idea to output a short test animation at your final render settings and run a test color-depth reduction to see how the 24-bit animation looks at 8 bits. Consider creating an 8-bit super palette in Equilibrium's Debabelizer. A *super palette* is an optimal palette that is based on the colors found in a range of different images, such as frames in an animation.

Debabelizer is an essential tool for batch processing animation files and creating optimal palettes. You also can automate repetitive processes using a macro utility such as QuicKeys. Daystar Digital's free Photomatic utility automates many Photoshop processes. You can download Photomatic from http://www.daystar.com/.

Animated 3D Objects

Animated 3D objects can add interest to your Director project. Animation in a 3D interface can make it easier to understand and use. A 3D animation can provide alternate views of a complex structure, such as a sculpture, a human heart, or a flower.

One way to provide multiple views of a complex object is to show the object rotating about an axis. It's easy to create object rotations in Extreme 3D. The following steps show how:

1. Select the object you want to rotate.
2. Select a key frame for the end of the animation. The number of frames for a full-circle rotation depends on the requirements of your project. Thirty-six frames generally provides a smooth rotation, but you might be able to get by with fewer frames.
3. Choose the Animate, Auto Rotate command in Extreme 3D and specify a rotation angle of 360 degrees for a full circle rotation. You might want to rotate about the object's Y axis (vertical axis), but it depends on how your 3D world and your object axes are set up.

4. Extreme 3D automatically creates an animation of the object rotating 360 degrees about its center point on the axis you specify.

If the object swings out of view or doesn't rotate the way you want it to, you might need to move the object's center point. To line up the object's center point with the axis of rotation, use the Object Center tool. Another trick is to link the object to a construction point you place on the axis of rotation. Then, use the Auto Rotate command to rotate the construction point. The object appears to rotate or orbit around the construction point.

You can output your animation as a QuickTime movie or a sequence of PICT images. You also can add interactivity with Lingo, enabling the user to rotate the object to the right or left. The movie HEART.DIR on the accompanying CD demonstrates one way to do this with an animation output as a sequence of PICT frames.

A *QTVR Object movie* is a special QuickTime movie format for 3D objects that enables you to manipulate and rotate photographic-quality objects in real-time on average desktop PCs. You also embed objects in standard QTVR scenes or panoramas. Although QTVR Object movies are easier to create than standard QTVR scenes, you still need the QTVR Authoring Tools Suite or the QTVR Object Tool available free at Apple Computer's Web site to create object movies, and the QTVR Xtra and QuickTime extension to view them in Director.

QD3D provides interactivity and fast, software-based rendering of objects saved in 3DMF format. With the QD3D Xtra and the QD3D system extension you can add fully interactive, rendered 3D objects to the Director cast and use them from within Director.

Navigable Environments

One of the most useful applications of 3D animation is to provide visualization of 3D environments that are impossible or too expensive to see in the real world. Adding interactivity enables the user to explore the 3D world using the computer keyboard and mouse. Interactive controls typically provide the capability to turn left or right, and move forward and backward within the 3D world.

QuickTime VR, the cross-platform "virtual reality" extension of QuickTime, provides photographic-quality imagery, sophisticated navigation features, embedded hot spots, and the capability to pick up and manipulate objects within the 3D scene. QuickTime VR movies are special QuickTime movies created with the QTVR Authoring Kit.

The animation features of most 3D programs enable you to create navigable environments fairly easily. You typically create animations for navigable environments by animating the camera in the 3D world:

- To simulate a panoramic effect in a 3D world, simply rotate the camera about its center point.
- To simulate a walk-through or fly-through in the 3D world, animate the camera along a prescribed path.
- You also can create animations with multiple panoramic views and multiple motion paths for a more immersive, virtual reality-type experience.

With some planning and a little work, you can create navigable 3D environments with Lingo in Director. If you have the QTVR Authoring Tools Suite, you can create QuickTime VR movies and play them back in Director with a full range of interactivity using XCMDs, XObjects, or Xtras.

Panoramas and Fly-Throughs

A *panorama* is a wide, typically 360-degree, view of a 3D world as seen from a single spot. This spot is sometimes called a *node*. Some 3D programs, such as Bryce, have a special panorama rendering mode that automatically creates 360-degree views of a 3D scene. By showing different pieces of the panorama, you can simulate the act of standing at the node and looking around in different directions in your 3D world. In other programs, such as Extreme 3D, you can place the camera at the node, rotate it 360 degrees, and create PICT-file animations or a QuickTime movie. Playing the animation simulates turning a full circle while standing in a single spot.

The Director movie PANORAMA.DIR on the accompanying CD is an example of using Lingo to produce an interactive panoramic effect.

Walk-throughs and fly-throughs simulate the act of moving through a 3D environment and are easy to create in Extreme 3D. You can turn any spline curve into a motion path for your camera. You also can use key-frame animation to animate the camera.

To use key-frame animation:

1. Open the Views browser and create a series of key-frame views or establishing shots.
2. Create a view for the beginning of the fly-through, the end of the fly-through, and any intermediate steps such as turns.
3. When you're done, set the current frame to zero in the Animation Control window.
4. Select the view that is the starting point of your fly-through in the Views browser.
5. Choose View, Align Camera, To View.
6. Change the current frame to the next key-frame and select the second view from the Views browser.
7. Choose View, Align Camera, To View again. Repeat this with every view until you reach the end of your fly-through.
8. From the Views browser, select the Camera view and play back the animation. If it looks OK, render the animation to disk.

If you render the fly-through as a QuickTime movie, you can use QuickTime's built-in controls or Lingo's digital video commands to move back and forth along the pre-defined path. Chapter 14, "Digital Video: The Movie within the Movie," discusses the use of digital video in Director. You also can render the animation as a sequence of PICTs, import them into the cast, and use the Cast to Time command to create the fly-through animation in the Director Score. You then can add interactivity using Lingo.

Views, Nodes, and Meshes

But what if you want to do more than just fly along a single path? How do you give the user the ability to look around, change directions and otherwise navigate through the scene? You can invest in QTVR authoring tools and production equipment, or you can use your 3D program to create views and animated motion paths, and use Lingo to control the navigation.

To create a fully navigable 3D environment requires some planning. You use the concept of a node, where the user is stopped at a single spot having the ability to look around, as well as the concept of a motion path that defines the paths that the user can take to move through your 3D world. Basically, you break down the navigation you want into nodes and motion paths, and map them out as animations in your 3D program.

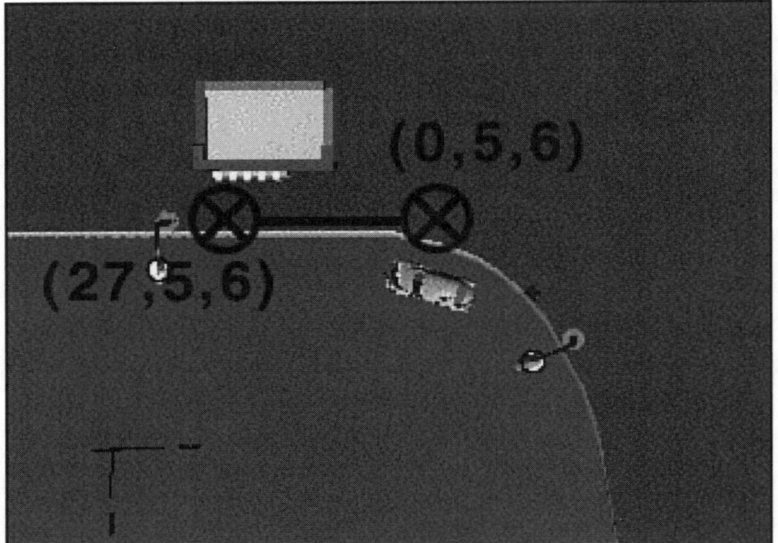

Figure 13.4

A birds-eye view of a 3D model with mapped out nodes and motion path of a simple navigable environment. There are two nodes in the environment at coordinates (27, 5, 6) and (0, 5, 6). There are four views at each node: north, east, south, and west.

1. Map out the motion paths in your 3D world. You might want to render your world from a birds-eye view and sketch the possible motion paths.
2. Select places along the motion paths where the user can stop and look around. These places are the nodes.
3. Decide how many views the user has at each node. For example, it might be possible to just have four views at 90-degree angles (forward, backward, left, and right). If you have only one motion path, the user can move forward and backward along the motion path at each node.

4. If you want the user to be able to move throughout your 3D world, you'll have to decide which directions the user is able to move at each node, such as right, left, up, down, right 30 degrees, and so on. Then, you can create more motion paths extending from that node.
5. As you add more motion paths, you quickly create a network of interconnected motion paths. This network is sometimes called a mesh.

A *mesh* consists of a web of nodes and motion paths in two or three dimensions. *Nodes* are places where the user can stop and look around. *Strands* of the mesh are the motion paths the user follows to navigate through your environment. To provide a navigable 3D environment, create animations that simulate looking around at each node and animations that simulate moving between nodes along each and every motion path.

- For planning animations and Lingo control, use a naming convention for nodes and views. For nodes you can use the X, Y, Z coordinates of the node in 3D space, for example (1, 2, 1). For the views you can use the cardinal positions, for example N, E, W, S, NNE, NE, ENE, and so on.
- Planning your camera shots and node positions on a spreadsheet is helpful. You can plan each key-frame or all frames. One way to organize the spreadsheet is to have each row represent the frame or key frame that you want to specify. In the columns of the spreadsheet enter the X, Y, Z coordinates of the node, the camera position and look-at point for each view, and the names of the nodes you can travel to from each view.
- Set the units of your 3D world to reflect the node structure, so that nodal coordinates fall on integers.
- Plan the number of animation frames for each view and motion path.
- If you have more than three or four nodes, you might want to create a navigable QuickTime movie.
- In a QuickTime movie, you create navigation by jumping to a frame using Lingo's digital video commands and playing a selected range of frames that simulate moving between nodes or looking around at the node.

- In your spreadsheet, include a column for the number or range of QuickTime frames for each view and motion path (see fig. 13.5).

Figure 13.5

A sample spreadsheet to help plan animations and QuickTime movies for the navigable environment illustrated in figure 13.4.

Street VR spreadsheet (SS)

A4 Frame

	A	B	C	D	E	F	G	H	I	J	K
1	Scene:		Street								
2											
3				Node			View(look-at points)			QuickTime Frame	
4	Frame		X	Y	Z	N	E	S	W		
5											
6	1-36	1	27	5	6	x37y5z6	x27y5z16	x17y5z6	x27y5z-4	n1e10s19w27n36	
7	37-77		Motion Path, Node 1-2							37-77	
8	78-114		0	5	6	x10y5z6	x10y5z16	x10y5z6	x0y5z-4	n78e87s96w105n	
9	115-145	2	Motion Path, Node 2-1							115-145	
10											
11											
12											
13											
14											
15											
16											
17											
18											
19											
20											
21											
22											
23											
24											

QTVR

QTVR provides a level of interactivity close to virtual reality, along with high-quality imagery and compressed files. You still have to map out your 3D world with a mesh of motion paths and nodes and then create the views at each node and the animations for each path, but QTVR handles compiling it into a single file and automatically provides the navigation controls. Look for this process to become easier as the technology matures. To create QTVR movies for playback from Director, you need the QTVR Authoring Tool Suite or the free QTVR Authoring Tools. Check out availability and pricing at http://qtvr.quicktime.apple.com.

Summary

The advent of faster processors, low-cost hardware acceleration, and system-level 3D support on desktop computers is bringing the capability to display high-quality 3D graphics and animation to a broad range of desktop systems. 3D graphics in Director can range from flying logos with 3D type to fully interactive and navigable "virtual reality" environments.

Although you still use your illustration and graphic design skills, creating 3D graphics is a different process than creating 2D graphics. The 3D objects you create exist in a fully realized 3D world in which you have detailed control of environmental features such as lighting and material properties. In some respects, 3D graphic design is similar to sculpture, set design, stage design, and architectural design except that your 3D environment exists inside a computer and represents an infinitely malleable and reusable graphic asset.

Creation of 3D graphics and animation usually involves learning a new, complex software program, but you also can use many of the 2D programs you are already familiar with to add dimensionality to graphics. Extreme 3D is a powerful yet easy-to-use 3D graphics and animation program that is integrated into the Macromedia's Director Multimedia Studio.

3D graphics can add interest to an otherwise "flat" Director project. 3D graphics and textures appeal to the tactile sense and enhance the feeling that you are directly manipulating objects on the computer screen. A well-designed 3D user interface can look better organized and give a clearer visual impression of interface functions. 3D animation can provide alternate views of a complex object or environment and more clearly illustrate a visually complex, dynamic process. One of the most useful applications of 3D animation is to provide visualization of 3D environments that would be impossible or too expensive to see in the real world.

Several developments make it easier to incorporate 3D graphics and animation into Director projects. In Director 5, Photoshop plug-in filters are used directly on cast members and 3D filter effects can be animated within Director. New Director 5 cast Xtras enable you to integrate QuickTime VR and QuickDraw 3D scenes and objects with a full range of powerful interactive and rendering features directly into your projects. Apple Computer is providing free, easy-to-use authoring tools for 3D artists, and Netscape Communications is integrating next generation VRML into their navigator for interactive 3D graphics on the World Wide Web.

Matt Davis

Digital Video: The Movie within the Movie

Since it's integration with digital video in version 3.1.3, Macromedia Director is probably the most popular "container" application for digital video. Digital video, however, is reputed to be a dark subject. It appears to be full of folklore, secret tricks, and many pitfalls to catch the unwary.

Digital video continues to provoke common complaints such as stuttering video clips; clips that suddenly fall silent; flashes of color; video simply not appearing when bidden; and an assortment of minor ills. Rather than being a fragile medium, digital video is a little understood one—both from a technical standpoint and from an aesthetic view. The former forms the basis of this chapter; the latter is for you to explore.

Director provides a great deal of control over this very powerful medium, far beyond the capability to display a "talking head" video clip. Many situations benefit from digital video:

- The use of digital video in a Director movie can solve problems with complex sprite animation; for example, by removing the performance hit of using many layers with many ink effects.
- Digital video can solve problems with timing; for example, synchronizing sprite animation with audio on a variety of machines).
- Digital video can help in asset management; for example, a collection of photographic images stored in a single QuickTime movie.
- Digital video incorporates compression, enabling 288 minutes of CD-quality stereo sound on a CD-ROM instead of 72 minutes of standard CD audio.

Director is a valuable digital video creation tool, too. The superior layering controls and ruthless optimization for on-screen use are invaluable to the world of digital video. Conversely, digital video can play back pre-recorded Director animation where Director might slow considerably—especially in high pixel depth (16-bit and 24-bit screens) and complex layering situations.

Director is not, however, a digital video *editing* application. This chapter refers to many specialist applications, which will be *briefly* described later in the chapter.

The following is a list of the major topics covered in this chapter:

- Introduction to digital video
- File formats
- Technical choices
- Sources for video
- Techniques for digital video
- Software tools
- Handling digital video in Director
- Helper applications

Three sample projects are included on the CD-ROM that comes with this book. In the Chapter 14 folder, you will find *Ellipse*, which demonstrates basic incorporation of digital video in a Director movie. *Pond* uses Lingo to control the playback of a digital video member.

Micons uses digital video created from Director movies. Be sure to read the documentation supplied with the files on the CD-ROM.

Introduction to Digital Video

What is digital video? Like multimedia, it is the result of a naming problem, because digital video need not be video at all. Digital video can—and frequently does—address speech, text, images, music, sequences, and their relationships with time.

On a more pragmatic level, the use of digital video in a Director movie can solve problems with complex sprite animation. Intricate Director animations containing a great deal of sprites, CPU draining ink effects, and so on might not play back as well on a typical end user system as it does on your development system. One solution to this problem is to convert the animation sequence to a single channel digital video member, giving all classes of computers a better chance to smoothly play the animation.

An example of this case is on the CD-ROM. The Micons movie depicts four "motion icons" from a much larger project. Originally planned for "film loops," I switched to using QuickTime and found the performance far better. Remember to copy the examples onto your hard disk.

Digital video is a blanket term that covers more than the files on your hard disk. It is important to remember the many "features" that are part of digital video can be isolated and used in their own right. This adds to the confusion, as its proponents seem to be saying, "It's a floor wax, and hey, it's a great dessert topping too!" Therefore, we can split digital video into two parts—time-based media and compression.

Digital video and Director may end up showing similar things, but they approach it in different ways. Director's method is about careful moment-by-moment direction and control (think of a puppeteer). A digital video is the finished performance—a *movie* of the puppetry.

Time-Based Media

Digital video is about time. Time is central and pivotal to digital video, because the key requirement is that a series of pictures should be synchronized to an audio signal and remain in synch from the second frame to the very last hour.

On the other hand, there is more to a time-based media than gluing pictures to sound. Digital video formats, such as QuickTime, will keep text and music stored as Musical Instrument Digital Interface (MIDI) together in a single file. This means that lyrics to a song can appear and disappear depending on the notes, rather than an arbitrary factor such as timings with a stopwatch. QuickTime takes many different media types, playing them back in synch.

This behavior is the *opposite* of Director. Director always plays every frame of its sprite animations, a very common occurrence is slower playback speed when played back on a computer less powerful than the developer's system. On the other hand, digital video normally gives timing priority, in order to play back a one-minute video on a slower system it will resort to skipping (dropping) frames as needed to maintain its predefined timing. Some describe the behavior as "sound priority," that is, the soundtrack of a digital video will—short of total overload—play normally, with no loss of quality, while the video stutters and jerks now and then in order to "keep up" with the music or speech.

To stop the digital video from dropping frames and adopt the normal Director behavior, open the member information panel for your digital video member and check the Direct to Stage and Play every frame options.

Think of a time base that is contained within your movie, but can run independently of it. You are in control of the user interface and you send messages to the digital video time base where necessary, allowing the mechanics of the digital video architecture to take care of the details. Alternatively, you can switch off the time base and concentrate on the second part of digital video—compression.

Compression

An often-said phrase is that "a picture is worth a thousand words." Well, that point is debatable. If that logic is pursued, then it is clear that an animation could be worth around a thousand pictures!

Sadly, this is precisely what animation is: hundreds, thousands, perhaps hundreds of thousands of pictures, each faithfully recorded in high resolution, taking up storage space.

The following is an example that might cause you to look at your VHS player in another light:

The U.S. video standard, NTSC, is known as a 525-line system, of which 480 are used for pictures. The 4:3 ratio gives us a corresponding 640 pixels across each row. If we multiply them together and then multiply that by three, we can work out the number of bytes required to store just one frame of NTSC video.

The number of bytes required for a 24-bit bitmap image of a single frame of NTSC is 0.9 MB of memory. (A single PAL frame would take about 1.29 MB of memory.)

PAL is the video standard throughout most of Europe. Exceptions include France and some countries in Eastern Europe that use SECAM.

The NTSC TV system displays 29.97 of those frames per second. As you watch the television, you are seeing about 26.9 MB (32.4 MB for PAL) flash past per second, and this does not include sound.

This is impressive because it represents the volume of data your digitizer board handles at the start of the pipeline and is the sort of data volume written to D1 and D2 video tape used in high-end video and film production.

The bottom line is that if you want video on your computer, you're going to have to cheat. Today's average personal computer is not capable of moving 32 MB per second of data from its disk drive to the screen as would be required to play a "raw" full-sized video stream. The relatively slow data rate of CD-ROM drives pose an even greater challenge. The data handling capability of systems is measured in Kilobytes Per Second (KBS) or Megabytes Per Second.

The magic of digital video is the clever data compression schemes devised to reduce the volume of the data stream to a manageable rate.

Temporal (Delta Change) Compression

If you put aside enough memory for just "a frame" in full—not lots of frames, just one big perfect frame—and then started off with frame one in its entirety, then frame two would be pretty much the same. So, instead of redrawing everything for frame two, you could simply paint over the things in frame one that had changed in frame two.

This is known as the *delta change* or *temporal* compression method. By recording the changes between frames, rather than the frames themselves, one achieves remarkable savings in certain circumstances. But it is not perfect—when you are panning or zooming, the whole scene changes from frame to frame!

Spatial (Including Run-Length Encoding) Compression

You can look at each frame individually and work out the areas where things are pretty much unchanging. (The "talking head" against a white background, for example, could be described as, "Here's a little white pixel; here's a little white pixel..." and so on for fifteen minutes until "Here's a light grey pixel; here's a dark grey pixel; here's a mousy brown pixel..." and so on until the pixels portraying somebody's hair had been analyzed until you reach the utter boredom of the background. The solution is to look at the line of pixels and generalize, as in "Here's about this many white pixels, then a grey, dark grey, brown" and so on.

This is an example of the *run-length encoding* method. By recording consecutive runs of colors, one can achieve high reductions in clean simple areas. However, in complex areas of detail, it is not efficient.

An alternative method is to use color space models, sharpening and edge detection algorithms in order to analyze an image so that large spaces of tone are described in sparse detail, and so that areas of contrast are described in fine detail, such as in JPEG compression.

Run-length encoding tends to be used for pictures with limited colors—8 bits (256 colors) or less. JPEG compression is designed to work with 16-bit (thousands of colors) or 24-bit (millions of colors) images.

These two concepts—temporal and spatial—are at the core of most compression schemes. Each is used in a greater or lesser extent to create two broad categories of compression methods: lossy and lossless.

Lossy Compression

This compression is known as *lossy compression* because information is quite literally lost, never to be retrieved. The reduction of bandwidth is significant, however, because compression ratios in the order of 100:1 are commonplace. Lossy compression is the only possible method of delivery of live-action footage.

The amount of compression is a variable under your control. There are levels of compression that govern what can be ignored and what should be recorded in both the frame-by-frame basis (delta or temporal) and the detail within the frame (spatial, q or Quality).

Lossy compression introduces artifacts to an image. In this case, an artifact is something in the image that wasn't there before, such as a by-product of compression. As the amount of compression increases and the files decrease in size, the artifacts become more severe. It starts with a slight loss of clarity, leading to areas of fine shading becoming blotchy. At high compression rates, areas of subtle detail, such as smudges on a painted wall whose loss may go unnoticed, are lost and become blotchy masses, and details and edges are picked out with aggressive image sharpening effects such as "ringing." (See figure 14.1.)

Figure 14.1

The effects of lossy compression.

Bear in mind that lossy compression is like instant coffee. We can reduce a handful of beans to a teaspoonful of powder (achieving remarkable compression) that can be almost instantly turned into a cup of coffee (superb decompression) and it provides most of the key properties that the original did (it looks like coffee, tastes like coffee, and so on). But it cannot be reverse engineered (it isn't quite like fresh coffee—the full range of subtle flavor cannot be reconstituted). You, the author/coffee brewer, should retain—and ideally work with—original material (coffee beans) stored in the next category of compression, which is lossless.

Lossless Compression

As the name suggests, the *lossless* compression method will reduce the file size without losing any information from the original file. This means that quality is preserved at all times, and that no matter how many processes the material goes through, a lossless compression scheme will faithfully retain all the information your material started out with.

The drawback is that although files can be a tenth of their original size (in extreme cases), for most of the time, the saving of space might amount to 50 percent of the original file. This might seem to be a great savings, but because the original files are very large, this method is suitable for archive material and special cases only—the resulting playback data rate is too demanding for most systems.

Data Rates

Compression is needed because there are restrictions and "bottlenecks" throughout a computer system. Limited RAM is a common factor, but there is often a backlog due to the rate at which data is transferred from storage device to processor—or from RAM to the screen, for example.

Digital video is synonymous with CD-ROMs—a major bottleneck.

The original CD-ROM drives spun their disks at 150 revolutions per minute, and this equated to reading about 150 KB from the disk every second. While it was theoretically possible that a CD-ROM drive *could* deliver 150 KB per second, it turns out to be unlikely. Unlike an audio CD player, the data wouldn't necessarily be accessed in sequential order and time would be spent moving the disc head to new locations. Furthermore, the computer needs time to decompress the data once read from the disc, and more time to display it.

The practical upshot is that although the theoretical maximum transfer rate was 150 KB per second, it became advisable to assume that—what with everything else happening in the computer—you can only hope to get two thirds of that. One hundred kilobytes per second is not a lot. Over time, we have seen the speed of CD-ROM drives increase to four times the original speed, and this can only increase in the future. (See table 14.1.)

Table 14.1

CD-ROM Performance Rate Specs: The Reality

Speed	Theoretical Rate	Maximum Rate	Safe Rate
150	150 KB/sec.	100 KB/sec.	90 KB/sec.
300	300 KB/sec.	200 KB/sec.	180 KB/sec.
600	600 KB/sec.	400 KB/sec.	360 KB/sec.

The preceding table shows the conservative end of digital video data rates for the original single speed drives, the double speed drives which dominated the market from 1993 to 1995, and the quad speed drives that took over from then on.

While the main factors of a digital video member—size, frames per second, and compression method—dictate the range of the playback rate, it is possible to improve these figures with some experimentation with cache settings and by balancing the compression with the power of the processor.

A more powerful processor can decompress a frame quicker, and therefore you can increase the data rate, and on the other hand, a faster CD-ROM drive means that less compression is required. These represent fine-tuning. If you move past the maximum rate in the table, then the results are related to the individual machine set up, rather than the average for a particular class of machine.

To meet the data rate limitations of the worst case target system, adjust the movie dimensions, frame rate, compressor type, and compression quality. Beyond the choice of compressor, the biggest improvements are made by reducing the dimensions of the movie.

Some authoring tools and utilities will automatically adjust compression quality and key frame rate to achieve a specified bandwidth. Reducing the number of frames per second will help a great deal. Beyond these controls, remember media prioritization.

Compression Schemes

Digital video is a nice, safe, catch-all phrase. It covers time-based media; it provides a unified file format for a wide range of media types; and it deals with a variety of compression methods. Of course, there are several "standards" to choose from, such as those from Apple, Microsoft, and the Motion Picture Experts Group.

Over the last few years, these three main offerings have settled down into their respective niches. Rather than being a test of allegiance, your decision has more to do with feature set, platform choice, and the reason for delivering content.

Microsoft has released tools for the Macintosh user to convert QuickTime movies into the Video for Windows format, and vice versa. The tools can be obtained from online services and the Microsoft Web site, or via Microsoft's developer scheme.

QuickTime

QuickTime, developed by Apple Computer, Inc., was released in December of 1991. At the time of release, and based on CD-ROM technology, QuickTime was capable of providing the traditional "postage stamp" movies (120×160 pixels) that would play at 12 fps (frames per second). Today, if one takes the same machinery and simply replaces the old QuickTime for the new, then it offers up to 320×240 pixel movies at 12 fps, or 240×180 pixel movies at up to 30 fps. That's the same equipment as in 1993—Mac IIvx, 030, 8 MB of RAM.

However, on today's equipment—a Power Macintosh, for example—QuickTime movies can measure 640×480 pixels and play at a super-smooth 30 frames per second from a quad-speed CD-ROM drive without hardware assistance.

As well as compressed video and audio, QuickTime 2.5 provides access to MPEG material—including the "White Book" standard (for example, CD-i) streams. MIDI also is built into QuickTime. The important thing to remember as Director developers is that these can be controlled in the same way, using the same Lingo we use for video today.

QuickTime is a very "cross-platform" technology. Not satisfied with MacOS, Windows 3.x, and Windows 95, QuickTime is moving into Unix—notably the Sun and SGI platforms used in high-end Internet server applications and in the world of television and film. Even a solution for OS/2 is available—should you feel so inclined. Thus, the unity of QuickTime becomes a major strength.

Historically, QuickTime creation has been a Mac-only affair. Applications that created QuickTime movies on the PC used to write out data in the Video for Windows (VFW) format and put a QuickTime wrapper around it. Features found on the Macintosh, such as multiple tracks of a similar type, were simply not possible on the PC.

QuickTime 2.5 achieves parity on both "sides." This is a significant achievement, because it requires a Windows version of SoundManager 3 (the Macintosh sound technology) and even a significant amount of QuickDraw (the Macintosh graphics technology) to be brought to the 32-bit Windows systems such as 95 and NT. Note that it is unlikely that this will be achievable on the 16-bit Windows systems.

Versions of QuickTime prior to 2.5 have some important differences between the Macintosh and Windows platforms. Windows files are limited to one video track and one audio track. No MIDI or text tracks are available.

Your Relationship with Apple

Although QuickTime is now considered part of the Macintosh system software, it is not so common on the Windows platform. In order to distribute the QuickTime components with your application, you must obtain a license from Apple Computer.

Your first step in licensing is to contact Apple's licensing department with your contact details, postal address, and the software you wish to license. For QuickTime, it's expedient to license for Macintosh and PC platforms regardless of actual destination. This will soon be extended to cover various flavors of Unix.

The traditional method of contacting the Apple licensing folks is via their generic e-mail address at SW.LICENSE@applelink.apple.com. For the most up-to-date information on Apple's software licensing, check their Web site at http://dev.info.apple.com/swl/swl.html. Alternatively, call them directly at 512-919-2645 or by fax at 512-919-2120.

Apple will send you copies of the license agreement that you then complete and return. When the papers are processed, Apple will return a copy for your records and include the official QuickTime logo artwork for packaging. The mammoth signing session need only be done once for QuickTime. As you release additional products requiring QuickTime, simply fax the details of your product to the legal department using the form provided. Similarly, the same agreement has covered revisions to QuickTime, requiring little or no action from you should a new version of QuickTime be released.

Amongst your obligations as a licensee, it is worth highlighting a few interesting points. Don't just provide the system extension or DLLs—you should include all the components for a QuickTime install—as provided on the Apple Web sites and on the QuickTime Software Development Kit (SDK).

The proper installation includes the simple player application and Apple's own software license agreement. Similarly, when providing QuickTime for Windows, the safest option is to include the installation provided by Apple. If you intend to write your own Installer, then be sure to read and follow the guidelines in your QuickTime Licensing Agreement.

Video for Windows

Microsoft's counterpart to Apple's QuickTime is Video For Windows (VFW). Director for Windows can use either QuickTime for Windows or VFW. As a rule for the sake of efficiency, cross-platform projects developed on the Macintosh will employ QuickTime for Windows in it's Windows incarnation, and that QuickTime for Windows will have to be included with the project.

Developers of corporate solutions for Windows (such as presentations, kiosks, and demonstrations) are often faced with the clients' requirement to use AVI rather than QuickTime. This can be worked round by using QuickTime tools to generate the digital video assets, and converting them to AVI using Microsoft tools. Note that QuickTime compressors such as "video" and "animation" must be recompressed with the Microsoft Video and Microsoft RLE components (available as a Macintosh plug-in to QuickTime). CinePak is part of both AVI and QuickTime.

Your Relationship with Microsoft

If you need to use Video for Windows, be aware that the raw components of VFW are a part of the Windows 95 installation, but not Windows 3.1 or 3.11 as standard.

In order to distribute VFW, you need to obtain a license from Microsoft. As with QuickTime, this does not involve a licensing fee.

However, unlike the QuickTime licensing process, you must be a part of the Microsoft Developer Network (membership must be at Level 2). This membership includes the right to distribute the VFW mechanism in your products.

MPEG

MPEG has been associated with the holy grail of computer video—Full Screen, Full Motion Video (FSFMV)—having stolen this crown from Digital Video Interactive (DVI).

It is the first compression scheme sophisticated enough to play quality full-screen video and high-fidelity sound from a single-speed CD-ROM. It is quite impressive that all this information can be squeezed in the same space used by the original audio only compact disc. To accomplish this, highly sophisticated mathematics are used—not only on the video but also to compress the audio. All this calculation just can't be handled by the average personal computer. As a rule, hardware is required for playback in the form of an MPEG card.

While we're knee-deep in acronyms, it might be worth mentioning that the Motion Picture Experts Group (MPEG) is part of the International Standards Organization (ISO) and that MPEG is similar in structure to the Joint Photographic Experts Group (JPEG). But both parties are not related to M-JPEG (Motion JPEG). There is no such group as the Motion Joint Photographic Experts Group—with or without a hyphen.

In the Windows camp, MPEG has found favor with the authors of kiosks specifically for this reason. It delivers FSFMV without fail, and at a quality level exceeding that of most VHS machines. MPEG has not made a great impression on the Mac camp due to its reliance on hardware—previously unavailable for Macintosh.

Digitizing video for MPEG playback is a black art. The best quality requires frame-by-frame compression. This involves a computer controlled VCR (usually a professional-quality format) outputting a single frame to video circuitry to clean the image. Each frame is then analyzed by the computer, with reference to the previous frame, and the results stored. Good MPEG digitization requires very specialized (and expensive) equipment.

Unlike the software compression methods, MPEG implementations on the 16-bit Windows platform can require a change of screen mode, resulting in an "all or nothing" capability. Because the video stream is written directly to the screen in both Macintosh and Windows incarnations, Director is unable to add graphics on top of it.

M-JPEG

Not to be confused with MPEG, this system uses the high-quality compression from the Joint Photographic Experts Group, and accelerates it to be able to work with video signals. As a result, Motion JPEG has the capability to both digitize and deliver *very* high quality video. Like MPEG, it is reliant on specialist hardware, but it is not designed to work with CD-ROM. In fact, most M-JPEG solutions require high-speed "AV" drives to both record and play back video.

The cost of digitizing hardware is much lower than for MPEG, which has lead to a lack of playback-only cards. Today, M-JPEG is the popular choice for digitizing video destined for CD-ROM playback using a software decompression system.

Technical Choices

Caveats aside, and before delving into practical demonstrations of digital video, it is necessary to clear up a few of the rather important technicalities behind digital video.

Basics

Over time, the digital video community uses the word *grab* to refer to the process of acquiring, scanning, or digitizing a video image or sequence. We "grab" some video just as we might "scan" a picture. An alternate term is video *capture*.

Digitizing (grabbing) video shares many principles with scanning artwork. If you are digitizing material from video tape, then you should endeavor to grab at the highest quality achievable in order to capture a complete unadulterated copy of the video sequence. You must be able to record every frame without wasting a fraction of a second in unnecessary compression. *Bandwidth-dependent compression* (in other words, compressing to a specific data flow such as 230 KB per second) should be a final step rather than an intermediate one.

Remember that video is just another media source—like pictures on a flat-bed scanner. It is sensible practice to scan pictures at 300 dpi in 24 bit, performing all scaling and balancing operations on this large file, and when complete, then (and only then) resample or scale to 72 dpi at 8 bits. Never the other way around!

Grabbing video is similar. Aim for as much quality as you can get with your equipment. The resultant movies are virtually unplayable without hardware assistance—this is a very good sign! It shows that there is far more information recorded than can be displayed in real time. Like a 24-bit picture on an 8-bit system, this file looks bad and is far too large and unwieldy for everyday use, but we need its content—which equates to quality—for editing.

Grab video with as little compression as your hard disk space can manage, and elect to "post compress" with applications such as "FusionRecorder." QuickTime choices include "Component" or "None," but these require a very fast hard disk and a powerful processor. For modest equipment, try Apple Video (set to high). On the other hand, best results will be obtained from one of the M-JPEG variants with hardware assistance.

Although the end product may be played using a software decompressor, such as CinePak, the capture and editing may all be done by a hardware compressor-based system, such as VideoVision Studio, using high-speed hard disk arrays (see the "Tools" section later in this chapter). Although the M-JPEG compression used by these systems is not lossless, the quality is superior to virtually all lossy software compressors. These systems also allow one to do editing with image sizes greater than the end product, helping to preserve the quality until the final preparation step when the video is compressed with a software compressor such as CinePak while simultaneously scaling it to the final size.

One exception is step-frame (or frame-by-frame) capturing from video-disk players under computer control, in which case the video can be digitized at a leisurely pace by a slow computer (as in the case for high-quality MPEG described earlier in this chapter).

Having obtained this high-quality material, it is important to preserve it during the editing process. When the assembly is complete, export the results as a stand-alone movie, correctly scaled, with the compression regime you require. Be prepared for a long wait...

Compression

For "quick-and-dirty" projects or prototypes, you might want to capture and compress the video all at once. Be aware that software-based compressors are asymmetrical—that is, it takes more time to compress the video than play it back. Some highly asymmetrical ones such as CinePak are simply not practical for real-time compression while capturing. Others, such as Apple Video, can compress while digitizing with a fast enough computer system.

NOTE

> CinePak and Apple Video are known as *codecs* because a codec comprises of a *co*mpression method and a *dec*ompression method.

It is important to compress to a lossy codec like CinePak only when your edit is complete. Compression is a lengthy process and involves great computational power. The more compression required, the more power required in the computer. CinePak, for example, is a 140:1 compressor. On average, every minute of video requires 140 minutes or longer to compress. Some material can take longer!

> To be technically accurate, CinePak's 140:1 ratio means that the video it can decompress in one minute would take 140 minutes to compress. It takes a *lot* of time, roughly a bit more time than originally allowed for.

However, there are other codecs that do not offer such good compression but can work to deadlines. The role call of the most-used codecs could run as follows:

- CinePak & Indeo
- Apple Video and Microsoft Video
- Animation
- YUV (Component)
- Graphics
- Sprite

CinePak and Indeo

CinePak and Indeo are 24-bit codecs, but when displayed on an 8-bit screen, they dither to the palette they find in operation (usually the system palette).

CinePak and Indeo *can* have a color palette which should override the current palette, but this will be *ignored* by Director. Director will use the palette it finds in the palette channel and, therefore, affect the palette designed for the movie.

If this causes problems, there are Xtras and XObjects to fix this, but it is easier to save your digital video as "24 bit" or "color" (not "256 colors") and force palettes created with deBabelizer from within Director.

Both codecs tend to be very lossy. CinePak was originally referred to as Apple Compact Video, but in subsequent revisions has become universally known as CinePak. The Indeo format includes a hardware-assisted version that can be used for digitization in real time from tape, but its real strength is in software playback in limited bandwidth situations, such as from CD-ROMs.

In the "software-only" form, neither are suitable as a master format, and introduce artifacts that degrade quality very quickly over edit generations.

Apple Video and Microsoft Video

These codecs are optimized for a 16-bit color space or an 8-bit grayscale space. They do not record actual colors in a Color Look Up Table (CLUT); they simply record color information as a separate, compressible signal to the luminance signal.

Unlike CinePak and Indeo, these codecs compress video quickly—perhaps only a half second per frame. They can compress video in a 4:1 to 10:1 ratio, and the highest quality settings approach lossless compression—albeit at the expense of bandwidth. If you're working with fast equipment but without the luxury of time or hardware acceleration, then these codecs provide a good compromise.

Both Apple video and Microsoft video work well with Director output when the animation codec cannot achieve the required bandwidth.

Animation

This Animation codec works at all color depths, including the Thousands+ and Millions+ depths, where the plus signs imply alpha or matte channels (also known as linear key signals to the video fraternity). Animation is a lossless compressor, good for archiving computer-generated (rendered) material.

A *matte* is a term held over from the film world. It used to be a picture painted on a sheet of glass, but in terms of digital video, it is the same as an "alpha channel"—a grayscale image "behind" the color image that makes a movie "transparent" in the matte channel's black areas, solid in the matte's white areas, and translucent in the gray areas.

Because it takes a lot of computational power to calculate the transparency, this is not a real-time effect. Yet.

Animation's modest compression is obtained though recording changes in frame—a similar, but more advanced, method to the PICS or FLI formats.

If you're using the Animation codec as a delivery format, then remember that it primarily records the changes between frames. Therefore, to obtain smooth results, a higher frame rate helps more than a slower frame rate—especially if you elect to use the "play every frame" method.

YUV (Component)

Component video is another 24-bit codec. YUV is not intended as a playback codec (without hardware assistance). As an acquisition format, it achieves superior quality with modest compression. More important, it understands the finer points about video—fields as opposed to frames, the 29.97 actual frame rate, and so on. YUV records no composite video artifacts, such as blurring and smearing, from component sources such as Betacam, which results in higher image quality than those based on composite (and even Y/C) video.

This codec is good as a master format and for archival uses. YUV makes an efficient editing format for FSFMV with appropriate hardware, though hardware assisted M-JPEG formats tend to be more popular outside the broadcast industry.

Graphics

Graphics works best in palletized environments (8 bits or less). The Graphics codec is a lossless compressor optimized for quick decompression of run-length encoded graphics.

> As QuickTime develops, keep your ears to the ground, because although Director is one of the most cosmopolitan applications on the market, it likes to offer the balance of features among operating systems. As QuickTime moves into a new phase with QT2.5, and the Mac features such as QuickDraw and the Sound Manager find Windows incarnations, support of the deeper features of QuickTime may surface.

Video Dimensions

Digital Video—especially lossy compressors—are optimized. Another way of putting it is that they assume that certain conditions are met in order to perform "as advertised." They are electronic engines, in that they can hit certain performance harmonics. What does this mean?

The answer is magic. Magic numbers. Throughout this chapter, numerically gifted readers will have noticed a preponderance of numbers that share a common link. These numbers are usually divisible by eight—sometimes by 16, but in almost all circumstances, divisible by four.

Resonant sizes are dependent on pixel depth, and herein lies the magic—and a reason for those "chunky" artifacts seen on heavily compressed digital video movies. A digital video must subscribe to a magic number according to the depth of the monitor it finds its self playing on. Both its size and position on-screen in relation to the top left corner of that screen must be cleanly divisible by that magic number. Cue table 14.2.

Table 14.2

Examples of Optimized Dimensions for Digital Video

Monitor Depth	Magic Number	Examples
4	16	160×120 256×192
8	8	248×186 240×176 (not 240×180!)
16	4	108×456

Interestingly, 240×180—which is known as one of the "common" digital video movies—is a legal size for 16-bit screen, but illegal for 8-bit screen (it is not cleanly divisible by 8), therefore leading to poor performance, such as dropped frames. If you have a movie that measures 240×180 that is likely to end up on an 8-bit screen, then it should be cropped (now) to 240×176. When you lose two pixels from the top and bottom of the video, it makes a big difference!

If in doubt, make 8 your magic number and ensure that both the dimensions of your digital video and the position in relation to the screen are cleanly divisible by it.

Remember, in order to enjoy the benefits of performance gain, both the location (in respect to the monitor, not the stage) and the size of the movie must be cleanly divisible by the magic number.

The magic number rule isn't actually an all-powerful route to digital nirvana, but it can help a great deal when in critical situations such as CD-ROM work. The biggest benefits from using magic numbers are on slower equipment.

Key Frames

Also known as *iFrames* in some codecs and compression systems, a *key frame* is a full-frame image that the codec will works from when deciding what has changed from frame to frame. Key frames are inserted periodically throughout a movie, commonly once a second or every 15 frames.

The importance of key frames can be illustrated in this example. A digital video of an interview shows a standard digital video controller, enabling the user to stop and start the video, and drag the control bar around. But if the codec records the changes between frames, in order to scroll backward, the digital video system would have to scuttle back to the very beginning of the video and track forward to the point selected by the user—a lengthy and messy procedure. By inserting key frames every 15 frames, the playback point is never more than 15 frames away from a full frame from which to work out the image. This saves time and processing power.

Key frames are a central part of most codecs, especially CinePak and Indeo. It is very easy to overlook the check box, as good results are regularly achieved by automatically using one key frame per second, but there is room for experimentation. The more key frames you use, the more stable the movie; the less key frames you use, the better the bandwidth.

Adding too many key frames will push the data rate up (possibly beyond the constraints of a CD-ROM drive) because the gains by delta compression are lost. But in a fast-moving video clip (action, dance, "punk" camerawork, and so forth), delta compression has little to work on. Every frame is pretty much different anyway. In this case, a higher key frame rate—two times a second, or every seven frames if the movie was 15 fps—will help the quality tremendously.

Conversely, using too few key frames (or none at all) will have the disk head hunting for the nearest key frame if it has to drop a frame, often causing it to drop that frame too, and thus the movie falls apart. Also, it makes skipping around in the movie a lengthy process. For short bursts, however, the lack of a big hefty key frame (or a key frame in the wrong place) keeps the data rate very low.

In balance, one key frame a second remains the safest option, but keep these questions in mind:

- Will the video be used with a controller? If not, then you can ease up on the key frames for more bandwidth.
- Will the video be stepped frame by frame in both directions? If so, then you need each frame to be a key frame.
- Will the video run backward? If you want a shuttle effect, then a key frame every second works well.

In these preceding examples, careful use of key frames is essential. Be prepared to experiment!

Controller movies prefer a key frame every 0.5–3 seconds, depending on the kind of movie (fast action means more key frames; head shot means less key frames).

If a movie will run backward (as in a rewind), the key frames are used for showing this. With a 15 fps movie that lasts 20 seconds, jumping from the end to the beginning plays the key frames at about 4 fps, lasting about five seconds. If you wanted the movie to play smoothly backward and forward, then the logical method is to make every frame a key frame. Don't do this! Cheat! Make two movies—the second version being a reversed copy of the normal one that appears to go backward when playing forward. Some Lingo programming and coinciding frame calculation may be required for interactive controlled movies.

Illustrative movies (where the movie will be browsed frame by frame—a slow motion car crash, for example) prefer more key frames—every half second or more.

If there is no sound associated with a movie, switch on "play every frame." If sound is required, synchronize an audio file in RAM (such as a fully imported sound member) to the video by checking the `movieTime` property and using the `puppetSound` command to start the audio on cue.

Playing a QuickTime movie and a spooled sound file (such as an AIFF) is not a good idea—especially on the CD-ROM.

Slideshow movies are a useful way to incorporate a large number of pictures that must be displayed in all color depths. They simply consist of a sequence of pictures, where each picture is in one frame of the movie. QuickTime handles the compression (and, therefore, the speed at which it can be read from the storage device), and dithers the 24-bit image and fits it to the palette in use if the monitor is set to 8 bit or less.

Slideshow movies require 60 frames per second and 60 key frames per second. As Lingo is used to control the movie and Lingo's `movieTime` deals with ticks or units of $1/60$ of a second, one can display still number 417 by setting the `movieTime` of sprite x to 417 and updating the stage.

Additional Tracks

QuickTime 2.5 handles four distinct track types within Director for both Macintosh and Windows 95, identified within Director by the four symbol types `#Video`, `#Audio`, `#Text`, and `#Music` (the latter referring to the MIDI tracks that can access the musical instruments built into the QuickTime mechanism. Prior to 2.5, QuickTime for Windows did not support multiple tracks, MIDI, or text.

Under the MacOS operating system, QuickTime defines a file format that can include a time track with many—not just one of each type, but many—separate items linked to it whether it be video, audio in English, audio in Italian, both, and so on, or 15 different songs on MIDI tracks.

The concept of multiple non-video tracks was part of the original QuickTime 1.0 but has taken time to filter through, due in part to the lack of easy access to tracks other than the video and audio. Because Director 5 now enables this, it is advisable to quickly summarize in the following sections the track types found in QuickTime in the following sections.

Video Tracks

This is the known entity as before. Windows users can access one video track per QuickTime movie. MacOS users, however, can include multiple video tracks and switch between them.

Why should one want more than one video track in a movie? One example is in the simulation of a TV studio with four cameras. The user could cut between cameras stored on separate video tracks and listen to the production talkback while mixing the actors voices with sound effects and music.

QuickTime contains the facilities to store the result as a "dependency" movie, which simply contains pointers to other movies from within its data fork and, therefore, takes up little space.

The new Lingo command `trackEnabled` within Director 5 enables MacOS users to select which video track to use at playback.

Audio Tracks

QuickTime's audio tracks can contain audio data at any sampling rate (11 KHz, 22.05 KHz, 48 KHz, and so on) and compression method (IMA, MACE, and so on). In the MacOS environment, you can selectively switch on or off multiple sound tracks stored within a QuickTime movie. The method is described later in this chapter.

This enables synchronization of multiple audio tracks to a single video track. The user can access these on the fly for multiple language translations of a group discussion, for example. The process of "remixing" a piece of music uses this method. Another, less glamorous use might be multiple descriptions of a single event, such as a road crash.

This requires sound mixing, which is looked after by the Sound Manager on the Macintosh. However, before QT2.5, the Windows platform had access to only one track at a time. This applies to both versions prior to 2.5 QuickTime for Windows and Video for Windows. Director provides multi-channel capability on the PC with the Wavemix library, but this is for sound members rather than audio tracks within a digital video file.

Text Tracks

The traditional role of the text track has been to provide subtitles to pop videos and, with the MIDI track below, karaeoke movies complete with synchronized text highlights. Now that the text track is accessible to the Director user, it can store Lingo data or handlers. By attaching handlers or lists to specific parts of a video, one can react to time-oriented media with tailored data. Because this data is manipulated at the same time as the video, audio and MIDI data, a great deal of control is delegated to the QuickTime mechanics, leaving Director to handle the moment-by-moment interface requirements and ideally increasing responsiveness.

Text tracks have sample points over time, where a string of up to 32 KB of text can be stored. For example, although a paragraph can be stored in one frame, the next frame can be the same thing (and therefore continue the same sample point) or it can contain a full `movieScript`. Or it can contain nothing at all.

To access the text, you can find the next or previous sample point from a given position within a movie—set with the `movieTime` if necessary—with the `trackPreviousSampleTime` and `trackNextSampleTime` properties, respectively.

Tools to build, edit, and create text tracks in QuickTime movies are supplied on the QuickTime SDK, available from the Apple Programmers and Developers Association (APDA). Macintosh users, however, can experiment with text tracks by creating them with SimpleText and MoviePlayer. (See the "Helper Applications" section later in this chapter.)

Music Tracks

The QuickTime "music" track provides an opportunity to provide a sound track supplied in the MIDI format played through either instrument sound samples that come in the QuickTime Musical Instruments extension or special instruments created by the developer. Unlike traditional MIDI solutions, QuickTime's MIDI track does not require hardware—it is a software-only solution.

The main feature of the music track is its minuscule size in comparison to a digitized audio file. MIDI does not record the sound of music. It concentrates on the note-by-note dynamics and passes responsibility of instrument selection to a synthesizer producing the instrument sound. In QuickTime, this is under developer control, too. You can lock the choice of instrument to your specific choice or, with the aid of an

XObject, pass this on to the user, thereby opening up wide opportunities for creativity or abuse!

The QuickTime musical instruments have included a subset of the 128 standard instruments (licensed from Roland, a manufacturer of MIDI keyboards); however, the full General MIDI instrument set is coming in future versions of QuickTime.

Kiosk developers might like to bear in mind that it is possible to create your own "instrument" samples, including properly multi-sampled instruments, all at CD quality if you wish (at the expense of RAM). Alternatively, rather than using the internal synthesizer, QuickTime Music tracks can be switched to function as part of an Open MIDI System (OMS) by connecting to external equipment via a MIDI interface on the serial port. Note that the Director developer is still dealing with a *QuickTime movie*, though!

Originally, the QuickTime Musical Instruments extension contained the MIDI instruments, which could pose problems to developers wishing to provide their own sounds on the user's machine. Instruments can now be stored as part of the QuickTime movie.

Tools for converting Standard MIDI files and for creating instruments are available on the new QuickTime SDK mentioned earlier.

Factors in Effective Compression

This section could be titled "what hurts compression and how to fix it." A recurring word so far has been "optimization." Beyond the technical *delivery* optimization—such as using the correct size, the correct color depth, and the correct codec—thought must be put into the technical origination of material.

In order to obtain the best performance from digital video, certain situations should be avoided. Due to the way many compressors work, defects and artifacts that are present in low-quality originals are emphasized and accentuated rather than glossed over. This means that a digital video movie with poor image quality will also achieve poor performance.

The following conditions are guaranteed to adversely affect performance:

- Noisy video
- Pans and zooms
- Hand-held shots
- Lighting effects
- Video dropouts
- Composite video
- Overoptimistic compression settings
- Wrong compressor
- Fragmented media on disk

Noisy Video

Avoid TV "snow" from poor reception of broadcast material or from electrical interference. Some video cameras are fitted with a "gain" control for poor lighting conditions. When used, this amplifies noise inherent in the camera system. Obscure sources of noise include long wavelength colors (for example, reds). Avoid deep red objects shot on VHS.

Codecs, such as CinePak, work by looking for broad areas of little change and compressing them, while also seeking out areas of high contrast (such as edges) and emphasizing them. Thus, every speck of noise is carefully and faithfully reproduced, which wastes bandwidth and makes the movie hard to compress.

In these circumstances, remember to grab big and apply a gentle Gaussian blur (like the "Despeckle" filter). Before editing continues, try cropping the edges of a video where those smudgy, flickering tracking errors are found, which are painful to digitize with a digital video editing program, such as Premiere.

Pans and Zooms

Though legitimately part of the vocabulary of television, pans and zooms guarantee every pixel is changing from frame to frame unless its against a studio *cyclorama*, a professional-quality backcloth.

On the higher end of the camcorder market, controls are offered for "shutter" speed. Use the slow "shutter" setting—probably indicated for dim light. Alternatively, switch on image stabilization to get a light blur on moving objects (motion blur). This is easier to digitize.

Do it slowly, using plain background if possible. If you must pan, then try to obtain a "fluid head" for your tripod. If you need to zoom, then remember the curse of the camcorder. All users go through what is called the tromboning phase, a cinematic style seen on home movies around the world.

Zoom Lenses: The Curse of the Camcorder.

We've all experienced it. Give somebody a camcorder, and they shoot long shots full of zooms—in and out, and in again, then out again… As well as adversely affecting compression, this adversely affects the viewers, too. This shooting style has been dubbed *tromboning*.

Treat zooms and pans as a special effect. Rather than simply zooming in on a subject, pick up the camera and place it closer to the subject. Where possible, shoot scenes twice from two angles rather than dart back and forth.

An example is the ad hoc interview. It is tempting to start your shot tight on the interviewer for the introduction, zoom out to show the interviewee, and then zoom in to the interviewee. Then if the interviewer asks a new question, you do a quick pan (possibly a sneaky zoom out) to catch it. It looks dreadful!

Instead, shoot the interview first, keeping on the subject. Then when the interview is over, shoot your "establishing shot"—the interviewee will be more relaxed now that its over. With the subject free to go, the interviewer can now repeat the questions into thin air for the benefit of the camera. Remember to include "reaction shots"—also known as "noddies," for obvious reasons—as these shots can be used to cover a multitude of sins (or simply to chop an overlong answer).

Hand-Held Shots

Hand-held shots should be justified. If you can't use a tripod, can you use a monopod? Is there any way of supporting the camera steadily? The reason is that digital video performance is degraded by hand-held shots. Each movement is like a mini-pan.

Use image stabilization if your camera has this feature. If not, lean against a wall. Steady the camera on a sturdy object. It helps to rest the camcorder on a small cushion or beanbag both to protect the camera and to help you align it.

Alternatively, consider begging or borrowing a SteadyCam!

You can emulate a SteadyCam in an emergency. Mount a camcorder onto a photographic tripod. Keep the legs folded up and fully extend the center post. Grasp the tripod under the pan and tilt head and hold it away from your body with your elbow bent. Try to keep it steady, but resist the temptation to tuck your elbow into your body. It is very tiring and you could develop some interesting muscles, but the results are surprisingly good.

Lighting Effects

Moving lights cast moving shadows. These might affect the whole image between frames, making it difficult to compress. Contrast lighting can aggravate things—lots of edges for CinePak to investigate. This slows compression, too. Fluorescent lights (strip lights) pulse with the alternating current. This means that you might experience *beating*, where the lights appear to fade up and down every second or so.

Flashes—from photographers' cameras, or lightning, for example—create two large jumps between frames—from standard to bright, and then from bright to standard. Double trouble from the compression viewpoint.

Video Dropouts

This can be as bad as noise. *Dropouts* are big blips on the screen that are caused by bits of magnetic stuff literally "dropping out"—or off—the tape. Like flashes, dropouts present double trouble as their entry and exit are recorded, plus the edge accentuation of a lossy compressor. The playback of a digital video containing a "carefully digitized" dropout may balk, causing dropped frames or a gap in sound. Due to the interleaving of sound and video, something has to give.

How much use is too much use for video tapes? Tapes that contain more than a dozen plays or tapes that are used in many different machines should probably be left on the shelf. The better the condition of your tape, the less likely it is for your tape to experience dropouts.

Composite Video

Composite video is always difficult because of the natural behavior of intense colors—especially reds—and the strange color effects caused by regular patterns of dark and light, known as *cross color* or *strobing*. If you can obtain a Y/C output (also known as S-VHS), then it will help remove some—but not all—of these artifacts.

One magic box that you should consider is the TimeBase Corrector (TBC). Although it can appear to be an expensive luxury (costing more than a Camcorder), it dramatically improves the quality of your video source by acting as a "laundry" to the video coming in from the tape before dispatching it neatly ironed to your digitization hardware. Although the full use of TBCs cannot be covered in this chapter, it will earn its keep in a busy studio.

Overoptimistic Compression Settings

Asking a movie compressor to compress a full-screen, full-motion video of hand-held VHS footage to 150 KB per second will take a long time, and will probably have the compressor drop most of your frames in order to compress it to the specified data rate.

The Wrong Compressor

In this chapter, it has been recommended to work with material in a high-quality format from acquisition all the way through to the production process. Comparable to a 24-bit stock photo image, it is big and unwieldy, but all the information it contains is required. The picture will be converted to a useable format at the last step of the delivery stage.

However, using CinePak during the editing process or Graphics on a photograph will not render good results, no matter how carefully the previous steps were taken.

Fragmented Media on Disk

Although not strictly a compression problem, the effects of fragmented media on disk can look very similar.

When a file is stored on a disk, it doesn't necessarily get stored in a contiguous line of bits (like a track on a record). The filing system of the computer often splits the file up into little bits so that it can fit a big file into lots of little holes. When the computer needs to read in the file, it consults a directory on the disk that contains a list of the physical location of the fragments of the file and reads them back in the correct order. The file is *fragmented*.

Digital video files are extremely sensitive to file fragmentation during playback. Time taken by the disk to consult the directory to find the next fragment is time *not* spent on reading and decompressing the video—resulting in dropped frames. When coupled with poor-quality material or optimistic compression settings, the movie may simply "die." The movie will appear to stop playing back as the time taken to catch up extends beyond the time left to play.

File fragmentation should not be confused with media prioritization. Media prioritization is concerned with the physical location of files on a disk. This is also extremely important for CD-ROM work.

Sources

It's all very well knowing the technicalities of your digital video delivery mechanism, but just what do you show? Where does all this stuff come from?

You easily can create your own digital video with Director. Remember that way back before QuickTime, Director—known then as VideoWorks—started life as an animation tool, creating movie files for applications such as HyperCard.

The main sources of digital video include (in rough order of cost)

- Director movies
- Clipmedia
- Video tape you shoot yourself
- Library material
- Video tape shot for you
- Broadcast material

Note that "video tape you shoot yourself" could mean using anything from a camcorder to a fully equipped, outside-broadcast truck.

Director Movies

As has been mentioned before, Macromedia Director is an excellent tool for creating animation-orientated digital video content. The frame-based metaphor and the superb control of sprites enable careful and structured composition of digital video movies.

In order to create successful digital video files from your Director movies, consider the limitations and methods of digital video. Unlike Director's "movie loops," digital video members tend to be constrained to a rectangular area. If you want your animation to occur on your Director background, then you must pre-matte the animation onto the designated area of the background in a separate application such as Premiere. This method is described later in the chapter.

Recording It Yourself

The "do-it-yourself" attitude is a grand subject. It can cover activities from the recording of a simple "hello world" voiceover with a computer's built-in microphone to a three-month shoot on 35 mm cine film, complete with a cast of thousands. Most people settle on the happy medium of a high-end consumer (increasingly known as "prosumer") Hi-8 or S-VHS camcorder complete with image stabilization and S-Video connectors. If budget or status allows, then Betacam equipment assures a significant boost in the quality of the end product (at the expense of expense). Conversely, the use of VHS equipment saves cash, but generously contributes to the time and trouble bills.

Aside from the mere technical considerations, remember that by writing, producing, and shooting your own content, you can bypass a great deal of hassle and expense over negotiations with asset providers and buying of rights to existing material. You might find yourself in the enviable position of being a content provider or "asset owner" yourself.

If you plan on using your own content, then the primary objective is to create material with the highest quality possible. As before, content quality is up to you. You can use a checklist approach for technical quality.

Assuming that your assets will be from real life, shoot on the highest quality format possible. If you don't use D1, then use BetaCam. If not Betacam, then C format one-inch tape. If not one-inch, then Hi-band U-Matic. If not Hi-band Umatic, then Hi-8. If not Hi-8, then S-VHS. If not S-VHS, then Video-8. If not Video-8, then buy a Video-8 deck rather than sink to VHS.

If you really must use VHS, then at least ensure that your VHS equipment is clean and the machine is newish and well cared for.

One-inch tape and U-Matic are falling into disuse with the new digital tape formats. D4 and the new Digital Cassette video systems are taking the higher end.

When shooting your own material, remember to check your legal position. Ensure that you obtain the correct permissions when shooting testimonials or *vox-pops*.

Vox-pops (short for vox populii—"the voice of the people") commonly involve popping down to the local mall and shoving a microphone under the nose of a member of the public in order to obtain an opinion. Talk to the mall folks first. Ensure all your interviewees know what the shoot is for and that you get their permission.

Obtaining Video from Elsewhere

When buying material, there are two major categories. These categories tend to represent the two extremes of the cost scale.

- Clipmedia (like clip art)
- Pre-existing material (such as TV shows and library material)

Clipmedia material is created with the express purpose of being used over and over again. Often this material is offered as "royalty-free" (note this does not mean "copyright free"), in that once you have purchased the material, you may use it in any manner you choose, usually with the exception of inclusion into a similar clipmedia product.

As with all clip material, the content is likely to be generic, designed for use on low-end machines, and the contents follow set themes. Unlike PostScript clip art, however, it will usually be provided "as is," with little scope for customization. What you see is what you get, and if what you get is not quite right, it can be frustrating if not downright impossible to edit. Often, the price of clipmedia is in not getting what you wanted.

However, clipmedia is one of the cheapest forms of obtaining digital video and often can provide material that would not be cost effective to use any other way. An example is Apple's QuickClips. QuickClips includes comic bursts of 1950s information films and B movies to create what can only be described as "video punctuation marks."

QuickClips does not, however, include the original "I'll be back" clip, nor anything in that genre. If you really want to use a famous clip of film, you have no other choice than to obtain the right to use existing footage.

Licensing pre-existing material involves expense, which may be considerable in the example of licensing a famous film clip. Furthermore, artists' contracts might mean that you need their permission in addition to the owner's permission.

On one hand, the right to use a clip of a commercial might be given for free of charge. If, however, the content is likely to add credence to your project, work with a lawyer and a negotiator. Talk to agents.

A golden rule is to never start using uncleared material and then seek clearance. Get clearance first for a better bargaining position. Obtaining clearance is the most difficult, fraught, expensive method of obtaining digital video assets, but you get exactly what you want and it could very well be central to the success of your project.

Unlike clipmedia, licensed material is rarely supplied predigitized, and although a choice of formats may be offered, AVI or QuickTime tends to not be one of them. Remember to budget for digitization on top of licensing costs. The benefit of doing your own digitization of licensed material is that you are in control of the quality. If you used the "Really, what was it?" clip from Apple's QuickClips, then you are limited to its 160×120 size and 8-bit sound. This was leading edge three years ago but is impractical today. If you had digitized it yourself (after having negotiated with the film's publishers), then you would be able to use the full-screen version and IMA 16-bit sound available today.

Techniques

Having decided to create your own material, what can you do to ensure a smooth-running, high-quality digital video movie? The answer depends on what kind of material you wish to use: traditional video (existing footage); the vox-pop or testimonial style video (usually an interview scene); a presenter or studio shoot; or computer-generated material—from 3D software or from Director itself.

Live Footage and Testimonials

The majority of material in this category can be labeled as the "Talking Head." Like most broad terms, it includes everything from the established professional presenter to the impromptu interview with, for example, mom coming out of the store with the kids in tow. There are two sides to this material: the technical and the content. Content is subjective, and is not covered here. For a quick guide in generating digitally friendly video, check the following:

- Use a tripod. Tripods need to be heavy. Make a tripod heavy by hanging your kit bag from the center post. If you want to raise the camera, try to use the leg extensions rather than the center post.
- When shooting a predominantly vertical shot (like a talking head), then turn the video camera on its side as you would a stills camera. Yes, this seems very silly to start with, but remember that you can rotate it in your video editing package later.
- Watch for distracting backgrounds. Backgrounds can be detailed, but should not move if compression is an issue (as it usually is). Beware of trees on windy days, as well as busy streets.

Although this chapter is not about the techniques of shooting video, the following list includes a few more pointers:

- If the subject isn't a seasoned presenter, he will not be comfortable looking directly into camera. Have the subject talk to someone to the left or right of the camera to avoid the "furtive, darting eyes" of someone trying to remember what comes next. Frame the shot so that the nose is centered and just a bit higher than the middle of the screen. On the Director stage, if the head is looking to your left, then place the movie to your right, giving your subject space to "look into."
- Remember that videotape is cheap. Shoot everything and shoot it well. You will not be digitizing all of it. Sometimes, those "by-the-way" comments are just what you want—even if they're wanted in a completely different section. Or project.
- By keeping the tape rolling, you can often get a far better performance from a subject who isn't used to the shiny end of a camera. Shouting "cut" might be good therapy for the director, but leads to more takes than doing a "keep-going" smile of encouragement. Factual presentations now use the "American Cut"—a quick mix that is the video representation of ellipses (...).

Color Separation Overlay (ChromaKey)

Color separation overlay (also known as ChromaKey) used to be the province of television studios and film special effects departments, but now is a feature in $400 digital video editing applications such as Premiere. Color Separation Overlay (CSO) is the generic name for the ubiquitous "blue-screen" method, but many know it by a brand name—ChromaKey. (There are others, including "Ultimatte" and "Digimatte."). However, the basic procedure of replacing a background color with another image source is the process of CSO.

CSO solves a lot of scenic problems and it is an established technique for a wide variety of situations—from flying superheroes to simply combining live action with computer graphics. This latter category is of most interest to the Director user—be it for weather maps or dramatic effect.

There is slightly more to good CSO than some blue paper tacked to a wall.

The trick is in even lighting—and lots of it. For this, you'll need space. Good ventilation makes for a happy working environment, because the number of lights used generate a lot of heat.

At least two lights are required for the background alone—probably four (see fig. 14.2). Using blue paper tends to be trickier to light than blue felt, because paper is in fact quite shiny and picks up highlights. Note that if you use felt, it is a very good idea to use the flame-retardant or flame-proof material.

Check for "hot spots" (abnormally bright areas) on the backdrop. Although a light meter is customary in these circumstances, you can sometimes get away with a squint test.

Place your subject so that the distance between it and the background is twice the distance between the camera and the subject. The real intention is to keep the subject as far away from the background as possible.

Due to the amount of light shining onto the background, some of the light will bounce back, illuminating the subject with a blue wash of light. Consequently, this causes horrible fuzzy edges where the CSO "half works." To make doubly sure that no blue light spills onto the subject, pour more light onto the back of the subject—this is known as a *backlight*—and then balance your subject's "key" and "fill" lights accordingly, watching for shadows on the background.

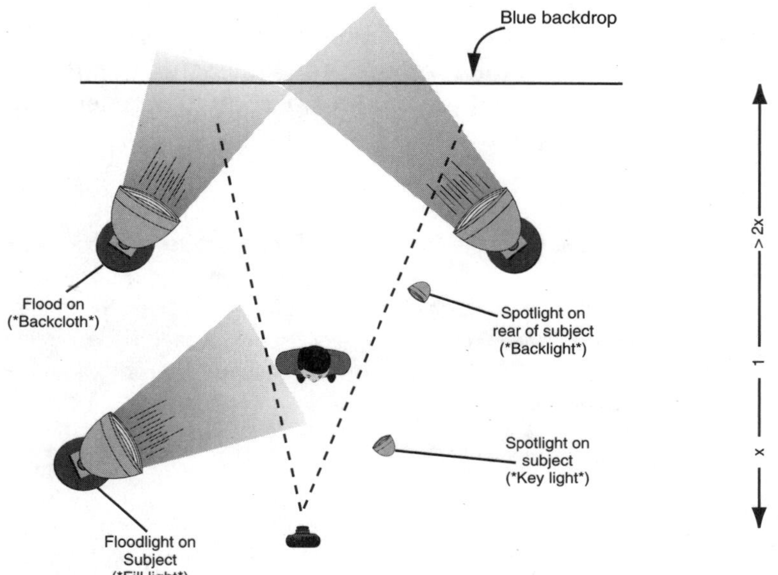

Figure 14.2

A CSO lighting plan.

It's handy to have your video digitizing computer wired to the camera to preview results. It also helps to check the background for hot spots by grabbing just the background, and use the Equalize command in an application such as Photoshop to show where the hot spots—and "black holes"—are located.

Blue creates the sharpest outline with composite video equipment. (Blue uses a higher frequency than red or yellow and, therefore, achieves better resolution). Blue is the most common choice because it is an "alien" color that contrasts well with all types of skin and hair color, but it is not the only color for CSO. Green is another good choice, because blue is a popular clothing color.

Animation

Working with animation-based digital video is a lot less time-consuming than working with analog video. By definition, such material is generated digitally, and the content does not suffer from any "pollution," such as noise from tape or artifacts from conversion to digital. Animation is "cosmetically perfect," so to speak. Animation raises the threshold of what is achievable in terms of frame rate and the area that a digital video can occupy on stage.

Although 320×240 at 12 fps is a theoretical limit for video via a double-speed CD-ROM in a home computer, the same setup might be able to achieve 20 fps at 320×320 by using a clean, computer-generated source untouched by analog dirt.

Digital video is not restricted to the 4:3 ratio of your television screen or monitor. A 640×120 movie contains the same amount of pixels as a 320×240 movie, therefore giving the appearance of full-screen animation. For an example, check out the "Pond" presentation on the accompanying CD-ROM. This movie is discussed in detail with other examples of digital video in Director later in this chapter.

Tools

This section briefly covers digitization hardware. Basic software tools are outlined that are required for digital video in the wider sense. When working with Director, however, some applications change slightly in their approach. The section titled "Helper Applications" explains the specific changes of focus of the following groups of software.

Digitizing Hardware

The Macintosh digitizing hardware comes in two varieties: built-in (as in the AV class machines) and third-party digitization cards.

Built-In Video

The AV class Macs, starting with the Quadra 840 AV and Centris 660 AV, have video and audio digitization built in to the hardware. Both composite and S-Video inputs are provided, and are able to cope with digitizing a 240×180 window at 12–15 fps with the built-in disk drive.

With clean material and a lean system folder, 320×240 can be achieved, but should not be relied upon.

The Power Macintosh AV systems can cope with larger window sizes, but FSFMV is still difficult to digitize.

An AV Macintosh can overlay graphics onto a video signal with the monitor set to 8 bits. A 640×480 monitor works best. Connect a video source to the Mac.

In the finder, launch Director. Switch back to the finder from the Application menu. Now launch either the Apple Video Player or Video Monitor application, and select the "large" size or full screen option. You should see your video playing. Switch back to Director.

Set the stage to the darkest green of the system palette via the Movie Properties dialog box.

You should now see your video playing on the stage. If it freezes, switch from Director to the Video Player and back again. The video freezes are due to Director drawing windows. Once in playback mode, it plays normally.

Digitization Cards

If you want to digitize video that fills the screen, at more than 12 fps, it is best to get a specialized card to do so.

There are digitization cards to suit every budget—from the entry level (but very effective) Video Spigot to the broadcast-quality VideoVision Telecast from Radius and the specialist Video Explorer.

A low-end card will cost about the same as a camcorder. High-end cards are in the family car budget. With both solutions, a very large hard disk is obligatory. When working with video hardware, use AV class or "non-thermo resetting" hard disks. Ordinary disks take a rest from their usual chores occasionally and recalibrate themselves. If you happen to be recording video at that time, the effect is disastrous. AV drives do not need recalibration.

If your demands are for broadcast quality, then an AV drive is not enough. You need a RAID (Redundant Array of Inexpensive Disks). Two hard disks (sometimes four) are controlled by a special card so that they work as one unit. This enables data to be written at a sustained 10 MB per second or more.

If you need to back up the raw digitized material, the only cost-effective way is to budget for a DAT drive, too.

Digitizing Software

Digitizing boards usually come with their own software or a limited version of commercial software that has been customized to their product. Computers with built-in video digitization facilities also come with a simple application to grab video.

These applications tend to have just one job in mind—to get video into your system. Functions such as editing and fine control over compression are not addressed.

Digitization software should offer a flexible frame rate, a flexible size of movie, a choice of sampling rates for audio, and the capability to record directly to disk or RAM and compress afterward (for a better frame rate). Some control over brightness and contrast is offered at this stage, but this is where a TBC comes in handy.

Think of this software as the equivalent of a scanner plug-in. Rather than devote processor power and RAM to fancy functions, you want to devote it to just one job: getting the video, the whole video, and nothing but the video.

> Don't forget audio. Sound engineers in the TV industry are often aware that video gets proportionately more attention than the audio.

Some board manufacturers create their software (or versions of their software) that work as a plug-in with applications such as Adobe Premiere.

Editing Software

Three broad categories of editing software are available: those suited to mixing traditional "analog" footage, such as Premiere; those that are oriented to composting digitally created material, such as After Effects; a catch-all "special effects" group that includes filter sets, such as Boris Effects; and transitions, such as Morph.

The first category blends metaphors of film editing, which has a useful graphic feel to it, with the terminology of video editing, which has historically been abstract. Such software also tends to offer "asset management"—because the number of clips can get large in a full edit—and tends to concentrate on longer sequences at the expense of layering control. These applications are happier putting together a 10-minute interview rather than a 10-second promo sting.

If your requirements are to matte a ray-traced 3D animation over a sequence of stills with a feathered drop shadow, then the editing moves beyond assembly into the realm of *compositing*, which is the domain of applications such as After Effects.

Features to be found in a compositing application are similar to a paint application on one hand—high-quality interpolation of pixels (in scaling and rotation operations) and exemplary anti-aliasing throughout the many layers of graphics. On the other hand, the features are similar to Director—layer control, trajectory control over time, tweening, and so on.

The major difference between applications such as After Effects and Director is that After Effects is not a real-time application. The movies it creates require rendering in addition to the compression stage.

The third category of editing applications covers the world of effects packages—some of which blur the line between application and plug-in, such as Boris Effects. Others, such as Morph, resolutely remain a one-trick pony—be it ever such a good trick.

Morphing software has thrown off its "flavor of the month" mantle, but it should still be a part of your tool kit. Morphing can be used for tricks such as color replacement, creating a non-looping sequence loop such as clouds, water, or flags. It helps 2D animation break into 3D—for example, sliding a face from profile to full face. It also continues to morph and caricature, of course (no longer a "special" effect!).

Utilities

The best source of QuickTime-oriented utilities is the QuickTime SDK. The SDK contains applets to perform tricks such as adding text tracks from documents, burning text onto the screen, converting MIDI files, setting copyright information, and so on. Buried deep in the CD are special "cleaning" applications that ensure your movies have the right number of key frames and that the poster frame is set correctly. Many of these applications are also available—at no cost—on the seeding and beta disks available to Apple developers. Some also are available via the Internet. The SDK, however, comes with full documentation, whereas the developer disk and Internet versions are "unsupported."

Handling Digital Video in Director

Digital video is a resource-hungry media, as is Director. It is remarkable how the two get along so well, considering that both are busily doing low-level stuff with the screen, each with strict adherence to their own, sometimes conflicting, time bases.

Planning a Movie within a Movie

The single biggest constraint in the use of digital video is the target playback platform. It is possible to achieve full-screen, full-motion video within a Power Macintosh computer or a Windows machine with an MPEG card of the correct type correctly installed. But unless you can guarantee these conditions, your authoring platform is likely to be far more powerful than the playback platform.

When planning your use of digital video, set a target platform and adhere to it strictly. Whenever possible, use a representative of your target platform and keep it available at all times, remembering the Director user's mantra of "Test Early, Test Often."

TETO, or the "Test Early Test Often" mantra, was first coined, I believe, by John Dowdell of Macromedia. It really should, in my humble opinion, be adopted as a chant over those Tibetan bells in the Director Access application, punctuated by the thwacking sound of heads against desks.

Examples

The following three examples refer to projects that are on the CD-ROM that came with this book. The projects are in the Chapter 14 folder. It is a good idea to check out the projects first.

Pond deals with simple control of digital video via Lingo. Ellipse describes the process of "matting" a digital video onto a background, and the final example explores the text track.

Pond—Controlling Digital Video with Lingo

Pond is a presentation template that depicts a water and pearl motif, where each presentation slide is punctuated with a rising pearl that hovers throughout the slide's duration as water ripples beneath it.

The animation, created in Specular Infini-D, comprises 45 frames of animation in a single movie measuring 480×128 pixels. The animation is divided into three parts: 15 frames of rising pearl, 15 frames of floating pearl, and 15 frames of exiting pearl. The ripples on the pond are synchronized with these three stages, and if frame accuracy is achieved, the animation should appear seamless.

Clearly, if each frame were imported into Director, complex frame handling would be required to achieve the seamless transition among the three states. More than 2 MB of RAM would be needed just for the strap, and the a slice of the available computing power would be devoted to just that task. As it stands, this movie will plays in an 030 class machine in a default projector's RAM allocation.

The Score contains three simple Lingo handlers to perform the following three tasks as follows:

- Between slides, the digital movie is allowed to run freely. We give it enough time to display at least 16 frames of the video.

  As a slide builds up and text appears, the first script checks the `movieTime` of the pearl video, and "catches" the pearl at the top of the screen and holds it there by "opening" the movie into frames 16–30, and whilst there, keeping it there.

- The second script performs a similar function but allows time for a mouse or key event to interrupt and move the playback head onward.

- The third script enables the movie to escape from the 16–30 loop and into frames 31–45, but as soon as the loop is exited, the handler lets the Score take over and the movie "runs free" until the playback head hits the next build-up.

The entire process can be bound up into one large Lingo handler, but this template was originally designed for use by Director users with little or no Lingo experience.

The QuickTime video in this example was originally saved in the QuickTime animation format set at 24 bits at the highest quality. In order to achieve the required bandwidth to play back on a humble Windows machine, it was compressed using CinePak at a quality and spatial setting of three.

Ellipse—Matting a Digital Video member

In this example, we will be using Premiere to composite a video onto a background from a director project.

Sample files are provided in the Ellipse folder inside the Chapter 14 folder of the accompanying CD-ROM. As well as the finished movie and digital video file, the original rendered animation with a matte channel is included in the subfolder.

The requirement is to place a rendered animation (in this case, a spinning globe) created in Infini-D at a size of 240×176 onto a full-screen background. The problem is that the animated globe is rendered with a matte (or alpha) channel. We want the globe to sit cleanly on the sky background, cut out from its current black background using the matte. The animation should be centered horizontally and in the upper part of the screen.

A third application is required, capable of using the matte channel to composite the globe on the background. In addition, we need a portion of the background where the digital video sits.

We need pixel accuracy in order to get the final composite video sprite to seamlessly superimpose on the Director background. It helps to have a calculator and some aspirin ready. Before the process begins, calculate the location and dimensions of the final digital video.

The coordinates you want to refer to are in the top left corner of your digital video in relation to the the stage. These coordinates shall be X and Y.

The movie you want to matte measures 240 pixels horizontally and 176 pixels vertically. These shall be known as X1 and Y1.

The stage measures 640×480, which shall be known as X2 and Y2 (see fig. 14.3). Therefore:

X=((X2-X1)÷2), Y=(Y2÷2)-((Y2÷2)-Y1)

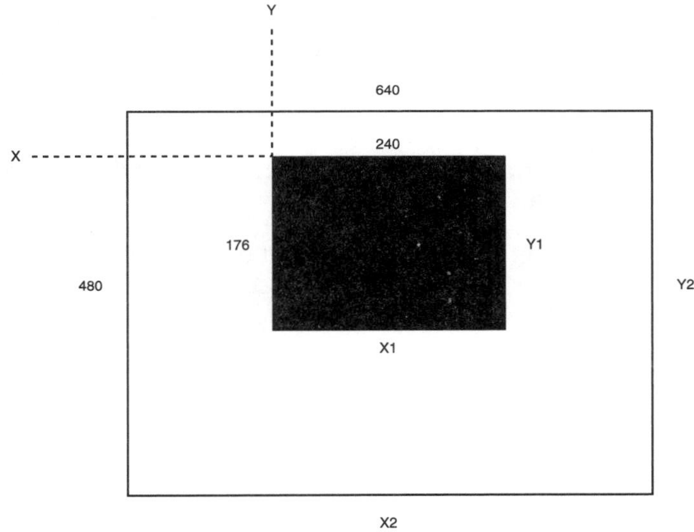

Figure 14.3

Diagrams are better than equations.

You need to isolate the portion of the background between X & Y and X1 & Y1 (which is the area between the stage coordinates 200, 64 and 440, 240). As you can see, catch-all equations are tempting to suggest, but diagrams and doodles are a great help in sorting out the relationships between numbers!

1. In Director, select all the items in the frame you want the digital video movie to sit on top of, and use the tweak window to dial in a negative value of X & Y. That means moving everything up 64 pixels (–64) and to the left by 200 pixels (–200).
2. Now set the stage size of your Director movie to that of the digital video (in this case, 240×176). This has isolated the exact area that is covered by the digital video movie.
3. Choose Export from the File menu and choose This Frame as PICT.
4. You can now quit Director and launch your video editing application, such as Premiere.
5. In Premiere, set the Project size and output movie to that of your render. In this case, the size is 240×176 which is probably not in the list of predefined project sizes.
6. Import the exported portion of background and the QuickTime movie.
7. Matte the movie over the background by placing the background in Channel A and the animation in the overlay channel. Drag the background end point to match the animation.
8. Select the animation and choose Transparency from the Effects menu. In this case, the movie has an Alpha channel, so choose this option from the pop-up menu and click on the OK button.
9. You now can make a movie by choosing Make Movie from the Make menu. Choose the following options: Whole movie, QuickTime Movie, with the compression settings set to Apple Video with a Quality of "50" at 15 fps and a key frame every 15 frames.
10. Press the Option key while dragging the Quality slider to set the Temporal quality (the delta change settings—how much needs to change in order to register it). Use a spatial setting of 75 (see fig. 14.4).

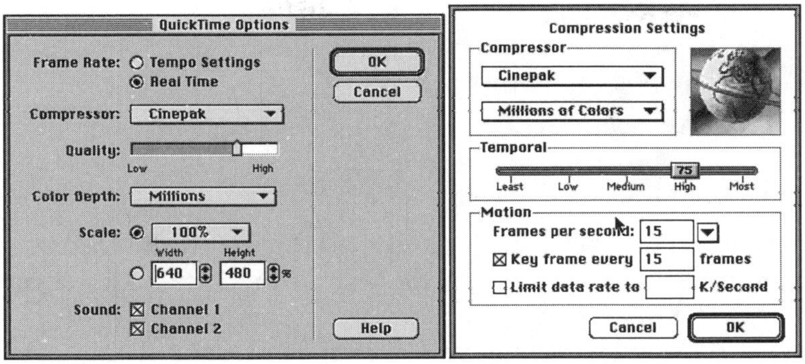

Figure 14.4

Temporal compression settings are not accessible in Director 5.

Note that the control over temporal settings can be accessed only when the key frame option is checked. Also, notice that the Director QuickTime Options dialog box does not have this control. To compress a Director movie with a lossy codec, export it from Director using the Animation codec and recompress in Premiere or a compression utility such as Apple's ConvertToMoov.

11. After you set the compression settings and the format, select a location and a name for the movie. A sensible location is in the same folder as your Director movie.
12. When this is complete, quit Premiere and relaunch Director with the movie you require the digital video animation on.
13. Import the movie by choosing Import from the File menu or pressing Command+R. Choose Digital Video from the pop-up menu. Locate your newly created digital video file from the standard file dialog box.
14. In the Cast window, select the Digital Video member, and click on the "information" button to set the attributes of the digital video.

    For best results and the highest performance for this kind of member, choose Direct to stage, Loop, and Play Every Frame. Switch off the Sound property because this movie does not use sound.
15. In the Score window, locate the frame in which you wish the animation to appear. From the Cast window, drag the digital video onto the stage.

16. Position the movie by using the Sprite Properties dialog box (Control-click the digital video and choose Sprite Properties from the pop-up menu).
17. Enter the X & Y coordinates (in this case `200` and `64`) and press Return. The digital video sprite is now positioned correctly, ensuring that the "magic numbers" are used.

An important point to keep in mind is that animation is sensitive to the area of movement—full-screen movement in digital video should be avoided. The worst case for a codec, for example, is four small sprites that chase around the edges of the screen. Here, delta change compression would render every frame entirely different. Sprite-based animation, such as the Director Score-based animation, is much more effective. Digital video can help out, but it isn't a universal panacea.

Micons: Using Director to Create a Composite Digital Video

This example demonstrates the use of Director to create a digital video for use within a different Director movie to reduce complexity of the Score and increase performance. It also demonstrates the loading of small digital video files into RAM so that several can play simultaneously.

> The term micon, or *motion icon*, was coined in 1989 by its inventor, Hans Peter Brøndmo. *Micons* are little, self-contained animations that represent an object or concept much as a traditional icon does. In fact, due to their ubiquity, many people group this class of interface elements into the generic "button" category.

Micons are captivating items, bringing life to otherwise static choice screens and providing encouragement to interaction. However, Micons pose an interesting challenge for the Director developer.

Consider the screenshot of the "micon" example on the disk shown in figure 14.5. This is from a typical kiosk application, designed to run from a hard disk in relatively cheap equipment. If you wish to try the example supplied, then please copy the "micon" folder from the accompanying CD-ROM to your hard disk first, and be sure to set your monitor to thousands of colors. Note that this movie is used as an illustration only, so the buttons will not work.

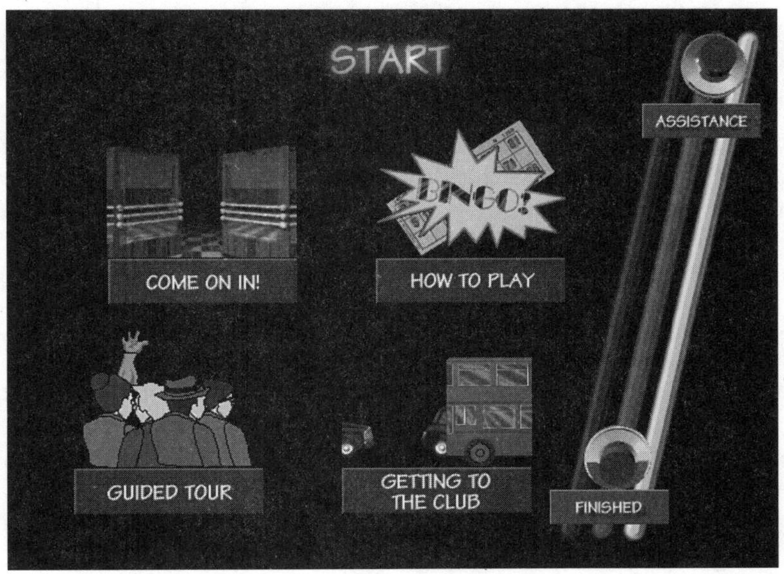

Figure 14.5
Multiple digital video members on stage.

Four distinct animations are built from a combination of traditional Director (sprite) animation and 3D animation. If it were done with bitmap sprites, then each member would need to be present in RAM for every frame of all the animations. This applies to animation in the Score, in a movie loop, or as a Director movie imported into the cast. In this case, using digital video helps performance a great deal.

Each micon was created separately in Director from original material from a diverse set of applications. For example, the bus was drawn in Deneba Canvas and colorized in Director. The taxi was drawn by hand in Photoshop, where the vibrations were added with the Wave filter.

For each micon, the digital video size is established by setting the stage size to 160×120, which offers a good balance between size and performance. When the design is complete, the movie is exported using the Animation codec and brought into the main movie as a digital video member.

Note the way in which each micon has a different duration. The animations slip in and out of synchronization with each other, obscuring the loop points. To do this by manual Score animation is virtually impossible—and is "a challenge" to do with Lingo if the performance hit of up to 48 puppetSprites and their control is acceptable. It is possible to import one director movie into another, but in these circumstances, it would add to the already complex matting going on, further degrading performance.

The endless and overwhelming complexity of managing numerous animation channels is reduced at a stroke to a single frame containing four sprites in it. The Lingo programmer needs only to look after button handling and branching options; the digital video looks after the animation.

Of course, it's not quite that simple. First, the micons are set to play every frame—Director will never drop a frame, thus loosing any synchronizing between the micons. Second, due in part to their small size and looped nature, the digital video micons will—when memory permits—load into RAM. This is very important. Third, the micons all want to spool off disk at the same time.

The first "pass" will be slow as each frame of each digital video is loaded into RAM. Performance improves thereafter. It is inappropriate to load digital video files greater than 1 MB into RAM.

Turn your attention to the case of the physical location of your digital video assets on your disk, mentioned earlier. In the case of playing four QuickTime movies simultaneously from disk, the files should be positioned close together. When playing from RAM, there is no longer a problem, but the *first* pass is from disk, where media prioritization helps a great deal.

Most disks and CD-ROM drives have caches and "read-ahead" buffers. These items are of use to kiosk developers, who have direct control over the playback platform. A correctly sized cache also can help unnecessary trips for the read head back to directory tables in the center of the disk to pick up the next location point.

Importing and Exporting Digital Video Members

Due to the relatively large size of digital video, all digital video members are imported into Director as a linked member. This means that the digital video remains external to your Director movie.

Remember that with linked assets such as pictures, sounds, and digital video, the Director movie refers to that asset with nothing more than a path name. In order to ensure proper operation of linked members consider the following:

- Ensure that you include all linked assets in addition to your projector, as well as Director movies if not built into the projector.
- Try to keep the same hierarchy when you move the completed project to another part of a hard disk or another disk entirely. This is part of asset management, but there is plenty of room to trip up.
- If your projector, director files, and digital video movies all reside in one folder, then the hierarchy is very simple to achieve. If, however, your digital video movies are kept on another disk from the Director files that call to them, care must be taken in planning the hierarchy. Consider, for example, a presentation stored on a hard disk that also uses video material stored on CD-ROM. Planning the hierarchy frequently requires the use of full path names and scanning connected drives.
- When protecting movies (converting from a DIR format to the impenetrable DXR format), Director does a final check of the internally held path names to your digital video. Beware. This very helpful trick has a very nasty sting to it. Although this is covered in the manuals, it should be reiterated.

When protecting movies, note their location and then move the DIR files that need to be converted *out* of their hierarchy. Select the destination in the Protect Movies dialog as being the place the movies originally came from. Do not, under any circumstances, do the human thing of sending the protected movies somewhere else and then manually move them back. All connections to your linked assets will be broken.

In fact, a Macintosh projector will probably survive the broken links. A Windows projector, on the other hand, will display dialog boxes asking for the location of your linked files. Remember to move your movies out of the hierachy and "protect" them back in again. The Director online community hears of this disaster about once a month. You have been warned.

Color Depth

As described earlier in this chapter, most of the Digital Video codecs are designed to work in higher color depths (thousands of colors), whereas others are designed for paletted environments (256 colors or 8 bit). At this point, the Director community can take a deep breath because Director's handling of digital video has significantly eased the nasty hairy problems associated with palettes and CLUTs.

From the introduction of Director 5, the use of 16-bit and 24-bit stages is no longer the exclusive realm of the Macintosh community. Director 5 opened high color depth to the world of Windows, thus removing the biggest source of anguish at a stroke. Due to the current specifications of the typical end-user system, a lot of development is still carried out assuming an 8-bit screen.

Codecs such as CinePak, Microsoft Video 1, Apple Video, and Indeo are all optimized for a 16-bit environment. If writing to an 8-bit display, the digital video system software performs on the fly, dithering to the palette currently assigned the stage, at the expense of the performance degradation. This is due to the extra "dither" processing required. (Any palette stored in the digital video member is *disregarded* by Director.)

Common Problems

Some common problems with digital video in Director include disappointing performance, a certain dogged persistence of movies, and a few tears caused when transporting digital video from Macintosh to Windows.

Logically, there has to be a slight difference in the maximum performance between a digital video movie playing in a simple player application and the same movie playing from within Director—even with it's Direct To Stage option set—because there are simply more things going on at the time when in Director. The difference usually means that your digital video movies are sailing too close to the limits of the technology. Although the CD-ROM drive imposes a limit on transferring material, another slice of the processor's time must be devoted to uncompressing and displaying that material, and that time must be obtained with your projector or Director itself contending for the processor's attention. As mentioned earlier in this section, playing 24-bit digital video in an 8-bit environment requires an extra computational process and more RAM in which to perform it.

The first step in curing performance ills is to check magic numbers (see table 14.2 earlier in this chapter). It is likely that the position of the digital video on stage may need to be altered or that the movie itself does not conform to the magic number rule. If both these conditions are met, then the solution in these circumstances is to recompress the movie with slightly more pessimistic settings, or investigate workarounds, such as cropping the movie slightly.

Testing early and testing often shows one artifact of using digital video that can phase the uninitiated: persistence, associated with the use of the Direct To Stage property.

The symptoms are easy to spot. Director plays the digital video as normal. When set to jump to a new frame without the digital video on the stage, an image from the movie remains. The image is obliterated if sprites pass over the area or a transition occurs. Colloquially speaking, digital video hangs around, bumping into things.

This effect happens because Direct To Stage cuts a hole in the Director stage and hands control of this area to the digital video mechanism, such as QuickTime. When the movie has finished, Director cannot "see" that the area needs to be "refreshed." In order to prevent a mess, you should make the stage redraw itself immediately following your use of digital video using one of the following methods:

- Replace the digital video sprite with an invisible draw rectangle.
- Add "Set the stageColor to the stage Color" to the frame script following the digital video.
- Add a full stage transition effect to the following frame—set the transition time to the minimum and the chunk size to the maximum.
- Write a handler that sets the visible of sprite X to FALSE (where X is the channel with the video in it) and calls `updateStage`.

Finally, it is well worth tidying up some QuickTime arguments which will, no doubt, continue unabated. QuickTime movies can be "flattened," and they can be "single-fork movies," which means that those movies are playable on non-Macintosh computers.

A flattened movie is not necessarily playable on non-Macintosh computers. A single fork movie is playable on a non-Mac and a flattened movie may or may not be playable on a non-Mac. Because of the confusion this creates, the term *flattening* is liberally applied to both.

The problem is that in some applications (such as MoviePlayer), both "Make movie self contained" and "make playable on non-Apple computers" check boxes may have to be set, whereas others (such as FlattenMovie) do both in one simple step.

If your Mac QuickTime video doesn't work with QuickTime for Windows, flattening and forks might be the cause.

Flattening a movie is to make the movie self contained. On the Macintosh, a QuickTime movie can contain actual movie tracks such as video and also can also store pointers to other movies. A movie can be composed of nothing but pointers to other movies, meaning that the pointer movie is minute—5 KB or so. If you moved that movie of pointers onto a different system, however, it cannot play because as the source movies are not available.

Making a movie from pointers to other movies enables the simulation of video editing with the capability to save many different versions without clogging up the hard disk. This is limited to the Macintosh with versions of QuickTime prior to 2.5.

In order for a Macintosh QuickTime movie to play on a non-Macintosh computer, it must be flattened and *then* have the header information taken out of the resource fork and integrated into the data fork. Just flattening the movie is not enough. Figure 14.6 shows the layout of a QuickTime movie in the three stages: unflattened, flattened, and single fork.

The structure of a QuickTime movie leads to another performance issue. When a movie is encountered by Director, the QuickTime mechanism spools to the end of the file to pick up some important information. This can take quite a while with a long movie. From QuickTime version 2.2, this information is stored at the head of the file, rather than the end. Digital video created with versions of QuickTime prior to 2.2 might benefit from this minor "tweak."

When porting from Macintosh, QuickTime for Windows will let Director know what is happening. A comprehensive listing of error codes and their meanings is available from the Macromedia Web site at http://www.macromedia.com. Search for Technote 3110TN.TXL.

In conclusion, a flattened movie does not depend on any other movies. A movie that is playable on non-Macintosh computers does not depend on any other movies and keeps the header information and the movie information in one fork.

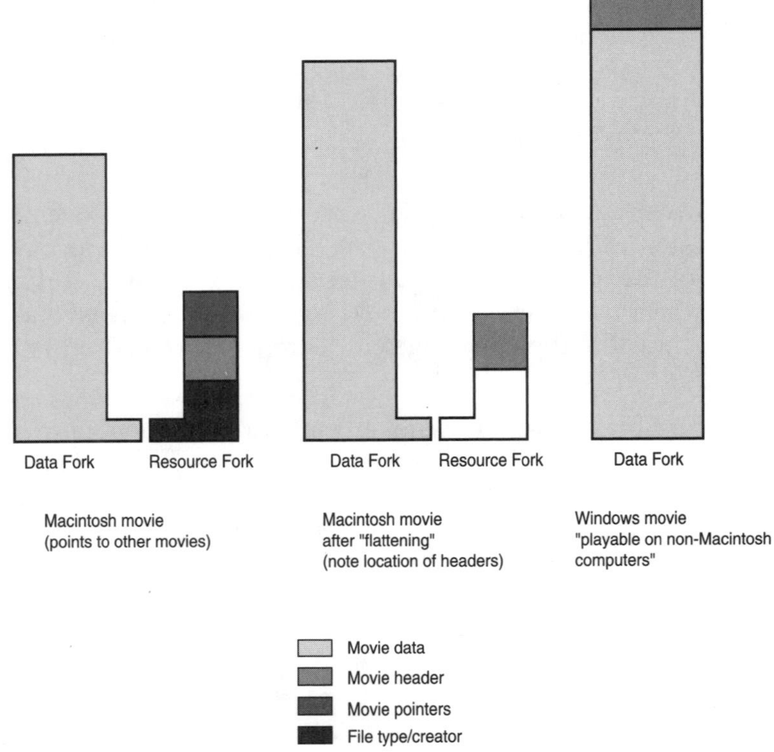

Figure 14.6

Digital video file structures.

Existing Controls

Although the Lingo functions for digital video seemed slim in previous versions of Director, they nonetheless provide a very flexible suite of functions.

MovieRate

The `movieRate` property is the equivalent of your VCR buttons. Setting the `movieRate` to 0 stops it; setting it to 1 plays it forward at normal speed; setting it to 2 plays the movie forward at double speed. You can set it to –2 and Director will attempt to play it backward at double speed.

MovieTime

The `movieTime` property is similar to a VCR tape counter or timecode track, with the added bonus of the being able to set the property, which achieves random access. The key thing to remember is that the `movieTime` has nothing to do with frames per second. `movieTime`—measured in ticks—is the standard Director time unit. There are 60 ticks in a second. Therefore, to make a movie jump to a point that is 37 seconds from the beginning of the movie, set the `movieTime` as follows:

```
set the movieTime of sprite X to (37*60)
```

For fairly loose timing, the preceding example is fine. When dealing with digital video generated by animation software and replayed as a "play every frame" movie, however, you want to refer to individual frames rather than the movie time *per se*. Knowledge of the exact frames per second setting is required, so that if you want to remain looping in the middle third of a 45-frame movie (frames 16–30), and you know that the movie is created with 15 fps, the ticks per second divided by frames per second will give the number of ticks per frame (60÷15=4 ticks per frame) and, therefore, the code reads as follows:

```
on exitFrame
 if the movieTime of sprite X > (4 * 30) then
  set the movieTime of sprite X to (4 * 16)
 end if
end
```

New Controls

Rather than act as a second take on a Lingo dictionary, the following sections represent a few of the high spots in the Director 5 Lingo in terms of controlling digital video. There is a short section dedicated to this is in the online help. Much of it concentrates on reading the properties of a digital video member, but the excitement is in the access to digital video "tracks." For those who work on cross-platform or Windows-only projects, please bear in mind the caveats regarding multiple track types noted earlier in this chapter.

DigitalVideoTimescale

The `digitalVideoTimescale` property indicates the timescale of the system it is played under. The `timeScale` property is for inquiry only. You cannot change the value, and it refers to the member, not the sprite instance of it.

The `digitalVideoTimeScale` sets the scale factor used by Lingo when reading and setting `movieTime` properties. By default it is 60. Setting the `digitalVideoTimeScale` to 1 enables you to deal with QT times in round seconds; setting it to `timeScale` of a member gives the highest possible resolution. Normally the QT times are truncated to the nearest 1/60 second.

In case you hoped that the `digitalVideoTimescale` might tell you the frames per second of a member, it does not. If you need to obtain the frames per second of a member, the `frameRate` of member X is the way you would expect to determine the normal rate. Unfortunately it is only a valid number when the member's Play Every Frame and Fixed Rate properties are set. Here's a way you *can* discern the framerate of a digital video:

If the digital video is known to be at first frame—by setting the `movietime = 0`), for example—the timeunits per frame = `trackNextSampleTime(sprite 1,1)`.

If the digital video is set somewhere in the middle of its duration, the timeunits per frame = `trackNextSampleTime (sprite 1, 1) - trackPreviousSampleTime(sprite 1, 1)`

TrackType

The `trackType` enables you to inquire as to the specific type of content in a particular track of a digital video member or a sprite of it on the stage (differing only in the way it is addressed). Also, it returns the type in the form of a symbol from the track types available: `#video`, `#sound`, `#text`, and `#music`—MIDI data.

```
on checkMemberTracks whichVideoSprite
 -- this puts the track details of a digital video
 -- member on stage into the message window.
```

```
  -- Remember to pass the sprite number!
  put the memberNum of sprite whichVideoSprite into targetMember
  put trackCount(member targetMember) into howMany
  put "Sprite" && whichVideoSprite && ", member "& targetMember
  repeat with i = 1 to howMany
   put "track" && i && trackType(member targetMember, i)
  end repeat
  put RETURN
end
```

TrackText

The `trackText` property extracts the text string that is present in the text track at the given `movieTime`. Remember that the text need not be visible on the movie (disabled with the `trackEnabled` property), so when used in conjunction with the following Lingo properties and the `movieTime`, you can progress through a digital video member and assemble a list of text strings to enable text searches of a video clip.

TrackNextSampleTime and TrackPreviousSampleTime

The `trackNextSampleTime` and `trackPreviousSampleTime` navigate between "events" in tracks such as the text track. Each sample combines a string of text with an *in-point* (when the text appears) and an *out-point* (when the text disappears), so you can locate adjacent text pages by examining the track Next/Previous SampleTimes.

TrackNextKeyTime and TrackPreviousKeyTime

The `trackNextKeyTime` and `trackPreviousKeyTime` Lingo commands find your choice of the key frame closest to current frame within a digital video member, which should provide a clean image and a convenient mid-movie start point. Note that QuickTime movies that have passed through applications such as MovieShop (described in the next section) might have additional key frames added at irregular intervals.

Helper Applications

Director is an excellent playback platform tool for digital video, and it also plays a valuable creation role. However, while it is just possible to work without a pile of widgets, Director is neither designed nor suitable for video editing.

Compressing Video with MovieShop and Movie Cleaner

MovieShop has been around a long time. Early in the history of QuickTime, MovieShop was the only "industrial strength" movie analysis and compression tool. Behind a fearsome interface, MovieShop constantly processed a movie to make it play back at a certain bandwidth by varying spatial and temporal compression on a frame-by-frame basis, inserting keyframes where necessary.

Today, MovieShop is used by a diminishing "die-hard" clique of developers, because many people have discovered Movie Cleaner from Terran Interactive.

Movie Cleaner provides the functionality of MovieShop and adds a raft of extra functions and enhancements that make it an essential utility. Movie Cleaner comes in two versions: a $15 shareware "lite" version available from the Terran Web site (www.Terran-Int.com) and a $200 "pro" version that adds batch process, Power Macintosh acceleration, and specialized features such as filters for "talking head" video.

Adding Transitions with Premiere

A fact of life is that due to the intense optimization for real-time smooth effects, Director's transitions are barely supported in digital video export.

NOTE

> Rather than patiently explain about rendering to off-screen buffers and writing them out directly to screen and the way in which this works on frame-by-frame video taping but not in writing out an image file such as a QuickTime movie (gasp)... the positive angle is to offer a workaround.

Exporting a Director movie to digital video is not a real-time thing. Each frame is created, snapped, compressed, and then recorded. You can simulate transitions with complex score animation that, while not working in real time, end up looking better than the original transitions. Still, this is a painstaking exercise. Why not cheat?

By exporting the Director movie in chunks of digital video and bringing them into Premiere, you can use many of the unique transitions that are a part of the basic Premiere package or experiment further with third-party extensions such as the TransJammer effects.

In the end, the best results come from compromise: simple wipes and transitions that cover the whole stage are created in Premiere, and transitions such as "reveal" and "push" are re-created with sprite animation.

Synchronizing Sound with SoundEdit

In a similar fashion, Director does not export its sound tracks in QuickTime movies. Remember that Director's design emphasis is on real-time animation performance—it's export function is somewhat limited.

SoundEdit, included as part of the Director studio, covers virtually all the features needed in a multimedia sound tool. In addition, its capability to synchronize sound with digital video has been enhanced for this very purpose.

Creating Text Tracks with MoviePlayer

Macintosh users with System 7.5 or later can start experimenting with text tracks right away. You can create and edit text tracks with two applications that are likely to be on everyone's Mac: SimpleText and MoviePlayer 2.1 or newer (with the authoring plug-ins). Create your text in SimpleText, using the Return key to separate each line of text. Subtitles should be kept short.

1. In MoviePlayer, open a QuickTime movie.
2. Choose Info from the Movie menu.
3. Switch back to the Finder and launch SimpleText. You might wish to arrange the windows as shown in figure 14.7 so that you can see MoviePlayer's Info window, the Movie window, and your SimpleText document at the same time.
4. Type a sentence of text in SimpleText, select it, and drag the text over the movie. The movie border should highlight (if it does not, then you need to install the drag-and-drop extension). A new text track is placed in the movie.
5. Clicking on the movie window and rewinding the movie to show the new text as a full frame. Notice that the left pop-up menu in the Info window now includes a text track. Choose this track.
6. In the righthand pop-up menu, choose the Text Replace option. You can click on the arrows to the right of the pop-up if you want.
7. Drag the same text from SimpleText to the area marked "Drag Style Here." The text area in the QuickTime movie now shrinks to the size of the text. Note that you can change the font, size, and style of the text in SimpleText and repeat the drag to change your subtitle style.
8. The subtitle window traditionally sits at the bottom of the frame, so it needs to be moved. Choose Size from the Info window of MoviePlayer and click the Adjust button. Drag the area to the bottom of the screen and click the "Done" button and switch to Text Replace in the righthand pop-up menu.
9. In the Movie window, select a portion of the movie to place text over. Drag the control bar to the start point, and while pressing the Shift key, drag the control bar to the end point.
10. Switch to SimpleText. Select the line of text you wish to insert and drag it to the area in MoviePlayer's Info window marked Drop Text Here. The text is now put into the text track of your movie. Note that if you drag more text to the MoviePlayer *display* window, an additional text track will be created.

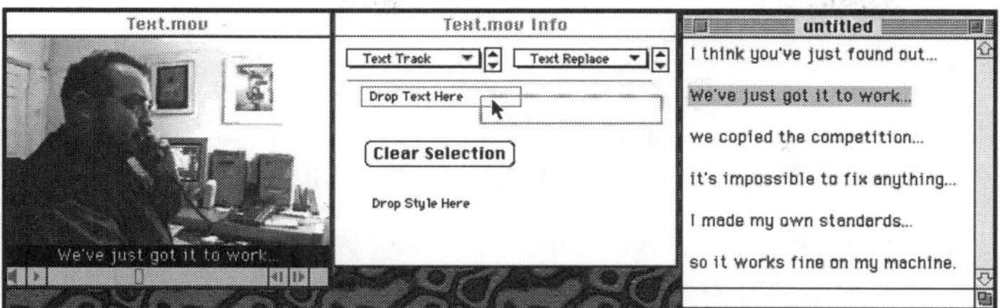

Figure 14.7

You can add text tracks with SimpleText and MoviePlayer.

11. Continue to add your text by selecting the timespan in MoviePlayer, then dragging the text into the "Drop Text Here" area in the Info window. If you make a mistake, select the timespan and click the Clear Selection button.
12. Save your movie, import into Director, and admire.

When you feel comfortable with this method, try creating a whole SimpleText document of subtitles, then import them into MoviePlayer. Clicking the Options button in the Import dialog box enables you to set the font, size, style, color, background color, alignment, and size properties directly.

This dialog also enables access to some special features of the text track:

- Text can be anti-aliased.
- Text can be keyed (a transparent background).
- Text can be hidden.
- Text can be prevented from scaling with the movie.

Summary

To fine-tune your movies:

- Plan for the end user's system configuration, especially the data rate.
- Magic Numbers: Make sure that your digital video dimensions and stage positions are divisible by the magic numbers—use 8 as a magic number when in doubt.
- Defragment your hard disk and prioritize media when possible.

To get the best quality:

- Use the best quality originals. Try to obtain the master tape if presented with a VHS. Record live action directly to hard disk, if you only have a VHS camcorder.
- Grab large, grab more, reduce later. Remember that it's like scanning pictures: you don't scan at 8 bit, 72 dpi—you'd go for 24 bit and at least 150 dpi, especially if it requires a lot of retouching and color balancing. Video is no different.
- Use applications such as Movie Cleaner to compress your digital video.

Beyond talking heads:

- Treat video as any other data type. Remember that digital video is a useful container for all sorts of media. Exploit the time-oriented nature as well as the superb compression.
- Use the new features of Digital Video controls in Director 5, such as access to QuickTime's text tracks, MIDI tracks.
- Watch cross-platform issues. Remember TETO (test early, test often).

Director as creation tool:

- Micons: Use Director-created digital video to exceed speed and composition limits and simplify the use of the Score.
- Watch out with transitions: If creating digital video with Director, do not rely on transitions and sound; design around them; add them later.
- Read the Technotes: 3110TN.TXL Tech note (from http://www.macromedia.com) that outlines the error codes for digital video in Director. This exhaustive list should be stuck to your wall within easy reach. It serves as a quick check on what went wrong or as an overview of what can go wrong.

And once again:

- TETO—test early, test often! Again!

John Chambers

Director in 3D

Well, this is where it all started many years ago. They called it VideoWorks, a very cool black-and-white program that enabled the user to move little objects around a tiny eight-inch screen, measured diagonally, of course. Years later, things just keep getting better.

Macromedia has added an arsenal of new features to Director 5. Throughout this chapter you will find many step-by-step instructions to help get you up to speed in creating cool animation quickly. Also included are some troubleshooting tips to help out with some of the more often made mistakes when creating animations in Director.

The basic areas covered in this chapter are as follows:

- Quick primer on animation principles
- How Director approaches animation
- Basic animation techniques
- Advanced animation techniques
- Troubleshooting

A Quick Primer On Animation Principles

Animation is actually a trick being played on our eyes. The process of animation is achieved by presenting a series of images in rapid succession. These images are offset by a small amount from one frame to another to create the illusion of motion. As the playback head advances over the frames, we see movement on the stage, like magic "Animation" is created. Whether you are creating animations for movies, videos, or computer presentations, all the information that the audience views is located in frames. Therefore the term *frames per second* (fps) is used to tell how fast a movie is being played. Basically, two different speeds for playback exist—24 fps for motion pictures or film and 30 fps for video tape.

The video tape category can be broken down even further. There are two different speeds and formats for video tape. The United States uses National Television Standards Committee (NTSC) format, which was developed in the early 1950s. The NTSC format runs at about 30 fps. Actually, the true speed of NTSC video is really 29.97 fps, but rather than explaining the technical reasons for such a strange speed, we rounded it off to 30 fps. The European standard is PAL, which runs at a speed closer to that of film at 25 fps. Director's playback head can travel at speeds ranging from one second per frame all the way up to 120 frames per second. With this wide range of speed settings, you can achieve just about any type of animation sequence.

NOTE

You need to keep in mind two things when you're creating animations. Objects placed closer together in adjacent frames will move slower than objects spaced farther apart. On the accompanying CD-ROM, open the file named "Speed Test" from the Chapter 15 folder. When the animation is played, the file shows two balls moving across the stage. The speed of the animation is 15 fps for the entire movie sequence, and both balls are moving at 15 fps. Notice the lower ball moves faster than the ball at the top, even though the movie stays at a constant 15 fps. Closer examination of the stopped file shows that the lower ball moves faster because of the spacing of the object in the frames. The faster object moves faster only because the spacing of the object is farther apart than the spacing of the lower object. So when trying to speed up an animation, speeding up the playback might not always be the answer. Object placement can be just as important.

How Director Approaches Animation

In its simplest form, Director advances the playback head over time and displays data contained in each frame to the screen. Sounds simple? Well it is, only what happens from frame to frame is a little more complicated. As the playback head advances over time, it encounters frames, channels, sprites, tempo changes, transitions, sound cues, palettes, Lingo scripts, and a few more pieces of information. Actually it might not be that simple, but it becomes easier to understand by actually working in the program and dealing with these elements one at a time.

When a movie starts, Director first looks at the movie script. The movie script tells Director what to do at startup, during the playback, and when the movie stops. The `startMovie` handler can contain the screen-depth settings for the monitor; it can adjust the volume of sound for the movie. It can do anything Lingo can do. As the playback head enters each frame, a list of 54 tasks must be followed before the playback head can advance to the next frame (see fig. 15.1). The items in this task list are called *channels*.

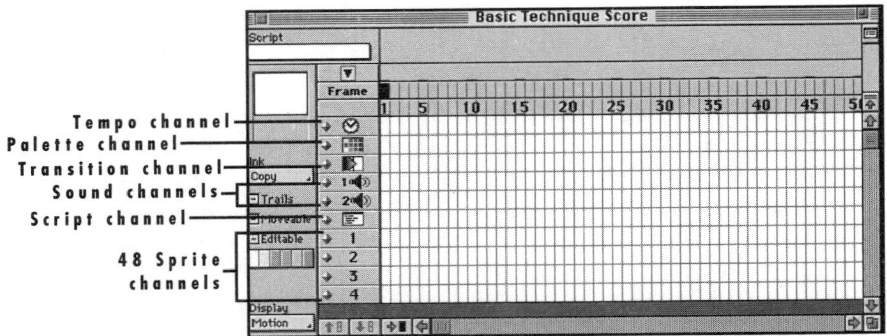

Figure 15.1

The channels in the Score window.

Frames

Frames are viewed in the Score window. The first frame is located on the left side of the window. A number 1 is displayed near the top of the Score window to mark the first frame (see fig. 15.2). The frame numbers increase as the playback head travels to the right. There is no upper limit to frames in a Director file, although you could get very tired of scrolling millions of frames. The playback head indicates which frame is currently being shown on the stage. The control panel also displays the current frame number as seen in figure 15.3. A frame runs up and down the Score window as a vertical column. Each frame column contains 54 channels. Channels hold all the stage information for the frame.

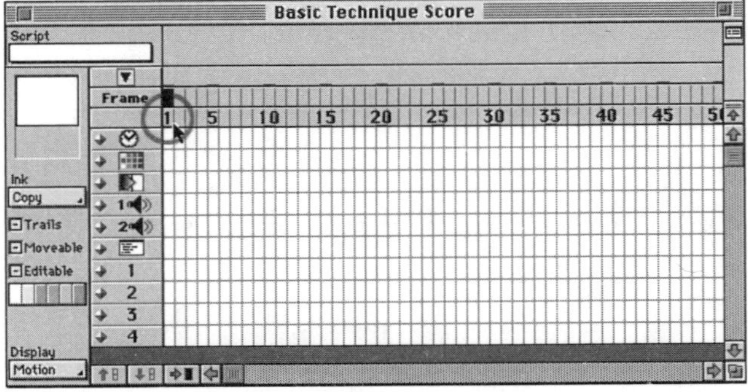

Figure 15.2

Showing the position of Frame 1 in the Score window.

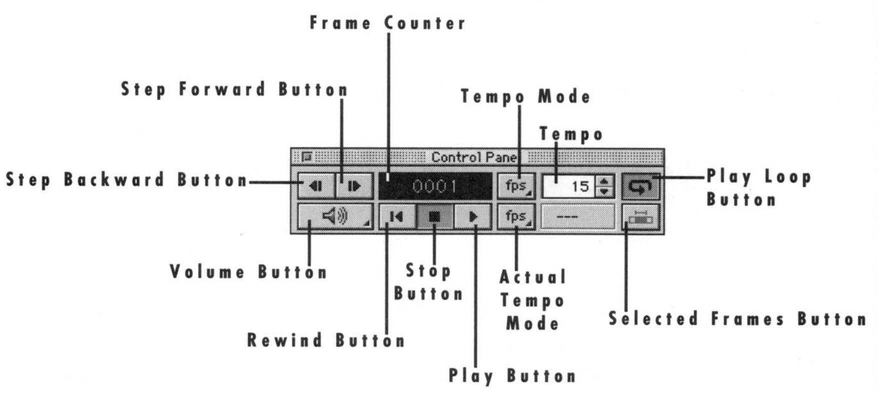

Figure 15.3

The control panel also displays the current position of the playback head.

Select Score from the Preferences pop-up from the File menu bar and check Playback Head Follows Selection in the Display options. This instructs the playback head to jump to the frame that is being edited. This feature should be left on to make the editing process easier. The position of the Playback Head corresponds to the images on the stage.

Channels

Channels are rows that run the entire length of a Director file. As the playback head passes over frames, all the channel layers affect the stage. The channel layers provide information about speed, palette settings, transitions, sounds, scripts, and the sprite locations of cast members on the stage.

As the playback head enters a frame, the channels are executed in order, starting from the top of the Score window, the Tempo channel, and continues down to channel 48, the last of the channels. The order of the channels is very important. Channel 1 is the first channel to be drawn on the stage, channel 2 is the second channel drawn on the stage, and so on. Sprites in higher numbered channels will be on top of sprites in lower numbered channels. In other words, channel 1 is located on the bottom of a stack visually and channel 48 is on top of the visual stack. The playback head then returns to the top of the next frame and travels down the next row of channels. This will happen for all the remaining frames of the movie.

Cels

A *cel* is the location in the Score window where a horizontal channel meets with a vertical frame. A cel can only contain one element at a time. The element can be one of many different things: a graphic, color palette, tempo setting, Score script, sound, or transition. The key here is that the cel can only contain one item per cel.

The term *cel* dates back to the days of painting cartoon characters on clear sheets of acetate or celluloid. The painted cels could be stacked up and photographed as one frame of an animation due to the fact that the clear part of the cels allow the underlying cel images to be seen.

Sprites

The term "sprite" can be confusing. A *sprite* is a cast member that has been placed on the stage. A sprite is not a cast member, but only the stage information pertaining to its cast member, such as which cast member it should be, the location on the stage, the location in regards to a previous frame, the ink effect, the blend amount, the visibility, and the script code. To draw a more visual analogy, let's say the cast member is a rubber stamp and the sprite is the ink impression that it leaves behind on the stage; the sprite—like the ink impression—shows up in a cel of the Score window.

Because a cast member can be used hundreds of times throughout a movie, deleting a cast member might not be a good idea because removing a single cast member can remove hundreds of sprites with a single key press. The delete key operates on the active or topmost window. Keep an eye on which window is active when deleting elements. A deletion in the Cast Member window will delete a cast member; a deletion in the Score window will delete a sprite.

NOTE

Sprites are controlled by the Score window. The channels tell the sprites where they are and what color they should be and so on. This control can be taken away from the Score window and given to Lingo by turning the puppetness of a sprite on. A puppeted sprite can then be controlled by Lingo. To create a `puppetSprite`, use the following Lingo code:

```
puppetSprite 4, TRUE
```

or

```
set the puppet of sprite 4 to TRUE
```

This script sets the `puppetSprite` of the sprite in channel 4. The script can be placed in a movie script, a Score script, or in a handler such as `on mouseUp` or `on mouseDown`. The puppeted sprite can now be moved to a new location by using `locV` and `locH` Lingo commands, changed to another cast member using the `castNum` command, or the blend amount of a sprite adjusted with the `blend of sprite` command. Remember to turn the `puppetSprite` off when finished by using the command `puppetSprite 4, FALSE` or the sprite will behave very strangely when Score window changes are made later in the movie to the sprite in the fourth channel.

The Control Panel

To play back the animations on the stage, you can use the Control Panel. This small, easy-to-use panel has all of the functions available to manipulate the playback head. Choose Control Panel from the Window menu or select Command+2 from the keyboard. Figure 15.3, shown previously, shows all of the Control Panel functions.

- **Step Backward and Step Forward buttons.** These two buttons will move the playback head forward or backward one frame. Holding either button down will quickly scan the movie in the corresponding direction.
- **The Frame Counter.** Displays the current position of the playback head. Entering a number in the frame counter and pressing the Return key will advance you to that frame.
- **Tempo Mode pop-up.** Determines how the Tempo is displayed. The choices are frames per second (fps) and seconds per frame (spf).

- **Tempo.** The area to the right of the Tempo Mode and left of the Loop Playback button. This is the actual speed of the selected frame in either fps or spf. Entering a new Tempo into the field and pressing return or clicking on the arrow buttons will change the Tempo.
- **The Loop Playback Button.** Sets the movie to play again after the last frame (down position) or to play only once (up position).
- **Volume Button.** This pop-up menu sets the volume for the entire movie.
- **Rewind Button.** Rewinds the movie to frame 1. You can also select Rewind from the Control menu or press Command+Option+R.
- **Stop Button.** Stops the movie on the current frame. Select Stop from the Control menu or press Command+. (period).
- **Play Button.** Plays the movie from the current frame. Select Play from the Control menu or Command+Option+P.
- **Actual Tempo Mode.** This pop-up list sets the display mode of the Actual Tempo to the right of this setting. The choices are frames per second (fps), seconds per frame (spf), and Running Total and Estimated Total. Running Total is the elapsed time since the start of the movie. Estimated Total is a more accurate (although slower) calculation of elapsed time.
- **Selected Frames Only Button.** Toggle this button on or off to set the movie to play only the selected frames in the Score window. A green line at the top of the Score channels will indicate the selected frames. If the movie is looped, only the selected frames will play over and over.

Basic Animation Techniques

Building an animation from scratch is the best way to learn how Director deals with objects in motion. The following will be a step-by-step walkthrough for creating a basic animation.

Elements Inside of a Director File

Any Director file can have two basic elements: bitmapped elements and shape elements. Descriptions follow:

Bitmapped Elements

All cast members that can be placed on the stage can be animated. Cast members can be imported from just about any application. If the image can be converted into a PICT, PICS, Text, or QuickTime file, then it can become part of your Director animation. This include scans, video captures, drawing, and clip art. Because Director has a built-in painting program, we will create our object within Director.

1. Open a new Director file.
2. Close any open windows.
3. Save the file as `Bounce Test`.
4. Open the Paint window by choosing Paint from the Window menu or press Command+5.

   When the Paint window opens, expand it to a larger working size.

Bouncing balls are great for animation demos for a number of reasons. They're fun to watch, easy to control, and most of all, easy to replace later with real images. If you prefer to create a more complex image for this demo, feel free to do so, just keep the image small—about the size of a quarter. The new image will be a bitmapped graphic.

5. In the Paint tool box select the Filled Ellipse tool.
6. In the Foreground Color chip of the Color Selector, press and drag out to a color in the palette and then release. The foreground color chip will update to this new color.
7. Press the Shift key and drag the mouse to create a circle about the size of a quarter. If you want to jazz up the image a little, add a small light-colored dot (created with the Paintbrush tool) to the ball for a highlight effect as seen in figure 15.4.

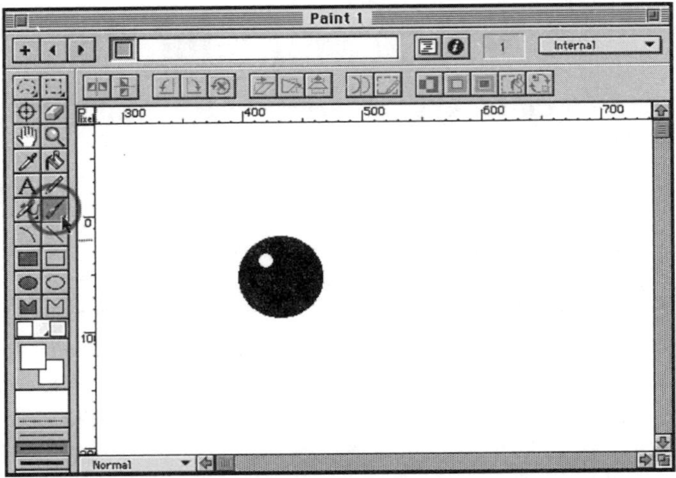

Figure 15.4

After creating a quarter sized ball, add a highlight to it with the Paintbrush tool.

A couple of actions have taken place behind the scenes as the ball was being created. Figure 15.5 shows the new ball artwork was added to cast member 1 and a registration point was added to the center of the new artwork in the Paint window. The registration point can be seen by selecting the Registration Point tool in the Paint window's Tool palette. Registration points are set to the center of a new image by default.

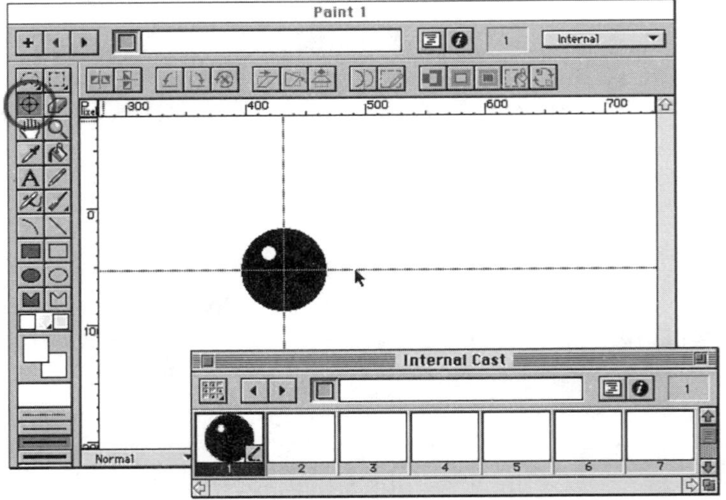

Figure 15.5

After the ball artwork is created in the Paint window, the artwork is added to the Cast Member window and registration point is added to the center of the artwork in the Paint window.

The next object we will create is a wall to bounce the ball against. This image will be a shape created with the Tool palette. The difference between the wall shape and the ball bitmap is that a bitmapped image is created with a bunch of pixels. The size of the image is set at time of creation and scaling up the image will distort the image with jagged stair stepped pixels around the outside. A *shape* is an object that can be resized without distortion. Shapes animate slower when compared with bitmapped images, but bitmaps use more RAM and disk space. Bitmapped images are best for motion; shapes work best as still images.

8. Close the Paint window and open the Tool palette from the Window menu or press Command+7.
9. Save the file with Command+S.

Shape Elements

Another big difference between bitmapped cast members and shape cast members is that bitmapped cast members are created in the Paint window and are moved onto the stage. Shapes are created directly on the stage. Both of these images will appear in the Cast Member window as cast members after they are created.

1. Select the Filled Rectangle tool and draw a profile of a wall. Draw the wall shape directly on the stage in about the same size as figure 15.6. Position your wall shape in the lower right corner of your screen. We will bounce the ball off this wall.

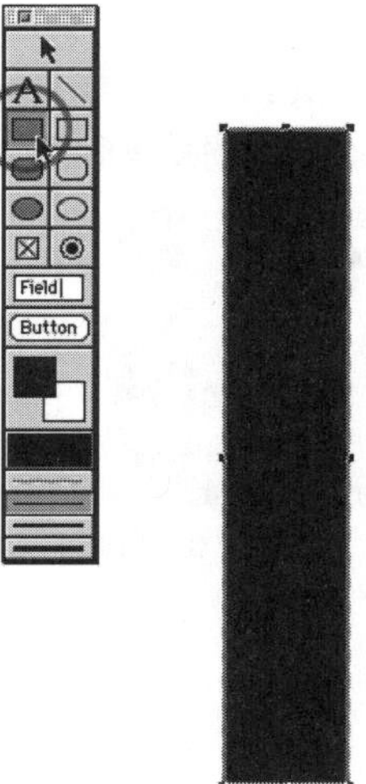

Figure 15.6

Drawing a shape directly on the stage.

2. Close the Tool palette by pressing Command+7.
3. Save the file by pressing Command+S.

Recording Animations

Three different examples will be used to explain the steps of the animation process. Open the Score window from the Window menu or press Command+4. In frame 1, channel 1 of the Score window, a cel has been selected. This is the sprite of the wall shape that was just created. The Display pop-up menu, located in the bottom left corner of the Score window, will enable you to view your sprites in different ways in the Score window. Set the Display pop-up to Member for this part of the demo (see fig. 15.7). The options for the Display pop-up menu are:

- **Member.** Shows the cast member of the sprite. The default setting shows the number of the cast member followed by the name if there is room in the cel. To change this setting so that the name of the cast member is displayed, select Cast from the Preferences pop-out from the File menu and change the Label pop-up to Name.
- **Script.** Displays either the script number associated with the sprite, a "+" to indicate a sprite with a cast member script or "00" to indicate a sprite with no script.
- **Motion.** Displays the direction the sprite has traveled from the previous frame. Also, a newly born sprite will display a letter. This letter corresponds to which type of sprite it is: B for bitmapped, Q (QuickDraw) for a shape.
- **Ink.** Displays the ink applied to the sprite from the Ink pop-up menu just above the Cast Display pop-up menu (see fig. 15.8).
- **Blend.** Displays the blend percentage as set in Sprite Properties from the Modify menu.
- **Extended.** Displays the cast member type, motion, blend and the cast member number, the ink code, the script code, the X and Y location, as well as changes in the X and Y location. To customize the Extended Display options, select Score from the Preferences pop-out under the File menu.

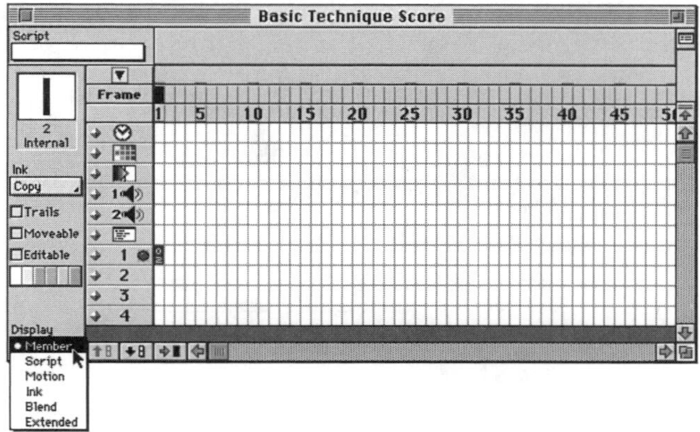

Figure 15.7

The Display pop-up enables a sprite to be viewed different ways.

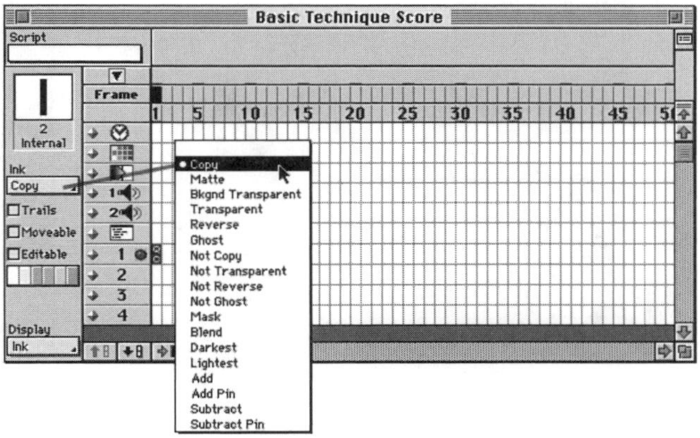

Figure 15.8

The applied ink effect can be seen on the sprites when the cast member Display pop-up is set to Ink.

If the Display pop-up menu is not visible in the lower left corner of the Score window, enlarge the Score window until it is visible.

Real-Time Recording

Like a tape recorder, Director can record all of the moves on the stage and record them to the Score window. This type of technique is really better for rough-draft animations. As seen shortly, real-time recording is a little difficult to control.

1. Close the Score window and open the Cast Member window. Position the Cast window in the top of the stage area and not blocking the wall sprite created earlier.

2. Select the ball cast member. The selected cast member is the target or moving object in the real-time recording demo.
3. Press and hold the Control key and spacebar at the same time.
4. Using the mouse, click on the stage away from the Cast Member window and drag the image of the cast member around the stage (see fig. 15.9).

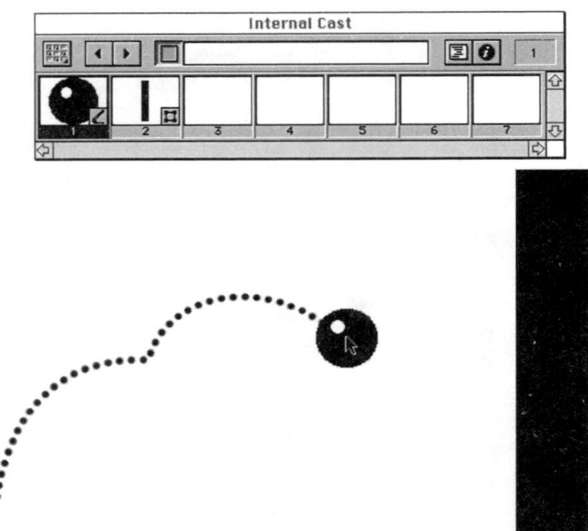

Figure 15.9

Dragging a cast member around the stage for a real-time recording session.

5. To stop recording, first release the keyboard and then the mouse.

The real-time recording option created new sprites in different locations of the Score window as the ball was dragged around the stage. Because the wall was in the frame where the animation started, duplicates of the nonmoving wall sprite were created for each of the new frames (see fig. 15.10).

6. Play the movie to see the results of the real-time recording. Close the Score window and select Play from the Control menu or choose Shift+Enter.

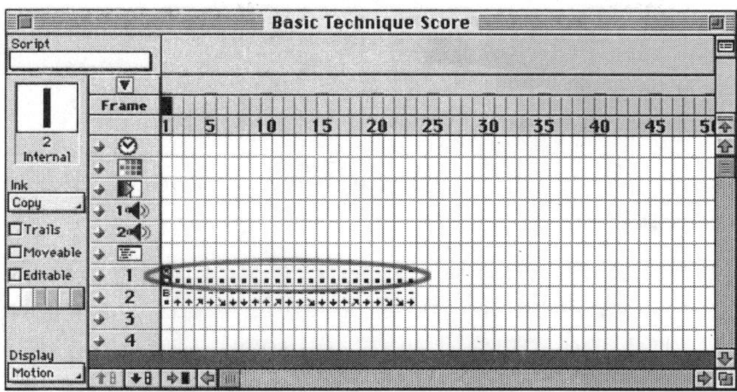

Figure 15.10

Because the wall sprite was located in the first frame of the real-time recording, the wall sprite was duplicated for the remainder of the frames.

Pressing Shift+Enter (not Return) will close all open windows and play the movie. Pressing the Enter key again stops the movie and returns all the open windows.

In additon to Shift+Enter, which plays the movie and hides all windows, Command+Option+P will play the movie without hiding windows.

Removing Unwanted Sprites

The only sprite needed for the next demo is the wall sprite in channel 1, frame 1. The remaining sprites need to be removed. The following steps show the easiest way to remove unwanted sprites from the Score window.

1. Double-click the number 2 in the beginning of the channel 2 (see fig. 15.11). Don't click the gray diamond to the left of the channel number. Double-clicking the channel number will select all of the sprites in that channel.

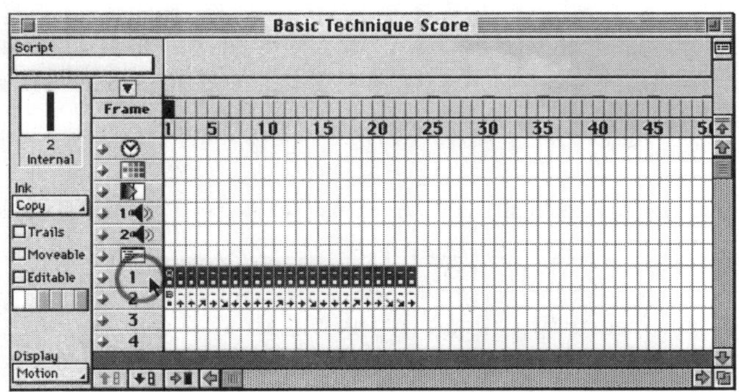

Figure 15.11

Double-clicking the channel number will select the entire channel.

The gray diamond to the left of the channel numbers turns the channel's visibility on or off.

2. Press the Delete key on the keyboard or choose Clear Cells from the Edit menu.
3. Double-click the number 1 in front of channel. This selects all of channel number 1. The first frame needs to remain for the next demo and should not be removed.
4. To deselect the sprite in frame 1 while leaving the rest of the sprites selected, press the Shift key and drag the cursor over the sprite in channel 1, frame 2.
5. Press the Delete key to remove the selected sprites.

Step Recording

The real-time recording option can be somewhat inaccurate at times. Step recording is a little slower and can be much more accurate than setting up each frame and recording the frames one at a time.

1. Close the Score window by pressing Command+4.
2. Open the Cast Member window by pressing Command+3.
3. Drag cast member 1, the ball, out of the Cast Member window and onto the bottom left corner of the stage. When the cast member is dragged onto the stage, its sprite appears and is placed in channel 2 of the Score window. Because channel 1 was occupied, any cast members moved to the stage will fill the channels in order.

If the dragged out cast member was placed in channel 6 of frame 1, the blank cel in frame 1 of channel 6 would need to be selected before the drag was executed.

4. Close the Cast Member window by pressing Command+3.
5. Open the Score window by pressing Command+4.

The red step-recording light is visible in the channels that contain newly placed cast members so the step-record light will be on for the ball sprite in channel 2. The light needs to be turned on for the wall sprite in channel 1. Do the following to turn on a step-record light:

6. While pressing the Option key, click in the area to the right of the channel number of the channel that is to be recorded. The red step-record light will appear.

Now, both channels are ready to step record.

7. Open the Control Panel by pressing Command+2.
8. Either press the 3 key on the keypad (not the number 3 above the W or E keys on the keyboard) or select the Step Forward button in the Control Panel to advance the playback head one frame. Both of the recording channels will duplicate into frame 2.
9. Move the ball to another position on the stage closer to the wall image. The wall will stay where it is.
10. Repeat step 8 above to continue the animation sequence as seen in figure 15.12, for a total of 15 frames.

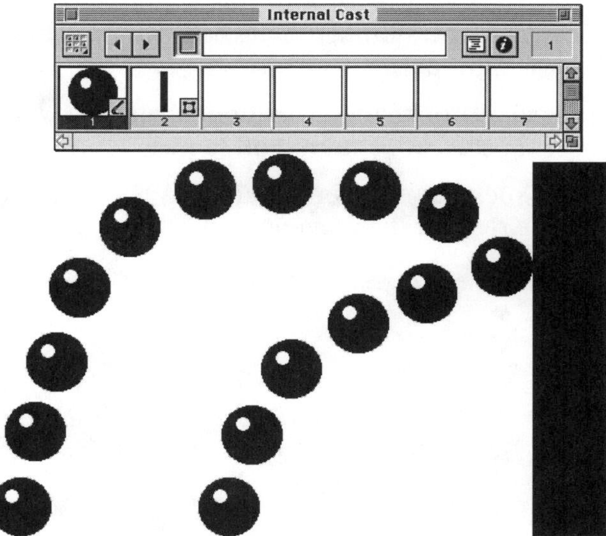

Figure 15.12

Place the ball sprite close to these positions when creating the Step Record movie.

11. Rewind and play the movie to see the step-record animation.

Space To Time

The step-recording option works very well to create accurate animations. The only drawback to step recording is that you cannot see the animation sequence as it is being created. Using Space To Time, a sequence of sprites can be set up in a single animation frame. Then, Space To Time is applied and all the sprites in the single frame move out over multiple frames.

The followng steps show how to remove the unwanted sprites for this next demo and leave the frame 1 sprites in channels 1 and 2.

1. Select frame 2, channel 1, and then press the Shift key and click on frame 15, channel 2 to select all of the unwanted sprites.
2. Press the Delete key.
3. Rewind your movie (Command+Option+R).

First, the entire animation sequence needs to be built up in frame 1.

4. Close the Score window and open the Cast window.
5. Drag cast member number 1, the ball, out onto the stage, above and to the right of the first ball.

Because the ball is not changing color or shape, we will use the same cast member for the entire animation sequence.

6. Drag cast member number 1 again, out onto the stage, above and to the right of the previous ball.
7. Repeat step 5, 11 more times until the stage looks something like figure 15.12.

For a more realistic-looking animation, sprites that need to move faster should be placed farther apart. Slower moving sprites are placed closer together.

All the animation sequence is in frame 1 and is actually more like a still life than an animation, but the entire path of the ball can be seen as it hits the wall and bounces back to the ground. The process of cutting and pasting the sprites in the correct channels and frames would take a long time. To shorten this time, Macromedia has built in a great function called Space To Time. This Space To Time option repositions sprites in consecutive channels and places them in the same channel over a period of time (see fig. 15.13).

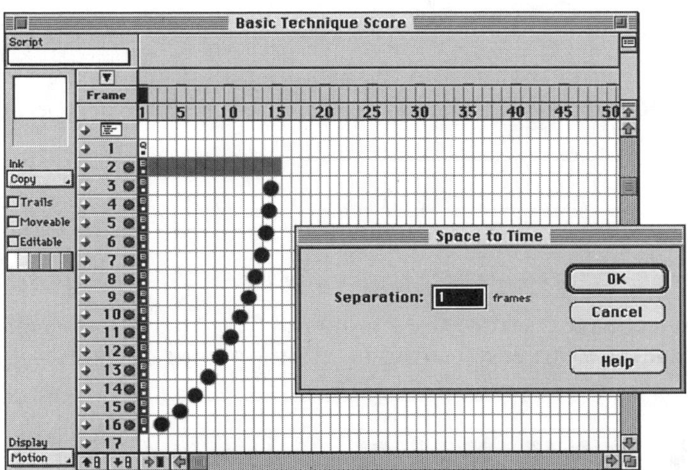

Figure 15.13

Space To Time repositions sprites from a single frame to multiple frames over time.

8. Open the Score window (Command+4).
9. Select channels 2–15 in frame 1 (the ball sequence) in the Score window.
10. Select Space To Time from the Modify menu. A dialog box asking for input dealing with the separation of the moving sprites will open.

The sprites need to be next to one another for this demo. A number of 1 in the Space To Time dialog box will keep the sprites together.

11. Enter the number **1** in the Space To Time dialog box and click OK.

The sprites in the channel of frame 1 will jump into the frames of channel 2. The sequence now travels over time. But where is the wall? When the selection was made earlier, the wall sprite was not included.

In-Between

The wall sprite will need to be included in all of the frames in the above sequence, not just the first frame. This could be done the hard way by selecting the sprite, and copying and pasting it into the other 9 frames. In-Between enables frames to be filled in with the same sprite over time.

1. Select the wall sprite in frame 1 of channel 2. While pressing the Shift key, click frame 15 of channel 1. The entire 15 frames of channel 1 should now be selected.
2. Select In-Between from the Modify pull-down menu or press Command+B.

The wall sprites will fill up the empty selected cels in channel 1.

3. Save, rewind, and play the movie to see a Space To Time and In-Betweened animation sequence.

The basic components of this movie will be needed for the next demo.

4. Select Save As from the File menu. Save this file as **`Bounce Special`** to an easy-to-find location on your hard disk.

In-Between Special

Now, let's bounce the ball on the wall a little differently. The first bounce demo was created by placing all of the sprites in the 1 frame. This time, a motion path will be created for the ball to follow. Key frames will be used along the motion path to keep from having to set up all of the individual sprite positions, as in the earlier demo.

The Bounce Special movie should be open with both the Cast and Score windows displayed.

1. Select all the sprites in channel 2 except the sprite in frame 1, the starting location. Delete sprites 2–15.
2. Drag cast member 1, the ball, into the Score window to channel 2, frame 5.

The cast members dragged to the Score will appear in the aligned center on the stage.

3. On the stage, drag this newly placed ball to a position about halfway to the wall as seen in figure 15.14. This will be a key frame, a position on the motion path.

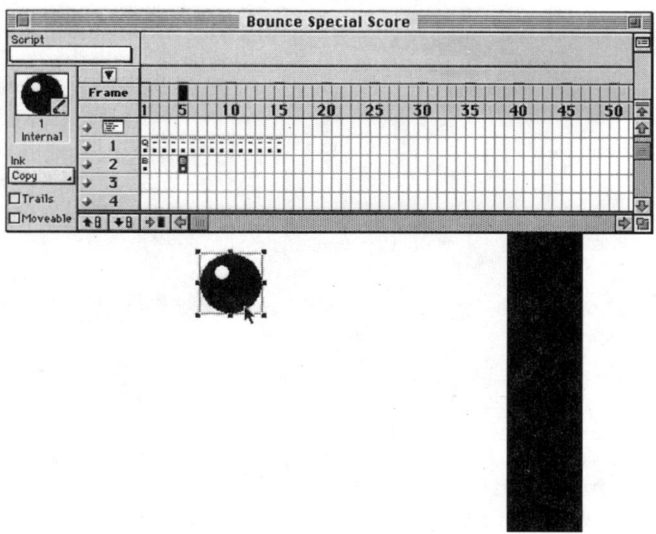

Figure 15.14

The second key frame in this animation is positioned halfway to the wall.

4. Drag cast member 1 into channel 2, frame 10 of the Score window.
5. On the stage, drag the ball located to a position touching the wall. This will be key frame 3.
6. Once more, drag cast member 1 into the Score window. Place the ball sprite in channel 2, frame 15.
7. On the stage, drag the ball to its ending location, on the ground in front of the wall. This will be the last key frame, number 4.

Now that we have all of the key frames in place, Director can set the In-Betweens.

8. Select all frames in channel 2, even if the cels don't contain sprites.

Two different In-Between effects could be applied to this group of key frames. Choosing In-Between would fill in the empty cel with evenly spaced sprites. The sprite would form a straight line from sprite to sprite. To create an arched motion path, the In-Between Special command will be used.

9. Select In-Between Special from the Modify menu (Command+Shift+B). The In-Between Special dialog box appears.

The In-Between Special dialog box options are expanded (see fig. 15.15).

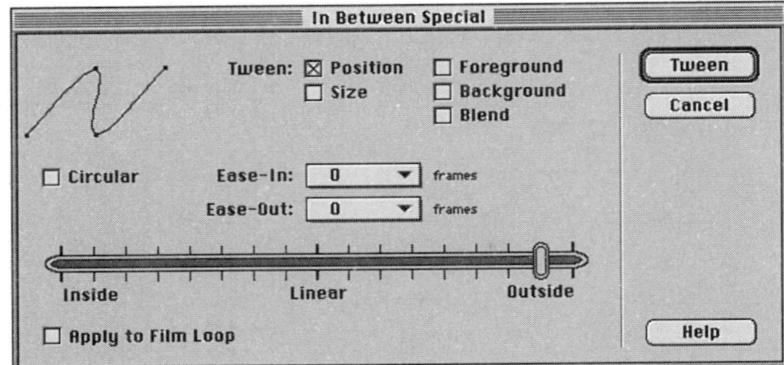

Figure 15.15

The In-Between Special dialog box options.

- **Circular.** If a sprite's start point and finish point are in the same location, checking the Circular option will cause the new path to move in a smooth circle.
- **Inside/Outside Slider.** Adjusts how closely the In-Betweened sprites stay to the original placement of the key frames. Outside will make a looser, larger motion path. Inside will make a tighter, smaller motion path. Linear will create a motion path with no curves, only straight line segments. This would be the same as selecting In-Between from the Modify menu.
- **Apply to Film Loop.** Enables the In-Betweened Special path that will be created to be applied to a looped cast member.
- **Tween Options.** These check boxes determine what attributes of the sprite are affected in the tween.
- **Ease-In/Ease-Out pop-up menus.** Can be used to make adjustments to the speed of the newly created path. These options don't change the placement of the key frames in the Score window, only the spacing of the new sprites.

10. After the adjustments are made to the In-Between Special dialog box, click the Tween button.

If the effect is not what you expected, choose Undo from the Edit menu and try again.

11. Save and play the movie to see the effects of In-Between Special applied to key frames.

Modifying a Sprite on Stage

Until now, the sprites have been used as is on the stage to create an animation. The next section will deal with changing the actual sprites on the stage.

The first Bounce Movie that was created earlier will be used for this sprite modifying demo. The movie should contain the bounce sequence of 15 frames.

1. Open Bounce Movie.
2. Close the Cast window (Command+3).
3. Open the Score window (Command+4).

The sprite that will be modified needs to be found. The Step Forward button in the Control Panel could be used by clicking the button until the correct frame is reached or the sprite could be found in the Score window by using the Display pop-up menu. To get a better understanding of the Score window, the latter technique will be used.

4. In the Score window, set the Display pop-up menu to Motion (see fig. 15.16).

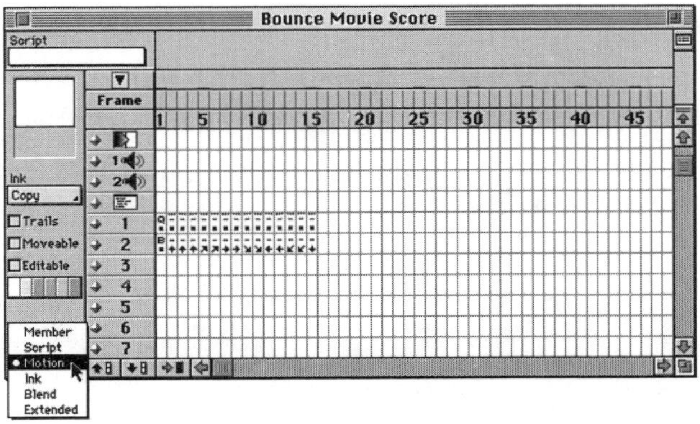

Figure 15.16

The Member pop-up display in the Score window set to Motion.

The Sprites in the Score window are now marked with arrows and lines. These indicators show the direction, if any, of the sprite in relationship to the previous frame. A straight line shows no movement; the wall sprite should have no arrows in its channel. The ball, on the other hand, should have arrows filling all of its channel except the first frame. The Q in the first frame of channel 1 indicates that the sprite is a shape or QuickDraw object. The ball displays a B for Bitmapped object.

5. In the Score window, select the last, right-pointing arrow—this should be the ball that touches the wall. The left arrows in this sequence show the ball moving away from the wall (see fig. 15.17).

Figure 15.17

The arrows in channel 2 show the movement of the ball.

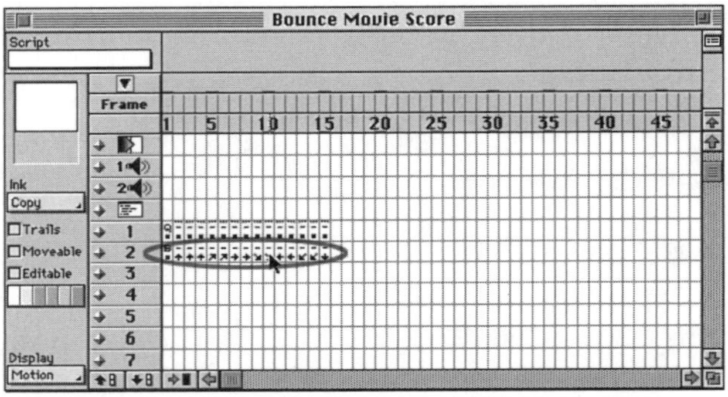

The effect that is going to be created will be the ball smashing against the wall. In the Score window, make sure the last, right-facing arrow is selected.

6. Close the Score window. To see the ball touching the wall object on the stage.

The ball is selected and is outlined in black dots. The outline has handles on all four sides and corners.

7. With the mouse, press and drag the leftmost handle toward the center of the ball. This will make the ball thinner. Release the mouse (see fig. 15.18).

In step 7, only the handle on the left is used to smash the ball. If a corner handle was used to make this distortion, the center point of the ball would shift to another location and misalign the sequence.

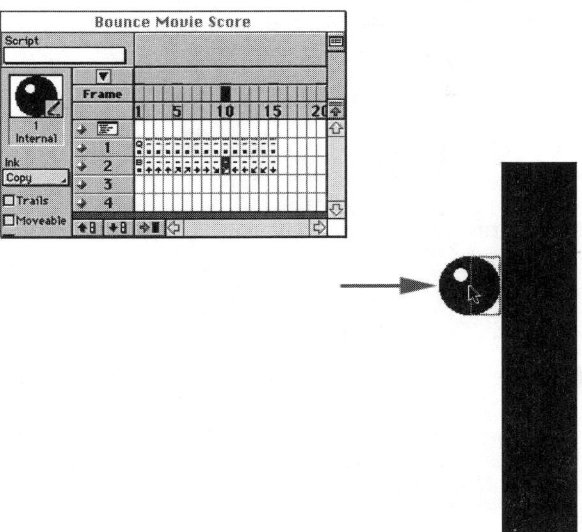

Figure 15.18

Using the left handle to distort the ball.

8. Next, use the handles at the top and bottom of the ball to expand it to make up for its lost volume. Actually, it just looks funnier this way. (See figure 15.19.)

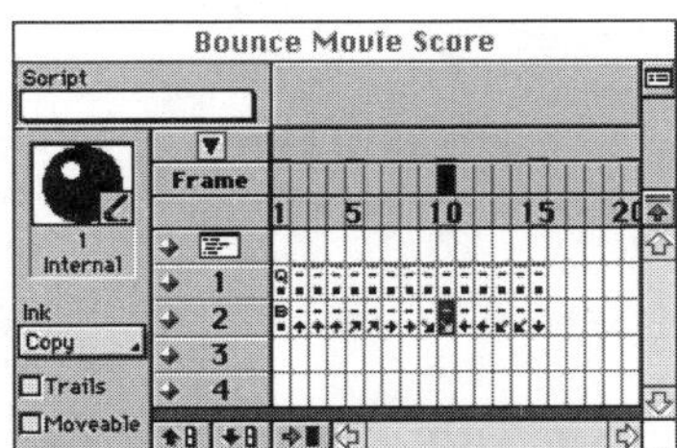

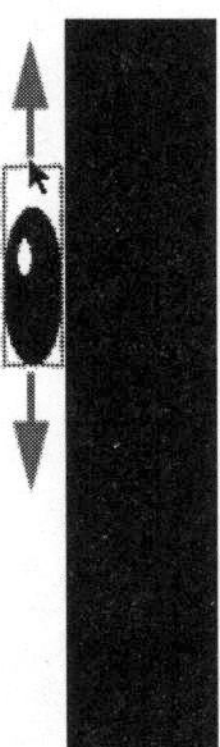

Figure 15.19

Using the top and bottom handles to distort the ball even more.

9. Save the movie as `Smashed Ball` and play the movie to see the effects of modifying sprites onstage.

Modifying a Sprite by Number Input

The above demo used a visual approach, by eye. But what if the ball had to be smashed exactly in half? You might not get it just right. Sprites also can be modified by numbers and percents. The following steps demonstrate how to repair the ball and return it to its original size.

1. Select the smashed ball sprite in the Score window (the last, right-facing arrow).
2. Choose Sprite Properties from the Modify menu. Select Properties from the Sprite pop-out from the Modify menu.

   The Sprite Properties dialog box will open (see fig. 15.20). The stage element (not the cast member) can be modified in the following way:

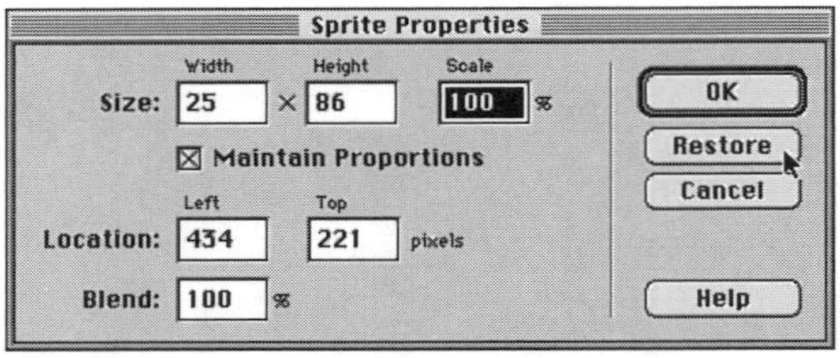

Figure 15.20

The Sprite Properties dialog box.

- **Size.** An exact amount can be entered for both the height and width of the selected sprite.
- **Scale.** The selected sprite can be reduced or enlarged by a percentage.

Remember that a bitmapped object scaled up will become very jagged. A shape will scale fine either up or down.

- **Maintain Proportions Check Box.** Keeps the left, right, top, and bottom proportions of the sprite equal.
- **Location.** These setting in pixels are the distance from the top and left sides of the stage. Use these boxes to exactly place a sprite on the stage.

- **Blend.** A sprite can have a transparency applied to it by setting a blend amount. A 50 percent blend would display a semitransparent sprite on the stage.
- **Restore Button.** Closes the Sprite Properties dialog box and restores the sprite to its original size, the size of its cast member.

3. Select the Restore button to bring the ball back to its original shape.
4. The ball's center position remains the same when restored. Use the left arrow key on the keyboard to return the ball to the correct position.

The Special Effect Channels

Above the sprite channels, the channels that contain all of the visual elements, are the special effects channels. These six special channels control the speed, color, scene changes, sounds, and script executions of each of the frames in the movie. Double-clicking on any of the following special effect channel cels will open that setting for that frame. Each special channel also has a pull-down menu item in the Modify menu. The following is a list of frame properties for each of the channels.

The Tempo Channel

With a cel selected in the Tempo channel, choose Frame Tempo from the Modify menu. This channel deals with time issues. Each time the playback head enters a frame, the Tempo channel instructs the movie to use one of the following actions. (See figure 15.21.)

Figure 15.21

The options of the Frame Properties: Tempo dialog box.

- **Tempo.** The playback speed of the movie. This speed can be seen in the Control Panel's Tempo display. The Tempo is set using frames per second (fps). The movie will play back at this set speed until another Tempo speed is encountered in a later frame. This speed is not a guarantee that the movie will play at the speed; large-moving or scaled images can cause the movie to play slower than the set Tempo speed.
- **Wait.** The playback head will wait or stall in this frame for the set amount of time. This wait setting is measured in seconds and ranges from 1–60 seconds.
- **Wait for Mouse Click or Key Press.** Without the use of Lingo commands, the playback head will wait until the mouse is clicked or any key is pressed on the keyboard. The function has its advantages over the Wait for Tempo setting above. For instance, when dealing with a screen of text or when reading a screen of text, a two-second wait might not be long enough and five seconds might be too long. The Wait for Mouse Click or Key Press enables the user to advance to the next frame when necessary.
- **Wait for End of Sound in Channel 1 or 2.** When a sound is playing in the sound channel and the playback head enters a frame with a Wait for End of Sound tempo setting, the playback head will stall in one of the two channels until the sound is finished. When the sound finishes the playback head will advance to the next frame.
- **Wait for End of Digital Video in Channel (number).** The function behaves the same as the Wait for Sound tempo setting above, except the wait deals with the playing of a digital movie. Because a digital video is a cast member, the number following the Wait for Digital Move to End setting can be set from 1–48, the sprite channels.

The Palette Channel

With a cel selected in the palette channel, select Palette from the Frame pop-up under the Modify menu. This channel sets up which color palette is to be used in the selected frame. Palettes also can be cycled. Cycling palettes are covered in the "Animating with Color Palettes" section later in this chapter. Only one palette per frame is allowed. The palette options are are shown in figure 15.22.

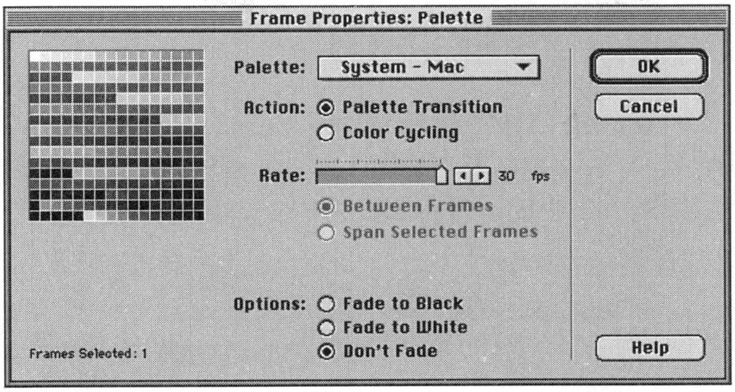

Frame Properties: Palette
Palette: System - Mac
Action: Palette Transition
Color Cycling
Rate: 30 fps
Between Frames
Span Selected Frames
Options: Fade to Black
Fade to White
Don't Fade
Frames Selected: 1
OK
Cancel
Help

Figure 15.22

The options of the Frame Properties: Palette dialog box.

Palettes only operate in an 8-bit (256 color) environment. A palette effect will not be visible with a monitor set to anything other than 256 colors.

- **Palette pop-up menu.** Standard and custom 8-bit palettes can be chosen from this list. Custom palettes that are created or imported are stored as cast members.
- **Actions: Palette Transitions.** As the playback head moves from one frame to another, different palettes can be applied to each frame.
- **Actions: Cycling Palettes.** Covered in the "Animating with Color Palettes" section later in this chapter.
- **The Rate.** The *palette rate* is the time it takes for the palette to display. The rate is set in frames per second.
- **Between Frames.** The default setting for the Color Palette dialog box. Between Frames tells Director to change to a different palette upon entering a frame. If, in the Score window, more than one frame is selected, the Span Selected Frames radio button will become available. The Span selection allows the palette to change over the selected frames.
- **Options: Fade to Black.** The entire screen will turn to black as the playback head enters the next frame in the Score. The rate slider sets the speed of the fade to black. A slow fade to black can make a very dramatic effect in a project.
- **Options: Fade to White.** Same as the Fade to Black setting above except the effect uses a white palette.
- **Options: Don't Fade.** This is the default. Believe it or not, this option won't do a fade.

The Transition Channel

With a cel selected in the Transition channel, choose Frame Transition from the Modify menu. This channel affects how the incoming frames will transition with the outgoing frames (see fig. 15.23).

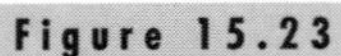

Figure 15.23

The options of the Frame Properties: Transition dialog box.

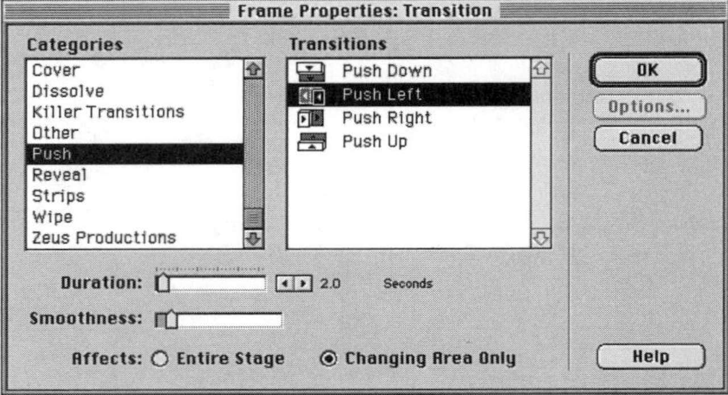

NOTE

A *transition* is the effect from frame to frame, not image to image. In other words, two images cannot transition with two different effects in the same frame. Only one effect can be applied to a single frame.

The standard Director transition palette contains 52 different transition effects. With the addition of Xtras, a plug-in technology, third-party software developers can write custom transitions for the Transition channel. Xtras may be stored in one of two places. Director-specific Xtras are stored in the Xtras folder in the application folder; shared Xtras are stored in the Xtras folder of the Macromedia folder, located in the System Folder.

The Frame Properties dialog box is divided into halves. The left half contains the categories of transitions and the right half is an item-by-item list of the selected categories. The All item in the categories side will display all of the transitions available.

- **Duration.** Sets how long a transition takes to complete in hundredths of a second. Click the right and left arrows from 0–30 seconds or use the slider to adjust the duration.
- **Smoothness.** When set to the left, executes a smooth transition. The slider set to the right executes a rough transition.

Smoothness is like a group of pixels. A setting of smooth will advance small increments of pixels throughout the transition. A setting of rough will advance in large increments of pixels throughout the transition.

- **Affects: Entire Stage.** The entire stage area will be included in the transition.
- **Affects: Changing Area Only.** Causes only the sprite that changes from frame to frame to be affected by the transition.
- **Options Button.** Active only when modification can be made to the transition. Third-party Xtras will enable fine-tuning to the transitions. The Options button is used to modify these options.

The Sound Channels

Sound cast members are dragged from the Cast Member window to either of the sound channels. The two sound channels enable two different sounds to be played in a Director project at the same time. The sound channel is covered in Chapter 12, "Sound: The Soundtrack."

Cast To Time

Director can automatically place a sequence of related cast members onto the stage. These cast members are placed over time with their registration points also aligned over time. The Director file named Pass Through located in the Chapter 15 folder on the accompanying CD will be used to try out the Cast To Time feature of Director.

The Pass Through is built of 15 individual cast members. All of the cast members need to be moved onto the stage to create an animation sequence. Cast To Time moves the cast members out to frames and automatically aligns them.

1. Open the Pass Through file and close all open windows.
2. Open the Paint window.

To view a quick flip-style animation in the Paint window, press and hold the Next Cast Member button to scan through the cast members.

3. Close the Paint window (Command+5).

4. Open the Cast window (Command+3).
5. Open the Score window (Command+4).

Set the window on the stage to match figure 15.24.

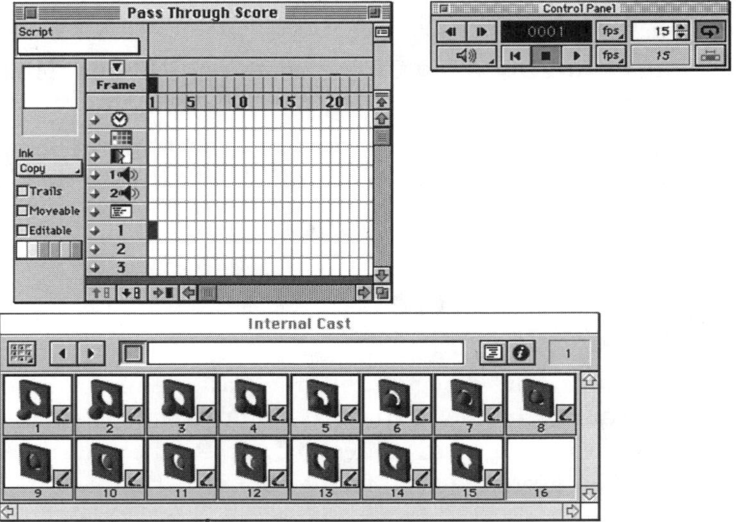

Figure 15.24
The window set up for the Cast To Time demo.

6. In the Cast Member window, select cast member 1.
7. In the Score window, select channel 1, frame 1. All of the cast members will be selected.
8. Hold the Shift key and select the last cast member—cast member 15—in the series.

This selected cel will be the starting position for the sequence.

9. Select Cast To Time from the Modify menu.

The selected cast members will be placed out onto the stage over time, in the same order as seen in the Cast Member window. These cast members are all aligned to one another, even though they are in different frames. Cast To Time places the entire sequence into the middle of the stage. To move the sequence, make sure all the sprites in channel 1 are selected.

10. With all sprites selected in the Score window, press and drag the stage image to the upper right corner of the stage.
11. Save and play the movie.

To have the movie play back and forth, the Reverse Sequence will be applied.

Reverse Sequence

The Reverse Sequence places selected sprites in their reverse order. To make the ball jump back through the block:

1. Select all of the sprites in channel 1.
2. Select Copy from the Edit menu.
3. Select frame 16 in channel 1, the next empty frame.

Only a single destination frame needs to be selected. When pasting multiple sprites from the Macintosh Clipboard, the sprites will fill in the channel to the right of the destination cel.

4. Select Paste Cells from the Edit menu.
5. Select frames 16–30 in channel 1.
6. Choose Reverse Sequence from the Modify menu.

Make sure all of the newly pasted sprites are selected before the Reverse Sequence command is given (see fig. 15.25).

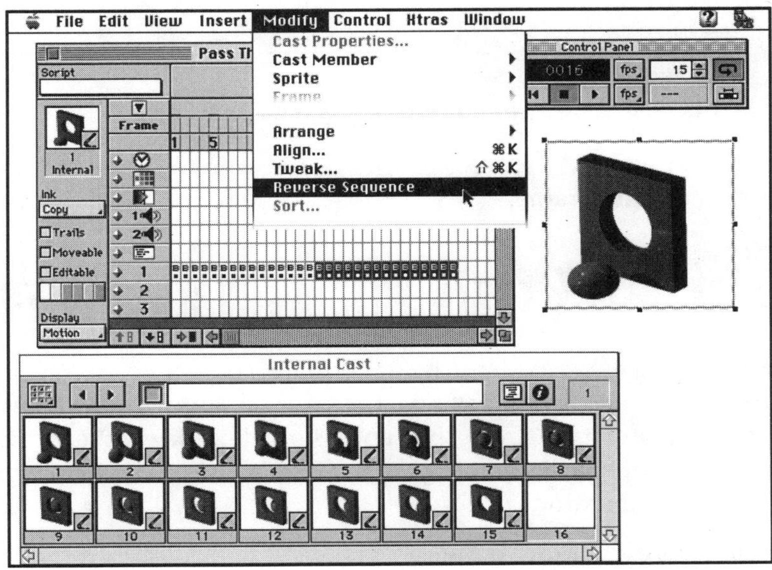

Figure 15.25

Selecting all of the sprites to be included in the Reverse Sequence.

7. Play the movie.

The movie has two hesitations in it—one in frame 16 and one in frame 30. Both of these frames are duplicates. To remove the stalled frame:

8. Select frame 16. Be sure the playback head in frame 16 is seleted also.

When deleting frames, the frame the playback head is in is the frame that will be removed (see fig. 15.26).

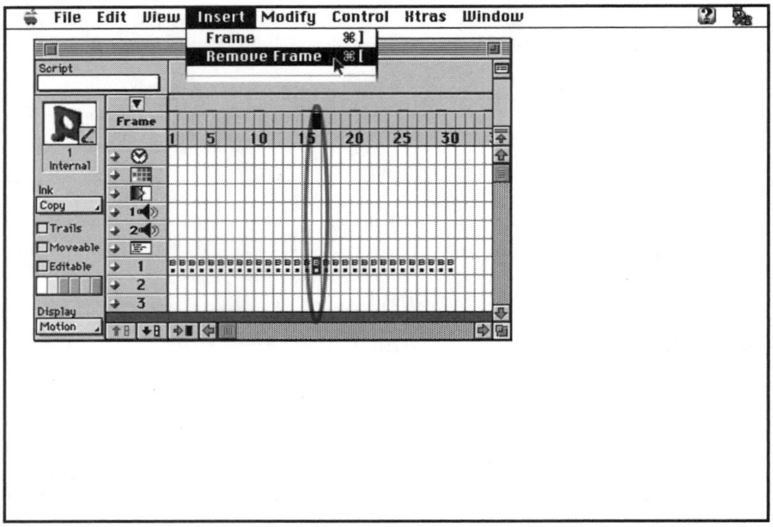

Figure 15.26

When deleting frames, the frame the playback head is in will be the frame that is removed.

9. Choose Remove Frame from the Insert menu.

Step 8 also should be applied to the last frame in the movie to remove the other stalled frame.

Quick Text Effects with Animation Wizard

Located in the Xtras menu is the Animation Wizard, a Movie in a Window, for creating quick text effects. Animation Wizard contains four anti-aliased text effects. Just enter some text, select the attributes, and there you have it—rolling credits for a movie or text effects for a business presentation.

To use the Animation Wizard:

1. Select a starting cel in the Score window. The Animation Wizard will use this cel as the starting point for any sprites it adds.
2. Choose Animation Wizard from the Xtras menu. (See figure 15.27.)

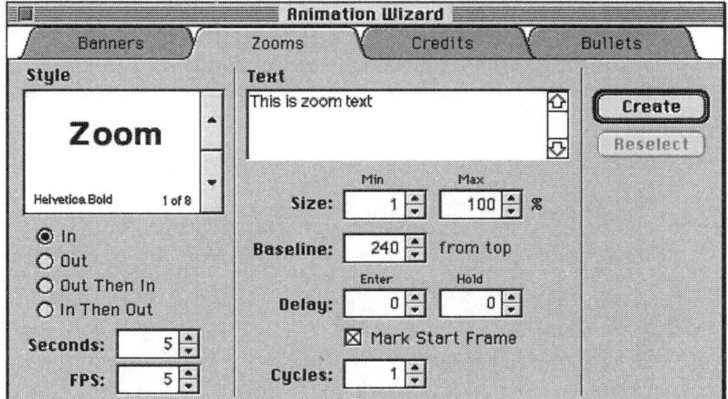

Figure 15.27

Some of the many options available in the Animation Wizard.

3. Select one of four text effects and adjust its attributes.

The following Animated text styles are available:

- **Banner.** Travels the text across the stage. The following options can be set: Font Style, the direction of travel, how long the sequence will last, the frames per second, placement on the stage, how long to wait before entering the stage, and how long to hold in the middle of the stage.
- **Zoom.** Expands or contracts text on the stage. The following options can be set: font style, how the text is to move, how long the sequence will last, the frames per second, the size of the text when the sequence starts and stops, placement on the stage, stage, how long to wait before entering the stage, how long to hold in the middle of the stage, and how many times it should repeat.
- **Credits.** Scrolling or fixed text is placed in the center of the stage. The following options can be set: font style, how long the sequence will last, the frames per second, how long to wait before entering the stage, and how long to hold in the middle of the stage.
- **Bullets.** Moves text onto the stage one line at a time. The following options can be set: font style, bullet style, how long the sequence will last, the frames per second, how long to wait before entering the stage, and how long to hold in the middle of the stage.

Once the text has been entered and the settings are made, the Create button will apply the text effect to the Score window at the position selected in step 1.

Ink Effects

How sprites are viewed on the stage doesn't stop at just their location. Setting the color attributes also plays a very important role. The following walkthrough will help to explain inks that are applied to sprites in the Score window.

Creating a Donut Demo

In the following demo, Sprite ink effects will be used to correct a few visual problems that could happen in an animation. (See figure 15.28.)

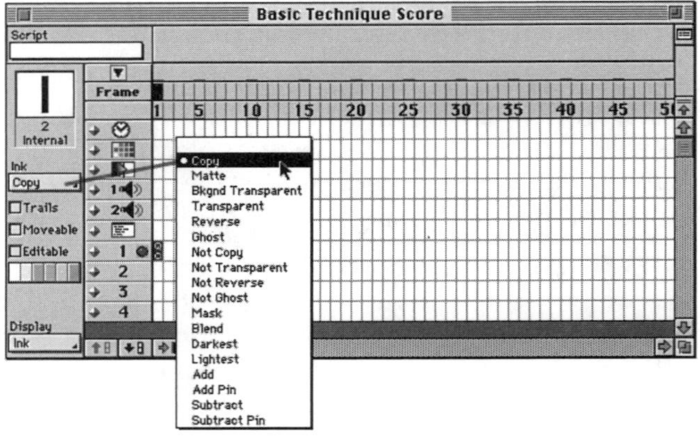

Figure 15.28

The Ink effect pop-up display in the Score window is used to change how the sprite appears on the stage.

1. Open a New Director file.
2. Save and name the file `Donut Demo`.
3. Close all windows except the Paint window.
4. Select the Filled Ellipse tool.
5. In the foreground color selector, press and drag out a dark color, and then release.

The foreground color chip will change to the selected color.

6. With the Shift key pressed, draw a medium-sized circle.

The Shift key constrains the Drawing tool and keeps the shape circular. This newly drawn element will be the outside of the donut. To put a hole in the donut:

7. In the foreground color selector, press and drag out to the white color chip (top left corner) and release.

For this demo to work, the center of the donut must be white; a light gray color will not work.

8. Select the Filled Ellipse tool again and drag a smaller white circle over the center of the larger circle. (See figure 15.29.)

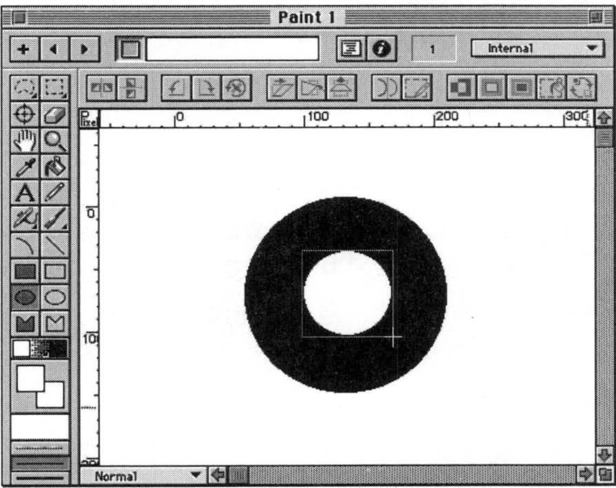

Figure 15.29
With the white foreground color chip selected, draw a smaller circle in the middle of the larger circle to make a donut hole.

Placing the center correctly takes some practice. Don't worry if the hole is not in the center. Even donut makers miss from time to time. With the foreground color chip still set to white, add sprinkles to the donut.

9. Double-click the Paintbrush tool and choose the small brush in the bottom left corner. Click OK.

10. With the paintbrush, draw a few short lines on the solid part of the donut.

11. Save the file.

For the demo the donut will need to sit on top of a table.

12. Click the New Cast Member button in the upper left corner of the Paint window. This will create a new canvas for the table art.

13. Choose a bright color from the foreground color chip.

14. Select the Filled Rectangle tool and draw a rectangle about twice the size of the donut in the previous Paint window.
15. Close the Paint window (Command+5).
16. Open the Score (Command+4) and Cast (Command+3) windows.

To understand the workings of channel layers, let's make a mistake and then correct it:

17. Drag cast member 1, the donut, onto the stage. The sprite will be placed in channel 1, frame 1.
18. Drag cast member 2, the table top, onto the stage and overlapping half of the donut.

Because we placed the donut on the layer below the table, we effectively placed the donut *under* the table. To change the order of the sprites, the table top could be cut and pasted to another place, then the donut could be cut and pasted into the table's original spot, then.... Well, we won't go through that hassle; we'll do it with a shuffle. *Shuffling* moves selected sprites up or down channels, changing their layering order.

19. Select the table top, the sprite in channel 2, and then select the Shuffle Up button (see fig. 15.30).

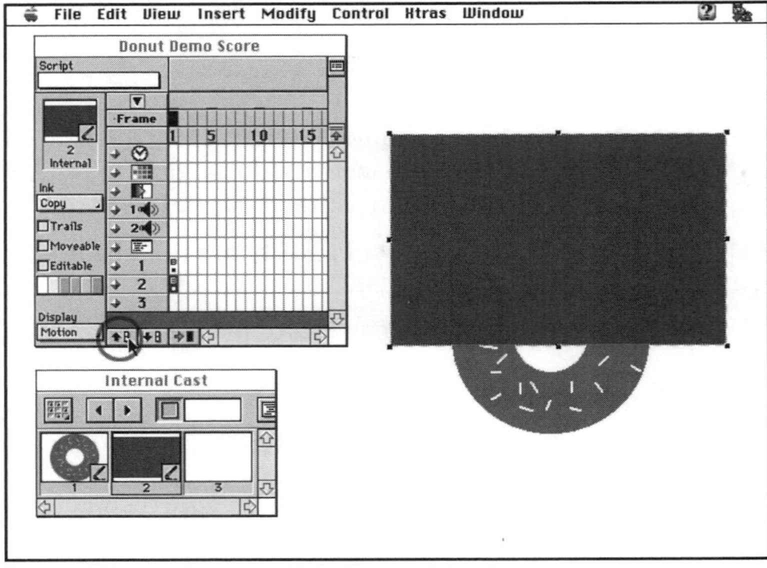

Figure 15.30

Choose the Shuffle Up button in the Score window to move the table top sprite underneath the donut sprite.

The Shuffle Down button also could be applied to the donut sprite in channel 1, moving the donut in front of the table top.

The table top moves up one channel (farther down the visual stack), and the donut is now on top, in channel 2.

The problem with sprites is that they are created on a white canvas in the Paint window. Applying an ink effect to the sprites will correct the problem of white knockouts. A Matte ink effect will be applied to change the white outside of the donut to clear, like acetate.

20. Drag the donut on the stage so that only half of it is setting on the table. The white knockout of the donut sprite can be seen. (See figure 15.31.)

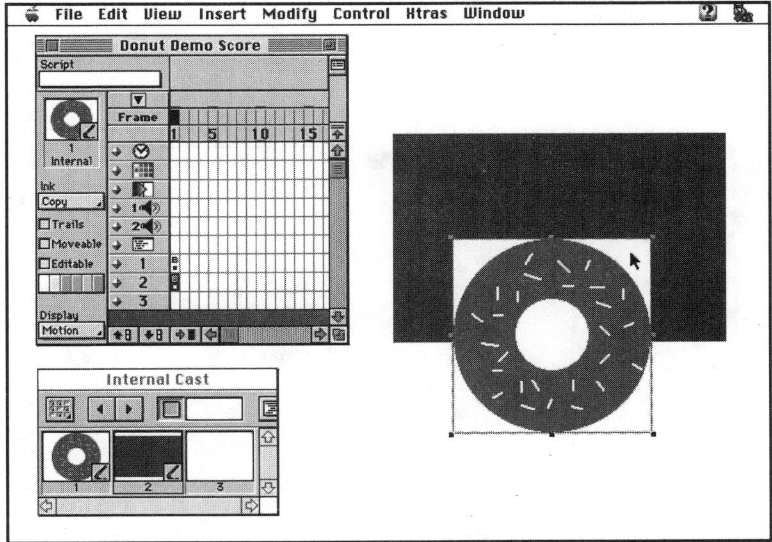

Figure 15.31

A white area of the donut sprite is visible with the ink effect set to Copy, the default setting.

21. Select the sprite in channel 2, the donut.
22. In the Score window, select the Ink pop-up menu and choose Matte from the list.

    The white edge will be removed from the donut. The Matte ink effect changes any white pixel outside of the sprite to clear.

To drop out the center of the donut:

23. In the Score window, select the Ink pop-up menu and choose Background Transparent from the list.

The center drops out. The Background Transparent ink effect changes any white pixel contained in the sprite to clear. The only problem is that the white sprinkles also are transparent.

Creating a Mask for the Donut

The problem of the transparent sprinkles can be fixed two different ways.

The first way is to change the sprinkles to the light gray color in the Paint window. Because only white pixels are affected in a Background Transparent, the light gray sprinkles will be visible. The second way to fix the problem of Transparent whites is to mask them out. Masks are 1-bit, black-and-white cast members used to block pixels.

To create a mask for the donut:

1. Move cast member 2, the table, to cast member 3. (See figure 15.32.)

Figure 15.32

Moving cast member 2 to cast member 3.

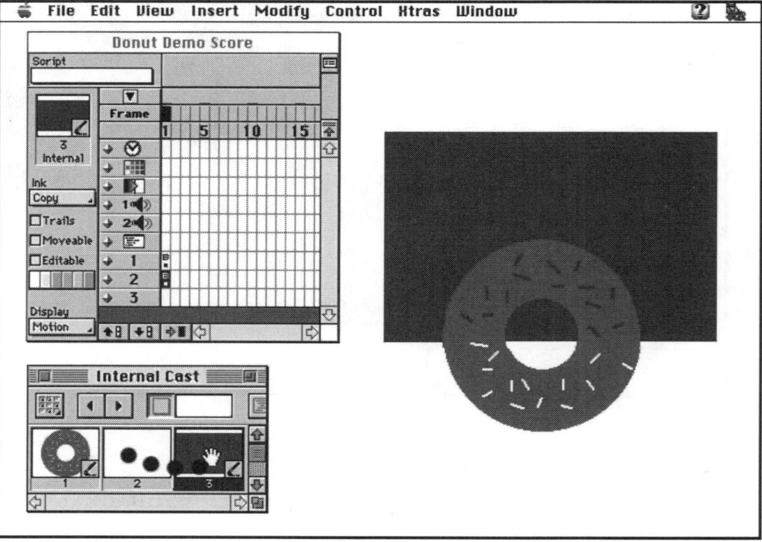

This leaves an empty cast member in the second cast member position. Masks must be placed in a position that is one cast member to the right of the cast member to be masked. Since the donut is in cast position, the mask needs to be in cast position 2. In addition to being a 1-bit cast member, a mask must be the same size as the masked cast member.

2. Select cast member 1, the donut. Choose Duplicate from the Edit menu or press Command+D to duplicate the donut to cast member 2.

This will ensure the mask is the correct size.

3. Double-click the donut mask, cast member 2.

The Paint window opens, showing the donut mask. The Paint bucket filled with black will help set the correct color of the mask.

4. Set the foreground color chip to black.
5. With the Paint Bucket tool, click on the donut artwork to change it to black.
6. With the Paintbrush tool also set to black, paint out the white sprinkles.

The finished image will be a black donut without sprinkles. The cast member looks black-and-white, but the palette is not. A 1-bit palette is needed for the mask to work.

To change the palette of the selected cast member:

7. With the donut mask selected, cast member 2, select Transform Bitmap from the Modify menu.
8. In the Transform Bitmap dialog box, set the Color Depth pop-up menu to 1 Bit (see fig. 15.33). Select OK to the alert message about the undo for this command.

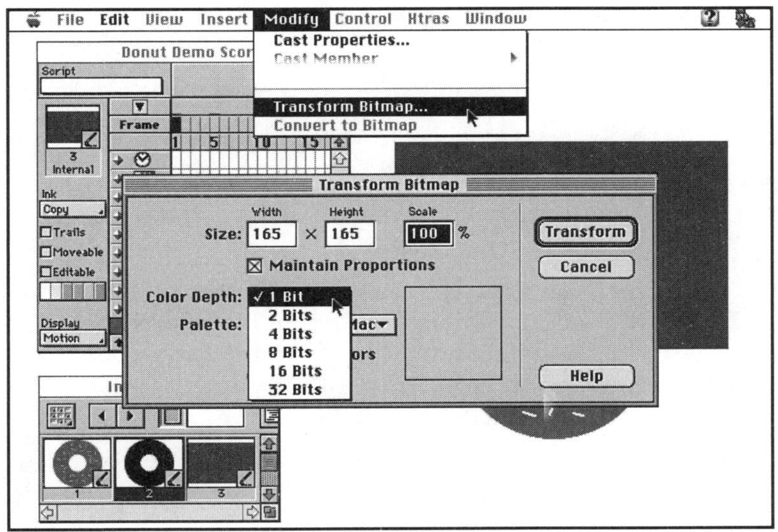

Figure 15.33

Using the Transform Bitmap dialog box to change the Color Depth of the donut mask.

The mask cast member is now the same size as the cast members to be masked and has a 1-bit palette. These are the two rules to creating a cast member mask.

9. In the Score window, set the Ink effect pop-up menu for the donut Sprite in channel 2, frame 1 to Mask.

The black area of cast member 2 (the Mask) is blocking out the transparency of cast member 1 (the Masked cast member).

10. Save the file (Command+S).

Other Ink Effects

The Ink pop-up menu contains 15 different effects that can be applied to sprites in the Score window. Copy is the default ink setting.

> The Matte and Background ink effects applied to a sprite will slow down an animation.

1. **Copy.** Displays the cast member as is. The rectangular bounding box of the image will show as white.
2. **Matte.** Sets the white pixels within a bounding box of a sprite to transparent.
3. **Background Transparent.** Sets all of the white pixels within an image to transparent.
4. **Transparent.** Makes all of the colors in a sprite transparent.
5. **Reverse.** Reverses all color in the sprite, sets white pixels to transparent.
6. **Ghost.** Changes black to white and white to transparent. Works best on 1-bit cast members.
7. **Not Copy/Not Transparent/Not Reversed/Not Ghost.** These ink effects are based on the four ink effects above. First, a reverse effect is applied to all colors in the sprite then the Copy, Transparent, Reverse, or Ghost ink effects (from above) is reapplied to the selected sprite.
8. **Mask.** Used in the previous demo. Uses the next cast member in the Cast window to block or unblock background colors.

Rules for a Mask are: must be the same size as the masked cast member, next cast member position in the cast window, and 1-bit.

9. **Blend.** Applies a blend to the sprite. The amount used in the blend is set in Sprite properties from the Modify menu.
10. **Darkest.** Compares pixels of the foreground and background colors. The Darkest ink effect displays only the darkest pixel found in the background and foreground colors.
11. **Lightest.** Compares pixels in the foreground and background colors. The Lightest ink effect displays only the lightest pixel found in the background and foreground colors.
12. **Add.** Creates a new color. The values of the background and foreground colors are added to one another. The sprite displays the combined values. If the color value exceeds the maximum visible color, the color will wrap around the color scale.
13. **Add Pin.** The same as Add with the exception that if the color value exceeds the maximum visible color, the maximum color is used.
14. **Subtract.** The opposite of Add with the exception that the minimum values are used. If the new value is less than the minimum visible color, the color will wrap around the color scale from the top.
15. **Subtract Pin.** The same as Subtract with the exception that if the color value is less than the minimum visible color, the minimum color is used.

The ink effects discussed in the list can be confusing. The best way to understand the effects is to try each one of them. The Copy, Matte, and Background Transparent ink effects will be used 99.9 percent of the time. But you never know when a strange ink accident might be just the thing you need.

Editing in the Score Window

The Score has to deal with a great many things such as cels, frames, channels, inks, and displays. The following are some handy things to know when editing in the Score window.

Cel Selections

To select a single sprite, click on it. A black reversed cel indicates the selection.

To move a single sprite to another position, cut the selected sprite, then select a new position in the Score window and paste.

To select a group of sprites, click on the first sprite in the group, then press the Shift key and click the last sprite in the intended selection. Black reversed cels indicate the selection.

To move the group of sprites, select and cut the sprites. Then select a new position in the Score window and paste. The sprites will be pasted from this position and fill to the right until all sprites are pasted. In other words, if a single cel is selected and six sprites are pasted, the single cel will be filled with the first sprite and then five more cels to the right of the single cel will be filled with the remainder of the sprite.

Drag-and-Drop Option

Cels can be moved around the stage without cutting and pasting. Select Score from the Preferences pop-out from the File menu. In the Display Options, select the Drag-and-Drop Enabled check box. To select a cel, click on it. To move the cel, press and drag the cel—a clutching hand cursor will indicate the moving process—to another location in the Score window and release. (See figure 15.34.)

In addition to using Drag-and-Drop to move cels, pressing the Option key while dragging will copy the cel to the new location.

To select a group of cels, press an unselected cel and drag to select the remaining cels. The key to this selection is that the first cel is not already selected. Trying to select a group of cels with the first cel already selected will only move that cel. If this becomes a problem, disable Drag-and-Drop through the Score preferences.

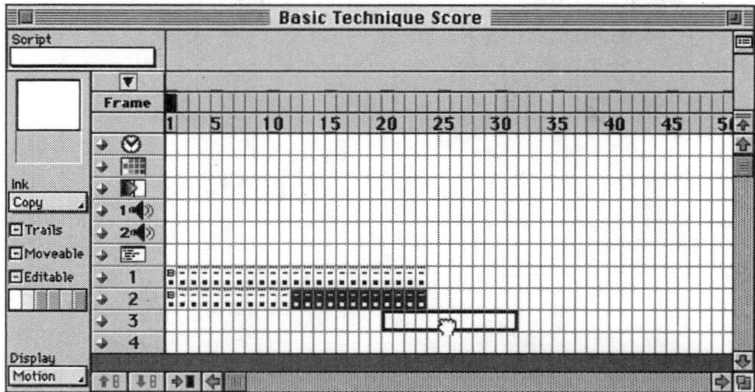

Figure 15.34

The Drag-and-Drop option enables the sprite to be moved around the Score window by pressing and dragging.

Inserting and Deleting Frames

Cutting cels from a channel will not shorten a movie. This will only remove images from a frame. To actually make the movie shorter, frames need to be removed. The position of the playback head is very important to the Delete Frame command. The frame where the playback head is located is the frame that will be removed when the Delete Frame command from the Insert menu is used.

The Insert menu's Frame command will add a frame to the movie. If any cels are located in the frame where the addition is to take place, the cels will be duplicated and moved one frame to the right.

Color Coding Cels

When working with a 100-frame movie, the actual available cels for this movie would be 100 frames × 54 channels or 540 active cels. Trying to find a single cel in a group of more than 500 can take some time. Cels can be arranged in colored groups. Moving elements could be blue, buttons could be red, and text media could be yellow. This makes spotting a cel or group of cels much easier.

To set the colors of cels:

1. Select Score from the Preferences pop-out from the File menu and choose Allow Colored Cells in the resulting dialog box. A small color palette will appear to the left side of the Score window when the dialog box is closed.
2. Select a cel or range of cels, then select a color from the cel color palette. The cel is now color coded. (See figure 15.35.)

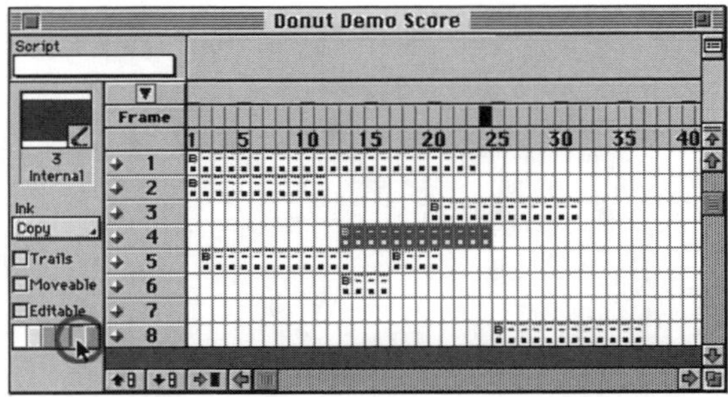

Figure 15.35

Select a range of cels and choose a cel color. Colored cels are easier to locate within the Score window.

The color of the cel will not affect the sprite on the stage.

Advanced Animation Techniques

This section of the chapter covers more advanced animation techniques using Director's built-in features such as film loops and Cycling palette. In Director, many of the traditional animation techniques have been condensed to a few keystrokes and mouse clicks. This provides more time to be creative and less time spent repeating steps.

The first demo that will be created will deal with Auto Distort and film loops. Auto Distort changes cast members, then applies the changes to multiple cast members to be used over time. Film loops are very useful for creating things such as flying birds and spinning tires on a car. A *film loop* is a sequence that repeats over and over and doesn't have to be baby-sat. Just place the looped cast member on the stage, and it does its thing. Individual cast members from the loop don't have to be bothered with once a loop is made. The following demo will make spinning clock hands.

Auto Distort

1. Open the Director file named Loop Demo.
2. Close all open windows, except the Cast window.

The Cast Member window contains two cast members: a clock face and a single clock hand.

3. Double-click cast member 2, the clock hand. The Paint window opens.
4. Close the Cast Member window.

The first thing that needs to be done is to spin the clock hand cast member. Here, the single cast member will be duplicated into many different positions by using Director's Auto Distort feature.

5. In the Paint window, select the Marquee tool with its option set to Shrink.
6. Drag a selection around the clock hand artwork. Upon releasing the mouse, the marquee will snap closely around the artwork (see fig. 15.36).

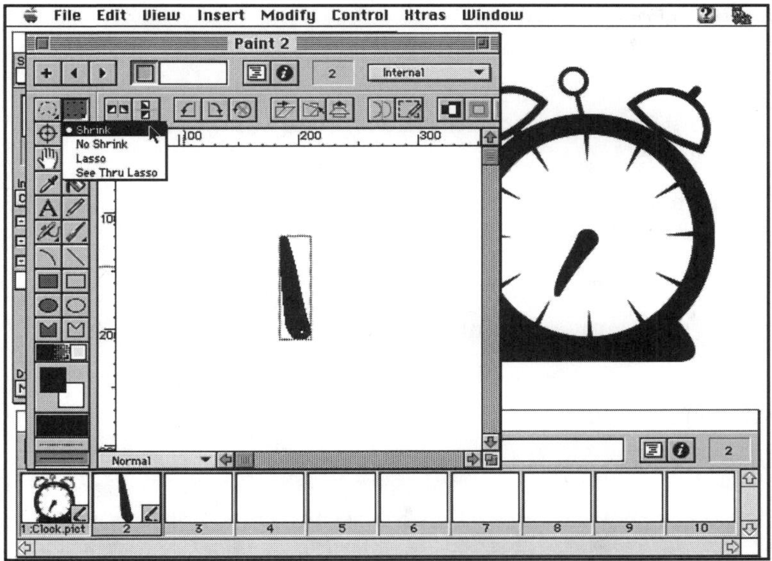

Figure 15.36

With the Marquee tool set to Shrink, drag a selection around the clock hand.

The clock hand will need to be rotated 360 degrees. The Paint window has a row of function keys for special effects. These effects will be combined with Auto Distort to create a spinning loop cast member.

To spin the artwork:

7. With the artwork selected, click the Rotate Right button four times to rotate the hands 360 degrees. *Don't deselect the artwork.*

The artwork is now in the process of distorting. Director knows the original position and the current position of the selected artwork.

8. Choose Auto Distort from the Xtras menu.
9. An alert dialog box displays, waiting for a number of new cast members to create. Enter **12** to create a total of 13 cast members. Click Begin to create the new cast members.
10. Close the Paint window.

The reason for making an extra cast member is to get the first and last positions lined up. Now, the duplicate cast member will be removed.

11. Open the Cast Member window and delete cast member 14, the last clock hand. Choose Cut Cast Member from the Edit menu or press Command+X.
12. Select the clock face cast member and drag it to the stage.

The In-Between command will be used to make the clock available throughout the entire movie.

13. In the Score window, channel 1, frame 1, the clock face sprite should be selected. Press the Shift key and click the cel in channel 1, frame 12.
14. With all 12 frames selected in the channel, choose In-Between from the Modify menu.

This fills channel 1 with the clock face.

15. Save the movie (Command+S).

Cast To Time will be used to place all 12 cast members onto the stage, aligned over time.

Notice where the playback head is located. The last mouse action in the Score window was selecting a range of cels from frames 1–12. If the Cast To Time command was given now, the clock hand sequence would replace the In-Between of the clock from step 14. The playback head needs to be moved to frame 1 of channel 2.

16. Select frame 1, channel 2. This will be the start position for the clock hands. This will put the playback head in frame 1.
17. Select all of the clock hands in the Cast window by selecting the first clock hand, pressing the Shift key, and selecting the last clock hand.

18. Choose Cast To Time from the Modify menu. The Score window now shows 12 sprites in both channels 1 and 2, the clock and hands. The Cast To Time automatically places all of the cast members to the center of the stage.

19. Select all the sprites in channel 2 of the Score window and set the ink effect to Matte.

Step 19 accomplishes two things. Selecting all the sprites in channel 2 ensures that when the artwork on the stage moves, all 12 sprites move. The Matte ink effect removes the white area around the clock hands.

20. With all of the sprites selected in channel 2, on the stage, drag the selected hand artwork to the center of the clock face (see fig. 15.37).

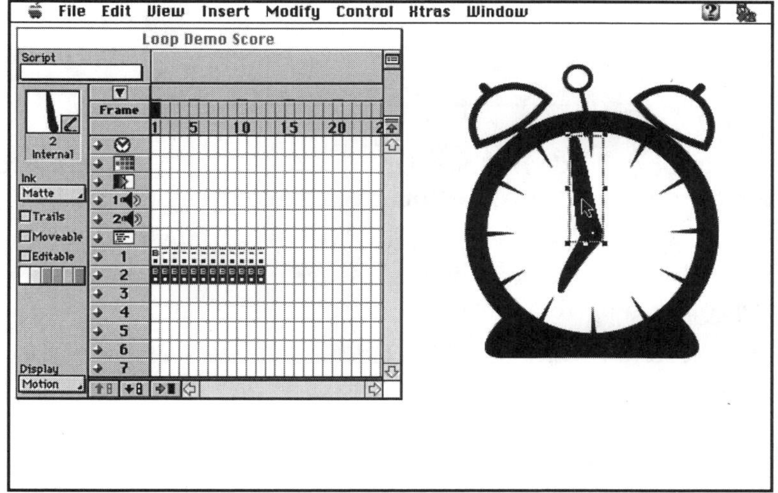

Figure 15.37

Set the ink effect to Matte and reposition the clock hand to the center of the clock face.

21. Save the movie, then play it.

The hands on the clock do not rotate correctly. They rotate from their own center and not the center of the clock. To recenter the hand without moving each individual sprite on the stage, the registration point will be changed in the Paint window.

22. Open the Paint window and click on the Next Cast Member button until cast member 2, the vertical hand artwork, is selected.

By default, the registration point is set to the physical center of the artwork. To reposition the registration point on the artwork:

23. Select the Registration tool in the Paint window toolbox. Click a new registration point on the white dot at the bottom of the artwork (see fig. 15.38).

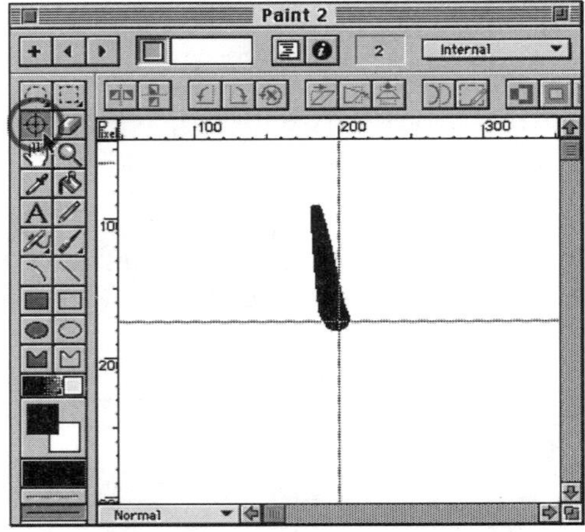

Figure 15.38

Use the Registration tool in the Paint window to register paint images.

The white dot was added to the original cast member to help easily find the rotation point. This white dot can be filled in later if needed.

24. In the Paint window select the Next cast member button to advance to the next clock had cast member and reposition the registration on this artwork.
25. Repeat step 24 until all of the clock hands are registered. (Do not change the registration on the clock artwork.)
26. In the Score window, again select all sprites in channel 2. On the stage, drag the clock hand back to the center of the clock face.
27. Close the Paint window and play the movie.

The hands now spin from the center of the clock face and only the registration points were moved to realign all of the sprites. Auto Distort has other options such as skew, warp, and perspective. These options are applied in the same fashion as the rotate steps above.

Film Loops

The above demo created spinning hands of a clock. The animation could stay as is and work just fine, until the animation sequence called for the clock to jump around as if it were ringing. The ringing animation would be a little harder to keep track of in the Score window due to the fact that multiple cast members would have to be aligned to a moving object. A film loop enables all of the hand cast members to be contained in a single cast member. Now when the clock jumps around, only a single cast member containing a series of events has to be dealt with.

Film loops are easy to create but sometimes difficult to understand why and when they're to be used. Generally, film loops are used when a repeating sequence is needed within a Director movie—a spinning tire on a car moving around the stage; a bird or birds flying around the stage; hands spinning around a clock face.

1. With the Score window open, select all of channel 2, the spinning hands.
2. Be sure the ink effect is set to Matte for all the sprites in channel 2.

Ink effects must be applied to the sprite before the loop is made. Otherwise, the ink effect is locked into the looped cast member.

3. Choose Cut Cells from the Edit menu.

The Clipboard now contains the placement and cast member number for each of the sprites.

4. Open the Cast window.
5. Select cast member 14, the next empty cast member position.
6. Choose Paste from the Edit menu. An alert dialog box appears.

The Cast window sees 12 incoming sprites, but the Cast window only holds cast members. A film loop is a cast member, except this loop cast member contains the location and cast numbers of the 12 sprites cut from channel 2. (See figure 15.39.)

> Never delete the original cast member used in the film loop. The film loop is using the originals to play back the loop. The original cast members can be modified. This modification will show in the film loop.

7. In the alert box, name the loop. Click OK.

The looped cast member will need to be placed back onto the stage.

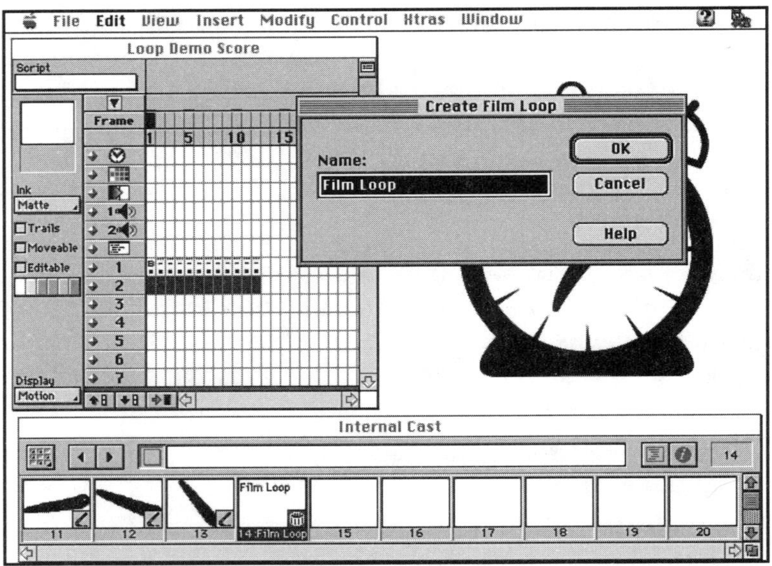

Figure 15.39

Pasting sprites into the Cast Member window will bring up the Loop Cast Member dialog box.

8. In the Cast window, drag the looped cast member out of the Cast Member window and onto the stage, align to the center of the clock.
9. Select from frames 1–12 in channel 2 and choose In-Between from the Modify menu.

This will fill in the remainder of the cel with the spinning hands.

10. Save the movie and then play it.

> The clock hands and the clock face also could be made into another loop. Loops within loops are acceptable. To bounce the clock around the stage now, only one sprite on the stage would need to be dealt with. This single sprite would contain the clock and the spinning hand all on one place for easy movement around the stage.

Animating with Color Palettes

Animated color palettes only work within an 8-bit palette. The monitor on the computer will need to be changed to 256. Refer to your Macintosh user's guide for instructions on changing to 256 colors.

A *color palette* is a grid of 256 available colors. Swapping or moving colors within a palette can cause some very interesting effects. In the next demo, a toaster will be made to look like it's becoming hotter over time using color cycling.

The demo is located on the accompanying CD-ROM in the Chapter 15 folder. The file is named Toaster Demo.

1. Copy the demo over to the current computer.
2. Open the file Toaster Demo from the hard disk.
3. Play the movie.

The movie contains all the cast members to make the movie except the palette to correctly animate the colors. In this demo, the toaster will start out as light blue, and as it heats, it will turn more red. Color cycling will be used to create this effect. The effect also could be done with lots of different colored cast members, but this would take up a great deal more disk space. Color cycling only needs to add 1 cast member, a palette.

1. Close all open windows.
2. Open the Color Palettes window (Command+Option+7) shown in figure 15.40.

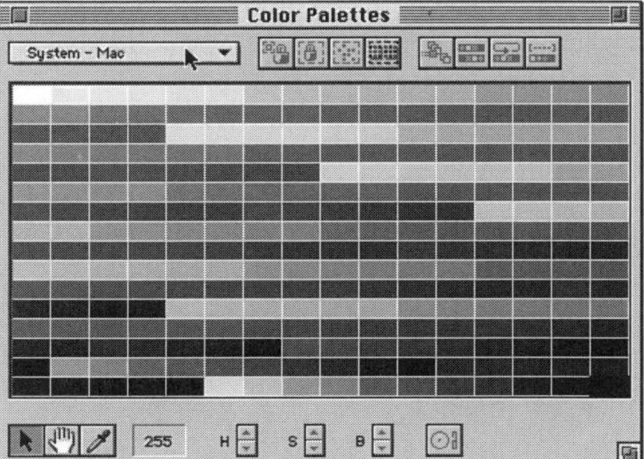

Figure 15.40

The Color Palettes window can be customized and stored in the Cast Member window.

The toaster is currently light yellow. Light yellow is chip 1 in the color palette. First, the color of the toaster will be changed to light blue. When you look at the color palette, you'll notice a light enough blue color is not available. You'll need to create a new color palette where the needed blue color chip will be created.

Chip 0, the white color chip, and chip 255, the black color chip can never be altered. The black-and-white chip is available.

3. Double-click on chip 1 of the Color Palette window. The Apple Color Picker will appear. (Chip 1 is actually the pale yellow chip to the right of the white chip, which is actually Chip 0.)
4. Press and drag around the color wheel until you find a light blue (see fig. 15.41).

Figure 15.41

Selecting a light blue color from the Apple Color Picker.

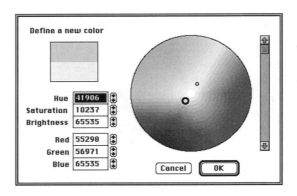

5. Click OK in the Apple Color Picker. An alert box appears.

The System-Mac palette cannot be changed. When a change is made to the System-Mac palette, a duplicated palette will be created.

A name needs to be given to this the new palette. The newly created palette will appear in the Cast window as an internal cast member.

6. Name the palette "Toaster palette."

If the movie is played now, no change will take place. The movie is still using the default system palette.

To change to the new Toaster palette:

7. Open the Score and Cast Member windows.
8. Drag cast member 6, the Toaster palette, out of the Cast Member window and into the Score window, palette channel, frame 1, as shown in figure 15.42.

On the stage the toaster will turn light blue. When working with the palette, Director only worries about one thing—the color of the chip in the cast member. Like a paint-by-number book, Director only sees the number of the cast member. If the palette being used has a yellow chip 1, the image will be yellow; if the palette being used has a light blue chip 1, the image will be light blue.

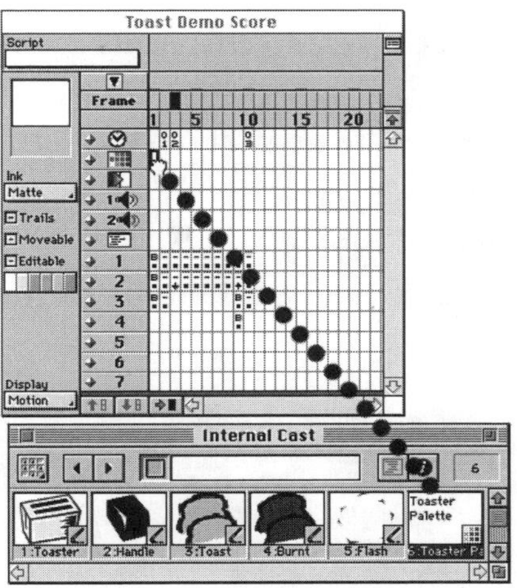

Figure 15.42

Applying the Toaster palette to the palette channel in the Score window.

9. Save and play the movie.

To make the toaster change colors gradually is a little more difficult. The program has to be told to swap color in and out of the current palette. Color cycling is used to change color over time.

10. Close the Cast and Score windows.
11. Open the Color Palettes window. In the upper left corner, select Toaster Palette from the Palette pop-up menu (see fig. 15.43).

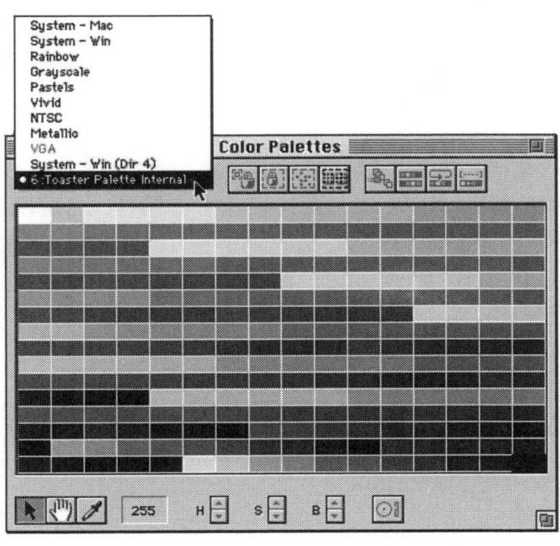

Figure 15.43

Selecting the Toaster palette in the Color Palette window.

The color change that will take place will be the toaster starting light blue and gradually growing more red as it appears to become hot. Using the color palette, a range of color will be set up to display one after another, a cycle. First, the color has to be added to the color palette.

12. Double-click on chip 8 and change its color to a bright red. Click OK.

The first and last colors are now set. To blend the 2 colors together:

13. With chip 8 selected, press the Shift key and click on chip 1, the light blue chip. All the chips in between will be selected.
14. Choose the In-Between button in the palette as shown in figure 15.44.

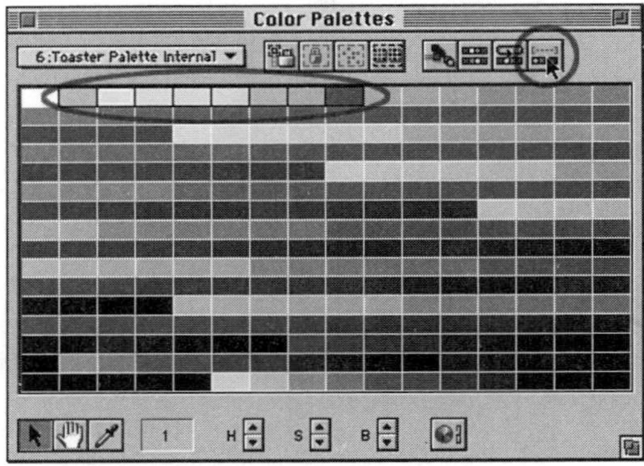

Figure 15.44

Selecting a range of color to In-Between in the Color Palette window. The In-Between button is visible at the top of the palette.

The light blue will blend into the red. This blend can be as long or as short as needed. Be careful not to blend past the eighth color chip. The ninth color chip is used in the toast in cast member 3. Changing this chip also will change the light toast. Now that the palette is correct, the Score has to know to cycle this toaster palette.

15. Close the Color Palette window.
16. In the Score window, double-click on the palette channel, frame 8. This frame is where the palette cycle will take place. The Frame Properties: Palette dialog box will open as shown in figure 15.45.

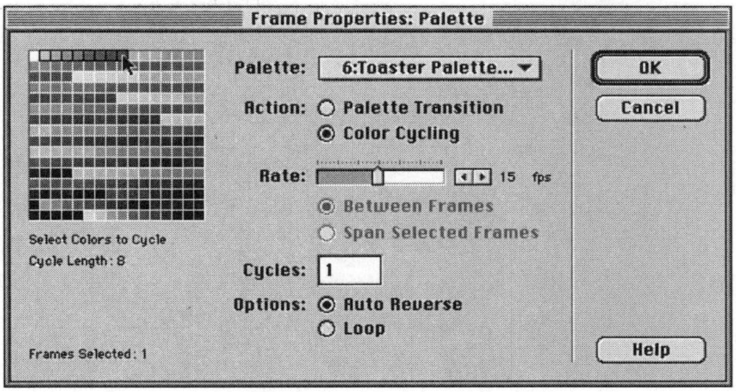

Figure 15.45

Setting the Properties in the Frame Palette dialog box.

To have the palette cycle, a range of color chips must be selected.

17. In the Frame Properties: Palette dialog box, Toaster Palette should be selected in the Palette pop-up menu. Press and drag over chips 1–8 in the chip mini-window as shown in figure 15.45. The cycle length at the bottom of the mini-window should be 8.
18. Select the Color Cycling radio button.
19. Set the Rate for the palette change; 15 frames per second is fine.
20. The effect will happen only once. The Cycle number should be 1.

To make the toaster heat up and cool down, a reverse will be applied.

21. Select the Auto Reverse radio button and click OK.
22. Save and play the move.

The toaster cast member changes colors without having to add any new cast members to the movie. The Palette options take time to understand and a little planning ahead is very helpful. Moving color chips around a palette before artwork is created is much easier than trying to recolor artwork to match up with a modified palette.

Troubleshooting

The following sections cover what to look out for when beginning or working in Director.

Saving

"If you save every two minutes, you can only lose two minutes of work. If you save every two hours, you can lose two hours of work." Can't stress this one enough. As a full-time instructor, I have seen literally hundreds, if not thousands, of system crashes. As much time as I spend preaching to my students, it always surprises me to walk around a room and see an untitled document or a document that is stored in temporary memory.

Some of the best times to save your work include:

- After you've opened a file and set up the parameters.
- After you've entered a line or paragraph of text.
- Before you print a document or run a movie.

Scaled Sprites

The number one cause of a slow-playing Director movie is generally a scaled sprite. A *scaled sprite* is a cast member that has been imported onto the stage at a different size than its original size. Cast members should always be imported at their intended size. Earlier in the chapter, the discussion on channel explains the process of putting a movie out to the stage. The playback head has to travel through 54 different channels of information (see the brief discussion on transitions later in this section). If in this lineup of information the playback head encounters a scaled sprite, the playback head literally calculates the differences in size and draws the object on the stage.

If the sprite is found to be the wrong size after importing, two things can be done to the cast member. First, return to the application and rework the master. (You did keep the master, didn't you?) Second, use Transform Bitmap from the Modify menu to resize the cast member (see fig. 15.46). The transform bitmap allows the cast member to be sized in two different ways—by percentage or actual pixel size. If a sprite has to be scaled, always scale down. In other words, import the image larger and scale down on the stage. The image on the stage will stay sharp, whereas an image scaled up will become jaggy and distorted.

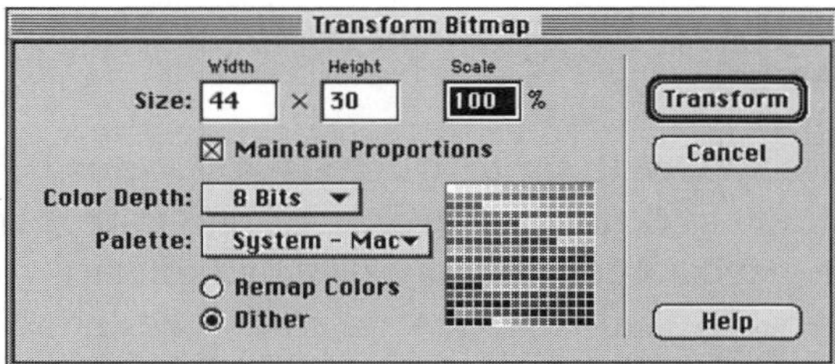

Figure 15.46

Use the Transform Bitmap dialog box to resize cast members.

To have the palette cycle, a range of color chips must be selected.

Bit Depth

The monitor controls the show. When a new Director document is opened, the first thing Director does is check the monitor's *bit depth*, the number of colors that will be displayed on the computer screen. For example, a client asks for a portfolio of quick color sketches and the portfolio has to be rather small to fit on leftover space on some type of removable media. You fire up Director and as soon as you can start creating some very nice illustrations, put them on the screen, and add some Lingo scripts to navigate through the imagery.

Upon finishing the project and quitting Director, you find a file that's megabytes in size instead of kilobytes. Funny, the images weren't that big—only a few colors here and there. When you use Director again to investigate, you find that the monitor was set to millions of colors. The image that was to be small is actually many times the size it should have been!

This problem can be fixed by using Transform Bitmap from the Modify menu and changing the bit depth of the drawings. The only problem is the 24-bit images will dither. (*Dithering* is the process of replacing pixels in an image.) The incoming pixels are from a palette of less colors. The dither puts these limited colored pixels in small groups to try to match the colors in the original full-color image. A dithered image will look speckled compared to the original. If the monitor was set to the correct setting before launching Director, the images would have been created in the correct palette in the first place—without having to dither the images.

Ink Effects

The ink effects applied to sprites can cause a slowdown in the playback speed. The Copy ink effect is the only ink effect that will not cause a slowdown in playback performance. The two killer inks, the effects that slow the playback the most, are Matte and Background Transparent. If possible, fill the whole of a cast member with the color it passes over. If the image moves over different colored backgrounds, then this technique will not work. A good rule of thumb is if the image doesn't move, it generally doesn't need an ink effect. Last, the sprite in channel 1, the lowest layer, never needs an ink effect other than Copy. If an ink effect is applied to the background, even though no effect is seen, the computer still processes the ink effect and slows the playback.

The Active Window

As people become more accustomed to applications, they tend to use keyboard shortcuts more and more. Just remember that in Director, cutting a cast member could remove many sprites. The Cast window and the Score window can be open at the same time, but only one of the windows can be active. The window with the title bar visible is the active window. Director does have a built-in safety—the program will bring up an alert box if two or more cast members are being deleted.

Transitions

Each time the playback head enters a frame, 54 channels of information are passed to the stage. A *transition* is an effect from frame to frame. When transitioning from frame 5 to frame 6, the actual transition information would occupy the transition channel of frame 6. The transition happens "between" frames 5 and 6. (See figure 15.47.)

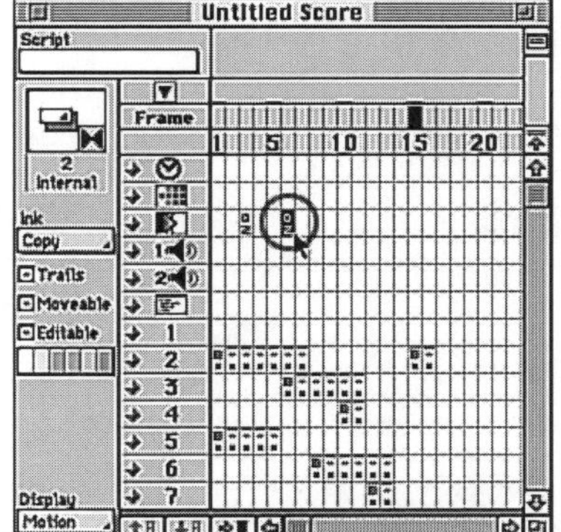

Figure 15.47

A Transition occurs between two frames. The playback head travels down one column of channels then advances to the next frame and travels down that column of channels. The transition happens between the frames.

Summary

Forty-eight channels of graphics, unlimited styles of transitions, more colors than the biggest box of crayons you had as a child, and multichannel sound mixing. Take all of these features, add complete control to it with Lingo scripts, and what you have is a very impressive and powerful package of goods. Regardless of whether these come from scans, drawings, video captures, stock photography, or are created internally in Director, stationary artwork literally jumps off the screen when put into motion. With Director's full palette of features, even people new to the tasks of animation can create very professional and extremely impressive animated presentations in a very short time.

PART IV

Lingo

Gretchen Macdowall

Lingo: The Basics

You can make useful movies in Director without typing a line of Lingo. Almost any movie that plays from start to finish, with occasional pauses to wait for a mouse click, can be created by using the Score alone. Linear Director movies work well for presentations.

Director movies that leave the navigation to the user rather than proceeding straight from start to finish are an entirely different story. You need Lingo to make your movies interactive.

Is Lingo hard to learn? No! The basic command set is very similar to HyperTalk—HyperCard's built-in language that turned programming over to "the rest of us" in 1985. Although the Lingo dictionary now contains more than 600 entries, the bulk of everyday coding centers around the 15 commands outlined in the "Essential Lingo" section of this chapter. Learn them and you're halfway there.

The bigger challenge is to understand how Lingo interacts with cast members and the Score, and where to place your scripts so they do what you want them to do.

You know by now—from working with the Score alone—that a Director movie that contains no Lingo plays from frame 1 straight through to the last frame, displaying and playing whatever cast members you have placed in each frame of the Score. When Lingo executes, it controls playback in place of the Score. A Lingo script can do the following:

- Jump to another part of the Score or to another movie
- Change the cast member and other properties of any sprite channel
- Keep a Director movie paused by looping continuously in one frame
- Detect and respond to a particular user action, such as a mouse click in a certain area of the screen, or a key press
- Generate new score frames on the fly and fill them up with members (new in version 5)

With the Score alone you can create movies that entertain your audience. With Lingo you can create experiences that include them. There are essential Lingo commands to learn and we'll get to those soon, but to use them effectively you must first understand a little about the Director environment.

Key Concepts

In an interactive Director movie the user runs the show. You can't tell from looking at a still screen, but behind the scenes Director is constantly checking to see whether the user has moved the mouse or typed a key. The bulk of Director programming lies in telling Director how to respond to the user. It can even include detecting when the user has done NOTHING for awhile and programming some enticement to continue.

This section takes you on a tour of the two sides of that environment—yours and the user's. On your side you have commands and functions. Those are the actions you can take. Most commands and functions work on objects in the Lingo environment such as sprites, cast members or windows. They make something happen that the user can see. On the user side are events and messages. Everything the user does (or doesn't do) with the mouse and the keyboard is an event that generates a Director message.

Your job is to use commands and functions to write message handlers that tell Director how to respond to messages. After reading this section you will understand Director's system for letting you know about user events, and you will know where to place your scripts to respond to those events.

Commands and Functions

Commands and functions are the building blocks of Lingo. Almost every line of code you write contains at least one command or function. *Commands make something happen.* The following lines of code all contain commands. In each line, the command is in bold. Each command line is followed by a *comment line* that explains what the command does.

```
sound close 1
-- stops the sound playing in sound channel 1
preLoad 12,15
-- loads any cast member in the score between frames 12 and 15
➥into memory
put " " into field "Question 1"
-- clears field "Question 1" by filling it with a space
```

Functions return a value that you can test, or store in a variable. Some functions require you to pass them values when you call them.

Functions that require values are documented with parentheses after them in the *Lingo Dictionary*. The following lines of code contain functions. In each line the function is in bold. The comment that follows each code line explains what it does.

```
if the stillDown = TRUE then go the frame
-- The stillDown function returns TRUE or FALSE
-- This line of code tests if the user is holding down the mouse
➥and continues
-- to loop in the same frame as long as the user is holding down
➥the mouse
put list( 4, 8, 12 ) into buttonSpriteList
-- The list function takes the values you pass in parentheses and
➥returns a
-- list containing those values - in other words the list command
➥makes
```

```
-- a list for you
-- This line of code makes a new list and saves it in the variable
-- buttonSpriteList for later use.
set nextFreeCast = findEmpty(member "ButtonZ")
-- The findEmpty function takes the cast member value you pass
➥in parentheses
-- and returns the number of the next empty cast slot.
-- This line of code sets variable nextFreeCast to the number of
➥the next empty
-- cast slot after cast "ButtonZ".
```

Inserting two hyphens in front of a code line creates a comment. Get into the habit now of documenting your Lingo as you go along. Not only do you make things easier for another person who might have to read your code, you help yourself as well. It's almost a given that you will have to revise what you create somewhere down the line. Months after the fact, when you're busy on new projects, you might find it hard to remember what a certain block of code in your old project is supposed to be doing. There is no performance penalty for heavily commented code. Comments are stripped from the code before it loads into memory and runs.

Now it's time to fire up Director and try some Lingo commands and functions out for yourself. Press Command+M to open the Message Window. The Message Window is an indispensable tool for testing out your Lingo code. Normally, you must play the movie to see your code in action, but the Message window enables you to test out just one line of code at a time, regardless of whether the movie is running or not.

The Message window opens with a commented line:

```
-- Welcome to Director --
```

All of Director's responses appear in the Message window as comments, making system responses easy to distinguish from your input.

Position your cursor under the `-- Welcome to Director --` line and enter the following:

```
put 5 + 3
```

After you press Return, Director evaluates your code and responds as follows:

```
-- 8
```

The `put` command evaluates the Lingo expression that follows it and displays the result in the Message Window.

Next, enter these two lines:

```
set myVariable = 4
put myVariable
```

Director responds as follows:

```
-- 4
```

The `set` command puts a value into a variable. When you use the `put` command on a variable, it shows you the variable's contents.

Now try a command and a function. Enter the following line:

```
put length("habitat")
```

Director responds as follows:

```
-- 7
```

The `length` function takes a string of characters as an argument and returns the length of the string. The `put` command displays the result of the `length` function. You could have entered just:

```
length("habitat")
```

and Director would have calculated the length of "habitat" but, without the `put` command, Director would have displayed nothing.

Figure 16.1 shows what the Message window should look like after you have entered the sample commands.

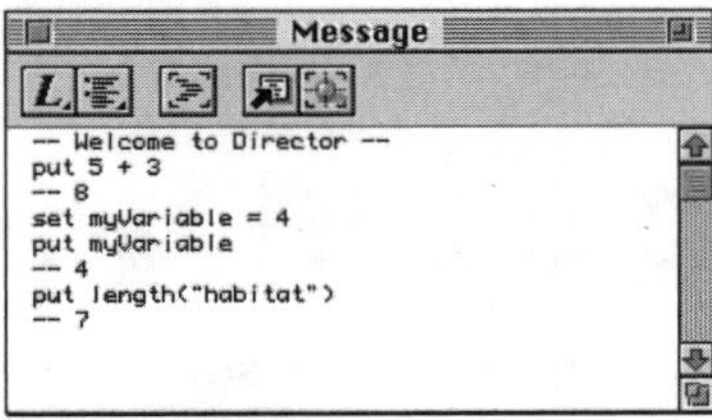

Figure 16.1

The Message window after you type the sample commands.

You can use the Message window for analyzing and debugging the code in your movies, as well as testing individual lines.

Objects and Properties

Objects are the parts of the Director environment that you can control using Lingo. *Properties* are object characteristics that you can check or change. The lion's share of Lingo coding involves checking and setting the properties of objects to change the action on the stage. Here are some lines of Lingo that get or set object properties. In each line, the object name is in bold and the object property is in italics.

```
set the locH of sprite 1 to 101
-- Moves sprite 1 to horizontal location 101 on the stage
set the boxTypeof member "Address" to #scroll
-- Changes the text field "Address" to a scrolling field
put the filled of member "Small Box"
-- displays whether or not the shape cast "Small Box" is filled
➥with a pattern
```

The Director environment itself is an object. To change one of the Director environment's properties, enter the following in the Message window:

```
set the stagecolor to 255
```

The stage turns black. `stagecolor` is one of the properties of the Director environment.

The built-in Director objects include sprites, cast members, and windows. In this chapter, you learn how to use Lingo to control Director's built-in objects by changing their properties. You also can create your own Lingo objects with properties you choose.

Chapter 20, "Object-Oriented Programming," covers creating and using custom Lingo objects.

Events, Messages, and Handlers

Everything in Lingo happens as the result of an event. Some events are user actions like `mouseUp` and `keyUp`. Others are generated by the system, such as `timeout`. Lingo recognizes the events listed in the following table:

Table 16.1

The Standard Lingo Events

Event	Happens When...
`mouseUp`	User releases the mouse button
`mouseDown`	User presses the mouse button down
`rightMouseUp`	User releases the mouse button while holding down the Control key
`rightMouseDown`	User presses the mouse button down while holding down the Control key
`keyUp`	User releases a key
`keyDown`	User holds down a key
`startMovie`	User launches a Director projector
	The Lingo command `play movie` is executed and the next movie loads
	The Lingo command `go movie` is executed and the next movie loads
	The first time the Lingo command `open window` is executed for a Movie in a Window
`stopMovie`	User presses Command+Q or Command+. (period)
	The Lingo command `quit` is executed
	The Lingo command `play movie` is executed and the current movie is unloaded
	The Lingo command `go movie` is executed and the current movie is unloaded
`activateWindow`	User clicks on a Movie in a Window that doesn't currently have the focus, bringing that movie to the front
`moveWindow`	User drags a Movie in a Window
`resizeWindow`	User resizes a Movie in a Window
`deactivateWindow`	User clicks on a Movie in a Window that does not currently have the focus, and the current movie moves behind the movie that now has the focus
`closeWindow`	User clicks the close box of a Movie in a Window. The Lingo command `close window windowName` is executed. The Lingo command `set the visible of window windowName to FALSE` is executed.
`enterFrame`	Playback head enters a frame in the Score

continues

Table 16.1, CONTINUED

Event	Happens When...
`exitFrame`	Playback head leaves a frame in the Score
`idle`	Director is not processing any events
`timeout`	The system property `timeoutLapsed` is greater than or equal to the system property `timeoutLength`

When Director senses that an event has happened, it creates an event message. It then looks through the Lingo scripts in the movie to find code that handles that message. A message handler is a block of code that starts with `on messageName`.

A Lingo script consists of one or more message handlers. Message handlers always start with `on` and end with `end`. They look like the following:

```
on messageName
   Lingo statement
   Lingo statement
   .
   .
   Lingo statement
end
```

The following are some simple examples of message handlers. Comments below each handler explain what it does:

```
on exitFrame
   go the frame
end

-- loops the playback head continuously in the same frame


on keyUp
   global score
   if the key = RETURN and field "Quiz Question 1" = "nuclear
   ➥reactor" then
      set score = score + 20
      alert "That's right!"
   end if
end
```

```
-- When the user presses RETURN, Director checks the text field
➥ "Quiz Question 1"
-- If the user has typed "nuclear reactor" into the text field
➥ the user's
-- score will be incremented by 20 and the system will display
➥ a dialog
-- box with the message "That's right!"
```

You can create your own events and event handlers in addition to the ones built into Director. Custom handlers fit the following basic mold:

```
on handlerName
   Lingo statement
   Lingo statement
end
```

Example:

```
on cleanUp
   puppetSprite 3,FALSE
   puppetSound 0
   updateStage
   sound stop 1
   set score = 0
end

-- returns a sprite to score control and turns off sound
-- in preparation to move to another part of the game
```

To call a custom handler, you simply use its name in your code. The following code generates a `cleanUp` event that goes to the `on cleanUp` handler.

```
on mouseUp
   cleanUp
   go frame "Game 2"
end
```

You might have been wondering, as you read these examples, how you control when and where a message is handled. How do you specify which frame should loop or which text field should check key presses for the Enter key? The type of script you place your handler in determines what messages it will receive. The next section describes how messages and scripts work together.

Introducing Scripts

The four different kinds of scripts in Director are sprite, cast member, frame, and movie. The kind of script in which you place the handler determines when and where it can handle a message. (There is also a fifth type of script—a parent script. Parent scripts do not receive messages about user events. Parent scripts are covered in Chapter 20, "Object-Oriented Programming.")

Sprite Scripts

A sprite script is linked to a cel in the Score. If the cel is occupied with a visible cast member, it receives a message when the user clicks on that cel or, if the cast member is an editable text field, when the user types into the field. You create a sprite script by highlighting that sprite's cel in the Score and clicking on the large rectangle above the Score (see fig. 16.2).

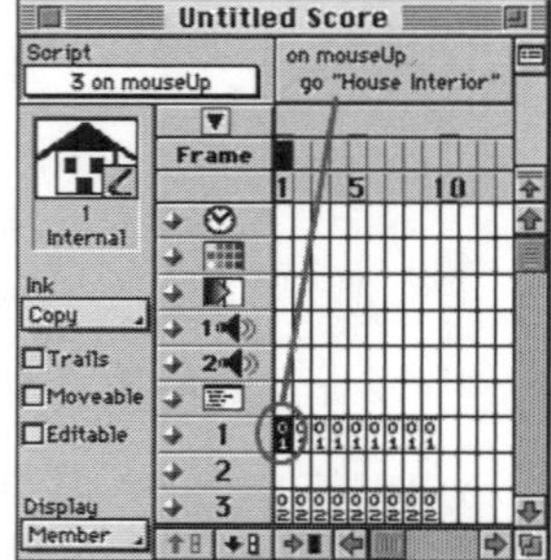

Figure 16.2

Create a sprite script by highlighting a cel in the sprite channel and clicking on the large rectangle above the Score.

Cast Member Scripts

A cast member script is linked to the cast member. It receives a message when the user clicks or types into that cast member, if the cel it occupies does not have a sprite script. If you want something to behave the same way everywhere you place it in the Score, use a cast member script. You create a cast member script by highlighting a cast member in the Cast window, clicking on the cast member properties button to bring up the Cast Member Properties window, and then clicking on the cast member's Script button (see fig. 16.3).

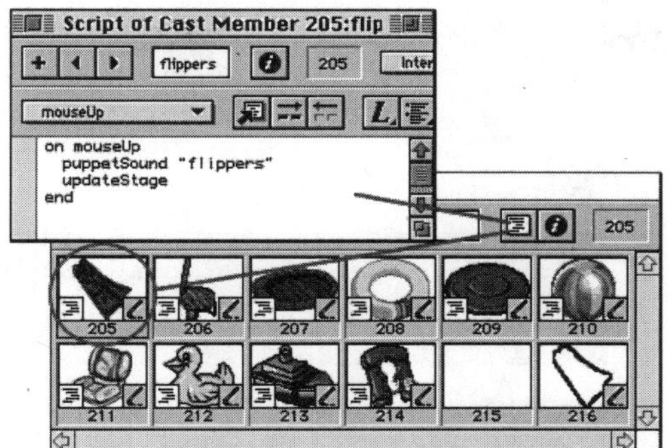

Figure 16.3

Create a cast member script by highlighting the cast and clicking on the script icon.

Frame Scripts

Frame scripts receive messages when the playback head enters or exits the frame they are on. They also receive any mouse and key-press messages not already handled by sprite or cast member scripts. The most common use of frame scripts is to keep the playback head looping over one frame or a series of frames. You create a frame script by double-clicking in the Score in that frame's Script channel (see fig. 16.4).

NOTE

> Macromedia's manuals use the term Score script to refer to a script attached to a frame.

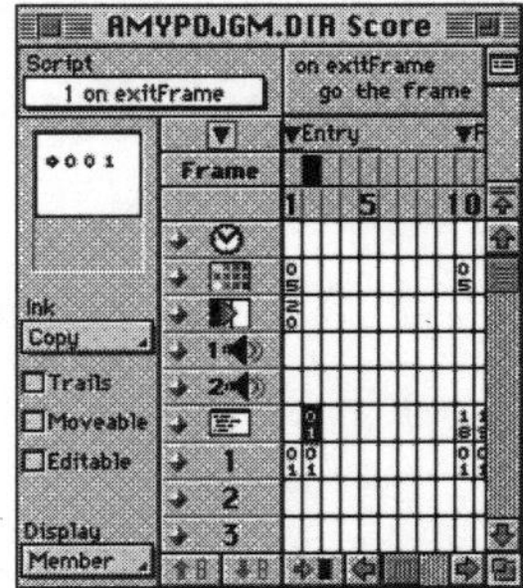

Figure 16.4

Create a frame script by double-clicking in the frame's Script channel.

Movie Scripts

Movie scripts receive all messages not already handled by sprite, cast member, or frame scripts. You create a movie script by choosing Window, Script from Director's menu.

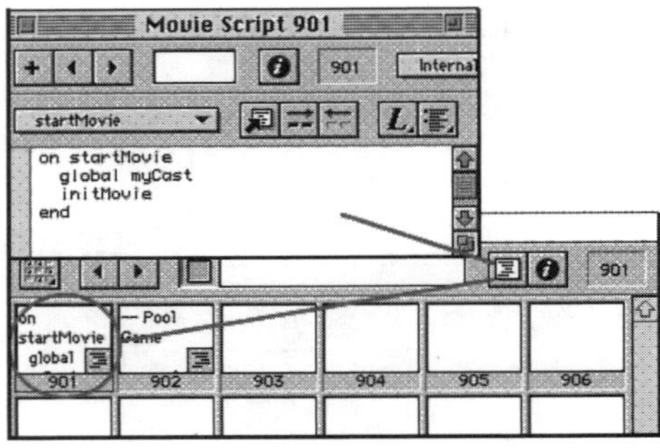

Figure 16.5

A movie script.

Movie scripts are a good place for default message handlers. Suppose you want the program to display an error message any time the user clicks on an area that's *not* hot. Normally, if you have two buttons on stage, each with a `mouseUp` handler, nothing happens if the user clicks on the stage anywhere outside the two buttons. If you place a `mouseUp` handler in the movie script, it catches any `mouseUp` messages that the buttons don't handle. The `mouseUp` handler in the movie script could display a message that tells the user where the active areas are.

Using Scripts to Make an Interactive Movie

Now, let's make a small movie that uses all four kinds of scripts. To begin, open the LITE.DIR movie from the Chapter 16 folder on the accompanying CD-ROM.

A light switch appears on stage because two cast members have already been placed in frame 1 of the Score. No scripts have been placed yet (see fig. 16.6).

Figure 16.6

The movie LITE.DIR.

You want this movie to do the following:

1. When the user clicks on the switch:
    - Make a click sound.

- If the switch is up, change it to the down position and darken the stage to make it look like the lights are off. If the switch is down, change it to the up position and lighten the stage to make it look like the lights are on.

2. When the user clicks anywhere else on stage, beep to let them know it isn't an active area.

Armed with a plan, you're ready to get started. The first thing you want to do is make the movie loop. If you play the movie now, it plays the first frame and stops because there are no more occupied frames. You must keep the playback head moving if you want the movie to continue playing. Frame scripts are a good place to put code that makes the movie loop.

1. Double-click in the Script channel over the frame and type the following script:

```
on exitFrame
    go the frame
end
```

   Now play the movie again. The movie continues to play indefinitely because the playback head is always directed back to the same frame it leaves. (Press the Stop button on the control panel when you want to stop the movie.)

   You now want to add some frame script code that runs only once. You can't put the code in the frame script that's looping because it would execute every time the frame looped.

   You need a new frame before the looping frame, in which to put the code you want to run only once.

2. Select sprite cels 1 and 2 in frame 1 and the same empty cels in frame 2 and In-Between them (Command+B), as shown in figure 16.7.

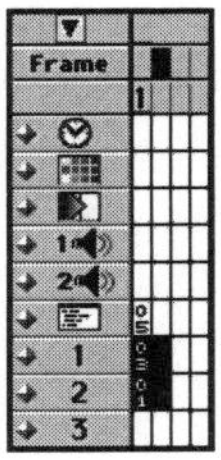

Figure 16.7

Select and In-Between cels 1 and 2 over frames 1 and 2.

Now, the switch plate and switch appear in frame 1 and frame 2:

- Select the frame Script left in frame 1 and drag it to frame 2. Now you can put another script in frame 1.
- Double-click in the Script channel over frame 1 and enter the following script:

```
on exitFrame
     puppetSprite 2,TRUE
end
```

The switch is in sprite 2. Here, you are going to use Lingo, rather than the Score, to animate the switch. You take control of a sprite channel by setting its puppetSprite property to TRUE. You only need to do it once. The property remains in effect over any number of frames until you turn it off by setting the puppetSprite property to FALSE.

`puppetSprite` is one of the essential Lingo commands covered in the next section.

Now you are ready to program the interactivity for the switch. First, you make it animate when you click on it so that it looks like it's up or down. You do this by switching the cast member that's in that sprite cel. When cast member 1, the ON switch, is in that sprite channel and the user clicks on it, you want to replace it with cast member 2, the OFF switch.

3. Open the cast script for cast member 1 by highlighting member 1 in the Cast window and clicking on the Script button. Enter the following script:

```
on mouseUp
     set the memberNum of sprite 2 = 2
     updateStage
end
```

This script changes the artwork in sprite 2 from the ON switch to the OFF switch when a user clicks on the ON switch. The `updateStage` command redraws the stage after you change the sprite with Lingo. Whenever you change things on the stage with Lingo, you must update the stage to show your changes. `updateStage` is another essential Lingo command covered in more detail in the next section.

Rewind and run the movie again. Now when you click on the light switch, it changes it to the OFF position. But when you click on it again (while it's off), it doesn't do anything. That's because cast member 2, the OFF switch, doesn't have a `mouseUp` handler—yet.

4. Open the cast script for cast member 2 and enter the following script:

```
on mouseUp
    set the memberNum of sprite 2 = 1
    updateStage
end
```

Rewind and run the movie. Now, clicking on the light switch turns it on or off, depending on the cast member you click on.

The code you were asked to enter into the cast scripts:

```
set the memberNum of sprite 2 = 1
```

works just fine, but if this were a real project, using sprite and cast numbers in your scripts wouldn't be a good idea because doing so makes changing things later difficult. If you refer to sprite 2 in many different places in your scripts and then later need to move that artwork to a different channel, you have to go back through your scripts and change the sprite number *everywhere* it occurs.

In Chapter 19, "Advanced Concepts," the section "Defensive Programming" explains in detail how to write your scripts so that you can change and reuse them easily. For now, you should just leave this code alone.

The next step is to make it appear as though the light is going off, which you can accomplish by changing the stage color of the stage from white to black. Add this line to the cast script for cast member 1, right after the `set the castnum` line:

```
set the stagecolor to 255
```

This code sets the color of the stage to position 255 in the color palette, which is black. You need another line of code to set it back to white. Put this line in the script for cast member 2 after the `set the castNum` line:

```
set the stagecolor to 0
```

The two cast scripts for the switch casts should look like this:

```
on mouseUp
   set the memberNum of sprite 2 to 2
   set the stagecolor to 255
   updateStage
end

on mouseUp
   set the memberNum of sprite 2 to 1
   set the stagecolor to 0
   updateStage
end
```

Now play the movie and click on the switch. The switch moves up and down and the light goes on and off.

The only thing absent is sound. You want the sound to play as soon as the user clicks, so you should include it in a `mouseDown` handler. You want the sound to play when the user clicks on sprite 2, whether the cast member in that channel is the On switch or the Off switch. A `mouseDown` handler in the sprite script for sprite 2 accomplishes just that. Highlight the two cels in channel 2 and click in the empty rectangle at the top of the score to open a Script window. Enter the following script:

```
on mouseDown
   puppetSound "click"
   updateStage
end
```

`puppetSound` puts a sound cast member under Lingo control. You must use `updateStage` after `puppetSound` to make the sound play. Play the movie again. The switch makes a clicking sound now.

Finally, you want to let the users know when they are clicking on an area that's not hot. You can make a movie script using a `mouseDown` message handler that catches all clicks falling outside the switch sprite.

5. Highlight an empty cast member and choose Window, Script from the menu bar to open a new movie script. Type the following:

   ```
   on mouseDown
      beep
   end
   ```

The `beep` command plays a system beep. Now play the movie. When you click on the light switch, the sprite script for channel 2 handles the `mouseDown` message, so it never gets to the movie script handler. When you click outside the light switch sprite, the movie script handles the `mouseDown`.

The movie LITEDONE.DIR in the folder for Chapter 16 contains the finished code for this example.

The Message Hierarchy

As you have just seen from building your movie, Director passes messages to the different kinds of scripts in a particular order, called the *message hierarchy*. The general message hierarchy order is Sprite, Cast, Frame, Movie—but not all messages go to every type of script. Only movie scripts receive all 17 messages. If you want Director to pass messages to your message handler, you must put it in the type of script that can receive that message. Table 16.2 shows the four script types and the list of messages that each receives. (To refresh your memory as to what user events trigger messages refer back to table 16.1.)

Table 16.2

The Four Script Types and the Messages They Can Receive

Script Type	Message List

Sprite	`mouseUp`
	`mouseDown`
	`rightMouseUp`
	`rightMouseDown`
	`keyUp` (editable-text sprite only)
	`keyDown` (editable-text sprite only)

Cast	`mouseUp` (not to editable-text sprite)
	`mouseDown`
	`rightMouseUp`
	`rightMouseDown`
	`keyUp` (editable-text cast only)
	`keyDown` (editable-text cast only)

continues

Table 16.2, CONTINUED

Script Type	Message List

Frame	`enterFrame`
	`exitFrame`
	`mouseUp`
	`mouseDown`
	`rightMouseUp`
	`rightMouseDown`
	`keyUp`
	`keyDown`
	`timeOut`

Movie	`enterFrame`
	`exitFrame`
	`mouseUp`
	`mouseDown`
	`rightMouseUp`
	`rightMouseDown`
	`keyUp`
	`keyDown`
	`idle`
	`startMovie`
	`stopMovie`
	`activateWindow`
	`moveWindow`
	`resizeWindow`
	`deactivateWindow`
	`closeWindow`
	`timeOut`

The Sprite Hierarchy

If a mouse event occurs and more than one sprite is under the mouse, Director sends the `mouseUp` or `mouseDown` message to all sprites under the mouse, in order from top (48) to bottom (1) until the message reaches a sprite that has a message handler for it. Messages pass right through sprites with no message handlers and sprites with their visible property off ("`set the visible of sprite 3 to FALSE`"). A script that consists only of the following is enough to intercept an event and not allow it to pass further down the hierarchy:

```
on mouseUp
end
```

Primary Event Handlers

The message hierarchy has one additional level, called the *primary event handlers*. Primary event handlers differ from the other event handlers (such as sprite, cast, frame, and movie handlers) in two ways:

- The other handlers do not receive messages until after they pass through all the other layers of the hierarchy. Primary event handlers grab messages first, before any other handlers.
- The other handlers "eat" any message that they receive. They do not pass it any further through the hierarchy. Primary event handlers act on a received message and then send it further down the hierarchy.

The primary event handlers are as follows:

- `the mouseUpScript`
- `the mouseDownScript`
- `the keyUpScript`
- `the keyDownScript`
- `the timeOutScript`

You can set a primary event handler from any script type by using the following syntax:

```
set the eventScript to "code line to execute"
```

Examples:

```
set the timeOutScript to "go frame 10"
set the mouseUpScript to "beep"
```

The code line to execute also can be a custom handler name:

```
set the mouseUpScript to "myMouseUpHandler"
```

The primary event handler remains in effect within that movie until you set it to a new line of code or disable it using the following syntax:

```
set the eventScript to EMPTY
```

Example:

```
set the mouseUpScript to EMPTY
```

Use primary event handlers when you want to temporarily intercept a message. Dissolve transitions, for example, take twice as long to finish if the user clicks while they execute. To work around this problem, you could set a primary event handler to ignore mouse clicks right before the transition, and then turn the primary event handler off right after the transition. The code would look like this:

```
set the mouseUpScript to "tempLockOut"


on tempLockOut
  dontPassEvent -- keeps primary event handler from passing the
  ➥mouseUp
                -- further down the hierarchy.
end
```

Without a primary event handler, you would have to add code to every sprite or cast on the stage to handle this temporary situation.

Another good use for a primary event handler is when you want to deal with an event in the same way throughout the entire movie. A movie might not have any text entry, for example, so it would not generally have any handlers for keyDown, except to check whether a user had pressed Command+Q to quit. That handler would look like this:

```
on checkQuit
   if the commandDown and the key = "q" then
      cleanUp
      quit
   end if
end
```

Setting the keyDownScript to checkQuit at the beginning of the movie handles keyDown events for the rest of the movie with no additional coding.

Pass and DontPassEvent

Normally, the first sprite, cast, or frame message handler to get a message "eats" the message and it does not get passed any further down the message hierarchy. But sometimes you want more than one script to receive a message. If you put a pass command in a sprite, cast, or frame handler (movie scripts are already at the bottom of the hierarchy), it acts on any message it receives and then passes it on to the next level of the hierarchy. In the following example, one button cast has been placed on the stage twice, creating two sprites. When clicked, each sprite plays the sound that its sprite script specifies. Then they both call on the same cast code to animate:

```
-- Sprite 2
on mouseDown
   puppetSound "horn"
   updateStage
   pass
end

-- Sprite 3
on mouseDown
   puppetSound "bagpipe"
   updateStage
   pass
end

-- Cast script for both sprites
on mouseDown
   set the locH of the sprite clickOn to the locH of sprite the
   ➥clickOn + 1
   set the locV of the sprite clickOn to the locV of sprite the
   ➥clickOn + 1
   -- make the button move slightly
   updateStage
end

on mouseUp
   set the locH of sprite the clickOn to the locH of sprite the
   ➥clickOn - 1
   set the locV of sprite the clickOn to the locV of sprite the
   ➥clickOn - 1
   -- return the button to original position
   updateStage
end
```

The `pass` command in a sprite script cannot pass a message to sprites in channels lower than the sprite that is clicked. The message gets passed to the next level of the hierarchy, which would be the cast script.

Primary event handlers do the opposite of what the other handlers do. Primary event handlers act on the event and then always pass it on. Using the `dontPassEvent` command in a primary event handler keeps it from passing the event.

Bypassing the Message Hierarchy

You can bypass the hierarchy completely and send an event message directly to any script by using the following syntax:

```
messageName(script "ScriptName")
messageName(script scriptNumber)
```

Example:

```
mouseUp(script "Exit Button")
```

If `"Exit Button"` is the name of the sprite or cast script for a button on the stage, the button behaves as though the user had clicked on it. This feature is convenient for making self-running tutorial demos that simulate user actions.

Deciding Where to Put Handlers

The message hierarchy sounds like a complicated system, but it actually makes your job easier by increasing your flexibility. There isn't always one "right" spot to place a script. You usually can accomplish the same thing in a couple different ways. Here are some guidelines you can use until you develop your own style:

- Put code that moves or changes sprites in sprite scripts.
- If a cast member should always behave the same way throughout the whole movie no matter where it appears in the Score, use a cast script instead of multiple sprite scripts
- Use frame scripts to keep the playback head looping in an area of the Score.
- Put your custom handlers in movie scripts.

Table 16.3 shows the order in which each Lingo event passes through the four layers of scripts. Draw a line from the event on the left, straight through the layers on the right to see which types of scripts receive that event message, and in what order.

Table 16.3

The Lingo Message Hierarchy

Event	Primary Event Handler	Sprite Script	Cast Script	Frame Script	Movie Script
enterFrame				on enterFrame	on enterFrame
exitFrame				on exitFrame	on exitFrame
mouseUp	the mouseUpScript	on mouseUp	on mouseUp	on mouseUp	on mouseUp
mouseDown	the mouseDownScript	on mouseDown	on mouseDown	on mouseDown	on mouseDown
rightMouseUp		on rightMouseUp	on rightMouseUp	on rightMouseUp	on rightMouseUp
rightMouseDown		on rightMouseDown	on rightMouseDown	on rightMouseDown	on rightMouseDown
keyUp	the keyUpScript	on keyUp	on keyUp	on keyUp	on keyUp
keyDown	the keyDownScript	on keyDown	on keyDown	on keyDown	on keyDown
idle					on idle
startMovie					on startMovie
stopMovie					on stopMovie
activateWindow					on activateWindow
moveWindow					on moveWindow
resizeWindow					on resizeWindow
deactivateWindow					on deactivateWindow
closeWindow					on closeWindow
timeOut	the timeOutScript				on timeOut
yourCustomEvent					on yourCustomEvent

In this section you have learned how to use commands to change the properties of Lingo objects. You now know how to write a handler, and where to place the handler to intercept a message. With these fundamentals of Lingo under your belt, you are now ready to learn about some essential Lingo commands in more detail.

Essential Lingo

With the new commands in version 5, the *Lingo Dictionary* now has more than 600 words. Fortunately, you don't have to be familiar with all 600 before you can begin working. In fact, the bulk of everyday Director programming centers around fewer than 20 commands and key words. In this section you'll build movies that use 14 of these essential commands.

The Chapter 16 folder on the accompanying CD contains two Marble movies: MARBLE.DIR and MARBLEDN.DIR. MARBLEDN.DIR contains the finished movie. MARBLE.DIR has all the cast members in place but includes only the movie script and a frame script that keeps the playback head inside the Main Menu section. MARBLEDN.DIR contains the finished movie. You can follow along using the finished MARBLEDN.DIR, or you can start with MARBLE.DIR and construct the movie yourself as you read along.

Open the movie MARBLEDN.DIR, a tiny movie with a main menu and two sections of "lessons" about marble (see fig. 16.8).

Figure 16.8

The MARBLEDN.DIR movie's main menu.

The marble movie is not a terribly interesting multimedia experience, but it does illustrate typical user-interface features that you will want to include in your projects. Check marks on the main menu indicate that a section has been visited. The cursor changes to a hand when a user moves it into clickable areas on-screen. Buttons provide feedback when a user clicks on them. The next section of this chapter uses code from the movie to show the most common Lingo commands in action.

Realistic Buttons—Controlling Sprites

When a user clicks in an active area onscreen, something should happen—and the sooner the better. Buttons that don't respond when a user clicks on them are lifeless and confusing. The buttons in the finished Marble movie depress and make a sound when the user clicks on them.

The buttons all share one cast and one `mouseDown` script. The code is attached to the `mouseDown` rather than the `mouseUp` to give the user the most immediate feedback. The code is in the cast script rather than the sprite scripts for each button, because the button should animate the same way everywhere it appears in the Score.

Open MARBLE.DIR, the unfinished version, and play it. The playback head stops on frame 2 because it contains a `go the frame` handler, but none of the buttons work yet. The following is the `mouseDown` handler for the button cast script:

```
on mouseDown
  set btn = the clickOn -- (a,b)
  puppetSprite btn,TRUE -- (c)
  puppetSound "Mouse Down" -- (d)
  set the loc of sprite btn = the loc of sprite btn - 1 -- (f)
  updateStage -- (e)
  repeat while the stillDown (g)
     updateStage
  end repeat
  set the loc of sprite btn = the loc of sprite btn + 1
  updateStage
  puppetSprite btn,FALSE
  puppetSound 0
end
```

Type this handler into the cast script for button cast (14). Now play the movie again. All the buttons now depress and make a sound when you click them. That's because they all share the same cast and the same cast script. The next section describes the Lingo commands used in the button cast script.

Set (a)

Syntax:

```
set variableOrProperty = value
set variableOrProperty to value
```

Example:

```
set score = 0
```

If you're familiar with other computer languages, you probably already know that a *variable* is a container that enables you to save data you want to use later. Variables you declare within a handler are *local*—they are discarded as soon as the handler finishes.

The first line of code sets the variable `btn` to the value of `the clickOn`, as follows:

```
set btn = the clickOn
```

Other lines in the handler can then use variable `btn`.

The ClickOn (b)

Syntax:

```
the clickOn
```

Example:

```
if the clickOn = 7 then go "Main Menu"
```

`the clickOn` is a Lingo function that returns the most-recently clicked on sprite channel. If the user clicks on the stage, `the clickOn` function returns 0. `the clickOn` makes it possible for the same cast script to work with multiple sprites, because it tells the cast script which sprite triggered it. The first line of code saves `the clickOn` into the `btn` variable, because `the clickOn` updates with every user click—even in a handler. If you refer to `the clickOn` at the beginning of a script and also further down, and the user clicks somewhere in between, the value of `the clickOn` changes.

By storing `the clickOn` in variable `btn`, you ensure that you are always working with the sprite that triggered the handler.

PuppetSprite (c)

Syntax:

```
puppetSprite channelNumber,TRUEorFALSE
```

Example:

```
puppetSprite 10,TRUE
```

The `puppetSprite` command places the specified sprite channel number under Lingo control—it no longer responds to the Score. Lingo programmers use the term "puppeting the sprite" to describe using the `puppetSprite` command on a particular sprite channel.

Since the Score does not control the channel after the `puppetSprite` command, whatever cast member is in the channel when you issue the `puppetSprite` command continues to display in the same position over subsequent frames until you use Lingo to change its properties or to move it. If you accidentally puppet a channel that doesn't contain a cast member, the channel remains empty over subsequent frames. Make sure you have a cast member in the channel before you puppet it. Use the following syntax to unpuppet the channel and return control to the Score:

```
puppetSprite channelNumber,FALSE
```

The following code line puppets the sprite channel that contains the button the user clicked, because this handler is going to use Lingo to move the button sprite:

```
puppetSprite btn,TRUE
```

After you do some experimenting, you might discover that you can use Lingo to change a sprite that isn't puppeted first. The change lasts, however, only for the current frame. Because the sprite isn't puppeted, control returns to the Score and your changes are wiped out as soon as the playback head enters a new frame.

PuppetSound (d)

Syntax:

```
puppetSound "castName"
```

Example:

```
puppetSound "Bird Call"
updateStage
```

The `puppetSound` command plays a sound that has been imported into the cast. The sound doesn't start to play unless you include an `updateStage` command after it or until the playback head enters the next frame. `puppetSound` takes control of sound channel 1 in the same way that `puppetSprite` takes control of a sprite channel—it ignores the Score. Once you play a `puppetSound`, any sound placed in the Score in sound channel 1 will not play— even after the puppeted sound has finished— until you return control of sound channel 1 to the Score with:

```
puppetSound 0
```

The following undocumented Lingo enables you to puppet any sound channel—not just channel 1:

```
puppetSound channelNumber,"castName"
puppetSound channelNumber,castNumber
```

Example:

```
puppetSound 3,"chirp"
puppetSound 4,8
```

No command corresponds to `puppetSound 0` to turn off puppeting for a channel other than 1. That's not a problem for sound channels 3 and 4, but if you use this command with sound channel 2, you have no way to return control to the Score.

The sounds you play with `puppetSound` must load completely into memory before they can play. `puppetSound` is good for button clicks and other sounds that aren't too large. The following code line plays the cast member sound "Mouse Down" in channel 1:

```
puppetSound "Mouse Down"
```

The `sound playFile` command is a better choice for large sounds. The syntax for `sound playFile` is as follows:

```
sound playFile soundChannel,"filename"
```

`sound playFile` streams the sound straight from the hard disk or CD rather than playing it from memory. You might experience a slight delay before the sound starts, especially if you play from CD, because Director has to find the file on disk and the disk head has to move to the file before it can play.

UpdateStage (e)

Syntax:

```
updateStage
```

Example:

```
puppetSprite 8,TRUE
set the forecolor of sprite 8 to 0
updateStage
```

Changes you make with Lingo to a puppeted sprite or to a puppeted sound channel generally do not register until you use an `updateStage` command. The command name `updateStage` implies that only visual changes update, but `updateStage` actually does more than that. `updateStage` redraws the sprites on stage to include your Lingo changes, plays puppeted sound, and updates digital video. If you plan to change several sprite properties at the same time over several lines of code, you can use one `updateStage` after all of them to display all of your changes at once. The following code plays the button click and moves the button at the same time when `updateStage` executes on the third line of code:

```
puppetSound "Mouse Down"
set the loc of sprite btn = the loc of sprite btn - 1
updateStage
```

You also could write the code as follows:

```
puppetSound "Mouse Down"
updateStage
set the loc of sprite btn = the loc of sprite btn - 1
updateStage
```

In this case, the button click would start a fraction of a second before the button moves, when the first `updateStage` executes.

The Loc of Sprite / Point() (f)

Syntax:

```
the loc of sprite whichSprite
point (horizontal, vertical)
```

Example:

```
set the loc of sprite 10 = point(100,120)
```

`the loc of sprite` is a sprite property that determines the location of the sprite on stage relative to the top left corner of the stage, which is point (0, 0). Director measures in pixels from point (0 horizontal, 0 vertical) to the sprite's registration point to determine the sprite's position. You set the registration point for a bitmap sprite in the Paint window. The registration point for shapes drawn with the tool palette, digital video, text fields and buttons, is the top left corner of the sprite (see fig. 16.9). `the loc of sprite` is stored as a special type of list called a point.

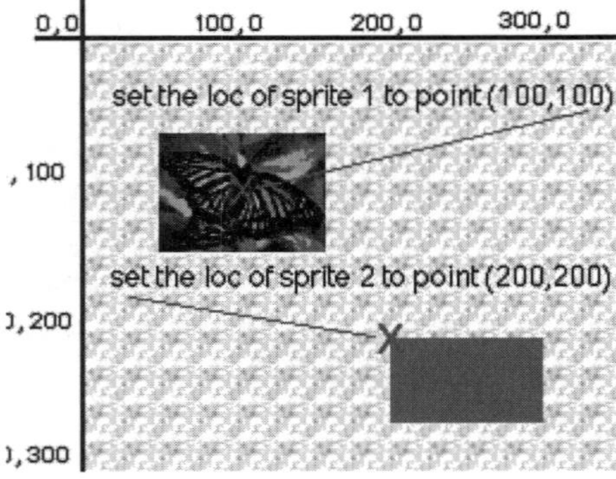

Figure 16.9

The registration point of the butterfly bitmap is in the middle of the image. The registration point of the shape is the top left corner.

Lists are Director variables that can store more than one piece of information. They are like arrays in other languages. Chapter 17, "Managing Your Data," covers lists in detail.

Highlight a sprite cel in the Score and type the following in the Message window:

```
put the loc of sprite 5 -- the number of the sprite you have
➥highlighted
```

Director returns the following:

```
point(100,200) -- the numbers will vary depending on where the
➥sprite is
```

The first number, `100`, is the *horizontal location*—the distance in pixels from the left of the stage. The second number, `200`, is the *vertical location*—the distance in pixels from the top of the stage.

The following code line takes advantage of a nice feature of Director lists. When you use a mathematical operation on a list, it applies the operation to every item on the list.

```
set the loc of sprite btn = the loc of sprite btn - 1
```

Subtracting 1 from point (100, 100) gives you point (99, 99). The code moves the button one pixel up and to the left, to make it look like it is depressing when it is clicked.

Repeat While (g)

Syntax:

```
repeat while condition
   statement
   statement
end repeat
```

Example:

```
repeat while soundBusy(1)
   go the frame
end repeat
```

`repeat while` executes the statements inside the loop until the *condition* is no longer TRUE. A repeat loop can stop the action on stage and grabs a big share of the processor while it runs. Including an `updateStage` or `go the frame` inside a repeat loop when possible keeps other animation and QuickTime moving. Repeat loops also lock out user mouse and keyboard events. To continue accepting mouse events within a repeat loop, include a test for the `mouseDown`, such as the following:

```
repeat while testCondition = FALSE and not the mouseDown
```

This repeat loop continues to loop as long as the user holds down the mouse button:

```
repeat while the stillDown
  updateStage
end repeat
```

The button sprite the user clicked on will remain in a depressed position as long as the user holds down the mouse.

You have all of the buttons responding to user clicks now. In the next section you will program the buttons to take the user to other sections of the movie.

Navigation and Keeping Track of Completed Sections

The buttons click in the Main Menu section, but they don't take you anywhere. The next code you need to add should contain the commands to take you to and from different parts of the movie. Here is where each button behaves differently, so the code must go into the sprite script of each button. Put the following handlers into the sprite scripts of the buttons (sprites 8, 9, and 10) in the Main Menu section (frame 2). Don't worry about what `puppetChecks` does yet.

```
-- put on History button
on mouseUp
  global gVisitedHistory
  -- unpuppet check mark sprites before going to a new section
  puppetChecks(FALSE)
  go "History"
```

```
  set gVisitedHistory = TRUE
end

-- put on Fun Facts button
on mouseUp
  global gVisitedFunFacts
  -- unpuppet check mark sprites before going to a new section
  puppetChecks(FALSE)
  go "FunFacts"
  set gVisitedFunFacts = TRUE
end

-- put on Quit button
on mouseUp
  puppetChecks(FALSE)
  go "AreYouSure"
end
```

Play the movie. When you click on any button in the Main Menu section, the button now takes you to another section of the movie. But right now, you still have no way to get back to the Main Menu. Add the following handler to button sprite 14's cast script. Don't worry about what `customCursorsOff` does yet.

```
on mouseUp
  -- turn off custom cursors before going to a new section
  customCursorsOff
  go "MainMenu"
end
```

Play the movie. Now, pressing the buttons on the All About Marble screen, as well as on the No button of the "Are You Sure?" screen, takes you back to the Main Menu. These buttons have no `mouseUp` sprite scripts, so they use the cast script. The buttons on the Main Menu have `mouseUp` sprite scripts that catch the `mouseUp` message before it gets to the cast script. The Yes button on the "Are You Sure?" screen also returns you to the Main Menu screen, but that's not what you want to happen. You want to quit when the user presses the Yes button. Add the following sprite script to the Yes button to override the cast script:

```
on mouseUp
  quit
end
```

Go to Frame / Play Frame

Syntax:

```
go [to] [frame] frameNumberOrLabel
play [frame] frameNumberOrLabel
```

Example:

```
go the frame
go to frame "Main Menu"
go "Help"

play frame "Baseball"
play "Kitchen scene"
```

The `go to frame` command moves the playback head to the frame label or frame number specified. Using frame labels rather than frame numbers is smart because the numbers change if you insert or delete frames.

If any commands follow the `go to frame` command in the handler, they still execute. `go to frame` moves only the playback head—it doesn't interrupt the script in progress—which is why you can set a global variable after the `go` command in the button scripts:

```
on mouseUp
  global gVisitedFunFacts
  puppetChecks(FALSE)
  go "FunFacts"
  set gVisitedFunFacts = TRUE -- still executes after the "go"
end
```

The `play` command, like `go`, also moves the playback head to another frame. The movie continues to play from that frame forward, until it hits a `play done` command. Then, if the playback head was called from a sprite script, it returns to the frame where `play` was called. If `play` was called from a frame script, however, the playback head returns to the frame that comes AFTER the frame that called it.

Unlike the `go` command, `play` suspends execution of any commands in a handler after the `play` until the playback head hits a `play done`. Then, and only then, do the rest of the commands in the handler execute.

```
on mouseUp
   play "SingALong"
   -- Handler is suspended here while the "SingALong" section
   ➥plays
   -- Playback head hits a "play done" in "SingALong"
   -- Playback head returns to the frame where this handler was
   ➥called
   -- The rest of the commands now execute
      puppetSound "All done"
      updateStage
      go frame "Time For Work"
end
```

The buttons on the Main Menu of the Marble movie could have used the `play` command to take the user to the Fun Facts and History sections. The return buttons in Fun Facts and History could have had `play done` scripts. But `play done` would not have returned the playback head to the frame labeled `Main Menu`, which has an important setup handler. Using `go Main Menu` for the return buttons ensures that the playback head always goes through `Main Menu`'s setup handler.

Notice that each section consists of two frames, a setup frame and a looping frame. The setup frame does work that only needs to be done when entering the section. The next frame traps the playback head in a looping frame.

Quit

Syntax:

```
quit
```

Example:

```
on enterFrame
  global timeAllowed
  if the timer - startTime > timeAllowed then
    cleanUp
    quit
  end it
end
```

`quit` terminates Director if you're in authoring mode, and terminates a projector. The Marble movie is too small to have any cleanup work to do, but it's a good idea to call a cleanup handler before you quit. The cleanup handler should dispose of any open Xtras or xlibs and return the user's system to the state it was in when your program started. Some externals misbehave if Director quits while they're still active, and it's only polite to leave things the way you found them on the user's system. If you have changed the user's monitor color depth for instance, you should restore it to its original settings.

Now that the buttons are all functioning, you can navigate to all sections of the movie, as well as quit. The movie is not, however, keeping track of where you go. No check marks appear, although the Score does contain sprites for them (sprites 5 and 6). Hey, where are they anyway? They don't appear on the stage.

When the movie starts, the check mark sprites are off-screen above the menu bar at a vertical position of –500. Positioning a sprite outside the stage enables you to place it in the sprite channel without making it visible to the user. Moving a sprite on and off stage to make it visible works better than using the `visible` property.

This code shows the sprite for a split second before making it invisible:

```
on enterFrame
   set the visible of sprite 5 to FALSE
end
```

Add the following handler to the first frame of Main Menu:

```
-- frame 1
on enterFrame
  displayChecks
  mainCursors
end
```

Play the movie. Now the check marks show for each section that you visit.

Version 5 gives you yet another way to hide a sprite with Lingo—by setting its member number to 0. The following code will make a sprite disappear by removing the cast member from the sprite channel:

```
on enterFrame
     set the memberNum of sprite 5 to 0
     updateStage
end
```

A sprite channel with a cast member number of 0 still executes sprite scripts if the user clicks over the area where the last cast member in the channel was.

Global

Syntax:

```
global variableName
```

Example:

```
global highScore
```

Declaring a variable `global` makes it available to all handlers in the movie. To use to a `global` in a handler, you must declare it before you use it, as seen in the following. For example:

```
on mouseUp
   global nextScene
   go nextScene
end
```

Refer to Chapter 17, "Managing Your Data," for more information on using and declaring globals.

The globals used in MARBLEDN.DIR are first declared in the `startMovie` script:

```
on startMovie
  global gDoneFunFacts,gDoneHistory
  global gCustomCursorList,gPointerCursor
  set gDoneFunFacts = FALSE
  set gDoneHistory = FALSE
.
.
end
```

Globals `gDoneFunFacts` and `gDoneHistory` are flags that keep track of whether the user has visited the Fun Facts or History section. Both globals are set to `FALSE` at the beginning of the movie because the user hasn't gone anywhere yet.

The initial frame of the History section sets global `gDoneHistory` to `TRUE`:

```
on enterFrame
  global gDoneHistory
  -- mark this section as visited
  set gDoneHistory = TRUE
  .
  .
end
```

When the user goes back to Main Menu, the first frame of Main Menu checks global `gDoneHistory`. If it is `TRUE`, then the History check mark is displayed by moving it from its place over the menu bar to a new position on stage:

```
on enterFrame
  displayChecks
  .
end

--Custom handlers in movie script

on displayChecks
  global gDoneFunFacts,gDoneHistory
  puppetChecks(TRUE)
  if gDoneFunFacts = TRUE then set the loc of sprite 6 =
  ➥point(39,137)
  if gDoneHistory = TRUE then set the loc of sprite 5 =
  ➥point(39,90)
  updateStage
end

on puppetChecks trueOrFalse
  puppetSprite 5,trueOrFalse
  puppetSprite 6,trueOrFalse
end
```

Custom Cursors

The last thing you want to add to the Marble movie is custom cursors., These will alert the user when the mouse rolls over a hot spot. Add the following line to the script for frame 1:

```
-- frame 1
on enterFrame
  displayChecks
  mainCursors -- add this line
end
```

Add the following scripts to the first frame of History, Fun Facts, and Are You Sure?:

```
-- frame script 10
on enterFrame
  -- give the button a custom cursor
  histCursors
end

-- frame script 20
on enterFrame
  -- give the button a custom cursor
  funFactsCursors
end

-- frame script 28
on enterFrame
  -- give the button a custom cursor
  areYouSureCursors
end
```

Play the movie. When the cursor rolls over a button, the cursor changes to a pointing hand.

The Cursor of Sprite

Syntax:

```
set the cursor of sprite channelNumber to list
```

Example:

```
set the cursor of sprite 9 to [4,5]
```

The `set the cursor of sprite` command makes a custom cursor appear over a sprite channel. The command applies to the entire channel, not just to one cast member. If you change the cast member in the channel, the custom cursor appears over the new cast member. You must keep track of custom cursors so that you can turn them off when you don't need them any more—otherwise you get cursors appearing in places they shouldn't. You turn off a custom cursor off by setting the cursor of sprite to `0`, like this:

```
set the cursor of sprite 10 to 0
```

When you set a custom cursor, you specify the cursor art you want to use as a list of two cast members. The first one is the cursor image and the second one is the mask image. Without a mask, the cursor artwork is transparent and hard to see. The mask travels behind the cursor art, keeping the stage from showing through the cursor. The cursor cast and the mask cast must be 1-bit (black-and-white) cast members, 16 pixels × 16 pixels in size. Cast members 19 and 20 are the custom cursor casts in the Marble movie. For detailed information on making cursor artwork, refer to Chapter 21, "How Do I...: The Top 20 Lingo Support Questions."

In the `startMovie` handler of the Marble movie, the custom cursor list is assigned to a global variable, as follows:

```
set gPointerCursor = [the number of member "HandCursor",the
➥number of member "HandCursorMask"]
```

You also could have coded it like the following:

```
set gPointerCursor = [19,20]
```

Using `the number of member castName` instead means that you don't have to change the code if you move those cast members to other cast member slots. Another global variable is set up in this line:

```
set gCustomCursorList = []
```

The movie is going to use `gCustomCursorList` to keep track of the sprite channels to which custom cursors are assigned. Each time the program goes to a new section, it uses the list to find the channels to which custom cursors are assigned and turn off the cursors before moving to a new section.

The following code sets up the custom cursors for the Main Menu section:

```
-- Custom movie script
on mainCursors
  repeat with buttonSprite = 8 to 10
    customCursorOn(buttonSprite)
  end repeat
end

-- Custom movie script
on customCursorOn whichSprite
  global gCustomCursorList,gPointerCursor
  set the cursor of sprite whichSprite to gPointerCursor
  append gCustomCursorList,whichSprite
end
```

The handler `customCursorOn` gives whatever sprite channel is passed to it, a custom cursor. The last line of `customCursorOn` adds the new sprite channel number to a list of sprite channels that have custom cursors assigned to them.

Append

Syntax:

```
append list, value
```

Example:

```
append groceryList,"lima beans"
put groceryList
-- ["ham hocks","lima beans"]
```

The `append` command adds the item you specify to the end of a list. If the list is empty, it puts one item in the list.

The custom handler `customCursorOn` assigns a custom cursor to a sprite channel. It then adds that channel's number to the custom cursor list. After the custom handler `mainCursors` finishes, `gCustomCursorList` looks like this:

```
[ 8, 9, 10 ]
```

Each of the buttons that goes to a new section calls the following custom handler `customCursorsOff` to turn off the current cursors. `customCursorsOff` uses the custom cursor list to find the sprite channels that have custom cursors:

```
on customCursorsOff
  global customCursorList
  repeat with listPosition = 1 to count(gCustomCursorList)
  set the cursor of sprite getAt(gCustomCursorList,listPosition)
to 0
  end repeat
  set customCursorList = []
end
```

Count

Syntax:

```
count(list)
```

Example:

```
put count(groceryList)
-- 2
```

The `count` command returns the number of items in a list. This code line repeats for each item on the list:

```
repeat with listPosition = 1 to count(gCustomCursorList)
```

GetAt

Syntax:

```
getAt(list,position)
```

Example:

```
if getAt(groceryList,2) = "lima beans" then beep
```

The getAt command returns the value of the list item at the position specified. The first time the following line executes, listPosition is 1:

```
set the cursor of sprite getAt(gCustomCursorList,listPosition)
to 0
```

If gCustomCursorList were to contain [8, 9, 10], then the value at list position 1 would be 8, so the custom cursor for channel 8 would be turned off.

Adding custom cursors to the movie was the final step. If you have been building the movie MARBLE.DIR, or following along with MARBLEDN.DIR, you now have the skills required for general Director programming and the foundation for learning how to construct more complex movies.

Summary

You've covered a lot of ground in this first Lingo chapter. First you learned about the parts of the Lingo environment—objects, properties, events, messages, and messages handlers. You learned that you can use commands and functions to build message handlers that respond to user events by changing object properties. Then you were introduced to the essential Lingo commands that almost every interactive movie requires.

In the next chapter, "Managing Your Data," you'll learn how to make a more intelligent interactive movie—one that can remember user responses to a quiz for example, or fetch information about a certain car model from a database.

Managing Your Data

Almost every Director movie must keep track of its own internal states and store information from the user. Sometimes you need to store one number just long enough to do a calculation. Other times you need to store a large amount of information, such as the essay answer to a test question, for the entire movie. This chapter outlines the many options for storing data in Director and provides some guidelines for using them.

The first part includes information on:

- Types of variables
- Options for temporary storage in Director, from simple variables to complex arrays

The second part covers:

- Permanent data
- Options for storing and reading data outside of Director

Types of Variables

The following sections discuss the various variable types, including local variables and global variables.

Local Variables

You declare local variables inside of handlers using the `put` command or the `set` command, as follows:

```
set [var] = [value]
```

or

```
put [value] into [var]
```

A local variable exists only for the life of the handler that declares it. The local variable is not available outside that handler; it doesn't save its value. Any number of scripts can each use the same local variable name. This makes several completely independent variables. Although the following scripts both use the local variable boundary, the two local variables are independent of each other. Setting one does not affect the other in any way.

```
on mouseUp
   set boundary = 320
   if the mouseH > boundary then
      put "You clicked in the right half of the screen."
   else
      put "You clicked in the left half of the screen."
   end if
end

on checkSprite
   set boundary = 50
   if the locH of sprite 3 >= boundary then
      puppetSprite 3,TRUE
```

```
    -- don't let sprite 3 move past a certain point on the screen
      set the locH of sprite 3 = boundary
      updateStage
    end if
end
```

You cannot use a local variable without first setting its value. If you do, you get a `variable used before assigned value` error.

Use local variables to hold temporary data that you don't need throughout your entire movie. The content of a local variable is purged after you exit a handler, whereas the content of a global variable is not. You save memory by using local variables where you can.

Global Variables

A global variable exists for the entire Director session. It can be examined or set from any handler and from any movie, including a Movie in a Window (MIAW). You declare a global as follows:

```
global globalname
```

Example:

```
global errorCode
```

You can declare a global inside or outside a handler. You do not have to assign a global a value before referring to it. Its initial value is `<Void>`.

If you declare a global inside a handler, any other handler that wants to get or set that global also must declare it. If you declare a global in one handler, then try to refer to that global without declaring it in another handler, Director assumes that you are creating a local handler variable with the same name.

In the following group of handlers, global `userEntry` is declared first in `startMovie` and then declared and used in `keyDown` and `userCheck`. The handler `wontWork` intends to check the length of the global `userEntry` but never declares it. In handler `wontWork`, `userEntry` actually refers to its own local variable `userEntry`. Since you must set local variables before they can be used, handler `wontWork` generates a `variable undefined` error.

```
on startMovie
  -- first declared here
```

```
   global userEntry
end

on keyDown
   global userEntry
   if the key = RETURN then put line 1 of field "UserName" into
userEntry
end

on userCheck
   global userEntry
   if voidP(userEntry) then
      put "No name has been entered yet."
   else
      put "The current user is: " & userEntry
   end if
end

on wontWork
   set tempName = userEntry -- variable undefined error
   if length(tempName) > 25 then
      beep
      put "Your name is too long"
   end if
end
```

If you declare a global variable outside of any handler at the top of a movie script, the global variable is available to any handler. If a global has been declared outside of a handler, handlers that use that global do not have to declare it. Here is how the same set of handlers would work with the global `userEntry` declared outside a handler. In the following movie script, global `userEntry` is declared on the first line, before the first handler—`startMovie`.

```
-- This is a movie script

global userEntry

on startMovie
   -- do some movie initialization stuff
end
```

```
on keyDown
   if the key = RETURN then put line 1 of field "UserName" into
userEntry
end

on userCheck
   if voidP(userEntry) then
      put "No name has been entered yet."
   else
      put "The current user is: " & userEntry
   end if
end

on willWorkNow
   set tempName = userEntry
   if length(tempName) > 25 then
      beep
      put "Your name is too long"
   end if
end
```

So why declare globals inside handlers? Declaring the globals you want to use in a handler makes it clear which variables are local to the handler and which variables are global. It could help someone reading your code. On the other hand, you can use a naming convention for global names, such as putting a "g" in front of them, to help you distinguish them from local variables:

```
global gPlatform, gColorDepth
```

If so, you might prefer to declare all your globals in one place, at the top of a movie script, once and for all.

Use global variables to hold data that must be available to all your movies throughout an entire Director session. You might want to store user preferences, for example, in a global because you would access this data at many different points throughout your movies.

You shouldn't use global variables for data that only one set of handlers or one movie uses. An unnecessary global, once declared, takes up memory for the life of your Director session. You can easily get confused about the purpose for each global when you have a big collection of them. In turn, you become more likely to accidentally use the same global name more than once for entirely different purposes.

Lists

Lists are containers for other variables. You use them to store several different values in one place. Lists do in Lingo what you would use an array for in another language, and more. A list can contain any kind and combination of Lingo variable types, including strings, constants, floats, integers, symbols, and even other lists. You can use the list itself as a local, global, or property variable.

The two kinds of lists are linear lists and property lists.

A *linear list* looks like the following:

```
[#Introduction,#MainMenu,#Health,#FunFacts]
```

The four elements in this list are all symbols. In this case, the list is being used to track the sections of a project the user has visited. After the user finishes a section, that section's name is added to the list.

A *property list* looks like the following:

```
[#Introduction:66,#MainMenu:88,#Health:152,#FunFacts:84]
```

Each element of a property list consists of a property, a colon, and the property's value. The list above is more useful as a property list. Each element now contains the name of the section the user visited as a property, and the score the user got on the quiz at the end of that section as the property's value. The list above tells us, for instance, that the user visited the "Introduction" section and scored a 66 on the quiz at the end of the "Introduction" section.

You create a linear list by using the `list()` function or by enclosing the elements with brackets. Both of these following statements create the same linear list:

```
set myList = list(1,2,3,4)
set myList = [1,2,3,4]
```

This statement creates an empty linear list:

```
set myList = []
```

The most common commands for working with linear lists are `getAt`, `setAt`, `append`, and `count`.

- `getAt`

  Syntax: `getAt` (*list, listposition*)
  Returns the value at the specified list position.

- `setAt`

  Syntax: `setAt` *list, listposition, value*
  Sets the value of a specified list position.

- `append`

  Syntax: `append` *list, value*
  Adds a list item to the end of the list.

- `count`

  Syntax: `count` (*list*)
  Returns the number of items in the list.

You can try out the commands above yourself. Open the Message window and enter the following to create the linear list `shoppingList`.

```
set shoppingList = ["eggs","milk","juice","cereal"]
```

Let's retrieve the second item on the list with the `getAt` function:

```
put getAt(shoppingList,2)
-- milk
```

Director returns `milk` because milk is the second item in `shoppingList`. Next, change the third item on the list using the `setAt` command.

```
setAt shoppingList,3,"bread"
put shoppingList
-- ["eggs","milk","bread","cereal"]
```

Director replaces the third list item, `"juice"`, with the new item `"bread"`. Now, add an item to the end of the list using the `append` command.

```
append shoppingList,"cheese"
put shoppingList
-- ["eggs","milk","bread","cereal","cheese"]
```

Director places the new item `"cheese"` after all of the other items in the list. Now retrieve the total number of items in the list with the count function:

```
put count(shoppingList)
-- 5
```

There are five items in the list.

You create a property list by enclosing the property value pairs you want to include in the list with brackets:

```
set myList = ["Russell":1,"Sarah":0,"Betty":1]
```

Enclose a colon with brackets to create an empty property list:

```
set myList = [:]
```

You can use any type of Lingo value for a property or a property value. All of the following lines contain valid property lists:

```
[ "dog" : 1, "cat" : 2, "bird" : 99 ]
[ 1 : 98.6, 4 : 98.7, 8 : 98.4 ]
[ #pink : #warm , #blue : #cold, #amber : #warm ]
```

The most common commands for working with property lists are `getProp`, `setProp`, and `getOne`.

- `getProp`

  Syntax: `getProp` (*list, property*)
  Returns the value of a property.

- `setProp`

  Syntax: `setProp` (*list, property, newValue*)
  Sets the value of a property.

- `getOne`

  Syntax: `getOne` (*list, value*)
  Returns the first property associated with a value.

Let's return to the Message window to create a property list. Enter the following line to create the new property list `myPropList`:

```
set myPropList = ["Russell":1,"Sarah":0,"Betty":1]
```

Find the value associated with property `"Russell"` by using the `getProp` function:

```
put getProp(myPropList,"Russell")
-- 1
```

Replace the value associate with property `"Sarah"`, by using the `setProp` command:

```
setProp myPropList,"Sarah",1
put myPropList
["Russell":1,"Sarah":1,"Betty":1]
```

Director replaces the previous value associated with property `"Sarah"` –0 , with the new value –1. Now use the `getOne` function to find the first property on the list associated with the value 1:

```
put getOne(myPropList,1)
-- "Russell"
```

The property `"Russell"` is the first property on the list with a value of 1.

Use lists to organize a series of items. Suppose you want to let a user backtrack through the areas she has visited by pressing a Back button. You can do this easily by using a list. If the following script is on the first labeled frame of each section of your movie, you can record the user's progress:

```
on recordLocation
   global locList
   if voidP(locList) then set locList = []
   append locList,the frameLabel
end
```

The code would make a list that looked like the following:

```
["Main","Chapter 1","Quiz","Chapter 5","Main"]
```

This handler in the script for your Back button would take you to the last section visited before the current section:

```
on goBack
   global locList
   set prevSection = count(locList) - 1
   -- the very last item is where the user is now
   go frame getAt(locList,prevSection)
end
```

Use lists to cycle through items quickly. You can keep a list of puppeted sprites, for example, which makes it easy for you to turn off puppeting for all of them when it is no longer needed. This code adds a sprite to the puppet list when it is puppeted:

```
on pup aSprite
   global pupList
   if voidP(pupList) then set pupList = []
   puppetSprite aSprite,TRUE
   updateStage
   if not getOne(pupList,aSprite) then
      append pupList,aSprite
   end if
end
```

This code unpuppets all the puppeted sprites:

```
on pupsOff
   global pupList
   repeat with x = 1 to count(pupList)
      set spriteNum= getAt(pupList,x)
      puppetSprite(spriteNum,FALSE)
   end repeat
   set pupList = []
end
```

Table 17.1 describes the syntax and use for all list commands:

Table 17.1

Director 5 List Commands: Syntax and Uses

Command	Linear List	Property List	Example Command and Result with Unsorted Starting Lists of:

			`linList`
			`["or", "is", "not"]`
			`propList`
			`[#cat:1,#dog:5,#bird:2]`

Use with Linear List			
`addProp`	Appends to end of unsorted list Inserts value into correct position of sorted list	No	`add linList,5` `["or", "is","not",5]`
`addAt`	Inserts value into specified position in list	No	`addAt linList,2,"Tree"` `["or","Tree","is","not"]`
	Appends to end of sorted or unsorted list	No	`append linList, 16` `["or","is","not",16]`
`list`	Creates a linear list	No	`put list (3,5,7)` `-- [3,5,7]`
Use with Property List			
`addProp`	No	Appends property: value to end of unsorted list and inserts property: value into correct postition of sorted list	`addProp propList, #color, "red"` `[#cat:1,#dog:5,#bird:2,#color:"red"]`
`deleteProp`	No	Deletes the first item with the specified property from the list	`deleteProp propList,#cat` `[#dog:5,#bird:2]`
`findPos`	No	Returns the position of the first occurence of the specified property on the list; returns <Void> if the property is not on the list	`put findPos(propList,#dog)` `-- 2`

continues

Table 17.1, CONTINUED

Command	Linear List	Property List	Example Command and Result with Unsorted Starting Lists of:
indPosNear	No	Returns the position of the property on a sorted list closest to the specified property; does not work on unsorted lists	sort propList [#bird:2,#cat:1,#dog:5] --1
getaProp	No	Returns the value of the property specified; returns <Void> if the property is not on the list	put getaProp(propList,#dog) --5
getProp	No	Returns the value of the property specified; gives a "handler not defined" script error if the property is not on the list	put getProp(propList,#dog) --5
getPropAt	No	Returns the property name at the specified position	put getPropAt(propList,1) --#cat
setaProp	No	Replaces the value of the specified property with a new value; adds a new property and value if the specified property doesn't exist	setaProp propList,#bird,8 [#cat:1,#dog:5,#bird:8]
setProp	No	Replaces the value of the specified property with a new value; gives a "handler not defined" script error if the specified property does not exist	setProp propList,#bird,8 [#cat:1,#dog:5,#bird:8]
Use with Both			
count	Returns number of items in list	Returns number of items in list	count(linList) --3 count(propList) --3
deleteAt	Deletes the	Deletes the item from that	deleteAt linList,1

Command	Linear List	Property List	Example Command and Result with Unsorted Starting Lists of:

	Item from that position in the list	Position in the list	`["is","not"]`
			`deleteAt propList,3`
			`[#cat:1,#dog:5]`

`getAt`	Returns the list item in the position specified	Returns the value of the list item specified	`put getAt(linList,3)`
			`--"not"`
			`put getAt(propList,3)`
			`--2`

`getLast`	Returns the last item	Returns the value of the last item	`put getLast(linList)`
			`--"not"`
			`put getLast(propList)`
			`--2`

`getOne`	Returns the position of the specified value; returns 0 if the value is not on the list	Returns the first property on the list associated with the value; returns 0 if the value is not on the list	`put getOne(linList,2)`
			`--"is"`
			`put getOne(propList,5)`
			`--#dog`

`getPos`	Returns the position of the specified value; returns 0 if the value is not on the list	Returns the position of the first item on the list that contains that value; returns 0 if the value is not on the list	`put getPos(linList,2)`
			`--"is"`
			`put getPos(propList,5)`
			`--2`

`listP`	Returns TRUE if the specified variable is a list	Returns TRUE if the specified variable is a list	`put listP(propList)` `--TRUE`

`max`	Returns the largest item	Returns the largest property value	`put max(linList)`
			`--"or"`
			`put max(propList)`
			`--5`

continues

Table 17.1, CONTINUED

Command	Linear List	Property List	Example Command and Result with Unsorted Starting Lists of:

`min`	Returns the the position specified	Returns the smallest property value	`put min(linList)`
			`--"is"`
			`put min (propList)`
			`--1`

`setAt`	Replaces the specified position in the list with the specified value; if the specified position is greater than the number of items in the list, adds items that contain 0 between the end of the list and the new item	Replaces the value of the specified position with a new value; gives an "index out of range" script error if the specified position is greater than the number of items on the list	`setAt linList,2,"be"`
			`["or","be","not"]`
			`setAt propList, 2,20`
			`[#cat:1,#dog:20,#bird:#2]`

`sort`	Put the list items in alphanumeric order; returns 0 if the value is not on the list	Puts the list items in alphanumberic order sorted by property if the value is not on the list	`sort (linList)`
			`["is","not","or"]`
			`sort (propList)`
			`[#bird: #2,#cat: 1,#dog: 5}`

List Math

You can use the arithmetic operators on lists to perform an operation on all the items in the list. Suppose you have a game in which you keep track of players and their points with a list like this called `scoreList`:

```
[#Mary:12,#Harry:15,#Paul:6]
```

The game has one bonus situation in which everybody gets 50 points added on to their score. You could use a repeat loop to iterate through all the items on the list and add 50 points to each one, or you could take advantage of list math and do it like this:

```
set scoreList = scoreList + 50
```

Director increments all the property values at once:

```
[#Mary:62,#Harry:65,#Paul:56]
```

Copying Lists

When you put a list into a new variable you are only setting the new variable to point to the list. You are not making a new copy of the list. After the following code executes, the variables `newList` and `oldList` both point to the same list:

```
set oldList = ["pig","dog","goat"]
set newList = oldList
```

If you make a change to `newList`, then examine `oldList`, you notice that `oldList` also shows your change:

```
append newList,"canary"
put oldList
-- ["pig","dog","goat","canary"]
```

The `duplicate` command makes a new independent copy of a list. If you substitute the `duplicate` command and use the same list example you now have two independent lists:

```
set oldList = ["pig","dog","goat"]
set newList = duplicate(oldList)
append newList,"canary"
```

```
put oldList
-- ["pig","dog","goat"]

put newList

-- ["pig","dog","goat","canary"]
```

Multidimensional Arrays

A list can contain lists, which also can contain lists, and so on, and so on. This is how you create a multidimensional array. Suppose you are writing a Tic-Tac-Toe game in which the user plays against the computer. You need to keep track of what each square already contains before you can calculate the next possible move. The first step is to come up with a numbering system for the squares. In this case, it's pretty easy (see fig. 17.1).

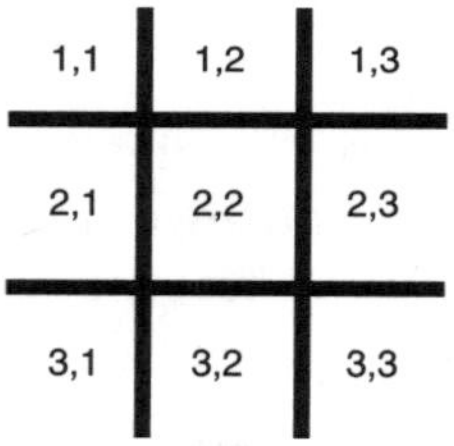

Figure 17.1

Numbering system for the positions on the game board.

1,1	1,2	1,3
2,1	2,2	2,3
3,1	3,2	3,3

The next step is to decide on a symbol for each possible state. You could use `#X`, `#O`, and `#none`. The third step is to build a list in which all the initial values of the squares are set to none:

```
on buildList
      global squareList
      set squareList = []
      repeat with row = 1 to 3
         set aRow = []
         repeat with column = 1 to 3
            setAt(aRow,column,#none)
         end repeat
         setAt(squareList,row,aRow)
      end repeat
end
```

Now you have a list called `squareList`, which contains three sublists—one for each row of your Tic-Tac-Toe board. Each row sublist has three items—one for each square in that row (see fig. 17.2).

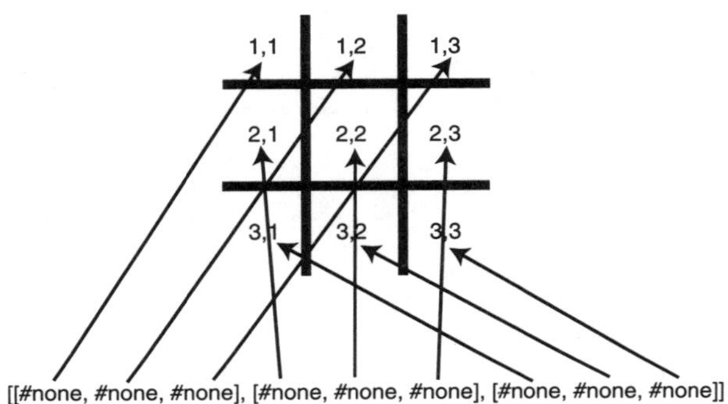

Figure 17.2

The list representing the game squares at the start of the game.

Now you need a handler that adds new moves to the list:

```
on newMove  row,col, XorO
   global squareList
   setAt  getAt ( squareList, row ), col, XorO
end
```

If the first player puts an "X" in the center square, you would call the handler with these arguments:

```
newMove (2,2,#X)
```

There are no placed game pieces to start, so the list looks like the following:

```
[[#none, #none, #none],[#none, #none, #none],[#none, #none,
➥#none]]
```

`GetAt (squareList,row)` refers to one of the sublists:

```
[#none, #none, #none]
```

If you substitute a sublist for the `getAt` statement and actual values for the argument names, the line of code in the `newMove` handler looks like this:

```
setAt  [#none, #none, #none] , 2 , #X
```

After newMove runs, squareList now looks like the following (see fig. 17.3):

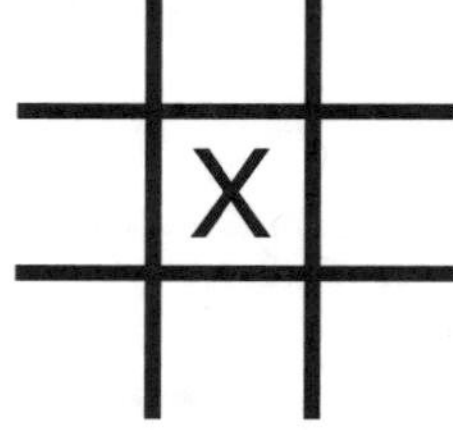

[[#none, #none, #none], [#none, #none, #none], [#none, #none, #none]]

Figure 17.3

The second sublist, which represents row 2 of the game board, shows an X in item 2. The items in the second sublist represent the three squares in row 2.

Open the movie LIST.DIR. It is a simple movie with a Tic-Tac-Toe board and a list keeping track of the spots on the board at the bottom of the screen. See if you can anticipate which item of the list will change before you click on a game piece.

The movies LIST.DIR and TICTAC.DIR are on the disc in the folder for Chapter 17, "Managing Your Data."

The movie TICTAC.DIR is a full Tic-Tac-Toe game that pits a human against the computer. It uses a list to keep track of where the pieces are so it can determine the remaining legal moves. Look at the code in TICTAC.DIR for more examples of the setAt and getAt commands at work. TICTAC.DIR uses a code object to organize the game code. Chapter 20, "Object-Oriented Programming," covers code objects in more detail. You may want to return to TICTAC.DIR again after reading that chapter.

Naming Variables

The kindest thing you can do for anyone who might have to read your code in the future (including yourself!) is to give significant variables meaningful names. What in the world does the following code do?

```
on whoKnows a,b
   global f,g
   set c = a * 12
   set d = b * 12
   set h = c - d
   if h > 0 then
```

```
      put f into field "r"
    else
      put g into field "r"
    end if
end
```

The following explains it:

```
on returnOnInvest oldMonthlyCost,newMonthlyCost
   set oldCostPerYear = oldMonthlyCost * 12
   set newCostPerYear = newMontlyCost * 12
   set savings = oldCostPerYear - newCostPerYear
   if savings > 0 then
     put "You'll save $" & savings & " with the new plan." into
     ➥field "Result"
   else
    put "You won't save with the new plan." into field "Result"
   end if
end
```

There is no significant space or performance penalty for using long variable names. When Director compiles your Lingo, it tokenizes the variable names. *Tokenizing* replaces the actual string with a compact, internal representation.

On the flip side, not every variable is significant. Scratch variables, like counters, don't need meaningful names. In fact, your code is more readable if you follow the common programming convention of using one-letter variables for these throwaways.

```
repeat with x = 1 to 100
   doSomething
end repeat
```

Code that uses meaningful variable names is almost self-documenting, but you can increase the readability even further by including comments. You create a comment line by preceding it with two hyphens. The following function is easy to understand at first glance because of the comments:

```
on stripChars inputString,charToStrip
   -- INPUT:   inputString - string to strip characters from
   --          EX: "beauty shop"
   --          charToStrip - which character to strip off
```

```
    --          EX: " "
    -- RETURNS: a string with the specified character
    --          stripped off
    ----------------------------------------------------------
    set ln = length(inputString)
    repeat with lastGoodChar = ln down to 0
       if char lastGoodChar of inputString <> charToStrip then
          exit repeat
       end if
    end repeat
    -- at the end of the repeat loop lastGoodChar will contain
    -- the number of the last character that is part of the
    -- string
    if lastGoodChar > 0 then
       return char 1 to lastGoodChar of inputString
    else
       return ""
    end if
end
```

The comments at the beginning of the handler explain what it does, what arguments it expects, and what it returns. This information is extremely helpful to others. Comments are stripped out of the code when the movie is compiled, so you don't have to worry about them taking up space or affecting performance.

Permanent Data

Suppose you are keeping track of user game scores in your application by storing them in a list. While your application is running, you can retrieve scores from the list, but as soon as your application quits, the scores are gone. If you want to save the game scores to use the next time you run the application, you need more permanent storage for the data. You can store permanent data in fields inside of the Director movie or write it to separate files outside the Director movie.

Storing Data in Fields

You can save information that the user enters into fields on stage, and you also can create fields that you never place on the stage just for storing data. You use the `saveMovie` command to save the contents of these fields with the movie. If you don't use the `saveMovie` command, the fields revert to their original state when you quit the movie. Any data entered during the session is lost.

You can read or write to the fields directly or use them to store lists that contain your data. If you have a very small amount of data, reading and writing directly to fields is easier. For larger amounts of data, reading the field contents into a list and using the list to access the data while the program is running is much faster. When it's time to quit the program, you can write the data back out to the field to store it.

Suppose you have a single-user application that needs to store a small amount of information about the user's preferences. You might want to keep track of where the user was when she quit last, so you can return her to that spot, as well as her current score.

You would create a field to directly store this small amount of data. The following code writes this user data to the field `User Information`:

```
on stopMovie
   global currentArea
   global score
   put currentArea into item 1 of line 1 of field "User
   ➥Information"
   put score into item 2 of line 1 of field "User Information"
   saveMovie
end
```

Now imagine that you have many people using your program rather than one user, and that you must store this information for every person. When the program is launched, you prompt each user to enter her name so that you can link the saved information to the right person.

One way to do this would be to have each line of the `User Information` field store the information for one person. An information line would be added to the end of the field for each new person.

But how would you retrieve one user's information under this scheme? You *could* read through each line of the field, examining the first item of the line (the user name) until you find the right entry. But this wouldn't be very efficient, for a couple reasons:

- If you look for the name of someone who was the 200th person to sign in, you have to cycle through 199 lines in the field before you find her.
- Chunk commands (`item`, `char`, `word`, `line`) are slow

A better solution is to use a property list. If you store each name as a property and use the `sort` command on the list, the user information is automatically indexed by user name. Now you can retrieve the entry you seek without having to cycle through all the others.

The following is a property list that contains the same information. The main list is a property list of user names. The value for each name in the main list is also a property list, containing the data for one user.

```
["David": [#currentArea: "Fitness Tips",#score:40],"Marlene":
➥ [#currentArea: "Quiz", #score:80], ... "Zane":
➥ [#currentArea: "Library",#score:99]]
```

You add an item to the list like this:

```
on addUser userName,area,score
   global userList
   if voidP(userList) then set userList - [:]
   set miniList = [:] -- sublist of one user's data
   setaProp miniList,#currentArea,area
   setaProp miniList,#score,score
   setaProp(userList,userName,miniList)
end
```

You retrieve user data from the list like this:

```
on getCurrentArea userName
   global userList
   set miniList = getProp(userList,userName)
   return getProp(miniList,#currentArea)
   -- you can nest list commands. Another way to
   -- write this would be:
   -- getProp(getProp(userList,userName),#currentArea)
end
```

Lists are only temporary storage. At the end of the Director session, you must store your list data to a field and do a `saveMovie` to preserve it. Fortunately, you don't have to write the list out item-by-item to the field. You can put the whole list into the field at once. Director converts the list to a string first and puts it into the field:

```
put myList into field "Storage Field"
```

A field can hold up to 32 KB of text. A list that you store this way must be able to fit entirely into the field. Otherwise, the data at the end of the list that doesn't fit gets cut off.

When you restart your program, you load the data back into a list from the field with code like this:

```
on loadList
   global myList
   put value(field "Storage Field") into myList
   sort(myList)
end
```

The `value` function converts the string in your storage field back into a list. Then you must sort the list to restore the internal indices that make searching fast. You lose these when you convert a sorted list to a string.

Using External Files

You can manage a small-to-moderate amount of permanent data just by using fields inside your Director movie. This is a good strategy for data that is not going to grow beyond the limits of a 32 KB text field. Although spanning data over multiple fields is possible, storing large amounts of data this way isn't practical. Data internal to the movie increases the movie's file size and memory requirements. Storing data inside the movie also makes it impossible for someone else to do data entry.

External files are a better choice for storing large amounts of data, because they keep your Director movie size small and reduce your memory requirements. You can retrieve data from a file one record at a time.

The FileIO XObject enables you to read and write to ASCII (text) files. This XObject is built into Director for Macintosh, so you don't have to have an `openXlib` command before you can use it—it's already open.

To find out which XObjects and Xtras are loaded and available to you, type `showxlib` in the Message window. XObject and Xtras are self-documenting. To get a list of all of an XObject's methods, type the following in the Message window:

```
XobjectName(mDescribe)
```

To list all the available methods for FileIO, you enter the following in the Message window:

```
fileIO(mDescribe)
```

The FileIO process is modal. If you open a file in Read mode, you must close it and reopen it in Write mode to write to it, and vice versa. Write mode wipes out the file if it already exists. To add information to an existing file, use Append mode. You open a file by creating a new instance of the FileIO XObject with the `mNew` command and assigning it to a variable. You can open multiple files. The following code opens a file that already exists and writes new data to it. Including the RETURN character at the end of a string signals the end of the record:

```
on appendMode oneRecord
   -- oneRecord is a string that looks like this:
   --   "Garden Hose,XRP2132,32.99"
   global catalogItems
   if objectP(catalogItems) then catalogItems(mDispose)
   -- if this file is already open then close it
   set catalogItems = fileIO(mNew,"append","cat.txt")
   -- "cat.txt" would need a full file path if it was not located
   ➥in
   --   the same directory as the calling movie
   catalogItems(mWriteString,oneRecord & RETURN)
   -- The RETURN character separates lines in the file. The
   --   mReadLine method reads up to a RETURN character (10).
   --   If you will be using mReadLine on the file, or you need
   --   to look at the data in the file with a text editor, you
   ➥should
   --   separate lines with the RETURN character
   put integer(field "Record Count") + 1 into field "Record
   ➥Count"
```

```
    -- keep a count in another field of the number of records in
    ➥ the file
    catalogItems(mDispose) -- close file
end
```

> Cross-Platform Alert!
>
> Mac text files use just the RETURN character (ASCII 13) to end lines, but PC text files use RETURN (13) and LINE FEED (10). FileIO uses the Macintosh convention to detect the end of a line on both platforms.
>
> If you write a file using FileIO that you are only going to read through FileIO on the PC, then you don't have to worry about this. If your PC users are going to use PC programs to view text files that you have created with FileIO, you should end lines with RETURN and LINE FEED.

The data file in the preceding example collects new catalog item data as it is entered, but the data won't be sorted by any data field. To get a particular item's record back out, you have to start at the beginning and read through each record until you come to the one you want. The more records you have in the file, the longer retrieving one record takes. You can speed things up considerably by maintaining an index to the file and by using the `mSeekPos` method to start reading at the beginning of the record you want.

In this example, the catalog items file is built by data entry. At the same time that you add a new catalog item record to the file, you can add an index entry to a list for the record. The index entry includes just the data field you want to use to retrieve records later and the number of the record. In this case, you would use an item number. This code adds an item number to the index:

```
on newIndEntry itemNumber
    global itemNumberIndex
    if voidP(itemNumberIndex) then set itemNumberIndex = [:]
    set lastRecord = integer(field "Record Count")
     setaProp(itemNumberIndex,itemNumber,lastRecord + 1)
    end if
end
```

The item number index list looks like the following:

```
["ARX111":1,"BT833":8,"LR222":55, ... "XR59393":200]
```

The index is much smaller than the data file because it contains only one data field's worth of data. You might, therefore, be able to use fields in your movie to store your index lists. Otherwise, you can write the index list out to a second file.

Having an index for a file that contains records of varying lengths only solves half the speed problem. To get to record 15, you still have to use `mReadLine` to read and discard records 1–14 before you arrive at 15. You can get around this by writing fixed-length records to your file and using the `mSetPosition` method to start reading at a particular place. `mSetPosition` positions the read before the character number specified. If you know that every record contains exactly 100 characters, for example, `mSetPosition(100)` positions you before character 101, which is the beginning of record 2.

The easiest way to write a fixed-length record is to pad the end of the string with a character that doesn't appear in your data. Here is a record padded out to a length of 50 with the "^" character:

```
Garden Hose,XRP2132,32.99^^^^^^^^^^^^^^^^^^^^^^^^^
```

If you make sure that the character you choose for the pad character doesn't occur in the data itself, using `the itemdelimiter` makes it easy to strip out the padding when you read in the record:

```
set the itemdelimiter = "^"
put item 1 of recordReadIn
Garden Hose,XRP2132,32.99
```

The record length you choose needs to be as large as the maximum length of all the fields. This means you limit the amount of characters the user can enter into a field at data entry. The RETURN character counts toward the length of the record. A 100-character record contains 99 characters of data and a RETURN character.

The following code uses a record number to read in a record from a file that contains fixed-length, 50-character records:

```
on getOneRecord recordNumber
   set recordLength = 50
      -- these records are padded out to character 50 with ^
   set catalogItems = fileIO(mNew,"read","catfile.txt")
```

```
        catalogItems(mSetPosition,recordNumber * recordLength)
        set record = catalogItems(mReadLine)
        set the itemDelimiter = "^"
        set strippedRecord = item 1 of record
        return strippedRecord
    end
```

The movie DATABASE.DIR contains the code above. It demonstrates the data entry and retrieval for a small fixed-length record database. The text file CATFILE.TXT contains the database.

The movie DATABASE.DIR is on the CD in the folder for Chapter 17. Copy DATABASE.DIR and its data file CATFILE.TXT into the same folder on your hard drive before you start working with it. If you run DATABASE.DIR from the CD it will not be able to write to the data file on the CD.

Large Databases

"What's the largest database Director can handle?" is a question that comes up often in Director support forums. The question doesn't have a hard-and-fast answer, because it depends on the size of one record, the projected size of the entire database, and what you want to do with the data. Because every situation is unique, the best way to test performance is to build a dummy text file that is similar in size and record length to your proposed database, and test access times using FileIO. Performance isn't the only factor, however. Other limitations include:

- The database itself can reside in a file outside of Director, but the indices must fit into Director's memory. If your database is static—included on a CD with your project, for instance—growth is not a concern. If your database will expand—you run the risk of overflowing memory or field size limits.
- You can't delete a record from an external file using FileIO, although you can flag records for deletion and write a maintenance program that periodically reads through the data file and writes it back out minus the deleted records.

- Report printing, using Director's `printFrom` command, requires that all the data you want to print per page fit into a field on screen.
- You have to write your own utilities in Lingo to handle data entry, database queries, and report generation.

Fortunately, there are other options if your database requirements go beyond what Director can handle. At this writing there are two Director Xtras, FileFlex and V12, that enable Director to create and manage an external database. The *Inside Director* CD includes information and fully functioning demos for both products in the Xtra Partners folder.

Summary

In this chapter you have learned that there are many ways to store and manage information with Director. Variables, lists, and fields help you organize data during a Director session. Lists are especially versatile. They enable you to sort and index many different types of data for quick retrieval.

If you want to save data between Director sessions you also have several options. You can save the data inside the Director file itself, write it out to a text file, or look into purchasing a database Xtra.

In the next chapter you will explore Movie in a Window, a feature that enables you to play several independent Director movies at once.

Gretchen Macdowall

Movie in a Window

Before Macromedia introduced the Movie in a Window feature in Director 4.0, Director could play only one movie at a time. The `go movie` and `play movie` commands were the only way to switch movies then, but these commands replace one movie on the stage with another. A *Movie in a Window* (MIAW) is a Director movie that opens in its own window and plays simultaneously with the movie on stage.

MIAWs are fully interactive Director movies that can execute Lingo scripts and play media independently of each other. You can open as many MIAWs as memory will allow. Playback performance depends on how many are open at a time.

Movie in a Window is a versatile Director feature that is only available through scripting. The size, location, appearance, and stacking order of MIAWs are all controlled through Lingo. You also use Lingo to pass messages back and forth between MIAWs and the stage.

Because MIAWs are self-contained and completely independent of each other and the stage, you can use them for special functions that you don't need for the entire session. This makes MIAWs great for help systems and programming utilities, especially because MIAWs continue to run independently of the stage movie, even when the stage movie is being edited. Because you can create windows that the users can position wherever they want on-screen, MIAWs are also a good way to implement tool palettes and controls. Finally, MIAWs are a more flexible alternative to Director's standard "alert" box. You can simulate a dialog box with an MIAW that accepts user choice input—something Director's `alert` command doesn't do.

In addition to the MIAW tools you can make for yourself, expect to see more commercial MIAW add-ons as well. With Director 5, you now can open protected MIAWs in the authoring environment. This feature enables third-party developers to write utility MIAWs, but still protect their code. The new Xtras menu will list any MIAW you place in the Xtras folder for easy access. Try placing the MEMMON movie from the CD there.

Take a look at the five sample MIAWs in the Chapter 18 folder on the accompanying CD-ROM to get an idea of the range of uses for MIAWs. They are listed below:

- **Clock.** A moveable window that displays the time.
- **Memmon.** A programming utility that loads and unloads cast and shows the memory freed by each action.
- **MixBot.** A programming utility that records and saves the sound volumes you set for sound channels as you play your movie.
- **Presentation Tools.** Windows that open alongside the main presentation that the speaker can use to navigate and take notes.
- **Dialog.** A generic dialog box that contains OK and Cancel buttons and adapts itself for Macintosh or Windows.

In this chapter, you will learn how to create and manage your own MIAWs. The Basics section covers the mechanics of creating and positioning one window. The sections on "Window Types" and "Panning and Scaling" contain information on customizing the appearance of your window. In the section "Managing Multiple Windows," you will learn how to juggle several open MIAWs at once.

The Basics

You can create an MIAW with one line of Lingo code, as follows:

```
open window "Movie File"
```

In one step this creates a new window, looks for the Director file Movie File in the default directory (the moviePath), assigns the Director file Movie File to that window, and opens the window. This is an easy way to open MIAWs via the message window for quick testing, but scripts that open MIAWs are more flexible if you separate the processes of creating and opening the window.

Creating a Window

Windows and movie files are two distinct Director elements. A *window* is a porthole through which the Director movie displays. When you create an MIAW, the movie and its window default to the same size. You can, however, change the size of the window and the area the movie plays within with the `rect of window` and `drawRect of window` commands. When you make the window assigned to a movie smaller than the movie itself, the window displays only the part of the movie that fits inside the window. Position the window outside the viewable desktop area and it disappears altogether. Don't be fooled, however. The Director movie assigned to that window remains in memory and continues to play, even though you can't see it anymore.

You create a window the first time you refer to it using the following:

```
window "windowName"
```

The string `windowName` becomes the window's name. If `windowName` is a valid path to a Director movie, the path becomes the window's name and the movie it points to is assigned to the window. Otherwise, the string just becomes the window's name and no movie is assigned to the window. Nothing will open if you use an `open` command on a window without a Director movie assigned to it because there's nothing yet to display.

Each of the following lines of Lingo, because they contain the phrase `window "`*`windowName`*`"`, will create a window—if a window by that name does not already exist. If there is no Director movie file named newWindow, the second line will create a window named newWindow that is not yet linked to any Director movie. If there is no Director movie file named helpWindow, the third will create a window named helpWindow that is not yet linked to any Director movie.

```
set helpWin = window "Macintosh HD : Project : HELP"
put window "newWindow"
set helpWin = window "helpWindow"
set the filename of window "aWindow" to "Macintosh HD: NAV"
```

Director has an internal list—called "the windowList"—to keep track of MIAWs. As soon as you create a window, even if the window hasn't been assigned a Director movie yet, it appears on the windowList with the name you assigned to it. Here is what the windowList would look like after the code in the preceding example runs:

```
[ window "Macintosh HD:Project:HELP", window "newWindow", window
➥"helpWindow", window "aWindow" ]
```

As you can see, windows with short names make it easier to decipher the windowList. It's a good idea to name your windows rather than use the file path name. If you don't assign a title to a window, the window name displays by default in the title bar. You probably would not want the file path to display there.

If your Director movies are going to play on Windows machines as well as Macs, you should name them from the start with DIR file extensions. You do not have to include file extensions when you specify a Director file name in your scripts. If you ask for movie HELP, Director will first look for movie HELP, then HELP.DIR, then HELP.DXR. If you don't include extensions in your code, you won't have to change anything later if you decide to protect the movies. Protected movies have a DXR extension.

Making constant references in your code to window "windowName" is very cumbersome. You can get around this by setting a variable to the phrase `window myWindowName`. If you make the window variable a global variable, you have the added convenience of making it available throughout your project.

```
global navWin
set navWin = window "Navigator"
```

You now can use the shorthand `navWin` anywhere you would have typed `window "Navigator"`. Each of the following two statements do the same thing:

```
moveToBack window "Navigator"
moveToBack navWin
```

Opening a Window

The Director movie assigned to an MIAW does not load into memory and begin to play until you open its window. The first two lines of the following code link a Director movie to a window and assign the window to global `helpWin`. The third line then displays the window.

```
global helpWin
set helpWin = window "Hard Drive: HELP"
open helpWin
```

So why would you separate these steps when you could? Why not just use the following:

```
open window "Hard Drive:HELP"
```

When you open a window, if you haven't specified any window properties, the window defaults to a non-modal, moveable window with close and size boxes, and opens in the middle of the desktop. If you want to customize any of these window properties, you should create the window, modify the window properties while it is still invisible, and then open it:

```
on newStatusBox
   global diaWin, miawPath
   set diaWin = window (miawPath & "DIALOG")
   set the windowType of window 1 to 1
   open diaWin
end
```

When you assign windows to files in one step and open them in another, you should find that they are easier to manage. Because assigning a Director file name to a window does not actually load the movie until you open the window, you can lump all of these assignments in one place at the start of your first movie. That way they are easy to locate and easy to change, should you change the names of the Director files:

```
on assignMIAW
   global miawPath
   set miawPath = "Hard Drive: MIAW:"
   global helpWin, dialogWin, paintPaletteWin
   set helpWin = window (miawPath & "TEMPH")
   set dialogWin = window (miawPath & "TEMPD")
   set paintPaletteWin = window (miawPath & "TEMPP")
end
```

All of the code outside of the `assignMIAW` handler can use the globals `helpWin`, `dialogWin`, and `paintPaletteWin` to refer to the MIAWs. Later on in production, if the file names of the Director files linked to these windows change, it's a simple matter to change them in one place in the `assignMIAW` handler.

Positioning a Window

The `rect of window` property specifies the window's size and its position in relation to the top left corner of the desktop. The following code creates a window 400 pixels wide by 300 pixels tall, and positions its top left corner 100 pixels away from the top left corner of the desktop (see fig. 18.1).

```
on quitDialog
   global quitWin,MIAWpath
   set quitWin = window (MIAWpath & "QUITDIA")
   set the rect of quitWin to rect(100, 100, 500, 400)
   open quitWin
end
```

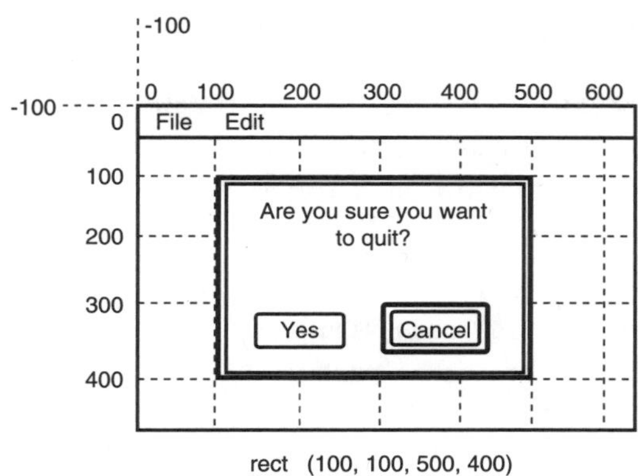

Figure 18.1

The dialog window has a `rect` *of (100, 100, 500, 400).*

The four values in an MIAW rect represent the following:

rect(A,B,C,D)

A Pixel distance of top left corner of MIAW from the left edge of the desktop

B Pixel distance of top left corner of MIAW from the top of the desktop

C Pixel distance of bottom right corner of MIAW from the left edge of the desktop

D Pixel distance of bottom right corner of MIAW from the top of the desktop

You can determine the size of an MIAW from its rect values as follows:

rect(A,B,C,D)

Width in pixels = C–A

Height in pixels = D–B

So, a window with the dimensions of rect (100, 100, 500, 400) would have a width of 400 (500–100) and a height of 300 (400–100).

By specifying negative coordinates, you can position a window above and to the left of the desktop—out of sight. You can use this no-man's-land coordinate space to stash windows that you want to load, but aren't ready to display yet.

Sometimes, there is a noticeable delay when you open a large MIAW that contains many sprites. That is because the movie is loading from the disk or CD, and then imaging on to the desktop. You can minimize the delay by using the `preLoadMovie` command to preload any cast that will appear in the first frame of the MIAW, and opening the window beyond the visible desktop. This part is transparent to the user.

```
on openLargeMovie
      global bigWindow,MIAWpath
      preloadMovie MIAWpath & "BIGWIND"
      set bigWindow = window (MIAWpath & "BIGWIND")
      -- the rect of bigWindow is rect(50,50,500,400)
      set the rect of bigWindow = the rect of bigWindow - 10000
      -- subtracts 1000 from each item in the rect
      -- the rect of bigWindow is now rect (-9950,-9950,-9500,-
      9600)
      open bigWindow   -- window opens outside of the visible
      ➥stage
end
```

Why a negative coordinate of 10000? The Macintosh system assigns the coordinate (0, 0) to the top left corner of the primary monitor. A second monitor placed to the left of the primary monitor in the monitor's Control Panel will be in the negative horizontal coordinate space. Using a high number like –10000 reduces the chance of the MIAW you are trying to hide showing up on the second monitor because you have specified negative coordinates occupied by that monitor.

When you are ready to display the MIAW, you reset the "`rect of window`" to the correct position on the desktop. Because the movie has already loaded from disk, it displays much faster.

```
on fastDisplay
   global bigWindow
   set the rect of bigWindow to rect(50,50,500,400)
   -- preloaded window appears on the desktop
end
```

Closing a Window

The `close window` command makes a window invisible, but does not unload the movie linked to it. The Director movie assigned to a closed window continues to play in the background. All you have done is hidden the window from view.

The `forget window` command removes the window and its associated Director file from memory. Use `close` or the `visible` property when you want to temporarily hide a window. This prevents a time-consuming reload of the movie from disk. Use `forget` when you want to clear a window from memory that you are not going to use again or when you need to free up memory.

Setting `the windowList` to an empty list as follows forgets all MIAWs:

```
set the windowList = []
```

Window Types

You can customize your MIAW window frames by setting the `windowType` property using the following command:

```
set the windowtype of window "windowName" to typeNumber
Ex: set the windowtype of window "Main" to 1
```

Director's Mac's built-in window types are the standard window types available in the Macintosh operating system. When you specify a particular window type, Director makes a call to the operating system to create that type of window. Window borders are decorative, but they also tell the user how that window is going to behave. Mac users quickly learn that a window with a title bar can be repositioned and that a solid border around a window signals a modal dialog box. Each window type behaves the same way across Macintosh applications, making it easy for users to get around. If you ignore interface conventions when you choose window types (for example, you create an alert box framed by a document window just to be "different"), you won't be doing your users any favors.

Table 18.1 lists Director's built-in window types.

Table 18.1
The Standard Window Types

Type	Description	Looks Like...
-1	Default Director window type	 name
0	Standard document	 name
1	Alert	
2	Plain	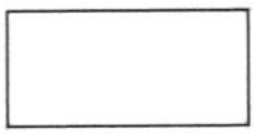
3	Plain with shadow	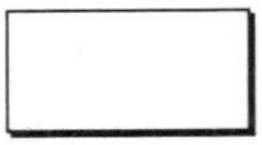
4	Document without size box	 name
8	Document with zoom box, with size box	 name

Type	Description	Looks Like...
12	Document with zoom box, no size box	name
16	Curved border	name

In addition to the standard window types, you also can also add custom window type resources, called Window Definitions (WDEFs), to your movies. Any application can use WDEF resources—not just Director—so you'll find some good collections of them online in Mac programming forums. The following are some good places to look:

World Wide Web	ftp://mirrors.aol.com/pub/info-mac/
America Online	Keyword: MDV (Macintosh Developers)
	Keyword: SUPERCARD
	Keyword: MHC (HyperCard and Scripting Forum)
CompuServe	GO APHYPER (HyperCard Forum)
	GO MACDEV (Macintosh Developers Forum)

You can add a new WDEF to your Director movies by opening a file containing a WDEF resource using Director's `openResFile` command. When you open a resource file containing a WDEF resource, you make a new window type number available to all of the movies in the Director session. When you set the `windowtype` of a window to the new number, you give it the new custom window type.

WARNING

Platform Alert: You cannot use Macintosh resources on the PC. Any custom window types, fonts, or other resources you add to your Macintosh movies will be ignored when you play the movie on the PC.

There are two parts to the process of adding a custom window type. First you must open the file containing the WDEF resource with ResEdit, Apple's free resource editing tool. (ResEdit is available from Apple at http://www.apple.com/.) ResEdit tells you the resource ID of the WDEF resource. You need this ID number to determine what `windowType` value to give your MIAW in Director. After you have determined the resource ID number, you can use the file containing the WDEF resource in Director by opening it with the `openResFile` command.

The following steps show how to use ResEdit to determine the WDEF resource ID number.

1. Open the WDEF resource file in ResEdit.
2. The WDEF resource file window contains icons for each of its resources. One icon is labeled WDEF (see fig. 18.2).

Figure 18.2

ResEdit displays the files resources, which include the WDEF resource.

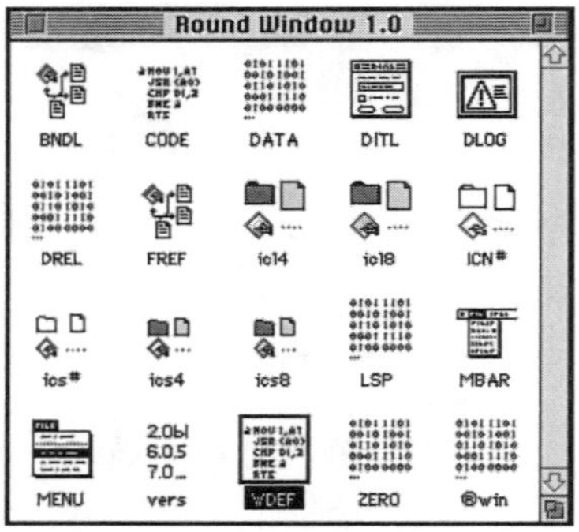

3. Double-click on the WDEF resource and note the ID number. The resource ID determines what `windowtype` you call in Director (see fig. 18.3).

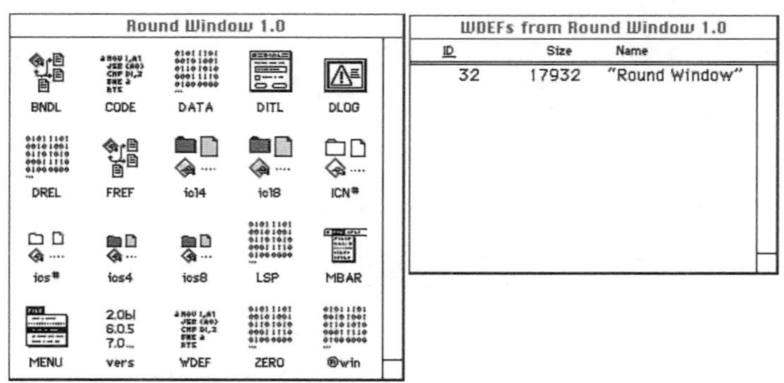

Figure 18.3

Double-click on the WDEF resource to open the window showing its ID number.

Now you are ready to use your new window type in Director. The window type is *not* the same as the resource ID. The following is the formula used to derive the window type:

```
Resource ID × 16 + variation
```

Some WDEFs include several variations. If so, the variation numbers are documented. Others include just one style. The primary style is variation 0. The WDEF installed in the preceding example has just one style—no variations. Plugging the resource ID of 32 into the formula, you'd get 512:

```
32 × 16 + 0 = 512
```

Now you are ready to use the WDEF resource file in Director. Close the WDEF file in ResEdit and launch Director. Use the command `openResFile` as follows to open up the WDEF resource file:

```
openResFile "resourceFileName"
```

For example:

```
openResFile "Round Window"
```

The WDEF resource in the resource file you opened is now available to Director. Use the number you derived from the WDEF resource ID to set `the windowType` property of a window to the new window type. The window should use your new `windowtype`:

```
set the windowType of "testWin" to 512
```

You can practice setting windowtype properties with the RoundWindow WDEF in the Chapter 18 folder of the accompanying CD-ROM.

Panning and Scaling

The previous section described using the `rect of window` to change the position of the movie on the screen. You also can use the two `rect` commands—`rect of window` and `drawRect`—of a window to create special visual effects by making the window larger or smaller than the size of the Director movie it displays.

Rect of Window

Setting the `rect of window` positions the window on-screen starting at the screen coordinate specified for the top left corner. The `rect of window` command aligns the top left corner of the Director movie with the top left corner of the window and displays as much of the Director movie as will fit inside the rectangle it defines. The `rect of window` command does not resize or reposition the Director movie within the window.

If the window rectangle is smaller than the size of the movie, part of the movie will be cut off (see fig. 18.4). You can use this feature to create a panning effect by sizing a window to show just part of the Director movie's stage, then moving a sprite that is under the viewable area.

If the window rectangle is larger than the size of the movie's stage, the empty space below and to the the right of the movie has a solid fill the color of the movie's stage color (see fig. 18.6).

Figure 18.4

The window at normal size (160×151), with top left corner at (100, 100)—rect (100, 100, 260, 251).

Figure 18.5

The window rect (100, 100, 200, 200) is smaller than the movie's rect.

Figure 18.6

The window rect (100, 100, 350, 350) is larger than the movie's rect.

DrawRect of Window

The `drawRect of window` positions and resizes the Director movie within the window relative to the top left corner of the window, which is (0, 0). If you set the `drawRect` smaller than the size of the Director movie stage, the Director movie stage will shrink to fit into the space (see fig. 18.7).

Figure 18.7

The movie's rect (0, 0, 100, 100) shrinks.

If you set the `drawRect` larger than the size of the Director movie, the movie expands to fill the space (see fig. 18.8).

Figure 18.8

The movie's rect (0, 0, 320, 321) stretches.

If you specify coordinates that do not start at (0, 0), the top left corner of the movie will display that distance away from the top left of the window (see fig. 18.9).

Figure 18.9

The movie's rect (75, 75, 175, 175) now begins 75 pixels away from the window's top left corner.

The `drawRect of window` does not resize the window; it resizes the Director movie that displays within the window.

Resizing a Director movie with `drawRect` impacts performance because the new size of every sprite must be recalculated with each frame. Resizing with `drawRect` is more effective on shape sprites than on bitmaps.

Window Messages

When a user interacts with a window, such as by bringing it forward or moving it, for example, Director sends a window event message to the window. You can trap for these events with `on eventName` handlers in your MIAWs. You might have an `on closeWindow` event, for example, that closes all open MIAWs if the user clicks the close box of one.

In most cases, user activity, not Lingo, generates Window messages. A Lingo resize of a window, for example, does not generate a `resizeWindow` message.

Table 18.2

Message	User Action
`activateWindow`	Clicks on a window that does not have the focus
`deactivateWindow`	Clicks outside of an active window
`closeWindow`	Clicks a window's close box (window types without a close box do not receive this message) (Lingo "close window " command sends this message) (Lingo "set the visible of window" command sends this message)

Message	User Action
moveWindow	Drags a window by the drag bar (windows without a drag bar do not receive this message)
resizeWindow	Drags in the resize box (only window types that allow resizing receive this message)
zoomWindow	Clicks in the zoom box (only windows with a zoom box receive this message)

Managing Multiple Windows

After you have learned to create and control MIAWs, you will think of many ingenious uses for them and will soon wind up with several MIAWs open at once. One common setup is the stage, a navigation palette, and a help window. You can ensure that all of the windows work together smoothly if you know some basics about how MIAWs interact with each other and with the stage.

The Stage Runs the Show

The stage isn't just another window—the stage is king. The stage establishes the palette and serves as communications central for all windows.

The `tell` command sends Lingo commands from the stage to a window or from a window to the stage. This enables you to control one window independently of another. (As the Director manual describes, you can use `tell` with other Lingo objects as well, but it is most useful for working with windows.) The syntax for using tell with windows is as follows:

```
tell window windowName to lingo statement
tell the stage to lingo statement
EX: tell window "Controls" to moveToBack
```

For a multiple-line `tell`, use:

```
tell window windowName
   lingo statement
```

```
      lingo statement
   end tell

   tell the stage
      lingo statement
      lingo statement
   end tell

   EX:
   tell window "Help"
      moveToFront
      puppetTransition 20,1,1
      set the locV of sprite 5 to 200
      updateStage
   end tell
```

One helpful way to use an MIAW is to use it as a navigation tool for a presentation. The MIAW displays a field with a list of all of the labels in the main movie. When the presenter clicks on one of the label names, the MIAW tells the stage to go to that frame. The following code, in the sprite script for the label field in the MIAW, communicates the requested label to the stage:

```
on mouseDown
   if the mouseLine > 0 then
      set ln = the mouseLine
      put line ln of field "Presentation Screens" into newLoc
      hilite line ln of field "Presentation Screens"
      tell the stage to go newLoc
   end if
end
```

You might have a situation where one MIAW needs to communicate with another MIAW. Although Lingo enables you to send a `tell` from one MIAW to another, it just doesn't work very well. The best way to handle communication between MIAWs is through the stage. If MIAW1 wants MIAW2 to do something, it should wrap the message in a `tell` to the stage, as follows:

```
tell the stage
   tell MIAW2
```

```
      message for MIAW2 here
    end tell
  end tell
```

Suppose you have added a window to the presentation described previously. This moveable window contains a text field for the presenter to record audience comments. Now when you use the navigation palette, you want the stage to go to a particular frame *and* you want the MIAW that displays the audience notes to display any comments that were recorded for that screen. You can expand the `tell the stage` section of the previous code sample to accomplish this:

```
on mouseDown
  if the mouseLine > 0 then
    set ln = the mouseLine
    put line ln of field "Presentation Screens" into newLoc
    hilite line ln of field "Presentation Screens"
    tell the stage
      go newLoc
      tell window "Audience Notes"
        go newLoc -- the "Audience Notes" MIAW uses the same
                              -- label names as the main movie.
      end tell
    end tell
  end if
end
```

The stage rules palette control as well as communications. Because only one palette can be active on-screen at a time, the stage "owns" the palette. When an MIAW opens—if it was created with a different palette than the stage movie's palette—its art will use the colors in the stage's palette. That means that an area of the image that uses the color in palette position 5 that was brown under the MIAW's palette, for example, could turn green if that is the color in palette position 5 in the stage's palette.

An MIAW can change the current palette, but only by telling the stage to do so:

```
tell the stage
  puppetPalette 14
  updateStage
end tell
```

Because only one palette can be active at a time, after the MIAW changes the palette, the MIAWs art will display correctly. But if the stage is visible, the stage art will look incorrect.

Another way to handle a situation where the MIAW has a different palette than the stage is to include code in the MIAW's `startMovie` that remaps the MIAW's artwork to the stage's palette. Instead of simply changing the colors of the artwork to whatever colors are in the same palette positions in the new palette, palette remapping tries to find colors in the new palette that are similar to those in the original palette. The following code, taken from a Macromedia tech note, enables palette remapping in an MIAW:

```
on startMovie
 set myName = getAt(the windowList, count(the windowList))
 -- This line puts the name of the Movie-In-A-Window (MIAW) that
 -- was just opened into a temporary variable called myName.

 tell the stage to tell myName to set the paletteMapping to TRUE
 -- We are telling the Stage to instruct the MAIW to enable its
 -- "Remap Palettes When Needed" option. For more information,
 -- see paletteMapping in the Help System.

 tell the stage to tell myName to updateStage
 -- Here we are telling the Stage to instruct the MIAW to refresh
 -- its playback area.
end
```

Event Handling

User event handling usually happens independently in each MIAW. A `mouseUp` event, for example, is trapped by the topmost MIAW under the mouse and is not passed to any other windows.

The following sections are a few exceptions to this that are worth noting.

MouseDown

If there is a QuickTime movie playing on the stage and the user holds down the mouse over a button or field in an MIAW with a `mouseUp` or mouseDown handler, the QuickTime on the stage stops playing until the user releases the mouse. This can be a problem if you included some kind of slider or moveable sprite on the MIAW that requires the user to hold down the mouse. You can get around this by inserting a repeat loop under the offending object in the MIAW that constantly updates the stage:

```
on mouseDown
   repeat while the stillDown
      tell the stage to exitFrame( script the frameScript )
   end repeat
end
```

Key Events

If you have an editable text field on the stage and an open MIAW, the key events are always trapped by the MIAW, making it impossible to edit the field on the stage. This happens in a projector, but not in authoring. It's best to avoid this problem by designing the interface so that editable text fields are always only displayed in one movie at a time.

If you must have the MIAW open while the user edits the field on stage, you can put a keyDown script in the MIAW that passes the typed key back to the stage's field, as follows:

```
on keyDown
   tell the stage
      put field "Input" & the key into field "Input"
   end tell
end
```

Rollovers

Unlike other user events, rollovers leak through MIAWs and are detected by the stage's rollover handlers if the MIAW is positioned over the stage. If you are going to be using rollover handlers and MIAWs, you should script the stage rollovers with this in mind.

Shared Resources and Events

Although MIAWs are generally independent of one another, they share parts of the Director environment. One movie's behavior can affect other movies, if it alters a shared resource.

Memory and Processor Cycles

Each MIAW uses memory and processor cycles—even when it is closed or invisible. Keep this in mind when you are planning multiple window projects. The number of open windows affects animation performance.

Globals

All movies running during a Director session, including MIAWs, have access to globals. Your MIAWs can use globals to pass information back and forth.

Objects

If you declare an object as a global, it resides in memory for the duration of the Director session and is available to all movies. You can create a new object from a script that resides in an MIAW and "forget" the MIAW afterward. The object remains accessible even after the movie script it was created from is not.

Scripts and Cast in Shared Linked Cast

If you link MIAWs and the stage movie to the same external cast, they will share the scripts and members from that cast. Changes to the cast by one movie, such as duplicating, copying, or changing the script text of members, are immediately reflected in other movies sharing the same cast members.

Timeout

Although each MIAW can have its own `timeoutScript`, user events in any movie reset the timeout. If there is a `timeoutScript` in Movie A and the user clicks on Movie B, the timeout is reset.

Idle

`Idle` events are sent to all resident MIAWs. MIAWs that have been closed but not "forgotten" still receive `idle` events and still execute their `idle` handlers.

The WindowList

`the windowList` is a list of all resident windows. `the windowList` is accessible to all movies. Windows that have been closed but not "forgotten" still appear on the list.

The Actorlist

Movies do not share `the actorlist`. Each movie has its own `actorlist`. MIAWs that have been closed but not "forgotten" still receive `stepFrame` events, and objects on an open MIAW's `actorlist` still execute `stepFrame` handlers.

Creating Reusable MIAWs

Most MIAWs are small movies built for a particular kind of task. Many of these tasks, such as dialog boxes, come up again and again in projects. If you spend a little extra design time up front, you'll be able to write your MIAWs once and reuse them in later projects with little or no modification. Try to design your MIAWs without dependencies on any external casts and with as few dependencies as possible on global variables set outside the MIAW. This will make it easier to plug them in to other projects later.

Window Commands Chart

Table 18.3

Command	Description
`open window`	Makes a window visible on the desktop if the window's `rect` coordinates are within the desktop.
`close window`	Makes a window invisible. The movie assigned to the window is still in memory and still processing, though not visible.
`forget window`	Unloads a window and the movie assigned to it from memory. The movie is no longer active.
`windowType of window`	Specifies the kind of frame and window controls (such as a zoom box) that the window should have.
`modal of window`	Specifies whether the movie should enable the user to click outside of it, or beep when the user clicks outside of it.
`filename of window`	Specifies the Director movie to display inside of the window. Multiple windows can have the same file name. Windows sharing the same file name display the same movie.
`name of window`	Specifies the text to use for window name. The default name of a window is the filepath to the MIAW. The title bar displays the window name if you do not set the `title` property.
`title of window`	Specifies the text to use in the window's title bar.
`rect of window`	Specifies the location and size of the MIAW relative to the desktop.

Command	Description
`the drawRect of window`	Specifies the location and size of the Director movie relative to its window. Can be set for the stage.
`the visible of window`	Specifies whether the window can be seen. Can be set for the stage.
`moveToBack`	Moves the target window behind all other windows. Can be sent to the stage.
`moveToFront`	Moves the target window in front of all other windows. Can be sent to the stage.
`the activeWindow`	Identifies the window name linked to the movie executing the line of code containing `the activeWindow`. Similar to the way other languages use `me`. Returns `(window` "*windowName*") for an MIAW. Returns `"the stage"` for the stage.
`the frontWindow`	Identifies the top window. Returns `(window "`*`windowName`*`")` for an MIAW. Returns "`the stage`" for the stage.
`windowPresent ("name")`	Reports TRUE if the window exists, whether it is "closed" or "open."

Summary

The Movie in a Window feature extends your interface options and enables you to create modular tools that you can easily share with others. In this chapter, you have learned that Movies in a Window are Director movies that operate independently of each other and the stage. You learned the basics of opening and closing one MIAW, then moved on to the details of coordinating communication between windows and the sharing of common resources. As you continue to experiment with MIAWs, you will undoubtedly find many uses for them in your projects.

This chapter, combined with the information in Chapter 16, "Lingo: The Basics," and Chapter 17, "Managing Your Data," have introduced you to the various parts of the Director tool set. In the next chapter, "Advanced Concepts," you learn how to apply that tool set to some of the most common development problems.

Gretchen Macdowall

Advanced Concepts

Chances are that if you are reading this book, you have a Director project already in mind. This chapter goes beyond the basics to cover the typically challenging areas in real-world Lingo programming.

Specifically, we'll discuss the following topics:

- Score animation versus Lingo animation
- Text entry
- HyperText
- Film loops
- Making games
- Making libraries and tools
- Performance and benchmarking
- Debugging
- Testing your code
- Coming to Lingo from C

Score Animation Versus Lingo Animation

After working with some of the sample movies, which stay within a few frames and do most of their animating in Lingo, you may be wondering if that is the "right" way to create all Director movies. This issue is something of a holy war in the online community of Director developers. On one side you have the hardcore Lingo-heads who proudly proclaim that all of their movies contain one frame and one frame only. Every pixel that is pushed is done in Lingo. They say that performance is better when you use Lingo instead of the Score. On the other side, you have folks who use the Score almost exclusively and only resort to Lingo when there's no other way. The less programming the better is their motto.

As is usually the case in life, the best answer lies somewhere between the two extremes. A Lingo approach is good for areas of your movie where sprites move or change the cast member as a result of user actions, especially if they don't return to the same state they were in before the user action.

For example, suppose you are tracking user progress through an adventure game. There are five objects to collect, but they don't need to be collected in any particular order. The list of collected objects should always be visible to the user and should appear in a corner of the screen. The list on the screen might look like the following:

```
[X] Amulet
[ ] Rope
[ ] Sword
[ ] Magic dust
[X] Loaf of bread
```

You could accomplish this without using any Lingo beyond making sections of the Score display each of the 32 possible combinations of checked-off items and branching to the correct section each time the user adds an object. Not only is this tedious to set up, but the process is prone to error as well. If you make any changes to one of the sections, such as changing the background sprite or adding another item to the list, these changes must be duplicated through all of the Score sections.

You'll find it is much easier to loop over one or two frames, using a sprite channel for each check mark and changing the cast of the sprite to an X when the user has picked up an object.

Another example that requires Lingo is a maze game like PacMan. Suppose PacMan starts out in the middle of the maze and the user can move him, with the arrow keys—up, down, left, or right. Again, the minimal Lingo solution requires a separate section in the Score for every possible move PacMan can make. But wait—what about the bad guys? They're moving in the maze, too. Now you need a separate Score section for every move that PacMan can make and every move the bad guys can make. It becomes impossibly complex. Using Lingo to move objects within the maze is the only way to solve this problem.

But every Director movie is not jam-packed with fast action. Some movies are presentations or sales support tools, with minimal user interaction beyond choosing the right section to play. Some otherwise interactive games contain heavily animated sequences that play from beginning to end. This is what the Score is made for. It doesn't make sense to duplicate linear non-interactive animation sequences in Lingo. Not only is this time-consuming, but it makes collaboration with artists difficult, because every modification requires you to change the code instead of changing a few cels in the Score.

If you want to control the action with Lingo, it's best to stay in as few frames as possible to minimize the number of frames in which you must carry changes over. Trying to keep everything in one frame is the ultimate Lingo holy grail, but it is not very practical. It makes more sense to run over two frames. In frame 1, include setup and initialization for that section, and then loop on frame 2.

Lingo animation within a repeat loop is much faster than Score-based animation. The following Lingo repeat loop moves a sprite across the stage one pixel at a time, 200 times, at a speed as fast as the computer can process:

```
on animateMe
   repeat with x = 1 to 200
      set the locH of sprite 5 = the locH of sprite 5 + 1
      updateStage
   end repeat
end
```

You could accomplish the same thing by placing the sprite on stage in frame 1 at the beginning location, and again in frame 200 at the destination location and tweening the sprite over the 198 frames in the middle. If you set the tempo at 120 and played this section of the Score, you would again be playing the animation as fast as the computer could process, because no consumer computer is really capable of playing animation at 120 frames per second.

If you timed the two methods you would find that the Lingo repeat loop method is 33 percent faster than doing the same thing over 200 frames in the Score. That is because the Score has some overhead that the Lingo repeat loop doesn't. At each frame the Score has to check to see which sprites have changed and need repainting, and whether the user has moved the mouse or typed a key. A movie playing from the Score can also be interrupted by other processes running on the computer such as network activity. A Lingo repeat loop, on the other hand, takes complete control. A Lingo repeat loop does not check to see whether the stage should be updated unless you include an `updateStage` inside it, and a Lingo repeat loop will ignore the user unless you include a check for mouse events inside it. A Lingo repeat loop also will refuse to surrender the CPU to any other processes. No wonder Lingo repeat loops are so fast!

There are disadvantages to using repeat loop animation. They are:

- A repeat loop buys its speed by ignoring user events and dominating the processor.
- The playback head does not advance during a repeat loop, so you must script all of the activity on stage during the repeat loop—not just the sprite you're interested in speeding up.
- Animation programmed within a repeat loop runs relatively faster or more slowly depending on the speed of the machine it's playing back on. Repeat loop animation is hard to synch to other events.

You can build in your own checks for user events inside of the repeat loop, and you can even build in a timer that displays the animation at a constant frame rate. You can do this by waiting a certain number of ticks between each repeat. The time expenditure required for this kind of wholesale rewrite of capabilities already built in to the Score makes sense only for the most demanding game applications.

Text Entry

In previous versions of Director there was one type of cast member for displaying text. The Director manuals called this type of cast member a "text field." You could use text fields to collect input from the user and evaluate it with Lingo.

Director 5 introduced a new type of cast member which the manuals call a "text" cast. The user cannot edit text cast members and you cannot use Lingo to search the text of text cast members. Text cast members are for displaying nicely formatted, anti-aliased text. You create a text cast member with the text button on the toolbar.

The type of cast member that was called a "text field" in previous versions of Director is now called a "field" cast member. "Field" cast members in Director 5 function the same way that "text field" cast members in previous versions did. Use "field" cast members to collect input from users and to manipulate text with Lingo. You create a field cast with the field button on the toolbar.

The editable property of a field cast member or a field channel in the Score gives the user the ability to edit text in a field on stage. (You set the editable property for a text field cast member in the cast member info dialog. You set the editable property for a sprite channel in the Score by highlighting the cels in the channel you want to apply the editable property to and clicking the "editable" checkbox to the left of the Score.)

The `autotab` property, which applies to field cast members only, moves the focus to the next field when the user presses the Tab key. Both of these properties also can be set in the cast member info dialog. Lingo is not required to set up text entry screens if you are not evaluating what the user enters into the fields. You do need Lingo if you need to check the fields for valid data, fill in some fields based on the values in others, or change the tabbing order.

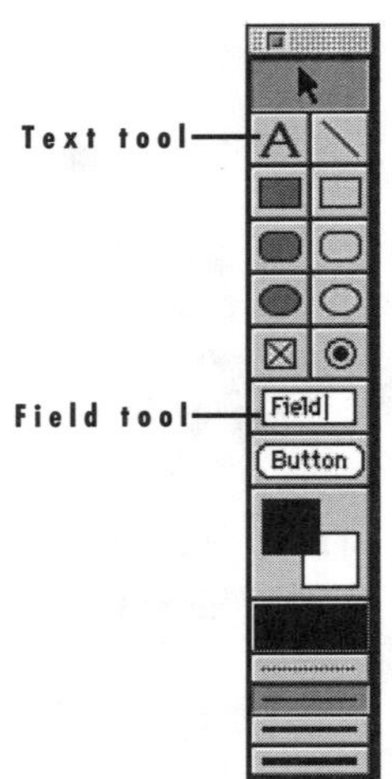

Figure 19.1

Use the Text tool for nice-looking static text. Use the Field tool for text-entry fields and fields that you want to control with Lingo.

Using the Key, CharToNum() and the Keycode

The best place for Lingo that evaluates a particular field, is in the `keyUp` or `keyDown` script of the field cast member. Inside of this script you will use the Lingo words `the key` or `the keycode` or the function `charToNum()` to search for certain key presses that you are interested in. When you detect the press of a Tab key, for example, you will know that the user is about to leave the field and that you should check over what they have entered.

`the key` and `the keycode` hold two different pieces of information about the last key that the user typed. The key tells what character the key typed; the keycode tells what key number on the keyboard the user pressed. Each key on the keyboard has its own unique keycode. Why do you need the keycode? Because some keys don't type anything printable—Escape and the arrow keys, for example. Some keys type the same thing—the numbers on the top row of the keyboard and the numbers on the numeric keypad, for example.

The keycode is dependent on the keyboard. The keycodes for some keys can vary between manufacturers and between the Mac and PC platform. For instance, the arrow keys have different keycodes on the Mac and on the PC. Using the keycode is the only way to distinguish between function key presses and between the numbers on the upper row of the keyboard and the numeric key pad.

The `charToNum()` function returns the ASCII value of any character you pass to it. (ASCII is a computer standard that represents each character with a number.) `charToNum(the key)` will return the ASCII value for the last key typed, even if the key typed is not a printable key. Because ASCII is a standard, the ASCII value of a key will not vary between keyboards or platforms. Use `charToNum(the key)` to detect Escape, the arrow keys, and other non-printing keys. `charToNum(the key)` won't work for detecting the difference between two keys that type the same thing—for instance the 8 on the row above the keyboard and the 8 on the numeric keypad, because the ASCII value for character "8" is the same regardless of which key typed it.

Use the movie KEYCODE.DIR on the accompanying CD to easily find the ASCII codes and keycodes that correspond to keys on the keyboard. You can copy the movie to Director's Xtra folder on your hard disk and open it via the Xtras menu in authoring for easy access. Close the Message window to direct key presses to the MIAW.

Some modifier keys, such as Control, Command, and Option, don't generate a keycode by themselves because they modify the behavior of other keys. The Lingo functions `the controlDown`, `the optionDown`, and `the commandDown` report TRUE when the user is currently pressing down one of these modifier keys.

Keycodes are dependent on the keyboard. Some of the keycodes vary between the Mac and the PC and a few keycodes vary among different keyboard manufacturers on the PC side. Be sure to test on a wide variety of platforms if your movie depends on keycodes.

Determining the Current Field

Lingo has no way to determine what field the user is currently editing. A function called the typeOn would be a nice addition to Lingo. In the meantime, the simplest thing to do is to include a sprite or cast script for each field that updates a variable on a `keyDown` that contains the current field.

```
on keyDown
   global currentField
   set currentField to "TotalCost"
end
```

Tabbing

When the current field has its Autotab property checked and the user presses Tab, the cursor automatically advances to the next field. The sequence of events is as follows:

1. keyDown event goes to the current field.
2. Text cursor advances to the next field.
3. keyUp event goes to the new field.

If you want to process the current field, you should check for Tab on the keyDown.

If you want to be kind to the user, you can make Return work like Tab. Make a list of the text field casts and their sprites. To move the text cursor to the next sprite on the list, set the editable property of that sprite:

```
-- Cast script for field
on keyDown
   global currentField,tabList
   set tab;ost + "Groceries",8:"Car repair",9:"Clothing"
   set currentField = "Groceries" -- hardcode to name of this
   ➥field
   if the key = RETURN then
     set cur = getPos(tabList,currentField)
     set newPos = cur + 1
     if newPos > count(tabList) then set newPos = 1
     set newSprite = getPropAt(tabList,newPos)
     set the editable of sprite newSprite to TRUE
   end if
end
```

Inserting Characters into a Field

There are some situations when you do not want to display exactly what the user types into the field. If you allow only five digits for a zip code field, for example, you might want the program to beep and refuse any input after the fifth digit. Or perhaps the field is a password field and you wish to display asterisks in the field instead of the password characters. You can control the content of the field by checking the key or keycode with each key press and appending the character to the field yourself. After you append the character to the field, you also must reposition the text cursor at the end of the line:

```
on keyDown
  global realPassword
  -- save the characters the user is typing in realPassword
  put realPassword & the key into realPassword
    -- show asterisks in the field
    put field "Password" & "*" into field "Password"
    set le = length(field "Password")
    -- set the selEnd at one character after the field
    -- set the selStart at two characters after the field
    -- this is a round-about way of getting the text cursor
    -- to display at the end of the field
    set the selEnd = le + 1
    set the selStart = le + 2
end
```

HyperText

You can implement HyperText in Director in two ways. One way is to draw invisible rectangles over the hot words in the field. This requires no Lingo, but it's not very flexible. Every time the text changes, you have to reposition the hot spots. If you want the same word to be hot, no matter where it appears on the field, you must draw a new hot spot for each occurrence. If you want a scrolling field—forget it.

Unless you have a very small list of hot words and you know your text isn't going to change, you're better off implementing HyperText using fields and Lingo. Lingo control only works with fields—not text cast members. You have to use invisible rectangle hot spots to define hot spots for text cast members.

The Lingo commands that help you determine what text chunk the mouse is currently over are `the mousechar`, `the mouseWord`, and `the mouseLine`. You compare the clicked text chunk to a list of hot words and determine what to do from there. If the list of hot words is very large, it's better to divide it into sublists. The sample list in the code that follows is small, but it's divided into the sublists to show how to handle this.

The following code, when placed into a field cast or sprite script, highlights the clicked word by changing the color of the word. If the word is found in the hotlist, it branches to the destination specified in the hotlist. The hotlist is a global and is set up as follows:

```
set hotlist = ["a":["aardvark":"ZooAnimals1","alternator":"
➥States1"],"b":["baby":"People2","button":"Tools2"]]
```

Each list item in the hotlist has a sublist of all of the entries beginning with that letter. When you search for a word in the list, you start by searching for the first letter to find the correct sublist. Then you search within the sublist.

```
on mouseDown
   global hotlist
  -- the mouseWord returns the word number in the field
  set wordNum = the mouseWord
  set fieldName = the name of member the memberNum of sprite
  ➥the clickOn
  set wrd = word wordNum of field fieldName
  -- length returns the number of characters in a string
  set len = length(wrd)
  set firstChar = char 1 of wrd
  -- get the ASCII value of this character with charToNum
  set asciValue = charToNum(firstChar)
  -- use the ASCII value to determine if the character
  -- is a capital letter. If so, convert it to lower
  -- case (upper case value + 32)
  if asciValue > 64 and asciValue < 91 then
    set firstChar = numToChar(asciValue + 32)
    set wrd = firstChar & char 2 to len of wrd
  end if
```

```
    set lastChar = char len of wrd
    -- strip punctuation
    if lastChar = "," or lastChar = "." then
      set wrd = char 1 to (len - 1) of wrd
    end if
    -- use the first character to find the right sublist
    set sublist = getProp(hotlist,firstChar)
    -- look up the word in the sublist
    set gowhere = getaProp(sublist,wrd)
    -- if the word was found then highlight it
    if not voidP(gowhere) then
      set the forecolor of word wordNum of field fieldName
      ➥to 35
      repeat while the stilldown
        -- keep other things going on stage while the mouse
        ➥is down
        updateStage
      end repeat
      -- set the word back to black when the mouse lifts
      set the forecolor of word wordNum of field fieldName
      ➥to 255
      -- go to the new marker specified for this hot word
      go gowhere
    end if
  end
```

When you're comparing a "word" returned by `the mouseWord` to the items on your hot list, there are a couple of things to watch out for. If your hot word starts a sentence, it will start with a capital letter. Rather than enter all of your hot words twice in the list—once beginning with capital letters and once beginning with lowercase letters—you can use Lingo to change the first letter of the word to lowercase before doing the comparison. The following code, taken from the preceding example, checks the first character for an ASCII value between 65 and 90 and substitutes the lowercase letter instead (uppercase ASCII value + 32).

```
if asciValue > 64 and asciValue < 91 then
  set firstChar = numToChar(asciValue + 32)
  set wrd = firstChar & char 2 to len of wrd
end if
```

You must also look for punctuation. If a user clicked on the word "today" in the following sentence, `the mouseWord` function would return `today.`

I walked my dog today.

Any group of contiguous characters is a *"word."* Because you can't include every combination of punctuation in your hotword list, you should look for punctuation at the end of any "word" returned by `the mouseWord` and strip off the punctuation character. The following code, taken from the preceding example, checks for punctuation characters and removes them.

```
set lastChar = char len of wrd
-- strip punctuation
if lastChar = "," or lastChar = "." then
  set wrd = char 1 to (len - 1) of wrd
end if
```

Scrolling Fields

Two commands that are new to 5, `scrollByLine` and `scrollByPage`, enable easy Lingo scrolling of a field. In fact, you can hide the scroll bar completely with a bitmap sprite, provide your own attractive controls, and use the following code to scroll the field with Lingo:

```
on mouseDown
  repeat while the stillDown
    -- 1 scrolls forward a line, -1 scrolls backward a line
    scrollbyLine member "myField",1
    updateStage
  end repeat
end
```

`scrollByPage` scrolls the field by the page-full, which is the number of lines of text that fit in the field on stage. To scroll the field back to the beginning, specify a negative number of pages greater than the pages the field contains:

```
on mouseDown
  repeat while the stillDown
    -- 1 scrolls forward a page, -1 scrolls backward a page
```

```
    -- -1000 will scroll this field back to the beginning if
    ➥it contains less than 1000 pages
    scrollbyPage member "myField",-1000
    updateStage
  end repeat
end
```

Film Loops

Film loops are wonderful, underutilized features of Director. You usually think of them in the context of animation, and they do make playback of animation easier. They also have a valuable hidden feature—you can use multi-channel film loops to break the 48 sprite barrier.

A film loop does not have to contain motion at all. You can make a film loop of several static sprites in one frame. If you fill 48 channels with sprites and make a film loop cast of the cels of that frame, you then can place the new film loop cast on stage and take up one channel where you previously were taking up 48 before. Sprites in a film loop retain their sprite and cast scripts.

Making Games

The kinds of games people create with Director fall into two categories—slower-paced children's educational games and action games. The graphics might differ, but when you dig through the code, you'll find the same underlying techniques in each type of game. The following sections highlight the essential coding areas of each type of game, but the example movies are too involved to reconstruct in detail on the page. There is one heavily-commented sample movie for each type of game on the *Inside Director* CD.

Before we get into specifics, the following are some general game coding tips to keep in mind:

- Be careful with repeat loops. A repeat loop stops all other motion on screen. Use repeat loops where smooth motion of one sprite is critical. In other circumstances, it's better to crank up the frame rate and loop over frames.

- Don't try to move too many large bitmaps around at the same time.
- When you program a particular type of game for the first time, try to break the code into small modules that aren't hard coded to particular sprites or cast numbers. If the code is generic enough, you'll be able to use it again for a similar game.
- Director script objects are especially helpful in game programming where you often have several game sprites that share basic behavior with some variations. The examples that follow do not use script objects because it would make the examples harder to understand. However, you could incorporate the sample code into script objects. Script objects are covered in detail in Chapter 20, "Object-Oriented Programming in Director."

Painting and Erasing

The Trails ink property is the ticket here. Trails causes the sprite to make copies of itself on every frame as it moves across the screen. Bump up your frame rate to make the sprite's trail as smooth as possible. Paths painted on the screen by sprites with trails turned on are erased when other sprites are moved over them. The bounding box of any sprite moved over the trailed sprites will erase your paintings. For the most realistic erasers, make your erasers rectangular.

The following code turns a sprite into a brush:

```
on mouseDown
  set brush = the clickOn
  puppetSprite brush,TRUE
  set the trails of sprite brush to TRUE
  set the forecolor of sprite brush to random(254)
  repeat while the stilldown
    set the locH of sprite brush to the mouseH
    set the locV of sprite brush to the mouseV
    updateStage
  end repeat
end
```

```
on mouseUp
  set brush = the clickOn
  set the trails of sprite brush to FALSE
  puppetSprite brush,FALSE
  set the forecolor of sprite brush to 255
  updateStage
end
```

The movie GENRAB.DIR on the accompanying CD is a children's painting program that uses Trails ink for the "paint."

Matching

Matching games present a jumble of game pieces, each hidden under a cover. As the user clicks on pieces, the covers of the pieces lift off to reveal the piece underneath. The object of the game is for the user to uncover matching pairs until all of the game pieces are matched.

This game wouldn't be very much fun if the objects always appeared in the same order on the game board. You need code to randomize the game pieces, code to keep track of which piece is in what spot, and code to detect whether the user has made a match.

The following handler takes a range of sprite channels and a range of cast members and returns a list of the sprite channels with cast members assigned in random order:

```
on scatter spriteList,castList
  set gamePieceList = [:]
  set counter = 1
  repeat while counter <= count(spriteList)
    -- pick a random position in the castList
    set randomCastListPos = random(count(castList))
    -- get the next channelNumber in the sprite list
    set spriteChannel = getAt(spriteList,counter)
    -- get the member at the random position of the castList
    set assignedCast = getAt(castList,randomCastListPos)
    -- put this sprite channel and random member on the
    ➥new list
    setaProp(gamePieceList,spriteChannel,assignedCast)
    -- delete the chosen member from the castList
    deleteAt(castList,randomCastListPos)
```

```
    set counter = counter + 1
  end repeat
  return gamePieceList
end
```

Next, you need code to make sure that the user can uncover only two pieces at any one time, as well as code to detect a match. You should place this code in the cast script of the cast that acts as the cover.

```
on mouseUp
  global gamePieceList,turnedOverList,coverCast
  -- gamePieceList: property list of sprites and the cast
  ➥that will
  --                be revealed when the cover is up
  --                EX: [6:23,7:45,8:23,9:45]
   -- turnedOverList: list of pieces that have already been
  ➥turned over
  --                 EX: [6:23,7:45]
  -- coverCast: cast number of the cast that acts as a door,
  ➥covering
  --            the member you are trying to match
  set mySprite = the clickOn
  puppetSprite mySprite,TRUE
  -- coverCast is set here for clarity. It would be better
  ➥to set
  -- this variable once in another script rather than every
  ➥time
  -- a game piece is clicked
  set coverCast = the memberNum of sprite mySprite
  -- reveal up transition, half-second duration, smallest
  ➥chunksize,
  -- changing area
  puppetTransition 15,2,1,1
  -- determine which member should be revealed
  set uncovCast = getProp(gamePieceList,mySprite)
  set the memberNum of sprite mySprite = uncovCast
  updateStage
  -- add this sprite to the list of turned over sprites
  addProp(turnedOverList,mySprite,uncovCast)
  -- will never have more than 2 sprites on this list
  if count(turnedOverList) = 2 then
```

```
      -- if there isn't a match then turn them back over
      if getAt(turnedOverList,1) <> getAt(turnedOverList,2)
      ➥then
        -- let user see the 2 uncovered sprites for a sec
        ➥before
        -- covering them back up
        wait(60)
        -- cover sprites back up
        repeat with x = 1 to 2
          puppetTransition 19,2,1,1
          set the memberNum of sprite getPropAt
          ➥(turnedOverList,x) to coverCast
          updateStage
        end repeat
      end if
      -- if they match then leave them uncovered but reset the
      ➥turned-over list
      -- to get ready for next match
      set turnedOverList = [:]
    end if
  end

  on wait numTicksToWait
    set startWait = the timer
    repeat while the timer - startWait < numTicksToWait
      -- keep other action going on stage during repeat
      updateStage
    end repeat
  end
```

The movie BRAIGAM on the accompanying CD is a concentration game where the object is to match the sense organ to something in the world that it can sense. For example, a nose matches to a flower.

Puzzle Game

The object of a puzzle game is to drag a sprite into the right area on the screen and drop it. For instance, you could have the outline of a map of the U.S. on one side of the screen and a pile of state sprites on the other. The user must drag and place the state sprites into their correct positions on the map.

The first thing you must do here is arrange the puzzle piece sprites on-screen in their final positions so that you can note their correct locations. You need a list containing the correct placement location for every piece to help you determine if the user has placed a piece correctly. Use the following utility handler to record the correct piece positions into a list.

```
on recordPositions startingSprite,endingSprite
  set positionList = [:]
  repeat with curSprite = startingSprite to endingSprite
    setaProp positionList,curSprite,the loc of sprite
    ➥curSprite
  end repeat
  return positionList
  -- looks like this - sprite number followed by correct hor
  ➥and ver position
  -- [3: point(78, 97), 4: point(138, 97)]
end
```

Call the handler as follows:

```
set correctPosList = recordPositions(5,15)
```

Make sure the movie is playing when you call the utility handler. If a movie is not playing, Lingo sometimes returns inaccurate sprite locations.

Then, arrange the pieces on-screen where they should be for their starting positions and record those positions into another list:

```
set startingPosList = recordPositions(5,15)
```

Next, you will want to enable dragging of the pieces. The easiest way to accomplish this is to use the `moveablesprite` property. When you turn this property on for a sprite, it follows the user's mouse after the user clicks on it, for as long as the mouse button stays down.

You also will want to have `mouseUp` handlers for the pieces that check whether the user drops the piece into the right spot. It's almost impossible to place a sprite with exact pixel accuracy, so you must have a placement *tolerance*—the number of pixels around the target location in which you'll accept the drop as a match.

The following startMovie code sets the moveableSprite property for the game sprites and the tolerance:

```
on startMovie
  global tolerance
  -- if the user drops this piece within 10 pixels of the
  ➥target it
  -- will be considered a match
  set tolerance = 10
  -- the puzzle pieces are in channels 3 through 6
  repeat with x = 3 to 6
    puppetSprite x,TRUE
    set the moveablesprite of sprite x to TRUE
    updateStage
  end repeat
end
```

The following code, when placed in the cast or sprite handlers for the pieces, checks whether the piece has been placed correctly:

```
on mouseUp
  -- startingPosList: list of the unplaced piece positions
  global startingPosList
  set mySprite = the clickOn
  -- check if where the user dropped the piece is correct
  if posOK(the loc of sprite mySprite) then
    puppetSound "that's right!"
  else
    -- find the position to send the sprite back to and send
    ➥it back
    set the loc of sprite mySprite to getProp
    ➥(startingPosList,mySprite)
  end if
end
```

The function posOK, called in the preceeding handler, should be placed in a movie script so that it is available to all of the sprite handlers:

```
on posOK aPoint
  global tolerance,correctPosList
  set mySprite = the clickOn
  -- get the exact point that is the correct position in the
  ➥puzzle for
```

```
    -- this sprite
    set exactPoint = getProp(correctPosList,mySprite)
    -- use list math to get the range around the correct
➥position that
    -- would still be a match
    -- For example point(100,100) - 20 = point(80,80)
    set lowerLimit = exactPoint - tolerance
    set upperLimit = exactPoint + tolerance
    if aPoint > lowerLimit and aPoint < upperLimit then
      return TRUE
    else
      return FALSE
    end if
  end
```

The movie SKELGAM on the accompanying CD has the user build a human skeleton by dragging bones from a pile.

Maze Chase

In maze chase games, the user moves an animated character, using the mouse or arrow keys, through a maze, avoiding bad guys and other hazards. The biggest challenge here is to keep the character moving in the direction the user specifies and inside the confines of the maze. You can define a maze in two ways:

- Lay out the maze onstage using transparent rectangle shapes. Then constrain the position of the sprite to stay within the shapes. The property `constraint of sprite` does most of the work for you here. The command

  ```
  set the constraint of sprite 5 to 7
  ```

  sets up sprite 7 as a containing sprite for sprite 5. The regpoint of sprite 5 will now always stays within the bounds of sprite 7. The constraint of sprite property overrides any sprite location you set with Lingo.

  ```
  on startMovie
    puppetSprite 2,TRUE
    set the constraint of sprite 2 to 1
    updateSTage
  end
  ```

```
on mouseDown
set the locH of sprite 2 = the locH of sprite 2 + 4
 updateStage
end
```

The transparent rectangle method is fairly easy to set up and also is easy to change, just by rearranging the rectangle shapes. You're limited, however, to 48 channels for the maze shapes and other game sprites.

- Lay out the maze logically by defining lists of points that represent the paths in the maze. With every move you can compare the sprite's position against the path lists to see whether or not it can continue moving in that direction. This does not limit you to 48 channels, but it's more time-consuming to code.

The core of a maze chase game is the code that moves the character sprite. Before advancing the sprite in the current direction, the code must check to see that the new position is inside the maze walls. The code also must check to see whether the sprite has hit any bad guys or other hazards. The best place for this code is in an `enterFrame` handler. Because the code executes with every frame, the challenge is to keep it spare so that it doesn't slow down the game.

The following code is the `enterFrame` handler for a simple maze that is constructed using the first method—a maze defined with transparent rectangle sprites:

```
on enterFrame
  global
characterSprite,badGuySpriteList,direction,curSegType
  -- characterSprite: the dot
  -- direction: current direction chosen by user
  ➥(up,down,left,right)
  -- badGuySpriteList: list of sprites that the dot can
  ➥collide with
  -- curSegType: is the current constraining rectangle
  ➥horizontal or vertical?
    repeat with listPos = 1 to count(badGuySpriteList)
      if sprite characterSprite intersects
      ➥getAt(badGuySpriteList,listPos) then
      -- check for collision first since that resets game
```

```
      gameOver
      exit
    end if
  end repeat
set savH = the locH of sprite characterSprite
set savV = the locV of sprite characterSprite
-- save old positions to see if move was successful
tryToMoveSprite(savH,savV)
-- advances sprite if it can stay within bounds of current
➥maze segment
-- otherwise sprite does not move
if (the locH of sprite characterSprite = savH and
➥curSegType = "H") then
  -- if the sprite didn't move check to see if it's at an
  ➥intersection and
  -- change current maze segment so it can continue moving
  checkCorner("Ver")
else if (the locV of sprite characterSprite = savV and
➥curSegType = "V") then
  checkCorner("Hor")
end if
```

The movie MAZE.DIR, found on the accompanying CD, is a simple sample movie that contains the code above. The movie HEARGAM, also found on the CD, is a more complex maze game. The object of the game is to guide a blood cell through the circulatory system ahead of the viruses that are chasing it.

Making Libraries and Tools (Movie)

As more people hop on to the multimedia bandwagon, business becomes more competitive—the deadlines get shorter and the expectations grow higher with each project. The best thing you can do to increase your productivity with Director is to build code libraries and tools that you can use over again.

Director 4.0 introduced the capability to link a movie to one shared cast. Director 5 expands on this capability by enabling links from a movie to several casts. This enables you to build an independent code

NOTE

library cast consisting only of movie script cast members and easily link it to any movie or group of movies.

To create a new external cast to store your library, choose File, New, Cast from the menu. Name it **`Code Library`** and choose External storage. Copy your code into the cast members of Code Library.

To link the code library cast to a movie, choose Modify, Movie, Casts from the menu and click the Link button. Choose Code Library from the file dialog box.

Time-Saving Library Handlers

Whenever you find yourself typing the same code over and over again, you should consider creating a library handler from it instead. How many times have you typed something like the following?

```
puppetSprite 1,TRUE
puppetSprite 2,TRUE
puppetSprite 3,TRUE
```

Everyone needs a utility handler for puppeting sprites. You can call the following handler with one sprite, a list of sprite channels, or the start and end points of a range of sprite channels:

```
pup(2,TRUE)
pup([5,6,9],TRUE)
pup(3,10,TRUE)
```

The handler evaluates the number of arguments passed to it and does the right thing, by using a new function in Director 5 called `paramCount()`. `paramCount()` returns the number of parameters that were passed to a handler.

```
on pup param1, param2, param3
  if paramCount() = 3 then
    -- called with pup(1,5,TRUE)
    -- want to puppet sprites 1 through 5
    repeat with spriteNum = param1 to param2
      puppetSprite spriteNum,param3
    end repeat
  else if listP(param1) then
    -- called with pup([4,6],TRUE)
```

```
        -- want to puppet sprite numbers 4 and 6
        repeat with listPos = 1 to count(param1)
          puppetSprite getAt(param1,listPos),param3
        end repeat
      else
        -- called with pup(4,TRUE)
        -- want to puppet just sprite 4
        puppetSprite param1,param2
      end if
    end
```

As you build your handler library, try to create handlers that will work everywhere—not just with certain sprite or cast numbers. It's also a good idea to limit the number of parameters a handler takes and to give it a simple name so that you can remember how to use it.

Making Tools with the New Score Generation Commands

In versions of Director prior to 5, Lingo gave the programmer control over the run-time environment and allowed permanent changes to the cast. There was, however, no way to permanently change the Score. The new Lingo command `beginRecording` enables you to make changes to existing sections of the Score or to populate completely empty sections with sprites.

Score generation can now automate what formerly were tedious manual tasks. For instance, in a large project where art is being continuously updated, it's possible to end up with a movie that includes one piece of art that appears in multiple cast slots. If these identical cast members are all used in different places in the Score, it wastes memory and uses up unnecessary space on the disk. Previously, the only way to remove these duplicate cast members from the Score was to highlight every occurrence and manually switch the cels to the correct cast member using the Edit, Exchange Cast Member menu command. You now can automate this and similar processes with Score generation.

You don't need to learn many new commands to use Score generation. It relies on familiar commands for setting sprite properties such as the `memberNumber of sprite` or the `forecolor of sprite`. During Score generation, you advance to the frame you want to create or change, make changes to sprite properties, and issue the new Lingo command `updateFrame` to save the changes.

You issue the command `beginRecording` to start making changes to the Score, and issue the command `endRecording` when you finish. The following handler uses Score generation to search through an existing Score for a list of cast members and replace them with either one member or a corresponding list of new members. You would call the handler with:

```
finddupes([2,5,8],[3,4,88],1,80)
```

which replaces cast member 2 with 3; 5 with 4; and 8 with 88 in frames 1–80.

Or you call it with

```
finddupes([2,5,8],[3],1,20)
```

which replaces cast members 2, 5, and 8 with member 3 in frames 1–20.

The following handler does the automated cast member replacement.

```
on finddupes lookFor,replaceWith,startFrame,endFrame
  -- lookFor: list of duplicate members to look for
  -- replaceWith: list of members to replace dups with
  --             If this list has one item then all dups
                 ➥will be replaced
  --             with the same member
  --             If this list has the same number of items
                 ➥as the list of
  --             duplicate member it will replace each item
                 ➥on "lookFor"
  --             with the corresponding item on
                 ➥"replaceWith"
  -- startFrame: frame to start looking in
  -- endFrame: frame to end looking
  --
  beginRecording
   set numMembers = count(lookFor)
   set numReplacements = count(replaceWith)
```

```
    if numMembers <> numReplacements and (numReplacements >
    ➥1) then
      alert "Replacement list has to have one item or the
      ➥same number of items as the list to search for."
      exit
    end if
    repeat with frm = startFrame to endFrame
      go to frame frm
      repeat with curSprite = 1 to 48
        -- cycle through every sprite channel
        repeat with listPos = 1 to numMembers
          -- see if this channel contains any cast in list
          ➥"lookFor"
          if the memberNum of sprite curSprite =
          ➥getAt(lookFor,listPos) then
            case (numReplacements) of
              1:set the memberNum of sprite curSprite to
              ➥getAt(replaceWith,1)
              otherwise:set the memberNum of sprite curSprite
              ➥to getAt(replaceWith,listPos)
            end case
            -- if there is only one replacement cast then use
            ➥it, otherwise find
            -- the corresponding cast member in list
            ➥"replaceWith" and use that
          end if
        end repeat
      end repeat
      updateFrame
      -- record the changes to the frame
    end repeat
  endRecording
end
```

Score generation is a powerful tool and is potentially lethal (to your Score anyway). If you run a handler that accidentally uses Score generation and you realize it immediately, you can use the menu command Edit, Undo Score to undo the changes. If you don't realize your mistake immediately and make other changes afterward, the Undo command won't work.

Performance and Benchmarking

Every year the average consumer machine becomes more powerful, and with the same regularity, new technology steps in to eat up the extra CPU cycles. Eight-bit color is slowly giving way to 24-bit color; 16-bit stereo sound is more common now; digital video movies are larger and display at higher frame rates than they did just last year. Multimedia programming is always a balancing act. You will get the best possible performance out of Director by understanding and minimizing the three major bottlenecks

- Load time
- Display time
- Processor time

Memory and Load Times

On the Mac, a Director projector must play within the memory partition allotted to it in the Preferred Size box of the Get Info dialog box. (Highlight a Macintosh application and choose File, Get Info from the menu bar to use the Get Info dialog box.) Director creates Standard Macintosh projectors with a Preferred Size of 4096 KB, but you can change the setting. In an ideal world, your entire movie and all of its media would fit into this 4096 KB partition and play directly from memory after an initial load. That's not usually the case, however. If all of your cast members cannot fit into memory, then Director unloads cast members when it determines that they are no longer needed, to make room for new ones.

Director's built-in memory management is very good for Score-based movies. Not only does Director anticipate in advance what cast members it will need and preload them, but it also writes internal cast members to the Director file in the order that they appear in the Score—not the order that they appear in the cast. Writing cast members to disk in Score order minimizes the distance the disk head has to travel during playback to load the cast members needed in any part of the Score. That is because they have all been written contiguously to disk. This is quite a performance help, especially for pieces destined for CD because CD reads are very slow. (Linked cast members will not get this performance boost. They are written to disk in cast member order.)

If you are using puppet commands to place cast members in sprite channels, Director will not know to preload those cast members because they don't appear in cels in the Score. You can still take advantage of Score-order optimization by reserving empty frames at the beginning of your movie and placing the cast you plan to preload and puppet in the empty frame cells in the order you are going to preload them. Your `startMovie` handler or the first frame of the movie can use a `go` to hop over the dummy frames to the first "real" frame where the action starts. The technique of using dummy frames to optimize loading order is affectionately known as "*Schusslerization*," named after creator Terry Schussler, former Director product manager.

Remember to take advantage of this feature at the end of the authoring cycle by performing a File, Save and Compact. All saves write the cast in Score order, but a Save and Compact gets rid of the dead space taken up by cast members that were deleted or moved around in the Score in the course of authoring.

No intelligent memory management scheme will do much about the load times for large cast members. The best way to handle this problem is to keep your media as small as possible. For graphics this still means 8-bit (256 color) casts, and 8-bit, 22 KB sound, or the use of compression. Some developers use QuickTime to display JPEG-compressed 24-bit still images and IMA 4:1 sound compression to play 16-bit, 44 KB stereo sound.

You can economize further by looking for places where you're wasting space. If a graphic is black and white, reduce it to a color depth of 1 bit. If a button-click sound only lasts for one second, try reducing it to an 11 KB sampling rate and see if you can tell the difference. If you have duplicates of any cast members, get rid of them. Use external AIF sounds with the `sound playfile` command whenever possible. `sound playfile` streams the sound from disk instead of loading it into memory. Sounds fully imported (not linked) into the cast and placed in the Score or played with `puppetSound` have to load into memory before they play.

If you have reasonably sized cast members (majority under 300 KB) and your movie is Score-based, you can probably let Director do all of the memory management for you automatically. If you have larger cast members or your movie relies on Lingo rather than the Score, you can take advantage of several Lingo features designed to make playback as seamless as possible.

Determining the Amount of Memory You'll Need

If your have a fairly small Director movie, you might be able to preload all of the cast members before you begin playing. (Choose Modify, Cast properties to set the `Preload` property for the cast to `Before Frame One` or `After Frame One`.) This requires a longer load time to start, but enhances playback performance because there are no further delays for disk access. Director stores cast members in a compressed form inside movie files. The movie file size in the Get Info dialog box is not the true measure of the actual space the movie will takes up in memory after it loads and the cast members have been decompressed. To determine the memory requirements of your movie, give Director as generous a memory partition as possible in Get Info, before launching Director and opening your movie. Temporarily set the preload properties of all casts to "Before Frame One." Play the movie through the first frame and stop it. Then choose Window, Inspectors, Memory from the menu bar to open the Memory Inspector window shown in figure 19.2.

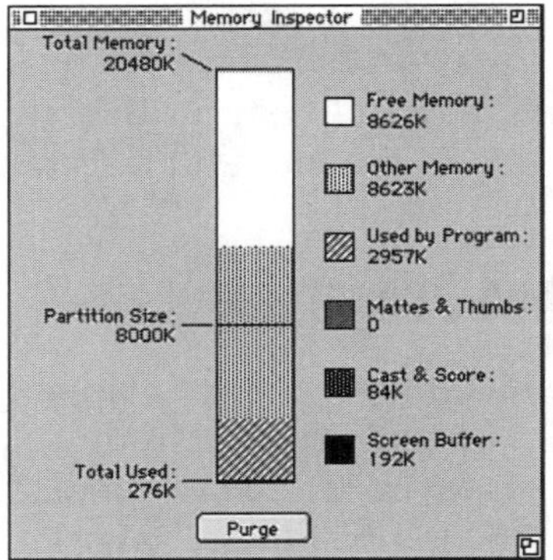

Figure 19.2

The Memory Inspector window.

The "Total Used" portion on the graph is the amount of memory your movie will take up when loaded. Add another 500 KB to 1 MB (depending on the type of projector) to this for the projector. The total is the amount of memory your projectorized movie will require for preloading all cast members.

You can find out how much memory an individual cast member will occupy in memory by clicking on the Info button in the Cast window. This brings up the Cast Member Properties window. The member size shown is the amount of memory the cast will occupy when loaded. The Lingo property `the size of member` also returns this information.

The `ramNeeded` command returns the amount of memory needed to display a particular frame or range of frames. This is useful in determining the minimum memory requirements for your movie, which is the amount of memory needed to display the frame with the largest size requirement, plus approximately 500 KB to 1 MB for the projector, depending on the type of projector.

If Director does not have enough memory to display the current frames, white boxes might begin to appear around graphics or some graphics could disappear altogether and sound might not play. The frame rate slows down as Director frantically tries to juggle the cast members needed for the current and immediately following frames.

Controlling Cast Member Loads

If you find that your movie is bogged down with too many loads in the same spot or has display problems caused by low memory, there are several Lingo commands and features that can help. The following sections describe these commands and features.

Cast Member Load Properties

You can adjust the loading properties of an entire cast, and fine-tune things for individual cast members with the load settings available in the property windows for casts and cast members. The Cast Properties window (selected with Modify, Movie, Casts, Properties from the menu bar) has a preload field to specify a preload option that applies to the entire cast. Programmers familiar with earlier versions of Director will recognize this as the old movie `preload` property. The Cast Properties dialog box is shown in figure 19.3.

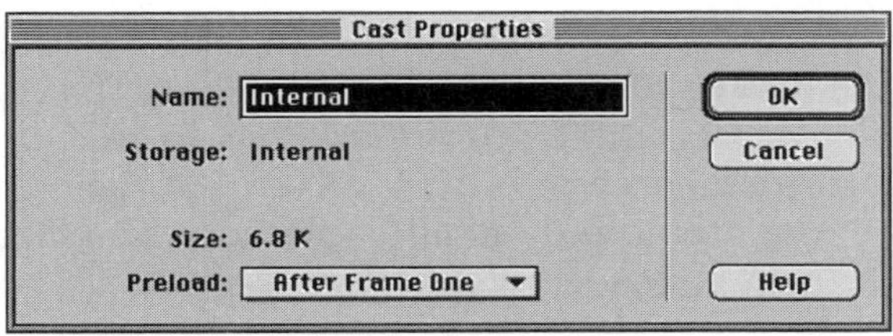

Figure 19.3

Set a general Preloading preference that applies to an entire cast in the Cast Properties window.

The choices for preload are Load Before Frame One, Load After Frame One, and Load As Needed. Load Before Frame One and Load After Frame One are for those rare situations where you can load the entire movie into memory. When you create a cast, the cast starts off with the default of Load as Needed, because that is the most likely situation. After you specify Load as Needed, Director preloads cast members on or before the frame where they first appear in the Score.

You adjust the unloading properties of individual cast members with the Unload field in the Bitmap Cast Member Properties window, as shown in figure 19.4.

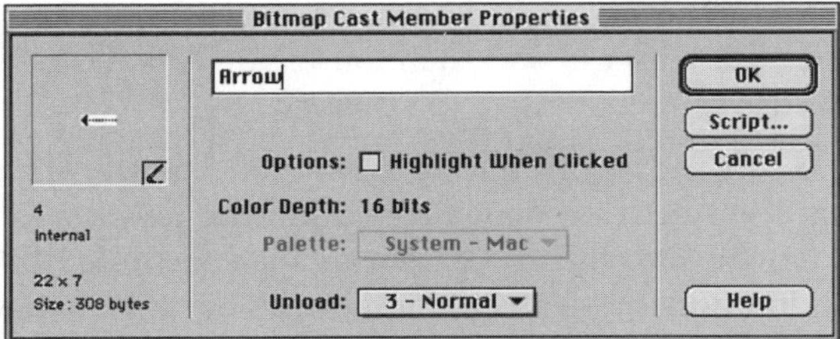

Figure 19.4

Adjust the amount of time you want a cast member to remain in memory after loading with the Unload field in the Bitmap Cast Member Properties dialog box.

The Unload options are Normal, Next, Last and Never:

- **Normal.** Leaves the unloading of the cast completely up to Director.
- **Next.** Places the cast member at the top of the queue for deletion as soon as the cast member no longer appears in a frame. Choose this option for a large cast member that only appears once in the movie.

- **Last.** Places the cast member at the end of the queue for deletion. Director does not remove the cast member from memory unless there are no more members on the queue with priorities of Normal or Next.
- **Never.** Retains the cast member in memory for the duration of the movie—if there is enough memory to keep all of the cast members with a priority of Never loaded. If you assign all cast members a priority of Never, but the movie does not have room to keep them all in memory, Director cannot keep them all loaded.

Preload Commands

If you are controlling your cast members through Lingo, you will have a better idea of when you are going to need them than Director does. In this situation, you can use Lingo `preload` and `idleload` commands to load the cast members you need.

The `preload` commands were available in previous versions of Director. They enable you to specify the loading of a cast member at a particular time. The `idleLoad` commands are new to Director 5. With `idleLoad` commands you can load a large cast member or a list of cast members while the user reads something on the screen or decides what to do next. Except for the tell-tale disk activity light, idle loads are transparent to the user. If the user moves the mouse, you can abort the load and return control immediately to the user.

`idleload` commands work during down time between frames. Each frame has a set duration dependent upon the frame rate. If a frame finishes drawing and finishes executing its `enterFrame` handler before the frame duration is up, Director just waits. The idea is to use this "idle" time to load cast members when the processor is not otherwise occupied.

These are the tasks that Director executes for each frame. Keep in mind that at a frame rate of 10 frames per second, all of this must happen in no more than six ticks. The durations next to the events are example times. The duration of any one event will depend on the movie and the machine its running on.

Table 19.1

EXAMPLE DURATIONS FOR THE EVENTS IN ONE FRAME

Task Number, Description	Time Required (in system clock ticks)
1. Director draws the frame	2 ticks including any transition
2. `enterframe` handler executes (if there is one)	.5 ticks
3. Idle period—idle messages sent repeatedly until the frame duration is over. Not much happening here unless there is an `idle` handler or there are `idleLoads` to perform	3 ticks
4. `exitframe` handler executes (if there is one)	.5 ticks

All of this must happen in the time allotted for the frame—6 ticks in this case. If the `enterFrame`, `exitFrame` or `idle` handler or `idleLoad` take longer than the time allotted per frame, it will slow the frame rate. The processor might be idle when you start an `idle` handler or an `idleLoad`, but if the `idle` handler takes too long, it will hold up the events that should happen after it.

PreloadMember

`preloadMember` loads a cast member or range of cast members into memory. The following command loads cast members 1–5:

```
preloadMember 1,5
```

Preload

`preload` loads all of the cast members needed for a frame or range of frames. The following command loads all of the cast members needed for frames 6–12:

```
preload 6,12
```

This command loads all of the cast members needed to build the frames from the current frame through frame 21:

```
preload 21
```

The Freeblock

`the freeblock` function returns the largest amount of contiguous memory available to load in a cast member. If `the freeblock` is smaller than the size of the cast member you are about to preload, Director will not be able to preload the cast member. The following code checks to see whether there is enough memory to preload a cast member:

```
if the freeblock > the size of member 4 then preloadmember 4
```

The IdleLoadMode

`the idleLoadMode` property determines whether cast members load immediately when you issue the `load` command, or wait for idle time to load. The default `idleLoadMode` is 0—idle loading is turned off. Under an `idleLoad mode` of 0 the following command immediately loads cast members 5–10:

```
preloadMember 5,10
```

If the group of cast members is large enough, playback pauses while they are loading. Instead, you might want to spread the loading out over idle periods until all of the cast members are loaded. To do this, you first turn on idle loading by setting `idleLoadMode` to 1, 2 or 3. Modes 1, 2, and 3 control the degree of frequency during an idle period that Director will attempt preloads.

idleLoadMode	***Effect***
1	Preloads during the idle period between enter and exit frame handlers
2	Ties idle preloads to the interval that was setfor other idle events with the `idleHandlerPeriod` property
3	Preloads during the idle period between enter and exit frames and again at exitFrame

Then you label the group of cast members or frames that you want to preload. Labeling groups you want to preload enables you to keep track of the progress of that group's loading. You can use any number for a label tag. The following code turns on idleLoading and sets it to the highest frequency. Then it creates the `idleLoadTag` 20, which applies to the cast members assigned to preload in the next line:

```
set the idleLoadMode to 3
set the idleLoadTag to 20
preLoadMember 100,102
```

The IdleLoadPeriod

`the idleLoadPeriod` controls the frequency in ticks, within the idle period between frames that Director attempts an `idleLoad`. The default value is 0, which attempts idle loads as frequently as possible during an idle period. If you set the `idleLoadPeriod` to 5, and you enter a frame with an idle period of 16 ticks, Director will attempt three idle loads—one every five ticks until the 16 ticks are up.

There might be times during the movie when you want to suspend idle loading temporarily—for instance, if you are about to play streaming media such as QuickTime or sound. Temporarily setting `the idleLoadPeriod` to an interval higher than the ticks per frame will effectively suspend idle loading.

IdleLoadDone

You can keep track of the loading progress of a labeled `idleLoad` group with the `idleLoadDone()` function. The following command returns TRUE, if cast members 100–102 (idleLoad group 20) are successfully loaded:

```
put idleLoadDone(20)
```

CancelIdleLoad

You can abort idle loading for an `idleLoad` group with the `cancelIdleLoad` command. The following line aborts idle loading for idle load group 50:

```
cancelIdleLoad(50)
```

FinishIdleLoad

The `finishIdleLoad` command loads whatever remains to be loaded from the idleLoad group all at once. The following line will finish loading idle load group 50:

```
cancelIdleLoad(50)
```

IdleReadChunkSize

The `idleReadChunkSize` property determines how much of a cast member Director will try to load during one idle read. The default value is 32 KB. If you find that idle loading is interfering with playback, you can decrease the `idleReadChunkSize`. This increases the number of idle loads it takes to load a cast member, but decreases the amount of time each load attempt takes. Macromedia does not recommend increasing the `idleReadChunkSize` beyond 32 KB because it will interfere with performance.

Preloadeventabort

When the `preloadeventabort` is set to TRUE, user activity such as clicking the mouse or pressing a key stops a preload event. If the `preloadeventabort` is set to FALSE, a long preload can lock out the user until the preload is finished. The `preloadeventabort` is turned off by default.

The TraceLoad

`the traceload` logs information to the Message window about cast members as they are loading. `the traceload` is set to 0—turned off, by default. Set `the traceload` to 1 to display cast members' numbers as they load. Set it to 2 to display more information, including the `fileSeekOffset`.

The *`fileSeekOffSet`* *number* is the distance in bytes that the disk head has to travel to load a cast member. The smaller the `fileSeekOffset` between cast member loads, the faster that group of cast loads. This is especially helpful in assessment of CD performance. The Schusslerization technique described earlier keeps `fileSeekOffsets` low because related casts are physically near each other in the movie file.

Display Time

Display time is the time it takes Director to composite all of the sprite layers and draw the finished image to the screen. For example, it can figure out which parts of a sprite with Matte ink ought to let the layers below show through. There are five variables are at work here:

- **Video card speed.** Accelerated graphics cards draw the screen faster. This especially helps with 24-bit images.
- **Screen technology.** PowerBook LCD (Liquid Crystal Display) screens display more slowly than regular desktop monitors.
- **Ink effects.** Some ink effects take more time than others to composite and display, especially when you use them on moving sprites. If a sprite (or sprites) takes more time to draw than the time allotted for the frame (four ticks per frame at 15 frames per second), the frame rate slows down to enable each frame time to draw.

  Copy, Matte, Background Transparent, and Transparent are the most commonly used inks. Of the four, Copy performs the best on moving sprites. The following chart uses Copy ink as a baseline and assigns it a value of 1. The values assigned to the other inks tell you relatively how much more time it takes to draw a sprite assigned that ink from one frame to the next. A sprite with Background Transparent ink, for example, takes 1.2 times as long to display from one frame to the next as the same sprite with Copy ink applied. The values below are examples and will vary slightly between processors and video cards.

Copy	1.0
Matte	1.5
Transparent	1.5
Background Transparent	1.1
Blend %50	4.3

- **Color depth.** 24-bit cast members not only take three times as much load time, but also require the video card to move around four times as much data.
- **Processor speed.** Director must take into account all of the sprite layers and determine which parts of overlapping sprites should be visible. A fast processor helps display speed.

Processor Time

Processor time is the amount of time the processor spends interpreting the Score and executing your Lingo code. If the processor cannot finish its work for a frame in the time allotted for the frame, the frame rate slows down. Fortunately, you can do several things to optimize your Lingo code.

Cast Member Name Versus Number

The first time you refer to a cast member by name, as in the following:

```
set the memberNum of sprite 7 to the number of member
"Turtle"
```

Director 5 creates an internal cross reference of cast member names and numbers. This can take awhile. Name references to cast members after the index exists are quite fast. However, if any cast member changes during the Director session—the user edits a field or you edit a cast member on the fly with Lingo, Director stops to create the index all over again.

If you find cast member name access bogging down, create a property list that links cast member names and numbers. Whenever you want to refer to a particular cast member by name, look it up in the list instead:

```
set the memberNum of sprite 3 to getProp(castList,"Turtle")
```

Repeat Loops

A long repeat loop locks out the user and prevents advancement of the playback head. To enable user actions to interrupt the repeat loop, you must build in detection for mouse events:

```
repeat while [condition] and not the mouseDown
```

Don't include lines of code in the a repeat loop that don't need to execute with every repeat. The following code, for example, is inefficient:

```
repeat while done = FALSE
    set counter = counter + 1
    set defaultName = "John " & "Smith"
    setAt aList,counter,defaultName
 end repeat
```

The third line sets the variable `defaultName` to a value that stays the same for every repetition of the repeat loop. It should be set outside of the repeat loop to speed things up:

```
set defaultName = "John " & "Smith"
 repeat while done = FALSE
    set counter = counter + 1
    setAt aList,counter,defaultName
 end repeat
```

Don't use an expression that must be evaluated as a counter in a repeat loop. In the following repeat loop, the number of words in field `"Story"` is evaluated with every repetition:

```
repeat with x = 1 to the number of words in field "Story"
  if word x of field "Story" = "Steve" then
    set nameCount = nameCount + 1
  end if
end repeat
```

Setting the end point of the counter beforehand eliminates this unnecessary repetitive calculation:

```
set numWords = the number of words in field "Story"
repeat with x = 1 to numWords
  if word x of field "Story" = "Steve" then
    set nameCount = nameCount + 1
  end if
end repeat
```

If/Then and Case

Place the most likely condition at the beginning of an if/then or case statement. An if/then or case statement stops executing as soon as it hits a matching condition. This is especially important when the if/then or case is executed repeatedly inside of a loop. The first two conditions of the following `exitFrame` handler will only be fulfilled for brief periods of time, and not until the video has been playing for eight minutes (`movieTime of 18000`). Because of the way the loop is structured, it will have to go through both conditions to get to the one that applies to the first seven minutes of the video.

```
on exitFrame
  if the movieTime of sprite 21 > 36000 and the movieTime of
  ➥sprite 21 < 36720 then
-- at 10 minutes into the movie, start animating a sprite
➥(puppeted elsewhere)
    set the castNum of sprite 6 to random(5)
  else if the movieTime of sprite 21 > 28800 and the
  ➥movieTime of sprite 21 < 29000 then
    -- at 8 minutes into the movie, animate another sprite
    set the castNum of sprite 4 to random(5)
  else
    -- from 0 - 8 minutes, loop a background sound
    if not soundBusy(2) then
      puppetSound "intro loop"
      updateStage
    end if
  end if
end
```

It is better to place the most likely condition first so that most of the time the loop exits before the other conditions:

```
on exitFrame
  if the movieTime of sprite 21 <28800 then
    -- from 0 - 8 minutes, loop a background sound
    if not soundBusy(2) then
      puppetSound "intro loop"
      updateStage
    end if
  else if the movieTime of sprite 21 < 36000 then
    -- between 8 and 10 minutes into the movie, animate
    ➥another sprite
    set the castNum of sprite 4 to random(5)
  else
    -- at 10 minutes into the movie, start animating a sprite
    ➥(puppeted elsewhere)
```

```
    set the castNum of sprite 6 to random(5)
  end if
end
```

Save Frequently Used Properties Into Variables

If code refers to a property more than once, save the property into a variable. This also makes the code less verbose. In the examples that follow, the first handler is less efficient than the second. In the first handler the `forecolor of the clickOn` has to be evaluated multiple times. In the second handler, it is evaluated once and saved into a variable for quick retrieval.

```
on mouseDown
  if the forecolor of the clickon <> 25 and the forecolor of
  ➥the clickon <> 13 then
    puppetSound "beep"
    updateStage
  end if
end

on mouseDown
  set fc = the forecolor of the clickOn
  if fc <> 25 and fc <> 13 then
    puppetSound "beep"
    updateStage
  end if
end
```

Fields

Parsing text in fields is one of the slowest operations you can do in Director. Read a large field first into a variable before performing chunk operations on it. The following code takes the text of a field called `"Story"` and replaces the placeholder `"insertName"` with the user's name. It reads the field into the temporary variable `temp` first, performs the text operation on temp, then writes temp back out to the field when it's done.

```
on insertName userName
  put field "Story" into temp
  set numWords = the number of words in temp
  repeat with x = 1 to numWords
    if word x of temp = "insertName" then put userName into
    ➥word x of var
  end repeat
  put temp into field "Story"
end
```

Symbols

When possible, use symbols instead of strings in property lists. Using the `getProp` command with items on the list that follows:

```
[#dog:1,#cat:2,#pig:3,#squirrel:4]
```

is faster than using `getProp` on this list:

```
["dog":1,"cat":2,"pig":3,"squirrel":4]
```

Testing the Efficiency of Your Code

Books and discussion groups on Director can only give you general guidelines for efficient coding efficiently. You can gauge the efficiency of various techniques by using Lingo's built-in timer to compare them.

- **the ticks.** A running tally of the elapsed time in ticks since the Director application launched.
- **the timer.** Also a running tally of the elapsed time in ticks since the Director application launched, or the elapsed time since the last `startTimer` command.
- **startTimer.** Resets the built-in timer to 0, similar to clicking a stopwatch. Make sure that only one handler is using the timer at a time, if you are using `startTimer`. If you need multiple timers, save each starting time to a variable and use `the ticks` instead. For example, see the following:

```
on stopWatch1On
   global watch1On
   set watch1On to the ticks
end
```

```
on stopWatch1Off
   global watch1On
   set elapsedTime = the ticks - watch1On
end
```

Testing Score-Based Techniques

You can test the effects of various Score properties such as sprite sizes, ink effects, and transitions by placing two animation sequences in the Score that are identical except for the variable you want to test. If you wanted to test and compare the animating speeds of Matte ink and Background Transparent ink, for example, you would place two identical animation sequences in the Score. You would give one or more sprite channels Matte ink in one sequence, and assign Background Transparent ink to the same sprite channels in the other sequence. Don't include the first or last Score frames in test sequences. Both of these frames have extra overhead that biases the test.

To test the performance of the two sequences, you would first maximize the frame rate to 120, and then time each sequence using the timer. Because few current machines are capable of playing multiple-channel animation at 120 frames per second, setting the frame rate to 120 plays the animation as fast as possible. If you set the frame rate to 120, any difference in the time it takes to play one sequence versus the other is due to the Score property you are testing.

Testing Lingo Code

It's hard to time the difference between a few lines of Lingo code because running three or four lines once might not register any elapsed time—you'll get a time of 0 ticks. You can still compare the two approaches by running them for the same number of repetitions inside of a repeat loop. The following two handlers compare the relative efficiency of setting the end point of a repeat loop to a variable before the repeat loop, or reading it with every repeat:

```
on propSetInsideRepLoop timesToRepeat
  set savtime = the timer
  repeat with y = 1 to timesToRepeat
```

```
      repeat with x = 1 to the number of words in field "Story"
        -- nothing
    end repeat
  end repeat
    put "Prop read inside repeat loop: " & the timer - savtime
  end

  on propSetBeforeRepLoop timesToRepeat
    set savtime = the timer
    repeat with y = 1 to timesToRepeat
      set numWords = the number of words in field "Story"
      repeat with x = 1 to numWords
        -- nothing
      end repeat
    end repeat
    put "Prop set before repeat loop: " & the timer - savtime
  end
```

Called from the Message window, the handlers produce the following output:

```
propSetInsideRepLoop(100)
-- "Prop read inside repeat loop: 22"
propSetBeforeRepLoop(100)
-- "Prop set before repeat loop: 1"
```

Testing Tips

To ensure the closest comparisons possible, preload all of the cast members your tests will use. That way, the first test run doesn't reflect the added overhead of loading the cast.

Run several repetitions of a test and average them to minimize the impact of extra overhead that might only happen the first time you run your test.

Defensive Programming

In the world of multimedia production, the only thing you can count on is change. There *will* be art and design changes and perhaps even the scope of the project will change. Suddenly, the original Mac-only floppy product demo has turned into a hybrid CD-ROM and trade show kiosk. Unexpected technical problems *will* crop up and make the whole thing a rush to the finish line. This section describes some ways to practice defensive programming—that creates code that is as easy to change, flexible, and modular as possible.

Don't Use Sprite or Cast Member Numbers in Your Code

Sprite numbers change whenever you have to rearrange channels to accommodate new art. Cast member numbers will change when you rearrange cast in the Cast window. If you refer to specific sprite numbers or cast member numbers in several places in your code, you then have to find all of those places and update the numbers. If you don't catch and change all of the places, this leads to errors. It's a much better idea to create a variable name for the sprite channel or cast member, set it once to the correct number, then use the variable name in place of the number. The following code references the same sprite channel several times within just one handler:

```
on animateKey
  global locked
  if locked = TRUE then
    puppetSprite 10,TRUE
    set the memberNum of sprite 10 to 9
    if inside(the clickLoc,rect(100,100,200,200)) then
      set the loc of sprite 10 to the clickLoc
    end if
  end if
end
```

Code is easier to change if you store the sprite and cast numbers in variables that are all set once in one place. The use of variables in place of sprite and cast numbers also makes the code more readable.

```
on startMovie
   global keySprite,lockArea,movingKey,memberList
   set keySprite = 10
   set lockArea = rect(100,100,200,200)
```

```
    set movingKey = getProp(memberList,"MKey1")
end

on animateKey
  global locked,keySprite,lockArea, movingKey
  if locked = TRUE then
    puppetSprite keySprite,TRUE
    set the memberNum of sprite keySprite to movingKey
    if inside(the clickLoc,lockArea) then
      set the loc of sprite keySprite to the clickLoc
    end if
  end if
end
```

Use a Small Separate Movie for Each Logical Section

Small movies load faster than large ones with many cast members, even if you specify the loading for each cast as Load as Needed. Thumbnails and header information are still loaded for each cast member at startup, even when Load as Needed is on.

If there is no backup and one large movie is corrupted, you lose everything. However, if you divide the movie into component movies, you lose only the corrupted component.

Finally, dividing a project over several small self-contained movies enables you to pass off part of the project to another person if you need help in finishing the job. Each person can work on one or two movies independently.

Don't Put Anything in Channel 48

If you fill channel 48, it's a Lingo golden rule that somewhere, late into the project, you'll need it. This means moving back sprite channels everywhere to free up channel 48. Always leave channel 48 free for such a contingency. It is even better to leave 43–48 free—if you can spare them.

Using the Debugger

Director 5 includes a long-awaited debugger. This is good news for developers who use Lingo extensively. You now can set breakpoints and watch variables as you step through your code line by line.

Setting a Breakpoint

You set a breakpoint in your code by placing the insertion point where you want the breakpoint and pressing the Set BreakPoint button in the Script window. A red dot appears beside the breakpoint, as shown in figure 19.5.

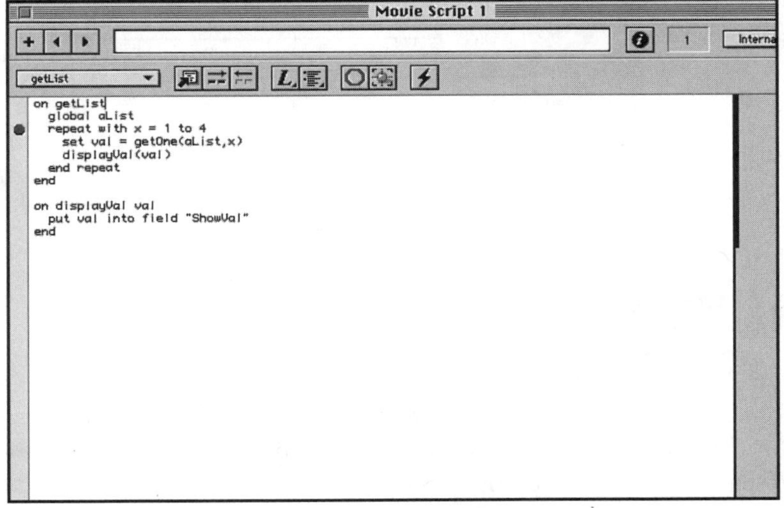

Figure 19.5

The Set Breakpoint button places a red dot next to the line of code where you want to break.

The next time you run the movie, Director stops at the breakpoint and opens the Debugger window. The top left pane of the Debugger window displays the calling list of handlers up to the breakpoint. The top right pane displays the values of variables within the scope of the current handler. The display updates with the current values as each line of code executes. In the bottom pane, the red dot shows the breakpoint and the green arrow shows the execution of the current line of code.

Stepping Through Code

Use the green step arrow buttons to step through the code line by line. The Step Script button steps through the lines of the current handler but does not step into any handlers called from the current handler. The Step Into Script button steps into handlers called from the current handler. In figure 19.6 the Step Into Script button would step into the handler `displayVal`, but the Step Script button would not.

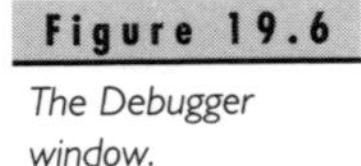

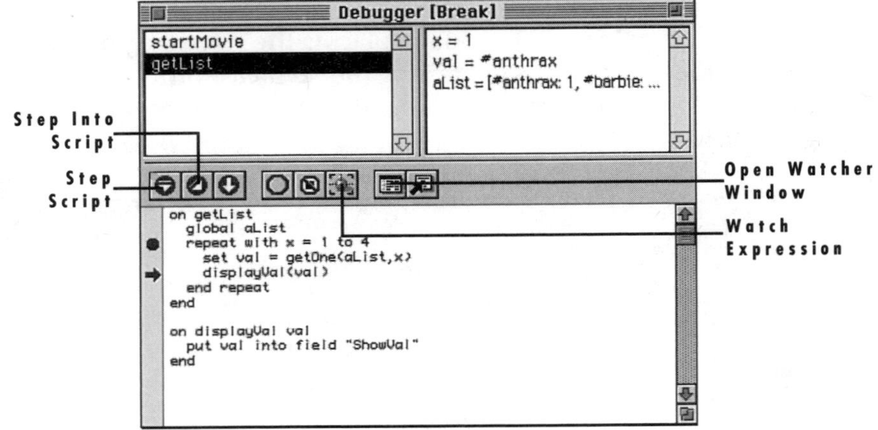

The Debugger window.

Watching and Altering Variables

You can monitor global variables and the values of expressions that are not variables by adding them to the Watcher window. You also can change the values of variables while your code runs and view the effects. Open the Watcher window by pressing the Open Watcher Window button in the Debugger Window or select Window, Watcher from the menu bar.

To add a variable or expression to watch that appears in your code, highlight the variable or expression and press the Watch Expression button. The expression and its current value appear in the Watcher window.

You also can watch an expression that's not necessarily available in the current code. Enter the expression into the Expression field of the

Watcher window and press the Add button. In figure 19.7 the expression `field "ShowVal"` is entered in the Expression field to add the field `"ShowVal"`. The expression `x * 20` in the fourth line does not appear in the code at all. Each time `x` increments in the code, the Watcher window displays the new value of the expression `x * 20`.

To change the value of a variable in the Watcher window, highlight the variable's line and type a new value for it in the Value field. In the following figure, to change the value of `aList`, you highlight the line for `aList`, type a new value in the Value field, and press the Set button to change that variable's value.

The Watcher window does not display the values of local variables outside of the current handler—their values display as `<Void>`. You cannot set a local variable in the Watcher that is outside of the current handler. The Watcher can display script object properties if the object is global.

Although you can add an expression to the Watcher, you cannot reset its value through the Watcher. You can only reset the values of variables and lists.

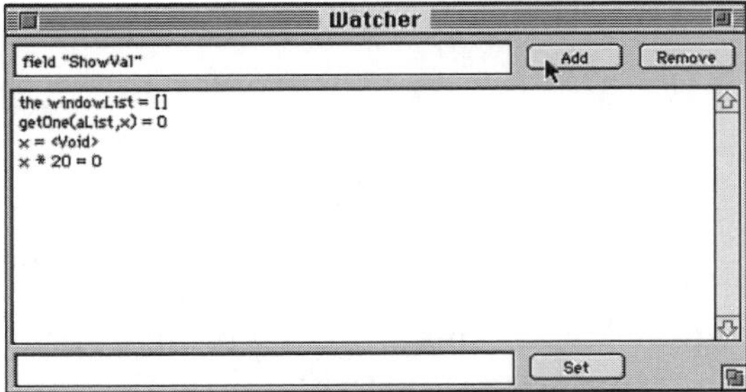

Figure 19.7

Enter an expression in the Expression field and press the Add button to add it to the Watcher window.

Debugging Tips

There's nothing worse than staring at your computer monitor wondering why something that should work, doesn't. If you are new to Director and you run across something that doesn't work as expected, try the following:

- Read about the command or feature in the manual, especially if this is your first time using that feature.

- Make a new movie that includes only the code or feature that doesn't work. Suppose you import a sound cast member, for example, but the sound won't play when placed in the Score. The first thing to try is to import the sound into an empty movie and see whether it plays there. If the sound doesn't play in the new movie, it probably means that the sound file was in the wrong format. If the sound does play in the new movie, you know that your original movie was at fault. Perhaps the sound was using too much memory, or maybe you accidentally turned off the volume of that particular sound channel in your code.
- Reboot the machine with all extensions off. Some extensions cause odd behavior in Director. (You can turn off your extensions by pressing the Shift key while you restart your machine.)

Figure 19.8

Highlight an expression, enter a new value for it, and press the Set button to change the expression's value.

If you have been using Director for six months or longer and you run in to a problem that can't be resolved by the preceding steps and you've been working on it for an hour or more, it might be a Director issue. Director is an amazing program with a lot of quirks. Online user forums, such as the Macromedia forums on CompuServe and America Online, and Web sites devoted to Director are your best source of information on quirks that could affect your work. See Appendix B, "Hot URLs: Favorite Director Web Sites," for a list of Director-oriented Internet resources.

Testing Your Code

After you import your last piece of art and type your last Lingo `end` tag, you might be tempted to breathe a sigh of relief and heave your project immediately out the door. Don't do it. Testing is an important part of the process. Thorough testing prevents support calls and unhappy customers later. The tips that follow will ensure that you test the broadest range of situations.

Test on a Full Range of Machines

Test on a couple of machines that represent the low and high end of the Macintosh line. If you tell users that your project runs on a Macintosh IILC with 4 MB of RAM and a single-speed CD player, make sure that you test that low-end configuration. Also, test on new machines. New system patches, extensions, and hardware sometimes cause unexpected problems.

Test the Playback of a CD-ROM

The load times of even a double-speed CD are very slow compared to the load times from hard disk. If your project is destined for CD, you should plan on creating a test CD no later than half-way through the project. CD performance might affect development decisions.

Stress Test

It's a good idea to test "extreme" usage because your project will face these situations with real users. If you design a project for children, use the mouse to click frequently all over the screen. When children get excited playing games, this is what they do. Leave the project running overnight to make sure there are no slow memory leaks. If you have text entry fields, test input at the low and high end of the range. What happens if the user types in 0 for a numeric field? What about when the user enters nothing in a text field? What if the user types 1,000 characters into a text field that only expects 20? You get the idea. Users don't mean to be devious, but they aren't always going to use your program in the way you expect.

Coming to Lingo from C

Darien Fitzgerald programs edutainment titles in Director for publisher Virtual Entertainment of Needham, Massachusettes. Darien came to Virtual Entertainment with several years of development experience in C and C++, and learned Director on the job. In this interview, he discusses some of the adjustments a C programmer makes when learning Director, and offers some tips for getting up to speed quickly.

What do you think you brought from your experience programming in C that helped you in Director?

The ability to organize my code and certain concepts in C such as modularization. Also, just by having programming experience, not necessarily C, there are a lot of problems which you end up solving in Director that you would also have to solve in C. You can pretty much apply the same algorithms.

Did working with an OOP language like C++ help you to understand Director's OOP concepts and terms?

I think the semantics they use are a little bit confusing—the parent, child, ancestor. They do mention in the manual that the ancestor is sort of like a base class and the parent would be the class which had inherited the base class. The big difference with Director is that you can actually change the base class on the fly. You can set the ancestor of me to one thing and then further down the line you can set the ancestor of me to another thing. You would never be able to do that in C. One of the problems is that you are more likely to have a situation where you would want to work in a C-like system where the base class could return a reference to the class that inherited from it.

What was difficult in the transition?

The first step was learning the relationship between all the components in Director. I think that's difficult for anyone whether they know C or not.

If Macromedia could have described their whole environment in more technical terms, I would have had a much easier time. If you just have a little information about what's going on behind the scenes, you have a better idea of what to do when something goes wrong. Instead of just thrashing about trying to get Director to work, you can take some sort of logical action.

Initially it's hard to know what is the most advantageous structure for your code. Normally if you're a C programmer you are setting up the environment, or you're using an API, but generally the API has few restrictions about what you're actually going to do and how you're going to set up your code.

As a C programmer I had a certain programming style which I was eventually but not immediately able to incorporate. One of the first thing you notice if you don't use objects and you're writing movie scripts—there's no scope for any of the global variables but you really want to have scope within one script. The work around for that is obviously to use parent scripts.

There are certain things in C that are just missing [in Director]—like data structures. There are two work arounds for that. One is to birth objects and use properties. The other is to use property lists with symbols. That's relatively fast. It's a pretty verbose way of referencing though, compared with C.

Another thing that caught me is that you can't pass strings by reference in Lingo. If you pass one as an argument you're really passing a copy. To change the string, you have to pass it back as a return value. If you're passing a string a lot, say in a repeat loop, it makes a copy every time and slows things down.

Do you have any tips for managing the transition?

Before you jump into coding, experiment with the Score. My tendency was to do everything in code instead of using the Score, when in fact often you can implement something much quicker just by jumping to different parts of the Score. And use the object features of Lingo as a method of modularizing your code.

It's been a year since you started using Director. You've shipped two titles and you're working on a third. How are things going now?

I eventually learned how to do just about everything I need to do in Lingo. When I was first starting, I would know exactly how to do what I wanted to do in C, and there would be apparently no equivalent way to do it in Lingo. I don't seem to be running in to that lately. Lingo turned out to be more powerful than I thought it was.

Summary

At first glance, this chapter might seem to be a hodge-podge of unrelated but useful tips on programming with Lingo. Actually, the underlying theme is efficiency—both in creating efficient movies that perform well and use resources wisely, and in leveraging your own programming time by building code libraries and learning to program "defensively."

The next chapter, "Object-Oriented Programming in Director," takes the idea of coding efficiency to a new level. Director script objects enable you to organize your code and to create a collection of self-standing Lingo templates that you can reuse in many projects.

Gretchen Macdowall

Object-Oriented Programming in Director

This chapter was written with one thought in mind—that there is nothing particularly mystical or complex about using code objects in Director. In fact, you can learn to use Director objects (also known as Parent/Child scripting in the Director documentation) without any prior experience with object-oriented programming.

If you are completely new to object-oriented programming (OOP), Director is a particularly gentle way to learn OOP concepts because, unlike traditional OOP languages, it enables you to use objects in your code to any extent that you want. You can design a project that consists only of objects, or you can just use objects here and there to organize sections of your code.

If you are coming to Lingo with experience in an OOP language like C++, it might take you some time to get your bearings. Lingo does not have a ready-made class library, imposes few rules about object structure, and uses its own unique terminology. The following is a table of OOP terms and their Lingo equivalents:

OOP Terms	*Lingo Equivalents*
Traditional OOP language	Lingo
Base class	Ancestor script
Class	Parent script
Instance variable	Property variable
Class instance / object	Child object
Method / member function	Method

The second section of this chapter, "Creating an Object in Lingo," teaches you how to create and use a single code object in Lingo. If you stop there and go no further, you still have added a valuable accessory to your Lingo toolbelt. The real power of code objects, however, lies in their capability to save you from repetitive coding. In the sections "Creating Multiple Objects from the Same Parent Script" and "Using Ancestor Scripts," you learn how to write code modules once that you can use again and again.

What Is an Object?

In Chapter 16, "Lingo: The Basics," the word "object" describes a thing in the Director environment that you can see and control with Lingo, such as a sprite channel, a cast member, a Movie in a Window, or the stage. You control objects in the Director environment by setting their properties. Objects respond to messages with the behavior you write for them in message handlers.

This chapter introduces you to a different kind of object—a code object. A *code object* is a self-contained unit of code in memory that keeps track of its own internal data. Code objects do share some traits with other Director objects. Code objects have internal variables called properties, and they too respond to messages with behavior you write for them. But unlike the other objects in the Lingo environment, you can't see a code object and they don't come ready-made. For the sake of brevity, the remainder of this chapter will use the word "object" to refer to "code objects."

In Lingo, you define an object template by writing a Parent script. You then create an object from that Parent script by sending a `new` message to the Parent script. You can create as many objects as you want from the same template. The Director manuals call the objects created from a Parent "Child objects."

You get a Lingo object to do something by sending it a message. The object's methods (*method* is a fancy word for handler) determine which messages it responds to. The following are some examples of messages you might send to Lingo objects to illustrate what kinds of things objects can do:

```
moveForward(badguy1)
```

`Badguy1` is the name of an object controlling the movement of a bad guy sprite chasing the main character in a maze. Inside `badguy1`'s code are property variables that keep track of the sprite number of the bad guy, where he currently is on the screen, the direction in which he's currently heading, and how many pixels he should move. The object's "`moveForward`" method handles the `moveForward` message. It checks the bad guy sprite's current position and moves him the specified number of pixels in the right direction. Two other objects—`badguy2` and `badguy3`—were created from the same Parent script template. They have different sprite number properties, so they control two other sprites on-screen. The property containing the number of pixels `badguy2` and `badguy3` can move at a time might be smaller or larger for either of those objects than `badguy1`'s property, so they will each move at different speeds. `Badguy1`, `badguy2`, and `badguy3` all share the same Parent script, yet their behavior is different because their property variables have unique values.

```
put returnFinalResult(quiz) into field "Quiz Score"
```

The quiz object keeps track—in its property variables—of the quiz questions, the correct answers, and the formula for coming up with the final score. The quiz object is like a black box. No code outside of quiz knows anything about how it comes up with its scoring. The code outside quiz knows only that sending a `returnFinalResult` message to quiz will return a value.

Keeping all of the details about quiz questions and scoring in one place inside of the quiz object makes it easy to add a question or change the scoring method. You can change these things in one place inside of the quiz without disturbing any other code.

The OOP word for code that manages its own data and shields its internal workings from the outside is *encapsulation*. Lingo objects are encapsulated.

The Top Five Reasons to Use Objects

The following five sections discuss reasons for using objects.

Reason 5: Objects Organize Your Code

Parent scripts contain code and the variables that the code relies on in the same place. If all of your code and variables related to printing a report or playing digital video, for example, is in the same place it's easier to maintain.

Reason 4: Object Properties Offer the Benefits of Globals without Cluttering Up the Global Space

Like globals, an object's property variables maintain their state over time; unlike globals, they are known only to the object maintaining them. This keeps them out of the global pool.

Suppose you have a catalog application. In each product section—Electronics or Clothing, for example—you are keeping track of the number of products the user has bought, the number of items he has looked at, and how long he has spent in each section, so you can track the user's buying preferences. All of these variables would have to be globals (or part of a global list) to be able to maintain their contents over time. You'd end up with a lot of global variables all named with some variation of a product section name and `counter` or `timer`, all available everywhere in the project. How long before you accidentally use the same global name twice for two different purposes?

Instead, you could make an object for each section with property variables for the number of products bought, the number of items looked at, and the time spent in that section. The Electronics object can have a `productsBought` property variable, and so can the Clothing object. Neither of these variables is part of the global pool because their scope is restricted to the object to which they belong.

Reason 3: You Can Test Objects Independently

An object is self-contained. Because it is not dependent on any code outside of itself, an object can be tested before other parts of the project are done. After you have finished coding an object, you should be able to test it by sending messages to all of its methods. If the methods set the right property variables and/or return the right values, then you know that the object is functioning properly and can be integrated into the larger project. Easy unit testing is another benefit of encapsulation.

Reason 2: Objects Make Code Easier to Change

A Parent script defines the methods any object created from it will have. There is another level of script called an Ancestor script. A Parent script can link to an Ancestor script. When a Parent script links to an Ancestor script, all of the Ancestor script's methods and properties become part of the Parent script. The Parent script then supplies any additional methods or properties that it needs. The OOP term for the capability of one script to incorporate the methods and properties of another script is *inheritance*.

Suppose you have written an object that controls a fish sprite in a game. The fish sprite moves randomly around the tank. If the fish comes near the tank wall, it turns around; if it gets near the bottom of the tank, it changes direction; if it is about to collide with another fish, it swims away. The fish object's methods might be named something similar to the following:

```
moveForward
nearWall
nearBottom
nearOtherFish
```

Next, you want to create a predator fish. The predator fish moves in the same random way as any other fish and also tries to avoid the walls and the bottom of the tank. When the predator fish gets near another fish, however, it eats the other fish instead of swimming away. The predator fish object's `moveForward`, `nearWall`, and `nearBottom` methods would be the same as the original fish object's methods. The only method that would be different would be the `nearOtherFish` method.

In this situation, you could create a new Parent script for the predator fish. The script would use the original fish script as its Ancestor. The predator fish Parent script would inherit all of the methods of the original fish script it had specified as an Ancestor. The only additional code you would have to write for the predator fish would be a new `nearOtherFish` method.

Reason 1: You Can Build a Library of Objects That You Use Over and Over Again

If you create your objects with reuse in mind, eventually you will have a library of objects that you can put together to handle much of your routine coding. Director 5 introduces the capability to link a movie to more than one cast. This enables you to maintain a code library cast containing library objects that you can easily link to any movie.

If you are convinced that coding with objects is a good idea, then it's time to get down to business and learn how to create them.

Creating an Object in Lingo

To learn about objects in Lingo, you start by building an object that contains the minimum necessary code to work. This minimalist object will not be very useful, except to illustrate what an object is made of.

Open the movie MINIMAL.DIR (see fig. 20.1). A button and a field have already been placed on stage for you, and there is a `go the frame` script to keep the movie running when you play it. There aren't any other scripts yet. The movie MINIMDN.DIR contains the finished scripts.

You can find the movie MINIMAL.DIR on the accompanying CD in the folder for Chapter 20.

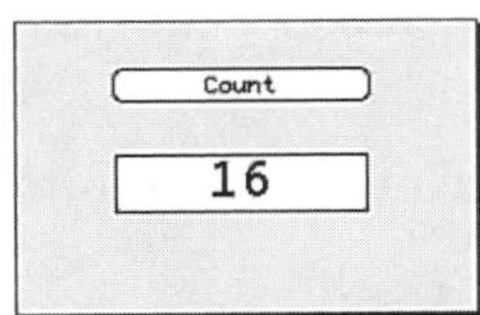

Figure 20.1

MINIMAL.DIR shows how to create a simple object.

You define an object's methods and properties in Lingo by creating a Parent script. Create a new, empty Parent script by clicking on the + button in the Script Window.

Click on the Info button in the Script window and use the Type pull-down menu to change the script's type property to Parent (see fig. 20.2). Enter the name **`minimal`** in the script's name field.

It's important to use the Parent script type for Parent scripts. If you accidentally create an object from a movie script and send it a message, Director will look through all of the movie scripts for a handler for that message. If you have a movie script handler with the same name as one of your object methods, the movie script handler will get the message instead of your object.

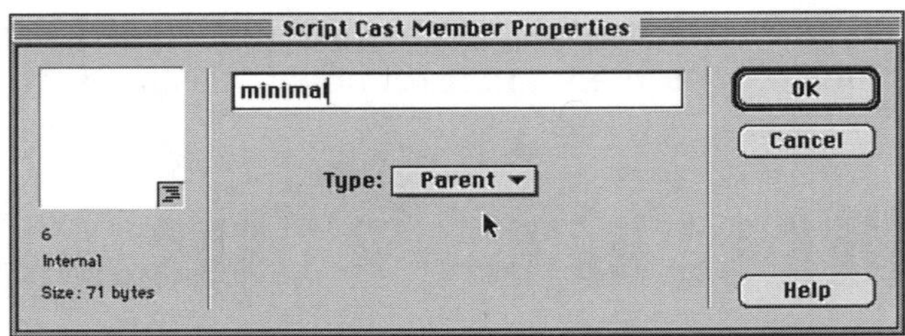

Figure 20.2

Use the Type pull-down menu to create a Parent script.

The New Method

The only required method in a Parent script is the `new` method. The `new` method creates a new object from a Parent script. A Parent script is like a template document in a word-processing program. Just like you can create any number of identical documents from one template, you can create any number of identical objects by calling the new method of a Parent script. Each time you send a parent script a `new` message it makes a new object from that parent script. (If you were working with objects in previous versions of Director you will recognize the `new` method as the old `birth` method.)

Enter the following code into your minimalist Parent script:

```
on new me
   return me
end
```

All object methods contain the word `me` in the `on` line. The variable `me` will contain a pointer to the object's location in memory after the object is created. The return line inside of the new method also is required. It returns a pointer to the newly created object. If you don't include a `return me` line, you will have no way of communicating with your object after you create it.

Compile the script by clicking on the lightning icon in the script window. Then enter the following in the Message window to create a new object from the script:

```
set minimalObj = new(script "minimal")
```

The code line you entered created a new object from the `minimal` script and put it in the global `minimalObj`. (Any variable you declare in the Message window is global.) It's a good idea to store your objects in globals so that they will be available to code anywhere in your movie that wants to use them.

Global objects, like any other global, persist across movies. After an object is created from a Parent script, it exists independently in memory. It no longer references the Parent script. If you `go to` another movie that does not contain the object's Parent script, the object will still work. The object is using its own copy in memory of the code defined in the Parent script. If you change a Parent script's code after you have created an object from it, you will not change the object already in memory. You must create a new object from the edited Parent script.

Enter the following in the Message window to see whether you did indeed create an object:

```
put minimalObj
```

Director returns the contents of the object variable, which confirms that the object was created successfully:

```
-- <offspring "minimal" 2 8daa90>
```

Object variables contain 3 pieces of information:

- **`offspring "minimal"`**—the Parent script from which the object was created.
- **2**—the number of references to the object. The Parent script always counts as the first, and the object created from it counts as the second. Any variable you set to the object will increase the number of references to it. For example, if you enter:

  ```
  set x = minimalObj
  put minimalObj
  ```

  Director will now return:

  ```
  -- <offspring "minimal" 3 8daa90>
  ```

- **`8daa90`**—the object's location in memory.

`minimalObj` was created successfully, but the object can't really do anything yet—it cannot receive any messages other than `new`, and it has no property variables to store data.

You will not want to have to create a new object by typing commands in the Message window every time you run the movie. Make a `startMovie` script that handles creating the object, as follows:

```
on startMovie
  global minimalObj
  set minimalObj = new(script "minimal")
end
```

This object is going to have a rather limited purpose. The object will increment a counter every time a button is pressed, and display the counter in a field. To keep track of the counter from one button press to the next, the object will need a property variable.

Declaring Property Variables

You declare an object's property variables at the top of the object script with the following syntax:

```
property varName, varName, varName ...
```

Open the minimal object script again and insert the following line at the very top, before the new method:

```
property counter
```

Now, recompile the script and play the movie to create a new object. (The startMovie script now contains code to create `minimalObj`.) Type the following in the Message window:

```
put the counter of minimalObj
```

The Message window returns:

```
-- <Void>
```

You can refer to an object's property variables from outside the object with the following syntax:

```
the property of object
```

The property variable counter has not been set by the object yet, so it returns <Void>. Go back to the `minimal` script and add the following line to the new method:

```
set counter = 0
```

The object script should now look like the following:

```
property counter

on new me
   set counter = 0
   return me
end
```

Recompile the script and play the movie. Look at the counter object property again by typing the following:

```
put the counter of minimalObj
```

Now the Message window returns:

```
-- 0
```

The object property counter is `0` because it was set in the `new` method as `minimalObj` was created.

The `minimal` object script is still not capable of doing anything yet. You need to give it two methods. Open up the `minimal` object script again and enter the following code after the new method:

```
on increment me
   set counter = counter + 1
end

on displayCounter me
   put counter into field "Show Counter"
end
```

Now the `minimal` object script can handle an increment message and a display message. Why two methods? The smaller and more single-purpose your methods, the easier they are to modify later.

Give the button cast a script that sends increment and display messages to `minimalObj` by entering the following code into the button's cast script:

```
on mouseUp
  global minimalObj
  increment(minimalObj)
  displayCounter(minimalObj)
end
```

Choose Control, Recompile All Scripts from the menu bar to record your changes. Rerun the movie. When you click on the button, the current value of `minimalObj`'s counter property displays in the text field. Every time you click on the button, it sends another pair of increment and `displayCounter` messages to `minimalObj`. `minimalObj`'s increment method handles the increment message by adding 1 to the property variable counter. `minimalObj`'s `displayCounter` method handles the `displayCounter` message by displaying the counter property variable in a field.

You have just created your first Director object and learned the following:

- An *object* is a self-contained unit of code and data.
- You define an object's characteristics by writing a Parent script. The Parent script declares the object's internal variables (properties) and contains the handlers (methods) to handle messages sent to the object by other scripts.
- You create a new object by sending a new message to a Parent script. All Parent scripts must have a new method. The Parent script's new method returns an object that you must store in a variable.

Creating Multiple Objects from the Same Parent Script

In the movie MINIMAL.DIR, you created one object from a Parent script template. There are going to be times when you want to create just one object to organize code and the variables related to that code in one place.

You also can create a Parent script template that generates many child objects. The child objects are alike in that they all contain the same methods, but each child object keeps track of its own property variables. If you have come to Director from a traditional OOP language, you can think of a Parent script as a class and a child object as an instance of a class.

The movie MULTI.DIR demonstrates a situation where creating multiple child objects saves coding. It's a fictional on-screen quiz of new cashiers on product codes (see fig. 20.3). The screen contains five fields where the user has to enter numeric data.

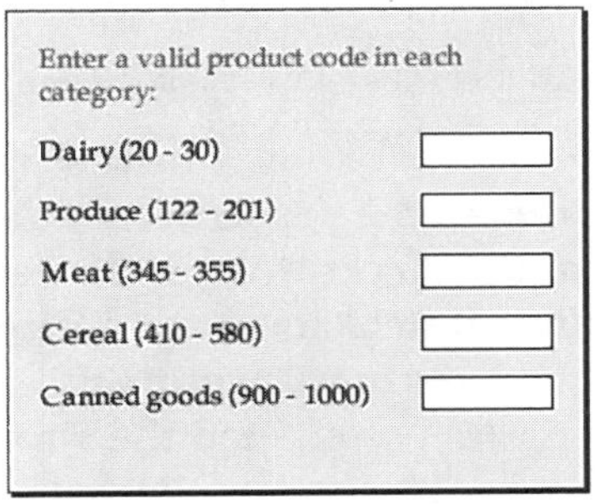

Enter a valid product code in each category:

Dairy (20 - 30)

Produce (122 - 201)

Meat (345 - 355)

Cereal (410 - 580)

Canned goods (900 - 1000)

Figure 20.3

The MULTI.DIR movie is a fictional quiz of cashiers on product codes.

The correct range for each question appears on-screen beside the question for convenience. If this was a real quiz screen, it obviously would not be a good idea to show the answers on the screen. Also, there is no way for the user to tab between questions. Adding the code to do that would make the example more complex, but any real product that includes data entry should let the user tab between fields. Chapter 19, "Advanced Concepts," explains how to handle tabbing in editable fields.

Suppose that on this screen you want to check that the number the user entered in each field is correct—in this case, "correct" means that the number falls within a certain numeric range. If it's wrong, you want to beep and erase the entry. After three wrong entries in any field, you want to prevent the user from entering any more data in that field to discourage random guessing.

There are only two differences between the fields. Each field has a different valid numeric range, and each field has to keep track independently of how many wrong guesses it has had. That means you can create one Parent script template to handle the code for the fields and use property variables to hold each field's valid range and wrong answers.

Open the movie MULTI.DIR. The screen and data entry fields are already laid out. There is a looping frame script to keep the movie running when you play it. It also already contains a Parent script, but there is no code to create child objects from the Parent script yet and no code to link the child objects to the fields.

The movie MULTI.DIR is on the accompanying CD in the folder for Chapter 20. The movie MULTIDN.DIR in the same folder contains the finished code for this example.

Now, let's break down the code in the Parent script.

```
property myField,validRange,wrongAnswers,limit
```

The first line of the code, as shown in the preceding line, sets the object's properties. Two of the properties, `myField` and `validRange`, are going to be passed to the object when it is created. This enables each object to check a different field and use a different valid range against which to check the field's entry. The property `wrongAnswers` is a tally of how many times the user has entered the wrong data into the field. `Limit` is the number of wrong answers allowed before the user is locked out of the field.

The second section of the code is as follows:

```
on new me,passedField,passedRange
  set myField = passedField
  set validRange = passedRange
  set wrongAnswers = 0
  set limit = 3
  resetField me
  return me
end
```

The first method is the `new` method. This `new` method is expecting to be passed a field number and a `validRange` list. A new message sent to this Parent script will look like this:

```
set fieldObject = new(script "FieldCheck",7,[50,120])
```

This would create a new object with a `myField` property of `7` and a `validRange` property of `[50,120]`.

The following shows the third section of code:

```
on checkValue me
  set aValue = integer(field myField)
 if aValue < getAt(validRange,1) or (aValue > getAt(validRange,2))
then
    set wrongAnswers = wrongAnswers + 1
    if wrongAnswers < limit then
      wrongAlert me
    else
      shutOffField me
    end if
  else
    rightAnswer me
  end if
end

on wrongAlert me
  beep
  put " " into member myField
end

on rightAnswer me
  set the backcolor of member myField to 114
end

on shutOffField me
  beep
  set the editable of member myField to FALSE
  set the backcolor of member myField to 255
end

on resetField me
  set the backcolor of member myField to 0
  set the editable of member myField to TRUE
  put " " into member myField
end
```

The `checkValue` method is the meat of this object. This handles the `checkValue` message sent from a field script. It evaluates the data in the field and decides what action to take. If the data is wrong, the object beeps. If the user has answered the same field wrong too many times (more than the property `limit`), the object locks the field, preventing further data entry. If the data is right, the object turns the field blue.

The rest of the methods are internal methods—they do not receive messages from outside of the object. They are called inside of the object itself. If you have come to Director from a traditional OOP language, you can think of these as private methods. But be aware that in Director, private methods will not generate errors if they are sent messages from outside of the object.

The first code to add is the code that creates a child object for each data entry field on the screen. You have five fields, so you need five objects. The field member numbers go from 7–11 in the cast. Create a new movie script and enter the following code:

```
on startMovie
  global field1Obj,field2Obj,field3Obj,field4Obj,field5Obj
  set field1Obj = new(script "FieldCheck",7,[20,30])
  set field2Obj = new(script "FieldCheck",8,[122,201])
  set field3Obj = new(script "FieldCheck",9,[345,355])
  set field4Obj = new(script "FieldCheck",10,[410,580])
  set field5Obj = new(script "FieldCheck",11,[900,1000])
end
```

Compile the script, rewind the movie, and play it. Type the following in the Message window:

```
put the validRange of field1Obj
```

Director responds:

```
-- [20, 30]
```

Now, try the same thing with the last object:

```
put the validRange of field5Obj
```

Director responds:

```
-- [900, 1000]
```

An object has been created for each field with unique property values for the field. The only thing left to do is to add code to each data entry field that sends the `checkValue` message to the object responsible for that field.

Give the first data entry field (in channel 7) the following sprite script:

```
on keyUp
  global field1Obj
  if the key = RETURN then
    checkValue(field1Obj)
  end if
end
```

Give the next data entry field (in channel 8) the same sprite script, but change the object name to `field2Obj`:

```
on keyUp
  global field2Obj
  if the key = RETURN then
    checkValue(field2Obj)
  end if
end
```

Do the same thing for each field sprite, making sure to change the object name each time. Now run the movie. Each field accepts a different range of correct answers, but behaves the same way after it detects a right or wrong answer.

In this section, you have learned the following:

- You can create many child objects from the same Parent script.
- Child objects operate independently and contain their own unique values for property variables.

Using Ancestor Scripts

Suppose you have finished programming your cashier quiz screen and your customer, the owner of the grocery store, reviews it. "Oh dear," she says. "We forgot to tell you about the special requirements we have for the Produce and Dairy fields." She goes on to tell you that Dairy is the most-entered category of product code—all cashiers should know Dairy inside and out. If a cashier taking the quiz gets Dairy wrong even once, the customer wants an alarm to sound and the screen to lock immediately. She'll have to let that cashier go. On the other hand, Produce codes are very difficult to remember. The customer wants the cashier to have no limit on the number of tries it takes to get that question right.

Do you have to rewrite entirely new scripts to handle these exceptions? No. You can make new Parent scripts for the Dairy field and the Produce field that use the original `FieldCheck` script as an ancestor. Objects created from the new Parent scripts will inherit all of the Ancestor script's methods. In each new script, you will only have to write one new method to make the requested change.

The following diagram shows a new object created from a Parent script that declares an Ancestor. The new object combines the properties and methods of the Parent and Ancestor. A method from the Parent replaces a method from the Ancestor with the same name.

Figure 20.4

An object created from a Parent script and Ancestor script.

```
Ancestor Script

property counter

on new me
 return me
end

on advance me
 soundAlarm me
 set counter = counter + 1
end

on retreat me
 set counter = counter - 1
end

on soundAlarm me
 beep
end
```

```
Parent Script

property alarmCnt, ancestor

on new me
 set alarmCnt = 10
 set ancestor = new(script "Ancestor Script")
end

on soundAlarm me
 beep(alarmCnt)
end
```

```
Child Object

Properties:

counter
alarmCnt
ancestor

Methods:

on new me
 set alarmCnt = 10
 set ancestor = new(script "Ancestor Script")
end

on soundAlarm me
 beep(alarmCnt)
end

on advance me
 soundAlarm me
 set counter = counter + 1
end

on retreat me
 set counter = counter - 1
end
```

Let's make the Dairy field changes first. The Dairy field must sound an alarm now and shut down all of the fields the first time it receives a wrong answer. Review the methods in the `FieldCheck` script to see whether you can find the method that you would have to change for Dairy:

```
on resetField me
  set the backcolor of member myField to 0
  set the editable of member myField to TRUE
  put " " into member myField
end

on checkValue me
  set aValue = integer(field myField)
 if aValue < getAt(validRange,1) or (aValue > getAt(validRange,2))
then
    set wrongAnswers = wrongAnswers + 1
    if wrongAnswers < limit then
      wrongAlert me
    else
      shutOffField me
    end if
  else
    rightAnswer me
  end if
end

on wrongAlert me
  beep
  put " " into member myField
end

on rightAnswer me
  set the backcolor of member myField to 114
end

on shutOffField me
  set the editable of member myField to FALSE
  set the backcolor of member myField to 255
end
```

It looks like the `wrongAlert` method would have to change, because that is the method that handles wrong answers. Create a new Parent script and name it Dairy Check. You will put the new `wrongAlert` method into this script. But first, you have to tell it where to get the rest of its methods. At the very top of the script, declare an ancestor property:

```
property ancestor
```

Ancestor is a reserved word in Director. Setting the *ancestor* property of one object to another object enables the first object to inherit the methods of the second.

A script declared as an Ancestor script can declare an Ancestor of its own. There is no limit to the number of Ancestors you can nest together. An object created from a Parent script with a chain of Ancestor scripts will inherit the methods of the Parent and all of the Ancestors. For example, if Script A declares Script B as an Ancestor, and Script B, in turn, declares Script C as an Ancestor, an object created from Script A will contain methods from Scripts A, B, and C.

If there is more than one method with the same name, the methods of the Parent script override the Ancestor methods of the same name. In the preceding example, if Parent Script A had a method called `display` and Ancestor Script B had a method called `display` as well, an object created from Parent Script A would use Parent Script A's `display` method.

If there is more than one Ancestor method with the same name, the methods of the Ancestor closest to the Parent script override the other Ancestors' methods. In the preceding example, if Ancestor Script B and Ancestor Script C both contained `move` methods, an object created from Parent Script A would use Ancestor Script B's `move` method.

Now, enter the following code for the DairyCheck's new method:

```
on new me,passedField,passedRange
 set ancestor = new(script "FieldCheck",passedField,passedRange)
  return me
end
```

The `startMovie` handler is going to be creating a new `DairyCheck` object for field 1 now instead of `FieldCheck`. Change that line in the `startMovie` handler:

```
set field1Obj = new(script "DairyCheck",7,[20,30])
```

The first line of the new method for `DairyCheck` is as follows:

```
set ancestor = new(script "FieldCheck",passedField,passedRange)
```

`DairyCheck` is creating a new `FieldCheck` object and storing it in its Ancestor variable.

The new `DairyCheck` object will pass the field and range arguments on to `"FieldCheck"` because `"FieldCheck"`'s new method will be looking for them.

We are setting the object's Ancestor property in the new method here, once and for all, but it is possible to change an object's Ancestor property to point to a new object at any time.

When you switch an object's Ancestor from one object to another, the object immediately inherits the methods of the new Ancestor object and loses the methods of its previous Ancestor. This capability to switch an object's ancestor on the fly is unique to Director. Most traditional OOP languages don't allow it.

At this point, `DairyCheck` has a new method and one property variable, but no other properties or methods of its own. Rewind and run the movie. The Dairy field behaves exactly like the other fields. The `DairyCheck` object inherited all of the methods from its Ancestor script.

Now it's time to add the method that you want to override. Open the `DairyCheck` script again and add a new `wrongAlert` method:

```
on wrongAlert me
  global field2Obj,field3Obj,field4Obj,field5Obj
  puppetSound "alarm"
  shutOffField me
  shutOffField field2Obj
  shutOffField field3Obj
  shutOffField field4Obj
  shutOffField field5Obj
end
```

The new `wrongAlert` method sounds the alarm. It then sends a `shutOffField` message to itself and the same message to all of the other field objects, causing them to shut off too.

Recompile the `DairyCheck` script and rewind and run the movie again. This time when you enter a wrong answer in the Dairy field, the `wrongAlert` method of `DairyCheck` gets the message and an alarm sounds.

Now you need to make a new Parent script for the Produce field and name it `ProduceCheck`. Give it the same property and new method as the `DairyCheck`:

```
property ancestor

on new me,passedField,passedRange
 set ancestor = new(script "FieldCheck",passedField,passedRange)
  return me
end
```

Change `field2Obj` in the `startMovie` handler to reference the new script:

```
set field2Obj = new(script "ProduceCheck",8,[122,201])
```

The Produce field must not put a limit on wrong answers. In this case, `ProduceCheck` will have to override the `checkValue` method. It omits the lines that keep a tally of `wrongAnswers` and compares the number of wrong answers to a limit. Add the following method to `ProduceCheck`:

```
on checkValue me
  set aValue = integer(field the myField of me)
 if aValue < getAt(the validRange of me,1) or (aValue > getAt(the
validRange of me,2)) then
      wrongAlert me
  else
    rightAnswer me
  end if
end
```

`ProduceCheck` inherits the property variables `myField` and `validRange` from the Ancestor `FieldCheck` object. You will notice that `ProduceCheck` has to use different syntax to get at the inherited properties. When an object refers to an inherited property, it must use the following syntax:

```
the propertyName of me
```

Again, recompile, rewind, and run the movie. The Produce field accepts any number of wrong answers because the `checkValue` method of `field2Obj` is overriding its Ancestor's `checkValue` method.

With a minimum of extra coding, you have been able to make the requested changes. As you can see, tapping the capability of an object to inherit behavior from an Ancestor object can save you time.

The ActorList

The objects you have created in the previous examples have all had one thing in common—their methods were triggered by messages sent when a sprite was clicked or keyed on stage. Don't get the idea that some kind of user action is required to send a message to an object. Another way you can send a message to an object is to put it on the `actorList`, which is a reserved list maintained by Director. Director sends a `stepFrame` message to objects on the `actorList` at every frame, before it sends an `enterFrame` message to the frame.

One very handy object you can create that makes use of the actorList is a timer object. It records a start time and the amount of time you want to wait, then keeps track of whether the time is up or not. You can use a timer for games with a time limit or for triggering events at particular intervals. Timer objects are more versatile than Director's built-in `startTimer` and `the timeOutScript` commands, which only enable you to have one timed event going at a time. Let's look at a timer script that is already built. Open the movie TIMER.DIR from the Chapter 20 folder of the accompanying CD-ROM (see fig. 20.5).

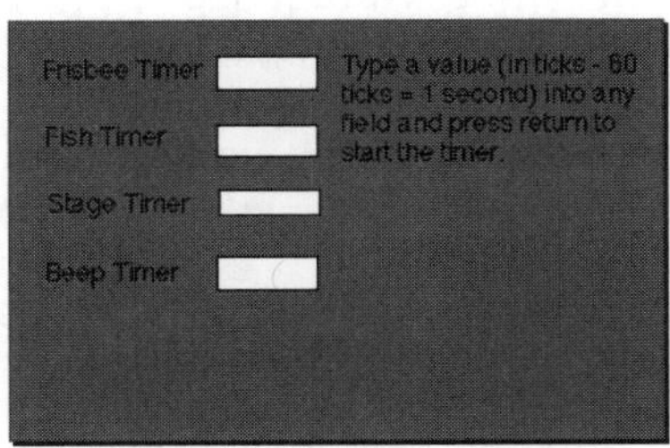

Figure 20.5

The TIMER movie.

The first member contains the timer Parent script. Let's look at the first section of code:

```
property startedAt, stopAfter

on new me
  return me
end
```

You should be pretty familiar with the `new` method at this point. The timer's `new` method takes no arguments, so we can create a `new` timer by saying the following:

`set stopWatch = new(script "timer")`

The next section of code follows:

```
on startTiming me,forHowLong
  set startedAt = the ticks
  set stopAfter = the ticks + forHowLong
  putMeOnActorList me
end
```

But `stopWatch` doesn't really start doing anything until it receives the `startTiming` message. The property `startedAt` gets set to `the ticks`. `The ticks` is a Director function that returns the number of ticks since the Director session started. You can try it by typing the following in the Message window:

`put the ticks`

Director returns the number of ticks since your session started:

```
-- 90201
```

The `forHowLong` argument passes in the number of ticks the timer should wait before going off.

The following code sends a `startTiming` message to `stopWatch`, telling it to go off after five seconds (5×60 ticks = 300 ticks):

```
startTiming(stopWatch,300)
```

The `stopWatch` object stores the time it started in the property variable `startedAt`, and the time it should go off in the property variable `stopAfter`.

After you have captured the starting time, you have to have some way of continually checking to see whether the timer should go off yet. That's where `the actorList` comes in. Once this object is on the `actorList`, its `stepFrame` method will be executed automatically at every frame. The `stopWatch` object will use its `stepFrame` method to check regularly to see if it should go off.

The next section of code follows:

```
on putMeOnActorList me
  takeMeOffActorList me
  append the actorList,me
end
```

`the actorList` acts like a global, but doesn't have to be declared as a global or a list. It's always available.

You manage `the actorList` with regular list syntax. You can add an object to `the actorList` with `append` or `setAt`, just like you'd add an item to any other list. The first line of the preceding method takes any old timer off of `the actorList` before adding a new timer.

`the actorList` persists across movies and between runs of the same movie when you're authoring. Objects remaining in `the actorList` trying to operate on sprites that don't exist in the current movie can wreak havoc. It's a good idea to clear `the actorList` in your `startMovie` handler like the following:

```
set the actorList = []
```

The next section of code follows:

```
on stepFrame me
  if the ticks >= stopAfter then
    timerDoneEvent me
    stopTiming me
  end if
end
```

After stopWatch is on the actorList, Director will send it a stepFrame message on every frame. (Because the stepFrame message is dependent on the frame rate, stopWatch will only be accurate within a few ticks. For example, if the frameRate is 15 fps, stopWatch will only get a stepFrame message every 4 ticks.)

StopWatch's stepFrame method checks to see whether the current time is past when the timer should go off.

The next section of code follows:

```
on timerDoneEvent me
  beep
end

on stopTiming me
  takeMeOffActorList me
end
```

stopWatch beeps when the time is up. Although the line of code in the timerDoneEvent method could easily have been included in the stepFrame, having it as a separate method will allow another object using this script as an Ancestor to override the timerDoneEvent with its own method.

The next section of code follows:

```
on takeMeOffActorList me
  set myPos = getPos(the actorList,me)
  if myPos > 0 then
    deleteAt the actorList,myPos
  end if
end
```

After the stopWatch object has gone off, it takes itself off the actorList by finding its position on the actorList and deleting itself.

The stopWatch object is not tied to any sprites on stage. You can try it out by playing the movie and typing the following in the Message window:

```
set stopWatch = birth(script "timer")
starTiming(stopWatch,180)
```

The timer beeps after three seconds.

You can customize the `timerDoneEvent` to stop a sound or play an animation in synch with a certain point in a music piece. Take a look at the `frisbeeTimer`, `fishTimer`, and `stageColorTimer` scripts to see how they have used the timer script as an Ancestor, but customized the `timerDoneEvent` method. Play the movie and enter values in the fields to send each object a `startTiming` event.

Escaping the Score

A criticism frequently leveled against Lingo is that you can never hope to do "real" object-oriented programming with it because Lingo is hopelessly tied to the Score. This just isn't true. The Score is a great tool for sequencing animation, but if you are more comfortable controlling everything through Lingo objects, you need put nothing more in the Score than one `go the frame` script.

Previous versions of Director required you to place a dummy place-holder cast in any channel you wanted to control with Lingo. Director 5 gives you two ways to fill empty sprite channels on the fly, as follows:

- You can puppet the sprite and use the `set the memberNum of sprite` command to place a cast member in an empty channel. (Note: You must set the forecolor of the sprite to 255 first for this to work.)
- You can use Score generation to place permanent cast members in the cells. Score generation is covered in Chapter 19, "Advanced Concepts," in the section titled "Making Libraries and Tools."

Open the movie NOSCORE.DIR. It contains one frame script and nothing else in the Score. Play the movie (see fig. 20.6). Forty-eight interactive sprites appear on stage and begin moving. Click on a sprite and it changes direction.

You can find the movie NOSCORE.DIR on the CD in the folder for Chapter 20.

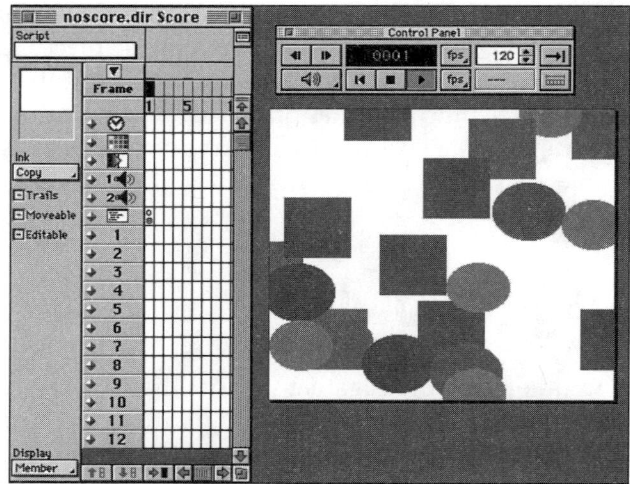

Figure 20.6

The NOSCORE movie.

Forty-eight objects created from the same Parent script control the appearance, movement, and interactivity of each sprite on the stage. Let's look at the part of the startMovie script that creates the objects:

```
on startMovie
   global objectList
   set objectList = []
   set the actorList = []
   repeat with x = 1 to 48
      setAt(objectList,x,new(script"genSprite",random(6),
      ➥random(30)))
      appear(getAt(objectList,x))
      append the actorList,getAt(objectList,x)
   end repeat
```

It's hard to come up with meaningful names for 48 objects that all do the same thing. And if you do come up with a naming scheme like circle1, circle2 ,circle3, and so on, it still makes sending a message to all of the objects in sequence difficult. If you have a group of like objects that you will be sending message to in sequence, it's more convenient to store them in a list than to name each one individually.

In the following line of code, the global objectList is the container list that will store each new object as it is created:

```
set objectList = []
```

In the following line of code, each position in `objectList` is filled with a new object created from script `"genSprite"`:

```
setAt(objectList,x,new(script"genSprite",random(6),random(30)))
```

The following lines of code are inside a repeat loop. The repeat loop makes it easy to send the appear message to all 48 objects and append each one to `the actorList`.

```
appear(getAt(objectList,x))
append the actorList,getAt(objectList,x)
```

The `appear` method of script `"genSprite"` finds an empty spot in the Score and fills it with a cast member:

```
on appear me
  set spriteNum = findSpace(me)
  puppetSprite spriteNum,TRUE
  set the forecolor of sprite spriteNum to 255
  set the ink of sprite spriteNum to 8 -- matte
  set the loc of sprite spriteNum to point(random(the stageleft),
  ➥random(the stagebottom))
  set the memberNum of sprite spriteNum to mymemberNum
  updateStage
end

on findSpace me
  repeat with x = 1 to 48
    if the memberNum of sprite x = 0 then
      return x
      exit repeat
    end if
  end repeat
  return 0
end
```

The following line of code calls the `findSpace` method and looks for an empty sprite channel in the Score to use. Empty sprites have a `memberNum` of `0`.

```
set spriteNum = findSpace(me)
```

The following line of code sets the forecolor of the sprite to black. If you place a cast member in an empty sprite channel by setting its member number, you must also set the forecolor of the sprite to 255 to make it work reliably.

```
set the forecolor of sprite spriteNum to 255
```

In the following line of code, setting the `memberNumber` of the sprite makes the sprite appear in the empty sprite channel.

```
set the memberNum of sprite spriteNum to mymemberNum
```

The objects in NOSCORE.DIR do not have complex behavior, but they all operate independently of each other and the Score. Who knows what imaginative and ingenious objects *you* can create.

Further Reading

OOP is a very popular subject for computer books these days. Visit any technical bookstore, and you will find several shelves devoted to OOP books. Unfortunately, most of them are very thick, and tend to describe in great detail a particular OOP methodology or language.

Designing Object-Oriented Software by Rebecca Wirfs-Brock, Brian Wilkerson, and Lauren Wiener (Prentice Hall) is a good choice for introductory reading because it explains the concepts underlying object-oriented design, and then presents several project design walk-throughs. It is not language-specific, so you can apply your new tricks to Lingo right away. All of this happens within a mere 233 pages of clear writing.

For more information about OOP, consider the following pages on the World Wide Web:

- *What Is Object-Oriented Software? An Introduction*

  By Terry Montlick

  http://www.soft-design.com/softinfo/objects.html

  Illustrated, humorous, down-to-earth explanation of what OOP is and what the benefits of OOP design are.

- *The IBM Smalltalk Tutorial: What is Object-Oriented Programming?*

  http://www2.ncsu.edu/eos/info/ece480_info/project/spring96/proj63/www/tutorial/oop.html

  Explains OOP concepts using diagrams. Very approachable. Not specific to Smalltalk.

- *The Object Orientation FAQ*

  http://iamwww.unibe.ch/~scg/OOinfo/FAQ/oo-faq-toc.html#TOC

  Exhaustive collection of information on OOP concepts, languages, books, and other resources. Not a good learning tool, but an excellent reference.

Summary

By now, you should have a solid understanding of how objects work in Director. In the process of learning how to use Director objects, you have been exposed to the following OOP concepts:

- **Encapsulation.** An object's properties and methods are together in one code unit. Code outside of the object can pass the object messages, but needs to know nothing about the internal workings of the object.
- **Inheritance.** An object can inherit the methods of an Ancestor script, and then must add its own methods only for any additional behavior it needs. In the MULTI and TIMER movies, you have seen how the use of Ancestor scripts can reduce the amount of coding you have to do to make design changes.
- **Polymorphism.** Two objects can respond to the same message in different ways because an object can choose to use a method it inherited from its Ancestor, or create its own method to override the Ancestor method. In the MULTI2 movie, you have seen how two of the fields respond differently to the `checkValue` message. In the TIMER movie, you have seen how you can produce completely different kinds of timers by creating a timer Parent script that inherits most of its methods from an Ancestor script, but contains its own `timerDoneEvent` method.

If you feel at home using Director objects, at this point, you might want to explore object-oriented design. Object-oriented design solves programming problems by defining them entirely in terms of cooperating objects. The resources in the previous section are a good starting point for learning how to "think in objects."

Gretchen Macdowall

How Do I . . .: The Top 20 Lingo Support Questions

Let's face it. You won't find the answers to all of your questions about using Director in the manuals, although the manuals are a good place to start. The following questions come up again and again in online support forums. If you're just getting started with Director, check this chapter first when a question comes up. It might save you a call to tech support.

Create a Custom Cursor?

There are two Lingo commands that will change the cursor graphic to an image you specify. One command changes the cursor graphic for the entire stage; the other command specifies the cursor graphic to use when the cursor passes over a particular sprite. The following command changes the cursor for the entire stage:

```
cursor numberOrList
```

Example:

```
cursor 4 -- changes the cursor to a watch
cursor [5,6] -- changes the cursor to cast member 5 with a
➥cursor mask in member 6
```

Changing the cursor to a number specifies one of the built-in system cursors in table 21.1.

Table 21.1

Macintosh System Cursors

Number	Name	Looks Like...
0	no custom cursor set	
–1	arrow	
1	I-beam	
2	crosshair	
3	crossbar	
4	watch	
200	invisible cursor	

Changing the cursor to a list uses the cast members in the list as artwork for the cursor—the first member is the cursor image and the second is the mask. When you change the cursor with the general cursor command, it remains in effect for the duration of the current movie until you turn it off with cursor 0.

The following command changes the cursor image over a particular sprite:

```
set the cursor of sprite spriteNumber to list
```

Example:

```
set the cursor of sprite 13 to [8,9]
-- changes the cursor for sprite channel 13 to the image in cast
➥member 8, with a mask image in cast member 9
```

The cursor of sprite command specifies the cursor image to use when the mouse is over that sprite channel. It remains in effect for the duration of the current movie, or until you turn it off with:

```
set the cursor of sprite spriteNumber to 0
```

If you change the cast member in a sprite channel that has a custom cursor, the custom cursor will appear when the mouse passes over the new cast member. To avoid this, you must turn off the custom cursor for a sprite channel that no longer contains a cast member.

You can set both a custom general cursor and individual custom cursors for sprite channels. For instance, you might set the general cursor to your own arrow artwork, but set `the cursor of sprite` to a hand image for two sprite channels containing draggable sprites. In that case, the cursor uses your custom arrow over most of the screen, but changes to a hand when over the two draggable sprites.

Cursor Artwork

The cast members you use for your custom cursor must be 1 bit (black and white). You can check this in the cast member's Info box. To transform a cast member to 1 bit, select the cast member and choose Modify, Transform Bitmap, Color Depth, 1 bit. If the cursor artwork is larger than 16×16 pixels, Director will only use a 16×16 portion of the cast member, starting at the top left of the cast member's bounding box. The registration point of a cursor cast becomes the cursor's hot spot.

You can create a custom cursor with one cast member. In that case you set the cursor to a one-item list like this:

```
set the cursor of sprite 9 to [8]
```

If you use one cast member for a cursor, the white parts of the cursor image are transparent, making the cursor hard to keep track of on the screen. The second cast member in a cursor list is the mask. The mask image is usually the same as the cursor image, with the parts of the cursor that should be opaque colored black. The left side of figure 21.1 shows a custom cursor without a mask. The right side shows the same cursor with a mask.

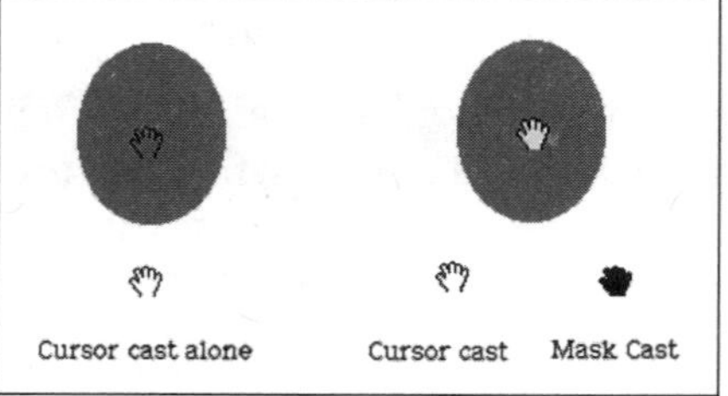

Figure 21.1

A cursor without a mask and a cursor with a mask.

Control a QuickTime Movie with Lingo?

If you want a QuickTime movie to appear onstage and immediately play from start to finish, you can accomplish that without using Lingo. Place the QuickTime cast member in a sprite channel in the Score where you want it to start, and then set the tempo channel to "Wait for end of digital video in channel." You must use Lingo commands to control the video sprite's properties if you want to do the following:

- Replace the standard QuickTime controller bar with your own start, stop, and play buttons
- Play sections of the video in response to user actions
- Synch animation on the stage to particular spots in the video

There are many new properties related to digital video with version 5, especially for handling QuickTime movies with multiple tracks. If you are a digital video buff, you'll want to explore all of the new QuickTime Lingo, but the two most-used QuickTime properties are `the movieTime` and `the movieRate`.

Setting `the movieRate` property of a video sprite plays or stops the video. It also can play the movie backward, play it faster than normal, or play it in slow motion, depending on the value you give `the movieRate`. Setting `the movieRate` to 0 stops the video; setting `the movieRate` to 1 plays the video at its normal frame rate.

Setting `the movieTime` property of a video sprite advances the video to the position specified. Movie time is measured in ticks. There are 60 ticks to a second. To advance to a position two seconds into a movie you would specify a `movieTime` of 120.

To prepare a digital video cast for Lingo control, select it in the cast window, choose Modify, Cast Member, Properties from the menu bar, and check the Paused checkbox. Normally when the playback head enters a frame with digital video cast, the digital video starts playing. The `Paused` property keeps the video paused on the first frame until you use Lingo to play it.

Place the video cast member in a sprite channel by dragging it to the stage or Score. Put an `exitFrame` handler of `go the frame` in the Script channel of the frame you want the digital video cast to play in. When you play the movie, the playback head advances to the frame the digital video is in and loops there. The first frame of the video displays, but it waits for Lingo instructions to play.

You must puppet a video sprite before you can control it. After you set a property, you must do an `updateStage` to make the property change take effect. The following code in a button script rewinds the digital video sprite in sprite channel 7 and begins to play it:

```
on mouseUp
   puppetSprite 7,TRUE
   set the movieTime of sprite 7 to 0 -- go back to the beginning
   set the movieRate of sprite 7 to 1 -- start it playing
   updateStage
end
```

You can use the startTime and stopTime properties to play a segment of the video. Suppose you know that a line of dialog starts three seconds into the video and ends at seven seconds. The following code in a button script plays just that piece of dialog:

```
on mouseUp
   puppetSprite 7,TRUE
   set the startTime of sprite 7 to 180 -- (3 times 60 ticks)
   set the movieRate of sprite 7 to 1 -- start it playing
   set the stopTime of sprite 7 to 420 -- (7 times 60 ticks)
   updateStage
end
```

The stopTime property must be set after the movie is already playing to work correctly.

Performance

If you want your QuickTime movies to play back smoothly, you must compress them at a data rate that your playback environment can handle. Movies playing off of CD should be compressed at a lower data rate than movies playing from a hard drive. The process of creating QuickTime movies is covered in detail in Chapter 14, "Digital Video: The Movie within the Movie."

The biggest performance boost you can give your movies once they're inside Director is to turn on the directToStage property in the Cast Property window for the QuickTime cast. In fact, the directToStage property makes such a difference that a newly imported digital video cast has the property turned on by default. Normally when Director draws a frame, it has to composite each sprite layer, figuring which parts of the sprite in lower layers will show through the transparent parts of sprites in upper layers. When a video sprite has directToStage set, its rectangle is not figured in to the composite—it sits on top of all the other sprites.

Turning on the directToStage property speeds up the performance of a video, but you can't place any other sprites over the video. Anything that overlaps the rectangle of the video sprite will not be drawn. Another disadvantage is that in some situations, an image of the video or part of the video remains on the screen after the sprite is no longer in the channel. You can use a transition to remove the unwanted image from the screen.

Some people recommend playing video in a tight repeat loop instead of looping over a frame in the Score:

```
on playvid spriteNum
   puppetSprite spriteNum,TRUE
   set the movieRate of sprite spriteNum = 1
   -- wait while the movie plays and the user isn't clicking
   repeat while the movieRate of sprite spriteNum > 0 and not
   ➥the mouseDown
      updateStage
   end repeat
end
```

The disadvantage of the repeat loop is that it prevents you from playing any other animation unless your script includes the animation in the repeat loop. It also makes handling mouse events a little more complicated. A mouse click exits the repeat loop and stops the movie, which might not be the behavior you want.

Contrary to the documentation, you can't preload an entire QuickTime movie. When you preload a QuickTime cast, you preload the header—a small amount of information about the entire movie, such as its time scale and duration—at the beginning of the QuickTime movie. Preloading a QuickTime video can slightly shorten the pause you get when you first play the video. Because memory management for QuickTime lies outside of Director, you have to preload fairly close to the time you want to play the QuickTime; otherwise, the preloaded QuickTime header might get knocked out of memory before you have a chance to play the video. The Enable preload box in a QuickTime cast member's Get Info box must be checked before you can preload that cast successfully. You'll want to experiment to see whether the effort required to preload is worth it for your project.

Custom Palettes

If you use QuickTime movies that require custom palettes, you'll need the FixPalette XObject by Dan Sadowski. Otherwise, all the QuickTime movies will use the palette under which the first QuickTime movie played. FixPalette only works with movies that have the `directToStage` property set.

The FixPalette XObject is on the accompanying CD in the folder for Chapter 21.

This is a Mac-only issue. There is no problem with custom palettes and QuickTime movies on the PC, hence, no need for the FixPalette XObject on that platform.

Have More Than 48 Hot Spots On-Screen at a Time?

You can either use a film loop to consolidate several sprites from several channels into one film loop cast that takes up one channel onstage, or you can use Lingo to get the coordinates of a mouse click and compare it with a list of the locations of hot spots. The film loop method enables you to have irregular hot spots, while the entirely Lingo method limits you to a grid of squares.

Film loops do not have to contain any motion or span multiple frames. You can make a film loop of one static frame. Any sprites with sprite or cast scripts retain the scripts in the film loop, but references to `the clickOn` will now refer to the film loop's channel instead of the individual sprites contained in the film loop.

The movie HOTSPOT.DIR in the Chapter 21 folder on the *Inside Director* CD-ROM demonstrates the film loop and Lingo methods of detecting more than 48 hot spots per screen.

Synchronize Sound and Animation?

You can use the Score to synchronize music and graphics events, but the synch varies somewhat from machine to machine. Differences in processor speed, available memory, video card speed, and hard disk or CD speed all have some effect on sound and graphics synch. If you can control the playback machine (in an in-house presentation situation, for instance) the following steps will ensure smooth playback every time:

- Give the projector enough memory in the Get Info box to preload all of the cast members. Chapter 19, "Advanced Concepts," describes how to estimate the amount of memory you will need. See the section titled "Memory and Load Times."
- Preload all of the cast members.
- Create the presentation in 8-bit color and make sure the monitor is set to 8 bit.
- Turn off unnecessary non-Apple extensions and control panels.
- Turn off virtual memory and networking.
- Quit all other applications and close all windows.

If you intend to play the movie on a variety of machines and there are important graphics events that need exact synchronization (for example, a certain graphic displaying exactly as the music reaches a crescendo), consider making QuickTime movies of these sections and reimporting them.

Another option that works very well is making a sound-only QuickTime movie of the music or narration. Note the number of ticks into the movie where the important event happens, then use Lingo to trigger the graphics event when the sound reaches that point. The following code synchronizes a list of points in the sound to switches of a graphics cast member. Because the code runs on an `enterframe` handler, it is important to have the frame rate set high to ensure that the handler is checking the `movieTime` frequently enough.

```
on startMovie
  global soundOnlyQT, graphicSprite, eventList
  set soundOnlyQT = 1
  set graphicSprite = 2
  puppetSprite graphicSprite,TRUE
  -- eventList: each item represents ticks:cast member number
  set eventList = [ 120:3, 240:4, 700:5]
end
```

```
on enterFrame
  global soundOnlyQT, graphicSprite, eventList
  if eventList = [:] then exit
 if the movieTime of sprite soundOnlyQT >= getPropAt(eventList,1)
➥then
   set the memberNum of sprite graphicSprite = getAt(eventList,1)
    -- as each event is passed it is deleted and the next event
    -- is now in position 1
    deleteAt(eventList,1)
  end if
end
```

Save User Data?

If you want to save the progress of a user through a test, save the user's entries in text fields, or save other user changes to the environment such as the positions of windows or moveable sprites, you have two options, as follows:

- You can record the changes to a text field and use the `saveMovie` command to save the changed movie.
- You can write the changes out to an external file using the FileIO XObject.

Chapter 17, "Managing Your Data," describes both of these approaches in detail in the "Permanent Data" section.

Launch or Communicate with Another Program from Director?

The `open` command opens another application, or opens a document with another application. The syntax is as follows:

```
open document with application
```

Or, you can use:

```
open application
```

Example:

```
open "index.html" with "Netscape"
open "HyperCard"
```

There are several ways to communicate with another open application. You can do the following:

- Have Director and the other applications communicate by reading and writing to an external file.
- Use the `copyToClipboard` and `pasteClipBoardInto` Director commands to exchange information with the other applications through the Clipboard.
- Use an Xtra that enables your projector to send and respond to Apple Events. The zScript Xtra enables your Director movies and projectors to communicate with other applications via Apple Events.

The zScript Xtra in the Chapter 21 folder on the accompanying CD enables you to send and receive Apple Events within Director movies and projectors. To use the Xtra from a projector, you must first open it with the following:

```
global aScript
set aScript = xtra "AppleScriptXtra"
```

For more information on working with Xtras, see Chapter 23, "Macromedia Open Architecture: All About Xtras."

Flush Clicks Out of the Buffer?

If you program any type of game that involves mouse clicks, eventually you will run into the problem of mouse clicks accumulating while the computer is busy doing other things. When the processor is free, all of the accumulated mouse clicks fire off, and the user has to wait and watch until they're finished. This is more of a problem on slow machines or in movies that make heavy use of repeat loops. It happens especially in children's games, where excitement generates a lot of frantic clicking.

The Mac system keeps track of user events in an event queue. Normally, Director is continually looking for mouse and keyboard events in the queue and passing them on to handlers inside your movie. If Director is busy processing a long handler or executing a repeat loop, it stops fetching events out of the event queue and they pile up. When Director is done processing, it starts handling the mouse and keyboard events that piled up in the queue when it was too busy to handle them.

One way to handle this is to avoid creating long event sequences that the user can't interrupt. You can make a list of handlers interruptible by enclosing the list in a dummy repeat loop like the following:

```
repeat while not the mouseDown
   handler1
   handler2
   handler3
end repeat
```

Another way to handle this in Lingo is to use this code before the start of a long handler:

```
set the mouseUpScript = "dontPassEvent"
set the mouseDownScript = "dontPassEvent"
```

and to put the following in an `exitFrame` handler when you want to resume mouse event processing:

```
set the mouseUpScript = EMPTY
set the mouseDownScript = EMPTY
```

Another alternative is the Johnny XCMD. Johnny is a code resource that flushes mouse and keyboard events from the event queue during the period that you specify.

The movie FlushEvent Movie test on the accompanying CD contains the Johnny code resource. The movie is a demo that demonstrates how to call Johnny after you have opened it as a resource. To use the Johnny code resource in your movie, put FlushEvent Movie test in the same directory and open it with the following:

```
openXlib "FlushEvent Movie test"
```

Code resources are Mac-specific. They won't work on the PC.

Code resources are the old way of extending Director with external code. The new way is through Xtras, which are described in detail in Chapter 23, "Macromedia Open Architecture: All About Xtras." Many of the old code resources (XCMDs and XFCNs), however, still work under Director 5 and provide valuable enhancements.

Create a Dialog Box with Choice Buttons?

The alert command displays a dialog box with an OK button and a message of your choice. It's good for displaying error messages, but you can't give the user any choices or get any feedback from the user. To display a dialog box with choice buttons, you can do the following:

- Create your own dialog box graphic and place it in a high channel so that it will display on top of your other graphics, for example, 40 or so. Position it above the menu bar so that it is invisible and move it onto the screen when you want to show it.
- Open a Movie in a Window containing the dialog and button graphics. The MIAW approach has the advantage of not taking up a sprite channel.

The movie ALERT.DIR in the Chapter 18 folder on the accompanying CD, Movie in a Window, is a dialog box MIAW that passes user input back to the main movie.

Create Hypertext?

There are two ways to implement hypertext in Director. One way is to draw invisible rectangles over the hot words in the field. This requires no Lingo, but it's not very flexible. Every time the text changes you have to reposition the hot spots. If you want the same word to be hot no matter where it appears on the field, you must draw a new hot spot for each occurrence. And if you want a scrolling field, forget it.

Unless you have a very small list of hot words and you know your text isn't going to change, you're better off implementing hypertext with Lingo. The Lingo commands that help you determine what text chunk the mouse is currently over are `the mousechar`, `the mouseWord`, and `the mouseLine`. You compare the clicked text chunk to a list of hot words and determine what to do from there. You can find more information about Lingo hypertext handling and a code example in Chapter 19, "Advanced Concepts," in the section titled "Hypertext."

Control Scrolling Fields?

To scroll a field to the top, put `EMPTY` before line 1 of field `"MyField"`.

To page or scroll through a field you can use two commands that are new in 5, `scrollByLine` and `scrollByPage`. The new commands enable you to hide the scroll bar completely with a bitmap sprite and provide your own bitmap scroll bars instead. You can find more information on handling scrolling text fields and code examples in Chapter 19, "Advanced Concepts," in the section titled "Scrolling Text Fields."

Hide the Stage?

You can hide and show the stage by setting its `visible` property. The following code hides the stage:

```
set the visible of the stage to FALSE
```

Show the stage again with:

```
set the visible of the stage to TRUE
```

Hiding the stage enables you to substitute a Movie in a Window for the main interface.

Keep the User from Quitting?

If the user presses Command+Q or Command+. (period), Director and most other well-behaved Mac applications will quit. You might want to prevent a keyboard quit in a children's game, where it can happen accidentally, or you might want to intercept the quit command so that you can do cleanup work or store user data before quitting.

There are two parts to intercepting a quit. You must do the following:

1. Prevent keyboard quit by setting the `exitLock` property to `TRUE`:

```
set the exitLock = TRUE
```

2. Watch for the combination of key presses that signal a quit, do your cleanup work, and use the Lingo `quit` command to quit when you're done.

```
on keyDown
  if the commandDown then
    case the key of
      "q","Q",".":cleanup
      otherwise pass
    end case
  end if
end

on cleanup
   -- dispose of open externals here
   -- restore the color depth of the monitor and any sound
   ➥settings you have changed
   -- write your user data out to a file or do a save movie
   quit
end
```

Determine the Size of the Monitor?

The deskTopRectList property, new with version 5, enables you to easily determine the screen space you have to work with. It lists the rect of the primary monitor first and any other monitors afterward. The deskTopRectList for one monitor, set to a resolution of 640×480, would looks like this:

```
put the deskTopRectList
-- [rect(0, 0, 640, 480)]
```

You can use the deskTopRectList to center a window on the primary monitor, without knowing its dimensions ahead of time, by using the following code:

```
on center windowRect
  -- windowRect: the rect of the window you want to center
  set windowWidth = getAt(windowRect,3) - getAt(windowRect,1)
  set windowHeight = getAt(windowRect,4) - getAt(windowRect,2)
  set primaryMonitor = getAt(the deskTopRectList,1)
  set screenWidth = getAt(primaryMonitor,3)
  set screenHeight = getAt(primaryMonitor,4)
  set a = (screenWidth - windowWidth)/2
  set b = (screenHeight - windowHeight)/2
  set c = a + windowWidth
  set d = b + windowHeight
  -- returns a centered rect
  return rect(a,b,c,d)
end
```

Make a Sprite Invisible?

Often, you will want to enter a frame with sprites initially invisible. You can use the visibility of sprite property or set the sprite location to be initially above the menu bar to keep it out of sight.

The visibility of sprite property doesn't work too well for this situation. If you set the visibility of a sprite to FALSE on the enterFrame of a frame, the sprite will be visible for a split second and then vanish.

It is better to place the sprite you want to be invisible onstage in the Score, then use the Sprite properties dialog box to change the sprite's vertical location to –500 or so. A negative vertical location places the sprite above the menu bar and out of sight. When your movie is running and you want to make the sprite visible, move it onstage by puppeting it and setting its vertical location to the place it should appear onstage.

Construct Lingo Commands on the Fly Based on Variables?

The `do` command enables you to execute lines of Lingo you construct using text strings. For example, the following line of code:

```
do "set x = 50"
```

does the same thing as

```
set x = 50
```

To include a text string in the command, use the keyword `QUOTE`. For example, the following line of code:

```
set newVar = "Potato"
```

would look like this when executed with the `do` command

```
do "set newVar = " & QUOTE & "Potato" & QUOTE
```

You cannot declare a global variable using `do`. The following code will execute, but the variable will remain undeclared:

```
do "global myGlobal"
```

You can get around this by temporarily inserting a script into a dummy cast member and executing the script. If you call the following code with

```
scriptset ("variable1")
```

it sets the script of cast member 2 to the following and executes it:

```
on makeGlobal
   global variable1
end
```

The following is the code for scriptset:

```
on scriptset whichVar
  set the scriptText of member 2 to "on makeGlobal" & RETURN
  ➥& "global " & whichVar & RETURN & "end makeGlobal"
  makeGlobal(script 2)
end
```

This enables you to declare a whole raft of globals by doing something similar to the following:

```
repeat with x = 1 to 50
   do "scriptset " & QUOTE & "gCityName" & x & QUOTE
end repeat
```

Randomize a List?

The random function is very useful for randomizing the order of pieces in a game or randomizing branching to create a varied experience for the user. One way to randomize a list is to create a new list. As you copy each item in random order from the old list to the new list, delete it from the old list:

```
on scramble oldList
  set newList = []
  set itemCount = count(oldList)
  repeat with x = 1 to itemCount
    set itemNumber = random(count(oldList))
    append newList,getAt(oldList,itemNumber)
    deleteAt(oldList,itemNumber)
  end repeat
  return newList
end

put scramble([1,2,3,4,5,6])
-- [3, 4, 6, 1, 2, 5]
```

Create an Array?

Lists in Lingo perform the same function as arrays in other languages. You make a multidimensional array by including lists as items in other lists. The following is an example of a two-dimensional array representing the squares on a 4×4 game board. Each sublist represents one row of four squares. Each item in a sublist represents one square. If an item is 1, the square is occupied; if an item is 0, the square is not occupied. Initially, all of the squares are empty.

```
set gameBoard = [ [0,0,0,0] , [0,0,0,0] , [0,0,0,0] ,
➥[0,0,0,0] ]
```

To change the status of the third square in the second row to be occupied, you would change that item on the list with:

```
set oneRow = getAt(gameBoard,2)
setAt oneRow 3,1
```

This would change `gameBoard` to look like the following:

```
put gameBoard
-- [[0, 0, 0, 0], [0, 0, 1, 0], [0, 0, 0, 0], [0, 0, 0, 0]]
```

Chapter 17, "Managing Your Data," contains a tic-tac-toe game board example that uses a list similar to the one in this example.

Pause a Movie for a Preset Amount of Time?

If you will not be playing animation in the frame where you want to wait, you can use the built-in controls in the tempo channel of the Score to wait a preset amount of time or wait for user response. If you want animation to occur in the frame while it is paused, you are better off scripting it in Lingo by looping on the `exitFrame` and using an `exitFrame` script to check the timer until the time period you want to wait is past.

Frame script:

```
on exitFrame
   if not timeUp(180) then
      go the frame
   end if
end
Movie script:
on timeUp timeToWait
  global gStartTiming
  if gStartTiming = 0 then
    -- set the start time the first time through
    set gStartTiming = the ticks
    return FALSE
  else
    set elapsed = the ticks - gStartTiming
    if elapsed >= timeToWait then
    -- if the time is up, reset gStartTiming so you can use the
    ➥handler again
    set gStartTiming = 0
    return TRUE
    else
      return FALSE
    end if
  end if
end
```

Go to the Next or Previous Frame Label, Regardless of the Marker Name?

The `next` and `previous` commands, which are new in version 5, move forward or backward through frame labels. The following code:

```
go next
```

advances to the next frame label, and

```
go previous
```

goes backward to the first frame label before the frame in which it is called.

If mouse clicks advance your movie through labeled frames in sequence, it's better to use the `next` and `previous` commands than hard code the frame label names, as follows:

```
go "Section 5"
```

If you change the frame label names, you also have to change code that refers to them. If your code uses `next` and `previous`, you don't have to change the code when you change frame label names.

Determine the Platform on which a Movie Is Running?

In previous versions of Director, the property of `the machineType` was the only way to determine the platform on which the movie was running. A `machineType` of 255 or less corresponds to some model of Mac. 256, which means the movie is running on a PC.

The new 5 property `the platform` provides additional information about the environment in which you are running. The platform can return these values:

Value	Corresponding Platform
Macintosh, 68 KB	Original 68 KB Macintosh
Macintosh, PowerPC	PPC Macintosh
Windows, 16	Windows 3.1 or earlier
Windows, 32	Windows 95 or WinNT

As of this writing, `the platform` function returns incorrect results under some projector options. The following table summarizes the behavior of `the platform` function under Director 5.

Projector Option	Running On	Returns
Windows NT and 95	Windows 95	Windows, 32
Windows 3.1	Windows 95	Windows, 16
Windows 3.1	Windows 3.1	Windows, 16
Power Mac Native	Power Mac	Macintosh, PowerPC
Standard Macintosh	Power Mac	Macintosh, 68 KB
Standard Macintosh	Non-Power Mac	Macintosh, 68 KB
All Macintosh Models	Power Mac	Macintosh, PowerPC
All Macintosh Models	Non-Power Mac	Macintosh, 68 KB

More Lingo Support

Do you still need an answer to your question, "How do I...?" Don't worry! There are many other Director resources from which you can choose. First stop—one of the Web sites devoted to Director listed in Appendix B, "Hot URLs: Favorite Director Web Sites." Most of them contain timely information compiled by users that you just won't find in the manuals. Next stop—one of the Macromedia forums on an online service. Both CompuServe and America Online have active, staffed Macromedia forums (keyword MACROMEDIA for both). Post your question online. It's likely that another forum user has run into the same problem or knows the answer to your question. Beginner questions in both forums are welcome.

After you've gotten some Lingo under your belt, you might try the Direct-L mailing list (subscription information is listed in Appendix B). Direct-L gets its share of beginner questions, but unless you're really thick-skinned, you should probably save those for an online forum.

The more interesting Direct-L discussion centers around advanced Lingo techniques and ingenious work-arounds that you won't read about elsewhere. Some Macromedia engineers contribute to Direct-L.

For face-to-face support and networking, find out if there's a user group in your area. Macromedia maintains a current list of user groups. Contact information for Macromedia is in Appendix D, "Contacting Macromedia."

PART V

The Final Phase: Beyond Director

Lee Allis

Delivering the Goods

When your Director production is complete, its scope might be that of a commercial software product, ready for the shelves of CompUSA. Now, delivering that product will take some marketing work. From a technical standpoint, delivering a Director project takes attention to many details—and practice. This chapter discusses some of the best-known tips for testing and delivering a Director production. It includes topics on testing your Director project, setting up the projector, and what you'll need to distribute with the Director projector.

Testing Your Director Project

Most everyone who's been online in the Director community will recognize the name John Dowdell. John is the senior technical support engineer at Macromedia and has taken many a Director author through troubleshooting all of the issues. John's famous quote is "test early; test often; test on all of your target machines." This testing section will cover tips to complete each one of these steps in detail.

Test Early

Test early. Don't wait until you're ready to ship your product to test what you've developed. Don't wait to take your movie over to the Windows platform until the end if your Director for Macintosh project will be cross-platform. The following are some suggestions to follow as you test your Director production.

Test the Media

From the very beginning of development, you will need to test the media elements you introduce to your Director movie. Make sure each cast member—after you import it—works well within Director.

If you import a sound, play the sound from the Sound Cast Member Properties dialog box; if you import a digital video file, double-click on the file in the Cast window and preview it in the Video window; if you import a graphic, take a look at it in the Paint window. If these elements don't perform or appear to your satisfaction within Director, you might need to take them back to the digital video editing, sound editing, or graphics editing tools they came from for further editing.

When you import cast members, be aware of their location on the hard drive. If you link a sound or graphic, or if you import a QuickTime file, be aware that the path to that cast member is recorded in its member properties. If you end up moving the linked media element on the hard drive, you will need to re-link, or re-import it at a later time.

Create Small Movies

Create small movies and test modules, rather than one large Director project. It is easier to work with small files: they take less time to save; they make troubleshooting easier; and they also will perform better on lower-end machines. If you divide your project into a series of smaller files, you can navigate among them with Lingo.

There is no limit to the size of a Director movie. This is part of the problem. If you are authoring for a 650 MB CD-ROM, you would never want your Director file to be 650 MB. Instead, you may want to create a series of 5–10 MB Director movies, all that call to each other with Lingo. The file size limit in Director 3.1.3 was 16 MB. This limitation is history now, but you should keep it as a general guideline. This guideline, of course, will change given your target machine.

If you have an idea, make it work in a small movie first. Say you'd like to create a custom slider for a QuickTime movie in Director. Try to make this work in a small, test movie. Write the Lingo code, use sample artwork, and make it work on its own, away from the large project. After you know that your test movie works, you can either copy and paste it into your main Score or keep it as a separate file among those that the project will be branching.

If you encounter problems implementing your ideas in a small file, it will be easier to test where the problems are. When you work in a small file, you reduce the number of places problems can occur. If you can narrow down the problem, you also can reduce the time it takes to solve the problem. Should it become necessary to call for technical support, for example, you only have to explain part of the movie to the person who is trying to help you rather than having to explain the movie from start to finish.

The best reason for creating small Director modules is that you can save the files for later use. If you would like to use the same functionality in your next Director project, you can repurpose the code. Eventually, you might have an entire portfolio of Director modules, reducing development time on future projects.

Save Often

Saving your work and making backup copies is imperative when working in any application, but it's even more important in Director. A Director authoring session might consist of editing ten different areas in the movie. You might work on the movie script; you might import twenty cast members; you might set the forecolor of six sprites with the Tools palette and set three transitions. Saving often will help eliminate the pains of re-creating hours of work.

You can select from four different Save commands with Director 5's File menu, and you'll need to understand the advantages of each. Regardless of which of the four Save commands you choose, however, you should remember that is important to save your work often.

When Director saves a file using the regular Save command, those changes are saved to the end of the file, leaving the empty space where the now unused version of the modified object used to be. This command takes very little time to execute and is useful when you're doing a lot of production work—importing many graphics, working on your Lingo scripts, and so on. However, use of the Save command can actually increase the size of your file.

When you're ready to test your file, you should issue the Save As command or the Save and Compact command. Both of these commands write a completely new copy of the file. The Save As command re-writes the existing file with a different name or gives you the option to replace the existing file. The Save and Compact command re-writes the existing file with the same name and optimizes the file internally. Both the Save As and Save and Compact commands will take longer to execute than a regular Save. Before you start any testing, you should use either the Save As or Save and Compact command, so the file you test is optimized and most like the final product you will deliver.

Another useful technique is to issue a Save As command every half-hour or so and save incremental versions of the same project. This way, if you would like to revert to a previous version of the project, or the power goes out, or one of your files becomes corrupted, you'll only lose thirty minutes of work.

You can use Director 5's new Save All command to save the movie and its multiple casts: internal and external, both linked and unlinked. If your movie uses multiple casts, you can issue this command to save everything at once. If this is the first time you are saving the cast, Director will prompt you to name it and to pick a location at which to save it.

Test Often

Testing often is implied throughout this section. The most important idea is not to wait until the last minute to test your production. Whether you test every day or at the end of every week, make sure you consistently test your work.

Testing along the way is most important for cross-platform development. If you're developing for the Macintosh and Windows—or for the Internet, where you won't be able to tell whether the end user has a Macintosh or Windows machine—you'll need to test your project on both platforms each step of the way. You can do most of your development on one platform or the other, but you'll need to open and thoroughly test the movie on the other platform from time to time to see how things look on the other side.

Test from a Projector

The true test of a Director movie is when it plays as an executable file, or what Director calls a *projector*. Testing your movie or series of movies within Director is important, but it's more important to test your production in the environment that your audience will have. In the theatrical metaphor, there comes a time when you need to run through the scenes of your show and have a dress rehearsal before the audience arrives.

The Director projector's run-time engine is much smaller than the Director application. This way, you can distribute small Director projects on floppy disks. What's important to understand is that the versatility of the projector is different. Playing back your movie within the Director application can support the movie playback, open windows, and other system calls. When you test from a projector, you'll be testing the true capability of the small executable your audience will have in the final production.

Many people create a *stub projector* for both testing and final distribution. This would be a projector with only one small movie in it that simply launches another Director movie, outside of the projector. Using a stub projector eliminates the need to re-create a projector each time you'd like to test the file in the run-time environment.

Creating a Stub Projector

To create a stub projector, follow these simple steps. You will find a projector named Stub, and two movies to work with, STUB.DIR and INTRO.DIR in the Chapter 22 folder on the *Inside Director* CD-ROM.

1. Create a new Director movie with the File, New command, and save it as STUB.DIR.

> The reason we've given this file a DIR extension is so that it will run on all of the Director playback platforms, including Windows 3.1. Windows 95 and Windows NT no longer require the DIR extension for a Director for Windows movie.

2. In the Script channel of frame 1 in the Score (see fig. 22.1), double-click and type:

```
on exitFrame
   go to movie "intro.dir"
end
```

Figure 22.1

This Lingo script will have Director go from the "stub" projector to the movie INTRO.DIR outside the projector.

3. Save the file again, and choose Create Projector from the File menu, adding the STUB.DIR file to the projector (see fig. 22.2).

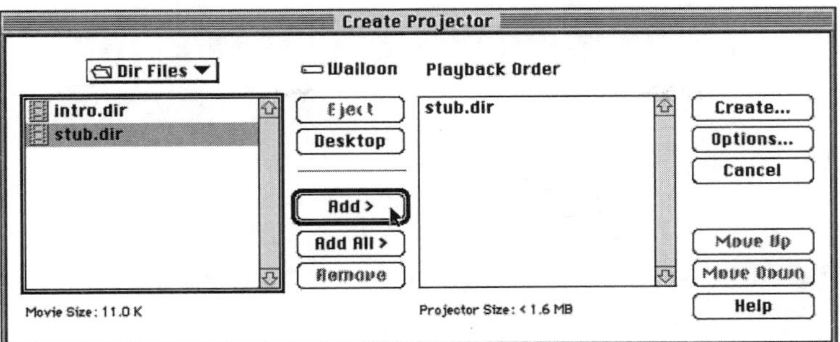

Figure 22.2

Add the STUB.DIR file to the projector list.

4. Click the Create button and Director will prompt you to name the file and ask for the location at which you would like to save it. Make sure that you save the projector in the same folder as the INTRO.DIR file.

As long as you have a movie file named INTRO.DIR, or the name you choose for your first movie, in the same folder as the stub projector, the stub projector will be able to run that movie file.

Stub projectors enable you to quickly and easily test Director movies from a projector during authoring. If you keep one around for testing, you will not need to create a new projector over and over. The following sections discuss how to set up projectors.

Testing on All of Your Target Machines

Testing your Director projects on all of your target machines is very important. If you are authoring for a multimedia kiosk, you only need to test on that single machine. The rest of this testing section is designed for those who are authoring a Director production for mass distribution and who are unsure of what target machine will be used.

Define the minimum system requirements your audience will need in order to run your project, then test your project using those minimum system requirements. Test your project on as many different configurations your audience will have as possible. The closer your testing environment is to the audience's machine, the better you can judge how the audience's experience will be.

Defining the Minimum Requirements

Director itself displays its minimum system requirements on the outside of the box. This saves customers' time and misconceptions as to what they will need in order to use the product. If you plan to distribute your Director project to a mass market, consider making one of these lists as well. This touches on the pre-planning issues covered in Chapter 5, "The Strategy."

When you write the minimum system requirements for your Director project, the intended platform, minimum available memory on the system, and processor speed are three of the most important issues to address.

Other important specifications include:

- Color depth setting
- System software
- Hard disk space
- Sound capabilities
- Monitor size
- Versions of QuickTime or Video for Windows
- Versions of the Sound Manager

These specifications might only be important if your project includes certain types of media.

Macintosh Guidelines

When you define the Macintosh guidelines for your Director project, review the Director for Macintosh authoring and playback requirements, defined by Macromedia.

The minimum authoring system requirements for Director 5 for Macintosh are

- 68040 processor or faster, including PowerBook, AV, and PowerPC
- System Software version 7.1 or higher

- Minimum 8 MB or more of RAM
- 40 MB available hard disk space

The minimum playback system requirements for Director 5 for Macintosh are

- 68020 processor or faster
- System 7.0 or higher
- 4 MB RAM (8 MB or more recommended)
- 9-inch monitor or larger

Depending on what you have included in your project and who your audience is, you might want to expand on this list or edit it in some way. Here are some suggestions:

- **Minimum processor.** This should remain the same. It's your choice if you would like your project to play on a 68020 or a 68040. The minimum cannot be below 68020, though.
- **System software version.** This should remain the same. If you require that your end user has the latest version of the system software, it will keep them up to date with the latest versions of the Sound Manager, Extension Manager, and other system inits.
- **Minimum RAM memory.** The amount of RAM your production requires depends on how you author your movie, and the machine your audience has. A basic Macintosh today ships with 8 MB of RAM. The system software might take 4–5 MB, leaving you with 4 MB of RAM or less for your Director project. If this is the case, test run your projector, allocating 3–4 MB to it. Chapter 17, "Managing Your Data," discusses authoring your Director project in a given memory requirement.

The following table shows the suggested, minimum, and preferred memory allocations for the Director for Macintosh projectors, by default.

Macintosh Model	Suggested Size	Minimum Size	Preferred Size
Standard Macintosh	4096 K	2048 K	4096 K
Power Macintosh Native	5034 K	2986 K	5034 K
All Macintosh Models	5034 K	2986 K	5034 K

The following steps show how to control the memory allocation to the projector:

1. Select the projector on the hard drive.
2. Get Info on it in the Finder, under the File menu, or press Command+I.
3. Adjust the memory allocation set for the Preferred size of the projector.

By testing your Director movie or series of movies from a projector, you will be able to gauge how much memory your projector will require. If items play back to your satisfaction, the allocation should be correct. If items are playing back poorly or are dropping out altogether, you will need to allocate more memory to the projector. Refer to Chapter 17, "Managing Your Data," for more information.

- **Minimum monitor capability.** Monitor requirements will depend on the stage size you've set for your movie.
- **Minimum free hard disk space.** This depends on the size of your project and supporting files. Find out the minimum amount of storage space your project requires, and relay that to the end user.

Windows Guidelines

The basic Windows guidelines for defining the system requirements for your Director for Windows projector are the same as the Macintosh. Take a look at the system requirements for authoring and playback for Director for Windows and customize it for your production.

This list is for Director developers creating cross-platform projects. If you are looking for a Windows-specific Director for Windows book, *Inside Director* has a sister book called *Inside Macromedia Director 5 with Lingo for Windows.*

The authoring system requirements for Director for Windows are:

- 486/66 or faster with 8-bit or higher video
- Windows 95, Windows 3.1, 3.11, NT 3.5.1, or higher

- 8 MB of RAM
- Hard drive with 40 MB free disk space.

The playback system requirements for Director for Windows are

- 386/33 or faster
- Windows 95, Windows 3.1, Windows 3.5.1, or higher
- 4 MB RAM (8 MB or more recommended)

Again, depending on what you have included in your project, and who your audience is, you might wish to expand on this list or edit it in some way. Here are some suggestions:

- **Minimum processor.** A Director for Windows projector requires a 386-enhanced processor or greater. Depending on your project, you might require your audience to have a 486 or higher. It's up to you.

  Animation speed and screen transition time are limited by processor speed. Be sure to test your project on the slowest recommended system to verify acceptable performance.
- **Minimum RAM memory.** For deciding on the RAM requirements for your Director for Windows projector, follow the same guidelines as the previous Macintosh scenario. You will want to test your projector in the lowest partition on the hard disk, and adjust the size of the temporary memory accordingly to decide on your recommendations.
- **Version of Windows.** When you create a projector with Director for Windows, it can be one of two types: Windows 3.x (16-bit) or Windows 95/NT (32-bit), but not both. If want to distribute a projector to all three of these Windows platforms, you will need to make two Windows projectors: one 16-bit and one 32-bit. An installation program, to install the projector to the end user's computer, will need to install either the 16- or 32-bit projector; but not both.
- **Minimum free hard disk space.** This depends on the size of your project and supporting files. Find out the minimum amount of storage space your project requires and relay that to the end user.

Deciding on Additional Recommendations

The following are some additional requirements you might want to require of the target machine:

- **Sound card.** Every Macintosh comes with built-in sound. If you'd like your end users to have a 16-bit sound card on the Macintosh, you might want to recommend it. On Windows, a sound card is not standard. You might recommend that your Windows end user install a sound card to hear the sound of your production.

If your Director movie plays sound and the machine does not have a sound card, there will not be an error message; the machine will simply not play the sound. A sound card might be a system recommendation rather than requirement. That's up to you.

- **CD-ROM drive.** If you distribute your Director project on a CD-ROM, your end user needs a CD-ROM drive. You might wish to specify a double- (2x), quad- (4x) speed, six- (6x) speed, or even an eight- (8x) speed CD-ROM drive for your project. Again, testing your project in this environment is the only true way of deciding on these specifications.

Testing Tips

If you're authoring for Internet distribution, you'll want to test download times on the slowest modem your audience might have. If you're authoring for CD-ROM distribution, you'll need to test from the CD, especially if your movies contain digital video. If you're authoring for floppy-disk distribution, test the projector from both the floppy disk, if it is a single, uncompressed projector, and from the hard drive if files are going to be installed. The results of these tests help define the system requirements for your projector and structure your instructions for the end user.

You might want to set up a beta test program for your Director project. This way, if your resources are limited, you will not need to do all of the testing yourself. Go online and see whether people will volunteer to help you test. Some Director developers take their CD-ROM titles to computer superstores to test their project on all of the different systems and video cards.

The results of your test can be put into a ReadMe file to accompany your project, or even a Help file to reduce the costs of technical support on your organization. Test, test, test. Doesn't sound like that much fun, does it? Then again, from those who have learned the hard way, this is the most important thing to do—from the very beginning.

Setting Up the Projector

Creating a Director projector is easy. You simply add the movie to the projector list and click the Create button. What takes more thought is how you should structure your Director project and how the projector works with the series of Director movies you've created. Like any software application, staging the delivery of the product onto the end users machines takes planning and testing to make sure the customer will experience what you intended.

Structuring Movies and Resources

When you create a Director projector, the Create Projector and Projector Options dialog boxes present you with many options. The choices you make in these dialogs depend on your production includes and your target machine. Once you save your movie, select Create Projector from the File menu (see fig. 22.3).

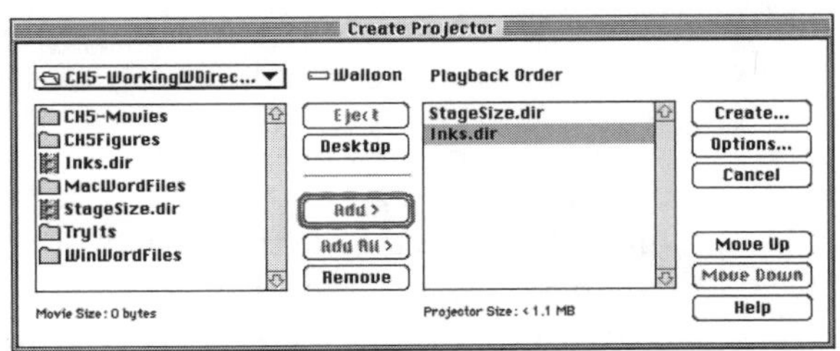

Figure 22.3

The Create Projector dialog box is where you add Director movies to a Director projector for distribution.

You can add one or many movies to your projector in the Create Projector dialog box. The Director projector plays the movies you add in the order you select. Deciding on which movies and how many movies to add to a projector is a crucial part of this final stage.

There are two categories of Director projects: (1) a simple, linear animation sequence and (2) an interactive project in which users will randomly jump between files. In the first case, you are safe to embed all of the movies in your project within the projector. Director will make its way through each one of them. In the second case, for large-scale, interactive projects, you will want to add only one file to the projector and store the remaining movies external to the projector. The following example describes this situation.

Say you're authoring a CD-ROM project and your target machine has 8 MB of RAM. Currently, the standard CD-ROMs hold 650 MB of data. Running a 650 MB projector through an 8 MB RAM partition is incredibly slow and much of the media will be purged from memory.

Instead, most Director developers create a stub projector, described earlier in this chapter. The movie in the stub projector will launch the first movie in the project with the `go` command. You then can seamlessly call between your first and subsequent Director movies with Lingo.

> An example of creating a stub projector is covered earlier in this chapter.

The Lingo used to navigate between movies is easy to use and is covered in detail in Chapter 16, "Lingo: The Basics." In short, to tell Director to go to another movie or to another frame in another movie, use the `go` command. To play specific movies or frames of specific movies and return at a later time, use the `play` command and the `play done` command.

When you set up your production for distribution, you might have a projector call to a subfolder or directory with 20–30 movies in it that call each other with Lingo. In a cross-platform project, one Macintosh and one Windows projector could call to the same folder of Director movies. Other folders can contain linked media elements, and the projector can launch the entire show.

Protecting Movies

Because most developers structure large projects in the hierarchy described above, it is common to protect the Director movies that remain outside of the projector. This is why Director 4 introduced the new capability of protecting movies. Director 5 enhances the protecting movies feature.

Protecting movies strips out all of the scripts and cast thumbnails of your Director movie. If you protect a movie, it can only be called from a projector; you can no longer open it from within Director. If you did not protect your files, anyone with Director would be able to open them. It is very important to be careful of your options when protecting movies.

Protecting movies is usually the last thing you'll do before you distribute your Director production. That is, of course, before you test it once again. To protect a movie or series of movies, select the Update Movies command from the Xtras menu (see fig. 22.4).

Figure 22.4

Protecting movies eliminates the cast thumbnails and scripts of your movie for distribution.

After you choose the Protect option in this dialog box, you can select a folder in which to save the backup of the movies. You also can delete the original files, but that is not recommended. You will always want to keep an unprotected archive of your master files.

The extension of a Director movie changes to DXR when you protect it. If you are authoring your movie for Windows 3.x, you might want to name your movie in the 8.3 naming convention: MYMOVIE.DIR. This file would then turn into MYMOVIE.DXR.

Understanding the change in filename extension is important when calling to new movies using Lingo. If a command looks for the `MOVIE2.DIR`, but you protect the movie, Director will not find it. Have your command look for `MOVIE2`—with no extension after the file name.

This way the projector can find the movie whether it has a DIR or DXR extension. The extension in the file name is not necessary for Director to find the movie.

Director 5 enhances the Protect Movies functionality, enabling you to protect an entire project with one command. Similar to the way the Update Movies command works now in Director 5, you can protect multiple movies at the same time and maintain their linked resources and directory structure.

Projector Options

The Projector Options dialog box offers many choices in how the projector plays when launched. It's easy to overlook this button when you create a projector, but this dialog box determines many important settings. The following sections cover each of the choices. To open the Projector Options dialog box, select the Create Projector command from the File menu, and choose the Options button (see fig. 22.5).

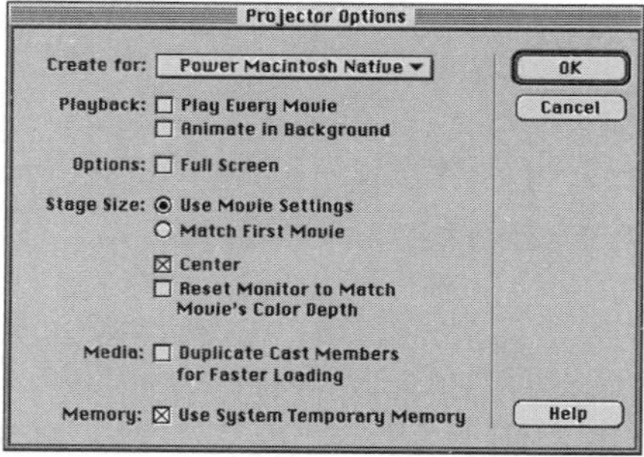

Figure 22.5

The Projector Options dialog box controls the playback settings for the Director projector.

Create for: The Operating System Option

The Macintosh enables you to decide whether your projector will run on a Standard Macintosh, Power Macintosh Native, or All Macintosh models. If you select the option for All Macintosh models or a fat-binary file, you should realize that the projector size will truly be "fat," or larger than, the other two options, because it includes resources for both types of processors. Experiment with all three of these types of projectors to preview the size of the projector. When you select each one of them, Director calculates the size of the projector in the Create Projector dialog box.

Playback: Play Every Movie

If you select Play Every Movie in the Playback options, Director plays back every movie you include in the play list. If this setting is not selected, Director only plays the first movie in the play list. If you are using a stub projector and include only one movie in the projector, you do not need to select this setting.

Playback: Animate in Background

The Animate in Background option tells Director to continue playing the movie if the user clicks outside of the movie window. If the user does not select this option, the movie stops playing when the user clicks outside of the stage area.

Animate in Background is especially useful if used in conjunction with Lingo's `open` command to launch another application from Director. When Animate in Background is selected, the Director movie continues playing while the user launches another application. When the other application plays and later closes, Director still plays in the background. If Animate in Background is not selected, the Director animation is suspended when the other application launches, and resumes playing when it quits.

When using the Animate in Background technique, loop the Director Score when the other application launches. Otherwise, the movie continues running to the end.

If you would like the movie to loop in one frame, you can use a `go to the frame` loop in the script channel of that frame. If you would like to loop the entire animation, you can use a `go to frame 1` loop in the Script channel of one of the last frames in the movie.

Options: Full Screen

The Full Screen option for projectors is a new feature for the Director for Macintosh version 5. When the user selects this option, Director covers the area surrounding the stage with the color of the stage in frame 1.

This is useful when the stage is smaller than the monitor and you want to cover up the desktop behind the presentation.

In Director 4.0.4, the Full Screen option was only available with Windows. Macintosh users had to use a Macromedia XObject, called Rear Window, or a commercial XObject called Finder Hider for achieving this functionality. Now, it's as easy as a click of a button.

Options: In a Window

The In a Window option is available in Director for Windows only. When selected, the Director stage will display in a normal window. It will not cover up the desktop behind the stage, like the full-screen option, and is not resizable.

Options: Show Title Bar

Show Title Bar is another projector option available in Director for Windows only. When the In a Window option is selected, Show Title Bar is available so that the window the stage occupies has a title bar. When the stage has a title bar, the window is moveable.

Stage Size: Use Movie Settings and Match First Movie

The first two settings under Stage Size—Use Movie Settings and Match First Movie—are important when you're using multiple Director movies. The projector follows those directions when it opens a new movie.

Stage Size: Center

The Center option displays the stage in the center of the playback monitor. If your projector plays back in the top left corner of the monitor, the problem most likely is that the Center option is not selected. You will need to verify performance of your projector on a screen larger than the stage size.

Stage Size: Reset Monitor to Match Movie's Color Depth

Reset Monitor to Match Movie's Color Depth is an option available on the Macintosh. (With Windows, you cannot explicitly change the color depth of the system; you need to select a different video driver and restart Windows.) When selected, this option changes the system setting for color depth in the monitor's control panel to match the movie's settings. The color depth of a Director movie is established by the bitmap cast member with the highest color depth.

An alternative technique to resetting the monitor to match the movie's color depth in this dialog box is to do it with Lingo. Lingo enables you to set the color depth to whatever you like, then set it back when the movie is over. This way, the user's Macintosh monitor returns to the original settings when your movie is done playing. The following is a sample handler:

```
on startMovie
   global oldColor
   --creates a global variable
   put the colorDepth into oldColor
   --puts the current colorDepth into the global variable
   if the colorDepth <> 8 then
   --checks if the colorDepth is < or > 8-bit
   set the colorDepth to 8
   --sets the colorDepth to 8-bit
   end if
   updateStage
end startMovie
on stopMovie
   global oldColor
   --calls the global variable from memory again
   set the colorDepth to oldColor
   --sets the colorDepth back to what it used to be
   updateStage
end stopMovie
```

Media: Duplicate Cast Members for Faster Loading

The Duplicate Cast Members for Faster Loading option, in the Projector Options dialog box, is a new feature of Director 5. When the user selects this option, Director duplicates cast members in the order the Score uses them. This makes the file larger, but speeds up loading cast members, especially off of a CD-ROM. It will be interesting how this new feature pans out to help the performance of Director productions. I would recommend testing your production both ways, with this option turned on and turned off, to see which performs better in your target environment.

If your Director project uses a Shared Cast, do not select the Duplicate Cast Members for Faster Loading option. You will be working against the way a Shared Cast works and will have troubles. Shared Casts are covered in Chapter 8, "Multiple Casts."

Memory: Use System Temporary Memory

The option to Use System Temporary Memory also is new in Director 5. This option is only available in the Projector options on Director for Macintosh, not Windows, because the two systems handle memory differently. When the user selects this option, Director takes advantage of available system memory when it uses up its own partition. If virtual memory is turned on, this option disables.

This setting is available in both the Projector Options and the General Preferences of the Director 5 for Macintosh application. It is helpful when Director needs more resources, but it also might slow down the system. If a user, or you, the developer, tries to launch another application in addition to Director, the system might run out of memory. Again, depending on what you are doing, whether your projector is running alone or with other applications, this option might or might not be what you want to use.

Deciding What to Include with Your Director Projector

You'll find that it is easier to distribute a finished product in Director for Macintosh than it is for Windows distribution. Many of you are creating productions for cross-platform distribution, so the requirements for both platforms are mentioned. This section also shows where to find the information you might need from Macromedia, Apple, and Microsoft for distribution of their products.

The two main issues to consider when you set up your final production are

- The files necessary to run your production
- The licensing permission required for distributing those files

Deciding What Files Are Necessary to Include with Your Projector

The following topics discuss staging your Director project: the projector, the Director movies, linked media, and supporting files. This section highly depends on what type of project you've created. And depending on what you've included in your Director project, the list of what you will need to distribute will change.

The Projector

First, include the projector file itself. This chapter discussed setting up the projector, and of course, don't forget it. If you have created a linear presentation, you may have a series of movies within the projector. If your project is interactive and offers the users random access to a series of files, the stub projector mentioned earlier can initiate a series of Director movies.

Director Movies

If your projector or main movie calls a Director movie, that Director movie needs to accompany the projector. These movies might be in the native DIR format or the protected DXR format. Most developers create one large folder that contains the projector and a subfolder of all of the Director movies outside of the projector that Lingo calls.

Director Casts

You need to distribute all externally linked casts in your Director 5 movie with the final projector. Take into account the link to the original Director movie that references them. Make sure to test the cast members and their links in the final staging area. The staging area might be an external hard drive you'll use to burn a CD-ROM or a place on your hard drive where the project is contained in one large folder. Linked casts and media should all be contained in subdirectories of the Director movies that call to them.

Linked Media

All media that links to the Director production must accompany your Director production, preferably in the same folder as the projector. Many developers create another subfolder for linked media elements. You will need to distribute any linked QuickTime, sound, graphics files, and media that you call to with Lingo along with your Director movie.

QuickTime files are always linked to the Director movie, so you will always need to distribute them with your movie.

The LINGO.INI File in Windows

The first file a Director for Windows projector looks for when it launches is LINGO.INI. The LINGO.INI is designed to inform Director for Windows what Xtras, XObjects, or DLLs should be loaded when launching Director. You can find an example of a LINGO.INI file in Director 5's directory. On Windows 95 and Windows NT, the text file is called "Lingo." Open this file to view its contents. The default LINGO.INI file that ships with Director 5 opens the FileIO XObject. If you do not wish to use FileIO, you can comment out those lines by adding two dashes (--) at the beginning of the lines.

You can use the LINGO.INI file for Windows to give instructions to your Director for Windows projector at any time. If, by chance, your Director for Windows projector comes across a LINGO.INI file from a different Director production first, it follows those instructions instead. Therefore, it is important to include a text file called LINGO.INI in the same directory as your Director for Windows projector. You can create this file with any text editor and save it as LINGO.INI. Even if you distribute a blank file, you bypass troubles with other previously installed LINGO.INI files on the users machine.

Xtras, XObjects, and DLLs

If you have used an Xtra, XObject, or DLL in your movie, it needs to accompany your projector as well. If you did not create the Xtra or XObject yourself, you need to obtain the permission of the author to use and distribute it. Most Xtras, XObjects, and DLLs, like the ones that ship with Director 5, come in a demo form. They all have ReadMe files, with the developer's contact information and notes on licensing.

Fonts

If you want the font you use in your Director movie to appear the same on every playback machine, you have three choices.

- ◆ You can use a system font that you know will be on the target machine.
- ◆ You can license the font from the font manufacturer and distribute it with your application—along with installation instructions.
- ◆ You can convert the font to bitmap, so it is appears the same on every computer. By converting the font to a bitmap graphic, however, the font is not editable.

With the rich text format (RTF) in Director 5, text cast members are displayed as bitmaps at run time, so you don't need to worry about distributing the font used in that type of cast member. These cast members are still editable within Director, at authoring time, but for distribution, you won't need to worry about fonts.

Third-Party Resources

In order to play QuickTime for Macintosh, QuickTime for Windows, or AVI files on any machine, the computer must have QuickTime or Video for Windows installed, respectively. You need to distribute the run-time version of these system extensions to your end users if your Director project includes digital video files. Ways to contact Apple and Microsoft about licensing their products are covered in the next section.

Licensing Considerations

Licensing issues come into play when you want to distribute materials—in part or in whole—that other parties create. This is important to understand for both the content of your movie, as well as the software components your movie uses.

All software applications come with licensing agreements that specify the terms under which you can use and distribute the application. If you are unsure of any of the terms, be sure to contact the software manufacturer.

In order to distribute QuickTime for Macintosh, QuickTime for Windows, or any other Apple Macintosh product, contact Apple Software Licensing. Currently, the phone number is 512-919-2645. Both QuickTime and QuickTime for Windows are royalty free, but you still need to contact Apple for complete information. On the Web, you can access QuickTime information at http://quicktime.apple.com/.

In order to distribute Video for Windows, contact Microsoft. The Microsoft Video for Windows Development Kit contains a royalty-free licensing agreement. On the Web, you can contact Microsoft at http://www.microsoft.com/.

For both QuickTime and Video for Windows, make sure to obtain the list of supporting files necessary to playback the version of the software you want to distribute. These lists are available from Apple and Microsoft, respectively.

Made with Macromedia

When you create a projector with Director for Macintosh or Windows, anything you create yourself belongs to you, such as your graphics, sounds, and scripts. Some parts of the projector still belong to Macromedia, mainly anything that enables the projector to run on other machines, without needing to run Director.

The Macromedia licensing agreement enables you to distribute your projectors freely as long as you do not charge any fees for them. If you wish to distribute your projector for a fee, the licensing agreement is a little different.

You do not have to pay Macromedia any royalty for projectors you create with Director. You do, however, need to do the following:

- Sign a Macromedia licensing agreement
- Agree to include the Made with Macromedia logo both somewhere in your software and somewhere on your exterior packaging (see fig. 22.6)

Figure 22.6

The Made with Macromedia logo.

- Agree to send two copies of your final product to Macromedia free of charge

For the most up-to-date information on the Made with Macromedia program, visit Macromedia's Web page at http://www.macromedia.com or call the Made with Macromedia FAQ hotline at 415-252-2171.

The latest version of the Made with Macromedia package, at the time of this publishing, can be found on the *Inside Director* CD.

Distributing the Movie

Chapter 3, "Configuration and Working Environment," covered which compression and installation tools most people use for their Director productions. Preferences for these, again, come with experience with the tools. The following sections list some of the most commonly used means for distribution of Director productions.

Compressors

If your Director project is simple and the projector fits onto one floppy disk, you can distribute your movie yourself by copying the projector file onto the floppy. If your project exceeds the 1.44 MB limit of a floppy, you have to compress it. Most Director projects are compressed with a third-party compression utility when distributing on floppies. If your project is still larger than 1.44 MB after compressing it, compression utilities allow you to *segment* (on the Macintosh) or *span* (on Windows) the file into a number of sub-files that are then distributed across multiple floppy disks.

On the Macintosh, most developers use Stuffit Deluxe from Aladdin Systems. You can find contact information for Aladdin Systems in the next section. CompactPro is a shareware counterpart to Stuffit.

On Windows, developers use WinZIP or PKZip, from PKWare. Feedback from the Windows community, however, is that end users are using more sophisticated installers. The next section covers commonly used installers as well.

Installers

Given the list of files you need to include with your Director projector, you most likely need to use an installation package to install your project on the end user's machine. The following are lists of the most common Macintosh and Windows installation packages at this time.

Macintosh Installers

On the Macintosh, Aladdin Systems offers Installer Maker and Stuffit, mentioned previously. Macintosh users are used to dragging a folder or file from a floppy or CD-ROM onto their hard drive. You can contact Aladdin at the following:

Aladdin Systems
165 Westridge Dr.
Watsonville, CA 95076
408-761-6200
408-761-6206 (fax)
E-mail: 75300.1666@compuserve.com or
Aladdin@aol.com

Windows Installers

You can choose from many options when selecting a Windows installation program. Users recommend many installers and often argue over which one is better. The following is a list of installers users recommend, along with company contact information. Depending on the scope of your project, you might prefer one over another.

- EDI Install Pro from Eschelon Development

  EDI Install Pro
  Eschelon Development
  24-2979 Panorama Dr.
  Coquitlam BC V3E 2W8, Canada
  205-880-8702
  CompuServe: 76625.1320@compuserve.com
  FTP: ftp.halcyon.com\local\dsmith\inspro.exe

- Freeman Installer by Freeman-Teresa Software

  Freeman Installer
  Freeman-Teresa Software
  GPO Box 712
  Braodway NSW 2007
  Australia
  tongk@arch.su.edu.au
  Web: http://www.jumbo.com:80/util/win/install/
  CompuServe: 100351.3364@compuserve.com

- InstallShield from Sterling Technologies

  InstallShield
  The Sterling Group
  172 Old Mill Dr.
  Schaumburg, IL 60193
  1-800-3-SHIELD
  1-800-374-4353

- Installit by Helpful Programs, Inc.

  INSTALLIT
  Helpful Programs, Inc. (HPI)
  600 Boulevard South, Suite 305
  PO Box 16078
  Huntsville, AL 35802
  205-880-8782
  800-448-4154
  Web: http://www.instalit.com
  FTP: ftp.instalit.com

- Setup Factory 3.0 by Indigo Rose Corporation

  Setup Factory 3.0
  Indigo Rose Corporation
  P.O. Box 2281
  Winninpeg, MB
  Canada, R3C 4A6
  800-665-9668
  204-668-8180
  204-661-6904 (fax)
  E-mail: support@indigorose.mb.ca
  Web: http://www.indigorose.mb.ca/indigo
  FTP: ftp.indigorose.mb.ca/pub/indigorose

- Wise Installation System from Great Lakes Business Solutions

  Wise Installation System
  Great Lakes Business Solutions
  39905 Lotzford, Suite 200
  Canton, MI 48187
  313-981-4970
  313-981-9746 (fax)
  Web: http://www.glbs.com
  CompuServe: go wiseinstall

You can find demo files of many of these installation programs on Macromedia's CompuServe and AOL libraries, their Web site at http://www.macromedia.com or at the online sites of the individual companies.

Summary

Remember that idea you had? Congratulations! It has just become a reality. Remember all of those chapters on Lingo, and animation, and sound? You will use them again in your next project. If you're not already online, go there! There is a community of Director developers waiting to share your ideas.

Whether you are just getting your feet wet in Director, or if you've successfully created a final Director production and distributed it, welcome to Director community. We look forward to seeing what you create.

Scott Kildall

Macromedia Open Architecture: All About Xtras

This chapter covers the following areas:

- What is Macromedia Open Architecture?
- Xtras versus XObjects
- Where to place Xtras
- Managing Xtras
- Lingo Xtras
- Transition Xtras
- Sprite Xtras
- Tool Xtras
- XObjects
- The big picture

What Is Macromedia Open Architecture?

Macromedia Open Architecture (MOA) is a set of structural interfaces incorporated into any Macromedia studio product, including Director, Authorware, SoundEdit, and FreeHand, which utilizes third-party extensions in the form of Xtras. Written in C or C++, an Xtra communicates with an MOA-compliant application such as Director 5 to add features and functionality normally not offered. This new technology uses cross-platform extensions and is used by different Macromedia applications, depending on its functionality.

Director 5 supports four types of Xtras, as shown in table 23.1.

Table 23.1

Director 5 Xtra Types

Xtra Type	Purpose
Lingo	Executes compiled C or C++ code directly from a Lingo script
Sprite	Offers the capability to define custom cast member types
Transition	Adds custom transitions
Tool	Adds commands to manipulate the Score, the cast, present Movies in a Window, saved casts, and more while in the Director development environment

You also might see Sprite Xtras referred to as *Media Asset Xtras*, *Asset Xtras*, or *Cast Xtras*.

Director 5 provides the means for Xtras to directly access cast member data, the Score, sound channels, QuickTime movies, Lingo scripts, and just about any other aspect of a Director movie. Coupled with the capability to create custom transitions and cast-member types, Xtras can transform Director 5 from a general-purpose authoring tool to an all-inclusive authoring tool. If you want to go beyond the packaged Director features, Xtras are the solution.

MOA guarantees the current interfaces will not be altered in future versions of Director, meaning that Xtras working in one version of Director are guaranteed to work in future updates.

In the future, it is likely that Authorware, another Macromedia authoring tool, will interface with some of the Xtras that Director uses, such as Sprite Xtras and Transition Xtras. Also, Macromedia will likely define entirely new Xtra types that Director will support.

Xtras Versus XObjects

Introduced in Director 2.0, XObjects were the external code format prior to Xtras. Though XObjects are now outdated, Director 5 still fully supports them. Due to the limitations of XObjects, future versions of Director might drop XObject support completely. Learning how to use XObjects is worthwhile, however, because there are numerous XObjects floating around, and the XObject Developer's Kit is far easier to learn and is more intuitive than the Director/Authorware XDK. Although Xtras are slowly emerging in the market, they offer superior capabilities over XObjects.

Table 23.2

Xtras Versus XObjects

Feature	Xtras	XObjects
Provides a way to extend Director's capabilities using C or C++	✓	✓
Has an easy learning curve for programmers		✓
Can be compiled as native PowerMac code	✓	
Development Kit is supported by Macromedia	✓	

continues

Table 23.2, CONTINUED

Feature	Xtras	XObjects
Development Kit is cross-platform	✓	
Many are available free of charge		✓
Can manipulate cast and Score data	✓	
Can do custom transitions	✓	
Can define custom cast member types	✓	
Can access QuickTime, text, and sound data directly	✓	
Will definitely be supported in future versions of Director	✓	
Can be used in other Macromedia studio applications	✓	
Provide global handlers to act as Lingo commands	✓	

Whenever possible, you should choose using Xtras over using XObjects. Even though compendiums of XObjects exist on CDs and on the Web for little or no charge, most of these provide limited features that usually do not work on both Macintosh and Windows. Because they are free of charge, they often are unsupported and have eccentricities in them that frustrate most Lingo users. While no Xtra is guaranteed to be problem-free, Xtras are more stable—in general. Another advantage to using Xtras is that they will operate in future versions of Director due to MOA's well-defined and versatile programmer's interface.

Before MOA was introduced, the telltale sign of a Director-generated product was a splash screen, followed by a pixel dissolve transition. Now, MOA offers the capability to create your own Xtras. Together with the numerous commercial Transition Xtras available, your movies can reflect your personal style without the Director look and feel.

Where to Place Xtras

Director automatically opens any Xtra located in one of the Xtra folders (described later in more detail), and Lingo Xtras can be accessed dynamically with the `openxlib` command. Different Xtra folders are accessed in authoring mode and in run-time mode as well.

In the Authoring Environment

In the authoring environment, there are three ways to access Xtras from Director, as follows.

- Place Xtras in the Xtras folder that is in the system folder. (When you install Director 5, a folder called "Macromedia" is created within the System folder. Within this "Macromedia" folder is a folder called "Xtras." The full path is as follows:

```
<System Folder>:Macromedia:Xtras
```

When you place Xtras in this folder, they become available to all movies and compiled projectors. Also, they become accessible by all other Macromedia applications that support that Xtra type. Placing a Transition Xtra in this folder, for example, makes it accessible to both Director and Authorware.

- Place Xtras in the "Xtras" folder in the Director 5 folder. The full path is as follows:

```
<Applications>:Director 5:Xtras
```

  Xtras in this folder are available to any movies in the authoring environment, but not to any other Macromedia applications.

When Director 5 launches, it searches both of the Xtras folders as well as any of its subdirectories for Xtras. This enables you to organize your Xtras into folders within the Xtras folder.

- Open Xtras directly through Lingo. This only applies to Lingo Xtras. With the `openxlib` Lingo command, you can open any Lingo Xtra (or XObject) that is on the hard drive. See the "Lingo Xtras" section later in this chapter for more information.

When opening an Xtra from the Xtras folder or through the `openxlib` command, Director 5 also can open aliases to the Xtra in place of the Xtra itself. In addition, Director can read Xtras that are marked invisible by resource editors such as ResEdit or Resourcer.

From a Projector

A compiled projector can access Xtras in three ways as well:

- As with the authoring environment, Xtras located in the System Folder/Macromedia/Xtras are available to the projector application. We do not recommend this method, because Xtras installed from your projector may conflict with Xtras installed by other applications or by the user. It also places a burden on the user to clean up his hard drive if he does not want to use a projector.
- If you create a folder called "Xtras" and place it in the same directory as the projector application, the Xtras are available to the projector. This is the recommended way to distribute Xtras with projectors.
- As with the authoring environment, you can open Lingo Xtras with the `openxlib` command.

Managing Your Xtras

The *Inside Director* CD contains a number of Xtras, but you will probably accumulate more as time goes on. Most Xtras come with sample files and instructions.

In the authoring environment, there are two Xtra folders in which you can place your Xtras: the one inside the System folder and the one inside the Director folder. Macromedia recommends placing all Xtras inside the Xtras folder residing in the System folder. Doing this makes them available to other Macromedia applications such as Authorware and FreeHand, and is a more permanent location on your computer.

Whichever method you choose, all future discussion of the "Xtras folder" refers to either one of these two folders.

You should remember a few factors when organizing your Xtras:

- Director's startup process slows down significantly with a large number of Xtras, so put only the ones you regularly use in the Xtras folder. This also applies to Photoshop filters that Director 5 uses. If you have 40 or 50 filters, Director takes an extra few seconds to launch, and the slower launch time can become irritating surprisingly quickly.
- When you view an Xtra through the Finder, there is no way to tell what type of Xtra it is. You might find it helpful to create folders inside the Xtra folder that denote the types of Xtras.
- All Director movies and cast files in the Xtras folder appear as Tool Xtras.
- Director performs alias-resolution, so you can keep a large library of Xtras on your hard drive and put aliases to the Xtra file on your hard drive.
- Director has the capability to search through subdirectories included in the Xtras folder.
- If Director encounters duplicate Xtras or duplicate aliases, it may display a warning that you are trying to use more than one Xtra of the same name.

Keeping this in mind, you should create an Xtra library that contains all the Xtras you might ever want to use, along with their instructions and sample movies. Furthermore, create folders for each Xtra type in the Xtras folder and move aliases of the Xtras that you want to use into those folders. By organizing your Xtras this way, you should run into fewer problems later.

The following scheme is set up with a few Xtras, some of which are installed with Director and some of which are included on the accompanying CD. These Xtras also will be used throughout the rest of the discussions in this chapter.

- PrintOMatic_Lite Xtra (installed with Director): a Lingo Xtra
- SharkByte Killer Transitions (on the accompanying CD): two Transition Xtras

- SimpleRedEye Xtra (on the accompanying CD): a Sprite Xtra that I wrote specifically for this book (which is, by the way, a cheap plug for my company)
- Palettes.cst (installed with Director): a cast of different palettes that is a Tool Xtra

To illustrate this organizational technique, we will now create four folders for each Xtra type inside the Xtras folder and put aliases of specific Xtras we want to use into the appropriate folders. For this example, we will use the Xtras folder inside the Director folder, but you apply the same procedure to the Xtras folder in the System folder instead.

For this project, you will need to install Director 5, if you have not already done so.

1. Open the Director 5 folder and create a new folder inside it called `Xtra Libraries`.
2. Open the Xtra Libraries folder you just created and create five folders inside it. Name them `Lingo Xtras`, `Sprite Xtras`, `Tool Xtras`, `Transition Xtras`, and `Other Xtras`.
3. Load the *Inside Director* CD into your CD-ROM drive. Then open the Chapter 23 folder.
4. Copy the SharkByte Killer Transitions folder into the Transition Xtras folder on your hard drive and copy the SimpleRedEye Xtra into the Sprite Xtras folder on your hard drive.
5. Open the Xtras folder found in the Director 5 folder. Select the files Animation Wizard, Palettes.cst, and PrintOMatic Lite. Then choose Make Alias from the File menu.
6. Reselect the files Animation Wizard and Palettes.cst and move them to the Tool Xtras folder on your hard drive.
7. Select the file PrintOMatic Lite and the FileFlex Xtra folder then move them to the Lingo Xtras folder on your hard drive.
8. Rename the Animation Wizard alias file as `Animation Wizard`, rename the Palettes.cst alias file as `Palettes Cast`, and rename the PrintOMatic Lite alias file as `PrintOMatic Lite`.
9. Open the Sprite Xtras folder and select the SimpleRedEye Xtra. Choose Make Alias from the File menu.

10. Move the SimpleRedEye Xtra alias to the Xtras folder and close the Sprite Xtras folder.
11. Open the Transition Xtras and SharkByte Killer Transitions folders.
12. Select TheJawsFAT and TheByteFAT, then choose Make Alias from the File menu.
13. Move the two new aliases to the Xtras folder on your hard drive.
14. Close the SharkByte Killer Transitions, Transition Xtras, and Xtra Libraries folders.
15. In the Xtras folder, create five new folders named `Other Xtras`, `Lingo Xtras`, `Sprite Xtras`, `Tool Xtras`, and `Transition Xtras`.
16. Rename SimpleRedEye Xtra alias as `SimpleRedEye Xtra`, rename TheByteFAT Xtra alias as `SharkByte - the Byte`, and rename TheByteFAT Xtra alias as `SharkByte - the Jaws`.
17. Move Animation Wizard and Palettes Cast to the Tool Xtras folder on your hard drive.
18. Move PrintOMatic Lite into the Lingo Xtras folder on your hard drive.
19. Move SimpleRedEye Xtra into the Sprite Xtras folder on your hard drive.
20. Move SharkByte - The Byte and SharkByte - The Jaws into the Transition Xtras folder on your hard drive.

> You can place any remaining Xtras or files in their appropriate folders. If you don't know what some of the files are or where they should go, you can always move them into the "Other Xtras" folder.

Although it might seem tedious to take the time to arrange your Xtras so meticulously, it saves time and averts a disaster in the future.

Your Xtras folder should now look similar to figure 23.1.

Categorizing Xtras by their type can be extremely useful when you are mastering a CD. For example, because Tool Xtras operate only under authoring mode, they should not be released in a compiled projector.

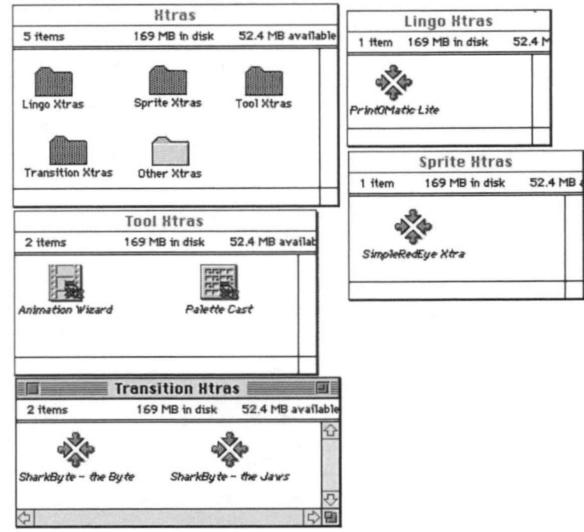

Figure 23.1

Organizing your Xtras folder.

Lingo Xtras

Lingo Xtras are by far the least intuitive Xtras to use. Most Xtras appear in various menus of Director, integrated as a part of the application; however, Lingo Xtras, as their name implies, are available only through Lingo scripts. Lingo Xtras are very similar to XObjects and execute C or C++ code directly from their handlers.

Opening Xtra Libraries

The easiest way to open a Lingo Xtra file is to place it in one of the Xtra folders described earlier. You can use the `openxlib` Lingo command to access a Lingo Xtra as well. The `openxlib` command requires the *full* path name unless the Xtra is located in the same folder as the movie from which you are opening it, in which case just the name of the file is required.

Examples of this include the following:

- The following script looks for an Xtra called Sound Xtra inside the Sound Xtra folder on the drive named Gamera:

```
openxlib "Gamera:Sound Xtra:Sound Xtra"
```

- This command searches for the Sound Xtra inside the Sound Stuff folder, located in the same folder as the movie file or projector:

```
openxlib (the pathname & "Sound Stuff:Sound Xtra")
```

- This would try to find the Sound Xtra inside the same folder as the movie file or projector:

```
openxlib "Sound Xtra"
```

Listing Available Lingo Xtras

Lingo provides a means to get a complete list of all of the available Lingo Xtras. You can create this list by completing the following steps:

1. Launch Director 5.
2. Open the Message window by selecting Message from the Window menu or Command+M.
3. Type **`showxlib`**.

The Message window outputs a list of the Xtras and the XObjects, as shown in figure 23.2.

All external libraries are listed after the `Xlibraries:` line. The prefix `Xtra:` precedes all Xtras, and the `XObject:` prefix, logically enough, precedes XObjects.

Unless you install additional Lingo Xtras, you should only see one Xtra listed—PrintOMatic_Lite Xtra.

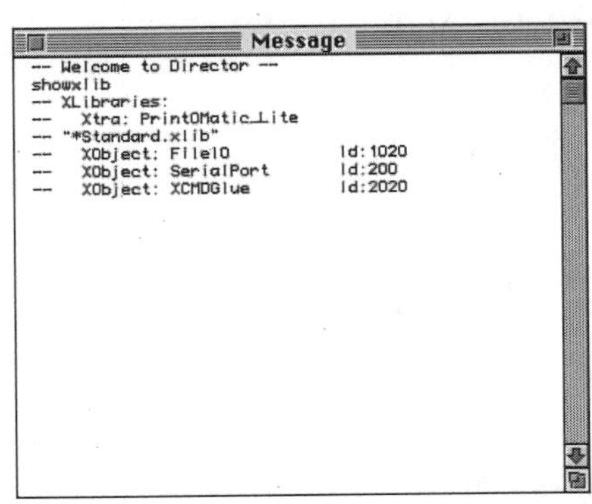

Figure 23.2

The showxlib command shows all Xtras and XObjects currently accessible by Director.

Referring to Lingo Xtras

You can reference all Lingo Xtras by their name as they appear in the `showxlib` output. This name may be completely different than the actual file name that was opened with `openxlib`. Xtras are their own variable type, similar to the cast type, and are referred to with the syntax

```
xtra <"Xtra Name">
```

such as

```
xtra "PrintOMatic_Lite"
```

You also can assign Xtras to variables—this saves time if you are creating multiple instances of Xtras. Rather than type the entire name, you can refer to the variable itself. For example, open the Message window and type

```
set printXtra = xtra "PrintOMatic_Lite"
```

followed by

```
put the name of printXtra
```

You also can determine the total number of available Xtras. Type the following in the Message window:

```
put the number of xtras
```

Finally, you can refer to Xtras by number. The term "Xtra 1" refers to the first Xtra that was opened, "Xtra 2" to the second Xtra opened; and so on. Referring to Xtras by number is helpful when you generate lists of Xtras, but it's not helpful when you use a specific Xtra.

In the Message window, type the following:

```
put the name of xtra 1
```

This line displays the name of the first Lingo Xtra opened by Director.

Getting the Method Table for a Lingo Xtra

Each Lingo Xtra has a *method table* that describes all of the handlers to which it responds, the parameters associated with each handler, and any additional information or instructions about the Xtra. You can obtain the method table using the `mMessageList` command with the following syntax:

```
put mMessageList( xtra "<xtra name>" )
```

Type the following in the Message window:

```
put mMessageList( xtra "PrintOMatic_Lite" )
```

If you assigned the PrintOMatic_Lite Xtra to the printXtra variable, you get the same result when you type:

```
put mMessageList( printXtra )
```

The Message window should look similar to figure 23.3.

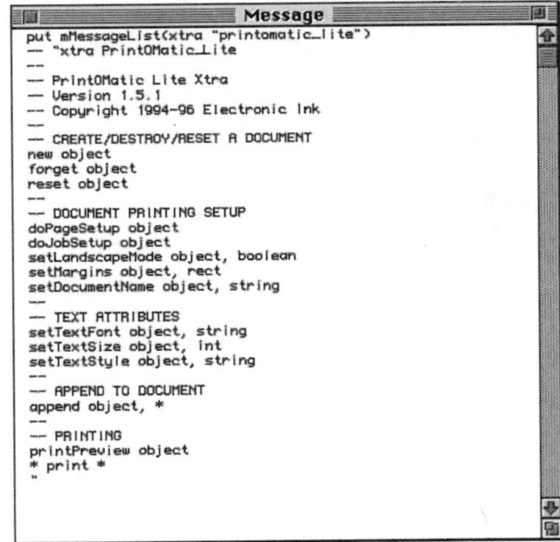

Figure 23.3

A Lingo Xtra method table, in this case for the PrintOMatic_Lite Xtra.

A double-hyphen denotes each comment line, giving information about the Xtra and its handlers. Each handler starts with an alphanumeric character and occupies a single line. The first two handlers, `new` and `forget`, are mandatory for all Xtras. The remaining handlers differ for each Xtra.

Each handler describes the parameters it takes by listing the parameter types in order, with the parameter types corresponding to the variable types (see table 23.3.)

Table 23.3

Xtras Parameter Names

Parameter Type	Corresponds
object	An instance of the Xtra*
string	A string of characters, e.g. "Natasha the Cat"
int	An integer, e.g. 3
boolean	A boolean value, i.e. true or false
float	A floating-point number, e.g. 3.41
symbol	A symbol type, e.g. #fred
rect	A rectangle
*	Any parameter

** In the case of the new method, the object parameter corresponds to the Xtra itself rather than the instance of an Xtra.*

Xtra Handler Types

Xtras can have three types of handlers:

- **Global handlers**. An asterisk (*) in front of the name denotes a global handler. In the case of PrintOMatic_Lite, the print method is a global method. They do not require an instance of the Xtra and function just like a Lingo command, enabling an Xtra to add commands to the Lingo vocabulary.
- **Parent handlers**. A plus character (+) precedes parent handlers. Also, parent handlers require the Xtra type as an argument. Technically, the `new` handler is a parent handler. Because it is a required handler, the `new` handler is an exception to the rule that plus signs precede parent handlers.
- **Child handlers**. These are the bulk of the handlers for most Xtras. In the method table, child handlers have no special characters preceding them. You can allocate an Xtra with the `new` command, which creates an instance of the Xtra. You call child handlers using a valid instance of the Xtra.

The PrintOMatic_Lite Xtra has one global handler, called `print`, and one parent handler. The required `new` handler and all of the rest of the methods are child handlers.

Global Handlers

Global handlers are powerful because they act as Lingo commands. In the case of PrintOMatic, it adds the `print` command to Lingo.

The print handler has the listing * print *. The leading asterisk indicates that this is a global handler, and the name of the handler is `print`. The handler has one parameter, an asterisk, meaning that the `print` command takes any parameter.

Let's try using the print global handler. If you have a printer, make sure it is hooked up to your computer correctly and is turned on. If not, just choose Cancel in all of the print dialogs.

1. Open the sample movie REDEYE.DIR from the *Inside Director* CD.
2. Open the Message window by choosing Message from the Window menu or pressing Command+M.
3. Type **`print "David Foster Wallace loves ice sculptures."`**.
4. When the Print Dialog box appears, select OK (or Cancel if you do not have a printer).
5. Type **`print member "red eye"`**.
6. When the Print Dialog box appears, again choose OK.
7. Close the Message window.
8. After you are done printing, close the file without saving the changes.

The `print` command is not a Lingo command, and without the PrintOMatic_Lite Xtra, what we just did would have given us script errors. The beauty of global handlers is that they function just like any other Lingo command without making you painfully aware that you are using an Xtra.

Creating an Instance of the Xtra

An *instance* of an Xtra is a variable of the Xtra type that corresponds to a specific implementation of that Xtra. With the PrintOMatic_Lite, for example, each of its instances represents a document to be printed. Multiple instances can be used at the same time with each one having its own data.

To initiate an Xtra, always use the new operator. By examining the method table for the PrintOMatic_Lite Xtra, notice that the new handler is listed as:

```
new object
```

The object parameter corresponds to the Xtra type. The new function always returns a valid instance of the Xtra unless an error occurs. By following the steps below, you can create two instances of the PrintOMatic_Lite Xtra. Each instance of this Xtra corresponds to a document to be printed. The instances are assigned to the variables document1 and document2.

1. Open the Message window by choosing Message from the Window menu or pressing Command+M.
2. Type **set document1 = new (xtra "PrintOMatic_Lite")**.
3. Type **set document2 = new (xtra "PrintOMatic_Lite")**.

Now, you'll test whether the instance of the PrintOMatic_Lite Xtra was allocated successfully.

1. Type **put document1**.
2. Type **put document2**.

What should appear is a line indicating that this is an instance of an Xtra, such as shown in figure 23.4.

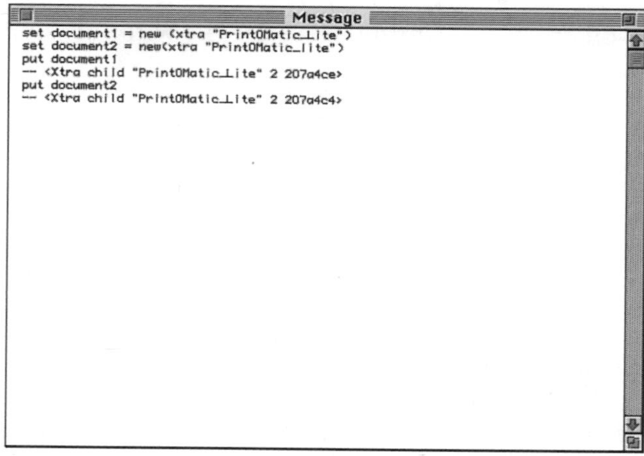

Figure 23.4

Instances of Xtras, in this case the PrintOMatic_Lite Xtra.

Whenever you allocate an Xtra from a Lingo script, you should verify that it was successfully created by using the `objectP()` function. The following steps take you through an example of this:

1. Open a movie script by choosing Script from the Window menu or pressing Command+Shift+U.
2. Type the following script:

```
on IsValidInstance theObject
     if objectP(theObject) then alert "This is a valid
     ➥instance of an Xtra or XObject."
     else alert "This is NOT a valid instance of an Xtra or
     ➥XObject!"
end IsValidInstance
```

3. Close the Movie Script window.
4. In the Message window, type **IsValidInstance(document1)**. This displays an alert box that tells you the instance of the Xtra was created successfully.
5. In the Message window, type **IsValidInstance(document2)**. You see same alert box you saw in step 4.
6. Save the movie onto your hard drive as **SAMPLE.DIR**.

The method listings may optionally supply an argument name after the parameter type. In PrintOMatic_Lite, the listing

```
new object me
```

would be equivalent to

```
new object
```

Other parameters can be passed in the `new` method, which you can ascertain from the method table listing. For example,

```
new object, int
```

or

```
new object me, int toasters
```

would take an argument of the Xtra name, then an integer.

Calling Child Handlers

Now that you have created two empty documents, try adding some content and printing them.

When you look at the method table for `setDocumentName`, you see it listed as the following:

```
setDocumentName object, string
```

The first argument of all child handlers is the instance of the Xtra itself. The second argument, in this case, is the name of the document that you see in the dialog box displayed while printing.

1. In the Message window, type **`setDocumentName(document1, "NDA")`**.
2. Next, type **`setDocumentName(document2, "Great Scotts")`**.

You can add material to the document with the `append` handler, which takes any argument type by adding one text field castmember to each document.

1. Type **`append(document1, member "NDA")`**.
2. Then type **`append(document2, member "Great Scotts")`**.

You also can preview the pages before you print them.

1. Type **`printPreview(document1)`**.
2. You should see some text on the page. Dismiss this window by clicking anywhere in it.
3. You can examine the second document by typing **`printPreview(document2)`**.

In addition, you can print both documents. Use the `print` global handler that accepts an instance of a PrintOMatic_Lite Xtra as one of its arguments.

1. Type **`print(document1)`**.
2. Type **`print(document2)`**.

If you have properly set up the printer to your computer, it will print a couple of pages of text that you should recycle as scratch paper.

Releasing the Xtra Instance from Memory

After you finish printing these two documents, you should free up the memory used by the two Xtra variables. Doing this is simple.

1. Type **`set document1 = 0.`**
2. Type **`set document2 = 0.`**
3. Close the Message window.

To release the instance of an Xtra from memory, set the Xtra variables to another value and the internal child handler `forget` is automatically called, releasing any memory that the instances occupied.

If the variable goes out of scope, which occurs in a local variable when its handler is exited and in a global variable when the movie ceases running, Director *automatically* releases the Xtra from memory. You can be slack about releasing Xtras from memory, but if you initiate an Xtra variable that has already been created, the first instance is automatically released from memory. Unlike memory management with XObject, Director 5 is very intelligent about disposing unused Xtras.

Never call the `forget` handler from Lingo such as:

```
forget(document1)
```

Not only does this fail to release the memory used by the Xtra, it might cause Director to crash. Director always calls the `forget` handler itself.

Transition Xtras

Transition Xtras operate exactly like the built-in Director transitions. They apply compiled graphics code to gradually show parts of a new frame over the existing frame. Once a Transition Xtra is in your Xtras folder, you can select it through the transitions channel.

1. Open the REDEYE.DIR file, if it is not already open.

2. Close all of the open windows, leaving only the Stage window visible.
3. Open the Score window by selecting Score from the Window menu or pressing Command+4.
4. Select the transition channel in frame 5.
5. Double-click your mouse and the Transition dialog appears. This dialog box enables you to select a transition that looks like figure 23.5.
6. Select Killer Transitions from the Categories list. These are all of the SharkByte transitions included in the Xtras folder.
7. Select The Byte from the Transitions list.
8. Press Options to view the Transition Options dialog box where you customize the transition (see fig. 23.6).

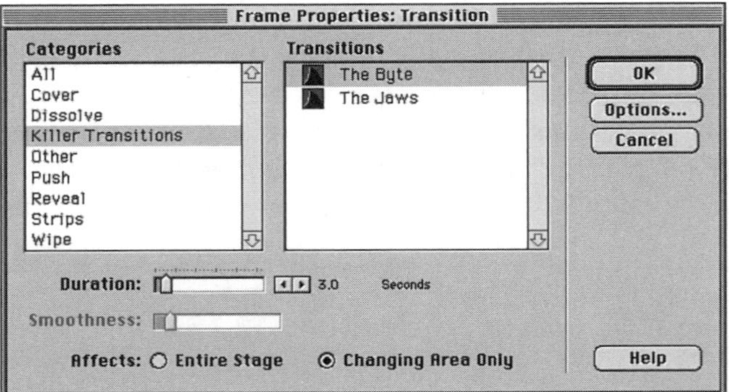

Figure 23.5

The Transition dialog box.

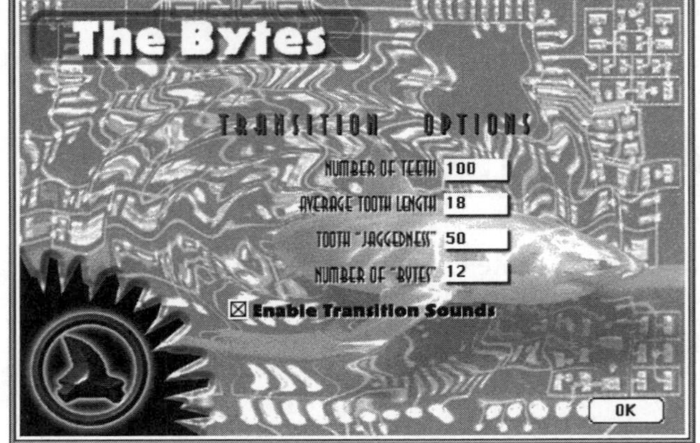

Figure 23.6

A custom transition by SharkByte.

9. Set the number of teeth to 100 and press OK.
10. Press OK once more at the Transitions dialog box and close the Score window.
11. Open the control panel window by selecting Control Panel from the Window menu or choosing Command+2.
12. Press the rewind button.
13. Turn the loop option off.
14. Press the play button and watch the transition.

Using Transition Xtras will transform your movies into more lively and original pieces. In time, you will probably see numerous packages of custom transitions on the market.

Sprite Xtras

Sprite Xtras are the most powerful of the new Xtras suite. Appearing as cast member types, they enable you to add new interface controls, graphical elements, video playback devices, 3D objects, and many more types of features to Director. From a programmer's standpoint, these are the most complex of the four Xtra types. Due to the complex nature of Sprite Xtras, no third-party companies were able to complete any for the Macromedia CD.

The following steps show the basics of using a Sprite Xtra by adding an extremely simple one to the Red Eye Software demo movie.

1. Open the REDEYE.DIR movie, if it is not already open.
2. Open the cast window by choosing Cast from the Window menu or pressing Command+3.
3. From the Insert menu, choose Red Eye Xtras, Simple Red Eye.

All custom Sprite Xtras appear in the Insert menu with a grouping (usually the company that makes the Xtra) and the Xtra name.

4. In the Cast window is a new cast member type with a Red Eye on it.

5. Double-click on the cast member, and the Xtra Cast Member Properties dialog box appears. This dialog box provides information about the cast member.
6. Click OK to exit the dialog box.

For more complex cast member types, you are able to access a few of the dialog boxes and use Lingo scripts to set custom properties or call custom functions.

- The About button presents an about dialog box that gives information regarding the capabilities of the Xtra.
- The Options button displays the properties of the cast member, which are set through the dialog box or through Lingo. A Sprite Xtra that plays custom sound formats can, for example, have an option to loop the sound as a property.
- Double-clicking on the cast member invokes a Media Editor, which is a dialog that edits and plays the data of the cast itself. The Media Editor can specify which sound file to play, for example, edit the sound file, and preview the sound of a sound-playing Xtra. If the Sprite Xtra does not have a Media Editor, double-clicking on the cast member displays the Xtra Cast Member Properties dialog box.
- Sprite Xtras can define properties set through Lingo or custom functions that are called by Lingo. Each Sprite Xtra should document how it is used with Lingo.

The following steps put a cast member on the stage and add a script, making it move to a random new location on the screen.

1. Open the Score window by choosing Score from the Window menu or pressing Command+4.
2. Select the cel in channel 4.
3. Select the cast window and drag the new cast member anywhere on the stage so long as its bounding box is completely visible.
4. Click on the Script button in the Cast window and type the following script:

```
on mouseUp
 set width = (the right of sprite the clickOn - the left of
 ➥sprite the clickOn)
 set height  = (the bottom of sprite the clickOn - the top
 ➥of sprite the clickOn)
 set the locH of sprite (the clickOn) = random(the
 stageRight - the stageLeft - width) + width/2
 set the locV of sprite (the clickOn) = random(the
 ➥stageBottom - the stageTop - height) + height/2
 updateStage
end
```

5. Close the Script window, then close the Cast window.
6. Copy the sprite from frame 10, channel 4 into frame 11, channel 4.
7. Open the Score script for frame 10 and type the following:

```
on exitFrame
  puppetSprite 4, true
end
```

8. Close the Script window.
9. Rewind the movie and play it. The sprite displays the name "Red Eye Software" letter by letter. When clicked on, the sprite changes position, changes the color of the sprite, and displays a Web address.

Tool Xtras

Tool Xtras run only in authoring mode. Their sole purpose is to assist in the design of your project. They appear in the Xtras menu and can be compiled as C or C++ Xtras, casts, or Director movies. Tool Xtras that are custom casts have a CST ending; Tool Xtras that are Director movies have a DIR ending. Director movies acting as Tool Xtras always appear as a Movie in a Window (MIAW).

Tool Xtras Installed with Director

Director automatically installs two Tool Xtras:

- Palettes.cst is a cast of various palettes.
- Animation Wizard is a movie that performs animation macros for text cast members.

We will use Palettes.cst, an external cast, to view and copy custom palettes provided by Macromedia.

1. Choose Palettes.cst from the Xtras menu.
2. When you see a cast with a series of palettes, select one of the palettes and open it by double-clicking on it.
3. You can open this cast file from Director and install custom palettes in it for future use.

Lingo Xtras, Sprite Xtras, and Transition Xtras can add items to the Xtras menu to enhance their interface. PrintOMatic_Lite offers an information box and access to a help file through the Xtras menu.

Creating Your Own Tool Xtras

You can create your own cross-platform Tool Xtras in just a few simple steps. There is a general procedure you should follow for creating a custom Tool Xtra.

1. Create a Director movie that does something useful, such as place text in a series of fields from a file; display a list of the sprites that are on the stage at a given frame with their visibility, position, and dimensions; output a log file of all of your frame markers with their names and frame number; and so on.
2. Make sure the movie's name conforms to the PC file conversion with a file name of no more than eight characters, followed by a three-character DIR extension. This ensures that the movie will be fully cross-platform.
3. Place the movie in your Xtras folder and launch Director.

The following steps show how to create a Tool Xtra that displays an image of a cat that, when clicked, meows.

1. Choose New, Movie from the File menu.
2. When asked to save changes to the existing movie, choose Save.
3. Choose Movie, Properties from the Modify menu.
4. Set the stage size to 96×100 and click on OK.
5. From the File menu, choose Import.
6. Select MEOW.AIF and click Add. Then select KITTY.PIC and click Add. Click Import.
7. Open the Cast window by choosing Cast from the Window menu or pressing Command+3.
8. Drag the image of the cat's head onto the stage so that it covers the entire stage area.
9. Make sure that the cat's head is selected in the Cast window, then click the script button.
10. Type the following:

```
on mouseUp
    puppetSound "MEOW.AIF"
end
```

11. Close the Script window. Then close the Cast window.
12. Open the Score window by choosing Score from the Window menu or pressing Command+4.
13. Select the script channel for frame 1 and open the Score script window.
14. Type `go to the frame` and close the script window.
15. Save the movie as MEOW.DIR and place it in the Tool Xtras folder inside the Xtras folder.

If you relaunch Director, the MEOW.DIR movie will show up as a Movie in a Window that will emit a cat's meow when you click on it.

XObjects

We do not cover the use of XObjects in very much detail because they are not extensions that work with MOA and are now outdated tools.

You may, however, run across some invaluable ones that do not have Xtra replacements yet, so we will cover the basics.

Overview

XObjects have very similar features as Lingo Xtras with only child handlers. They are manipulated completely through Lingo, with instances being created and each instance having its own data.

Table 23.4

Lingo Xtras Versus XObject Syntax

Lingo Xtra Syntax or Action	XObject Syntax or Action	Purpose
`openxlib`	`openxlib`	Opens the Xtra or XObject file*
`closexlib`	`closexlib`	Closes the Xtra or XObject file
`mMessageList`	`mDescribe`	Displays the method table
`new`	`mNew`	Creates an instance of the Xtra or XObject
assign the Xtra instance to zero	`mDispose`	Releases the Xtra or XObject instance from memory
child handler	`XObject method`	The term for a function used by an instance of the Xtra or XObject
`objectP()`	`objectP()`	This function may be used to determine whether a variable is a valid Xtra or XObject instance.
the number of Xtras	no equivalent	Lists the number of available Xtras

* *If the Lingo Xtra is in the Xtras folder,* `openxlib` *and* `closexlib` *are not necessary.*

We will use the FileIO XObject, which is built into Director, as an example XObject. This XObject lets you create, read, and write files.

You can access XObjects in one of two ways:

- Use the openxlib command.
- Paste the 'XCOD' resource into the Director application, your Director movie, or your projector file.

> You *cannot* open the XObjects automatically by placing them in the Xtras folder. The FileIO XObject and SerialPort XObject are built into Director; therefore, we do not cover `openxlib` and `closexlib` in this example.

We will use the FileIO XObject in the message window to write a list of high scores to a text file. This versatile XObject can be used for any file storage of data including product localization, a simple database engine, or preferences for a compiled projector.

1. Launch Director 5.
2. Open the SAMPLE.DIR file you modified earlier.
3. Open the Message window by choosing Message from the Window or pressing Command+M.
4. In the Message window, type **`showxlib`**.
5. One of the lines is

   -- **XObject: FileIO Id:1020**
6. Now type **`FileIO(mDescribe)`**.

The method table of the FileIO XObject shown explains some of its features. The mNew and mDispose XObjects are required methods that create and delete instances of the XObject respectively.

Letter codes precede XObject methods. These codes indicate the return type and parameters it uses. The first letter corresponds the return value, the second letter to the first parameter, the third to the second parameter, and so on.

Table 23.5

XObject Letter Codes

Letter Code	Variable Type
X	none (is only used with return values)
I	integer or Boolean
S	string
P	picture; for example, the picture of cast "Grits"
O	an instance of an XObject
V	variable argument list; can have different return types and/or different parameters

Creating an XObject Instance

Each instance of the FileIO XObject corresponds to a file that is accessed in some way. The following is from the method table listing for mNew:

```
ISS       mNew, mode, fileNameOrType
```

mNew requires two parameters: a string that describes the access mode and the name of the file or the file type, depending on whether you'll be displaying a dialog box. The return value for mNew is an XObject instance when successful or an error number when unsuccessful.

The syntax for mNew is as follows:

```
set <xobject instance> = <XObject name>(mNew [, arguments])
```

The following steps create a text file on the hard drive and write text to it.

1. Type **set highScoreFile = FileIO(mNew, "?write", "High Scores").**
2. A standard Save dialog box appears. Choose a convenient location for the file on your hard drive and click Save.
3. Type **put highScoreFile** and the Message window returns a variable representing an object type.
4. Now type **IsValidInstance(highScoreFile)** and a message box appears confirming that the instance is a valid XObject.

XObject Methods

Using XObject methods differs slightly from using child handlers with Lingo Xtras. The syntax for using child handlers with an instance of an Xtra is

```
<child handler>(<xtra instance> [, arguments])
```

such as, with the PrintOMatic_Lite Xtra

```
SetDocumentName(printDocument, "Fred's term paper")
```

where printDocument is the instance of the Xtra.

With XObjects the syntax is

```
<xobject instance>(<xobject method> [, arguments])
```

If you are using a PrintOMatic_Lite XObject, this would probably be

```
printDocument(mSetDocumentName, "Fred's term paper")
```

where `printDocument` is the instance of the XObject.

Now you can try out a few XObject methods with the FileIO XObject instance you just created.

1. Type **`put highScoreFile(mFileName)`**. The Message window indicates the full path name of the file.
2. Type **`put highScoreFile(mWriteString, "Susan Faludi: 90,000" & RETURN)`**. This writes this line to the file and returns an error number (zero means that no error occurred).
3. Type **`put highScoreFile(mWriteString, "Antonio Gramsci: 85,635" & RETURN)`**.
4. Type **`put highScoreFile(mWriteString, "Mark E. Smith: 82,500" & RETURN)`**.

Releasing XObject Instances from Memory

Unlike instances of Xtras that automatically are released from memory if not in use, XObject instances *must* be freed explicitly by Lingo. The `mDispose` method, which is mandatory for all XObjects, does this. In the case of the FileIO XObject, this also closes the file.

1. Type **`highScoreFile(mDispose)`**.
2. Open the high score file in a text editor and view three lines of text for the top three scores.

The Big Picture

You have covered the basics of using Xtras, but this should give you an idea of their capabilities and a taste of what to expect in the future. Although a small number of Xtras are currently available, as the XDK becomes more widely understood and used, we expect that the Xtras market will rapidly expand and that a number of companies will sell Xtras commercially or develop them in-house.

For anyone who is frustrated by the limitations of Director, desires a more original interface, or wishes to speed up the production process, Xtras provide the solution. Xtras are supported by Authorware, SoundEdit, and FreeHand, and will likely be incorporated into the Shockwave technology. Macromedia Open Architecture guarantees Director's place as the most powerful authoring tool on the market.

PART VI

Appendices

Director on the Internet: Shockwave!

Shock wave: *n* 1: a compressional wave of high amplitude caused by a shock to the medium through which the wave travels. 2: a violent, often pulsating, disturbance or reaction.

Shockwave is Macromedia's technology that enables you to publish Director movies on the World Wide Web. In essence, Shockwave is Director's playback engine plugged into a World Wide Web browser application. This exciting technical advance merges the engaging and creative power of Director's interactive multimedia with the dynamic, far-reaching, and rapidly expanding delivery channel of the Internet.

The Internet, particularly the Web, has become a significant mass medium in its own right. Shockwave is a key enabling technology in the maturation of the Web medium. With Shockwave, an astonishing set of services and tools now can be packaged into a rich media interface and fully integrated into the Web for narrowband delivery.

Going far beyond the mere addition of a new file type to the HTML standard, Shockwave represents a fundamental shift in the way the medium of the Web can be used. As soon as they appeared on the Web, Shockwave movies began to remove some basic limitations previously intrinsic to the Web.

For Web designers, Shockwave heralds a great leap forward in the possibilities, as well as the standards, of their Web offerings. Shockwave raises the stakes for Web site design and opens a significant new mass market and demand for the services of Net-savvy, skilled Director developers.

Speaking of Net-savvy, skilled Director developers, we, Sasha Magee and Noel Rabinowitz, the authors of this appendix, and partners of InfraRed Communications, have been a cutting-edge Shockwave production team since before the beginning of Shockwave.

Shameless self-promotion aside, we have found that a great Shockwave development team needs to be well-versed in the broadest array of design techniques and conventions, scripting methods, user preferences, financial issues, and competitive arguments. We have structured this appendix as a microcosm of the issues you will encounter along Shockwave's critical development pathway, starting with commitment and ending with delivery of Shockwave content on the Web. For greater production details, tips, and tricks, we invite you to read *Macromedia Shockwave for Director User's Guide*, our introductory book on Shockwave, also from New Riders Publishing. For a deeper look at site-based design solutions that take full advantage of Shockwave for Director, Shockwave for Freehand and Authorware, streaming and broadband delivery, look for our second New Riders book, *Shockwave Power Solutions*.

At the time of this writing, Shockwave for Director 5 was announced and an early alpha version put together. Much of the specific implementation of Shockwave for Director 5 has not yet been determined or is preliminary. Therefore, we present some specific implementation for first generation Shockwave and some for Shockwave for Director 5, but we place more emphasis on basic design and development considerations, which are not likely to change.

The best thing you can do to obtain the most current versions of Shockwave software and documentation is to download them, free of charge, from Macromedia's Web site. A Director 5-compatible Shockwave plug-in and Afterburner beta will be available at the time of this book release. The final version should be ready a couple of months later. Check out Macromedia's Web page for your free download at http://www.macromedia.com.

The Shockwave Process

In this appendix, we break down the Shockwave development path into four stages:

- Commitment to Shockwave
- Production and optimization of Shockwave movies
- Serving Shockwave
- End-user delivery of Shockwave

The key challenges faced at each stage are identified in this appendix and resources are outlined to help you meet those challenges. When taken together, this appendix gives you much of what you need to know to be a trailblazer of the critical pathway of Shockwave development.

It seems obvious that gaining the commitment of your client or department to develop Shockwave should be the first stage. What is not obvious, however, is how much of your attention you will need to focus on this stage of the game. To successfully gain the commitment to develop with Shockwave, you must be familiar with all the pros and cons of Shockwave, how it works, its current and potential uses, and yes, the Shockwave jargon. Even when commitment is guaranteed, understanding the cost-benefit picture of Shockwave development versus other solutions will help your overall design effort.

With commitment settled, production and optimization follow. The first hurdle is to create movies that work and satisfy your design goals. Within this context, your key challenge will be to maximize the richness of your media and interactivity, while minimizing the bandwidth required to transmit your movie. We discuss briefly the mechanisms Shockwave uses to reduce file sizes and provide checklists to help you accomplish maximum bandwidth utilization. Because it also is important to know Shockwave's Net-specific Lingo and the details of embedding Shockwave movies into the Web page, we have included references on these aspects.

Configuring Web servers to dish out Shockwave is the main hurdle in the stage of serving your Shockwave movies on the Web. This straightforward process is detailed for several major Web servers.

The challenge of the end-user stage is installation of the Shockwave plug-in into the Web browser. We suggest resources to make it easy for your end users to download the appropriate plug-ins and configure their systems.

Shockwave for Director jargon:

Shockwave: *n.* Macromedia's cool name for its technologies that incorporate multimedia content into Web pages. Shockwave technology currently exists for Director, Authorware, and Freehand.

Shockwave movie: *n.* Any Director movie played by the Shockwave plug-in running under a Web browser. Shockwave movies are optimized for minimum bandwidth and then compressed using Afterburner. "Director movies are cool. Huh huh. Yeah, Shockwave movies are cool. Huh huh."

Director movie: *n.* A Shockwave source file.

shock: *v.* To design and incorporate Director movies into Web pages. "What, you're not going to shock your Web page?" or "Yes, I can shock your Web site for a very reasonable price."

shocked: *adj.* The term for Web pages that contain embedded Shockwave movies. "Check out the shocked version of our Web site."

Shockwave plug-in: *n.* Director's playback engine running within a Web browser. The Shockwave plug-in running under Netscape 2.0 and other Web browsers enables users to view the embedded Director (DIR) or compressed Director (DCR) files. "You can't see our Shockwave movie? Just download the plug-in."

burn: *v.* To compress your Director files in Afterburner for the purposes of Web delivery. This turns DIR files into DCR files. "Wowie zowie, that 170 KB DIR file burned down to a 50 KB DCR file."

Afterburner: *n.* Macromedia's post-compressor application used to shrink Director file sizes. Afterburner discards nonessential data and compresses the bitmap cast members by applying run-length encoding. Burnt files are played by the Shockwave plug-in with no loss in performance.

Commitment to Shockwave Is Really a Commitment to Director's Technology

Since its earliest version in 1985—as VideoWorks 1.0—Director's technology has been a driving force in the multimedia industry explosion. Building on Director's technological legacy, Shockwave is nearly an ideal platform for Internet-delivered multimedia. Shockwave for Director has the winning combination in the key efficiency areas of bandwidth, performance, platform neutrality, Net-aware functionality, and development costs.

Thanks to Director's easy-to-learn, yet powerful, scripting language, Lingo, you can add tremendous interest, interactivity, and variety to your Shockwave movie without adding much to the file size. Lingo was made to order for the needs of Web scripting.

A strategic strength of Director is its cross-platform file compatibility. Director movies move gracefully between the Macintosh and Windows platforms and can be packaged for playback on 3DO and OS/2 as well. By the time this book hits the shelves, it undoubtedly will be on several other platforms. The capacity for cross-platform playback has been a crucial part of Director's success, and now that this technology is embodied in Shockwave, it serves as an ideal multimedia engine for the multiplatform landscape of the Internet.

Shockwave inherits nearly all of the tremendous multimedia power of Director. Some minor issues need be considered in designing movies that run under a browser, and there are some limitations placed on

Shockwave for security reasons. But the vast majority of Director's features are supported in Shockwave. Now, with the beta and upcoming full release of Shockwave for Director 5, advanced features such as Xtras, multiple cast libraries, and linked media will be supported.

The major performance issue for multimedia on the Web is download time. For fast downloads, you need small file sizes. Because Director dates from the days of single-sided disks, it is a natural for a world of 14.4 and 28.8 Kbps modems. With the addition of Afterburner, Director's built-in compression program, thriftiness with disk space becomes downright miserly. This stinginess with disk space, though, doesn't come at the price of power.

Usually when people think multimedia, they think of CD-ROMs and huge file sizes, so the notion of publishing multimedia on the Internet might seem a bit absurd. With Shockwave for Director, however, you can provide media-rich content with file sizes that are consistent with current Web-page norms. Delivering great content under 100 KB is no problem.

Director's sprite-based animation architecture is extremely powerful and efficient. A *sprite* is a bitmap that is given a position on the screen at a particular moment in time. A series of sprites can be shown in rapid succession, thus creating animation. In Director, multiple sprites based on the same bitmap can be displayed at once. Sprites also can be stretched, blended, or given color effects. Text can be rendered to the screen in real time with whatever sizes, fonts, and color effects you assign. You also can add QuickDraw (vector-based) objects such as lines, circles, and rectangles.

Because Director uses sprite-based animation, it gives you a wide range of tools to animate images using very little file size to do so. You might even say that Director is built on an inherent compression scheme, but it works in the opposite way as popular compression schemes such as QuickTime or Video for Windows. QuickTime and Video for Windows take a series of frames and a continuous soundtrack and work backward, removing visually redundant information within or between these frames to reduce file size. Director works the other way. It starts compactly and, taking your cast of small bitmap images and sounds, Director expresses or composes them as sprites on the screen in real time to create animated motion. There is no need to remove redundant information from between the frames; that's inherent in how Director works.

Director is a time-tested and comprehensive authoring tool. It has been used for many years to author games, marketing tools, CD-ROM titles of every kind, corporate presentations, speaker support, simulations, prototype interfaces, movie storyboarding, and much more. Now with Shockwave, you can leverage much of this mountain of content—with a little elbow grease—for publication on the Internet. And with Shockwave, you are poised for a very smooth ride when bandwidths scale up dramatically with the spread of cable modems and other broadband delivery systems.

Shockwave Lets Director Bring True Multimedia to the Web

Director is an interactive, multimedia, cross-platform authoring tool. Content made with Director is multimedia because it combines text, animation, sound, and video, orchestrating these elements as they play out in time. It is interactive because it can be designed to behave differently based on input from the user via the keyboard, mouse, and so on. Director enables you to provide user control over navigation, ask for responses from your user, and generate feedback based on this interaction.

Navigation control, user response, and feedback all help to make Director an interactive multimedia tool. Shockwave brings these benefits to the World Wide Web. But doesn't the Web do this without Shockwave? Strictly speaking, the World Wide Web already is an interactive multimedia environment. Yes, Web pages can contain text and bitmapped graphics together, but sound and video files are downloaded and played back separately within helper applications. And yes, hot spots, menus, and query fields all provide interactivity, but this type of interactivity cannot be compared to the instantaneous feedback of even the simplest kiosk or computer game! Fast feedback, present in Director movies but absent in the unshocked Web, draws in users, giving them the almost tactile sensation of affecting their environment. And, of course, Shockwave adds animation and sound to the Web.

Without integral sound, motion, and tactile interaction, the communication potential of the Web has been seriously hampered. Before

Shockwave, multimedia on the Web was more like multiple personality disorder. Text and bitmaps were integral on the page, but sound and video lived isolated in their lonely windows, unsynchronized, disintegrated, and out of context. Animated or sync-sound messages could be offered only via QuickTime or Java. Large QuickTime downloads are slow and nonresponsive at best, and at worst are not an option at all for most users. Java applets are very costly to author, and Java's implementation of multimedia is limiting.

Shockwave bursts through these barriers by utilizing Director's power to drastically shrink both the development costs and the network bandwidth needed to convey sound and motion on the Internet.

Nailing the Arguments for Using Shockwave

The following are what we have found to be the most compelling arguments in favor of using Shockwave to deliver multimedia content on the Web:

- Shockwave enjoys excellent market penetration and is running under the most popular browsers. It is, therefore, a strategic mass medium in its own right. As of this writing, Macromedia has had well over one million downloads of the Shockwave for Director Plug-in.
- Shockwave adds to existing Web technology by being HTML-compliant. This feature makes it easy to enhance existing Web pages with Shockwave content.
- Shockwave uses the Director development environment and playback engine for the best Internet multimedia with the least-expensive and fastest development.
- Shockwave adds rich media to Web pages without devouring big bandwidth.
- By adding deep interactivity, animation, and sound to Web pages, Shockwave enables many new Web applications.
- As more and more sites begin to use Shockwave, sites that don't will be left behind.

The World Widespread Web

All the most popular Web browsers will incorporate the Shockwave plug-in. At press time, the Shockwave plug-in has been implemented or announced for Netscape, SGI's WebFORCE, the Microsoft Internet Explorer, and CompuServe. This represents 80 percent of all users of the Web, or an estimated 15 million users.

Utilizing Current Web Technology

Director movies with their DIR file extension are recognized in the HTML standard. DIR files have their own MIME type. There is a new HTML tag, `<embed>`, which references the URL of your Director movie and positions the playback stage within your Web page.

Incorporating DIR files into your HTML is just as easy as embedding a GIF or any bitmap. In fact, much of the work to be done in shocking the Web is immediate replacement of static bitmaps with animated versions of your familiar billboards and logos. In terms of updating your HTML, it couldn't be easier. To include a GIF image in a Web page, for example, you could use the following line:

```
<img src="fish.gif" height=48 width=64 alt="Fish image">
```

The process of embedding a Director movie is just as simple:

```
<embed src="fish.dcr" height=48 width=64>
```

Director Is the Standard

There are more than 250,000 multimedia developers already using Director. Director was designed to be approachable as well as powerful, and is being used in many diverse settings, including in-house corporate communications departments, interactive titles development, game development, and more. It has proven to be the most enabling technology for multimedia in general.

In contrast, Sun Microsystems' Java development language is significantly more complex. Whereas Java is a tremendous advance for the

Internet, it is not the best choice for multimedia. Because Java is a full-blown programming language, it has a much higher learning curve. Just as not everybody can learn to use C++, not everyone can afford the commitment to learn Java.

The second advantage Director has over Java for multimedia is its robust multimedia feature set. In Director's 10 years of evolution, Macromedia has included a large number of built-in multimedia features that make development of animations or interactive multimedia pieces downright easy, and often even fun. Director takes care of the dirty work, handling things like layering, interpolated motion, and timing, leaving you free to actually communicate. From basic buttons to fully implemented applications, multimedia takes many times longer to develop in Java than in Director, even after you learn the language.

Rich Media, Thrifty Bandwidth

Shockwave is perfect for adding rich media to your Web pages. By using sound and animation, shocked Web sites command more attention, have more impact, and are more memorable.

Every Web user has had the experience of waiting for a graphic-laden page to download. With the advent of motion-based media such as QuickTime, this problem only gets worse. Shockwave, however, makes very efficient use of bandwidth, often better than static images.

It's not just what you say, it's how you say it. Why is integrated multimedia so much cooler than scattered partial-media? Because you get the following:

- A TV-like experience (in the *positive* sense!)
- Sound
- Helpful eye-grabbers to guide the user
- Better user feedback
- Complex behaviors

New Capabilities Means New Applications and New Expectations

With the new capabilities Shockwave adds to the Web, new applications become possible. Things like complex navigation, deep interfaces, real-time graphing, games, and puzzles are things you can create with Shockwave today. Shockwave developers have only scratched the surface of the new possibilities, however, and the near future will bring many new uses as yet undreamed of.

As more and more sites are shocked or Java-enhanced, users will come to expect motion and rich interactivity. Sites that use only static graphics will seem like all-text sites do today—old-fashioned.

Production and Optimization

This section contains several useful items that will give you some easy-to-refer-to tools to use as you create Shockwave movies. There are three checklists:

- Starting a new Director movie
- File size reduction
- Things to avoid

There also is a reference of Net-specific Lingo and new features of Shockwave for Director 5, as well as a reference for the `embed` HTML command.

Checklist for Starting a New Director Movie for Shockwave

- Set default palette to System-Windows in the Movie Info dialog box (choose File, Movie Info).

- Set your monitor's color depth to 256 colors (8 bits) if you are using a Macintosh.
- Set your stage to the desired height and width in the Preferences dialog box (choose File, Preferences). All other preferences are overridden when you compress the file in Afterburner.

Checklist for File Size Reduction

- Remove all unused cast members from the cast.
- Only use very short sounds sampled at 8 bits, 11.025 KHz, mono.
- Reduce the bit depth of bitmapped cast members as far as possible; 1 bit is preferred.
- Use QuickDraw objects for all lines, circles, rectangles, and textures.
- Reduce large textured areas to a mosaic of tiled bitmaps if possible.
- Use ink and color effects and scaling instead of adding cast members.

Checklist of Things to Avoid in Your Movies

Though major limitations have been removed, some limitations still remain. The following are a summary of things that are either not supported in Shockwave or are perilous to use on the Web and therefore should be avoided.

- Functions other than tempo settings in the time channel don't work (Wait For commands don't work).
- Palette cycling is tweaky and annoying to most users.
- Don't use nonstandard audio sampling rates (use 11.050 or 22.1 KHz only).

- Make sure any QuickDraw text in your movie uses only standard fonts.
- Don't use long repeat loops because they tie up the system while they execute. Use short repeat loops or loop by moving between frames instead.
- Don't use Movie in a Window.
- Don't use fileIO commands.

New Lingo for Shockwave

Several new commands are available for accessing the network from Director Lingo scripts. This section lists each of these new commands and functions and explains their usage.

Because the network is essentially an asynchronous place—that is, it takes time to get things from the Net, and in the meantime, Director can continue to interact with the user—most of the network commands involve starting an operation, checking to see whether it has completed, then getting the results. This is different from most Lingo commands, which immediately return the result.

Three commands are available to start asynchronous operations, and one to preload into cache. Note that a uniform resource identifier (URI) is a more general specification than a uniform resource locator (URL). But for practical purposes, they can be considered identical.

- **GetNetText uri.** This command starts the retrieval of an HTTP item, to be read by Lingo as text. The uri parameter is a uniform resource identifier that specifies the HTTP item to be retrieved. At present, only HTTP URLs are supported as valid uri parameters.
- **PreloadNetThing uri.** This command starts preloading an HTTP item into the local file cache. The uri parameter is a uniform resource identifier that specifies the HTTP item to be referenced. At present, only HTTP URLs are supported as valid uri parameters.

  In general, an item that has been preloaded can be accessed immediately, because it is taken from the local disk cache rather than from the network. However, it is impossible to determine when an item may be removed from the local disk cache.

Two functions enable a Lingo script to determine the state of the asynchronous operation:

- **NetDone().** This function returns true when the asynchronous network operation is finished. Until that point, it returns false.
- **NetError().** This function returns the empty string until the asynchronous network operation is finished. Then it returns OK if the operation completed successfully, or a string describing the error if it failed to complete successfully.

After an asynchronous operation has finished, three functions are available to retrieve the results:

- **NetTextResult().** This function returns the text result of the operation. For a GetNetText operation, this is the text of the HTTP item.
- **NetMIME().** This function returns the MIME type of the HTTP item.
- **NetLastModDate().** This function returns the last modified date string from the HTTP header for the item.

  Note, however, that the `NetTextResult`, `NetMIME`, and `NetLastModDate` functions can be called only from the time `NetDone` or `NetError` report that the operation is complete until the next operation starts. When the next operation starts, the results of the previous operation are discarded in order to preserve memory space.

One command can be used to abort a network operation that is in progress:

- **NetAbort.** This command aborts a network operation without waiting for a result.

It is possible to have more than one operation active at a time. When two operations start, however, the Lingo script needs a way to identify them. After an operation starts and until the next operation begins, the following function can be called to retrieve a unique identifier for that operation:

- **NetOperationID().** This function returns a unique identifier for the last asynchronous operation that was started.

Each of the functions NetDone, NetError, NetTextResult, NetMIME, NetLastModDate, and NetAbort take as an optional parameter the unique identifier of an operation unique identifier returned by NetOperationID.

In addition, there are two more asynchronous commands:

- **GoToNetMovie uri.** This command retrieves and goes to a new Director movie from the network. The uri parameter is a uniform resource identifier that specifies the HTTP item that contains the movie. At present, only HTTP URLs are supported as valid uri parameters.
- **GoToNetPage uri.** This command opens an arbitrary URI, whether it is a Director movie or not. Because this involves invoking the Internet browser to determine the type of item being opened and to handle it appropriately, it is a less efficient operation than GoToNetMovie, which assumes that the item must be a Director movie, and which therefore handles the entire operation within the Director Player.

Some Prior Limitations of Shockwave Have Been Removed

The major limitations of the first generation Shockwave—no linked media and no XObjects—have been removed. Shockwave for Director 5 supports several types of external files, including Xtras, linked media, and external casts.

Xtras are a new type of application extension in Director 5, created using the Macromedia Open Architecture (MOA). Director supports all three types of Xtras that can be used at playback time: Transition Xtras, Sprite Xtras, and Lingo Xtras. Like Director 5, Shockwave continues to support the earlier XObject extensions.

Additionally, Shockwave for Director 5 supports linked files and external casts. Linked files provide ways to support media too large to stream in real time during playback, such as large bitmapped images, sounds, and QuickTime movies. External casts provide ways to dynamically update and expand a movie.

New in Shockwave for Director 5

Shockwave for Director 5 supports nearly all the new features in Director 5, and adds some enhanced features of its own.

- **Support for Director 5 Features.**
- **Multiple Cast Support.** Shockwave for Director 5 provides authors the opportunity to utilize multiple casts in the design of the shocked content. Multiple casts can be downloaded separately and stored in the Shockwave "support" folder. Once installed, Shockwave movies can access different cast alternatives based on user's selection while interacting with the movie. Taking advantage of multiple casts, authors can incorporate Score templates into the design of their content, which enhances the interactivity for the user and offers improved development efficiency for the author.
- **Linked Media Support.** Shockwave authors will, for the first time, be able to take advantage of linked media in the design of the shocked content. Linked media may be downloaded separately and stored in the Shockwave "support" folder and then accessed during the playback of Shockwave content.
- **Rich Format/Anti-Aliased Text Support.** Shockwave for Director 5 carries over the built-in support for rich text formatting (kerning, tracking, line spacing, tabs, and indents) and anti-aliased text featured in Director 5. This enables Shockwave authors to enhance the presentation of text elements in their shocked movies.
- **Extended Lingo Commands.** Shockwave for Director 5 provides access to the variety of new Lingo extensions available with Director 5, with the exception of commands and expressions disabled to ensure "safe playback" over the network.
- **Xtra Support.** Shockwave for Director 5 offers support for Lingo, cast, and transition Xtras. This feature enables Shockwave developers to take advantage of the broad range of Lingo, transition, and tool Xtra's being created for Director 5 and the Macromedia Open Architecture. In the future, developers can look forward to the release of Xtras targeted at the needs of Shockwave developers (that is, Xtras that offer support for streaming audio and video).

- **Afterburner as a Tool Xtra.** Afterburner for Director 5 has been integrated into the Director 5 authoring environment as a tool Xtra, which simplifies the process of creating Shocked movies.
- **Director 4.0 Compatibility.** Shockwave for Director 5 will play DIR, DXR, and DCR files created using Director 4.0. This backward compatibility smooths the transition from 4.0 to 5 by permitting site developers to distribute a single plug-in for both their existing collection of Director 4.0-based shocked movies and for their new content created using Director 5.
- **Improved Playback Performance.** Like Director 5, Shockwave for Director 5 offers up to a 50-percent improvement in the execution of Lingo scripts, which results in higher performance, more responsive playback, and interactivity.
- **Background Color Support.** Authors can set the background color of the embed rectangle (for example, the set the embed tag parameter) that appears while a movie is being downloaded, which provides a smooth transition to the Shockwave movie when it arrives.
- **Added Security.** Shockwave for Director 5 disables specific Director features to further ensure unauthorized access to files on the user's file system.

Writing HTML for Shockwave—Quick Reference

The HTML tag to embed a Shockwave movie is the following:

```
<embed>
```

The parameters are as follows:

<TC Mini> **Parameter**	***Description***	***Example***
src	url of the movie	src="Movies/movie.dcr"
height	height of the movie	height=300
width	width of the movie	width=400

When writing HTML for shocked Web pages, remember to specify the height and width of the movies. This speeds up the layout of the page and omitting this can have unpredictable effects.

Finally, embed no more than three Shockwave movies in a single page and avoid multiple movies with audio on the same page.

Shockwave for Director 5 supports embed tags that set the background color and color palette of the user's screen. See your Shockwave for Director 5 documentation for specific implementation.

File Compression in Shockwave

Compression is a term applied to all methods of reducing file sizes or bitstreams. Compressing digital files has the benefit of reducing the bandwidth needed to store or transmit that file. In designing Shockwave, Macromedia understood that download time, and thus file size, is of paramount importance in Internet multimedia.

Typical Download Times by Content and Channel Speed

Tables A.1, A.2, and A.3 provide details of typical download times for common modem throughputs, ISDN throughput for a single B channel, and representative throughput on a shared 10.0 Mbps cable.

Table A.1

Common Modem Throughputs

Channel Speed	Typical Content	Size	Download Time
14.4 Kbps	Small graphics and animation	30 KB	20 seconds
14.4 Kbps	Small complete title	100–200 KB	1–2 minutes
14.4 Kbps	Short video clip	500 KB	8–10 minutes
28.8 Kbps	Small graphics and animation	30 KB	10 seconds
28.8 Kbps	Small complete title	100–200 KB	30–60 seconds
28.8 Kbps	Short video clip	500 KB	2–3 minutes

Table A.2

ISDN Throughput When Using a Single B Channel

Channel Speed	Typical Content	Size	Download Time
56 Kbps	Small graphics and animation	30 KB	5 seconds
56 Kbps	Small complete title	100–200 KB	15–30 seconds
56 Kbps	Short video clip	500 KB	1 minute
56 Kbps	Full-size title	1 MB	2 minutes

Table A.3

Representative Throughput on a Shared 10.0 Mbps Cable Modem or Ethernet LAN

Channel Speed	Typical Content	Size	Download Time
1.5 Mbps	Small graphics and animation	30 KB	less than 1 second
1.5 Mbps	Small complete title	100–200 KB	1 second
1.5 Mbps	Short video clip	500 KB	3 seconds
1.5 Mbps	Full-size title	1 MB	6 seconds
1.5 Mbps	Title with full video	2 MB and sound	12 seconds
1.5 Mbps	MPEG video stream	–	Continuous

Note: 1.5 Mbps is also roughly the throughput of a single-speed CD-ROM.

As mentioned earlier, Director is highly bandwidth efficient to begin with. Its built-in file structure can be thought of as an inherent compression scheme. Director's use of sprite-based animation, vector font support, QuickDraw objects, scaling, and ink effects enables you to build complex motion and imagery without creating a huge file.

Shockwave takes compression one step further. Shockwave contains a dedicated file compression technology for Shockwave called Afterburner. With Afterburner, you can reduce download times by 40–70 percent. Conversely, Afterburner enables you to include much more content within a file the same size as an unburnt movie.

Using Afterburner

Afterburner couldn't be easier to use. If you are using the first generation Afterburner, open your DIR from the Afterburner application. You are prompted with a standard Save dialog box. Just tell it which folder to save into and give it a file name. As the default file name, Afterburner presents the name of the active movie with the extension DCR. Another, even simpler, way to burn is to drag your file over the Afterburner icon and follow the same procedure.

In Shockwave for Director 5, Afterburner runs as an Xtra. Select Afterburner from the Director 5 Xtras menu. (To appear in this menu, Afterburner must be installed in the Xtras subdirectory within the directory containing the Director 5 application.) Note that the Afterburner Xtra works on the currently active Director movie.

How Afterburner Works

Every form of compression has a CODEC (COmpressor/DECompressor) algorithm that enables computers to shrink or compress file sizes and then expand or decompress the file later. In Shockwave, Afterburner acts as the compressor and the Shockwave plug-in acts as the decompressor.

Afterburner takes in Director movies (DIR files), crunches them down in size, and spits them out as DCR files (for Director CompRessed). These DCR files are zapped across the Net, then decompressed and played back by the Shockwave plug-in. The process is often referred to as *burning a file*, and the resulting compressed files are often called *burnt files*.

In Shockwave, Afterburned files play back just like the uncompressed original Director file. There is no loss of performance. The only thing you lose is another excuse to take a coffee break while waiting to download uncompressed files.

The first release of Afterburner simply compresses graphics files. Future releases, however, will include audio compression and more graphics compression options.

Afterburner opens up a whole world of creative possibilities to Director developers designing for the Web because it gives you approximately twice the bandwidth to play in. This will enable much more detailed images, more sound, and more involved interactivity.

Interestingly, Afterburner has proven in many cases to be a more compact technique for compressing static bitmaps than GIF or JPEG. One test, for example, revealed that a Director movie that contains just an 8-bit PICT image of 132 KB can be turned into a 44 KB DCR. Imagine that! The same image saved as a GIF is 77 KB.

As Shockwave is becoming a standard for the well-equipped Web user, it makes sense to use Afterburned movies not only for animations and sound, but for simple static images as well. Of course, compression will vary case by case, but in general, the compression ratios in Afterburner are phenomenal.

How Good Is Compression with Afterburner?

In evaluating the usefulness of any compression scheme, you have to ask several questions. What is the compression ratio? Is it lossless or lossy? What are the processing requirements for both compression and decompression? The following sections answer these questions.

Compression Ratio

Comparing the size of the uncompressed Director file with the compressed Afterburner file yields what is known as the compression ratio for Afterburner. There are several factors that determine how small a Director movie will burn. For one thing, Afterburner does not yet compress the audio portion of the DIR file (the sound cast members). It is a real winner, however, in compressing the bitmapped cast members.

Compression Schemes: Lossy and Lossless

In general, compression schemes are either lossless or lossy (no better words have been invented, unfortunately). *Lossy compression* shrinks file sizes by permanently removing nonessential, irrelevant, or redundant information. The resulting file is forever degraded. This is an acceptable compromise for many kinds of media files for which quality is happily sacrificed for a commensurate reduction in file size. There are many sophisticated lossy compression schemes, such as MPEG, JPEG, and Cinepak, but we are not so concerned with them here.

The most direct method of lossy compression is to simply throw out information, a technique called *bit reduction*. Reducing the bit depth or the resolution of bitmapped images, for example, dramatically reduces file size, as does reducing the sampling frequency or bit depth of audio files. For images, dithering can be used to lessen the degradation that results, and lost color information can be restored or simulated later using other techniques. We use these methods frequently when authoring Shockwave movies.

Lossless compression reduces file sizes without degradation or change to the file. PKZIP and StuffIt are examples of tools used for lossless compression (in fact, they use a very similar algorithm to Afterburner's). Lossless compression is extremely important for compressing data that cannot lose even one bit of information, or it becomes useless. Director files made for Shockwave contain precise information for animation, as well as Lingo code for interactivity and so on, so lossy compression schemes cannot be used on Director movies.

The process that PKZIP, StuffIt, and Afterburner use to compress a file is too complicated to go into in any detail here, but a quick summary will give you an idea of what compression ratios to expect.

The compressor looks for repeated patterns of data and keeps what is essentially a glossary of each of those patterns. It then replaces each pattern with the index reference, which is, in general, much smaller. In addition to the compression of Afterburner, Director itself deals with a string of repeated values (such as in a solid-color portion of an image). An uncompressed series of four red pixels in an 8-bit image would require four 8-bit bytes of data, because it would be represented as red, red, red, red. Compressed, however, that same series of pixels would take only two bytes of data, because it would be represented as four red. This compression process is called *run-length encoding*. As you work with Shockwave, you will discover that images with large areas of solid colors compress very well.

Serving Up Shockwave

Before you dive into Shockwave, you first need to be familiar with some basic World Wide Web concepts and terminology. A brief explanation is given about how Shockwave fits into the architecture of the Web, followed by steps to configuring your Web server. Of course, you can experiment with your Shockwave movies without a configured server by simply opening the files locally from your hard disk. But you will need to configure your server in order to serve Shockwave movies across the Web.

Being Part of Open Architecture Browsers

The plug-in architecture of Netscape Navigator, SGI's WebFORCE, and other plug-in-compatible browsers enables new features to be added to HTML. When the Shockwave plug-in is installed, most of the more popular browsers will recognize the `<embed>` tag, and from what the server tells them is embedded, will be able to pass that information along to the plug-in.

The process by which HTTP (HyperText Transport Protocol—what the Web is based on) deals with different file types is this.

The server has a MIME-type table that tells it that files of a given extension are a certain type of file. Files with a GIF extension are type image/gif, for example; files with a JPG extension are image/jpeg; and files with a DCR or DIR extension are application/x-director.

The plug-in architecture enables Shockwave-compatible browsers to treat DIR and DCR files like just another file type, such as GIF or JPEG. Just like embedded GIFs or JPEGs, your Shockwave movie files download with the Web page, then the Shockwave plug-in plays your movie in the page. Easy as pie.

Basic Web Terminology

The URL is the standard address for anything on the Internet and has three parts:

- The first part is the name of the Internet protocol. Examples of this include FTP, gopher, and HTTP.
- The second part is the name of the Internet host. Examples of hosts include the following:
  - www.macromedia.com
  - ftp.macromedia.com
- The address includes the folders your browser has to go through to find the file you're searching.

Our shocked home page, for example, is located at http://www.eline.com/Infrared/Shocked. In this URL, the name of the protocol is HTTP, the server is www.eline.com, and the path to the file is /Infrared/Shocked.

An HTTP server is a computer that delivers World Wide Web data across the Internet. In response to a request specifying a URL, the HTTP server returns a block of data, plus the type of that data. The data type is called a MIME type.

A *MIME* (Multipurpose Internet Mail Extensions) *type* is a specification of the type of a block of data. It was originally proposed and used for enriching the content of mail messages. In the context of the Web, and HTTP in particular, MIME types specify what type of data is returned from a server. MIME types can include text, graphics of various types (GIF, JPEG, PNG, and so on), sound, or Director movies. A MIME type consists of two parts: the content type and the content subtype. The content type specifies a major category, such as image, audio, or application; the subtype specifies a particular data type within that category, such as MIME type of image/jpeg. In the case of a Director movie, the MIME type is application/x-director.

Configuring Your Server

Because Shockwave is an evolving technology, the steps detailed here might change. We suggest you confirm the exact steps for your system by checking the Macromedia Web site at http://www.macromedia.com.

To successfully serve Shockwave movies, your HTTP server must be configured to recognize and handle Shockwave movies. Most servers are Unix-based platforms, although some servers use Macintosh HTTP or WebSTAR software. This section covers configuration for Unix, MacHTTP, and WebSTAR servers.

Configuring Unix Servers

Have your system administrator create an entry in the file that registers MIME types. The administrator will need the following information:

MIME type: application
Sub Type: x-director
Extensions: DCR, DIR, DXR

Configuring Macintosh Servers

Macintosh Web servers come in two flavors: MacHTTP, which is shareware, and WebSTAR, which is a commercial product. Although WebSTAR is based on MacHTTP, they have different configuration processes.

Configuring MacHTTP Servers

If you are running a MacHTTP-based HTTP server, you need to modify the file MacHTTP.config. Add the following lines to the file:

```
BINARY .DIR TEXT * application/x-director
BINARY .DXR TEXT * application/x-director
BINARY .DCR TEXT * application/x-director
```

Configuring WebSTAR Servers

If you are using WebSTAR, perform the following configuration steps:

1. Run the application WebSTAR Admin.
2. Locate and select your server in the Pick A Server window (your server must be running).
3. Choose Suffix Mapping from the Configure menu. The Suffix Mapping dialog box appears.
4. Specify the following settings:

Action:	BINARY
File Suffix:	DCR
File Type:	TEXT
Creator:	*
MIME Type:	application/x-director

If you are providing DIR or DXR movies, repeat the process for each suffix you want to add.

Configuring the Client

The following are instructions for installing the Shockwave plug-in under Netscape for Windows and Macintosh. The first step is to download the Shockwave plug-in, Afterburner, and documentation from Macromedia's Web site at http://www.macromedia.com. Follow the links to the appropriate Shockwave resource page. Naturally, you will want to download the version for the platform and browser you are running on. And, of course, apply the standard provision that you should consult the installation instructions in the README file because these procedures might have changed.

Macromedia provides several standard buttons that you can add to your Web page to make it easy for users who don't have the Shockwave plug-in to get the appropriate version. These are available on the Macromedia Web site.

Configuring Shockwave for Windows

1. Locate your Netscape directory and then locate the Shockwave EXE package you just downloaded. Double-click on it. This extracts the compressed files in a DOS window. Close the window when it's finished.
2. Locate your Netscape directory and double-click on the file called SETUP. There are two files named SETUP, so make sure that you choose the one with the little computer icon next to it.
3. After the installer has launched, read the instructions on the Setup for Shockwave License Agreement. Choose NEXT if you accept the terms of the agreement. If not, choose EXIT. On the second screen, under destination directory, choose NEXT. Shockwave for Director will be installed.
4. This installs the Shockwave Plug-In into the default directory, which is listed under "Destination Directory."
5. If there is no text under the "Destination Directory," choose BROWSE and select the directory where netscape/plug-ins resides. Then choose NEXT to continue the installation.
6. If you are installing the Shockwave for Director 5 beta or final version, you should drag the Afterburner file into the Director Xtras folder.
7. Read the README.TXT information. If, after completing this process, you get error messages from Netscape while viewing a "shocked" Web page, try re-extracting the Shockwave Package you downloaded and follow the "Extracting" instructions again.

Configuring Shockwave for Macintosh

1. Double-click on the Shockwave self-extracting archive application you just downloaded. Select a folder in which to extract it.
2. Drag the Shockwave file into the Netscape Plug-ins folder.
3. If you are installing the Shockwave for Director 5 beta or final version, you should drag the file Afterburner into the Director 5 Xtras folder.

Let the Shocking Begin!

You now are ready to win commitment for Shockwave development, then produce and optimize Shockwave movies, serve, pull down, and view shocked Web sites. We suggest you visit Macromedia's Shockwave Gallery to see all the hottest shockers around and, of course, you should visit http://www.eline.com/Infrared/Shocked for your dose of brain damage. This brief introduction to the critical path of Shockwave development is a mere glimpse at key design and technical issues. It is up to you as a Director 5 developer to bring your cutting-edge work out on the wild, wild Web. Once you shock, you won't want to stop.

Hot URLs: Favorite Director Web Sites

If you have a World Wide Web browser and Internet access, you can tap into a wealth of Director-related information at any time. This appendix gives you a jumping-off point for finding more Director resources, but remember that the Web is a dynamic medium; it's always changing. Therefore, some of the addresses for these sites are liable to change.

Each site is listed with a general descriptor, a descriptive quote from the site (where applicable), and the site's address (its URL).

General Director-Related Web Sites

Director—Maricopa

Site quote: The strands of this Web are for users of Macromedia Director, the most powerful authoring software in the universe. This Web is a subset of our Multimedia Authoring Web.

URL: http://www.mcli.dist.maricopa.edu/director/

Director FAQ Index

Site quote: The Director FAQ: Frequently Asked Questions. This page features the short index to the FAQ main sections. The full index lists all of the questions for each topic. You can also conduct a search over the FAQ.

URL: http://www.mcli.dist.maricopa.edu/director/faq/index.html

Director OOPs?

Site info: (Almost) everything you need to know about Object-Oriented Programming in Director.

URL: http://www.mcli.dist.maricopa.edu/director/oops.html

Director FAQ?

Site info: Same Web site as the FAQ index (above).

URL: http://www.mcli.dist.maricopa.edu/director/

Direct-L Mailist

Site info: Recent Macromedia Director messages sorted by date. View by: DATE—REPLY COUNT—SUBJECT, or SEARCH THIS LIST

URL: http://asearch.mccmedia.com/direct-l/

updateStage

Site quote: Gretchen Macdowall's own Web site! Very popular. "A biweekly harvest of info-nuggets on Macromedia Director and multimedia development culled from online discussion groups and from my own Director adventures."

URL: http://www.xensei.com/users/gcm/

Kurt Cagle's Lingo/Code Page

Site quote: This page is essentially devoted to code fragments contained in articles I write, or even full-blown code. It should be considered *thinkware* — These samples are not guaranteed for accuracy, and I assume no liability if they do not work. They are meant principally as objects of study.

URL: http://www.blarg.net/~cagles/lingo/index.html

Yahoo: Computers: Multimedia

Site info: Yahoo's search page for multimedia Web sites.

URL: http://www.yahoo.com/Computers/Multimedia

Index to Multimedia Information Sources

Site info: The title above says it all…

URL: http://viswiz.gmd.de/MultimediaInfo/

Multimedia-Related Links

Site info: Another invaluable resource to multimedia-related Web sites.

URL: http://www.rst.fi/~riku/mmedia.htm

Welcome to Netscape

Site info: The home page for Netscape and its products, including the Navigator web browser. Plenty of info on Navigator plug-ins as well.

URL: http://home.netscape.com/ndx.html

Apple Computer

Site info: You're a developer; this is Apple's home page; enough said...

URL: http://www.apple.com/

Microsoft Corporation

Site info: You're a developer; this is Microsoft's home page; enough said...

URL: http://www.microsoft.com/

QuickTime Continuum

Site info: Information on Apple QuickTime...

URL: http://quicktime.apple.com/

sharedcast at HCCS

Site info: Mac-related Director shareware.

URL: ftp://sharedcast.hccs.cc.tx.us/Director/

Pangea/Esmedia at Stanford

Site info/quote: Director-related shareware. "This directory contains material related to Macromedia Director... It is a partial mirror of the site maintained by Marvyn Hortmann at ftp://sharedcast.hccs.cc.tx.us/.

"All material is presented as is, without expressed warranties, and is not supported in any official or semi-official way by Macromedia or Stanford University. Comments or questions regarding this site should be directed to [co-author of *Inside Director*] Dave Miller, davem@pangea.stanford.edu."

URL: ftp://pangea.stanford.edu/pub/esmedia/programs/Director/

Macromedia!com

Site info: Macromedia's home page.

URL: http://www.macromedia.com/index_in.html

Macromedia: Interactive Gallery

Site info: See how other developers use Macromedia software.

URL: http://www.macromedia.com/Gallery/index.html

Macromedia Meta Index

Site info: This unofficial guide is intended to provide quick and easy access to all known Macromedia-related information on the Internet.

URL: http://www.pce.net/sales/petert/macromedia.html

Academic Macromedia Software

Site quote: Diskovery Educational Systems is proud to provide affordable software to over 2,000 educational customers throughout the country. Our innovative and cost-saving approach to software sales and service has made us a leading education dealer. We have developed a strong relationship with software publishers and have showed them the benefits of discounting to the academic community. Throughout the country, hundreds of schools, community colleges, and universities are confident that they can obtain the latest, most advanced software by taking advantage of Diskovery's ability to secure and sell nationally known computer products.

URL: http://www.diskovery.com/EPG/Indices/Software/ByPublisher/Macromedia.html

Anton's FreeHand Page

Site info: Peripheral links to all things Macromedia and multimedia...

URL: http://www.euro.net/ecompany/afpindex.html

Xtra Developers

Sound/PrintOMatic/PopMenu Xtras

Site info: Gray matter design has a suite of royalty-free Xtras for Macromedia's flagship authoring tool, Director. The products, which will evolve to support Macromedia's recently announced open development architecture, MOA, offer multimedia developers critical utilities that manage sound, printing, and interface design.

URL: http://www.gmatter.com/gmd/102995pr.html

FileFlex Headquarters

Site quote: FileFlex is the relational database in many popular multimedia products. Designed specifically for multimedia CD-ROMs, kiosks, and interactive productions, FileFlex, a full-featured database engine, provides behind-the-scenes data access and storage services for multimedia developers.

URL: http://www.component-net.com/fileflex/fileflex-hq.html

Gray Matter Design

Site quote: This Web site provides you with detailed information on gray matter design and Macromedia products, access to cool multimedia technologies and lots of other useful resources for multimedia CD-ROM and Internet developers! If you are a user of Macromedia Director,

Authorware, SoundEdit, Deck II, Extreme 3D, FreeHand, and especially Shockwave, this Web site is the place to be!

"You can start by taking a look at our very cool interactive catalog, showcasing our multimedia add-on products, including The Media-Book CD for Director and our first suite of Xtras for Director and Authorware! Then you can check out our other useful information and FREE goodies!

We have much here to share with you, so please take your time and browse around!

URL: http://www.gmatter.com/

Rollover Xtra

Site quote: Rollover Toolkit Xtra for Director 5.0: If there's just one Xtra you add to your toolchest, make sure it's the Rollover Toolkit from Penworks Corporation! Detect, and be notified of, sprite rollover starts and ends! Easy to use, and try before you buy! Author for free, runtime just $25/platform. No royalties! The single most valuable Xtra you can get!

URL: http://www.penworks.com/rtkinfo.htm

Shockwave

Shockwave: Welcome to Macromedia!

Site info: Macromedia's Shockwave home page.

URL: http://www.macromedia.com/Tools/Shockwave/Gallery/Shocked.sites/Macromedia/index.html

Macromedia Shockwave Gallery

Site info: More on Macromedia's Shockwave.

URL: http://www.macromedia.com/Tools/Shockwave/Gallery/index.html

Macromedia Shockwave Vanguard

Site info: How a diverse range of developers are using Shockwave.

URL: http://www.macromedia.com/Tools/Shockwave/Gallery/Vanguard/index.html

Macromedia Shockwave Epicenter

Site info: More cool Shockwave sites, including Macromedia's Shocked Site of the Day.

URL: http://www.macromedia.com/Tools/Shockwave/Gallery/Epicenter/index.html

Shockwave Technology

Site info: Tools, support, and other indispensable tech stuff about Shockwave, from Macromedia.

URL: http://www.macromedia.com/Tools/Shockwave/index.html

Selected Publications

Macromedia: New Media Magazine

Site info: Selected multimedia-related articles from *New Media Magazine*, presented by Macromedia.

URL: http://www.macromedia.com/Brain/New.media/index.html

New Riders: Shockwave User's Guide

Site quote: *Shockwave for Director User's Guide* is the first book to cover the hottest technology to hit the Web. This book includes step-by-step design and implementation techniques to get Shocked files up and running on your Web site quickly. Your personal guides through this book are the creators of the first Shockwave file ever produced outside of Macromedia." Authors Noel and Sasha did the Appendix B on Shockwave for *Inside Director*; okay, enough about New Riders...

URL: http://www.mcp.com/newriders/multimedia/shock.html

The MediaBook CD for Director

Site info: SRP of US $299 gets you an impressive array of Director-related learning materials from gray matter design.

URL: http://www.gmatter.com/gmd/products/MBCD.html

Lingo User's Journal

Site quote: The *Lingo User's Journal* is the only publication dedicated to Lingo and XObject/Xtra programming! The *Lingo User's Journal* is an excellent technical resource whether you're a beginner, intermediate, or advanced programmer. We run articles for all levels, from beginner articles explaining variables, handlers, and strings to advanced articles on asynchronous callbacks, multiple timer facilities, encryption handlers, and objects.

URL: http://www.penworks.com/LUJ/lujinfo.htm

Macromedia User Journal

Site quote: The *Macromedia User Journal* brings you the most detailed information on improving your performance using Macromedia software, including Director, Authorware, and MacroModel. It is filled with solutions and workarounds that save you tons of time and loads of frustration. The MUJ is the most helpful publication in the field... a combination of completely concrete, detailed information on Macromedia techniques as well as interesting perspectives on the field as a whole. This newsletter is extremely useful for insider programming tips... it's also useful for getting a peek inside the industry that you can't get elsewhere.

URL: http://www.hyperstand.com/MUJ/mujsub.html

The Apple Multimedia Program

Site quote: This site is your gateway to multimedia at Apple Computer. Whether you're an aspiring or established multimedia developer, involved in any area of new media—from title development to video digitizing to online publishing—we invite you to explore the wealth of information on this site.

URL: http://www.amp.apple.com/

Remarkable Titles

Total Distortion—Pop Rocket

Site quote/info: Multimedia done very well… Pop Rocket is a publisher and developer of entertaining and thought-provoking interactive media… The company has received considerable critical acclaim for (their game) Total Distortion and has thousands of dedicated fans that say Total Distortion has put all other interactive entertainment to shame.

URL: http://www.poprocket.com/welcome.html

MediaBand—Canter Technology

Site info: Mark Canter and Company bring you more of the cool stuff that's on the *Inside Director* CD-ROM: Meet Media Band!

URL: http://www.mediaband.com/

Haight-Asbury in the Sixties—Rockument

Site quote: An Interactive Media Publisher based in Northern California. Rockument has just released its first CD-ROM title, Haight-Ashbury in the Sixties! This incredible sight and sound extravaganza features the *S.F. Oracle* psychedelic newspaper, the Drop Out game, hundreds of images, and music by the Grateful Dead, the Jefferson Airplane, Big Brother and the Holding Company with Janis Joplin, and Tom Constanten. Be sure to check it out!

URL: http://www.rockument.com/

Communication Technology Laboratory

Site quote: Includes the Breast Cancer Lighthouse mentioned in chapter one of *Inside Director*. "The Michigan State University Communication Technology Laboratory celebrates technological augmentation of the human spirit. As individuals, we embrace the computer as esteemed accomplice to extend our potential in art and learning, science and creativity, and communication and contemplation. We develop information products which use emerging technologies in innovative ways to address the needs of our times."

URL: http://commtechlab.msu.edu/

New Lingo Terms in Director 5

Lingo has expanded and changed in many ways in Director 5. There are more than 100 brand-new terms—many have changed slightly and some have new functionality. Large groups of terms are introduced for brand-new functionality, including Score generation, QuickTime track control, background loading of animation, and scriptable authoring. As with each new release of Director, the older terms are still supported, but they become obsolete and should be avoided.

This appendix includes the following:

- New Lingo terms in Director 5
- Lingo changes
- New Lingo terms by category, including what has changed in each category
- Outdated Lingo

New Lingo Terms in Director 5

activeWindow
alignment of member
autoTab of member

beginRecording
border of member
boxDropShadow
boxType of member
buttonType

cancelIdleLoad
case
castLib
the castLibNum of sprite
changeArea of member
channelCount of member
charPosToLoc
chunkSize of member
clearFrame

deleteFrame
desktopRectList
digitalVideoTimeScale
digitalVideoType of member
dropShadow of member
duplicate(list)
duplicateFrame

editable of member
emulateMultiButtonMouse
end case
endRecording

fileName of castLib
filled of member
finishIdleLoad
font of member
fontSize of member
fontStyle of member
frameLabel

framePalette*
frameSound1
frameSound2
frameScript*
frameTempo*
frameTransition
frontWindow

idleHandlerPeriod
idleLoadDone
idleLoadMode
idleLoadPeriod
idleLoadTag
idleReadChunkSize
insertFrame

keyPressed

lineCount of member
lineHeight of member
linePosToLocV
lineSize of member
loc of sprite
locToCharPos
locVToLinePos

margin of member
media of member
member
memberNum of sprite

name of CastLib
new
number of CastLib
number of castLibs
number of members of castLib

on activateWindow**
on closeWindow**
on moveWindow**
on resizeWindow**
on rightMouseDown
on rightMouseUp
on zoomWindow**

```
on openWindow
otherwise

pageHeight of member
paletteMapping
paletteRef of member
pattern of member
the platform
preLoadMode of CastLib
preLoadMovie

rightMouseDown, the
rightMouseUp, the

sampleRate of member
sampleSize of member
save castLib
score
scoreSelection
scriptsEnabled of member
scriptType of member
scrollByLine
scrollByPage
scrollTop of member
selection of castLib
shapeType of member
sound of member

timeScale of member
trackCount(member)
trackCount(sprite)
trackEnabled
trackNextKeyTime
trackNextSampleTime
trackPreviousKeyTime
trackPreviousSampleTime
trackStartTime(member)
trackStartTime(sprite)
trackStopTime(member)
trackStopTime(sprite)
trackText
trackType (member)
trackType (sprite)
```

transitionType of member
type of member

unloadMovie
updateFrame
updateLock

windowPresent
wordWrap of member

* *Not new term, new functionality*
** *Not documented until Director 5*

Changes in Lingo

The following terms have been updated to match new Director functionality. Specifically, the term "cast" is replaced by "member" wherever possible. The older terms are still supported, but they will become obsolete and should be avoided.

Director 4.0 Term	Director 5.0 Term
backColor of cast	backColor of member
cast	member
castmembers	number of members
castNum of sprite	memberNum of sprite
castType of cast	type of member
center of cast	center of member
controller of cast	controller of member
crop of cast	crop of member
depth of cast	depth of member
duplicate cast	duplicate member
duration of cast	duration of member
erase cast	erase member
fileName of cast	fileName of member
foreColor of cast	foreColor of member

continues

Director 4.0 Term	Director 5.0 Term
frameRate of cast	frameRate of member
height of cast	height of member
hilite of cast	hilite of member
loaded of cast	loaded of member
loop of cast	loop of member
modified of cast	modified of member
move cast	move member
name of cast	name of member
number of cast	number of member
number of castmembers	number of members
palette of cast	palette of member
picture of cast	picture of member
preLoad of cast	preLoad of member
preLoadCast	preLoadMember
purgePriority of cast	purgePriority of member
rect of cast	rect of member
scriptText of cast	scriptText of member
size of cast	size of member
sound of cast	sound of member
text of cast	text of member
textAlign of field	alignment of member
textFont of field	font of member
textHeight of field	lineHeight of member
textSize of field	fontSize of member
textStyle of field	fontStyle of member
video of cast	video of member
width of cast	width of member

New Lingo Terms by Category (Plus What's Changed in Each Category)

Director includes several new Lingo terms that can be divided into categories. The following sections list these terms as well as their categories. Where changes have occured, an additional list including the changes follows.

Buttons and Shapes

```
buttonType

filled of member
lineSize of member
pattern of member
shapeType of member
```

Cast Members

```
digitalVideoType of member
editable of member
filled of member
media of member
member
new
paletteRef of member
scriptsEnabled of member
scriptType of member
scrollTop of member
shapeType of member
sound of member
transitionType of member
type of member
wordWrap of member
```

What's Changed: Cast Members

Director 4.0 Term	Director 5.0 Term
backColor of cast	backColor of member
cast	member
castType of cast	type of member
center of cast	center of member
crop of cast	crop of member
depth of cast	depth of member
duplicate cast	duplicate member
erase cast	erase member
fileName of cast	fileName of member
foreColor of cast	foreColor of member
height of cast	height of member
hilite of cast	hilite of member
loaded of cast	loaded of member
modified of cast	modified of member
move cast	move member
name of cast	name of member
number of cast	number of member
palette of cast	palette of member
picture of cast	picture of member
preload of cast	preload of member
preLoadCast	preLoadMember
purgePriority of cast	purgePriority of member
rect of cast	rect of member
scriptText of cast	scriptText of member
size of cast	size of member
sound of cast	sound of member
text of cast	text of member
textAlign of field	alignment of member
textFont of field	font of member
textHeight of field	lineHeight of member
textSize of field	fontSize of member

Director 4.0 Term	Director 5.0 Term
textStyle of field	fontStyle of member
video of cast	video of member
width of cast	width of member

Casts

```
castLib
fileName of castLib
name of CastLib
number of CastLib
number of castLibs
number of members of castLib
preLoadMode of CastLib
save castLib
selection of castLib
```

What's Changed: Casts

Director 4.0 Term	Director 5.0 Term
number of castmembers	number of members

Code Structures and Syntax

```
case
end case
otherwise
```

Digital Video

```
digitalVideoTimeScale
digitalVideoType of member
timeScale of member
trackCount (member)
```

```
trackCount (sprite)
trackEnabled
trackNextKeyTime
trackNextSampleTime
trackPreviousKeyTime
trackPreviousSampleTime
trackStartTime (member)
trackStartTime (sprite)
trackStopTime (member)
trackStopTime (sprite)
trackText
trackType (member)
trackType (sprite)
sound of member
```

What's Changed: Digital Video

Director 4.0 Term	Director 5.0 Term
controller of cast	controller of member
duration of cast	duration of member
frameRate of cast	frameRate of member
loop of cast	loop of member
sound of cast	sound of member

External Files

```
fileName of castLib
```

What's Changed: External Files

Director 4.0 Term	Director 5.0 Term
fileName of cast	fileName of member

Fields

```
alignment of member
autoTab of memeber
border of member
boxDropShadow
boxType of member
charPosToLoc
dropShadow of member
editable of member
font of member
fontSize of member
fontStyle of member
lineCount of member
lineHeight of member
linePosToLocV
locToCharPos
locVToLinePos
margin of member
pageHeight of member
scrollByLine
scrollByPage
scrollTop of member
wordWrap of member
```

What's Changed: Fields

Director 4.0 Term	Director 5.0 Term
textFont of field	font of member
textFont of field	fontSize of member
textStyle of of field	fontStyle of member
foreColor of cast	foreColor of member
height of cast	height of member
text of cast	text of member
textAlign of field	alignment of member
textHeight of field	lineHeight of member
textSize of field	fontSize of member

Frames

See also the "Score Generation" section later in this appendix.

```
clearFrame
deleteFrame
duplicateFrame
frameSound1
frameSound2
frameTransition
insertFrame
updateFrame
```

What's Changed: Frames

```
frameLabel        changes in functionality
framePalette      changes in functionality
frameScript       changes in functionality
frameTempo        changes in functionality
```

Lists

```
duplicate(list)
```

Memory Management

```
cancelIdleLoad
finishIdleLoad
idleHandlerPeriod
idleLoadDone
idleLoadMode
idleLoadPeriod
idleLoadTag
idleReadChunkSize
preLoadMode of CastLib
preLoadMovie
unloadMovie
```

What's Changed: Memory Management

Director 4.0 Term	Director 5.0 Term
loaded of cast	loaded of member
preLoadCast	preLoadMember
preload of cast	preload of member
purgePriority of cast	purgePriority of member

Movie Control

```
score
scoreSelection
updateLock
```

Movie in a Window

```
activeWindow
frontWindow
on activateWindow
on closeWindow
on moveWindow
on openWindow
on resizeWindow
windowPresent
```

Palettes

```
paletteMapping
paletteRef
```

Parent Scripts

```
new
```

What's Changed: Parent Scripts

Director 4.0 Term	Director 5.0 Term
birth	new

Score Generation

```
beginRecording
clearFrame
deleteFrame
duplicateFrame
endRecording
frameLabel
framePalette
frameScript
frameSound1
frameSound2
frameTransition
frameTempo
insertFrame
updateFrame
updateLock
```

Sprites

```
the castLibNum of sprite
loc of sprite
memberNum of sprite
paletteRef
```

What's Changed: Sprites

Director 4.0 Term	Director 5.0 Term
castNum of sprite	memberNum of sprite

Sound

channelCount of member
sampleRate of member
sampleSize of member

What's Changed: Sound

Director 4.0 Term	Director 5.0 Term
sound of cast	sound of member

System

activeWindow
desktopRectList
digitalVideoTimeScale
emulateMultiButtonMouse
frontWindow
keyPressed
the platform
rightMouseDown, the
rightMouseUp, the

Transitions

changeArea of member
chunkSize of member
transitionType of member

User Interaction

emulateMultiButtonMouse
keyPressed
on rightMouseDown
on rightMouseUp

rightMouseDown, the
rightMouseUp, the

Outdated Lingo

Outdated	What to Use Instead
birth	new
factory	parent scripts
instance	property
closeDA	outdated after System 7
method	lists, parent scripts
openDA	outdated after System 7
when…then constructs	if…then constructs

Contacting Macromedia

The following sections provide ways to contact Macromedia, both in the U.S. and abroad.

Office Locations

Macromedia has offices in the U.S., Europe, Japan, Asia Pacific, and Latin America.

Macromedia U.S.
600 Townsend, Suite 310W
San Francisco, CA 94103
Phone: 415-252-2000
Fax: 415-626-0554
Web page: http://www.macromedia.com

Macromedia Europe (including Europe, the Middle East, and Africa)
Pyramid House
Easthampstead Road
Bracknell
Berkshire RG12 1NS
United Kingdom
Phone: 44-1-344-458600
Fax: 44-1-344-458666

Macromedia Japan
2F Deer Plaza Akasaka
4-3-28 Akasaka
Minato-ku, Tokyo
Japan 107
Phone: 81-3-5563-1980
Fax: 81-3-5563-1990

Macromedia Asia Pacific
East Kew, Victoria
Australia 3102
Phone: 61-3-9859-8325
Fax: 61-3-9859-4162

Macromedia Latin America
600 Townsend Street
San Francisco, CA 94103
U.S.A.
Phone: 415-252-2000
Fax: 415-626-0554

Sales

Domestic Sales: 800-288-4797

Product Upgrades: 800-457-1774

International Sales: contact your local distributor

Customer Service

For customer service questions:

Phone: 800-470-7211

Product Information

For product literature or the Showcase CD:

Phone: 800-326-2128

Source & Center

Contact Source & Center for training, consulting services, purchasing Priority Access technical support, referrals for multimedia development, referrals to user groups, and authorization programs for trainers, developers, and service bureaus.

Phone: 800-396-0129 or 415-252-7999

Macromedia International User Conference

Phone: 415-252-7999

Success Stories

World Wide Web: pr@macromedia.com
Fax: 415-626-1502

Product Suggestions and Feedback

Contact the Director Product Team with product suggestions and feedback about Director.

E-mail: director@macromedia.com
Fax: 415-626-0554

Made with Macromedia Program

Macromedia offers Director 5 developers the capability to distribute applications created in Director without paying royalties. The new Macromedia licensing policy enables you to distribute your Director projects royalty-free, provided you include the Made with Macromedia logo as described in the guidelines.

FAQ voice mail: 415-252-2171
World Wide Web: http://www.macromedia.com/

Technical Support and Resources

For Online Services

Information about Director is available from Macromedia's forums on CompuServe, America Online, Microsoft Network, and also at various sites on the Internet. For an up-to-date list of all the resources available online, call MacroFacts, Macromedia's 24-hour fax information line, and request document 3503. In the United States and Canada, call 800-449-3329. Outside the U.S.A. and Canada, call 415-863-4409.

CompuServe

To reach the Macromedia forum on CompuServe, use the command GO MACROMEDIA.

On CompuServe, Macromedia provides message areas for discussion of multimedia development and support of all their products, as well as libraries that contain useful utilities and examples—including drivers, models, DLLs, XObjects, and Xtras.

America Online

In the United States, to reach the Macromedia forum on America Online, type the keyword `Macromedia`.

On America Online, Macromedia provides message areas for discussion of multimedia development and support all of their products, as well as libraries that contain useful utilities and examples—including drivers, models, DLLs, XObjects, and Xtras.

Microsoft Network

To reach the Macromedia forum on Microsoft Network, type the command `Goto Macromedia`.

On Microsoft Network, Macromedia provides message areas for discussion of multimedia development and support for all of its products, as well as libraries that contain useful utilities and examples—including drivers, models, DLLs, XObjects, and Xtras.

Resources in Faxable Formats

Macromedia's 24-hour fax information line provides instant access to techNotes on all of Macromedia's products and services. Currently, there are almost 100 Director and multimedia techNotes available.

MacroFacts Automated Fax-on-Demand System

Phone: 800-449-3329 (United States and Canada)
Phone: 415-863-4409 (elsewhere)

Technical Questions or Problems with Macromedia Products

Phone: 415-252-9080
Fax: 415-703-0924

For assistance by fax or phone internationally, contact the vendor or the distributor from which you acquired Director.

The *Inside Director 5* CD-ROM

Many thanks to the parties who've contributed to the *Inside Director 5* CD-ROM. More copyright and trademark information is available on the next-to-last page of this book.

What follows is a brief description of technical details for the CD-ROM; after that is a listing of the CD-ROM's contents.

About This CD-ROM

The *Inside Director 5* CD-ROM is a hybrid; it's designed to run on more than one platform. In this case, the CD will run on Macintosh computers or on Windows-based PCs.

Table E.1

Operating Systems That Run the *Inside Director* CD-ROM

Environment	Operating System
Macintosh	System 7 System 7.5
Windows	Windows 3.1x Windows for Workgroups Windows 95

Technically, the same CD-ROM is used in both *Inside Director 5 for Mac* and *Inside Director 5 for Windows*. And while most of the material is identical from one platform to the next, some platform-specific material might not be available on either the Mac or the Windows section of the CD-ROM. This is not due to error.

We've tried to make it as easy as possible to access the contents of this CD-ROM. Check out the rest of this appendix to find out how to get to the stuff you want!

If You Have a Mac

Yes, of course, you'll likely have a Mac, because you're using *Inside Macromedia Director 5 with Lingo for Macintosh.*

1. Insert the CD-ROM in your CD-ROM drive.
2. Click on the READ ME file for details about the CD-ROM and its contents. The READ ME program describes all of the software in detail, and provides push-button installation options for each program.

Macintosh Software Overview

When you insert the disc into a Macintosh, you can access the folders discussed in this section:

Project Files Folder

This directory contains the author's Director project files. You can open files directly from the CD-ROM or copy files to your hard disk.

Macromedia Demos Folder

This directory contains working-model versions of Director 5, Extreme 3D, and xRes. Be sure to read the READ ME files in this directory before installing the software.

Macromedia Demos: Director 5 Folder

Contains the working model edition of Macromedia Director 5. Double-click on Director 5 Demo Install to implement the program on your Macintosh.

Macromedia Demos: Extreme 3D Folder

Contains the working model edition of Extreme 3D. Double-click the E3D Demo Installer icon to set up the software.

Macromedia Demos: xRes Mac Folder

This folder contains the working model demo of Macromedia xRes v2.0. xRes 2.0 is an excellent tool for creating and editing high-resolution images. xRes 2.0's many new features, including the Macromedia User Interface (MUI); path import from FreeHand; Web file formats such as GIF89a, Progressive JPEG, and PNG; Export and Acquire module support; direct editing of smaller images; and new brushes, gradients, and textures make creating in hi-res fun for the Adobe Photoshop user. This demo is available only for the Mac. There is no equivalent software on the PC side of the CD-ROM.

The demo version enables you to explore most of the functionality of xRes with the following exceptions:

- Save, Save As, Export, Render, and Print are disabled.
- Color library support is not included.
- You can copy and paste within xRes, but you cannot copy out to the Finder.
- The Batch Conversion Xtra is disabled.

To install the software, double-click on xRes(tm) 2.0 Demo Installer.

KPT 3.0 Demo Folder

Kai's Power Tools 3 is a collection of extensions that plug into Adobe Photoshop or any paint application that fully and correctly subscribes to the Adobe Plug-in architecture. To install the software, double-click on the KPT3 Install.1 icon. KPT has also provided equivalent software for Windows users.

Big Top Productions Folder

This folder contains the Mac versions of Big Top's Cartoon Toolbox. The toolbox consists of four demo programs that were developed in Director.

Felix Cartoon Toolbox, Awarded Best of Show at MacWorld 95 by the Boston Computer Society, enables kids and adults to easily create their own professional-looking cartoons. It's packed with hundreds of character animations, special effects, props, sound effects, music, and more. All the characters from the original TV series are also here: The Professor, Poindexter, Rock Bottom, Master Cylinder, Vavoom, and Felix. See the README.TXT for information concerning system requirements.

The Cartoon Toolbox is so easy to use, you'll be able to make great cartoons the first time you use it! Standard editing concepts are presented in a manner that anyone can grasp immediately. You can edit frames, characters, backgrounds, music, and effects. Simple visual tools enable you to add or delete at any time. You also can save and edit up to 8,949 cartoons, plus export them to a disk and share them with friends without the Cartoon Toolbox software.

To really appreciate the Cartoon Toolbox, you have to play it. This interactive demo will give you a good idea of the scope of the Cartoon Toolbox. We've included animation clips from almost every character, as well as props, special effects, and one background and music loop. To run the demo from the CD-ROM, double-click on the BIG TOP icon. To exit from the running demo at any time, press Command+Q. A Windows version also is available on the CD-ROM.

Passage to Vietnam Demo Folder

This folder contains the demo version of "Passage to Vietnam" by Against All Odds Production. Winner of the "best of show" 1995 *NewMedia* INVISION award, Passage to Vietnam is one of the most highly-acclaimed interactive reference pieces created with Director.

The Passage to Vietnam CD-ROM is based on Rick Smolan's most recent book with the same title. Smolan, best known for his *Day in the Life* book series, took 70 of the world's best photojournalists to Vietnam to document this little-known country for the first time in 20 years.

The project has been responsible for a large format coffee-table book and HDTV documentary special. To run the demo from the CD-ROM, double-click on the 60meg Demo icon. This software is for the Mac only. The CD-ROM does not contain a Windows version of this program.

IB&C 3.0 Demo Folder

This folder contains a demo of Instant Buttons and Controls v3.0. StatMedia and ArtBeats have teamed up to produce a comprehensive toolset containing thousands of design elements optimized for multimedia and Web page design. This demo version enables you to sample some of the icons, bars, sounds, buttons, and seamless patterns (tiles) available for Mac and Windows. (Note that only a Macintosh demo of this product is included on the CD-ROM.) To run the demo, double-click on the IB&C 3.0 Demo icon.

Headbone Interactive: BugzDemo Folder

Headbone Interactive uses Director to produce its critically-acclaimed "What the Heck Will Elroy Do Next?" CD-ROM series. This directory contains a demo of Headbone's "Elroy Goes Bugzerk" product. According to Headbone Interactive, Elroy Goes Bugzerk, the first episode of the Elroy series, is an Interactive Comic Adventure for ages 7–97.

Elroy Goes Bugzerk won *PC Gamer*'s "Best Educational Software Title of 1995," the *MacUser* list for Top 50 CD-ROMs of the Year, and critical acclaim from many publications, including *PC Gamer*: "...this is the best I've seen. Because of its fresh and clever graphics style as well as its well-told story, Elroy Goes Bugzerk takes the prize."

You can run the demo version of "Elroy Goes Bugzerk" directly from this CD-ROM. To start the demo, double-click on the Bugzerk Demo icon. To exit the running demo at any time, press Command+Q. The CD-ROM also contains a Windows version of this program.

Headbone Interactive: PaveDemo Folder

The latest title in the Elroy series is "Elroy Hits the Pavement." You can run the demo version directly from this CD-ROM by double-clicking the Pavement Demo icon. To exit the running demo at any time, press Command+Q. The CD-ROM also contains a Windows version of this program.

Mattel Folder

This folder contains Mattel's Hot Wheels demo. Mattel, Inc. is using Director to develop some of its creative marketing tools. The Hot Wheels Marketing and Design groups at Mattel wanted to produce an interactive computer disk that would be sold with a Hot Wheels car.

They asked Mattel's in-house Digital Studio Services department to design and produce it. The result was a very enthusiastically received demo for Mattel's Pre-Toy fair. Double-click HOTWHEELS DEMO.MAC to run the demo. To exit the demo at any time, press Command+Q. The CD-ROM also contains a Windows version of this program.

Equilibrium: DeBabelizer Lite LE Folder

Equilibrium has provided two DeBabelizer programs for this CD-ROM. DeBabelizer Lite LE is a fully functional subset of Equilibrium's flagship product, DeBabelizer Toolbox. A demo version of DeBabelizer Toolbox is provided, along with the fully functional Lite version. Please note that DeBabelizer is available only for the Macintosh.

With its numerous graphics readers and writers, DeBabelizer Lite is perfect for simple image translation and slideshow functions. Its compatibility with Photoshop Filter, Acquire, and Export plug-ins also provides an extremely cost-effective filtering solution.

For bitmapped, scanned, or Paint files, DeBabelizer Lite offers nearly the same translation capabilities as DeBabelizer Toolbox without the internal scripting, image processing, or palette manipulation. Slideshow creates on-screen thumbnails of a folder full of images that can all be translated automatically. DeBabelizer Lite intelligently maintains maximum color integrity and quality to and from each format and platform. To install DeBabelizer Lite LE on your Macintosh, double-click the DeBabelizer LiteLEdir5.sea icon.

Equilibrium: DEBABELIZER V1.6.5 DEMO Folder

This folder contains a demo version of DeBabelizer—the Graphics Processing Toolbox.

DeBabelizer Toolbox is an essential tool for anyone working with computer graphics. This award-winning product combines graphics processing, palette optimization, and translation in one program. With easy "Watch Me" scripting and batch features, thousands of images can be processed automatically to specifications.

A true production powerhouse, DeBabelizer translates among more than 70 bit-mapped graphics, animation, and digital video formats, including DOS/Windows, Amiga, Sun, XWindows, Alias, Electric Image, SoftImage formats, and more.

DeBabelizer supports Photoshop and third-party Acquire, Filter, and Export plug-ins, as well as AppleScript. It includes dozens of image editing and palette manipulation tools, including SuperPaletteTM, which automatically creates the best palette for a series of images. DeBabelizer complements all paint, scan, and image processing programs.

Installation Tip: Equilibrium recommends that you restart your Macintosh and press the Shift key (so that all extensions will be turned off) before installing the demo.

When you run the install program for the demo, it prompts for the location of an archive file. When asked to "install the final portion of the archive," open the Equilibrium folder, and then open the DEBABELIZER V1.6.5 DEMO folder. Then select DeBabelizer 1.6.5 DEMO.#2 and press the Load button.

If You Have a Windows-Based PC

As mentioned previously, you can run this CD-ROM on a Windows machine as easily as you can on a Mac (well, almost). There are two ways to explore the Windows side of the CD-ROM. One way is to browse the CD using File Manager. If you choose this method, please note that the directory organization of the disc is documented in this chapter (and also on the READ1ST.WRI file in the root directory of the CD-ROM). We have documented exactly what programs you need to run in order to set up each software.

The other, more convenient method of exploring this CD-ROM is to install and run the included "Guide to the CD-ROM" program. Guide to the CD-ROM makes it easy to browse files directly from the disc and to install software from the CD to your hard drive.

The Guide to the CD-ROM program has been tested with Windows 3.1, Windows 95, and Windows NT v3.51. Please note that the "Guide to the CD-ROM" program may not be compatible with future releases of NT. If you have NT 4.x running (which has not shipped at the time of this writing), we advise that you explore this CD-ROM using File Manager or an equivalent program.

Because Microsoft is continually upgrading DLLs and other resources used by Windows, your system might host system resources that are newer than those installed by the Guide to the CD-ROM setup program. If during installation, you are prompted to overwrite a newer version file, we recommend that you choose not to replace newer files with older versions.

To install system resources required to run Guide to the CD-ROM, here's what to do:

1. Start Windows.
2. From Windows File Manager, double-click on SETUP.EXE. This runs a setup program that installs files required to run Guide to the CD-ROM. Setup creates a program manager group containing icons for running and removing Guide to the CD-ROM. SETUP.EXE need only be run once.
3. Open the program group and double-click the Guide to the CD-ROM icon. When the banner program appears, press the Continue button. Then follow the instructions that appear on-screen.

Windows Software Overview

This section documents the directory organization of the CD-ROM, for those of you who elect not to install the Guide to the CD-ROM program.

\ (root) directory

The root directory contains the setup program for installing the Guide to the CD-ROM program. If you are exploring the CD-ROM manually using File Manager, the main program of interest in the root directory is CODECOPY.EXE, which copies Director project files from the CD-ROM to your hard drive.

\CDGUIDE directory

The CDGUIDE directory contains the Guide to the CD-ROM program files.

\SOURCE directory

This directory contains the author's Director project files, as discussed in the book. You can open files directly from the CD-ROM, or copy files to your hard disk. A program that copies files to your hard disk has been provided. To use it, run CODECOPY.EXE from the root directory of the CD-ROM.

\SOURCE\APPENDXB Subdirectory

If you have an Internet Web browser installed on your machine, you will want to open the HTML document in this directory to explore Web sites on the Internet that pertain to Director, Macromedia, and Multimedia in general.

Start your Web browser and open \source\appendxb\appndxb.htm. Once opened, the local file acts just like any other Web document. Just point and click to go there.

All links were operational at the time this book went to print. However, the Web is a dynamically changing environment, and Web pages could change without notice. When you run \CODECOPY.EXE to copy project files to your hard drive, this file is copied also.

\3RDPARTY Subdirectory

This directory contains utilities, product demos, and software from vendors of multimedia products. Each product resides in its own subdirectory beneath the \3rdparty directory.

\3RDPARTY\ANDROM\SERIES1 Subdirectory

Contains Andromeda Software's Series 1 Photography Filters and provides the Best in Optical Lens Effects. This fully functional filter is compatible with any paint program that supports Photoshop plug-in filters. Use the cMulti and sMulti Filters to create versatile circular or straight, multiple lens, kaleidoscopic effects. To install, run w1demo.exe.

Please note that at time of publication, Andromeda did not have Macintosh filters ready. The CD-ROM contains the Windows version only. By the time you read this, Andromeda may have released Macintosh filters. Point your Web browser at http://www.andromeda.com.

\3RDPARTY\ANDROM\SERIES2 Subdirectory

Andromeda's Series 2 3D Filter provides true 3D surface wrapping, viewpoint control and shading. This is a demo filter. To install, run w2demo.exe.

\3RDPARTY\ANDROM\SERIES3 Subdirectory

Andromeda's Series 3 PC Screens Filter converts grayscale into pure line art, mezzoblends, mezzotints, and other specialty screens. It's Digital engraving for the '90s. This is a demo filter. To install, run w3demo.exe.

\3RDPARTY\BIGTOP Subdirectory

The BIGTOP subdirectory contains Big Top's Cartoon Toolbox. The toolbox consists of four demo programs that were developed in Director.

Felix Cartoon Toolbox, awarded Best of Show at MacWorld 95 by the Boston Computer Society, the Cartoon Toolbox lets kids and adults easily create their own professional-looking cartoons. It's packed with hundreds of character animations, special effects, props, sound effects, music, and more. All the characters from the original TV series are also here: The Professor, Poindexter, Rock Bottom, Master Cylinder, Vavoom, and Felix.

See README.TXT for information concerning system requirements.

The Cartoon Toolbox is so easy to use, you will make great cartoons the first time you use it! Standard editing concepts are presented in a manner that anyone can grasp immediately. You can edit frames, characters, backgrounds, music, and effects. Simple visual tools enable you to add or delete at any time. You can also save and edit up to 8,949 cartoons, plus export them to a disk and share them with friends without the Cartoon Toolbox software.

To really appreciate the Cartoon Toolbox you have to play it. This interactive demo will give you a good idea of the scope of the Cartoon Toolbox. We've included animation clips from almost every character, props, special effects, and one background and music loop. To run the demo from the CD-ROM, run btdemo.exe. To exit from the running demo at any time, press CTRL-Q. A Mac version of this software is also included on the CD-ROM.

\3RDPARTY\BRENDA Subdirectory

This directory contains Brenda—The Batch Renderer v2.20.

Many developers use editing tools from outside Director to make a common palette, or "super palette," that the images in a multimedia presentation can share.

Brenda is a batch-oriented image processing utility developed primarily to create VGA-friendly palettes and to efficiently remap images to VGA-friendly palettes. It does some other things, as well. When you press the Install button, Brenda's installation routine will prompt for a path. Respond with

d:\3rdparty\brenda

where d is the letter of your CD-ROM drive.

Brenda is "TollWare"

Brenda is made available as a new concept in software exchange: TollWare. Brenda is not a product and cannot be bought or licensed. Brenda is a timed-release, digital assistant and, as such constitutes a service, hence the term TollWare. You will use it as you would a bridge or (*shudder*) Information Superhighway. If you have a job to do and if Brenda helps you do that job, you are obligated to pay the toll: $5.00 (U.S.). If you use it twice, you are obligated to pay the toll twice, and so forth. If you expect to use Brenda a lot and would like to avoid repeated, endless tolls, you can purchase an unlimited use service contract for $60.00 (U.S.). For more information, see BRENDA.WRI after you have installed the product.

Brenda * The Batch Renderer is a Windows-only product. On the Macintosh side, please check out the DeBabelizer software for similar functionality.

\3RDPARTY\HEADBONE\BUGZDEMO Subdirectory

Headbone Interactive uses Director to produce its critically-acclaimed "What the Heck Will Elroy Do Next?" CD-ROM series. This directory contains a demo of Headbone's "Elroy Goes Bugzerk" product. According to Headbone Interactive, Elroy Goes Bugzerk, the first episode of the Elroy series, is an Interactive Comic Adventure for ages 7–97.

Elroy Goes Bugzerk won *PC Gamer*'s "Best Educational Software Title of 1995," the *MacUser* list for Top 50 CD-ROMs of the Year, and critical acclaim from many publications, including *PC Gamer*: "...this is the best I've seen. Because of its fresh and clever graphics style as well as its well-told story, Elroy Goes Bugzerk takes the prize."

You can run the demo version of "Elroy Goes Bugzerk" directly from this CD-ROM. To start the demo, run bugzdemo.exe. To exit the running demo at any time, press Control+Q. A Macintosh version of this software also is available on the CD-ROM.

\3RDPARTY\HEADBONE\PAVEDEMO Subdirectory

The latest title in the Elroy series is "Elroy Hits the Pavement." You can run the demo version directly from this CD-ROM by executing pavedemo.exe. To exit the running demo at any time, press Control+Q. A Macintosh version of this software is also available on the CD-ROM.

\3RDPARTY\KPT\DISK1 Subdirectory

KAI'S POWER TOOLS 3 DEMONSTRATION VERSION

Kai's Power Tools 3 is a collection of extensions that plug into Adobe Photoshop or any paint application that fully and correctly subscribes to the Adobe plug-in architecture.

More than two years since its 1.0 release, KPT again is pushing the envelope of possibilities with version 3.

This demonstration version of Kai's Power Tools will allow you to explore the entire set of filters, enabling you to see all the features in action before you buy. You will be able to open and run all of the features, but your changes will not be applied to your image.

For more information, please open README.WRI. To install the software, run setup.exe. A Macintosh version of this software is also available on the CD-ROM.

\3RDPARTY\MACROMED\DIRECTOR Subdirectory

This directory contains a working model version of Macromedia's Director 5 product. Director 5, the most powerful authoring tool for multimedia and the Internet, has the power, performance, productivity, and platform support every multimedia developer needs. Director 5 enables you to quickly and easily import and integrate media elements such as 2D and 3D graphics, animation, sound, and digital video from a wide variety of sources.

With Director you provide timing and interactivity for those media elements and then create stand-alone interactive applications. Director is the only tool that allows you to develop on Windows 95, NT, 3.1, or Macintosh OS and then deliver files on Windows 95, NT, and 3.1; Macintosh OS; Enhanced CD, and the Internet using Shockwave.

This save-disabled edition of Director enables you to explore all main features of the program, but you cannot save your work. To install the software, run setup.exe. A Macintosh version of this software is also available on the CD-ROM.

\3RDPARTY\MACROMED\E3DDEMO Subdirectory

This directory contains Macromedia's Extreme 3D Working Model, v1.00. Extreme 3D is a powerful 3D solution for design and multimedia. This demo version of Extreme 3D includes all the major features of the full product. You can use this demo version to get the feel of Extreme 3D, but you cannot save or export your work.

For more detailed product information, visit Macromedia online at http://macromedia.com/Tools/Datasheets/index.html.

Recommended System Configuration:

- MPC 486/25SX or faster
- 8 MB of RAM
- Windows 3.1 or higher
- 640×480 256 color display
- Double Speed CD-ROM drive

Be sure to open the READ_ME.TXT file, because it contains important information concerning installation, Win32's, memory, performance, and other eratta pertaining to this product. To install the software, run setup.exe. A Macintosh version of this software is also available on the CD-ROM.

\3RDPARTY\MATTEL Subdirectory

This directory contains Mattel's Hot Wheels demo. Mattel, Inc. is using Director to develop some of its creative marketing tools. The Hot Wheels Marketing and Design groups at Mattel wanted to produce an interactive computer disk that would be sold with a Hot Wheels car.

They asked Mattel's in-house Digital Studio Services department to design and produce it. The result was a very enthusiastically received demo for Mattel's Pre-Toy fair. Run hwdemo.exe to view the demo. To exit the demo at any time, press Control+Q. The CD-ROM also contains a Macintosh version of this software.

Symbols

A

D

E

F

G

I

M

N

O

P

Q

R

S

T

U

V

W

X

Y

Z

Fold Here

NO POSTAGE
NECESSARY
IF MAILED
IN THE
UNITED STATES

BUSINESS REPLY MAIL

FIRST-CLASS MAIL PERMIT NO. 9918 INDIANAPOLIS IN

POSTAGE WILL BE PAID BY THE ADDRESSEE

NEW RIDERS PUBLISHING
201 W 103RD ST
INDIANAPOLIS IN 46290-9058

REGISTRATION CARD

Inside Director 5 with Lingo for Macintosh

Name ______________________ Title ____________

Company ______________________ Type of business ____________

Address ______________________

City/State/ZIP ______________________

E-mail/Internet ______________________ Phone ____________

Would you like to be placed on our preferred mailing list? ❑ yes ❑ no

Have you used/purchased New Riders books before? ❑ yes ❑ no

Where did you purchase this book? Check one.

❑ Bookstore chain ❑ Independent bookstore ❑ Computer store
❑ Wholesale club ❑ College bookstore ❑ Other ____________

What influenced your decision to purchase this title? ______________________

____

____

Which of the following operating systems do you use? Check all that apply.

❑ Windows 3.x ❑ Windows 95 ❑ Windows NT
❑ Macintosh ❑ SGI ❑ Other ____________

What are the names of the software programs you use currently? ____________

____

____

Which of the following best describes your work environment? Check one.

❑ Self-employed ❑ Small business ❑ Large business

Which of the following do you create/develop for? Check all that apply.

❑ Games ❑ Motion pictures ❑ Web sites
❑ Print ❑ Other

What online services and Web sites do you visit on a regular basis? ____________

____

What trade shows do you attend? ______________________

What computer book titles do you consider your most valuable sources of information?

____

What applications/technologies would you like to see us publish in the future?

____

Copyright Information for the *Inside Director* CD-ROM

zScript ™ ©1996 Zeus Productions. All Rights Reserved.

Brain Game from Body Park, Skeleton Game from Body Park, Heart Game from Body Park, and Paint Movie from Biggs and Rabble CD ©1994, 1995 Virtual Entertainment, Inc. Virtual Entertainment, Inc., 200 Highland Avenue, Needham, MA 02194 (www.virtent.com) 800-301-9545. **NOTE:** *Users may use the code associated with these games, but may not use the images in other projects.*

HOT WHEELS and associated trademarks are owned by and used with permission of Mattel, Inc. ©1996 Mattel, Inc. All Rights Reserved.

Passage to Vietnam demo ©1996 by ad*hoc Interactive, Inc., 221 Chaledonia Street, Sausolito, CA 94965; Passage to Vietnam created by Rick Smolan, Against All Odds Productions.

Andromeda Filters demos ©1996, courtesy of Andromeda Software, Inc. 699 Hampshire Road, Suite 108. Thousand Oaks, CA 91361.

DeBabelizer Lite LE and DeBabelizer Toolbox 1.6.5 demo ©1996 by Equilibrium, Inc., 3 Harbor Drive, #111, Sausolito, CA 94965.

Memmon, a Memory Management Utility, ©1996 by Alex Zavatone. Check out the *Director Developer's Toolkit!* Tools to aid the developer in Director title production. Includes Parent/Child object browser, inspector Miaws, Hypertext, Shockwave tutorials, projector tracer and debugger, added functions and more.

Publisher: Audio Images
Price: List at $299.00
Goal: Produce a toolkit that Director developers really want to use with tools to aid Director movie creation for the professional developer.
Web Site: www.blacktop.com/zav/toolkit

Disc Install Information

If You Have a Mac

1. Insert the CD-ROM in your CD-ROM drive.
2. Click on the READ ME file for details about the CD-ROM and its contents.

If You Have a Windows-Based PC

1. Insert the CD-ROM in your CD-ROM drive.
2. Use Windows File Manager (Windows 3.1x) or Explorer (Windows 95) to find the CD-ROM's files.
3. Click on the READ1ST.WRI file to find out more about the CD-ROM and its contents.
4. You can automate the *Inside Director* 5 CD-ROM by double-clicking on SETUP.EXE (INSTALL for Win 95). You can then install or uninstall any of the programs on the CD-ROM from there.

Please refer to Appendix E, "The Inside Director 5 CD-ROM," for more information.